American Popular Music

Rhythm and Blues, Rap, and Hip-Hop

American Popular Music

Blues
Classical
Country
Folk
Jazz
Rhythm and Blues, Rap, and Hip-Hop
Rock and Roll

General Editor: Richard Carlin

Editorial Board:

Barbara Ching, Ph.D., University of Memphis

Ronald D. Cohen, Ph.D., Indiana University-Northwest

William Duckworth, Bucknell University

Kevin J. Holm-Hudson, Ph.D., University of Kentucky

Nadine Hubbs, Ph.D., University of Michigan

Craig Morrison, Ph.D., Concordia University and McGill University

Albin J. Zak III, Ph.D., University at Albany (SUNY)

American Popular Music

Rhythm and Blues, Rap, and Hip-Hop

Frank Hoffmann

Foreword by Albin J. Zak III, Ph.D.
University at Albany (SUNY)

An imprint of Infobase Publishing

Rhythm and Blues, Rap, and Hip-Hop

Facts On File, Inc.
An imprint of Infobase Publishing
132 West 31st Street
New York NY 10001

Library of Congress Cataloging-in-Publication Data

Hoffmann, Frank W., 1949–
   American popular music : rhythm and blues, rap, and hip-hop / Frank Hoffmann; [Richard Carlin, general editor ; foreword by Albin J. Zak III].
      p. cm.
   Includes bibliographical references (p.   ), discography (p.   ), and index.
   ISBN 0-8160-5315-4 (hc : alk. paper)
   1. Popular music—Encyclopedias. 2. Rhythm and blues music—Encyclopedias. 3. Rap (Music)—Encyclopedias. I. Carlin, Richard, 1956– II. Title.
   ML102.P66H6 2005
   781.643'0973'03—dc22   2005004762

Facts On File books are available at special discounts when purchased in bulk quantities for businesses, associations, institutions, or sales promotions. Please call our Special Sales Department in New York at (212) 967-8800 or (800) 322-8755.

You can find Facts On File on the World Wide Web at http://www.factsonfile.com

Text design by James Scotto-Lavino
Cover design by Nora Wertz

Printed in the United States of America

VB 10 9 8 7 6 5 4 3 2 1

This book is printed on acid-free paper.

Contents

Foreword

A signal feature of any encyclopedia is its presentation of the elements of a historical mosaic unassembled. The only organizing narrative force is the alphabet. From this leveled landscape, a reader is often led to unlikely observations of affinity and confluence among the encyclopedia's disparate entries. Because chronological sequence is not a factor, we wander as through a museum, forming our own impressions of the connections among the things we observe. Encyclopedias are, of course, especially useful in directing us to a particular topic. But it is also instructive simply to read through a few entries in succession. Start at the beginning. Reading the first four entries—"Paula Abdul," "Above the Law," "Herb Abramson," "a cappella"—we cover most of the historical time frame this book represents. A cappella is the unaccompanied singing style favored by early rock-and-roll vocal groups of the 1950s. Paula Abdul represents the 1980s pop diva for whom the dance was at least as important as the voice. Above the Law takes us into the 1990s, when hip-hop became king. And Herb Abramson was one of the founders of Atlantic Records, perhaps the premier R&B label, with a history stretching from the late 1940s to today, the home, over the years, to the likes of Ray Charles, The Drifters, Aretha Franklin, Wilson Pickett, Chic, and Lil' Kim.

Reading through a succession of apparently unrelated topics may feel disorienting at first, but gradually, among the kaleidoscopic wealth of information, common themes emerge, connecting many of the entries to one another in various ways. A great many of the artists cataloged in this book, for example, owe their early musical training to the churches they attended as youngsters. Sam Cooke, Aretha Franklin, Teddy Pendergrass, and Whitney Houston are but a tiny sample of artists schooled in the musical and expressive traditions of black gospel music. And each of these artists came to national prominence in a different decade, from the 1950s to the 1980s, a clear indication of the church's continuing influence. Indeed, the foundations for the style shared by hundreds of doo-wop groups of the 1950s was laid in black churches. And the vocal stylings common to all modern R&B divas are connected intimately to a long-standing tradition of gospel expression.

It is the connections to a traditional past and the continual, dynamic reshaping of tradition that gives this music its vitality, its strength, and its wide appeal. As the past is invoked, it informs the present with something familiar, and as traditional elements are transformed, they become fresh. The Orioles, and dozens of subsequent doo-wop groups, built on the sound of the Ink Spots and the Mills Brothers but transformed their elders' smooth, sophisticated pop, with its perfect Hollywood-movie diction and subtle jazz inflections, into a more youthful, unpolished sound with the lead singer's voice barely able to contain a sense of emotional transport. Prince, in forging an eclectic mix of R&B, pop, and rock elements, demonstrates, in his early work, a clear affinity for Sly Stone while offering up a blend that is all his own. And hip-hop culture, with its widespread use of sampling, makes connections with a musical past that range from sound fragments to extended quotations, such as Dr Dre's chorus for "Let Me Ride" (1992), which is taken from Parliament's "Mothership Connection (Star Child)" (1976), or Missy Elliott's revision (in 1997) of Ann Peebles' "I Can't Stand the Rain" (1974). Furthermore, the origins of rap in the 1970s as a street music requiring no instruments are essentially similar to those of doo-wop in the late 1940s, where groups of kids had only to gather on a neighborhood street, using nothing but their voices to make music that would, eventually, develop worldwide appeal. Such connections demonstrate the continued presence of a musical ancestry in the work of succeeding musical generations, through which develops a sense of stable and enduring tradition.

Another common thread running through the encyclopedia is the medium that represents and transmits the music, namely, recordings. The emergence of R&B coincided with an unprecedented increase both in record sales and in records' presence on radio (increasingly displacing live broadcast performances). Records became, as never before, the music industry's coin of the realm. And as they circulated, they allowed black music to travel in ways that were often forbidden to black musicians in a segregated and racist society. And as records developed an unprecedented economic potency, as increasing numbers of them were produced for the growing market, recording studios and record companies sprang up across the country, many little more than a couple of rooms in a storefront or warehouse. Making records became an attainable aspiration for thousands of young musicians who would have had no such opportunity with the large established record companies. With the recording field expanding exponentially, the range of sounds and production techniques expanded as well, sometimes through conscious creativity, other times by accident, luck, or happenstance.

With the recording field so densely and variously populated, different ideas arose of how a record should sound, what it should get across. If the records released by the small independent record labels lacked the polish of the majors, they held an undeniable emotional energy, and that was key. As these often rough-hewn, yet affecting, recordings became successful, that is, as they became part of people's lives, they contributed to the development among artists and the public of what we might call recording consciousness—a sense that records have a uniqueness about them, something different from live performance. The studio culture that would build over the years in now legendary studios such as Hitsville U.S.A. (Motown), Stax, and Atlantic has become fundamental to how music is produced and what listeners expect. Disco, Detroit techno, and other types of electronica are altogether studio-based genres. And hip-hop, despite its street roots, has thrived on the creative efforts of an array of producers making records that both tap into tradition and bring forth ever-new approaches to sonic expression. Indeed, the vast accumulation of records made over the past 60 years is itself a kind of encyclopedia. Thus, Public Enemy's Hank Shocklee says that his brother, coproducer Keith, "knows records like an encyclopedia." The records themselves are repositories of knowledge, experience, and tradition. It is fitting, then, that they provide not only pleasurable listening but pedagogic resources for thousands of young musicians, who learn their craft by listening, and nodes of collective memory for successive generations.

In the history of American popular music, the contributions of black Americans far outweigh their proportional presence in the overall population. It is striking that the *American Popular Music* series has two other volumes devoted primarily to black music: *Jazz* and *Blues*. In fact, the influence of black music is so pervasive that many white musicians, in their most impressionable years, develop an affinity for black music that forms the basis of their later careers. Elvis Presley, the songwriters Jerry Leiber and Mike Stoller, the Rascals, and Eminem are a representative few of the many white musicians irresistibly drawn to black musical styles in search of their own black-inflected voice. The pervasiveness of the musical influence makes as good a case as any that, while this music may originate with a particular segment of the population, it is ultimately transcendent. That is, while it is certainly the music of black Americans, it has become also the music of all Americans, which explains the iconic status of so many black performers. Sam Cooke, Ray Charles, Otis Redding, Jimi Hendrix, Aretha Franklin, James Brown, the Supremes, Prince, Michael Jackson, Tupac Shakur, and Lauryn Hill are among the many stars, representing various musical genres, whose impact has been felt throughout the culture and proved lasting.

Moreover, African-American musical influence is international. There was a time when black music was only available to African Americans, when record companies marketed "race" records only in African-American communities, and radio all but ignored the music. Mainstream media companies felt sure that the appeal of the music was limited. But in the era represented by this volume, black music proved its power to cross boundaries of social demarcation and geographic distance, including oceans. After all, the young English musicians who seemed to come out of nowhere in the 1960s in fact had deep roots in American R&B, blues, and rock and roll. They,

too, had learned from records. The Beatles recorded reverential cover versions of the Marvellettes' "Please Mr. Postman," Smokey Robinson and the Miracles's "You've Really Got a Hold on Me," and Barrett Strong's "Money (That's What I Want)", and the Rolling Stones, before they learned to write their own songs, lived on the legacy of their heroes—Muddy Waters, Howlin' Wolf, and Chuck Berry.

The *Rhythm and Blues, Rap, and Hip-Hop* volume of *American Popular Music* is both an informative resource and a celebration of a musical tradition. While it is necessarily selective, it points beyond its own boundaries in several directions—to other musical genres covered elsewhere in the series, to a historical past whose legacy is the foundation of the music represented here, and to more detailed stories of the artists, songs, songwriters, arrangers, records, disc jockeys, radio stations, record labels, producers, and entrepreneurs whose collective presence hovers over this project. As such, it is a starting point for further exploration both of a complex and fascinating cultural history and of an astonishing wealth of musical achievement.

Albin J. Zak III, Ph.D.
University at Albany (SUNY)

Preface

American popular music reflects the rich cultural diversity of the American people. From classical to folk to jazz, America has contributed a rich legacy of musical styles to the world over its two-plus centuries of existence. The rich cross-fertilization of cultures—African-American, Hispanic, Asian, and European—has resulted in one of the unique musical mixtures in the world.

American Popular Music celebrates this great diversity by presenting to the student, researcher, and individual enthusiast a wealth of information on each musical style in an easily accessible format. The subjects covered are:

Blues
Classical music
Country
Folk music
Jazz
Rock and Roll
Rhythm and Blues, Rap, and Hip-Hop

Each volume presents key information on performers, musical genres, famous compositions, musical instruments, media, and centers of musical activity. The volumes conclude with a chronology, recommended listening, and a complete bibliography or list of sources for further study.

How do we define *popular music*? Literally, any music that attracts a reasonably large audience is "popular" (as opposed to "unpopular"). Over the past few decades, however, as the study of popular music has grown, the term has come to have specific meanings. While some might exclude certain genres covered in this series—American classical music leaps to mind—we felt that it was important to represent the range of musical styles that have been popular in the United States over its entire history. New scholarship has brought to light the interplay among genres that previously were felt to be unrelated—such as the influence of folk forms on classical music, opera's influence on jazz, or the blues' influence on country—so that to truly understand each musical style, it is important to be conversant with at least some aspects of all.

These volumes are intended to be introductory, not comprehensive. Any "A to Z" work is by its very nature selective; it's impossible to include *every* figure, *every* song, or *every* key event. For most users, we hope the selections made here will be more than adequate, giving information on the key composers and performers who shaped each style, while also introducing some lesser-known figures who are worthy of study. The Editorial Board and other outside advisers played a key role in reviewing the entry lists for completeness.

All encyclopedia authors also face the rather daunting task of separating fact from fiction when writing short biographies of performers and composers. Even birth and death dates can be "up for grabs," as artists have been known to subtract years from their lives in their official biographies. "Official" records are often unavailable, particularly for earlier artists who may have been born at home, or for those whose family histories themselves are shrouded in mystery. We have attempted to draw on the latest research and most reliable sources whenever possible, and have also pointed out when key facts are in dispute. And, for many popular performers, the myth can be as important as the reality when it comes to their lives, so we have tried to honor both in writing about their achievements.

Popular music reflects the concerns of the artists who create it and their audience. Each era of our country's history has spawned a variety of popular music styles, and these styles in turn have grown over the decades as new performers and new times have arisen. These volumes try to place the music into its context, acknowledging that the way music is performed and its effect on the greater society is as important as the music itself. We've also tried to highlight the many interchanges between styles and performers, because one of the unique—and important—aspects of American cultural life is the way that various people have come together to create a new culture out of the interplay of their original practices and beliefs.

Race, class, culture, and sex have played roles in the development of American popular music. Regrettably, the playing field has not always been level for performers from different backgrounds, particularly when it comes to the business aspects of the industry: paying royalties, honoring copyrights, and the general treatment of artists. Some figures have been forgotten or ignored who deserved greater attention; the marketplace can be ruthless, and its agents—music publishers, record producers, concert promoters—have and undoubtedly will continue to take advantage of the musicians trying to bring their unique voices to market. These volumes attempt to address many of these issues as they have affected the development of individual musicians' careers as well as from the larger perspective of the growth of popular music. The reader is encouraged to delve further into these topics by referring to the bibliographies in each volume.

Popular music can be a slave itself to crass commercialism, as well as a bevy of hangers-on, fellow travelers, and others who seek only to make a quick buck by following easy-to-identify trends. While we bemoan the lack of new visionary artists today like Bessie Smith, Miles Davis, Pauline Oliveros, or Bob Dylan, it's important to remember that when they first came on the scene the vast majority of popular performers were journeymen musicians at best. Popular music will always include many second-, third-, and fourth-tier performers; some will offer one or two recordings or performances that will have a lasting impact, while many will be celebrated during their 15 minutes of fame, but most will be forgotten. In separating the wheat from the chaff, it is understandably easier for our writers working on earlier styles where the passing of time has helped sort out the important from the just popular. However, all the contributors have tried to supply some distance, giving greatest weight to the true artists, while acknowledging that popular figures who are less talented can nonetheless have a great impact on the genre during their performing career—no matter how brief it might be.

All in all, the range, depth, and quality of popular musical styles that have developed in the United States over its lifetime is truly amazing. These styles could not have arisen anywhere else, but are the unique products of the mixing of cultures, geography, technology, and sheer luck that helped disseminate each style. Who could have forecast the music of Bill Monroe before he assembled his first great bluegrass band? Or predicted the melding of gospel, rhythm and blues, and popular music achieved by Aretha Franklin during her reign as "Queen of Soul"? The tinkering of classical composer John Cage—who admitted to having no talent for creating melodies—was a truly American response to new technologies, a new environment, and a new role for music in our lives. And Patti Smith's particular take on poetry, the punk-rock movement, and the difficulties faced by a woman who leads a rock band make her music particularly compelling and original—and unpredictable to those who dismissed the original rock records as mere "teenage fluff."

We hope that the volumes in this series will open your eyes, minds, and, most important, your ears to a world of musical styles. Some may be familiar, others more obscure, but all are worthy. With today's proliferation of sound on the Web, finding even the most obscure recording is becoming increasingly simple. We urge you to read deeply but also to put these books down to listen. Come to your own conclusions. American popular music is a rich world, one open to many different interpretations. We hope these volumes serve as your windows to these many compelling worlds.

Richard Carlin,
General Editor

Introduction

American popular music owes much to the contributions made by African-American musicians. Many of the genres that continue to dominate the entertainment industry today—from forms originating in the 19th century, including the minstrel tradition, the blues, and ragtime, to the post–World War II idioms that constitute the primary focus of this book (rhythm and blues and its stylistic offshoots: rock 'n' roll, soul, funk, disco, and hip-hop)—evolved from black culture. In fact, it could be argued that rhythm and blues, rather than jazz, was the most important musical form of the twentieth century. In addition to providing the foundation for the aforementioned styles, it helped rejuvenate predominantly European-based styles (e.g., country, bluegrass, Tin Pan Alley pop) as well. It ultimately reached far beyond its core African-American constituency, informing the work of blue-eyed soul interpreters like the Righteous Brothers and the Rascals, as well as genre trailblazers like techno innovators Beck and Goldie.

The term rhythm and blues (R&B) emerged as the most acceptable designation for the music that had developed out of pre–World War II blues styles, for the most distinctive new element in this genre was the addition of a dance beat. The expression first appeared in formal usage in the late 1940s as the name of RCA's division that served the black audience; other alternatives at the time included "ebony" (MGM) and "sepia" (Decca and Capitol). Prior to the rise of rock 'n' roll, R&B had already evolved into a wide variety of subgenres, including:

1. self-confident, assertive dancehall blues which, in turn, encompassed
   a. big band blues (e.g., Lucky Millinder, Tiny Bradshaw)
   b. shout, scream, and cry blues (e.g., Wynonie Harris, Big Joe Turner, Big Maybelle, Ruth Brown, LaVern Baker, Roy Brown)
   c. combo blues or jump blues, which possessed a number of regional strains in addition to the cosmopolitan style exemplified by Louis Jordan: West Coast (e.g., Roy Milton, Amos Milburn, T-Bone Walker), Mississippi Delta (e.g., Ike Turner's Kings of Rhythm), New Orleans (e.g., Fats Domino, Professor Longhair), and East Coast (e.g., Chuck Willis, Wilbert Harrison);
2. more subdued club blues (e.g., Charles Brown, Cecil Gant, Ivory Joe Hunter);
3. country-tinged bar blues (usually centered in either the Mississippi Delta or Chicago) whose chief exponents included Muddy Waters, Howlin' Wolf, Elmore James, Lightnin' Hopkins, and John Lee Hooker;
4. vocal group singing, which was subdivided into
   a. the cool style (e.g., The Orioles, The Cardinals, The Spaniels)
   b. the dramatic style (e.g., The Moonglows, The Flamingos, The Platters)
   c. the romantics (e.g., The Harptones, The Flamingos)
   d. the cool style with a strong blues emphasis (e.g., The Clovers, The Drifters)

e. the sing-along novelty approach geared to mainstream pop acceptance (e.g., The Crows, The Penguins, Frankie Lymon & the Teenagers); and

5. gospel-based styles, which possessed three major strains:

   a. spiritual singing, with the focus upon the quality of the voice (e.g., Mahalia Jackson)

   b. gospel singing, with its concentration on the interplay between voices, which were often deliberately coarsened to stress the emotional conviction of the singers (e.g., Rosetta Tharpe, The Dixie Hummingbirds)

   c. preacher singing, with its tendency to speak the message in an urgent near-shout which often revealed the phrasing and timing of singing minus the melodic dimension (e.g. Reverend C. L. Franklin).

It soon became evident, musically speaking, that "rhythm and blues" was a less than satisfactory name for at least two of the most important stylistic innovations of the 1950s: the various vocal group styles and the gospel-based styles. These were to become increasingly popular as rock 'n' roll began to siphon off the unique spirit of previous R&B forms. For instance, the new vocal groups invariably based their approach on the style of two African-American ballad-singing aggregates that had proven successful with the easy-listening audience, the Mills Brothers and the Ink Spots. Both groups sang in the close harmony, or "barbershop" style, accompanied by a light rhythm section. They were linked because of the ease with which they timed their harmonies, and the purity of their voices.

Of course, these characteristics were a far cry from those comprising the classic R&B style. Therefore, the term "rhythm and blues" became most useful as a market designation; i.e., an indication that the performer was black or recording for the black audience. As noted by Charlie Gillett, there was ample justification—at least until 1956—for classifying the black market separately. The black audience was interested almost exclusively in

black performers; only five recordings by white acts reached the R&B Top Ten between 1950 and 1955, and three of those were rock 'n' roll records (Bill Haley's "Dim the Lights" and "Rock Around the Clock," and Boyd Bennett's "Seventeen"). Few white singers had either the interest of the cultural experience necessary to appeal to the black audience's taste—until rock 'n' roll changed the equation, resulting in a new type of white performer.

Lacking the financial resources and industry connections of established white pop acts, R&B artists displayed impressive persistence and creativity. The Harptones' doo-wop rendition of "The Shrine of St. Cecilia" represents a case in point. Taking a well-known tune, the group overcame the shortage of studio resources by intoning the "tick-tocks" of a clock and "ding-dongs" of bells; the sincerity of the delivery managed to make dated lyrics sound relevant and meaningful.

Motown Records played the pivotal role in the development of R&B into a mainstream genre. The product of the vision of one man, owner and founder Berry Gordy, the label sculpted a mainstream pop sound out of gospel and blues roots which reflected the vision of upward mobility and wholesome fun held by young blacks in the 1960s. Motown's stars were groomed to offend no one; the songs they sang had romantic lyrics that could appeal to practically anyone; and the music itself was rarely demanding, or even aggressive in the tradition of southern soul. The closest thing to an overt political statement released by Motown in the mid-1960s was Stevie Wonder's "Blowing in the Wind."

Although the assembly-line approach employed by Motown led to criticisms for monotony, the label released a remarkably diverse array of recordings, varying in sound, arrangement, and feel. This diversity—reinforced by Motown's mainstream commercial success—proved to be the launching pad for many of the black music styles that evolved after the mid-sixties. Virtually all black musicians were in some way influenced by the Motown Sound.

A host of regional independent labels producing soul music in the 1960s sought to control production values and nurture available talent with an eye to the long-term payoff, including Vee-Jay and Chess/Checker (Chicago), Stax/Volt/Enterprise, Goldwax, and Hi (Memphis), Philadelphia International, Philly Groove, and Avco (Philadelphia) and FAME (Muscle Shoals, Alabama). Funk, disco, and the dance-oriented styles of the eighties such as go-go music also owed much to Motown.

Hip-hop music—and its vocal offshoot, rap—represents the most significant innovation in African-American popular music during the final decades of the twentieth century. The genre—which drew heavily from dance club culture, black street poetry, and the dub music of reggae deejay toastmasters—remained a spontaneous under ground phenomenon (largely centered in metropolitan New York City) throughout much of the 1970s. Although classic soul and disco records provided the core soundtrack for the pioneering MCs—who continually experimented with scratching and other rhythmic flourishes—much of what was preserved from hip-hop's gestation period was limited to rough audiocassette transfers. The release of "Rapper's Delight"—recorded by the Sugarhill Gang, a collection of session players gathered together by the Sugar Hill label expressly to capitalize on the street buzz being generated by hip-hop—proved to be a watershed development. While experimental work of hip-hop deejays has continued to elude mass market acceptance, a wide array of rap styles—including the cartoon humor of the Fat Boys and DJ Jazzy Jeff with the Fresh Prince, the political diatribes of Grandmaster Flash and Public Enemy, the dance-inflected verse of Tone Loc and MC Hammer, and the gangsta rap of N.W.A., Tupac Shakur, and Ice-T—has achieved crossover success.

Despite the continued cultural dominance of hip-hop at the onset of the twenty-first century, African-American popular music encompasses a broad range of styles, from the torch ballad tradition of Anita Baker and Whitney Houston to a kaleidoscopic succession of ambient and techno-infused dance genres. The latter forms include

1. trip-hop: slow-motion breakbeat music melding rap, reggae dub, and film noir–influenced soundtrack samples, accented by audio loops and vinyl scratching;

2. jungle (or drum and bass): a fragmented, speeded-up blend of reggae afterbeats, hardcore techno, hip hop, soul, and jazz;

3. house: featuring insistent bass figures, looping drums, and erotic vocals. Although originating in Chicago, it would—by means of incessant cross-fertilization—give rise to acid house, disco house, deep house, ambient house, progressive house, power house, pop house, handbag house, and countless other subgenres;

4. techno: first identified with Detroit, an instrumental-based variant of electronica characterized by darting keyboards and impatient rattling drums; and

5. trance: a late 1990s hybrid of techno, ambience, and house consisting of processed, computer-generated extended compositions built around the repetition of keyboard arpeggios, octave leaps, pitch-shifts, lengthy drum breaks, and steadily rising crescendos.

The rich diversification of styles and comparatively rapid rate of change characteristic of black popular music in the post–World War II era stands in bold contrast to the chief white-dominated genre indigenous to the United States, country music. In *The Sound of the City* Gillett offers the following rationale for this situation:

This is partly because several white southern styles have never been widely popular with the national American audience, so that singers did not continually have to invent styles that would be special to their local audiences—those invented thirty or forty years ago were still special to a local area, or to the white south.

In contrast, almost every black southern style has proved to have universal qualities that attract national and international audiences, and this situation has placed continual pressure on singers to come up with new styles that are not already widely known and that the local audience can feel to be its own. And invariably, musicians and singers have responded positively to such pressure.

This predisposition for change has proven to be at once a strength and a weakness. It has enabled R&B to remain a dynamic genre, ever responsive to the needs and interests of its core audience. However, it has also discouraged participation on the part of the uninitiated, who are confused by the rapid succession of fads and fashions.

This work attempts to provide an overview of R&B, rap, and hip-hop—their key artists, recordings, record labels, and stylistic branches—via an encyclopedic format. While it would be impossible to cover all the nuances of the evolution of these musical genres during the past 60 years in a single book, this volume of *American Popular Music* should inspire the reader to listen to the recordings of the artists profiled here and seek out additional material relating to their music.

A-to-Z Entries

Abdul, Paula (b. 1962) *dancer and singer*

Paula Abdul's career success had everything to do with timing—and the MTV phenomenon. She studied dance throughout her childhood, and after attending college at California State, Northridge, became a Los Angeles Lakers cheerleader. Jackie Jackson noticed Abdul's skills in planning dance routines and hired her to choreograph the Jacksons' "Torture" video. She went on to work in television and films as well as assisting many other artists in video production, most notably JANET JACKSON, Duran Duran, the Pointer Sisters, and ZZ Top.

Abdul joined the roster of Virgin Records artists in the late 1980s. Her first album, *Forever Your Girl* (Virgin, 1988), became one of the decade's best-sellers (seven million copies in the U.S.), topping the *Billboard* Top 200 chart and producing four number one singles: "Straight Up," "Forever Your Girl," "Cold Hearted," and "Opposites Attract." Despite widespread criticism of her singing, the LP succeeded due to catchy FUNK arrangements and flashy videos that effectively captured her stylish, energetic dance moves and girlish charm.

To capitalize on Abdul's success, Virgin released an album of dance remixes of her hit recordings entitled *Shut Up and Dance* (Virgin, 1990). The next album, *Spellbound* (Virgin, 1991), maintained her upward career trajectory, reaching number one and spawning five hit singles. Subsequent releases have been less successful, but Abdul remains active both as a performer and choreographer, most recently appearing as a judge on the popular television series *American Idol.*

Above the Law

Above the Law were responsible for a somewhat incongruous blend of breezy dance-floor beats, sampled in large part from the classic soul era, and harsh, slice-of-life verses. Formed in the late 1980s, in Pomona, California, the gangsta rap group employed keyboards, guitar, and bass as well to accompany so-called hustlers Cold 187um (b. Gregory Hutchinson; aka Big Hutch), K.M.G. the Illustrator (b. Kevin Dulley), Total K-Oss (b. Anthony Stewart), and Go Mack (b. Arthur Goodman; he left the act in late 1993).

Above the Law's debut album, *Livin' Like Hustlers* (Ruthless, 1990), co-produced by label head EAZY-E and DR DRE, featured the Mega (depictions of street violence) and Ranchin' (graphic sexual settings) sides. Although it sold moderately well, follow-ups, including the mini album *Vocally Pimpin'* (Ruthless, 1991), *Black Mafia Life* (Ruthless, 1993), and *Uncle Sam's Curse* (Ruthless, 1994), met with a less enthusiastic public reception. At this point, Cold 187 (his modified moniker) had also become involved in outside projects, most notably Kokane's first album, *Funk Upon a Rhyme* (Ruthless/Relativity, 1994).

Following Eazy-E's tragic death in 1995, the group moved to the TOMMY BOY label. Releases like *Time Will Reveal* (Tommy Boy, 1996) and *Legends* (Tommy Boy, 1998) revealed Cold 187's growing skills as a G-funk producer. Above the Law went on to establish their own label, West World, assisted by a distribution deal with Street Solid. Although *Forever: Rich Thugs* (Street Solid, 1999) was arguably their finest effort, crammed full of infectious grooves, Cold 187—while nominally still a group member—shifted his energies to a solo career, recording his debut, *Executive Decisions* (Street Solid, 1999), and becoming the house producer and musical director at Suge Knight's DEATH ROW RECORDS. Although Above the Law recorded an album, *Diary of a Drug Dealer,* for that label, its release date was continuously postponed due to Cold 187's production assignments, leading to speculation that the group had broken up.

Abramson, Herb (1920–1999) *producer and record company executive*

Brooklyn native Herb Abramson, along with AHMET ERTEGUN and his brother Nesuhi, founded Atlantic Records in 1947. Their partnership was fueled by a shared love of jazz, blues, and gospel recordings. In the early 1940s, Abramson started promoting jazz concerts in New York and Washington, D.C. in addition to financing the short-lived Jubilee and Quality labels with Ahmet Ertegun and record retailer Max Silverman. Between 1944 and 1947 he produced the likes of Billy Eckstine, BIG JOE TURNER, and the RAVENS for National Records.

Although Atlantic's initial releases focused on jazz, it soon found commercial success with rhythm and blues artists such as RUTH BROWN, LAVERNE BAKER, CLYDE MCPHATTER and the DRIFTERS, and RAY CHARLES. After a military stint from 1953–55, Abramson administered the subsidiary label Atco, whose early roster included WYNONIE HARRIS, the COASTERS, and Bobby Darin.

In 1957, he sold his Atlantic holdings for $300,000 and concentrated on developing his own record companies—Blaze, Festival, and Triumph—with limited success. He would go to work as an independent producer for Elmore James, DON COVAY, Gene Pitney, Louisiana Red, Titus Turner, and other pop/R&B performers. His biggest hit came with Tommy Tucker's 1964 single, "Hi-Heel Sneakers." The Rhythm and Blues Foundation gave him its Pioneer Award in 1998 in recognition of his achievements.

a cappella

The concept of singing without instrumental accompaniment was derived from religious singing during the medieval period of European history. Within the context of American popular music, it refers to a spin-off of DOO-WOP, limited to vocals only (whether a solo or group setting) rather than with instrumental accompaniment. Although various artists have employed the device on rare occasion (Prelude enjoyed considerable success with an a cappella rendition of Neil Young's "After the Goldrush"), the PERSUASIONS enjoyed the greatest success utilizing this approach on a consistent basis within the R&B field.

Ace, Johnny (1929–1954) *singer, keyboardist and composer*

Born John Marshall Alexander, Jr., on June 9, 1929, the Memphis native joined the B. B. KING band, and then formed the Beale Streeters with King, BOBBY BLAND, and Earl Forest, Roscoe Gordon, and Willie Nix in 1949. The group placed three singles in the R&B Top Ten, including the chart-topping "My Song" and "The Clock," before Ace opted for a solo career in 1953. He remained a top recording act up until his death backstage at Houston's City Auditorium, December 24, 1954, while paying Russian roulette. Two posthumously released singles, "Pledging My Love" (number one for 10 weeks on the R&B charts) and "Anymore," were big hits in 1955.

acid jazz

Acid jazz represents a synthesis of jazz fusion, FUNK, HIP-HOP, and urban dance music. Its improvisational, percussion-heavy, and predominantly live orientation came largely from jazz, whereas its dedication to an ongoing rhythmic groove was borrowed from the latter three genres. The term entered the vernacular in 1988 when adopted as the name of a U.S.-based independent record company and, at the same time, employed as the title of an English compilation series consisting of reissued 1970s jazz-funk material. The evolution of the form is closely aligned with the continuing cross-fertilization of a wide range of related styles, most notably alternative dance, ambient house, DRUM AND BASS, club/dance music, HOUSE, jazz-rap, soul-jazz, trip-hop (see introduction), and trip jazz.

Due to this ongoing cross-pollination, acid jazz artists bring many different perspectives to their recorded work. One of the most popular bands within the genre, the Stereo MC's, moved from British hip-hop in the late 1980s to a more organic, jazz-inflected amalgam of hip-hop and soul-funk with the release of their most popular LP, *Connected* (4th & Broadway, 1992). Courtney Pine came from the opposite side of the fence, bringing his hardcore jazz sensibilities directly into African-American dance culture; his *Underground* (Talkin' Loud, 1997) melded steamy live grooves with a battery of technological effects.

Other important recording artists associated with acid jazz include the Brand New Heavies, the Coolbone Brass Band, Corduroy, Count Basic, D'Influence, D*Note, DJ Greyboy, Dread Flimstone, Galliano, the Grassy Knoll, Greyboy, Greyboy Allstars, Groove Collective, Incognito, JAMIROQUAI, the Jazz Warriors, Jhelisa, Ronny Jordan, A Man Called Adam, Marden Hill, Mondo Grossom Outside, Palm Skin Productions, Gilles Peterson, Red Snapper, Sandals, Slide Five, James Taylor (Quartet), and United Future Organization.

AD

A Brooklyn, New York-based rock/RAP fusion group, AD was a vehicle for lead vocalist Anthony DeMore's strong sense of political alienation. DeMore (b. 1969, Brooklyn) became interested in a music career while performing as MC AD in high school. He hooked up with guitarist David Tarcia at Bard College, and they went on to recruit bassist Aaron Keane and drummer Mervin Clarke. Despite the promise of a highly polished debut release, *AD* (Sage, 1993), they have maintained a low profile in the years since, making it apparent their days as a performing act are done.

Adams, Faye (b. circa 1925) *singer*

Faye Adams, known as "Atomic Adams" in recognition of her dynamic blues style, became a star quite by accident. Born Faye Tuell, in Newark, New Jersey, she started out singing gospel at age five with two older sisters as the Tuell Sisters. After marrying Tommy Scruggs in 1942, she adopted the performing name of Fay Scruggs.

She joined the Joe Morris Blues Cavalcade in late 1952, recording with the group briefly for Atlantic. On the lookout for a new label, Morris secured an audition with Al Silver, then head of Herald Records. Silver was particularly impressed with Adams, and decided to sign her as a solo act instead of as part of the Morris ensemble.

Her first hit came in 1953 with the gospel-inflected Morris composition, "Shake A Hand." Although Adams never so much as creased the pop charts again, she remained hot as a rhythm and blues singer into the late 1950s, scoring with singles like the rousing "I'll Be True," "Hurts Me to My Heart," and "Keeper of My Heart." She later concentrated on gospel singing.

Adams, Oleta *singer*

Brought up singing gospel in Yakima, Washington, Oleta Adams formed a soul trio in the early 1980s. She recorded two self-funded LPs for a Kansas label, but they failed to catch on with the public. After catching her cabaret act in a Kansas hotel bar, Roland Orzabal and Curt Smith—better known as the group Tears for Fears—recruited her to supply vocals on tracks used for their neo-psychedelic album, *The Seeds of Love* (Phonogram, 1987). She continued to work with them, both live and in the studio, eventually landing a contract with the duo's record company.

Adams' *Circle of One* (Phonogram, 1990), produced by Orzabal, who also composed the lead single, "Rhythm of Life," topped the U.K. chart and made the U.S. Top 20. It featured the Grammy-nominated single, "Get Here," adopted as the unofficial anthem for those with loved ones overseas during the Gulf War. Her career lost considerable momentum when the follow-up LP, *Evolution* (Mercury, 1993), failed to sell well. However, she continued to make recordings, releasing *Moving On* (Polygram, 1995) and *All the Love* (Bedrock, 2002).

ADC Band

A solid meat-and-potatoes FUNK act modeled after the more grounded side of the music troupe headed by GEORGE CLINTON, the Detroit-based ADC Band enjoyed a measure of success at the peak of the DISCO era, ultimately suffering from no discernable identity of its own. The group consisted of core members Audrey Matthews (lead vocalist) and Artwell Matthews (drums)—children of Detroit music entrepreneur Johnnie Mae Matthews—complemented by trombonist Sam Burns, lead guitarist Curtin Hobson, keyboardist Mike Judkins, singer/percussionist James Maddox, and bassist Mark Patterson. Audrey and Artwell, together with Patterson, formed Black Nazty, which signed with the STAX imprint, Enterprise, in 1971. With little to show for their efforts with the label other than the near-miss 1974 single, "Talking to the People," they moved to Mankind Records in 1976. Now known as Nazty, they finally creased the R&B charts with "It's Summertime," in addition to releasing an LP, *Nazty's Got the Move* (Mankind, 1976).

The act morphed into General Assistance and the ADC Band in 1977, and recorded an album, *Looking for My Roots* (Northern, 1978), for a label owned by Johnnie Mae Matthews. After shortening their name and signing with Cotillion, the group made waves with "Long Stroke" (Cotillion, 1978; number six R&B), followed by a string of lesser hits through 1982 before disappearing from view.

Afros, The

Dedicated to lampooning 1970s culture such as hairstyles and blaxploitation films, the short-lived New York–based act included the clean-shaven Hurricane and Koot Tee, who provided a visual contrast to the Afro-wearing DJ Kippy-O. Hurricane had previously been a deejay for the BEASTIE BOYS, and recorded briefly for their Grand Royal label. In their debut LP, *Kickin' Afrolistics* (CBS, 1990), the Afros leavened their sight gags and witty asides with more serious political commentaries. The music itself was unabashedly traditional, featuring call-and-response verses sung over FUNK-styled backbeats.

Aladdin Records

Aladdin Records was established in late 1944 by the Mesner brothers, Eddie and Leo. The Los Angeles-based label was initially named Philo; however, a lawsuit forced a name change in 1946.

Although releases spanned jazz (on the Jazz West and Intro subsidiaries), gospel, and classical (on Orefeo), Aladdin focused on rhythm and blues. Its artist roster included Amos Milburn, Charles Brown, BIG JOE TURNER, Shirley & Lee, and the FIVE KEYS. The label's album and singles releases are among some of the most highly valued among record collectors. The scarcity of many Aladdin, Jazz West, and Intro LPs is due in part to the Mesners' formation of budget subsidiary Score in 1957. Many jazz and R&B recordings remained in print for a relatively short time prior to being deleted and reissued on Score with a retail price of $1.98. It is likely that a number of albums intended for Aladdin instead debuted on Score.

Although the Aladdin name has remained in use, the company ceased to exist as a business entity when the Mesners sold their catalog to Imperial in 1962. The rights to these recordings now belong to the EMI Records Group; in fact, many LP compilations have featured material culled from Aladdin, Imperial, and Capitol.

Allen, Annisteen (1920–1992) *singer*

One of the most respected female vocalists of R&B's early days, Annisteen Allen is largely forgotten because her biggest hits came as a member of the band fronted by LUCKY MILLINDER. Born Ernestine Allen, on November 11, 1920, in Champaign, Ohio, she was greatly influenced by Ella Fitzgerald during her formative years in Toledo. She was discovered by LOUIS JORDAN, who recommended her to Millinder. Her soulful style became a distinctive trademark of Millinder's touring band and recordings for Queen/King, Decca, and RCA Victor between 1945 and 1951.

Allen went on to record solo for King/Federal (1951–53), Capitol (1954–55), Decca (1956–57), and a number of independents in the late 1950s, including Todd, Warwick, and Wig. She recorded a highly regarded debut LP, backed by KING CURTIS' band, entitled *Love for Sale* (Tru-Sound, 1961), but public indifference hastened her retirement from show business shortly thereafter. She died August 10, 1992, in New York City.

ALT (b. 1970) *rapper*

ALT—derived from his real name, Al Trivette, as well as standing for "Another Latin Timebomb"—was born and raised in Rosemonte, a Latin community immediately east of Los Angeles, California. A first-hand witness to the social problems caused by drugs and violence, he was signed by Atlantic at a time when the company was tentatively branching out into hardcore street rap. His eponymous debut (East West/Atlantic, 1991), however, was marred by dictates to steer clear of profane language. Concerned with artistic freedom issues, ALT switched to a more credible independent, Inner City. His first release for the label, the 1993 single "Riding High," documented a day in his Latin neighborhood. The ensuing album, *Stone Cold World* (Inner City/Par, 1993), offered more of the same slice-of-life material.

Andrews, Lee, and the Hearts

The Hearts were one of the more polished African-American harmony groups in the 1950s. Their most successful configuration consisted of lead singer Lee Andrews (born Arthur Lee Andrew Thompson, a North Carolina native who relocated to Philadelphia at age two), first tenor Roy Calhoun, second tenor Thomas Curry, baritone Ted Weems, and bass Wendell Calhoun. Their first hit, "Long Lonely Nights," which reached number 11 on the R&B charts in 1957, remains a classic ballad of the DOO-WOP era.

The group members began singing together while in high school at local venues in Philadelphia by 1953. Record executive George Goldner was sufficiently impressed to help them secure a contract with the Rainbow label the following year. When "Long Lonely Nights" began generating considerable regional attention, the master was sold for national distribution to the Chicago-based Chess Records. The group enjoyed even greater success with "Teardrops," before moving on to United Artists in early 1958. After clicking with another smooth ballad, "Try the Impossible," the group lost the hit-making touch.

Andrews went on to open a clothing boutique in Philadelphia. By the early 1970s, he was also appearing—initially backed by a couple of young female singers—in periodic rock revival shows billed as Lee Andrews and the Hearts.

Antoinette *rapper*

Although she failed to achieve pop stardom, Antoinette was one of the earliest female rappers of note. Born in Queens, New York, she surfaced on Hurby "LuvBug" Azor's compilation LP, *Hurby's Machine*, which described her as a "tough-talking RAP mama." Antoinette tried to live up to this characterization on her debut album, *Who's the Boss* (Next Plateau, 1989); although a measure of verve and spontaneity managed to come across, the incessant gangsta-speak ultimately dragged it down. The follow-up, *Burnin' at 20 Below* (Next Plateau, 1990), represented a quantum leap forward, featuring her sexually liberated testimonials backed by a dazzling array of musical styles, including FUNK, go-go, HOUSE, and contemporary HIP-HOP. More releases have not been forthcoming, however, and her promise remains largely unrealized.

Ashford & Simpson

The husband and wife singing/songwriting team consisting of Nickolas Ashford (b. May 4, 1942, Fairfield, South Carolina) and Valerie Simpson (b. August 26, 1946, New York City) first attracted attention writing for artists such as Maxine Brown and Chuck Jackson. In the late 1960s, they were hired by Motown, where they wrote and produced for many of the label's artists.

Simpson recorded briefly as a solo act in 1972 before the duo embarked on a performing career the following year. They remained steady, if unspectacular, hit-makers until their first Top Ten R&B success, "Don't Cost You Nothing," early in 1978, which initiated a decade-long string of best-selling recordings. Despite their laid-back, melodic sound, Ashford & Simpson only managed to crack the pop Top 40 on two occasions: "Found a Cure" (1979) and the R&B chart-topper "Solid" (1984).

Atkins, Juan (b. 1962) *producer*

Juan "Magic" Atkins is one of the "Detroit mafia" who pioneered the TECHNO genre in the latter half of the 1980s. Seminal tracks like "No UFO's," "Ocean to Ocean," "The Chase," and "Electronic"—later included in the anthology, *Classics* (R&S, 1993), credited to Model 500—blended his production skills with over-the-top science fiction concepts, greatly influencing 1990s acts like KLF and Black Box.

Atkins maintained a low profile in the early 1990s before resurrecting his trailblazing Metroplex label as part of the Submerge organization. He also reversed his former policy of shunning remix projects, working on Eon's "Spice" and Inner City's "Let It Reign," among others.

Atlantic Starr

The funk-based band was formed in 1976, in White Plains, New York, by brothers David, Jonathan, and Wayne Lewis. The early edition of Atlantic Starr, which included members Clifford Archer, Sharon Bryant, Porter Carrol, Joseph Phillips, Damon Tntie, and William Sudderth, became a fixture on the R&B charts, with such hits as "When Love Calls," "Circles," and "Touch a Four Leaf Clover." Despite a significant reorganization in 1984, now featuring the Lewis brothers, Phillips, and vocalist Barbara Weathers, the band remained a top-notch recording act through the decade with Top Ten R&B singles like "Freak-A-Ristic," "Secret Lovers," "If Your Heart Isn't in It," "Always" (a number one pop and R&B smash), and "One Lover at a Time."

Babyface See REID, L. A., and BABYFACE

Bad Boy Records
Bad Boy was the brainchild of PUFF DADDY (Sean Combs), who struck paydirt in the 1990s with his own patented blend of HIP-HOP and old-school R&B. Combs first made an impact in the music business as an A&R executive for New York-based UPTOWN RECORDS in the early 1990s. When Uptown fired Combs he formed Bad Boy. Thanks largely to his street-level contacts and production talents, the label became a dominant force in the hip-hop/R&B marketplace by the mid-1990s. At its peak, the Bad Boy roster included rappers Craig Mack and the NOTORIOUS B.I.G., as well as updated R&B acts like Total and Faith Evans.

The company lost momentum as a result of the fallout emanating from a high-profile East Coast/West Coast feud with DEATH ROW's Suge Knight. The media speculated that this rivalry played a role in the 1996–97 drive-by murders of both Death Row artist TUPAC SHAKUR and Bad Boy's B.I.G. Combs was also plagued by various legal problems, beginning with a lawsuit resulting from an April 15, 1999, incident in which he allegedly assaulted Interscope Records executive Steve Stoute, and followed later in the year by an illegal firearms possession charge as well as a personal injury suit initiated by his chauffeur. Bad Boy took a more direct hit when Arista voided their prior distribution agreement and added Evans to its own roster in spring 2002. Nevertheless, the company soldiered on, owing much to the earning power of its leading artist, Puff Daddy.

Bailey, Philip (b. 1951) *singer and percussionist*
Born May 8, 1951, in Denver, Colorado, Philip Bailey first achieved success after joining the funk juggernaut, EARTH, WIND & FIRE, as co-lead singer and percussionist in 1972. He departed for a solo career in the early 1980s, recruiting fusion star, George Duke, to produce his debut LP, *Continuation* (Columbia, 1983). His second album was a breakthrough smash, due in large part to pop-friendly production work by Phil Collins, who also played percussion and co-wrote the infectious duet single, "Easy Lover," which reached number two on the U.S. and topped the U.K. pop charts. His career momentum was greatly slowed when the next release, *The Chinese Wall* (Columbia, 1985), perceived as out-of-step with prevailing post-disco R&B trends, was only a modest seller.

Baker, Anita (b. 1958) *singer*
An exponent of traditional rhythm and blues vocalizing, Baker's restrained intensity and subtle coloring attracted widespread media attention and pop mainstream success in the mid-1980s. Born in Toledo and raised in Detroit, she began her professional career as lead singer for the R&B group, Chapter 8, from 1976 to 1984. Her moderately successful debut album, *The Songstress* (Beverly Glen, 1983) was followed by the commercial breakthrough release, *Rapture* (Elektra,

1986), which included the single, "Sweet Love," a Top Ten hit reputed to have sold more than four million copies. Her subsequent albums, most notably the chart-topping *Give You the Best That I've Got* (Elektra, 1988) and *Compositions* (Elektra, 1990), have all been bestsellers. Baker's 2004 release, *My Everything,* was nominated for two Grammy Awards Best—R&B Album and Best Traditional R&B Vocal Performance for "You're My Everything."

Baker, LaVern (1929–1997) *singer*

One of the finest female rhythm and blues singers of the post–World War II era, LaVern Baker's greatest commercial success came from teen novelty recordings, most notably "Tweedlee Dee" and "Jim Dandy"/"Tra La La." Unable to make the transition to the adult market with any degree of lasting impact, she finally achieved widespread public acclaim in the 1990s following a 20-year hiatus in the Philippines—where she eventually became entertainment director at the Subic Bay Naval Base—for health reasons.

Born Delores Williams on November 11, 1929, Baker first sang professionally in the nightclubs of her native Chicago billed as "Little Miss Sharecropper." Her early recordings for National, RCA, Columbia (as "Bea Baker"), OKeh, and King attracted little attention; she became an R&B chart fixture—then known as "The Countess"—after signing with Atlantic in 1953. Her hits included "Bop-Ting-A-Ling," "Play It Fair," the soulful waltz-tempo ballad "I Cried a Tear," the gospel rave-up "Saved," and a searing update of the Chuck Willis ballad, "See See Rider." Well aware of Baker's protean talent, the label backed the ambitious project, *LaVern Baker Sings Bessie Smith* (Atlantic, 1958). Although her gospel-inflected treatment of classic blues material was every bit as effective artistically as ELLA FITZGERALD's songbook series devoted to notable popular composers, the album sold poorly. She moved on to the Decca subsidiary, Brunswick, in 1965. Although failing to return to the charts, she continued to perform live.

Baker's revival was spurred by her selection in 1990 to replace RUTH BROWN in the acclaimed Broadway revue, *Black & Blue.* Later that year she was voted into the Rock and Roll Hall of Fame and received a career achievement award from the Rhythm & Blues Foundation. A flurry of recordings for Sire, DRG, and Rhino followed, complemented by numerous reissues of her classic R&B tracks. She remained active until her death on March 10, 1997.

Ballard, Hank, and the Midnighters

Through a combination of bad luck and ill-advised career moves, the Midnighters, one of the great rhythm and blues vocal groups of the 1950s, just missed the big league status attained by contemporaries like the PLATTERS and the DRIFTERS. Nevertheless, they played a vital role in the development of popular music prior to the British Invasion.

The Detroit-based group, whose members included lead singer and songwriter Hank Ballard (born November 18, 1936), baritone Lawson Smith (b. 1936), bass singer Norman Thrasher (b. 1936; replaced by Charles Sutton), tenor Henry Booth (b. 1935; replaced by Sonny Woods), and guitarist Billy Davis (b. 1936; replaced by Arthur Porter), formed as the Royals in 1952. Signing with Federal Records, in Cincinnati, they first made the R&B charts in 1952 with the Johnny Otis composition, "Every Beat of My Heart," which was revived by GLADYS KNIGHT & THE PIPS in 1961.

Ballard received his first break from Otis when he signed as part of the Little Esther Revue and then joined the Royals in 1953. Shortly thereafter, the group became known as the Midnighters when their parent label, King Records, issued a recording contract to the "5" Royals. Their first hit following the name change, "Get It," was banned by many radio stations due to sexually explicit lyrics. The following year, Ballard's "Work With Me Annie," which borrowed thematically from "Get It," achieved even greater success, spawning a best-selling answer song, ETTA JAMES's "Wallflower," and a long string of

Hank Ballard and the Midnighters in performance (Frank Driggs Collection)

"Annie" songs (e.g., "Sexy Ways," "Annie Had a Baby") recorded by the Midnighters.

Ballard went solo in late 1958, releasing his material on King. His composition, "The Twist," spurred the rise of a new teen dance despite being released as the B-side of "The Letter." *American Bandstand* host, Dick Clark, sensing the commercial potential for the song, pitched it to the Cameo-Parkway label, which ultimately brought in up-and-coming vocalist, CHUBBY CHECKER, to produce a highly derivative cover version. Although few people were aware of his role in the creation of one of the most successful recordings of the rock era, Ballard did go on to produce a few pop hits of his own, most notably, "Finger Poppin' Time" and "Let's Go, Let's Go, Let's Go."

Bambaataa, Afrika (b. 1960) *rap DJ*

While DJ Kool Herc is widely credited with creating HIP-HOP, Afrika Bambaataa led the way in disseminating it worldwide. His vision incorporated deejays, rappers, singers, studio producers, breakdancers, and graffiti artists into one youth culture movement. Born Kevin Donovan on April 10, 1960, in the Bronx, he took the name of a nineteenth-century Zulu chief meaning "affectionate leader." Known as the "Master of Records," due to his unrivaled disc collection, he experimented with recorded musical elements such as Latin rock, European DISCO, FUNK, punk, and German electro bands such as Kraftwerk in order to create the ultimate dance environment. Although his primary creative medium was the club and street dances, he produced many important 12-inch singles and albums during the 1980s, most notably "Planet Rock" with Soulsonic Force, "Renegades of Funk" with Soulsonic Force, "Unity" with JAMES BROWN, *Planet Rock: The Album* (Tommy Boy, 1986), and *Warlock and Witches, Computer Chips, Microchips and You* (Profile, 1996). While no longer in hip-hop's innovative vanguard, he has remained in high demand as an elder statesman of the genre, working parties and raves and often making radio station appearances.

Banks, Darrell (1937–1970) *singer*

Born Darrell Eubanks on July 25, 1937, in Mansfield, Ohio, he issued a string of critically lauded soul singles before being tragically shot to death on February 24, 1970, during a dispute with an off-duty policeman who was having an affair with his girlfriend. His 1966 debut release, "Open the Door to Your Heart," has been termed "one of the finest non-Motown releases to emerge from Detroit." By 1967, he moved on to Atlantic, releasing the LP, *Darrell Banks Is Here* (Atco). Two years later, he switched to STAX, where he recorded the album, *Here to Stay* (Volt, 1969). Although Banks's ability to develop a distinctive style appears to have been hampered somewhat by his continued label jumping, he continued to produce classic songs up to his death, most notably, "I'm the One Who Loves You" and "No One Blinder (Than a Man Who Won't See)."

Banton, Buju (b. 1973) *reggae singer*

Buju Banton is one of the most important artists in the REGGAE field today, equally adept at romantic fare (albeit, marked by raw chauvinistic posturing) and social protest. Born Mark Myrie, in Kingston, Jamaica, he was raised in nearby Denham Town. He began learning the DJ trade as a 13-year-old with the Rambo Mango and Sweet Love sound systems. A mentor, DJ Clement Irie, recruited Robert French to produce Banton's 1986 debut single release, "The Ruler."

He next teamed with Dave Kelly, resident engineer at Donovan Germain's Penthouse Studio, to record a string of local club hits. Kelly not only shared songwriting credits, but made Banton's "Big It Up" the inaugural release on his Mad House label. Banton's success was led by a U.S. distribution deal with Mercury. The ensuing LP, *Voice of Jamaica* (Mercury, 1993), revealed an increasing preoccupation with cultural concerns such as Kingston's curfew laws ("Operation Ardent"), violence ("Murder"), and political warfare in his native country ("Tribal War"). His success, limited largely to England and the West Indies in the early 1990s, had become truly international in scope by the end the decade.

Bar-Kays

Formed by Al Jackson (drummer with BOOKER T. & THE MGs), the vocal/instrumental band, originally consisting of bassist James Alexander, organist Ronnie Caldwell, trumpeter Ben Cauley, drummer Carl Cunningham, saxophonist Phalon Jones, and guitarist Jimmy King, quickly established itself as a frontline act in 1967 on the strength of crossover hits like "Soul Finger." The Bar-Kays were temporarily placed on hold when all members except Alexander and Cauley were killed in the same October 10, 1967, plane crash that claimed the life of OTIS REDDING. Alexander eventually re-formed the group, and they became chart fixtures during the 1970s and 1980s in addition to doing extensive session work for STAX artists until the company went bankrupt. The band switched to the Mercury label in the mid-1970s, for which they recorded such Top Five R&B hits as "Shake Your Rump to the Funk," "Move Your Boogie Body," "Hit and Run," and "Freakshow on the Dance Floor" (the latter track appearing in the 1984 film *Breakin'*).

Barnes, J. J. (b. 1943) *singer*

J. J. Barnes is one of the great unrecognized talents of Detroit-based soul music. Although his energetic, intensely sung releases (many of which had much in common with early MARVIN GAYE singles) rarely achieved more than marginal sales, he became an extremely popular fixture in the northern British soul scene more than a decade later.

Born James Jay Barnes on November 30, 1943, in Detroit, he first made his mark as a member of the Halo Gospel Singers. He began his solo career in 1960 with the Kabel label, later releasing singles on Mickay and Ring. He reached a creative peak with Ric Tic in the mid-1960s, most notably, on "Please Let Me In," "Real Humdinger," and the GEORGE CLINTON production of the Beatles song, "Day Tripper." He then recorded a 1966 Top Ten R&B hit, "I'll Love You Forever," as part of the Holidays, a one-off assemblage also including future hitmaker EDWIN STARR and Steve Mancha.

MOTOWN purchased his contract and Ric Tic masters in 1966, but decided against issuing any of his recordings. He switched to the Groovesville label the following year, enjoying some success with "Baby Please Come Back Home" and "Now That I Got You Back." He failed to chart on the companion label, Revilot, in the late 1960s, and didn't resurface until the late 1970s, when he began recording in Great Britain to capitalize on his popularity among northern soul fans. He returned stateside in 1991 to release a couple of singles and an album, *Try It One More Time,* for Ian Levine's retro Motor City label.

Barrow, Keith (1956–1983) *singer*
Keith Barrow's career remains one of largely unfulfilled promise. A Chicago native and son of Willie T. Barrow, a minister who served as national executive director of Operation Push, an African-American civil rights initiative, Keith Barrow started out singing gospel. He possessed a rich, gentle falsetto heard to best effect on his two notable R&B hits, "You Know You Wanna Be Loved," a seamless blend of sweet soul singing and DISCO instrumentation, and the churning dance number, "Turn Me Up." Barrow also recorded three albums—*Keith Barrow* (Columbia, 1977), *Physical Attraction* (Columbia, 1978), and *Just As I Am* (Capitol, 1980)—before dying of AIDS on October 22, 1983.

Basehead
Alternately described as playing alternative dance or progressive RAP, Basehead was formed in 1991 in the Washington, D.C. area by Michael Ivey (vocals, guitar, songwriter, producer), who recruited guitarist Keith Lofton, bassist Bill Conway, and DJ Paul "Unique" Howard. The debut LP, *Play with Toys* (Émigré/Imago, 1991), recorded on a shoestring budget for a small independent label, featured a laid-back amalgam of rap, R&B, REGGAE, and FUNK. The follow-up, *Not in Kansas Anymore* (Imago, 1992), retained a pronounced slacker ethic in its commitment to spontaneous musical invention, although the results seemed more tentative in nature. *Faith* (Imago, 1996) staked out a more mystical, spiritual terrain; its limited airplay and sales seem to have shifted Ivey's attention to other projects.

Battiste, Harold (b. 1931) *producer*
One of the great unsung producers in the R&B/rock fields, New Orleans native Harold Battiste started out as a jazz pianist. He moved into production work in the early 1950s with the Los Angeles–based independent, Specialty Records. He returned to his hometown in 1956 to run a new branch for the label, but the needed support was not forthcoming.

Battiste jumped to Ric in 1960; his notable accomplishments there included producing Joe Jones's "You Talk Too Much" and arranging sessions for LEE DORSEY, one of which yielded the 1961 hit, "Ya Ya." When conflicts over distribution hastened the label's demise, he returned to Los Angeles to work as an arranger for Phil Spector. There he became reacquainted with Sonny Bono, a former associate at Specialty. He assisted Bono in producing the latter's early solo releases as well as the first Sonny and Cher recordings; however, the two parted ways over Battiste's contention that he wasn't receiving sufficient credit for his contributions.

Battiste next hooked up with fellow New Orleans expatriate Mac Rebennack, helping fashion the latter's Dr. John persona. Their successful formula, which blended voodoo incantations, Crescent

City–flavored rhythms, and Rebennack's distinctive husky drawl, resulted in a string of critically acclaimed albums, most notably, *Gris Gris* (Atco, 1968). In 1998, the city of New Orleans honored him with a Harold Battiste Day.

B-Boy Records

Formed in 1987 in the Bronx by Jack Allen and Bill Kamarra, B-Boy was one of the first independent labels specializing in RAP music. It attracted international attention shortly thereafter with the release of Boogie Down Productions' *Criminal Minded* (1987). Other roster artists of note included the Cold Crush Brothers, J.V.C.F.O.R.C.E., KG The All, Michael G, Levi 167, Spyder D, and Sparky D. On the brink of sustained success, however, Kamarra was incarcerated and the firm languished from a lack of leadership.

Beastie Boys

The Beastie Boys were widely attacked by the music press and the RAP establishment alike at their outset, largely due to the group's origins as a hardcore act when formed in 1981. The group members—MCA (Adam Yauch, b. August 5, 1965), Mike D (Mike Diamond, November 20, 1966), and Ad-Rock (Adam Horowitz, October 31, 1967; replaced Kate Schellenbach and John Berry in the early 1980s)—steadfastly protested accusations of musical piracy, arguing that rap was part of the post-punk cultural underground.

Hailing from well-to-do families in New York City, they acquired seasoning playing area youth clubs. In 1982, they recorded a seven-inch EP, *Pollywog Stew,* on the indie imprint, Rat Cage, followed in 1983 by the 12-inch rap single, "Cookie Puss," which was based on a crank call they made to Carvel Ice Cream. They were signed by DEF JAM in 1985, with their debut single for the label, "She's on It"—a track from the *Krush Groove* soundtrack that sampled AC/DC's "Back in Black"—becoming an underground hit. Some degree of national exposure was gained by opening for MADONNA's Virgin Tour and RUN-D.M.C.'s Raisin' Hell trek.

Their first album, *Licensed to Ill* (Def Jam, 1986)—which combined old school rap rhythms, metal guitar riffing, and b-boy humor viewed from a satirical perspective—became Columbia's fastest-selling debut album ever and the most successful rap LP of the decade, attracting considerable industry comment. However conservative elements censured the record's violence, sexism, rebellious posturing, and shallow party-hearty stance. With Def Jam attempting to assert greater control over the group's affairs, the Beasties relocated to California in late 1988 and signed with Capitol. Forming a working alliance with the British production team, the Dust Brothers, the group convinced them to apply their cut-and-paste sampling approach to *Paul's Boutique* (1989), a kaleidoscopic psychedelic-FUNK masterpiece that almost single-handedly created the alternative HIP-HOP genre. While media observers recognized the visionary features of the album, it experienced a considerable drop-off in sales, reaching only number 14 on the *Billboard* Top 200.

Check Your Head (1992), released on the group's new imprint, Grand Royal, offered yet another radical innovation, that of positioning rap verses on top of lo-fi grooves built around their own performances of an eclectic blend of styles, including hardcore punk, nu metal, 1970s dinosaur rock, jazz-soul fusion, updated lounge motifs, and dance-floor funk. Now embraced by college and alternative rock radio audiences, the record would debut in the Top Ten. For much of the decade, the Beasties seemed content to nurture this Gen-X following, reissuing their early indie material in *Same Old Bullshit* (Grand Royal, 1994); using *Ill Communication* to flesh out the ideas first explored in *Check Your Head;* and collecting the instrumental jams from the third and fourth LPs—enhanced with a couple of new tracks—for *The In Sound From Way Out!* (Grand Royal, 1996).

Hello Nasty (Grand Royal, 1998) found the group probing the boundaries of their tried-and-true formula, however, building densely layered hip-hop arrangements (complete with freestyle verses, call-and-response vocal refrains, and turntable scratching) on a retro electro-funk foundation. Like *Ill Communication,* it quickly rose to the top of the charts. Recent years have found the Beasties again treading water with *The Sounds of Science* (Grand Royal, 1999)—an exhaustive double-disc compilation encompassing not only album releases, but B-sides, non-LP singles, and EPs—and the painstakingly documented two-DVD *Video Anthology* (Voyager, 2000). In 2004 the trio released *To the 5 Boroughs* (Capitol).

Bee Gees, The

Many pop music artists have parlayed an eclectic blend of musical styles to achieve commercial success, but the Bee Gees are one of the few to remain on top despite a complete image makeover. Whatever genre assayed by the group, be it British Invasion pop, Baroque ballads, rhythm and blues, DISCO, or adult contemporary, their recorded output has been distinguished by immaculate three-part vocal harmonies, flawless arrangements and production work, and songwriting of the highest order.

Although the group (particularly in the late 1960s) has sometimes included added personnel, the primary members have always been the three Gibb brothers, Barry (born September 1, 1947) and the twins, Robin and Maurice (b. December 22, 1949). They first performed in public at an amateur talent show in Manchester's Gaumont British Theatre in 1955 as "The Blue Cats." After the family emigrated to Brisbane, Australia, in 1958, the trio began performing live as well as appearing on radio and television. Within two years the brothers were awarded a weekly TV series and secured an eighteen-month residency at Beachcomber Nightclub in Surfers Paradise. Their popularity with Australian youth led to a contract with Festival Records in late 1962. The group's first single, "Three Kisses of Love" (available on *Bee Gees: The Early Years, Vol. 2,* 1980), was released in January 1963, making

Australia's Top Twenty. A string of hits followed, climaxed by three number one hits in 1966: "Wine and Women," "I Was a Lover, a Leader of Men" (both on *Bee Gees: The Early Years, Vol. 1,* 1980), and "Spicks and Specks" (*Rare Precious & Beautiful,* 1968).

Primed to achieve international popularity, the family relocated to England in February 1967. The early months there were spent recording *The Bee Gees' First* (Atco, 1967), which included three U.S. Top Twenty singles: "New York Mining Disaster—1941," "To Love Somebody," and "Holiday." The album also earned them the "Beatles imitators" label; in the liner notes to *Bee Gees: The Early Years, Vol. 2,* the group's father, Hugh Gibb, refuted the charge, noting, "In actual fact we began recording before the Beatles . . . we came from Manchester, which is only 30 miles from Liverpool. It is rubbish to say we copied the Beatles' sound, it wasn't their sound, it was an English sound that began with Tommy Steele and skiffle."

Despite such criticisms, the group enjoyed a long run of hit singles, including "I Gotta Get a Message to You," "I Started a Joke," "Lonely Days," and "How Can You Mend a Broken Heart," and moderate selling LPs, most notably, *Horizontal* (Atco, 1968), *Idea* (Atco, 1968), *Odessa* (Atco, 1969), *Best of Bee Gees* (Atco, 1969), *2 Years On* (Atco, 1971), *Trafalgar* (Atco, 1971), and *To Whom It May Concern* (Atco, 1972). The band's progress was interrupted only by Robin's brief departure in 1969 to pursue a solo career. By 1974, however, sales of their increasingly over-produced recordings had dropped off to the point where their label demanded a stylistic change more in tune with the contemporary music scene. The resulting release, the R&B-disco flavored *Main Course* (RSO, 1975), placed the Bee Gees squarely into the pop mainstream with the help of three Top 20 singles, including the chart-topper, "Jive Talkin'." During the latter half of the 1970s, no act enjoyed greater chart success. Three of the group's contributions to the *Saturday Night Fever* soundtrack (RSO, 1977)—"How Deep Is Your Love," "Stayin' Alive," and "Night Fever"—spent a total of fifteen weeks at the top of the *Billboard* Hot 100. At one point the

Bee Gees had five of their compositions in the Top Ten (including songs recorded by Samantha Sang and brother Andy Gibb). The soundtrack remained number one on the album charts for twenty-four weeks; it was estimated at the time to be the best-selling LP in history. They also earned five Grammys for their work on the film soundtrack project in 1978.

Faced with the unenviable task of trying to top their hitherto unprecedented success, the Bee Gees moved away from disco with *Spirits Having Flown* (RSO, 1979), which included three number one singles: "Too Much Heaven," "Tragedy," and "Love You Inside Out." However, album releases of new material from that point forward exhibited a marked decline in sales. While songs such as "The Woman in You" and "You Win Again" continued the group's tradition of beautiful melodies, lush harmonizing, and polished production work, they appeared predictable compared with earlier cutting-edge releases. Furthermore, Top 40 radio stations seemed less inclined to place new Bee Gees records in rotation. On the other hand, they have remained a fixture within the adult contemporary format. In January 2003 Maurice Gibb died after undergoing abdominal surgery, and Barry and Robin retired the Bee Gees name forever.

Bell, Archie, and the Drells

Archie Bell (b. September 1, 1944, in Henderson, Texas) formed the Drells in the mid-1960s. The band members, who'd first sung together at Leo Smith Junior High School in Houston, included Huey "Billy" Butler, Joe Cross, and James Wise.

The group's number one hit, "Tighten Up," was originally recorded as a demo in 1964. After several years of limited success, Bell received his draft notice on May 12, 1967. When bandmate and roommate Butler found Bell in a funk over the imminent tour of duty in Vietnam, he tried to cheer him by performing an impromptu dance called the "Tighten Up." With a studio session already scheduled for the following day in order to stockpile recordings, Bell and Butler decided to do an updated version of their old song. Bell included an introduction, stating that the group was from Houston, Texas, because "when (John F.) Kennedy was assassinated, I heard a disc jockey say, 'nothing good ever came from Texas,' so I wanted people to know that we were from Texas and we were good."

When "Tighten Up" achieved hit status in Texas, it was picked up for national distribution by Atlantic Records. It took several months—until March 30, 1968—for the song to enter the *Billboard* Hot 100 as the label initially felt that the flip side, "Dog Eat Dog," possessed the greatest potential. By that time, Bell was stuck in a West German hospital recovering from a leg wound sustained in Vietnam. While he managed a 15-day pass which enabled him to record the follow-up singles, "I Can't Stop Dancing," "Do the Choo Choo"/"Love Will Rain on You," and "(There's Gonna Be a) Showdown," the group was unable to tour in support of the early Atlantic releases.

Bell received a military discharge on April 19, 1969, and immediately reunited with his group, which now included Wise, Lee Bell, and Willie Parnell. However, they now found it harder to make commercially successful records. They parted with Atlantic in 1970; their last charting single for the label was "Wrap It Up," which was revived by the Fabulous Thunderbirds in 1986. They moved on to Glades, where they reached the mainstream charts for the last time with "Dancing To Your Music."

The Drells were able to regain some measure of their R&B audience after signing with Philadelphia International in 1975. Working with the renowned producers, Kenny Gamble and Leon Huff, they recorded seven more hits through 1979, including "Let's Groove." The appearance of a DISCO version of "Tighten Up," which generated little interest, seemed to indicate that they were running out of creative ideas. By 1981, Bell was recording on his own for the Becket label. However, the group would remain popular as part of the Atlantic Coast "beach" music scene during the 1980s.

Bell, Thom (b. 1941) *producer and songwriter*

Thom Bell was an arranger, producer, and songwriter best known for the lush, dramatic settings he provided for Philly soul artists like the DELFONICS, the O'JAYS, and the STYLISTICS. Born in 1941, the Philadelphia native began a lifelong association with Kenny Gamble in 1959, first in a vocal duo, and then in the latter's DOO-WOP group, the Romeos. At age 19, he began arranging and conducting CHUBBY CHECKER's song repertoire, sometimes contributing original material as well. When Checker's production company failed, Bell caught on with the performer's record company, Cameo-Parkway, as a session pianist. While there he hooked up with the Delfonics, producing their sweet soul masterpieces, "La La Means I Love You" and "Didn't I Blow Your Mind This Time."

In the early 1970s, Bell was reunited with Gamble, who had formed the Philadelphia International label with Leon Huff. The symphonic scale of his productions, which were intensely soulful without lapsing into shallow displays of sentimentality, attracted major artists from outside the Philly soul circle, including the SPINNERS, the BEE GEES, and Johnny Mathis.

Bell, William (b. 1939) *singer and record company executive*

Born William Yarborough on July 16, 1939, the Memphis native joined the Rufus Thomas band in 1953. He went on to form the R&B vocal group, the Del Rios, along with tenor Harrison Austin, baritone Melvin Jones, and bass David Brown. He joined the Phineas Newborn band in the late 1950s before serving in the U.S. Army from 1962 to 1966.

Bell signed with STAX in 1966, recording a dozen hits for the label over the next decade, including the Top Ten R&B single "I Forgot to Be Your Lover." After signing with Mercury in 1976, he produced his biggest record, the R&B chart-topper and crossover Top Ten pop hit "Tryin' to Love Two." Although he continued to record throughout the 1980s, Bell increasingly focused on running his own labels, Peachtree and Wilbe.

Benson, George (b. 1943) *guitarist and singer*

Born March 22, 1943, Benson first attracted attention as a vocalist, winning a singing contest at the age of four. He would sing on the radio as "Little Georgie Benson" and with numerous rhythm and blues bands around his native Pittsburgh. Although Benson took up the guitar as an eight-year-old, he did not play in public until age fifteen. Shortly thereafter, he began playing sessions in studios outside Pittsburgh. While still a teenager, his groups, the Altairs and George Benson and His All-Stars, recorded for Amy Records. Moving to New York in 1965, he went on to record a series of widely admired, albeit moderate-selling, instrumental jazz albums for Columbia, A&M, and CTI.

Signing with Warner Bros. in late 1975, Benson was encouraged to sing for the first time as a recording artist. His debut LP for the label, *Breezin'* (Warner Bros., 1976), won three Grammy awards and reached number one on the *Billboard* Hot 100. Its triple platinum sales were driven by "This Masquerade," the first single ever to reach number one on the jazz, R&B, and pop charts. His next seven albums—*In Flight* (Warner Bros., 1977), *Weekend In L.A.* (Warner Bros., 1978), *Livin' Inside Your Love* (Warner Bros., 1979), *Give Me the Night* (Warner Bros., 1980), *The George Benson Collection* (Warner Bros., 1981), *In Your Eyes* (Warner Bros., 1983), and *20/20* (Warner Bros., 1985)—all went gold, and three achieved platinum status. His easygoing pop-funk style also led to more hit singles, including "On Broadway," "Give Me the Night," and "Turn Your Love Around."

Since the 1980s, Benson has divided his time between mainstream jazz projects (including live work with Dizzy Gillespie, Lionel Hampton, and Freddie Hubbard) and more pop-inflected recordings. His ability to navigate a middle course is reflected by chart-topping contemporary jazz albums such as *Tenderly* (Warner Bros., 1989), with pianist McCoy Tyner, and *Love Remembers* (Warner Bros., 1993).

Benton, Brook (1931–1988) *singer*

One of the premier song stylists of the late 1950s and early 1960s, Brook Benton fused the latter-day crooner tradition with the mellower side of rhythm and blues best exemplified by the likes of CLYDE MCPHATTER and SAM COOKE. His rich, velvety baritone stood out during an era dominated by higher-pitched tenor voices. Furthermore, he was a songwriter of considerable repute.

Born Benjamin Franklin Peay on September 19, 1931, in Camden, South Carolina, he sang with the Camden Jubilee Singers during his teens. He relocated to New York in 1948, joining another gospel

Brook Benton publicity still (Frank Driggs Collection)

group, Bill Landford's Langfordaires, shortly thereafter. Benton moved on to the Jerusalem Stars in 1951, before recording more secular fare under his own name for OKeh two years later. Later in the decade he teamed with songwriter Clyde Otis; their early collaborative successes included McPhatter's "A Lover's Question," the Diamonds' "The Stroll," and Nat King Cole's "Looking Back."

Benton continued to pursue a solo singing career, recording for the Vik label and then signing with Mercury in 1958. He found mainstream acceptance with "It's Just a Matter of Time," a song he cowrote with Otis and Belford Hendricks. He would go on to have eighteen gold records, including the Benton-Otis compositions, "Endlessly," "Kiddio," "The Boll Weevil Song," "Baby (You Got What It Takes)," and "A Rockin' Good Way," the latter two being duets with DINAH WASHINGTON.

The latter half of the 1960s, which included stints with RCA and Reprise, was a fallow period marked by few hits. He would return to prominence in 1970, however, with the Tony Joe White–penned "Rainy Night in Georgia." When follow-up releases failed to take off, he drifted into religious music, his most notable collaboration coming with the Dixie Flyers. He died April 9, 1988, of complications from spinal meningitis.

Berry, Chuck (b. 1926) *singer, guitarist, and songwriter*

Chuck Berry was one of the first artists whose earliest recordings reflect a fully developed rock 'n' roll style. Although he had one foot solidly planted in the rhythm and blues tradition of Muddy Waters, Howlin' Wolf, and other early electric pioneers, he also possessed a clear-cut affinity for the vocal phrasing and melodic structure of country music. More importantly, he was the greatest song poet of the pre-rock era; although he was almost thirty years old before achieving his first hit, his lyrics articulated a teen world of cars, dance hops, and growing sexual awareness, complete with humor and a deft hand at character development.

Born Charles Edward Anderson Berry, on October 18, 1926, in San Jose, California, he relocated to St. Louis with his family as a youth. When he went to Chicago in the mid-1950s in search of a music career, it was Waters who introduced him to record executive Leonard Chess. One of the songs he'd written, "Ida Reed," led to a contract with the Chess label. Renamed "Maybellene," after the cosmetics giant, Berry's recording topped the R&B charts for eleven weeks in 1955 (also reaching number five on the combined pop lists). Along with LITTLE RICHARD and FATS DOMINO, he was one of the first black artists to sell records consistently to white teenagers on the strength of classics like "Roll Over Beethoven," "School Day," "Rock and Roll Music," "Sweet Little Sixteen," and "Johnny B. Goode."

Berry's career was suspended in the early 1960s when he was sentenced to prison for transporting a teenage prostitute across state lines (a violation of the Mann Act). Upon his release in late 1963, he continued to place songs like "Nadine," "No Particular Place to Go," and "You Never Can Tell" high on the charts. When the focus in popular music shifted from the 45-rpm disk to the album in the mid-1960s, he signed with Mercury, releasing a string of concert jams recorded at venues like the Fillmore, San Francisco. Ironically, his biggest pop hit, "My Ding-A-Ling" (which topped the Hot 100 in late 1972), stalled at number 42 on the R&B charts. It would be his last charting single of any kind.

Although Berry's days as a commercial and creative force are well behind him, he continues to perform. He was one of the first artists elected to the Rock and Roll Hall of Fame, and was the subject of a major film documentary, *Hail! Hail! Rock 'n' Roll*, in 1987.

BG The Prince Of Rap *rapper*

BG's brief success abroad is a testament to the talent void in the European RAP scene. The Washington, D.C., native—not to be confused with the New Orleans–based artist known as Baby Gangsta—initially gravitated to the go-go scene that thrived along the Eastern seaboard during the mid-1980s. Introduced to HIP-HOP by an army associate, he began participating in rapping contests after his regiment relocated to Germany.

After catching his act, producer Jam El Mar, part of the famous Jam and Spoon team, helped BG record "Rap to the World," which became a major German club hit. The follow-up, "This Beat Is Hot," did even better, making the German Top 20. Columbia Records jumped on his bandwagon, promoting him as the "most exciting dance/rap act to emerge from Germany since Snap!" His debut album, *The Power of Rhythm* (Columbia, 1992), was something of a commercial and aesthetic disappointment, spurring one reviewer to christen him the "Prince of Wack."

Big Maybelle (1920–1972) *singer*

One of the foremost exponents of the blues shouting style, Big Maybelle has sometimes been called the female counterpart to BIG JOE TURNER. Born Mabel Louise Smith, May 1, 1920, in Jackson, Tennessee, she was recruited by Dave Clark to sing in his Memphis-based band after he discovered her singing in church. When Clark moved into record promotion, she caught on with Christine Chatman's orchestra. She made her first recordings with that organization on Decca in 1944, before doing solo work for King three years later.

After signing with Columbia's OKeh subsidiary in 1952 as Big Maybelle, she enjoyed a string of R&B hits, most notably, "Gabbin' Blues," "Way Back Home," and "My Country Man," as well as making the first recording of "Whole Lotta Shakin' Goin' On," later a smash single for rockabilly artist JERRY LEE LEWIS. Despite a prestigious appearance in *Jazz on a Summer's Day* (1958), a film of that year's Newport Jazz Festival, her work on such notable labels as Savoy, Brunswick, Scepter, and Chess failed to do well. Big Maybelle's switch to Rojac in 1966 brought about a change in direction; label brass there encouraged her to record recent pop hits like the Beatles' "Don't Pass Me By" and ? [Question

Mark] & the Mysterians' "96 Tears," which led to brief chart success. However, ongoing drug problems took their toll, contributing to her death on January 23, 1972.

Big Youth (b. 1949) *reggae deejay*

Big Youth—born Manley Buchanan in Kingston, Jamaica—became the most prominent "toaster" (a disc jockey ad-libbing over prerecorded instrumental tracks) of the early 1970s. His approach, which featured his scatting and street poetry accompanied by previously released recordings edited to submerge the original vocals and enhance the bass and percussion lines, would exert a strong influence on the emerging HIP-HOP genre.

Starting out as a cabdriver, Big Youth became as disc jockey in his early twenties, breaking out with the single, "Ace 90 Skank," in 1972. He often tackled current events in his songs, and, following his conversion to Rastafarianism, veered toward social commentary (e.g., "House of Dreadlocks"). Another overtly political release, "When Revolution Come," produced by Prince Buster, initiated a string of number one Jamaican hits in the mid-1970s.

He turned increasingly to a more traditional mode of singing, recording his own material and touring the U.S., Europe, and elsewhere with a band. Now something of a REGGAE institution, he remains active as a performer to the present day.

Black Radical Mk II *rapper*

Born Felix Joseph, in South London, England, he fell under the spell of progressive REGGAE acts such as BOB MARLEY, Steel Pulse, and Peter Tosh as a youth. However, the political rap of Boogie Down Productions, PUBLIC ENEMY, and others inspired him to try a recording career. Although his technical facility for composing verse remained somewhat awkward in early releases like the *This Is War* EP and his debut LP, *The Undiluted Truth* (Mango/Island, 1991), Joseph—a university graduate who'd majored in economics—revealed a strong

commitment to social causes like women's rights. By the mid-1990s, his recording career took a back seat to film projects, most notably the all-black production *Welcome to the Terrordome*.

Blackwell, Robert A. "Bumps" (1918–1985) *producer*

One of the leading arranger/producers of the rock 'n' roll era, Robert A. Blackwell played a significant role in furthering the careers of many seminal R&B artists. Born May 23, 1918, of mixed French, African-American, and Indian descent, he started out as a bandleader in his hometown of Seattle, Washington. In 1949, he relocated to Los Angeles to study classical composition at U.C.L.A. He tried his hand at writing a series of stage revues, called *Blackwell Portraits,* that failed to catch on with the public.

By the early 1950s, Blackwell had found a new line of work, arranging and producing gospel and R&B records for Guitar Slim, Lloyd Price, and others. He soon took charge of the A&R department at Specialty Records, where he bought LITTLE RICHARD's contract from Peacock and spurred the singer to record a cleaned-up version of "Tutti Frutti" in a New Orleans studio in 1955. He helped write some of Little Richard's follow-up hits such as "Reddy Teddy," "Rip It Up," and "Long Tall Sally," as well as handling production and becoming his personal manager. He also played a role in launching the pop music careers of former gospel stars SAM COOKE and Wynona Carr.

He left Specialty in the late 1950s to help establish Keen Records; while there he worked closely with Cooke and Johnny "Guitar" Watson. The hits proved somewhat elusive beyond this point, but as late as 1981 he coproduced the title track of Bob Dylan's *Shot of Love* (Columbia) LP. He died of pneumonia on March 9, 1985.

Bland, Bobby "Blue" (b. 1930) *singer*

Born January 27, 1930, in Rosemark, Tennessee, Bland sang with the Memphis-based gospel group the Miniatures in the late 1940s. He was a member of the Beale Streeters, in addition to JOHNNY ACE, Earl Forest, Roscoe Gordon, B. B. KING, and Willie Nix, in 1949, and was a driver/valet for King and a part of the Johnny Ace Revue in the early 1950s.

Bland first recorded as a solo artist for Modern in 1952, before establishing himself as a consistent hit-maker with Duke Records. He would record 45 hits with the label through 1972, including the R&B chart-toppers "Farther Up the Road," "I Pity the Fool," and "That's the Way Love Is." He would maintain his success with ABC/Dunhill, and then rejuvenate his career by teaming with King on a succession of recordings beginning in 1977.

Blenders, The

The Blenders arose out of the fact that second tenor Ollie Jones was not a good vocal fit with the legendary RAVENS. When the Ravens found a replacement, Maithe Marshall, who better met their needs for a soaring first tenor, Jones—after touring for almost a year with the 4 Notes—decided to start his own group. Relying heavily on the advice of the Ravens' Jimmy Ricks, Jones opted for a similar bass-lead sound. In short order, he recruited bass singer James DeLoach, baritone Tommy Adams, first tenor Abel DeCosta, and arranger/pianist Herman Flintall.

Ricks also helped the Blenders obtain bookings (the Ravens were unable to take on all offers that came their way), and he brought them to the attention of National Records owner, Al Green. They recorded four songs with the label around September 1949, two of which—"I Can Dream, Can't I" and "Come Back Baby Blues"—were released the following month. They met National A&R man Lee Magrid, and he became their manager and arranged a record deal for them with Decca subsidiary, Coral (although subsequent releases would be issued on the parent label) in March 1950.

In the meantime, the Blenders added guitarist/tenor Ernie Brown, while arranger/pianist Teddy Brannon took Flintall's place within the group. They recorded two years for Decca, without any notable commercial success. New manager Rita

Don then took them to independent producer Joe Davis, who recorded at least six sides on March 27, 1953 (followed by two more on April 17). Three songs from the first session—"I Don't Miss You Anymore," "That's the Way You Want It Baby," and "You'll Never Be Mine Again"—would be eventually issued by MGM. In June 1953, Davis started his own record company, Jay-Dee, releasing two of the sides recorded on March 27—"You'll Never Be Mine Again" and "Don't Play Around with Love"—in August of that year.

With the group's recordings failing to catch on with the public, and bookings becoming increasing harder to find, personnel—with the exception of mainstays Jones and DeCosta—came and went. When they decided to terminate the group in early 1954, Jones concentrated on songwriting, demos, and background singing. He began working with record producer Jessie Stone, who was interested in utilizing standardized vocal arrangements behind featured soloists. Stone enlisted Jones and DeCosta, now known as the Cues, with a host of Atlantic stars, including RUTH BROWN (billed as the Rhythmakers), BIG JOE TURNER (the Blues Kings), Charlie White (the Playboys), LAVERN BAKER (the Gliders), and Ivory Joe Hunter (the Ivorytones). They also recorded as the 4 Students on the Groove label.

Davis continued to release the Blenders' old masters with his own Davis label (as the "Millionaires") in 1955 and with Kelway, which featured the disc jockeys–only release, "Don't Fuck Around with Love," a raunchy version of Jay-Dee 780 (re-issued in Davis in 1973 as a one-sided record). By the 1960s, all former members of the group had left the music business, leaving only a legacy of fine music that, with a little luck, might well have achieved best-selling status.

Blige, Mary J. (b. 1971) singer

At the onset of her career, Mary J. Blige was alternately called the new CHAKA KHAN or new ARETHA FRANKLIN, due to the fresh approach and intensity she brought to the R&B genre. Her record company,

Mary J. Blige performing (Rebecca Cook/Reuters/Landov)

MCA, played up Blige's bad girl image, which was accentuated by her bleached blonde hair, combat boots, and street tough posturing. Born January 11, 1971, in Savannah, Georgia, Blige moved with her mother and older sister a few years later to the Schlobohm housing projects of Yonkers, New York.

A karaoke recording of ANITA BAKER's "Caught Up in the Rapture," made at a White Plains, New York, shopping mall after Blige had dropped out of high school, was passed on to UPTOWN RECORDS CEO, Andre Harrell, by her stepfather. The label signed her to a contract; the debut LP, *What's the 411?* (MCA, 1992), would carve out a new hybrid category: HIP-HOP soul. Her follow-up albums—*My Life* (MCA, 1994), *Share My World* (MCA, 1997),

Mary (MCA, 1999), and *No More Drama* (MCA, 2001)—have revealed a rapidly maturing artist, unafraid to address adult themes in a direct, inherently honest way. Her earlier street tough attitude has been replaced by sleek, sophisticated persona, projected by a husky, powerful voice that has few equals in the pop music scene.

Bloods and Crips

A one-off RAP project spurred by the 1991 Rodney King beating at the hands of Los Angeles police and ensuing riots in black areas, the Bloods and the Crips—rival street gangs—joined together to record their take on these events, each gang taking one side of an LP entitled *Bangin' on Wax* (Dangerous, 1993). In retrospect, the recording is more important for its social message than any intrinsic musical value.

Bloom, Bobby (d. 1974) *singer*

Bobby Bloom is best remembered for the scintillating "Montego Bay," which blended calypso, pop-rock, and bubblegum styles into a seamless whole, reaching the Top Ten in both Great Britain and the United States in 1970. Prior to his breakout solo hit, the New York–based artist had worked in the mid-1960s as a songwriter/producer for the Buddah/Kama Sutra company. His tentative solo forays at the time, including "Love Don't Let Me Down" and "Count on Me," failed to click. He went on to team with composer/producer Jeff Barry, contributing material to the likes of the Monkees. With the release of *The Bobby Bloom Album* (1970) and a second successful single, "Heavy Makes You Happy," he seemed poised to become a major star when he was killed in an accidental shooting on February 28, 1974.

Blossoms, The (Darlene Love & the Blossoms)

The Blossoms are one of the great unknown groups in pop music history. They performed yeoman's duties for "wall-of-sound" producer Phil Spector, but did not receive label credit for their best efforts.

The group formed in 1954 while members Fanita James, Gloria Jones, and twins Annette and Nannette Williams were still enrolled in Fremont High School, Los Angeles. During their first year together, they recorded for Flair Records without making any commercial impact. By the early 1960s, they had been teamed with Darlene Wright (aka Darlene Love) by Spector for studio sessions with his Philles label. For reasons which are still not entirely clear, Spector chose to use the Blossoms, with Love on lead vocals, to record two legendary singles that would be credited on the label to the Crystals, "He's a Rebel" and "He's Sure the Boy I Love." In addition, James and Love would be teamed with Bobby Sheen to record as Bob B. Soxx & the Blues Jeans.

The group's work with Spector enabled them to land regular appearances, along with Love, on the hit television show, *Shindig*, beginning in 1965. When Spector temporarily retired from the record business in 1966, the Blossoms were free to sign with another label, and opted to join the Reprise roster of artists the following year. They would have one minor 1967 hit, "Good, Good Lovin' " before fading into obscurity. They were able to work the oldies revival circuit to a small degree, while Love became a prominent session singer as well as acting in Hollywood feature films like *Lethal Weapon* (1987).

Blow, Kurtis (b. 1959) *rapper*

Born Kurt Walker in New York City, Blow was one of HIP-HOP's seminal pioneers. While a student at Harlem's City College of New York, he began rapping at the "Force" parties organized by future DEF JAM RECORDS founder Russell "Rush" Simmons, frequently working with the likes of GRANDMASTER FLASH and Joey "Run" Simmons (Rush's younger brother, soon to form RUN-D.M.C.). The Simmons family enlisted *Billboard* writers Robert "Rocky" Ford and J. B. Moore to compose and subsidize Blow's debut single, "Christmas Rappin'." Released

in December 1979 by Mercury, it was the first RAP track to be distributed by a major label.

Signed to a long-term contract with Mercury, Blow recorded the hard-biting social commentary, "The Breaks," which sold more than 500,000 copies in late 1980. Unfortunately, his albums—including *Kurtis Blow* (Mercury, 1980) and *Ego Trip* (Mercury, 1984), were the only two to make the pop charts—were uneven affairs at best. Faced with competition from a host of up-and-coming young rappers by the mid-1980s, Blow soon disappeared off the public's radar screen. He managed to ride the crest of the 1990s nostalgia craze, promoting and performing at revival concerts showcasing the genre's founding fathers.

bluebeat   See REGGAE.

Bobbettes, The

The Bobbettes were something of a throwback to the Tin Pan Alley heyday that included close harmony singing groups such as the Andrews Sisters and Chordettes. Despite a shot of jazz and rhythm and blues influences, these GIRL GROUPS were not that far removed in style from the barbershop quartets that dominated pop music in the early decades of the twentieth century.

The Bobbettes—consisting of Heather Dixon, Jannie and Emma Pought, Helen Gathers, and Laura Webb, all of whom were born in New York City between 1943 and 1945—began singing together as a group for parties in the mid-1950s while attending P.S. 109. A friend in the neighborhood, James Dailey, became their manager, hooking them up with Atlantic Records in early 1957. Their debut single, "Mr. Lee," written by the group as a tongue-in-cheek tribute to their fifth-grade teacher and featuring the Reggie Obrecht Orchestra, quickly rose to the top of the R&B charts. Furthermore, the song become something of a phenomenon, inspiring such fare as saxophonist Lee Allen's wailing instrumental, "Walkin' With Mr. Lee." Nevertheless, the Bobbettes proved unable to prolong their early commercial momentum, and were dropped from the Atlantic roster after follow-up releases all failed to generate any sales activity of note.

The Bobbettes went on to place several more singles into the lower reaches of the pop charts. These included a sequel to their first hit, "I Shot Mr. Lee," "Have Mercy Baby," "Dance With Me George," and "I Don't Like It Like That," an answer song responding to a New Orleans Sound classic, "I Like It Like That," by Chris Kenner. By the time the group members reached adulthood, their show business careers were effectively over. However, "Mr. Lee" remains popular an oldies radio stations, and has been updated by a number of rock acts over the years.

Bonds, Gary U. S. (b. 1939) *singer*

Gary U. S. Bonds created some of the best rave-up rock 'n' roll during the Brill Building Era, a period best known for its smoothed-out, or processed, interpretations of the seminal rockabilly and R&B of ELVIS PRESLEY, JERRY LEE LEWIS, LITTLE RICHARD, and other 1950s originators. The appeal of these recordings lies in the singer's raucous shouting, projected over a simulated party atmosphere, consisting of a murky blend of honking sax, pounding rhythms, and (seemingly) random background of youthful whooping and chattering.

He was born Gary Anderson, on June 6, 1939, in Jacksonville, Florida. His family relocated to Norfolk, Virginia, where he practiced DOO-WOP on street corners with a group known as the Turks. In 1960, producer Frank Guida, the new owner of the failing Norfolk Recording Studios, recruited Anderson (as a last-minute substitute for another performer allegedly possessing a "bad attitude") to do the lead vocal on a song he'd cowritten with a shoe salesman named Joe Royster. Anderson changed the country feel of the song to R&B, adding a chorus and thumping backbeat, and "New Orleans" became a Top Ten smash for the Legrand label. When the single first hit the streets, Anderson was perplexed to find it credited to

Gary U. S. Bonds in the early 1960s when he was a consistent hit-maker (Frank Driggs Collection)

"U. S. Bonds." It appears that Guida got the idea from the posters in the delicatessen located next door to the studio. When Anderson insisted on the addition of his first name for future releases, fans were initially confused, thinking U. S. Bonds referred to a group.

After the second Bonds release failed to click, Guida went back to the formula established in "New Orleans." He hooked Bonds up with another Legrand act, the Church Street Five, who were having trouble getting an instrumental piece, "A Night with Daddy G," to jell. A group member, Gene "Daddy G" Barge, encouraged Bonds to write lyrics on the spot. In a matter of minutes, the verses were ready and the musicians started working out an arrangement. Sources differ as how the resulting song, the number one smash, "Quarter to Three," ended up on tape. Some rock historians state that it was recorded by accident, although Bonds would go to claim that he knowingly turned on the recorder. One critic, Dave Marsh, posits that Guida added five overdubs of party sound effects in his quest for just the right ambience. A follow-up album, *Dance 'til Quarter to Three* (Legrand, 1961), did surprisingly well for a so-called teen release, reaching number six and remaining on the charts for 28 weeks.

The Bonds-Guida team continued to mine a similar vein with success through 1962, resulting in "School Is Out," "School Is In," "Dear Lady Twist," "Twist, Twist Senora," "Seven Day Weekend," and the aptly named "Copy Cat." He then receded back into the club and oldies circuits (one of his songs, "Friend Don't Take Her," would be a country hit for Johnny Paycheck in 1972) until Bruce Springsteen, long an admirer of the classic Bonds recordings, offered to produce his next LP, *Dedication* (EMI America, 1981), along with bandmate Steve Van Zandt. The album would yield a couple of hit singles, "This Little Girl" and the reworked Cajun classic, "Jole Blon."

Another Springsteen-Van Zandt production, *On the Line* (EMI America, 1982), including the single, "Out of Work," also achieved commercial success. Bonds then moved on to an independent label, Phoenix, producing his own LP, *Standing in the Line of Fire.* However, by then he had once again fallen out of favor with the public in the face of the new romantics and techno-pop acts then benefiting from heavy MTV rotation.

Booker T. & the MGs

Although best known for a series of tight, funky instrumental hits released in the 1960s, Booker T. & the MGs exerted a far greater influence as the house band for all STAX/Volt recording artists. In addition, two members, keyboardist Booker T. Jones and guitarist Steve Cropper, handled key songwriting, arranging, and production duties for the label. Cropper wrote such hits as OTIS REDDING's "Dock of

the Bay," WILSON PICKETT's "In the Midnight Hour," and ARETHA FRANKLIN's "See Saw."

The band's core members, which in addition to Jones and Cropper included drummer-guitarist Al Jackson, Jr., and bassist Donald "Duck" Dunn, coalesced around the Stax studios in Memphis as backup musicians during the early 1960s. One of the informal jam sessions led to a decision to record "Green Onions," jointly composed by Booker, Cropper, Jackson, and bassist Lewis Steinberg. The single reached number one on the R&B charts, and then crossed over to become a number three pop hit. Booker T. & the MGs continued to produce best-selling singles, including the Top 40 hits "Hip Hug-Her," "Groovin'," "Soul-Limbo," "Hang 'Em High," "Time Is Tight," and "Mrs. Robinson." The group's LPs were also commercially successful. Eleven of them, including *Green Onions* (Stax, 1962), *Hip Hug-Her* (Stax, 1967), *Back To Back* (Stax, 1967), *Uptight* (Stax, 1969), *The Booker T. Set* (Stax, 1969), and *Melting Pot* (Stax, 1971), made the pop album charts.

The first phase of Booker T. & the MGs ended with Jones's decision to relocate to Los Angeles in 1970 following a dispute with Stax. He recorded

Booker T. & the MGs strike a pose in 1964. (Frank Driggs Collection)

albums in the 1970s with his wife, Priscilla Coolidge, and did production work for Rita Coolidge, Earl Klugh, Willie Nelson, and BILL WITHERS. In the meantime, Cropper became in-house producer at TMI Studios. The band reorganized as the MGs in 1973 around Jackson and Dunn; new members included Bobby Manuel and Carson Whitsett. When Stax went out of business in 1975, plans were made to reconstitute the original quartet. Eight days later, however, Jackson was killed in a shooting incident. The others decided to go ahead with the reunion, bringing in drummer Willie Hall, a Stax alumnus who'd worked with the Bar-kays and ISAAC HAYES. Over the years, the band has continued in a low-key mode, combining recording and performing as a group with separate activities by individual members.

Boyz II Men

Boyz II Men have proven that a mainstream pop group emphasizing ballads is capable of outselling more trendy alternative rock and RAP competitors. Their sound—a blend of DOO-WOP, the 1960s MOTOWN singing groups (particularly THE TEMPTATIONS), and 1970s Philly soul, accented by contemporary vocal nuances—appears unlikely ever to seem dated.

Formed in 1988 at Philadelphia's High School for the Creative and Performing Arts, the quartet, comprised of Michael McCary, Nathan Morris, Wanya Morris, and Shawn Stockman, was championed during their formative years by NEW EDITION's Michael Bivins. Their debut LP, *Cooleyhighharmony* (Motown, 1991), driven by three Top 20 singles, ultimately sold more than nine million copies. A single from the film *Boomerang*, "End of the Road" (Motown, 1992), had—up to that time—the most successful chart run ever during the rock era, remaining number one on the *Billboard* Hot 100 for 13 weeks. The group's other albums—*Christmas Interpretations* (Motown, 1993); *II* (Motown, 1994), which sold over 13 million copies; *Remix Collection* (Motown, 1995); *Evolution* (Motown, 1997); and

Nathan Michael Shawn Wanya (Universal; 2000)—maintained the group's hot streak, despite competition from countless imitators, most notably 'N Sync and the Backstreet Boys.

Assisted by state-of-the-art video clips and a romantic, non-threatening image, Boyz II Men have also gone on to become one of the top singles groups of all time. According to Joel Whitburn's *The Billboard Book of Top 40 Hits*, they have recorded three of the six most successful songs since 1955: "One Sweet Day," with MARIAH CAREY, remaining number one for 16 weeks in 1995; "I'll Make Love to You," which topped the charts for 14 weeks; and "End of the Road." Other hits have included "It's So Hard to Say Goodbye to Yesterday," "On Bended Knee," "4 Seasons of Loneliness," and "A Song for Mama."

Bradley, Jan (b. 1943) *singer*

Born Addie Bradley on July 6, 1943, in Byhalia, Mississippi, she was discovered in 1961 by Don Talty, who was managing guitarist Phil Upchurch at the time. He got her a recording contract with Chess Records, and hired THE IMPRESSIONS' Curtis Mayfield to supply song material. Mayfield's first contribution, "We Girls," was a local Chicago hit in 1962. He then came up with "Mama Didn't Lie," a mid-tempo dance number that attracted radio play across all major genres of the day, including pop, R&B, and country. Bradley's follow-up releases failed to click, and she left the entertainment business in the late 1960s to become a social worker. "Mama Didn't Lie," however, remains a staple on oldies radio playlists.

Brenston, Jackie (1930–1979) *singer and saxophonist*

Born August 15, 1930, in Clarksdale, Mississippi, Brenston received label credit (for contractual reasons) as leader of the Delta Cats for the chart-topping (five weeks in 1951) rhythm and blues recording, "Rocket 88," which many experts consider to be the first rock 'n' roll hit. Brenston was actually vocalist/

saxophonist for IKE TURNER's Delta Rhythm Kings, which cut the track for Sam Phillips's Memphis Recording Service. The song—a paean to the automobile—was based on the jump blues styles then popular on the West Coast. However, it cut new ground with Turner's overamplified, fuzztone-styled guitar figure and wild saxophone solo (by Raymond Hill) over a standard boogie-woogie groove. The highly influential guitar sound was reputedly achieved when Phillips, seeking a temporary sound fix, jammed paper in a speaker cone damaged when Turner's amplifier fell off the top of the car en route to a recording session.

Brothers Johnson

The Los Angeles–based duo, made up of real-life brothers George (b. May 17, 1953) and Louis (April 13, 1955) Johnson, were, along with EARTH, WIND & FIRE and the Commodores, exponents of the 1970s soft funk school. They started out while in grade school as the Johnson Three + 1, along with brother Tommy and cousin Alex Weir. The Brothers Johnson played in Billy Preston's band until going out on their own in 1975. They were consistent hit-makers in both the R&B and pop fields for the A&M label from 1976 through the 1980s; their biggest successes—"I'll Be Good to You," "Strawberry Letter #23," and "Stomp"—not only topped the R&B charts, but made the pop Top Ten.

Brown, Bobby (b. 1969) *singer*

By the late 1980s, Bobby Brown was widely hailed as the king of New Jack Swing. Although not a particularly gifted singer or charismatic personality, he appears blessed with sound commercial instincts and the good fortune to have worked with some of the best studio producers in the business.

Born Robert Beresford Brown, February 5, 1969, in Boston, he first made an impact as part of teen idol sensations, NEW EDITION. He made a rather tentative start as a solo artist with *King of Stage* (MCA, 1986), produced by Larry Blackmon and

John Luongo. However, his next LP, *Don't Be Cruel* (MCA, 1988), with Teddy Riley, L. A. Reid, and Babyface manning the boards, was a major smash, including the number one crossover hit, "My Prerogative." Film roles (e.g., *Ghostbusters II*), video releases, a storybook marriage to singing superstar WHITNEY HOUSTON, and more best-selling recordings, including *Dance . . . Ya Know It!* (MCA, 1989) and *Bobby* (MCA, 1992), followed, all of it marred by later allegations of drug abuse and public marital discord.

Brown, Charles (b. 1922) *singer and pianist*

The Texas City, Texas, native taught high school before relocating to Los Angeles in 1943. He was a founding member of Johnny Moore's Three Blazers in 1944 before moving on to form his own band in 1948. He placed a dozen singles on the R&B charts from 1949 to 1952, most notably "Trouble Blues" (number one for 15 weeks in 1949) and "Black Night" (number one for 14 weeks in 1951). He is best remembered, however, for the seasonal classic "Please Come Home for Christmas," a minor crossover hit when first released in 1960. Married to R&B singer Mabel Scott from 1949 to 1951, Brown remained active as a performer well into the 1980s.

Brown, Chuck, and the Soul Searchers

Organized in the mold of an old-school R&B revue, Chuck Brown and the Soul Searchers recorded spirited dance music with a loose, spontaneous live feel as opposed to the processed, studio confections typifying the DISCO output dominating the charts during their heyday. Based in Washington, D.C., Brown's support band consisted of John Buchanan, trombone/vocals; Skip Fennell, keyboards; Leroy Fleming, saxophone/ flute/timbales; Gregory "Bright Moments" Gerran, congas/percussion; Chris Johnson, organ; Donald Tillery, trumpet/vocals; Ricardo "Tricky Sugar" Wellman, drums; Jerry "Wildman" Wilder, bass; and Le Ron Young, guitar.

Brown and his cohorts burst onto the R&B scene in a big way with the rousing 1979 chart-topping single, "Bustin' Loose, Part 1." Follow-up releases failed to do as well, and the group jumped to the Future label, issuing four critically acclaimed EPs and a final R&B hit in 1984, "We Need Some Money (Bout Money)." They continued performing and making records sporadically, most notably, *This is a Journey into Time* (1993), well into the 1990s.

Brown, Clarence "Gatemouth" (1924–2005)
singer, guitarist, and fiddler

Clarence Brown was a fine singer and extraordinary instrumentalist, comfortable interpreting a wide range of genres, including the blues, cajun, country, big band, and jazz fusion. Born April 18, 1924, in Vinton, Louisiana, he was raised in Orange, Texas (near Beaumont), where his father taught him to play the guitar and fiddle. He was recruited to play drums with a traveling show prior to serving in the military.

Once discharged he became a well-known guitarist in the San Antonio area, spurring music entrepreneur DON ROBEY to offer him a job at his Houston nightclub. Robey was sufficiently impressed with the reception Brown received there to arrange for a recording session with the Los Angeles–based ALADDIN label on August 21, 1947. When Robey established Peacock Records in 1948, he had Brown regularly do sessions until 1961; many are now regarded as Texas blues guitar classics.

During the 1960s, Brown began negotiating a wider range of genres, recording country-inflected material for Chess (finally issued as an LP, *The Nashville Session 1965*, in 1989) as well as jazz and rock hybrids. While amassing an impressive studio legacy, he recorded for the French-based Black and Blue and Barclay labels, as well as Red Lightnin', MCA, Rounder, Blues Boy, and Alligator. Countless other labels, including Ace and Evidence, have reissued his vintage early work. Brown released his last album, *Timeless*, in 2004.

Brown, Foxy (b. 1979) *rapper*

Born Inga Marchand in Brooklyn, New York, she won a talent show in 1994 based on her freestyling abilities. As a result, the Trackmasters asked her to guest on the track, "I Shot Ya," which they were producing for L. L. COOL J's *Mr. Smith* album. When the song became a hit in 1995, she was quickly asked to record with artists like Total, Toni Braxton, and Case, in addition to being recruited by NAS to join the Firm posse.

Caught up in a major-label bidding war at the outset of 1996, Brown signed with DEF JAM RECORDS in March. Her in-your-face delivery on such topics as fashion, sex, and the Mafia boosted her debut LP, *Ill Na Na* (Def Jam, 1996), to number seven in the *Billboard* Top 200. Her follow-up albums, the chart-topping *Chyna Doll* (Def Jam, 1999) and *Broken Silence* (Uptown/Universal, 2001), offered comparable fare. She now finds herself at something of a career impasse; despite her vibrant personality and attempts to interject a degree of sensitivity and introspection into her recordings, there is a heightened imperative to grow beyond the crass materialism and explicit sexuality which have become a Foxy Brown trademark.

Brown, James (b. 1928) *"The Godfather of Soul"*

James Brown—often billed as "The Godfather of Soul" and "The Hardest Working Man in Show Business"—has been the most successful R&B recording artist from the institution of the *Harlem Hit Parade* on October 24, 1942 up to the present day. He also played a major role in the evolution of both the soul and FUNK genres. Furthermore, he served as an important role model during the civil rights movement in his positive affirmation of black pride and the rich cultural legacy of African Americans.

Born May 3, 1928, in Macon, Georgia, Brown was raised in nearby Augusta. After forming his own vocal group, the Famous Flames, he cut a demo of the self-composed "Please, Please, Please" in November 1955 at radio station WIBB, Macon, which led to a recording contract with the King/Federal company. The hits continued unabated into the 1990s, although he rarely made the pop charts after the mid-1970s. While his biggest pop hit was "I Got You (I Feel Good)" (which reached number three in late 1965), he topped the R&B charts with "Try Me," "Papa's Got a Brand New Bag (Part I)," "It's a Man's Man's Man's World," "Cold Sweat," "I Got the Feelin'," "Say It Loud—I'm Black and I'm Proud (Part 1)," "Give It Up or Turnit A Loose," "Mother Popcorn," "Super Bad (Part 1 & Part 2)," "Hot Pants (Part 1)," "Make It Funky (Part 1)," "Talking Loud and Saying Nothing (Part I)," "Get on the Good Foot (Part 1)," "The

Payback (Part I)," "My Thang," and "Papa Don't Take No Mess (Part I)."

Brown's album releases also sold well, particularly his live sets, which revealed strong gospel, blues, and jazz elements alongside his unerring pop sense. Having achieved icon status by the 1970s, he made cameo appearances in the popular films, *The Blues Brothers* and *Rocky IV,* and was one of the first artists voted into the Rock and Roll Hall of Fame. Although troubled by legal problems related to domestic violence and substance abuse in the 1980s, Brown has remained a major concert attraction well into the twenty-first century.

James Brown strikes a well-known concert pose in 1964. (Frank Driggs Collection)

Brown, Peter (b. 1953) *singer and producer*
Vocalist/keyboardist/producer Peter Brown is closely identified with the DISCO era. His mastery of studio technology enabled him to function as a one-man band in the manufacture of slick, uptempo dance material.

Born on July 11, 1953, in Blue Island, Illinois, Brown attended the Art Institute of Chicago in the mid-1970s. He recorded a series of dance hits, most notably, "Do You Wanna Get Funky with Me," "Dance with Me," "You Should Do It," and "Crank It Up (Funk Town), Pt. 1," which crossed over to the pop charts at the height of the disco craze. When dance-oriented music retreated to the underground in the 1980s, Brown continued to release recordings, albeit less commercially successful, for RCA and Columbia.

Brown, Roy (1925–1981) *singer and pianist*
Born September 10, 1925, in New Orleans, he helped pioneer the Crescent City's R&B sound. He formed a gospel group, the Rookie Four, as a twelve-year-old. After relocating to Los Angeles to box professionally in 1942, he revived his singing career several years later. Brown would place 15 singles on the R&B charts for DeLuxe between 1948 and 1951, including his classic composition, "Good Rockin' Tonight" (later covered by ELVIS PRESLEY on the Sun

label), and the chart-toppers, "'Long About Midnight" and "Hard Luck Blues." He would release a couple more hits in 1957 for Imperial, a cover of Buddy Knox's "Party Doll" and "Let the Four Winds Blow," redone with even greater success by Fats Domino in 1961. He was able to take advantage of the blues revival before passing away May 25, 1981, in Los Angeles.

Brown, Ruth (b. 1928) *singer*

Along with DINAH WASHINGTON, Ruth Brown was the leading black female pop singer of the 1950s. The best-selling Atlantic artist of the decade, she helped the label gain a foothold as one of the most successful independents of the rock era.

Born Ruth Weston on January 30, 1928, in Portsmouth, Virginia, she sang in her father's church choir as a youth. Turning professional in 1946, she worked for a short time with LUCKY MILLINDER's band. Moving to Washington, D.C., she established a residency at Blanche Calloway's Crystal Cavern nightclub. Calloway recommended Brown to Atlantic, which signed her in 1948. Her debut single, "So Long"—not recorded for almost one year due to an automobile accident—became an R&B smash, and was followed in quick succession by "Teardrops from My Eyes," "5-10-15 Hours," "(Mama) He Treats Your Daughter Mean," the LEIBER AND STOLLER-penned "Lucky Lips," and the Bobby Darin composition, "This Little Girl's Gone Rockin'."

Although some of Brown's later singles became crossover pop hits, she had trouble maintaining her commercial momentum during the rock 'n' roll era. Following a dry spell, she switched to the Phillips label in 1962. When no immediate hits ensued, she

Ruth Brown live at the Brooklyn Paramount Theatre in 1958 (Frank Driggs Collection)

opted to retire from show business. She returned to the public eye in the 1970s, issuing blues-oriented albums and embarking on an acting career which spanned television sitcoms, film (most notably, *Hairspray* in 1988), and theater. Brown garnered a Tony for her performance in the Broadway musical, *Black and Blue* (she was also featured on the original cast album, released on DRG in 1989), and was inducted into the Rock and Roll Hall of Fame in 1993. She won a protracted battle to recover royalties earned from her early Atlantic recordings; she was eventually awarded $2,000,000, which she used as seed money to establish the Rhythm and Blues Foundation, a nonprofit organization geared to assisting older artists and helping perpetuate their artistic legacy.

Browne, Tom (b. 1959) *trumpeter and bandleader*

Trumpeter Tom Browne was a precursor of the SMOOTH JAZZ movement that peaked in the 1990s. His laid-back blend of pop, FUNK, and jazz became a fixture on the R&B singles and album charts in the early 1980s.

A native of Queens, New York, Browne started out performing classical music at New York City's High School of Music and Art. He worked professionally with Weldon Ervine in 1975, before hooking up with Sonny Fortune and the Fatback Band in 1976. Opting to go solo, he made a big splash in 1980 with the R&B chart-topper "Funkin' for Jamaica (N.Y.)," followed by hits like "Thighs High (Grip Your Hips and Move)," "Fungi Mama (Bebopafunkadiscolypso)," and "Rockin' Radio." His albums continue to sell well on the jazz and pop charts to the present day.

Bryson, (Robert) Peabo (b. 1951) *singer and record producer*

One of the most respected black contemporary song stylists to come along in recent decades, Robert Peabo Bryson was born April 13, 1951, in Greenville, South Carolina. He first surfaced with Al Freeman & the Upsetters in 1965, before joining Moses Dillard & the Tex-Town Display from 1968 to 1973. Bryson's early solo work for Bang in 1970 failed to find an audience, but his stint as lead vocalist for Michael Zager's Moon Band was marked by a string of R&B hits, most notably "Reaching for the Sky" and "I'm So into You." From 1979, he split his time between solo recordings and duets with a succession of smooth female vocalists such as Natalie Cole, Melissa Manchester, Roberta Flack, and Regina Belle. Although many of his recordings have failed to become pop hits, his polished delivery generates crossover appeal in a variety of genres, including adult contemporary and film soundtracks.

See also ZAGER, MICHAEL & THE MOON BAND (FEATURING PEABO BRYSON).

Burke, Solomon (b. 1936) *singer*

Solomon Burke was hardly a household name to mainstream pop fans; he had only five Top 40 records, the most successful being the R&B chart-topper, "Got To Get You Off My Mind," which reached number 22 on the Hot 100. However, he was a major architect of 1960s soul, infusing post–World War II R&B with the gospel roots honed during his days as the "Wonder Boy Preacher."

From 1945 until 1955, Burke headed "Solomon's Temple," founded by his grandmother, located in his native Philadelphia. He first recorded on the Apollo label in 1954, but went on to mortuary school in the late 1950s. He returned to the music business in 1960, signing with Atlantic. He remained a fixture on the R&B charts throughout the decade, recording such Top Ten hits as "Just Out of Reach (Of My Two Open Arms)," "Cry to Me," "If You Need Me," "You're Good for Me," and "Tonight's the Night." Even his lesser releases left their mark; the Rolling Stones redid his "Everybody Needs Somebody to Love" (which only reached number 58 on the combined pop and

Atlantic Records publicity shot of Solomon Burke in the early 1960s (Frank Driggs Collection)

R&B charts in mid-1964) on their third LP, *The Rolling Stones Now!*

While his charting singles had slowed to a trickle in the 1970s, he has continued performing as an elder statesman of soul into the twenty-first century. The December 4, 2004, issue of *Rolling Stone* magazine featured him in a sidebar of its survey of the 500 greatest songs of the rock era.

Butler, Billy (b. 1945) *singer*

Billy Butler's primary claim to fame is a result of happenstance relating to birth. He was the youngest brother of one of the leading exponents of the Chicago soul tradition, JERRY BUTLER. Nevertheless,

he had a solid, if lackluster, career of his own as a singer, songwriter, and guitarist.

Born June 7, 1945, in Chicago, Butler began performing professionally with his backup group, the Enchanters, while still a student at Wells High School. He began recording for the Columbia subsidiary, OKeh, in 1963, under the guiding hand of producer Curtis Mayfield. His group, which changed its name to The Chanters in 1964, consisted of tenor Earl Batts and baritone Jesse Tillman. They released a couple of hit singles, "I Can't Work No Longer" and "Right Track."

When OKeh lost interest in the group, they disbanded. Butler would revive his fortunes by forming Infinity in 1969. With his new unit, which included Batts, Phyllis Knox, and Larry Wade, he placed several singles on the lower reaches of the R&B charts between 1969 and 1973 on the Fountain, Memphis, and Pride labels. Butler would go solo in 1974, but failed to achieve further commercial success as a recording artist.

Butler, Jerry (b. 1939) *singer*

Jerry Butler's suave soul style, together with his desire to be a chef and ice sculptor while taking restaurant management courses in trade school as a youth, earned him the nickname, "The Iceman." Although only moderately successful within the pop field, chart historian Joel Whitburn rated him one of the fifteen most popular rhythm and blues recording artists during the 1942–88 period.

Born in Sunflower, Mississippi, on December 8, 1939, Butler moved to Chicago with his family as an infant. After graduating from high school in June 1957, he met Curtis Mayfield and Sam Gooden at the Traveling Souls Spiritualistic Church, and they performed in a series of vocal groups, most notably The Northern Jubilee Gospel Singers and the Roosters. The latter group, which also included the brothers Arthur and Richard Brooks, recruited Eddie Thomas as manager later in the year. Thomas changed their name to the IMPRESSIONS, and a personal appearance shortly thereafter at a local fashion show led to a recording contract with VEE-JAY's Falcon subsidiary (renamed Abner in June 1958, after Vee-Jay general manager Ewart Abner, when it was found that a Falcon label already existed in Texas).

Butler remained with the group long enough to pen the classic, "For Your Precious Love," before embarking on a solo career. Although Mayfield took over lead vocals for the Impressions, he also supplied many hit songs to Butler during the 1960–66 period. Their joint composition, "He Will Break Your Heart," would remain Butler's biggest success, spending seven weeks at the top of the R&B charts. During this productive run, Butler would also find

Jerry Butler appears lost in thought waiting in the wings before performing in the late 1950s. (Frank Driggs Collection)

success with outside material such as Felice and Boudleaux Bryant's "Let It Be Me," recorded as a duet with BETTY EVERETT, originally made popular by the Everly Brothers.

Although Butler continued to produce hits following a switch to Mercury Records in mid-1966, his releases veered ever closer to mainstream pop. His work with the Philadelphia production team of Kenny Gamble and Leon Huff resulted in two albums, *The Ice Man Cometh* (Mercury, 1969) and *Ice on Ice* (Mercury, 1969), and best-selling singles such as "Hey Western Union Man," "Only the Strong Survive," "Moody Woman," and "What's the Use of Breaking Up" that returned him to the center of the soul constellation.

Butler was no longer a pop force by the early 1970s, but continued to produce R&B hits (albeit at the lower reaches of the charts) until 1983. However, he had found new challenges by this time, establishing Fountain Records in 1980 and serving four four-year terms as a Cook County Commissioner. Still active as a performer, he was inducted, along with the Impressions, into the Rock and Rock Hall of Fame in 1991, and received the Rhythm & Blues Foundation's Pioneer Award in 1994.

Byrd, Donald (b. 1932) *trumpeter and bandleader*

One of the more commercially successful jazz-rock artists of the 1970s, Donald Byrd also left his mark as an educator and bop trumpet stylist. Born December 9, 1932, in Detroit, Michigan, he studied trumpet and composition in the early 1950s and performed during his military service. He performed and recorded with many of the most prominent bop interpreters later in the decade, including Art Blakey, Kenny Clarke, John Coltrane, and Sonny Rollins. After teaming with Pepper Adams for several years, he returned to his studies in Europe in 1961. He would begin a career as a jazz educator in the mid-1960s, serving at a number of prestigious American universities of the years such as Rutgers and Howard.

Byrd continued his recording activities in the 1960s, working extensively with saxophonist Dexter Gordon, among others. During the 1970s, he began integrating soul and FUNK elements into his work, most notably with a group of Howard University students who became the Blackbyrds (named after the seminal 1973 Byrd LP on Blue Note, *Blackbyrd*). Their single, "Walkin' in Rhythm," from the best-selling LP, *Flying Start* (Fantasy, 1974), became a Top Ten crossover pop hit. Although his flirtations with fusion offended many jazz purists, he continued to garner praise for his extraordinary technique and lovely tone as a trumpeter.

Byrd, Gary (b. 1954) *deejay*

A self-styled "disc journalist," Gary Byrd is widely recognized as a pioneer in the evolution of the RAP genre. Born in Buffalo, New York, he became a radio disc jockey at age 15 (allegedly the youngest in the state at the time). He became a close associate of STEVIE WONDER, contributing lyrics to two tracks on the singer's epic three-disc set, *Songs in the Key of Life* (Motown, 1976).

In the mid-1980s, Wonder also provided the multitrack accompaniment (billed as the GB Experience) to Byrd's extended single, "The Crown," which surveyed black history from ancient Egypt to Malcolm X. Although hardly noticed in the United States, it was a chart smash in both England and many other European countries. He gained further notice in Great Britain as the presenter for *Sweet Inspiration,* a 1985 BBC series devoted to gospel music. He was best known stateside as the chat show host and inquisitor on the nationally syndicated radio program, *Star Quiz.*

Cadets/The Jacks, The

Versatility defined this group that recorded in the 1950s as both the Cadets and the Jacks. The original lineup—first tenor Aaron Collins, second tenor George Hollis (later replaced by Willie Davis), tenor Lloyd McCraw, baritone Ted Taylor, and bass Will "Dub" Jones—began as a spiritual quintet in Los Angeles in 1947. Signing with the RPM/Modern company as the Jacks, they initially concentrated on romantic ballads. Their reputation is based largely on one of their early releases, "Why Don't You Write Me?" which peaked at number three on the R&B charts in 1955; like most material recorded by the Jacks, it featured Davis, something of a throwback to the heyday of the crooners, as the lead singer.

When follow-up singles failed to chart, the group—with Prentice Moreland replacing Taylor, who went on to a solo career—opted to cover the JAYHAWKS' novelty hit, "Stranded in the Jungle," as the Cadets. Their reading was considered superior due to improved production values and the animated interplay of group voices. When their version outperformed the original at retail outlets, in jukeboxes, and on the radio, they continued recording covers of contemporary R&B hits (featuring either Collins or Davis as the lead), albeit with less success.

Failing to recapture lightning in a bottle, the group fragmented in the late 1950s. Jones would become part of the reconstituted COASTERS in early 1958, one of the most popular vocal groups of the Brill Building Era. Collins, Davis, and Hollis—

along with bass Tommy Miller—would form the FLARES, who would make a singular contribution to the early 1960s dance craze fad with "Foot Stompin' — Part 1."

Cadillacs, The

The Cadillacs were one of the most beloved rhythm and blues vocal groups of all time; Dave Marsh's *Rock Book of Lists* placed them number one among black DOO-WOP ensembles. The group's polished stage show—complete with choreographed dance steps and flashy outfits—greatly influenced acts following in their wake (particularly the Motown artists; The TEMPTATIONS and the FOUR TOPS would even hire the Cadillacs' choreographer, Cholly Atkins). Although many of their classic tracks were recorded prior to the rock era and, therefore, had little chance of crossing over to a mainstream pop audience, the original recordings continue to be coveted by collectors.

The group—originally including Harlem P.S. 139 schoolmates Robert Phillips (born 1935), Laverne Drake (b. 1938), Johnny "Gus" Willingham (b. 1937), and lead singer Earl "Speedy" Carroll (b. November 2, 1937)—started performing together in 1953 as the Carnations. An audition the following year spurred manager/composer/musical arranger Esther Navarro to sign them to a personal recording contract. She encouraged them to add another singer known as James "Poppa" Clark (b. 1937) and to change their name, ultimately deciding on the Cadillacs, after the luxury automobile, due to the preponderance of groups with bird names at the time.

In 1954, Navarro booked them into New York City's Beltone Studios to record four songs featuring backing by Rene Hall's band: "I Want to Know About Love," "I Wonder Why," "Gloria," and "Wishing Well." The ballad "Gloria"—written by Navarro about another client, singer Gloria Smith—was released as a single on Josie, a subsidiary label of a leading R&B record company of the early 1950s, Jubilee. Featuring an extraordinarily sensitive lead vocal by Carroll, the song became a minor R&B hit.

Despite the defections of Willingham and Clark—replaced by Charles Brooks (b. 1937) and Earl Wade (b. 1937), respectively—the Cadillacs went on to achieve even greater success with another Navarro composition, "Speedo," which reached number three on the R&B charts in 1956. One of the best-loved recordings of the doo-wop era, its appeal owes much to the dynamic interplay of group voices providing a backdrop for Carroll's swaggering lead, which updates a longstanding blues tradition. A novel reworking of the Christmas chestnut, "Rudolph the Red-Nosed Reindeer," backed (as was "Speedo") by the Jesse Powell Orchestra, just missed the R&B Top Ten a year later. The group also had success with "Peek-A-Boo" and "What You Bet."

While active well into the 1970s, the Cadillacs ceased to be an artistically important act when Carroll left in 1961 to replace Carnell Gunter in the more commercially successful COASTERS. The group had already lost credibility in the late 1950s when members split into two factions, both of whom recorded and performed as the Cadillacs. After a period of inactivity in the 1970s, the Cadillacs re-formed with Carroll and Phillips in the early 1980s.

The ABC-TV program *20/20* spotlighted Carroll's life and work in the early 1990s. Despite his music activities, he worked steadily as a custodian within the New York City public school system, where he was universally loved by students and staff who knew nothing about his legacy as a musician.

Cameo

Formed in 1974 as the New York City Players by drummer Larry "Mr. B" Blackmon and keyboardist Gregory "Straps" Johnson (both formerly with East Coast), the hard-edged soul-funk group was a major force on the R&B charts during the 1980s. Augmented by Eric Curham, Gary Dow, Anthony Lockett, and brothers Nathan and Arnett Leftenant, Cameo's hit recordings included the chart-toppers "She's Strange," "Word Up," and "Candy." The ensemble enjoyed little crossover success, however, with only the latter two singles breaking into the pop Top 40.

C+C Music Factory

C+C Music Factory is the nom de plume used by New Yorker Robert Clivilles (born 1960) and Tennessean David Cole (b. 1962) when they aren't remixing songs for artists like NATALIE COLE ("Pink Cadillac"), Lisa Lisa & Cult Jam, Sandee, and Seduction. The duo first recorded as 2 Puerto Ricans, a Black Man and a Dominican with "Do It Properly," issued on their own label in 1987. By the time "Gonna Make You Sweat (Everybody Dance Now)," featuring rapper Freedom Williams—who had previously recorded with Grace Jones and New Kids on the Block—became an international hit in 1990, they had honed their formula to perfection, hiring vocalists and musicians as needed in addition to programming the backbeat. They would go to score six more American Top 40 singles during 1991–92, utilizing such singers as Deborah Cooper (ex-Fatback Band, Change), Q Unique, and Martha Wash (Weather Girls). While riding high, a collection of their production work for other acts was issued on the album, *Greatest Remixes, Vol. 1* (Columbia, 1992), credited to Clivilles and Cole. Their fruitful collaboration came to an untimely end with Cole's death from spinal meningitis in 1995.

Carey, Mariah (b. 1970) *singer*

Mariah Carey belongs to the same torch-singing, ballad tradition that spawned Barbra Streisand, Dionne Warwick, and WHITNEY HOUSTON. Like these singers,

The most successful female artist of the 1990s, Mariah Carey (Frank Driggs Collection)

in all during the decade. Her albums—particularly the eponymous debut (Columbia, 1990), which was number one for 11 weeks and spent 113 weeks on the charts; *Music Box* (Columbia, 1993); *Daydream* (Columbia, 1995); and the hip-hop–influenced *Butterfly* (Columbia, 1997)—also sold well. She was the most successful artist on the pop charts in the 1990s by a substantial margin. While Carey's vocal tools (including a seven-octave range) are considered above reproach from a technical standpoint, some critics have characterized her choice of material as bland at best. While she remains firmly in control of her career, making substantial contributions as a songwriter and producer, cracks have appeared in the firmament in recent years. After signing a lucrative recording contract with Virgin in early 2001, the disappointing performance of her first release—the *All That Glitters* soundtrack—led to rumors that the company was trying to void the deal. Furthermore, her productivity had allegedly been compromised by personal problems. However, she returned to the spotlight with *The Emancipation of Mimi* (Island, 2005).

Carey's florid style owes more to bel canto stage and mainstream pop conventions than rhythm and blues, gospel, and rock influences—all of which are nevertheless discernable in her recordings.

Born March 27, 1970, in Long Island, New York, she was groomed for a singing career by her mother, Patricia Carey, a former member of the New York City Opera. Carey's rise to fame was meteoric. In addition to winning the 1990 Grammy for Best New Artist, she enjoyed eight number one singles—"Vision of Love," "Love Takes Time," "Someday," "I Don't Wanna Cry," "Emotions," "I'll Be There," "Dreamlover," and "Hero"—during her first four years as a Columbia recording artist, 14

Carlton, Carl (b. 1952) *singer*

The Detroit native was something of a prodigy, first recording for Lando in 1964. He enjoyed five moderate R&B hits from 1968 to 1970 on the Back Beat label as "Little Carl Carlton" before dropping the diminutive reference. He remained a chart fixture through the mid-1980s for a succession of labels, including ABC, 20th Century, RCA, and Casablanca. However, although only two of his singles cracked the pop Top 40, "Everlasting Love" (1974) and "She's a Bad Mama Jama (She's Built, She's Stacked)" (1981).

Carter, Clarence (b. 1936) *singer*

Born January 14, 1936, in Montgomery, Alabama, Clarence Carter first made an impact as part of a blind duo, Clarence and Calvin (aka the C and C Boys), who released seven singles in the early 1960s.

When partner Calvin Thomas was seriously injured in an auto accident in 1966, Carter opted for a solo career. Beginning in early 1967, he recorded a string of hits produced at FAME's MUSCLE SHOALS studio, including "Thread the Needle," "Looking for a Fox," "Slip Away," and "Patches," which reached number four in the United States and number two in England. Carter's music was notable for an idiosyncratic guitar style perfectly suited to his earthy vocals; he also frequently contributed keyboards, compositions, and arrangements to his recordings as well those of others, including wife Candi Staton.

He shifted to ABC Records in 1974, but his dynamic style seemed anachronistic during the DISCO era. In the 1980s, he attempted comebacks with Venture, Big C, and Ichiban. Although no longer a chart fixture, his work continued to find a loyal following well into the 1990s.

Carter, Mel (b. 1943) *singer*

Born April 22, 1943, in Cincinnati, Ohio, Carter was singing on local radio by age four. At age nine he worked with the likes of Lionel Hampton, and later with Jimmy Scott and Paul Gayten's band. He won a national award as the best choral tenor in 1957. Two years later, Carter formed a gospel group, the Carvetts, and signed with Mercury Records. After relocating to California in 1960, where he performed on the club circuit, he entered military service.

Upon his discharge, Carter resumed his singing career full-time, enjoying one minor hit, "When a Boy Falls in Love," in 1963. He moved to the Imperial label in 1965, and went on to record a string of best-selling romantic ballads, including "Hold Me, Thrill Me, Kiss Me," "(All of a Sudden) My Heart Sings," and "Band of Gold."

In the 1970s, Carter recorded for Romar, enlisting producer Bob Marcucci, head of Chancellor Records, and the manager of teen idol Frankie Avalon. Although failing to return to the charts, he has continued to perform his smooth blend of pop-soul into the twenty-first century.

Castor, Jimmy (b. 1943) *funk bandleader and singer*

Jimmy Castor is best remembered for a few comic FUNK masterpieces in the 1970s. His career, however, spanned much of the second half of the twentieth century (as well as the styles popular at the time).

Born June 2, 1943, in New York City, he formed a DOO-WOP group, Jimmy Castor and the Juniors, on the verge of his teens. In 1956, they recorded one of his compositions, "I Promise to Remember," which was easily outstripped by Frankie Lymon and the Teenagers' cover version. Since they possessed comparable singing styles, Castor was often tapped to sing with the Teenagers in Lymon's place.

Castor went on to finish school before forming the Jimmy Castor Bunch in the mid-1960s. They produced a minor 1967 hit, "Hey Leroy," before slipping back into obscurity. The Jimmy Castor Bunch—now including percussionist Lenny Fridie, Jr., bassist Doug Gibson, guitarist Harry Jensen, drummer Robert Manigault, and keyboardist Gerry Thomas—returned for their most successful commercial run, starting with the release of "Troglodyte (Cave Man)," which reached number six on the pop charts in 1973. In addition to two more pop hits of note—"The Bertha Butt Boogie (Part 1)" and "King Kong (Part 1)"—Castor and his associates released at least thirteen LPs of original material through 1983.

Chandler, Gene (b. 1937) *singer*

A prime exponent of the Chicago soul school during the 1960s, Gene Chandler was greatly influenced by the post–World War II rhythm and blues vocal group genre. He particularly admired the Windy City–based quintet, the Spaniels, which featured the caressing lead vocals of "Pookey" Hudson.

Born Eugene Dixon on July 6, 1937, in Chicago, Chandler formed the Gaytones in 1955 while attending Englewood High School. He briefly joined the Dukays (whose members also included tenors Shirley Jones and James Lowe, baritone Earl Edwards, and bass Ben Broyles) in 1957 before serving in the U.S. Army during 1957–60. His first break came in 1960 when—back singing with the Dukays—a local talent scout, Bill Sheppard, helped them secure a recording contract with the Nat label. After hearing a group recording session in late 1961, which featured the tracks "Nite Owl" and "Duke of Earl," Vee-Jay Records executive Calvin Carter convinced Chandler to go out on his own. He re-recorded his composition "Duke of Earl"; his distinctive post–DOO-WOP vocals helped drive the single to the top of both the R&B and pop charts.

While his later chart success was intermittent at best, Chandler maintained his career for decades, placing thirty-six discs on the *Billboard* R&B singles charts alone. His most popular recordings

Vee-Jay Records publicity photo of Gene Chandler in the early 1960s (Frank Driggs Collection)

included "Rainbow" (he followed the 1963 hit with a live version, "Rainbow '65 [Part I]," which reached number two on the R&B charts), "Nothing Can Stop Me," "I Fooled You This Time," "To Be a Lover," "Groovy Situation" (duet with Barbara Acklin), and "Get Down." In addition to performing and studio work (also for the Brunswick, 20th Century, Salsoul, and FastFire labels, among others), he directed his own record company, Mr. Chand, and was active as a songwriter and studio producer.

Channels, The

The Channels are best remembered for the 1956 R&B vocal group classic, "The Closer You Are." They were also one of the more accomplished exponents of DOO-WOP ensemble singing, with all members of the quintet playing a major role in the exposition of musical ideas rather than focusing on backup harmonizing.

The Channels formed in the mid-1950s in New York City. When two members left in early 1956, the remaining core—first tenor Larry Hampden, second tenor Billy Morris, and baritone Edward Doulphin—were joined by lead vocalist Earl Lewis (born February 11, 1941) and bass Clifton Wright, both formerly with the Latharios. After securing a recording contract with the local independent label Whirlin' Disc, they recorded their debut, "The Closer You Are," that following summer. Featuring Lewis's distinctive soaring falsetto set off by the group's active ensemble singing, the song became a big East Coast hit, spawning a string of less notable follow-up singles, including "The Gleam in Your Eye," "That's My Desire," "Bye Bye Baby," and "Our Love Will Never Die."

With mainstream pop acceptance continuing to elude them, the group members decided to call it a day in the early 1960s. The oldies revival, however, kept their music alive via countless LP anthologies. In order to capitalize on offers to tour the nostalgia circuit, Lewis would assemble a new edition of the group (now billed as Earl Lewis and the Channels) in the 1970s, consisting of Jack Brown, John Felix, and John Fernandez.

Chantels, The

Although the SHIRELLES are widely recognized as the first GIRL GROUP to achieve substantial chart success during the rock era, they ventured down a path already taken by the Chantels. That group's lead singer, Arlene Smith, possessed one of the most dynamic voices ever recorded.

The Chantels—consisting of Sonia Goring, Lois Harris, Jackie Landry, Rene Minus, and Smith, all of whom were born in the Bronx, New York, between 1940 and 1943—were formed in 1956, when the members sang in the St. Anthony of Padua school choir. Their group name was taken from a rival basketball team, St. Francis de Chantelle. They soon came to the attention of Richard Barrett, then on the A&R staff at Gone Records, who signed them to one of the label's subsidiaries, End.

Most of the group's early hits—"He's Gone," "Maybe," "Every Night (I Pray)," and "I Love You So"—were composed by Smith and featured her expressive leads. "Maybe" spent 18 weeks on the pop charts, and is generally believed to have sold well over one million copies. Following this initial wave of popularity, their record sales experienced a significant drop-off. In an attempt to recapture their past success, they sang with Barrett on "Summer Love" in mid-1959. In 1961, the Chantels—now a foursome minus Smith—signed with Carlton Records. They enjoyed a brief return to the charts with a Top Ten R&B hit, "Look in My Eyes," and "Well I Told You," both of which featured close group harmonies up front rather than a lead/support harmonizing format. Their final hit, "Eternally," reached number 77 in early 1963.

Smith went on to teach in the Bronx, while the other members also continued to reside in the New York area. By the late 1960s Smith would revive the Chantels with two new girls in order to perform at rock revival shows.

Charles, Ray (1930–2004) *singer and bandleader*

One of the most distinctive and durable performers in American music history, Ray Charles excelled at a wide range of styles, including R&B, small combo jazz, soul, country, and updated big-band pop. He was also set a precedent for black music entrepreneurship, gaining control of his recorded output in the early 1960s, leasing tracks to ABC-Paramount through his own company, TRC.

Born Ray Charles Robinson, on September 23, 1930, in Albany, Georgia, he moved with his family to Greenville, Florida as an infant. He began losing his vision in his sixth year, becoming totally blind at age seven due to glaucoma. After studying classical piano and clarinet at the State School for Deaf and Blind Children, Saint Augustine, Florida, (1937–45),

Ray Charles performing in the 1970s (Frank Driggs Collection)

he began playing in area Florida groups. Relocating to Seattle in 1948, Charles formed the Nat King Cole–influenced McSon Trio (later known as the Maxim Trio and Maxine Trio) with guitarist G. D. McGhee and bassist Milton Garred. They reached number two on the R&B charts the following year with the Downbeat single, "Confession Blues."

Following a solo turn with Swingtime Records, he signed with Atlantic in late 1953. He released a string of classic tracks for the label through the decade, including the R&B chart-toppers "I've Got a Woman," "A Fool for You," "Drown in My Own Tears," and "What'd I Say (Part I)." Interested in interpreting a wider range of musical styles, he switched to ABC-Paramount in 1960, where he placed more than 50 recordings on both the pop and R&B charts through 1973, including the number one hits "Georgia on My Mind" (later designated the Georgia state song), "Hit the Road Jack," and "I Can't Stop Loving You." The latter single, culled from the immensely successful 1962 LP, *Modern Sounds in Country and Western Music*, was instrumental in changing public perceptions of what black artists could record.

Although the hits stopped at the onset of the 1980s, Charles remained in demand as a live performer, achieving virtually every honor possible for a pop musician, from Grammys—including Best Male R&B Vocal in 1975 ("Living For the City") and Best R&B Duet in 1990 ("I'll Be Good to You," with CHAKA KHAN)—to induction into the Rock and Roll Hall of Fame. He also found success within the music industry via investments in the record label Crossover, music publishing, and a recording studio. Shortly after his death on June 10, 2004, a major film devoted to his life and career, entitled *Ray,* appeared to rave reviews and substantial box office activity.

Charms, The (Otis Williams & the Charms)

The Cincinnati-based vocal group, the Charms, possessed genuine crossover appeal. Like many of their peers, however, they were victimized by the cover phenomenon. Their biggest pop hits—

"Hearts of Stone" (number one on the R&B charts for nine weeks) and "Ivory Tower"—were overtaken by three Top Ten cover versions: the Fontaine Sisters' "Hearts of Stone," Cathy Carr's "Ivory Tower," and Gale Storm's "Ivory Tower."

The Charms—consisting of Rolland Bradley, Richard Parker, Donald Peak, Joe Penn, and lead singer Otis Williams—first recorded for the Rockin' label in 1953. Their debut hit, "Hearts of Stone"—one of the biggest R&B singles of the 1950s—was followed by a string of chart successes: "Ling, Ting, Tong"; "Two Hearts"; "That's Your Mistake," the first release to be billed as "Otis Williams and The Charms"; "Ivory Tower"; and "United." The group moved on to King Records where they creased the lower rungs of the pop charts with "Little Turtle Dove" and "Panic." With their hit-making days behind them, Williams switched to the country field as a solo act with little success.

Checker, Chubby (b. 1941) *singer*

A native of South Carolina, Ernest Evans grew up in Philadelphia performing for classmates along with friends such as future teen idol Fabian Forte. The owner of the meat market where Evans worked after school arranged a private recording session with *American Bandstand* host, Dick Clark. As Evans completed a FATS DOMINO imitation, Clark's wife asked him his name. When he indicated, "My friends call me Chubby," she playfully responded, "Like in Checker?" That episode of humorous wordplay inspired Evans' professional name.

The resulting Christmas novelty, "The Class" (which featured impressions of popular singers by Checker), attracted the attention of the Cameo-Parkway label, which decided to release the record commercially in 1959. His breakthrough came when Clark advised Cameo-Parkway to record "The Twist," a dance number written by R&B singer HANK BALLARD and released as the B-side of "Teardrops on Your Letter" with his group, The Midnighters, in 1959. Checker sang his parts over an already recorded instrumental track; released in

Chubby Checker looking svelte after many nights of demonstrating the twist (Frank Driggs Collection)

June 1959, the record took nearly fourteen months to reach the charts. Checker's nonstop itinerary of interviews, TV dates, and live appearances (he is said to have lost thirty pounds during one three-week stretch of demonstrating the Twist) ultimately paid off, however, when the single reached the top of the *Billboard* Hot 100 in September 1960.

The Twist phenomenon inspired a rapid succession of additional dance fads. Due to his close relationship with Clark and a savvy record label, Checker was well positioned to continue as the King of Dance. His dance hits included "The Hucklebuck," "Pony Time," "Dance the Mess Around," "Let's Twist Again," "The Fly," "Slow Twistin'," "Limbo Rock," "Popeye the Hitchhiker," "Let's Limbo Some More," "Birdland," and "Twist It Up."

When the dance craze subsided, Checker managed to record additional hits, most notably "Loddy Lo," "Hooka Tooka," and "Hey, Bobba Needle." However, his popularity was ultimately eclipsed by the British Invasion and American Renaissance styles such as surf music, soul, and folk-rock. Checker has continued to perform extensively, occasionally attempting large-scale comebacks.

Cherry, Neneh (b. 1964) *singer*

In the late 1980s, Neneh Cherry surfaced with a series of edgy dance hits, helped immeasurably by heavy rotation on MTV, which recognized her street-smart demeanor and photogenic good looks as an unbeatable combination. Born March 10, 1964, in Stockholm, Sweden, the stepdaughter of avant-garde jazz trumpeter Don Cherry, she sang with the British postpunk act, Rip, Rig and Panic, in the early 1980s, before forming Float Up CP with several members of that band. She next provided backing vocals for the likes of the Slits and The The.

A talented composer—she cowrote the hits "Buffalo Stance," "Manchild," and "Kisses on the Wind" with husband Cameron McVey—Cherry maintained her creative momentum with a video release, *The Rise of Neneh Cherry* (1989), and a series of internationally successful LPs, including *Raw Like Sushi* (Circa, 1989), *Homebrew* (1993), and a collection of studio remixes, *Buddy X* (1993). She achieved further public attention via brisk poster sales, the use of "Buffalo Stance" in the film *Slaves of New York,* and the inclusion of her rendition of Cole Porter's "I've Got You Under My Skin" on the AIDS charity collection, *Red Hot and Blue.* Having mothered a child well before achieving stardom, Cherry has appeared content to maintain a low profile since the mid-1990s.

Chic

The brainchild of record producers Bernard Edwards (bass) and Nile Rodgers (guitar), Chic—augmented by vocalists Norma Jean Wright (replaced by Alfa Anderson in 1978) and Luci Martin and drummer Tony Thompson—enjoyed a string of disco-styled hits from 1977 to 1983, most notably, "Dance, Dance Dance (Yowsah, Yowsah, Yowsah)," "Le Freak" (number one on the R&B and pop charts), "I Want Your Love," "Good Times" (also a crossover chart-topping smash), and "Rebels Are We." By 1983, Edwards and Rodgers had shifted their focus to producing other acts, the former working with the Power Station, and the latter assisting David Bowie on his *Let's Dance* album (EMI America, 1983) as well as becoming a member of the Robert Plant-fronted Honeydrippers.

Chiffons, The

The Chiffons—along with acts like the SHIRELLES and the CHANTELS—helped define the GIRL GROUP sound of the early 1960s. And, like their peers, they found hits harder to come by when American popular music was by and large squeezed off of the radio by the British Invasion recording artists beginning in 1964.

The Chiffons—consisting of Barbara Lee (born May 16, 1947), Patricia Bennett (April 7, 1947), Sylvia Peterson (September 30, 1946), and lead singer Judy Craig (1946), all of whom were natives of New York City's Bronx borough—were formed in early 1960 by music entrepreneur Ronald Mack. With Mack serving as their manager, they worked as back-up singers in various studio sessions before being offered a recording contract by Big Deal Records later in the year. Following a minor 1960 hit, "Tonight's the Night," and a string of commercial failures, the group moved on to Laurie, a growing label that had enjoyed hits by Dion, Dickey Lee, and other teen idols. They immediately captured lightning in a bottle, taking the Mack-penned "He's So Fine" to the top of the pop charts for four weeks in early 1963.

They would remain successful for a time with much the same formula—Craig's sweet, tremulous lead vocals framed by the group's DOO-WOP styled harmonies—on hits like the Gerry Goffin–Carole King composition, "One Fine Day," "A Love So Fine," "I Have a Boyfriend," and "Sweet Talkin' Guy." At their peak, they also recorded as the Four Pennies, creasing the charts with "My Block" and "When the Boy's Happy (The Girl's Happy Too)" in 1963. Although relegated to a marginal existence within the music industry with the rise of new trends such as soul music, folk-rock, and the surf sound, the Chiffons—down to a trio minus Craig by the 1970s—have continued to perform intermittently in the New York area.

Chi-Lites, The

The Chi-Lites are living proof that, if a group excels at a particular style and sticks with it, ever-changing public tastes may eventually nudge it into the mainstream. During the 1960s, an era dominated by political rhetoric and musical experimentation, the group continued to specialize in poignant love ballads, finally breaking through to mass public acceptance in the early 1970s with hits like "Have You Seen Her" and "Oh Girl."

The group formed in 1960 out of a merger of former members of two Chicago-area vocal groups, the Desideros (baritone Marshall Thompson and bass Creadel "Red" Jones) and the Chantours (tenors Eugene Record, Clarence Johnson, and Robert "Squirrel" Lester). Calling themselves the Hi-Lites, they recorded a single, "Pots and Pans," for the Chicago-based Mercury Records. When it failed to sell, however, the label nixed the deal and, to make matters worse, they were forced to give up their moniker because it was already taken.

Adding a "C" to the front of their name to emphasize their Chicago origins, Marshall and the Chi-Lites, their name briefly in 1963–64, developed a regional following with a string of singles for James Shelton, Jr.'s Daran and Ja-Wes labels. By the mid-1960s, they took another stab at big-time success by re-signing with Mercury; however, when two releases on the Blue Rock subsidiary flopped, the group was cut loose once again.

Things began to turn around after the group, now known simply as Chi-Lites, hooked up with the Dakas production company, which facilitated a recording contract with music industry giant, MCA. With Record assuming a dominant role as songwriter, producer, and lead singer, they established themselves as consistent hit-makers. Although the Chi-Lites typically recorded melodic, sentimental fare featuring Record's soaring falsetto, it is somewhat ironic that their first pop Top 40 single was a rare excursion into social protest, the forceful "(For God's Sake) Give More Power to the People."

The group peaked a year later with "Oh Girl," in which a plaintive harmonica underscored Record's stark portrayal of male vulnerability—an extremely rare approach for a male pop artist of that era. Despite such unquestioned artistry, the Chi-Lites' sometimes overdone pathos failed to click with the public following the release of the vibrant "Stoned Out of My Mind." Jones would leave in 1973, while Record would detour off into a solo career with Warner Brothers three years later. The group soldiered on (re-forming with all of the original members in 1980), achieving modest success in the R&B field (41 charting singles in all), recording with Mercury (again!), Chi-Sound, 20th Century, Larc, and Private I up through the mid-1980s.

Chords, The

The Chords were one of the more notable victims of covering which—in its most frequent manifestation—consisted of remakes of black R&B recordings by white pop music artists. The Bronx-based group emerged in 1951 out of the remnants of three Morris High School ensembles—lead vocalist Carl Feaster and his brother, baritone Claude Feaster, from the Tunetoppers; first tenor Jimmy Keyes of the Four Notes; and second tenor Floyd "Buddy" McRae of the Keynotes—who hooked up with bass William "Ricky" Edwards, then with an outfit called the Chords. After a failed audition for Bobby Robinson's Red Robin Records, Atlantic signed them to their Cat subsidiary in 1954.

The Chords' debut single, the group-composed "Sh-Boom," was actually the B-side of their cover rendition of the Patti Page hit, "Cross Over the Bridge." Although their version, released in 1954, was a big crossover hit—reaching number five on the pop charts—they lost a substantial number of sales to the Crewcuts' major label release on Mercury. They had trouble following up this success, due in part to the need to record under another name because a group called the Chords was already recording for Gem. As a result, many fans did not realize that both the Chord Cats and the Sh-Booms were the same group as the original Chords.

When Atlantic lost interest in the group, they moved to the Vik label in 1957, and Roulette in 1960. By this time, the Chords were in the midst of personnel upheavals, with McRae being replaced by Arthur Dix, Edwards by Joe "Ditto" Diaz (formerly with Dean Barlow and the Crickets, as well as the Bachelors), and Claude Feaster by Bobby Spencer. Keyes would go on to form the Popular Five in 1963 along with Dix.

Clark, Dee (b. 1938) *singer*

Dee Clark was one of the distinctive exponents of the Chicago soul style. An extremely versatile singer, while his warm tenor voice—very much reminiscent of SAM COOKE's early pop period—was best suited for low-key ballads, he was also convincing with more intensively dramatic material, as typified by his biggest hit, "Raindrops."

Born Delectus (some sources say "Delecta") Clark, in Blythsville, Arkansas, on November 7, 1938, he moved to Chicago with his family in 1941. In his early teens, he was a member of a vocal trio, the Hambone Kids, who recorded briefly with OKeh Records in 1952. He moved on to another group, the Goldentones (later known as the Cool Gents), the following year. After the group won a

Chicago talent contest in 1955, deejay Herb Kent brought them to the attention of the local VEE-JAY label. The company would credit their 1956 recordings to "the Delegates."

Vee-Jay encouraged Clark to go solo, signing him to their subsidiary, Falcon (renamed Abner Records in 1958). Despite a number of commercially unsuccessful releases, he obtained the services of the Upsetters when the band's frontman, LITTLE RICHARD, entered the ministry. Shortly thereafter, Clark broke into the national spotlight in late 1958 with "Nobody But You." He remained a consistent hit-maker until the onset of the British Invasion, most notably with "Just Keep It Up," "Hey Little Girl," "How About That," and the Clark–Phillip Upchurch composition, "Raindrops."

With Vee-Jay experiencing financial difficulties, Clark jumped to the Constellation label. While he remained active for a time as a performer, however, his dance number, "Crossfire Time," released in fall 1963, would be his last charting single.

Clinton, George (b. 1940) *bandleader*

One of the most innovative forces in black popular music during the rock era, George Clinton's restless muse could not be confined for long within any particular genre. Establishing his first group, the Parliaments, in order to perform DOO-WOP, Clinton would utilize a wide array of artistic settings in addressing soul, psychedelia, FUNK, fusion, DISCO, and HIP-HOP, among other styles.

Born July 22, 1940, in Kannapolis, North Carolina, Clinton formed the Parliaments while growing up in Newark, New Jersey. Beginning in 1955, the group recorded sporadically with a number of labels, including Hull, Flip, Symbol, USA, MOTOWN, and Golden World. By the mid-1960s, the group included vocalists Clarence "Fuzzy" Haskins, Raymond Davis, and Grady Thomas. After adding lead guitarist Eddie Hazel, rhythm guitarist Tawl Ross, bassist Billy Nelson, organist Mickey Atkins, and drummer Tiki Fulwood in 1966, the Parliaments enjoyed a moderate pop hit, "(I Wanna) Testify."

Following more failed releases, Clinton was forced to change the group name by Motown writers Holland-Dozier-Holland. Strongly influenced by Jimi Hendrix–styled acid rock, the proto-funk exemplified by SLY AND THE FAMILY STONE, and the radical polemics of white working-class bands like the MC5 and the Stooges, he redirected the core of his band, now called Funkadelic, toward progressive rock. The skewed social commentaries and extended jams of Funkadelic's early albums—*Funkadelic* (Westbound, 1970), *Free Your Mind . . . And Your Ass Will Follow* (Westbound, 1970), *Maggot Brain* (Westbound, 1971), *America Eats Its Young* (Westbound, 1972),

George Clinton performing live in August 1979 with Funkadelic (Frank Driggs Collection)

Cosmic Slop (Westbound, 1973), and *Standing On The Verge Of Getting It On* (Westbound, 1974)—would sell moderately well to both young urban blacks and white hard rock fans. In the meantime, Clinton, getting back the rights to the Parliaments name, changed it to Parliament (while continuing to use most of the Funkadelic personnel) and produced a string of recordings—most notably, *Chocolate City* (Casablanca, 1975), *Mothership Connection* (Casablanca, 1976), *The Clones Of Dr. Funkenstein* (Casablanca, 1975), and *Funkentelechy vs. The Placebo Syndrome* (Casablanca, 1977)—emphasizing a dance-floor funk groove. Parliament's success, in turn, stimulated further interest in Funkadelic, which peaked with the release of *One Nation Under A Groove* (Warner Bros., 1978).

Clinton's P-Funk collective would grow to include more than 35 musicians and additional spin-off acts like Bootsy Collins' Rubber Band, Parlet, and Horny Horns. These wide-ranging activities appear to have sapped Clinton's creative energy and, by 1982, he had decided to focus on a solo career, with an on-again, off-again collaborative side project known as the P-Funk All Stars. With the exception of the LP *Computer Games* (Capitol, 1982)—including a single, "Atomic Dog," which received heavy exposure in clubs and on cable TV as a video clip—his post-1970s work has been lackluster at best. However, other artists (e.g., ICE CUBE, Primal Scream) still recruit his services in the recording studio, and his Parliament-Funkadelic material continues to be widely sampled within the hip-hop community.

See also HOLLAND, BRIAN, LAMONT DOZIER, AND EDDIE HOLLAND.

Clovers, The

The Clovers were one of the classic 1950s vocal harmony groups, equally at home with romantic ballads and uptempo jump material. They served as a missing link between the classic post–World War II rhythm and blues sound and the newly emerging rock 'n' roll genre.

The members—dual lead tenors John "Buddy" Bailey and Billy Mitchell (joined 1953), second tenor Matthew McQuater, baritone Harold "Hal" Lucas, Jr., bass vocalist Harold Winley, and guitarist Bill Harris—all hailed from the Washington, D.C., and Baltimore metropolitan areas. Entepreneur Lou Krefetz discovered the group performing at Washington, D.C.'s Rose Club in the late 1940s, when they were still enrolled in high school. After signing on as manager, he garnered a recording contract with Atlantic Records in 1950.

The Clovers' first R&B hit, "Don't You Know I Love You," released in 1951, was written by label president AHMET ERTEGUN. Many more popular releases followed, including "Fool, Fool, Fool," "One Mint Julep," "Ting-A-Ling," "Hey, Miss Fannie," "I Played the Fool," "Crawlin'," "Good Lovin'," "Lovey Dovey," "I've Got My Eyes on You," "Your Cash Ain't Nothin' but Trash," "Blue Velvet," "Nip Sip," "Devil or Angel," "Love, Love, Love," and "From the Bottom of My Heart." Their biggest pop hit, "Love Potion No. 9," followed a prolonged dry spell. They were unable to build on this success, however, and the group was relegated to the nostalgia circuit by the mid-1960s. Covers of their hits—most notably, Bobby Vee's "Devil or Angel," Bobby Vinton's "Blue Velvet," and the Searchers' "Love Potion Number Nine"—have assured them of a place on oldies playlists. Anthologies of their best-selling singles continue to appear on a regular basis.

Club Nouveau

Club Nouveau was the brainchild of Sacramento producer Jay King, who brought Samuelle Prater together with former members of a local vocal group, the Timex Social Club—Denzil Foster, Thomas McElroy, and Valerie Watson—to record for his own King Jay label. The group's debut LP, *Life, Love and Pain* (1986)—comprised of slick post-disco club fare—was a major hit, due largely to the release of a cover version of BILL WITHERS' chart-topping hit, "Lean on Me," as a single. A huge international smash, the song also made the Top

Ten in most European countries. The second album, *Listen to the Message* (1988), and a string of singles proved far less successful. The departure of McElroy and Prater—despite the infusion of new blood in the persons of David Agent and Kevin Irving—failed to reverse Club Nouveau's declining fortunes.

Coasters, The

The Coasters were—along with the PLATTERS and the DRIFTERS—one of the first black rhythm and blues vocal groups to find consistent success on the mainstream pop charts. Their entrée consisted of satirical commentaries on American popular culture, particularly the teen lifestyle, supplied by the legendary songwriting/production team of LEIBER AND STOLLER.

The group formed in Los Angeles in 1947 as the ROBINS, finding success with the uptempo R&B classics, "If It's So, Baby" and "Smokey Joe's Café." Eyeing the rapidly emerging rock 'n' roll market, the members—tenor Carl Gardner, baritone Billy Guy, tenor Leon Hughes, bassist Bobby Nunn, and guitarist Adolph Jacobs—assumed the name of the Coasters (a reference to their West Coast home base) and smoothed out the bluesy, rough edges characterizing the Robins' releases. The group

The early Coasters bringing their humor to the stage in 1956 (Frank Driggs Collection)

signed with Atlantic Records in 1956 and the label immediately assigned Leiber and Stoller to the band. The Coasters—now including tenor Cornell Gunther and bassist Will "Dub" Jones in place of Hughes and Nunn—enjoyed a long string of brilliantly arranged hit singles, including "Down in Mexico"; the private-eye send-up, "Searching," backed by "Young Blood"; a diatribe on parental authority, "Yakety Yak"; "Charlie Brown," which featured—like "Yakety Yak"—an inventive sax break by KING CURTIS; a spoof on TV western heroes, "Along Came Jones"; "Poison Ivy"; and "Little Egypt." The animated vocal interplay between group members (undoubtedly a by-product of the Leiber and Stoller studio arrangements) played a large role in the success of these records. Like many teen-oriented artists of the time, their albums sold in limited quantities.

The Coasters split up in the mid-1960s after the hits dried up. However, they reunited later in the decade due to opportunities presented by the rock 'n' roll revival vogue. In addition to numerous LP reissues of their classic tracks, they returned to the studio with Leiber and Stoller to recut old material on *Sixteen Greatest Hits* (Trip, 1973). The group—featuring various personnel configurations led by Nunn, Gardner, and Hughes individually, and Guy and Jones together—has continued to perform live. They were inducted into the Rock and Roll Hall of Fame in 1987.

Cold Chillin' Records

A RAP-oriented record label, Cold Chillin' became a working reality in 1987 when prime movers Tyrone Williams and MARLEY MARL signed a distribution deal with Warner Bros. The arrangement had Williams handling administration matters and Marl producing much of the music, with oversight by Warner A&R man Ben Medina. Street slang for "really kickin'," Cold Chillin' was a commercial success right out of the box with strong-selling albums such as Biz Markie's *Goin' Off* (1988), MC Shan's *Down By Law* (1988), Marl's *In Control Volume 1*

(1988), and Big Daddy Kane's *It's a Big Daddy Thing* (1989). The company lost momentum shortly thereafter, however, due largely to its failure to find artists of a comparable commercial stature in the 1990s.

Cole, Cozy (1907–1981) *percussionist*

Cozy Cole enjoyed one major hit during the rock 'n' roll era, the big-band-influenced instrumental, "Topsy, Part II." Few fans of that single, however, realized that Cole was a veteran jazz performer whose career stretched back to the early days of electrical recording.

Born William Cole in East Orange, New Jersey, October 17, 1907, he played in a variety of jazz ensembles as a youth before making his recording debut with Jelly Roll Morton in the late 1920s. He would go on to work with Cab Calloway and Louis Armstrong's All-Stars, among others. He teamed with big band percussionist Gene Krupa to form the "Krupa and Cole School of Drumming" in New York in the 1950s. His 1958 single, "Topsy, Part II," was allegedly the first recording built around a prolonged drum solo to become a million seller. Follow-up singles—the most successful of which was "Turvy, Part II"—failed to achieve a comparable impact. He died of cancer on January 29, 1981, in Columbus, Ohio.

Cole, Natalie (b. 1950) *singer*

As hard as it may be for hardcore pop music fans to fathom, Natalie Cole has been active as a recording artist for a longer period than her legendary father, jazz pianist/vocal crooner Nat "King" Cole. Born February 6, 1950, in Los Angeles, she began singing professionally at age 11. Signed by her father's longtime label, Capitol, in the mid-1970s, Cole placed eight singles in the R&B Top Ten in less than three years, including the chart-toppers "This Will Be," "Inseparable," "Sophisticated Lady (She's a Different Lady)," "I've Got Love on My Mind," and "Our Love."

Natalie Cole in the 1970s (Frank Driggs Collection)

During the 1980s, her recordings—including collaborations with such balladeers like PEABO BRYSON and Ray Parker, Jr.—languished in the lower reaches of the R&B charts, sometimes finding greater acceptance with a pop mainstream audience. However, Cole's career underwent a critical and commercial revival in the 1990s, prompted by 1991's *Unforgettable, With Love,* a collection of her father's hits that she sang as duets due to new recording technology, propelling her album releases to consistent best-seller status, a trend that continues to the present day.

Color Me Badd
Consisting of college students from Oklahoma—including Bryan Abrams (born November 16, 1969),

Mark Calderon (b. September 22, 1970), Kevin Thornton (b. June 17, 1969), and Sam Watters (b. July 23, 1970)—Color Me Badd were discovered by KOOL AND THE GANG's Robert Bell while performing as a live support band. Bell brought them to New York City, where—with Dr. Freeze providing an arranging assist, they recorded "I Wanna Sex You Up." Combining an improbable blend of spirited R&B harmonies and teen gangsta posing, the track was featured on the film soundtrack to *New Jack City.* They continued on a commercial roll with the singles, "I Adore Mi Amore" (Giant) and "Heartbreaker" (Giant), and the eponymous debut LP (Giant, 1991).

The dichotomy of effervescent pop and hoodlum posing seemed even more contrived with the appearance of *Time & Chance* (Giant, 1993), which utilized the production talents of both David Foster—best known for his work with the likes of WHITNEY HOUSTON and Barbra Streisand—and ICE CUBE associate DJ Pooh. Intensely concerned with the group's street credibility, their label enlisted Ice Cube himself to direct the video to the album's title-track (and first single). Nevertheless, Color Me Badd soon faded in the wake of a new wave of gangsta rappers and teen idols.

Combs, Sean   See PUFF DADDY.

Compton's Most Wanted
Gangsta rap practitioners combining hardcore lyrics and state-of-the-art production values, the group features lead rapper MC Eiht (which stands for "Experienced in Hardcore Thumpin'") and DJ Slip, who has produced a number of acts, including DFC. Their debut LP, *It's a Compton Thang* (Orpheus, 1990), was so heavily laced with obscene language that a censored version was deemed necessary by the record company. Follow-up releases—*Straight Checkn 'Em* (Orpheus, 1991), *Music to Driveby* (Orpheus, 1992), and *We Come Strapped* (Epic, 1994), *When We Wuz Bangin'* 1989–1999:

The Hitz (Capitol, 2001), *Represent* (Half Ounce, 2001)—toned down the rhetoric somewhat, despite the continued reliance on cultural shock tactics.

Con Funk Shun

The band was originally formed in Vallejo, California, in 1968, as Project Soul by two high school friends, lead vocalist/guitarist Mike Cooper and drummer Louis McCall. Relocating to Memphis in 1972, the group, whose personnel included Peto Escovedo (son of jazzman Pete Escovedo and brother of SHEILA E.), Karl Fuller, Paul Harrell, Cedric Martin, Felton Pilate II, and Danny Thomas, would eventually do session work for the STAX label. Con Funk Shun's first records were released by Fretone in the mid-1970s. Signed with Mercury in late 1976, the band produced 25 R&B hits, most notably the chart-topper "Ffun," between 1977 and 1986, few of which crossed over to a pop audience.

Contours, The

The Contours possessed an exuberant, gritty style that withstood MOTOWN's repeated efforts to smooth out the rough edges in search of a more radio-friendly sound. Despite the relatively primitive production values of the early 1960s, the raw intensity and rhythmic drive of their singles made them dance-floor staples.

The group—originally comprising Joe Billingslea, Sylvester Potts, Billy Gordon, and Billy Hoggs, while all were still in their teens—formed in Detroit in 1958. Their big break came when a later addition, Hubert Johnson, brought them to the attention of his cousin, JACKIE WILSON. Wilson then used his show business connections to secure them a record contract with Motown in 1961. On the verge of being dropped from the label a year later for lack of commercial potential, the Contours hit the top of the R&B charts with a Berry Gordy, Jr., composition initially earmarked for the then unknown TEMPTATIONS, "Do You Love Me." The track would

become a classic covered by a wide range of artists, most notably the Dave Clark Five, who reached the Top Ten with their version in 1964.

Although never again achieving the million-selling success of "Do You Love Me," the group creased the charts with "Shake Sherry," "Can You Do It," "Can You Jerk Like Me," "That Day When She Needed Me," "First I Look at the Purse," "Just a Little Misunderstanding," and "It's So Hard Being a Loser." When the hits stopped, later member Dennis Edwards moved on to the Temptations in 1968.

Continuing to tour the club and oldies revival circuits, the Contours—with charter members Billingslea and Potts—enjoyed one last hurrah when "Do You Love Me" returned to the Hot 100—reaching number eleven in 1988—due to its prominent inclusion in the smash film *Dirty Dancing*, starring Patrick Swayze.

Cooke, Sam (1935–1964) *singer and songwriter*

Sam Cooke was one of the prime architects of soul music. His voice was rivaled only by CLYDE MCPHATTER as one of the purest tenors of the early rock 'n' roll era. Largely in control of his recorded output throughout much of his solo career, he has been viewed as a role model for subsequent generations of African-American artists attempting to break into the business.

Born January 22, 1935, in Chicago, Cooke—the son of a Baptist minister—began singing in church choirs before he entered school. Following a stint with the gospel group, the Highway Q.C.'s, he became the lead singer for the Soul Stirrers from 1950 to 1956. His first tentative stabs at recording secular material came under the moniker Dale Cooke with Specialty in 1956. One track, "I'll Come Running Back to You," would top the R&B charts in late 1957, following his breakthrough on Keen with the number one crossover ballad "You Send Me."

Following several years of consistently placing singles on the pop and R&B charts, Cooke signed with RCA in 1960, where he recorded such classics

One of the most famous photos of Sam Cooke (Frank Driggs Collection)

success, however, they found themselves casualties of changing trends within the pop music industry.

Formed in Brooklyn, the Cookies—consisting of Ethel "Earl-Jean" McCrea, Dorothy Jones, and Margaret Ross—recorded for Lamp (a subsidiary of ALADDIN RECORDS) in 1954 after winning an Apollo Theater Amateur Night contest. Famed A&R man Jesse Stone brought them to Atlantic the following year. After releasing three singles—including "In Paradise," which reached number nine on the R&B charts in 1956—and supporting the likes of BIG JOE TURNER and CHUCK WILLIS in various recording dates, they were recruited to be RAY CHARLES's backing group, the Raeletts.

While continuing to do sessions for Neil Sedaka, Ben E. King, Tony Orlando, Carole King, Little Eva, and Eydie Gorme (including the latter's big 1962 hit, "Blame It on the Bossa Nova"), a revamped edition of the Cookies—including McCrea, Margie Hendrix, and Pay Lyles—returned to the charts with several Carole King–Gerry Goffin compositions: "Chains," "Don't Say Nothin' Bad (About My Baby)," "Will Power," and "Girls Grow Up Faster Than Boys." When the hits stopped coming, McCrea recorded as Earl-Jean, cracking the Top Forty with "I'm into Somethin' Good" before the British Invasion group, Herman's Hermits, covered it a few months later.

With work harder to find, the Cookies would eventually dissolve in the late 1960s. However, some former members reformed the group in the late 1990s to perform on the oldies circuit.

Cooley, Eddie, & the Dimples

New York–based singer/songwriter Eddie Cooley had two brief brushes with pop music fame. He cowrote, along with the legendary R&B composer, Otis Blackwell, "Fever," a major hit for Little Willie John, Peggy Lee, and the McCoys. He would record another one of his songs, "Priscilla," with three women known as the Dimples singing backup. In the single, which reached the Top 20 in 1956, Cooley came across as something of an anomaly: a

as "Chain Gang," "Twistin' the Nite Away," "Bring It on Home to Me" (with vocal accompaniment by LOU RAWLS), "Another Saturday Night," and the posthumously released double-sided hit, "Shake," backed by "A Change Is Gonna Come," one of the most transcendent protest songs of all time. At the peak of his game—holding steady in the face of the onslaught of British Invasion acts—he was fatally shot on December 11, 1964, by a female motel manager under circumstances that remain unexplained to the present day.

Cookies, The

The Cookies reflect the struggle faced by many GIRL GROUPS—seeking frontline recognition, but typically relegated to backup status live and in the studio—during the early years of the rock 'n' roll era. When they finally achieved a taste of big-time black man performing in a rockabilly style. Although "Priscilla" was a hit, he would return to obscurity when his follow-up singles—"A Spark Met a Flame," "Hey You," and "Leona"—failed to generate much commercial interest.

Coolio (b. 1963) *rapper*

Born Artis Leon Ivey, Jr., in Compton, California, Coolio recorded one of the first Los Angeles RAP records, "Whatcha Gonna Do." He worked with DR DRE as part of the World Class Wreckin' Crew, but his creativity suffered due to cocaine abuse. After a prolonged rehabilitation period and a stint serving as a firefighter, he joined forces with WC and DJ Alladin as part of WC & The MADD Circle, before moving on to the 40 Theivz, a loose HIP-HOP collective consisting of producers, rappers, and dancers. Coolio next embarked on a solo career with the assistance of a sidekick known as "Wino." His productive mid-1990s output included the single, "County Line," which recounted his experiences on welfare, and two critically acclaimed albums, *Home Alone* (Tommy Boy, 1994) and *Fantastic Voyage* (Tommy Boy, 1994).

Cornelius Brothers and Sister Rose

A soft-soul family trio—originally consisting of Carter, Edward (the principal songwriter), and Rose Cornelius—hailing from Dania, Florida, their lilting, immaculately produced, hook-laden material was more typical of the music coming out of northern urban centers than the gritty, down-home output typifying deep South recording centers. They became a major act almost overnight in the early 1970s with two million-selling hit singles, "Treat Her Like a Lady" and "Too Late to Turn Back Now," the latter including the addition of a second sister, Billie Jo. Album releases—*Cornelius Brothers and Sister Rose* (United Artists, 1972), *Big Time Lover* (United Artists, 1973), and *Got to Testify* (United Artists, 1974)—and follow-up singles, however, were increasingly less successful.

The group disbanded in 1976 when Carter joined a Miami-based Black Hebrew Israelites sect, taking on the name Prince Gideon Israel. He spent the next 15 years writing and producing the organization's music and videos. His plans to return to the pop music field were cut short when he died suddenly on November 7, 1991.

Cortez, Dave "Baby" (b. 1938) *organist and bandleader*

Along with BILL DOGGETT and COZY COLE, Dave "Baby" Cortez was one of the early stars of the R&B instrumental genre. A native of Detroit, he was born David Cortez Clowney on August 13, 1938. His father introduced him to the piano, which he played for a decade before switching to the organ while attending Northwestern High.

After high school, he relocated to New York, where he was in considerable demand as a session player and sang with the Pearls from 1955 to 1957. He first recorded as David Clowney for Ember in 1956. In late 1958, Clock Records offered Cortez a recording contract as an instrumentalist. In short order, he wrote and recorded the bouncy instrumental, "The Happy Organ," which topped the charts on the strength of its pop crossover appeal. Immediate follow-ups suffered from a cookie-cutter sameness of sound, and sold poorly.

Cortez would return to the charts in dramatic fashion, however, with the garage rock-styled classic, "Rinky Dink," a Top Ten hit in the summer of 1962. He drifted back into obscurity in the face of the British Invasion, but has continued to perform and occasionally record over the years. He would enjoy a brief return to the R&B charts in June 1973 with a noninstrumental single, "Someone Has Taken Your Place."

Covay, Don (b. 1938) *singer*

For a time during rock 'n' roll's Brill Building–dominated period, Don Covay was one of the more talented songwriters and performers plying their trade within the music business. Due to a combination of unfortunate timing and bad luck, he never was able to rise above journeyman status.

Covay first attracted attention singing around his native Washington, D.C., in the mid-1950s with the Rainbows, a talented group whose membership also included future stars MARVIN GAYE and BILLY STEWART. He would go on to write, sing, and play behind many of the top rhythm and blues artists of the late 1950s. He also recorded singles for Atlantic briefly under the name of Pretty Boy.

During the early 1960s, Covay bounced around from one independent label to another, looking for his big break. With the dance craze movement in full swing, he managed to make a few ripples on the recording scene with "Pony Time" and "Popeye Waddle." The former disc was hurt by the early 1961 release of a CHUBBY CHECKER song bearing the same name, which rocketed to the top of the charts.

His mid-1960s releases—most notably, "Mercy, Mercy" and "Take This Hurt Off Me"—were submerged by the output of the heavily hyped British Invasion artists. He continued to record intermittently into the 1970s, achieving minor success with "I Was Checkin' Out, She Was Checkin' In." Later in the decade, with DISCO dominating the pop landscape, he performed with a shifting array of former hitmakers such as WILSON PICKETT, SOLOMON BURKE, and JOE TEX as the Soul Clan.

Crook, General (b. 1945) *singer and producer*

Born February 28, 1945, in Mound Bayou, Mississippi, General Crook (his real name) grew up in nearby Greenville before relocating to Chicago in 1963. Greatly influenced by JAMES BROWN and other seminal funk artists, he made his recording debut with Capitol in 1969. He made the R&B charts shortly thereafter with "Gimme Some" and "What Time Is It?" He moved on to the Wand label, where he released his eponymous debut LP (Wand, 1974) and a string of old-school funk singles. When commercial success was not forthcoming, Crook chose to concentrate on producing, eventually helping Willie Clayton and Syl Johnson achieve hits.

Crows, The

Many pop music historians feel that the Crows' DOO-WOP classic, "Gee," which reached number two on the R&B charts (simultaneously a number 14 pop hit), was the first rock 'n' roll–styled recording to achieve national popularity. Certainly, it was one of the first rhythm and blues songs to cross over to the pop charts, in the process becoming a staple on white radio playlists.

The Crows—consisting of New York City natives Daniel "Sonny" Norton, lead vocals; Harold Major, tenor; William Davis, baritone; and Gerald Hamilton, bass—formed a group in the late 1940s along with guitar accompanist/tenor Mark Jackson. Their name was inspired by the rash of R&B vocal ensembles then popular that featured bird monikers, most notably the RAVENS, the Orioles, and the Cardinals. Following a period spent honing their craft on Harlem street corners, they secured the services of talent agent/manager Cliff Martinez, who first caught their act at one of the Wednesday night amateur shows put on by the Apollo Theater. Martinez would bring the band to George Goldner's fledgling Rama Records in early 1954.

The mainstream success of the Davis-penned "Gee," the group's debut record released in March 1954, spurred Goldner to establish Gee—a label geared to the rapidly emerging teen market—in January 1956. The Crows, however, never returned to the charts, despite producing a string of high-quality doo-wop singles through 1955, including "Heartbreaker," "Untrue," "Miss You," "Baby Doll," and "Mambo Shevitz." They disbanded in the mid-1950s; unlike many of their peers, they never re-formed to take advantage of the nostalgia boom in later decades.

Crudup, Arthur "Big Boy" (1905–1974) *singer and guitarist*

Born August 24, 1905, in Forest, Mississippi, Arthur Crudup was one of the seminal post–World War II blues shouters. He sang gospel music with the Harmonizing Four in the 1940s while recording secular material as a solo artist for Bluebird as early as 1941. He placed a half-dozen singles in the R&B Top Ten between 1945 and 1951—most notably, "Rock Me Mama," "Keep Your Arms Around Me," and "So Glad You're Mine"—while touring with such blues legends as SONNY BOY WILLIAMSON (II) and Elmore James.

Following almost a decade of inactivity, he recorded for Fire in 1959, a session allegedly set up by Elvis Presley, who counted him as a leading influence (Presley's first commercial release, "That's All Right, Mama," was a Crudup song). He found a new audience for his work during the 1960s blues revival, touring with Bonnie Raitt shortly before his death from a stroke March 28, 1974.

Crystals, The

The Brooklyn-based Crystals, consisting of Barbara Alston, Lala Brooks, Dee Dee Kennibrew, Mary Thomas, and Patricia Wright, were discovered by producer Phil Spector, who signed them to his fledgling Philles label in 1961. The group recorded six Top 20 hits, most notably, "He's a Rebel," "Da Doo Don Ron (When He Walked Me Home)," and "Then He Kissed Me," prior to being overwhelmed by the British Invasion acts. In a typically inexplicable Spector move, the Gene Pitney–penned "He's a Rebel" and "He's Sure the Boy I Love" were actually recorded by Darlene Love & the BLOSSOMS while the Crystals were out on tour.

Cymone, Andre *singer and bassist*

Born Andre Simon Anderson, Cymone was part of the Minneapolis punk FUNK vanguard enjoying commercial success the early 1980s. The Minneapolis native first attracted attention as the bass player in PRINCE's band, The Revolution. He opted for a solo career in 1981, recording a string of R&B hits—most notably, "Make Me Wanna Dance" and "The Dance Electric"—assisted by Prince's tour support and promotional video expertise. Although he remained active on the live circuit, his last chart single came in early 1986.

Cypress Hill

The first Latino act to make an appreciable impact within the HIP-HOP market, Cypress Hill were also instrumental in bridging the gap with followers of both alternative rock and heavy metal. Furthermore, they pioneered a new strain of stoned FUNK—featuring slow, rolling DRUM AND BASS loops, spacey sound effects, and mind-bending samples—which complemented their endorsement of marijuana use. Although long-term popularity eluded them, they were influential in the development of a number of 1990s styles, most notably, West Coast G-funk and English trip-hop.

Formed in Los Angeles in 1988, the group—consisting of DJ Muggs and rappers B-Real and Sen Dog—achieved success out of the box with their eponymous debut (Ruffhouse/Columbia, 1991), which reached number 31 on domestic album charts. Cypress Hill's uneasy blend of gangsta posturing and cartoonish humor took on a darker tint with the chart-topping *Black Sunday* (Ruffhouse/Columbia, 1993). However, the engaging craftsmanship characterizing the first two LPs had degenerated into the uninspired recycling of old ideas on *Cypress Hill III: Temples of Boom* (Ruffhouse/Columbia, 1995) and *IV* (Ruffhouse/Columbia, 1998).

In an attempt to win over a new generation of youth taken with the RAP-metal of Kid Rock, Limp Bizkit, and the like, the group recorded a double-CD set, *Skull & Bones* (Ruffhouse/Columbia, 2000): one CD devoted to hip-hop, the other to guitar-driven hard rock. Although the rock selections tended to be devoid of hooks and catchy riffs, the strength of the rap tracks—which approached the quality of *Black Sunday,* with funky, evocative arrangements accented by fluid rhymes—helped propel the release into the Top Five. However, *Live at the Fillmore* (Ruffhouse/Columbia, 2000), which reinterpreted their early 1990s material within a riff-rock format, and *Stoned Raiders* (Ruffhouse/Columbia, 2001) were commercial disappointments, leaving Cypress Hill's future very much in question.

Daddy-O (b. 1961) *rapper and producer*
Daddy-O has been termed the "Quincy Jones of RAP." He has spoken at a number of college seminars and provided community service to further the A.F.R.I.C.A. program, which included an anti-apartheid album and study guide.

The Brooklyn native helped form Stetsasonic, and when the group disbanded in 1990, he was recruited to remix dance-pop hits such as MARY J. BLIGE's "Real Love" and Shante Moore's "Love's Taken Over." He soon became one of the busiest producers in the record industry, his clients spanning HIP-HOP (e.g., Audio Two, K9, QUEEN LATIFAH), R&B (Jeffrey Osbourne), REGGAE (Third World), and alternative rock (Red Hot Chili Peppers, They Might Be Giants). He was also hired to produce jingles for the likes of Alka Seltzer, Casio Electronics, and Pepsi.

He began work on an overtly political rap album, but ultimately shelved it in favor of a more R&B-flavored set, *You Can Be a Daddy but Never Daddy-O* (Brooktown/Island, 1993). The debut single, "Brooklyn Bounce," became a moderate club hit.

Dana Dane *rapper*
Dana Dane will always be remembered as the first HIP-HOP artist to apply his name to a fashion line or retailer, a practice that was widely imitated in the 1990s. A graduate of New York City's High School of Music and Art, he also made mainstream-oriented music, his quasi-British accent backed by pronounced East Coast–styled beats and DJ Clark Kent's polished production touches. He recorded two moderately successful albums, *Dana Dane with Fame* (Profile, 1987), which included the crossover hit, "Cinderella," and *Dana Dane 4 Ever* (Profile, 1990).

Danderliers, The
A highly underrated R&B vocal group formed in the mid-1950s, the Chicago-based Danderliers—comprising Dallas Taylor, tenor and jump lead; James Campbell, tenor and ballad lead; Bernard Dixon, first tenor; Walter Stephenson, baritone; and Richard Thomas, bass—excelled at romantic ballads, most notably "My Autumn Love" (B-side to "Chomp Chomp Boom"), "May God Be with You," and "My Love." Ironically, though, their one major national hit, "Chomp Chomp Boom," which reached number ten on the R&B charts in 1955, was a rousing uptempo number. The Danderliers' chance at crossover pop success, however, was undercut by the Crewcuts' rush release of a competing cover version. Eugene Record was allegedly inspired to form his highly successful soul group, the CHI-LITES, after hearing the Danderliers' singles.

Davis, Tyrone (b. 1938) *singer*
A masterful interpreter of laid-back romantic ballads, Tyrone Davis effectively bridged the gap between R&B and mainstream pop in the 1970s. Even when the hits dried up, his elegant, sophisticated style enabled him to tour—and occasionally record—with success into the 21st century.

Born May 4, 1938, in Greenville, Mississippi, Davis and his family moved to the rust-belt city of Saginaw, Michigan, when he was 14. In 1959 he was employed as a steelworker in Chicago, where he began performing at area clubs. He served as valet and chauffeur for blues guitarist FREDDIE KING in the early 1960s. A local star, Otis Clay, introduced him to producer Harold Burrage, who dubbed him "Tyrone the Wonder Boy" and made records with him for the Four Brothers and Hit Sound labels.

Davis finally achieved nationwide recognition in 1968 with the number one R&B hit, "Can I Change My Mind"; the restrained lead vocal, accented by piercing horn charts, formed the template for follow-up releases. For the next fifteen years, he was a fixture on the R&B recording scene—as well as crossing over to the lower reaches of the pop charts—with hits like "Is It Something You've Got," "Turn Back the Hands of Time," "I Had It All the Time," "Without You in My Life," "Turning Point," "Give It Up (Turn It Loose)," and "Are You Serious." His albums also enjoyed a measure of success, seven reaching the middle range of the *Billboard Top LPs* listing. He later recorded for the Ocean Front and Future labels in the 1980s, and Ichiban, Rhino, and Malaco in the 1990s.

Day, Bobby (b. 1932) *singer*

Bobby Day had only one hit record of note, but oh, what a record! The double-sided single, "Rock-in Robin"/"Over and Over," not only was a major best-seller in 1958 (the A-side went number two on the Hot 100 and topped the R&B charts for three weeks) and remains in heavy rotation on oldies radio playlists, but has been widely covered, most notably, the Dave Clark Five's "Over and Over" and MICHAEL JACKSON's "Rockin' Robin."

He was born Robert Byrd on July 1, 1932, in Ft. Worth, Texas. Day moved to the Watts area of Los Angeles in 1948, where he formed the R&B vocal group, the Hollywood Flames—also known as The Flames, Four Flames, Hollywood Four Flames, Jets, Tangiers, and Satellites—a couple of years later.

They went through many personnel changes over the years; their lineup consisted of Earl "Jackie" Nelson, David Ford, Clyde Tillis, and Curtis Williams (formerly of the Penguins and composer of the DOO-WOP classic, "Earth Angel") when "Buzz-Buzz-Buzz" became a crossover hit in 1957.

Although the group continued to record into the 1960s, Day moved on to a solo career in 1958. He wrote—and recorded the original version of—"Little Bitty Pretty One," which became a Top Ten crossover hit for Thurston Harris. He also supplied the backing vocals for "Pretty Girls Everywhere," by Eugene Church and the Fellows.

Following several more minor solo hits, Day would form a duo, Bob & Earl, with former group mate Nelson in 1960. However, he had moved into other areas of the music business (his place being taken by Bob Relf) by the time the duo released their first chart record, "Harlem Shuffle," in 1963.

Death Row Records

Widely considered the definitive gangsta rap label, Death Row was formed out of the ashes of N.W.A., when former member DR DRE joined forces with entrepreneur Suge Knight in 1991. Success followed in short order when Dre's debut solo album, *The Chronic*, released in 1992, achieved multiplatinum sales. During the mid-1990s, the company enjoyed a string of successes, with recordings by SNOOP DOGGY DOGG and TUPAC SHAKUR, among others, becoming top sellers.

At its commercial peak, Death Row began receiving considerable negative press as a result of a feud between Knight and Sean "PUFF DADDY" Combs, head of the BAD BOY label. Their standoff filtered down to the artists employed by both firms, most notably Death Row's Shakur and Bad Boy's NOTORIOUS B.I.G. Shakur's drive-by shooting death in Las Vegas on September 13, 1996, was linked by many observers to B.I.G.'s equally mysterious murder in Los Angeles on March 9, 1997. In the meantime, Dr Dre became disillusioned with Knight's hardball policies, and left to form his own label,

Aftermath, in 1996. Knight himself was convicted of racketeering in 1997; after briefly serving time in prison, he changed his label's name to The Row.

DeBarge

One of the major teen groups of the 1980s, the group was on the verge of becoming a major pop phenomenon when lead singer Eldra (EL) DEBARGE opted for a solo career. Formed in 1978, the Grand Rapids, Michigan–based family group—consisting of Eldra, a sister, Bunny, and three other brothers, James, Mark, and Randy—were signed the following year by MOTOWN, who marketed them as the next Jackson Five.

Their debut album, *DeBarges* (Motown, 1981), did not set the world on fire; however, "I Like It," released in late 1982, became a best seller both on the R&B and pop charts. From this point onward, DeBarge became an unstoppable force, producing one hit after another, including "All This Love"; "Time Will Reveal"; "Rhythm of the Night," from the film, *The Last Dragon,* in which they appeared; and "Who's Holding Donna Now?"

Bunny chose to remain with Motown when the remaining three DeBarge brothers signed to Striped Horse Records in 1987. The final blow to the group's declining fortunes came when their other brothers, Chico and Bobby DeBarge, were arrested and convicted on cocaine trafficking charges in 1988.

DeBarge, El (b. 1961) *singer*

Born June 4, 1961, in Grand Rapids, Michigan, Eldra (El) DeBarge was the lead singer for DEBARGE—which included a sister and three other brothers—from its formation in 1978 until he decided to go solo in 1986. His debut LP, *El DeBarge* (Gordy, 1986), was a hook-laden fusion of pop-R&B poured in the MICHAEL JACKSON mold. He maintained his momentum with the 1986 hit single, "Who's Johnny?," the theme song for the blockbuster film, *Short Circuit,* followed by "Real Love."

El DeBarge publicity still from the late 1980s (Frank Driggs Collection)

In order to prolong his career, he chose to expand beyond his teen idol base, focusing on the adult contemporary market with albums like *Heart, Mind & Soul* (Warner/Reprise, 1994).

Def Jam Records

Def Jam was founded in New York in 1983 by producer Rick Rubin and Russell Simmons, who'd gotten involved with HIP-HOP culture as a manager for artists like RUN-DMC. Roughly a year following the release of its debut recording—L. L. COOL J's "I Need a Beat" (Def Jam, 1984)—the label achieved platinum sales for two albums: the BEASTIE BOYS' *Licensed to Ill* (Def Jam, 1986) and L. L. Cool J's *Radio* (Def Jam/Columbia, 1986).

As RAP broke into the pop music mainstream during the 1980s, Def Jam continued to grow, achieving both commercial and artistic success with PUBLIC ENEMY—*It Takes a Nation of Millions* (Def Jam, 1988), *Fear of a Black Planet* (Def Jam, 1990), and *Apocalypse 91 . . . The Enemy Strikes Back* (Def Jam, 1991; number four)—Warren G, among others. Seeking greater creative control, Rubin left to establish his own imprint, the Los Angeles–based Def American.

Polygram purchased 60 percent ownership of the company in 1993. Taking note of Def Jam's $40 million in profits for 1998, Seagram acquired Polygram's interest in the label the following year. In 2000, Seagram bought Def Jam's remaining shares for approximately $100 million, renaming their record company holdings the ISLAND/Def Jam Music Group, including the subsidiaries American, Def Soul, Lost Highway, Murder Inc Records, Roadrunner Records, and Roc-A-Fella Records.

Delfonics, The

With their falsetto leads, high-pitched harmonies, and lush arrangements, the Delfonics helped pioneer the Philadelphia soul sound in the late 1960s. The formation of the group, however, was inspired by the mid-1950s recordings of Frankie Lymon and the Teenagers.

The founding members—brothers William and Wilbert Hart and friend Randy Cain—started out performing DOO-WOP covers as the Philadelphia-based Veltones, along with a succession of other teenagers in the neighborhood. When Cain enrolled at Lincoln University in Oxford, Pennsylvania, the Harts continued to perform around their hometown of Philadelphia, incorporating dance steps into their act. With the return of Cain in 1965, the threesome added Ritchie Daniels (who left for military service in 1968) to form the Four Gents; changing their name to the Delfonics the following year, they achieved local hits with "He Don't Really Love You" and "He's Been Untrue."

The William Hart composition, "La-La Means I Love You"—built around words his young son would exclaim each morning—made the Delfonics international stars in 1968. It was followed by a succession of best-selling singles, most notably "Didn't I (Blow Your Mind This Time)," which won a Grammy for the top soul hit of 1970. The group also placed five LPs on the *Billboard* Top 200, the most successful being *The Delfonics* (Philly Groove, 1970).

When Cain departed in early 1971, he was replaced by MAJOR HARRIS. Harris had broken in with the Teenagers, before moving on to the Jarmels—singing on the 1961 hit, "A Little Bit of Soap"—and the Nat Turner Rebellion. He would embark upon a solo career when the hits stopped coming for the Delfonics in the mid-1970s.

Delicious Vinyl

The Los Angeles–based label was co-founded in 1987 by two New Yorkers, Matt Dike and Mick Ross, both DJ/promoters attempting to fill the demand for high-quality HIP-HOP recordings to program for club nights. In attempting to emulate the laid-back sampling/breakbeat approach popularized by artists like ERIC B. AND RAKIM, they would ultimately be credited with establishing the "new West Coast sound."

Delicious Vinyl first achieved commercial success with YOUNG M.C. and Tone Loc, whose salacious "Wild Thing" (composed by Young M.C.) went triple platinum. The company built on this foundation with best-selling releases by Pharcyde, Master Ace, and the British-based Brand New Heavies. After inking an international distribution deal with East West in 1994, Dike and Ross continued to uncover new talent of note, including the Wascals, the RAP/club music hybrid Born Jamericans, and Angel (the first signing on their subsidiary, Brass Records).

Dells, The

One of the most successful R&B vocal groups of the rock era, the members—lead singer Johnny Funches (replaced by Johnny Carter, formerly of the Flamingos), tenors Marvin Junior and Verne

Vee-Jay promo shot of the Dells (Frank Driggs Collection)

Allison, baritone Mickey McGill, and bass Chuck Barksdale—got together while attending Thornton Township High School in Harvey, Illinois. They first recorded as the El-Rays in 1953 for the Chess label, and achieved a degree of prominence when the Vee-Jay single, "Oh What a Nite," reached number four on the R&B charts in 1956. After a decade of obscurity, the Dells resurfaced in the mid-1960s as an archetypal Chicago Soul ensemble, enjoying crossover success with such hits as "There Is," "Stay in My Corner," "Always Together," "I Can Sing a Rainbow"/"Love Is Blue," and a reworking of "Oh, What a Night." The group remained an R&B force until the mid-1980s, although pop success eluded them following the early 1970s.

Dell-Vikings, The (Del Vikings)

The Dell-Vikings were one of the first integrated groups to achieve success during the rock 'n' roll era. Due to legal entanglements, however, they failed to realize the promise of their debut release, the million-selling classic "Come Go With Me."

The group was formed in Pittsburgh, Pennsylvania in 1955 where the members—originally consisting of lead vocalist Norman Wright, first tenor Corinthian "Kripp" Johnson, second tenor Donald "Gus" Bakus, baritone David Lerchey, and bass Clarence Quick—were stationed while serving stints in the Air Force. The name came from perusing books at the library about the exploits of the Vikings; the addition of the word "Dell" was agreed upon simply because they liked how it sounded. After winning the Air Force–sponsored "Tops in Blues" contest, they decided to pursue a professional performing career in earnest. They first recorded for the Luniverse label in 1956 without success.

While practicing at the Air Force Serviceman's Club in late 1956, Quick introduced them to a song he'd composed at the piano, "Come Go with Me." A friend, Pittsburgh disc jockey Barry Kaye, let them use his primitive basement recording studio; due to its small size and acoustic limitations, some of the group members were required to sing in a nearby closet to achieve the desired sound. Leased to the Pittsburgh-based Fee-Bee label, the recording became an overnight local smash. When Dot Records picked up national distribution rights in early 1957, it would become one of the top hits of the year.

Dot immediately signed the Dell-Vikings to a long-term contract; however, Mercury Records, which also wanted to obtain rights to the group, argued that since none of the members were 21—except for Johnson—they weren't legally bound to Dot. As a result, the other members jumped to Mercury when offered a more lucrative contract, bringing in William Blakely to replace Johnson. In the meantime, Johnson put together his own version of the Dell-Vikings with Dot. For a brief time in mid-1957, both labels had Dell-Vikings records on the charts; Dot had the bigger success with the crossover Top Ten smash, "Whispering Bells," while Mercury had "Cool Shake," featuring Bakus singing lead, which reached number nine on the R&B charts.

By December 1957, Mercury had obtained exclusive rights to the group name. As a result, the Dot group would record as the Versatiles for Fee-Bee; one member, Chuck Jackson, would go on to achieve solo fame as a soul singer for Wand Records. However, the Mercury edition (now spelled "Del Vikings") failed to score another hit, eventually disbanding in the mid-1960s. The group—featuring a rapid succession of singers,

including, at various times, Wright, Quick, Lerchey, and Johnson—would re-form to perform at oldies revival shows in the 1970s. In addition to having their classic material frequently reissued on vinyl and compact disc, the Del Vikings were still releasing new recordings as late as the 1990s.

Demon Boyz

A product of the English underground music scene, the Demon Boyz developed a "wiggedy diggedy" style of delivery that has influenced American acts like Das-EFX. The duo—consisting of Mike J. and Darren, known as "Demon" because of his pointed ears—started out performing at the Rebel MC's Broadwater Farm sound system parties. They soon developed an affinity for the club scene as well with singles like the breakbeat-heavy "Dett," and trailblazing "Jungle-ist." Their debut LP, *Recognition* (Music of Life, 1989), was followed by *Original Guidance – The 2nd Chapter* (Tribal Bass, 1993), which revealed an increasing fascination with REGGAE accents. Seemingly on the verge of wider public acceptance, the Demon Boyz disappeared from view.

Destiny's Child

One of the most popular recording acts at the onset of the 21st century, the Houston-based group—originally consisting of lead singer Beyoncé Knowles, second lead vocalist Kelly Rowland, alto LaTavia Roberson, and soprano LeToya Luckett—came together in 1993 and adopted their name from the book of Isaiah. Beyoncé's father, Music World Management's Mathew Knowles, steered the quartet from early local impact opening for best-selling rhythm and blues artists to international recognition after signing with Columbia in 1997.

Their initial success came with the inclusion of "Killing Time" in the top-grossing 1997 film, *Men in Black*. They built up further momentum with the release of their eponymous debut LP (Columbia, 1998), which featured production assists from leading urban R&B/hip-hop producers R. KELLY,

TIMBALAND, MISSY "MISDEMEANOR" ELLIOTT, and Wyclef Jean. The latter's collaboration with the quartet, the infectious dance number "No, No, No (Part 2)," reached number one on the R&B charts. Their second album, *The Writing's on the Wall* (Columbia, 1999)—while including producers Elliott, Kevin "She'kspere" Briggs, Rodney Jerkins, Chad Elliot, and Dwayne Wiggins of Tony! Toni! Tone!—provided more opportunities for creative input by group members. The anti-male anthem, "Bills, Bills, Bills," headed up the R&B charts for nine consecutive weeks in 1999.

Despite personnel problems—Roberson and Luckett were, according to a lawsuit settled July 24, 2002, allegedly forced out by Mathew Knowles after refusing to accept his legal guardianship—Destiny's Child, bolstered by the additions of Farrah Franklin and Michelle Williams in February 2000, emerged as the leading female R&B vocal act. With Beyoncé Knowles now dominating songwriting and production, the group released a steady stream of hits, most notably, the albums *8 Days of Christmas* (Columbia, 2001) and the platinum-selling *Survivor* (Columbia, 2002)—winner of the 2002 Grammy Award for Best R&B Performance by a Duo or Group with Vocal—and the number one singles "Say My Name" and "Independent Women, Part 1," the latter of which appeared in the *Charlie's Angels* soundtrack. In late 2001, the group—now a trio following the departure of Franklin that August—announced a hiatus to work on solo recording projects. During the interim, they released *This Is the Remix* (Columbia, 2002), consisting largely of old hits—ranging from street-smart hip-hop to torchy R&B-tinged ballads—reworked by producers such as Timbaland, Maurice Joshua, and the NEPTUNES.

At this point in time, the group members branched off into solo projects; Rowland released an LP in 2003, but Knowles garnered even more critical and commercial success the following year with her own album. Williams concentrated on making gospel recordings; her "churchified" twang was given a higher profile than ever before in the group's reunion CD, *Destiny Fulfilled* (Sony BMG, 2004).

Destiny's Child (from left, Kelly Rowland, Beyoncé Knowles, and Michelle Williams) (Albert Ferreira/Reuters/Landov)

Diddy   See PUFF DADDY.

Digable Planets

The Digable Planets grew out the psychedelic jazz rap pioneered by the likes of De La Soul and PM Dawn. This is reflected in their spacey word play and sinuous jazz riffs, along with their whimsical pseudonyms—Butterfly, Doodle Bug, and Ladybug—allegedly an outgrowth of their admiration for the community structures of insects. Their debut LP, *Reachin' (A New Reflection of Time and Space)* (WEA, 1993), featured the smash single, "Rebirth of

Slick (Cool Like Dat)" and also displayed a pronounced political take on contemporary life, as expressed in the track "La Femme Fetal," an indictment of pro-life lobby stratagems like the firebombing of abortion clinics.

Digital Underground

Although distinctly a part of the hardcore RAP movement, the Digital Underground are notable for the depth of vision and comic sense they have brought to the genre. The strong influence of the P-Funk sound pervades their music, beginning with the debut LP, *Sex Packets* (Tommy Boy, 1990), which includes as its subtext a mad scientist's scheme to market a drug causing wet dreams.

The Oakland-based Digital Underground was formed in the mid-1980s by Shock-G (born Gregory E. Jacobs, vocals/keyboards) and Chopmaster J (samples programmer/percussion). Other core members would include DJ Fuse (b. David Elliot, October 8, 1970, Syracuse, New York), Money B, and Eddie "Humpty Hump" Humphrey (an alter ego of Shock G), who capitalized on an unfortunate kitchen mishap by donning an outrageous false nose onstage and creating a series of tribute recordings (e.g., the "Humpty Dance" routine, regarding the ability to get his hooter into the pants of whomever he desires).

The group was invited to contribute tracks to the film comedy, *Nothing But Trouble* (1991), in which they also appeared. The songs were also released on *This Is An EP* (1991), which was followed by a string of successful albums, including *Sons of the P* (Tommy Boy, 1991) and *The Body-Hat Syndrome* (Tommy Boy, 1993), which included the addition of DJ Jay Z, Clee, and Saafir (aka the Saucy Nomad) as well as a guest appearance by former member TUPAC SHAKUR on "Wussup With the Luv," a diatribe against drug dealers selling to children.

Dirt Nation

The rap trio Dirt Nation provided a mellow, soul-inflected alternative to the dominant gangsta style of the mid-1990s. The group—consisting of New Jersey native E Depp, JB (born in Brooklyn), and KD (a native of Jamaica)—met while attending school in Maryland, and moved their home base to Manhattan in order to secure a recording contract more easily. They achieved immediate success in 1993 with their debut single, "Khadijah," a tuneful tribute to the distaff sex that quoted material by MARVIN GAYE, Curtis Mayfield, and JIMMY McGRIFF. The album that followed, *Three the Hard Way* (1994), offered similar fare while utilizing the talents of GANG STARR's Guru Keith E and Biggie Smalls.

disco

Disco returned dancing to the forefront of pop music, and it did so with a verve and drive fueled, at least in part, by a disregard for many of the conventions held dear by rock enthusiasts. This perceived slight on the part of rock establishment would ultimately elicit a widespread negative reaction sufficient to drive the movement back underground.

The genre emerged out of an urban subculture in the early 1970s. Discos had been quietly serving their core audience for years. They originated as settings where one could dance to recorded music. The deejay deploying two turntables, a mike, and a PA system was a fixture in black communities. Whites deployed a similar arrangement for dances featuring oldies in church basements and community centers. Discotheques such as the Peppermint Lounge in New York City helped popularize the Twist and countless spin-off dances in the early 1960s. For a short time, even wealthy jet-setters found it hip to mix with the masses in New York hot spots.

By the 1970s, however, discos promised escapism and release. With music and lighting choreographed to manipulate the mood of the dancers, the experience melded 1970s self-absorption with a 1960s sense of community. In this setting, the person playing the records was often more important than the identity of the records.

The genre appears to have received its impetus from venues such as The Loft in Manhattan and

The 10th Floor on Fire Island because gay men had trouble securing live acts to perform at their social soirées. These places combined the functions of private clubs, dance parties, and avant-garde hangouts. In short, gay cultural circumstances in the 1970s, partially out of the closet but still not welcome in mainstream society, played a significant role in the evolution of disco.

In light of these social forces, disco may well have been the first pop music form dictated by consumers; if dancers related to a record at these venues, it was classified as disco. The style was rooted in smooth black urban pop best exemplified by Gamble and Huff's Philly sound and the seductive raps of Barry White, ISAAC HAYES, and the like. However, it also incorporated a quirky, unpredictable side: left-field oddities sometimes went on to mainstream success by way of the discos; e.g., Manu Dibango's 1973 release, "Soul Makossa," considered by some to be the first true disco hit. By 1974 the dance club scene was regularly responsible for breaking major hits; within another year it was helping determine the way records were made. Album-sized singles were introduced to fill deejay needs; these "disco singles" became so popular that a large number of them were released commercially. In addition, many pop recordings were issued in a "disco version," most notably, new arrangements of show-biz oldies, rock chestnuts, soul classics, and classical music's greatest hits.

The disco version's extended length, use of musical drama, and emphasis on instrumental texture rather than vocal personality or verbal complexity predisposed the genre to a strong European influence. European composers and arrangers were instrumental in freeing disco from its tendency to cannibalize the past by developing forms that were more appropriate to its dance imperatives. Rather than lengthening conventional pop songs with gimmicks, studio wizards such as Munich-based Giorgio Moroder developed long, structured compositions calculated to fill an entire album side with music that ebbed and flowed in one beat-driven, but melodically varied, cut. DONNA SUMMER's "Love to Love You Baby" typified this approach, with its avoidance of the widely used verse-chorus–instrumental break–verse-chorus format in favor of an extended track suggesting a compressed movie soundtrack (perhaps even a classical music work) with its different movements. This spin-off form, known as Eurodisco, could be, in Ed Ward's words, as light (or shallow) as French pop, as dramatic (or pompous) as a German symphony, as cerebral (or cold) as experimental avant-garde music, or as minimalist (or repetitive) as a chant (or ad jingle).

Disco ultimately secured mainstream acceptance through the success of *Saturday Night Fever*. Released in 1977, the film cut across all demographic lines, while the soundtrack—featuring the BEE GEES and an assortment of minor dance hits—became the best-selling LP in pop music history. Up to this point in time, the disco scene had remained outside the pop mainstream because (1) few real discos existed anywhere other than in the major urban centers, (2) music that was specifically disco (in contrast to crossover hits) continued to be boycotted by many pop radio stations, and (3) the absence of recognizable stars meant there was no handle by which less informed fans could sort through the disco section in record stores.

In the wake of disco's breakthrough, established artists (e.g., Rod Stewart, the Beach Boys, the Rolling Stones)—even new wave trendsetters Blondie—rushed to cash in by recording in this style. Radio stations did not just add disco cuts to their playlists, they often went all-disco. Record companies competed to hire disco insiders and artists.

After a brief run as the top pop music genre in 1978–79, disco began to lose its patented dance groove. In addition, its success stimulated a cultural backlash from the more reactionary elements of the white establishment. "Disco sucks" dominated bumper stickers and graffiti of the day. There were disco record bonfires and anti-disco protests that occasionally degenerated into riots (e.g., at a Comiskey Park baseball game in 1979). The rock press widely criticized the genre.

By 1980, the best dance music was again coming from its original source, black pop. Disco was absorbed back into the underground, to be resurrected in the 1980s as dance-oriented rock (DOR), alternative dance, HOUSE, go-go, electronic dance music, and, ultimately, TECHNO. Summer was the only notable disco artist to maintain past chart successes.

Disposable Heroes of Hiphoprisy, The

The Disposable Heroes of Hiphoprisy were notable advocates of multiculturalism, open-mindedness, and tolerance, setting themselves in direct opposition to widespread HIP-HOP values such as homophobia, misogyny, and racism. Formed in 1990, the duo—consisting of Michael Franti and Rono Tse—were ex-members of the San Francisco–based avant-garde industrial jazz collective, the Beatnigs.

Franti's idealistic verses—best heard on their only LP, the ambitious *Hypocrisy is the Greatest Luxury* (4th & Broadway, 1992)—made them a favored opening act for the likes of Arrested Development, PUBLIC ENEMY, Nirvana, and U2. In the end, however, the Heroes were unable to attract a sizable African-American audience. Some RAP community constituents dismissed them as a ploy to ease white America's fears over the prevailing gangsta rap ethic. After working with beat visionary William S. Burroughs on *Spare Ass Annie and Other Tales* (1993), the duo called it quits. Franti went on to form the funk-oriented Spearhead, while Tse joined forces with the Bay Area–based rap group Mystik Journeymen.

Dixie Cups, The

The Dixie Cups typified the GIRL GROUP genre: attractive teenage females with pliable voices and personalities, molded to suit the artistic and commercial priorities of a handful of record label executives and studio producers. This trio stood apart from their peers, however, because they sang on one of the rock era's most memorable recordings: the rock-steady

paean to idealized romance, "Chapel of Love." In addition, the song was selected as the first release by JERRY LEIBER AND MIKE STOLLER's highly regarded (for its high ratio of hits to releases) Red Bird label.

The Dixie Cups—consisting of New Orleans natives Joan Marie Johnson and sisters Barbara Ann and Rosa Lee Hawkins—were introduced to Leiber and Stoller by singer Joe Jones, who'd decided to manage them after catching their act at a local talent show. Providing them with an alternative name to Little Miss and the Muffets, Leiber and Stoller placed them with the songwriting/production team of Jeff Barry and Ellie Greenwich, who'd recently provided material for the Phil Spector acts, the Ronettes and the Crystals, and had recorded as the Raindrops. The couple, who had married October 29, 1962, felt that "Chapel of Love"—which they cowrote with Spector and placed on the 1964 album, . . . *presenting the fabulous Ronettes featuring Veronica*—possessed hit potential. Over Spector's objections, they brought in the Dixie Cups to reinterpret the song with an arranging assist from Jones.

The trio enjoyed a brief run of lesser chart entries in 1964–65—including "People Say," "You Should Have Seen the Way He Looked at Me," "Little Bell," and "Iko Iko"—before Red Bird went out of business in 1966. The Dixie Cups jumped to ABC Records, but failed to record another hit.

Dixon, Willie (1915–1992) *singer, bassist, and producer*

After rising to house producer for Chess Records in 1954, Dixon wrote, arranged, produced, and played bass on the recordings of CHUCK BERRY, Buddy Guy, Howlin' Wolf, Little Walter, OTIS RUSH, Muddy Waters, SONNY BOY WILLIAMSON (II), and others. He was a key force in the development of the post–World War II Chicago blues scene. Many of his compositions have become blues standards, including "Back Door Man," "I Can't Quit You Baby," "I Just Want to Make Love to You," "I'm Ready," "I Ain't Superstitious," "The Red Rooster," "The Seventh Son," and "Wang Dang Doodle."

Born July 1, 1915, in Vicksburg, Mississippi, Dixon revealed an aptitude for writing poetry as well as a deep, rich voice developed in church prior to moving to Chicago in 1937. He first made his mark as a professional boxer before becoming a singer/bassist with a jazz-pop combo, the Five Breezes, in 1940. The group would record for Bluebird that year without commercial success; sessions with Mercury in the early 1940s, as a member of the Four Jumps of Jive, also failed to produce any hits. Together with pianist Leonard Caston and guitarist Bernardo Dennis, he then founded the Big Three Trio, whose jazz-R&B-pop amalgam was waxed by Columbia in the late 1940s. Their most popular recording, "You Sure Look Good to Me," reached number ten on the 1948 *Billboard* R&B charts.

He began working as a producer for Chess Records in 1951, proving his worth on a series of tracks with guitarist Robert Nighthawk. While producing Chess sessions well into the 1970s, Dixon found time to pursue many other activities, including production work for the Chicago-based Cobra label, recording as the featured artist, promoting new talent (e.g., Little Wolf, Margie Evans), managing a record company (Yambo), and live performing, first with Memphis Slim in the early 1960s and, beginning in 1967, as head of his own band, the Chicago Blues All-Stars. Dixon's only solo hit, "Walking the Blues," reached number six on the R&B charts in 1955.

Following the 1987 settlement of a two-decade dispute with Led Zeppelin over the failure to credit his contribution to the composition of "Whole Lotta Love" (based largely on his "You Need Love"), Dixon established the Blues Heaven Foundation, an organization dedicated to preserving blues music and culture as well as helping secure copyrights and ensuing royalties for other songwriters and recording artists. Despite a relative lack of success as a recording artist, much of his work has been reissued on compact disc, from the Big Three Trio to 1970s albums by the Chicago Blues All-Stars. His most enduring legacy, however, remains the classic Chess tracks he helped create in a supporting role. Many of them are available in a three-CD compilation, *The Willie Dixon Chess Box* (Chess, 1992).

DJ Hollywood (b. 1954) *rapper*

DJ Hollywood is one of the lesser-known names in RAP, despite his seminal contributions to the genre, including coining the term "HIP-HOP" and originating the practice of delivering extensive rhymes over recorded music, the very essence of hip-hop. His legacy appears to have been shortchanged due to the location of his home base (Manhattan), the records he utilized (DISCO), and his audience (reportedly in large part downtown hustlers).

Born December 10, 1954, he formed his own singing group as a fourteen-year-old. By 1971, he was in demand as a DJ in Harlem clubs such as the Charles Gallery. During the disco era, he added record mixing—a technique he picked up from a club owner—to his arsenal, enabling him to focus on the most danceable portions of the records. His mastery of the turntables at the Apollo Theater in the mid-1970s would influence up-and-coming artists like KURTIS BLOW and the Fatback Band.

A major DJ until the mid-1980s, he dropped out of sight for a time due to drug addiction. He made a comeback in the early 1990s, working in the greater New York area with old-time associate Lovebug Starski. Albums like *Hollywood's World* (Tuff City, 1995) and *Rarities* (Ol Skool Fava, 1995) provide a representative look at his style.

DJ Screw (1970–2000) *rapper and producer*

DJ Screw developed a novel mixing style which involved pitching down his recordings to foot-dragging tempos. The effect was mildly trippy, with his popularity growing from a strictly local phenomenon—he started out selling mix cassettes at his Houston-based record store, Screwed Up Records and Tapes—to a nationwide scale during the 1990s.

Born Robert Earl Davis, his music was closely tied in with the advocacy of "syrup sippin'," a southern rap practice of consuming codeine-infused cough syrup to induce a hallucinatory state during which time seems suspended and the senses swirl. This was reflected in some of his tape titles: *Syrup & Soda, Syrup Sippers,* and *Sippin' Codeine.* Soon his home studio, the Screw Shop, became the operations center for the Screwed Up Click, made up of several dozen Houston-based artists, including Big Pokey, Hardheadz, Lil' Keke, and Mobb Figgaz. Fans began recording the mixes and trading them on the Internet; imitators sprang up offering "screwed" remixes of rap hits and other classic R&B fare. DJ Screw also issued commercial CDs, including *3 in the Mornin', Part 1* (Big Tyme, 1995), *3 in the Mornin', Pt. 2* (Big Tyme, 1996), and *All Work, No Play* (Jam Down, 1999), the latter two of which championed local rap material.

He was found dead in his studio of a codeine-induced heart attack on November 16, 2000. Although Houston's rise as a southern rap center was dealt a severe blow, DJ Screw's mixing technique has continued to flourish, most notably through works issued on the Swisha House and Beltway 8 labels.

DJ Smurf *rapper and deejay*

A product of Atlanta's bass music scene, producer DJ Smurf is best known for his work with club/dance and HIP-HOP artists such as MC Shy D and DJ Kizzy Rock. His own albums—including *Versastyles* (Wrap, 1995), *Collipark Music* (Benz, 1997), *Dead Crunk* (Benz, 1998), and *NonStop Booty Shake* (Fortune Entertainment, 1999)—are best defined as dirty RAP or party rap, exhibiting a tendency toward bawdy lyrics and hook-laden grooves.

Doggett, Bill (1916–1996) *keyboardist and bandleader*

Pianist/organist Bill Doggett is best remembered for the first notable instrumental hit of the rock 'n' roll era, "Honky Tonk," which topped the R&B charts in early 1956. However, his career as a bandleader, accompanist, and music arranger spanned more than a half-century, from the mid-1930s through the 1980s.

Born February 16, 1916, in Philadelphia, Doggett first played professionally with Jimmy Gorman and His Orchestra before forming his own band in 1938. When the demands of overseeing a large organization became too much to handle, he sold it to LUCKY MILLINDER. Relocating to Los Angeles in 1947, he found work as an arranger for such jazz luminaries as Louis Armstrong, Count Basie, and Lionel Hampton as well as performing with the Ink Spots, ELLA FITZGERALD, Coleman Hawkins, Illinois Jacquet, LOUIS JORDAN, and countless other pop and rhythm and blues artists.

Doggett put together a combo in 1952, signing with the King label shortly thereafter. They became one of the most successful R&B bands of the decade, with hits like "Slow Walk," "Ram-Bunk-Shush," and "Hold It."

By the 1970s, Doggett had relocated to Long Island, where he occasionally performed at area rock 'n' roll revival shows. He died in New York City on November 13, 1996.

Domino, Antoine "Fats" (b. 1928) *singer and keyboardist*

Fats Domino was one of the most consistent rhythm and blues hit-makers of all time. He wrote and recorded rock standards years before "rock 'n' roll" became a household word. His engaging, inimitable style helped facilitate the transition of popular R&B artists to the pop charts at the outset of the rock era.

Born February 26, 1928, in New Orleans, Domino taught himself the popular piano techniques of his day, including the blues, boogie woogie, and ragtime. In the mid-1940s, local band leader Dave Bartholomew hired him as his regular pianist. This job led to his 1949 recording contract with the Los Angeles–based Imperial label, and the Domino-Bartholomew songwriting partnership.

His debut single, "The Fat Man," was a Top Ten R&B hit in 1950. For a dozen years, Domino would

Fats Domino exhibiting his distinctive piano style in 1957 (Frank Driggs Collection)

release at least one Top Ten single every year; his number one R&B releases included "Goin' Home," "Ain't That a Shame," "All by Myself," "Poor Me," "I'm in Love Again," "Blueberry Hill," "Blue Monday," "I'm Walkin'," and "I Want to Walk You Home." Despite the drop-off in chart singles by the early 1960s, he remained in demand as a theater and nightclub attraction. Furthermore, his albums continued to sell well. When he moved to ABC-Paramount in 1963, Imperial retained many of them in its catalog, most notably *Rock and Rollin' With Fats Domino* (Imperial, 1956), *Fats Domino–Rock and Rollin'* (Imperial, 1956), *This Is Fats Domino!* (Imperial, 1957), and *Million Sellers by Fats* (Imperial, 1962). He recorded for a number of other labels as well in the 1960s, including Mercury, Sunset, and Liberty/United Artists.

By the 1970s, Domino had cut back sharply on his concert tours, limiting his out-of-town work largely to Las Vegas and Lake Tahoe. His recordings were more widely available in England and Europe than at home; American fans often found it necessary to seek out import anthologies. He has continued to record and perform intermittently in recent years. His first major-label LP release in 25 years, *Christmas Is a Special Day* (1993), received critical acclaim but had limited sales.

Don and Juan

At a time when DOO-WOP music was becoming increasing idiosyncratic due to a barrage of weird vocal effects aimed at keeping the style commercially relevant, Don and Juan exemplified a more traditional form of rhythm and blues group singing. Despite a relatively short career, they enjoyed two different flirtations with fame, having first appeared on the music scene as members of the Genies, best known for recording the clever up-tempo hit, "Who's That Knocking" (Shad 1959).

Lifelong residents of New York City, Don (Roland Trone) and Juan (Claude Johnson) met in 1961 while working as house painters in an apartment building. Their practice of singing together on the job led a tenant to contact agent Peter Paul about them. After becoming their manager, Paul arranged an audition with the Big Top label, then on a roll with a roster that included pop star Del Shannon. The Johnson-penned "What's Your Name," a 1962 single that reached number seven on the pop charts, was followed by a string of failures—of which only "Magic Wand" charted—before the twosome decided to retire from show business. Beginning with the Royal New York Doo Wop Show in May 1981, Don and Juan returned to performing on an intermittent basis for oldies revival fans. "What's Your Name," a romantic ballad built around the duo's gorgeous two-part harmonies, remains extremely popular on oldies radio playlists.

doo-wop

Doo-wop, the popular name for vocal group rhythm and blues, includes the following musical qualities: group harmony, a wide range of vocal parts, nonsense syllables, an uncomplicated rhythm, light instrumentation, and simple music and lyrics. Above all, the focus is on ensemble singing. Single artists fit the genre only when backed by a group (the possibility that the group may not be mentioned on the record label is immaterial). Typically, solo billing simply means that this individual is more prominently placed in the musical arrangement (e.g., Dion, BOBBY DAY, Thurston Harris), unlike typical group productions.

Doo-wop emerged in the urban ghettos from the blending of rhythm and blues, gospel, and popular black vocal group music in the post–World War II era. The style represented the culmination of many hours spent by teens—usually black males—practicing vocal harmonies in school gyms, on street corners, and at subway entrances. These young groups sought a piece of the American Dream via crossover success in the music business. From their perspective, the more direct route to success meant adapting white pop standards to contemporary

Sonny Til and the Orioles in the early 1950s (Frank Driggs Collection)

black vocal styles. In other words, they attempted to replicate the formula employed a generation earlier by black groups like the Mills Brothers and the Ink Spots. The pronounced gospel and R&B traits within their work reflected the influences from childhood (church, social activities, etc.) that formed the core of their music education. Doo-wop features began emerging in African-American pop music during the 1948–51 period. They can be discerned in R&B hits like the Orioles' "It's Too Soon to Know" and the Dominoes' "Sixty-Minute Man." The doo-wop era began around 1952—a time when the key musical qualities of the genre were all clearly in evidence—and remained artistically and commercially viable until the early 1960s. This time frame can be subdivided into several phases of stylistic development.

Paleo–Doo-Wop (1952–1954) This subgenre retains many visible features of its stylistic ancestors; e.g., R&B in the DRIFTERS's "Money Honey"; gospel in "The Bells of St. Mary's," by LEE ANDREWS AND THE HEARTS; and black pop vocal groups in the PLATTERS's "Only You." These traits had yet to be synthesized into a truly singular style. Other notable records from this period included the CADILLACS's "Gloria," the CHORDS's "Sh-Boom" (the cover by the Crewcuts became one of the biggest hits of that year), the CROWS's "Gee," the Drifters's "Honey Love," the Harptones's "A Sunday Kind of Love," the Jewels's "Hearts of Stone," the Orioles's "Crying in the Chapel," and the Penguins's "Earth Angel."

Classic Doo-Wop (1955–1959) This phase featured tight and sweet harmonies; however, the lead singers lost much of the smoothness typifying paleo–doo-wop recordings. Bass singers were given a more prominent role; in the past they had tended to function merely as part of the background harmony. The performers were generally quite young, featuring lyrics primarily concerned with young, idealistic love. Nonsense syllables were employed in the majority of songs. Instrumentation remained in the background, albeit with a heavy backbeat. Key recordings included the Cleftones's "Little Girl of Mine," the DELL-VIKINGS's "Come Go with Me," the El Dorados's "At My Front Door," the FIVE SATINS's "In the Still of the Night" (1956), the FLAMINGOS's "I Only Have Eyes for You," the Heartbeats's "A Thousand Miles Away," the Monotones's "Book of Love," the Rays' "Silhouettes," the SILHOUETTES's "Get a Job," and the Willows's "Church Bells May Ring."

The classic period saw the development of a wide array of spin-off styles, in part a response to newly devised marketing strategies. These included:

1. Schoolboy doo-wop. The focal point here was an ultra-high tenor, usually a male in his early teenage years. While Frankie Lymon was the definitive interpreter from the standpoint of both commercial success and singing prowess, he had many imitators, including brother Lewis Lymon (the Teenchords), the Kodaks, the Schoolboys, and the Students. Among the notable hits were LITTLE ANTHONY & the IMPERIALS's "Two People in the World," Frankie Lymon and the Teenagers's "Why Do Fools Fall in Love," and the Schoolboys's "Shirley."
2. Gang doo-wop. Lead singers studiously avoided being smooth; rather, they seemed to swagger as they sang. Likewise, harmonies, though intricate, were rough in approach. Major hits included the CHANNELS's "That's My Desire," the Charts's "Desiree," and the Collegians's "Zoom Zoom Zoom."
3. Italo–doo-wop. Like African Americans, Italian Americans accorded music a prime place in their upbringing through church. Although isolated white groups had appeared in the early 1950s (e.g., the Bay Bops, the Neons, the Three Friends), the first major wave of white doo-wop acts surfaced in 1958. This variant was distinguished by even tighter group harmonies, roughly hewn tenors pushing their upper registers to produce a "sweet" sound, and the prominence of bass singers (the latter a precursor of the neo–doo-wop phase). Notable recordings

Frankie Lymon and the Teenagers publicity still (Frank Driggs Collection)

included the Capris's "There's a Moon Out Tonight," the Classics's "Till Then," the Elegants's "Little Star," and the Mystics's "Hushabye" (1959).

4. Pop doo-wop. Heavily influenced by the commercial mainstream going as far back as turn-of-the-century barbershop quartets, this style had little in common with classic doo-wop other than tight harmony. Practitioners developed a number of ploys geared to making inroads into the pop market, most notably (a) cover records, (b) softening the doo-wop sound in order that it might reach a broader range of age groups, and (c) jazzing up adult-oriented standards so as to appeal to youth. Among the more popular records in this vein were the Duprees's "You Belong to Me," the Echoes's "Baby Blue," the Fleetwoods's "Come Softly to Me," The Temptations's "Barbara" (not the MOTOWN group), and the Tymes's "So Much in Love."

Neo–Doo-Wop (1960–1963) The impetus for this phase was the oldies revival (largely focused on doo-wop), which began in 1959. Although neo–doo-wop maintained the simple melody lines and preoccupation with love lyrics typifying the classic phase, the distinctive features of doo-wop were greatly exaggerated; e.g., a greater preponderance of falsetto leads, and heavier and more pronounced bass singing. Instruments also figured more prominently in song arrangements. Notable hits included GENE CHANDLER with the Dukays' "Duke of Earl," the Devotions's "Rip Van Winkle," Dion with the Del Satins' "Runaround Sue," Curtis Lee with the Halos's "Pretty Little Angel Eyes," the PARADONS's "Diamonds and Pearls," the Reflections's "(Just Like) Romeo and Juliet," the Regents's "Barbara Ann," and the STEREOS's "I Really Love You."

The absorption of new talent from a variety of backgrounds spurred the development of new stylistic subcategories, including

1. Tin Pan Alley doo-wop. Exposed to doo-wop as well as schooled in music composition, young songwriters (e.g., Gerry Goffin/Carole King, Barry Mann/Cynthia Weil, Jeff Barry/Ellie Greenwich) and producers (Phil Spector) created their own formula. They melded doo-wop conventions (e.g., tight harmony, pronounced bass, nonsense syllables) with more complex melodics, augmented instrumentation, and thoroughgoing production values. Key recordings included the CHIFFONS's "He's So Fine," the Crystals's "Da Doo Ron Ron," the Raindrops's "The Kind of Boy You Can't Forget," Randy and the Rainbows's "Denise," and the Tokens's "Tonight I Fell in Love."

2. Distaff doo-wop. With few exceptions (e.g., the CHANTELS, the BOBBETTES, the SHIRELLES, and fronting male groups such as the PLATTERS), women did not play a prominent role in doo-wop until the Tin Pan Alley variant achieved popularity. Notable hits included PATTI LABELLE and the Bluebelles's "You'll Never Walk Alone," the COOKIES's "Don't Say Nothin' Bad About My Baby," and Reperata and the Delrons's "Whenever a Teenager Cries."

3. Garage band doo-wop. This category denotes material recorded on substandard equipment. Representative examples included the Laddins's "Did It" and the Contenders's "The Clock."

4. Novelty doo-wop. Almost without exception, this genre encompasses humorous, uptempo material. Themes covered include fantasy (e.g., the ETERNALS's "Rockin' in the Jungle," the CADETS's "Stranded in the Jungle"), rebellion (e.g., the COASTERS's "Yakety Yak"), fads (e.g., the Royal Teens's "Short Shorts"), and media heroes (e.g., Dante and the Evergreens's "Alley Oop").

5. Pseudo–doo-wop. This category refers to the doo-wop style minus the vocal group format. Major strains have included solo efforts (e.g., Ron Holden and the Thunderbirds's "Love You So," Rosie and the Originals' "Angel Baby") and duos (e.g., Skip and Flip's "Cherry Pie," DON AND JUAN's "What's Your Name," Robert and Johnny's "Over the Mountain").

Post–Doo-Wop (1964–) For all practical purposes, the genre ceased to function in a creative sense as elements associated with it virtually disappeared from recordings. With few exceptions, words replaced nonsense syllables as background responses, harmony receded into the background, falsetto appeared less frequently, the bass was used less as a separate voice, instrumentation took on much greater importance, and melodies exhibited a much greater degree of variation. A number of groups—most notably the Drifters, the Four Seasons, and Little Anthony & the Imperials—crossed over into the pop mainstream. The primary innovations in vocal group singing now took place within the A CAPPELLA genre.

Dorsey, Lee (1924–1986) *singer*

One of the underrated exponents of New Orleans–based rhythm and blues, Lee Dorsey would record a half-dozen 1960s classics. Before embarking upon a singing career, however, he was an accomplished professional boxer who contended for the light-heavyweight title.

Born Irving Lee Dorsey in December 24, 1924, in New Orleans, he relocated as a 10-year-old to Portland, Oregon, with his family. He was known by the fighting name of Kid Chocolate before serving four years in the Navy. Returning to boxing after the service, he met renowned songwriter/producer Allen Toussaint at a party in New Orleans. Toussaint was influential in getting Dorsey into a recording studio. His first hit came in 1961 with the self-composed nonsense song, "Ya Ya."

After a moderately successful follow-up in much the same vein, "Do-Re-Mi," Dorsey disappeared from the charts for several years. He would regain the hit-making touch in mid-1965, with a new take on an early 1960s dance step, "Ride Your Pony." He continued on a roll with "Get Out of My Life, Woman," the Toussaint-penned "Working in the Coal Mine," and "Holy Cow"—all featuring Dorsey's engagingly animated vocals.

Although he remained active as a performer, Dorsey's recordings rarely made much of a commercial impact from that point onward. Working without the production team of Toussaint and Marshall Sehorn in the 1970s, his last charting single was "Night People," released in early 1978. He died of emphysema in New Orleans on December 1, 1986.

Dozier, Lamont   See HOLLAND, BRIAN, LAMONT DOZIER, AND EDDIE HOLLAND.

Dr. Alban *rapper*

Alban Nwapa, a Nigerian-born rapper, was a major force behind what has been termed "JUNGLE REGGAE HIP-HOP." After moving to Stockholm to study dentistry, he launched the Alphabet Club as a vehicle for his attempts to "toast" over the dance records (the venue later spawned a record and clothing outlet). The Swemix label offered him a recording contract. His debut single, "Hello Afrika," was a huge international dance hit in 1990, as were

follow-ups like the anti-drug "No Coke" and brotherhood anthem, "U & Mi." Produced by Denniz Pop, these recordings offered an innovative blend of Euro-TECHNO, African rhythms (highlighted by Nigerian percussive effects), and Dr. Alban's distinctive Afro-Swedish patois backed by dance-hall chanting.

Dramatics

The group initially recorded for Wingate in 1966 as the Dynamics. Following a minor hit with Sport the following year, the Dramatics, including lead vocalist Ron Banks, Larry Demps, Willie Ford, William Howard, and Elbert Wilkins, signed with the STAX imprint Volt in the early 1970s, where they found notable success with Top Ten pop singles like "Whatcha See Is Whatcha Get" and "In the Rain" (which topped the R&B charts for four weeks). The group (with ex–Chocolate Syrup singer L. J. Reynolds and Lenny Mayes replacing Howard and Wilkins in 1973) switched to the Cadet label in 1974 and then to ABC in 1975. With Reynolds (1981) and Banks (1983) opting for solo careers, the Dramatics ran out of steam, although they continued to enjoy intermittent success through the mid-1980s.

Dr Dre (b. 1965) *rapper and producer*

Andre Young, better known as Dr Dre, played a major role in steering RAP away from its preoccupation with partying, politics, and the exploration of new sonic effects to a celebratory form of gangsta rap. As a record producer, he modified the influential GEORGE CLINTON school of FUNK into a stretched-out, lazier variation which he termed "G-funk." He was also a high-profile label executive; first with DEATH ROW RECORDS—co-founded in 1992 with Suge Knight, it provided the template for HIP-HOP aesthetics in the mid-1990s—and, in the late 1990s, Aftermath Records.

Born February 18, 1965, Dr Dre first attracted attention in the early 1980s working South Central Los Angeles house parties and clubs as part of the

World Class Wreckin' Cru. By 1986, he had teamed with ICE CUBE to supply compositions to Ruthless Records. The label's owner, rapper EAZY-E, together with the twosome, formed N.W.A. (aka Niggaz With Attitude). The group released two albums, *N.W.A. and the Posse* (Marcola/Rams Horn, 1987) and the double-platinum smash, *Straight Outta Compton* (Ruthless/Priority, 1989). The latter release also attracted widespread publicity due to its incendiary lyrics, most notably on the heavily censored track "Fuck tha Police." With the departure of Ice Cube, N.W.A. released two more million-selling records—the EP *100 Miles and Runnin'* (Ruthless/Priority, 1990) and *Efil4zaggin* (Ruthless/Priority, 1991)—featuring Eazy-E's comic-book lyrics set to Dre's thickly textured funk arrangements.

Intent on pursuing a solo career, Dre released his debut solo album, *The Chronic* (Death Row, 1992), which profoundly modified the hip-hop landscape with its G-funk sound. He then shifted his focus to production work, providing the music to several film soundtracks—most notably, *Above the Rim* (1994) and *Murder Was the Case* (1994)—and assisting protégé SNOOP DOGGY DOG with *Doggystyle* (Death Row/Interscope, 1993), as well as Warren G, Blackstreet, and others.

Alienated by the gangster behavior of his Death Row partner, Knight, Dre severed all ties in summer 1996 and formed Aftermath. While the new label was not an immediate success, Dre slowly returned to public favor with a more mainstream pop approach on the albums *Dr Dre Presents . . . The Aftermath* (Aftermath/Interscope, 1996, featuring his production work with various artists) and *2001* (Aftermath/Interscope, 1999; also issued in "clean" and "instrumental" versions).

See also EMINEM.

Drifters, The

With the possible exception of the Dells, the Drifters were more successful in adapting to stylistic changes within the pop music scene than any other DOO-WOP group. Beginning as a rhythm and blues act in the early 1950s, they shifted to a more pop-oriented sound to remain leading hitmakers throughout the classic rock 'n' roll era, and were still regularly denting the charts at the peak of the British Invasion, folk-rock, and MOTOWN soul.

CLYDE MCPHATTER, formerly lead singer with Billy Ward's Dominoes, formed the Drifters in 1953 with second tenor Gerhard Thrasher, baritone Andrew Thrasher, and bass Bill Pinkney. Before McPhatter entered the Army in the mid-1950s, the group enjoyed a string of R&B hits featuring his smooth, sexy tenor voice, most notably "Money Honey," "Such a Night," "Lucille," "Honey Love," "Bip Bam," "White Christmas," "What 'Cha Gonna Do," "Adorable," "Steamboat," and "Ruby Baby."

Following a period of diminished record sales—and various personnel changes—the group disbanded in 1958. Because the Drifters had signed a multiyear

Early 1960s publicity photo of the Drifters (Frank Driggs Collection)

contract with New York's Apollo Theater, their manager recruited another group, the Five Crowns, to fill the void. Assisted by the songwriting/production team of LEIBER AND STOLLER, the new Drifters quickly outstripped their predecessors with releases like "There Goes My Baby," reputedly the first R&B recording to utilize a sophisticated string arrangement; "Dance with Me"; "This Magic Moment"; "Save the Last Dance for Me"; and "I Count the Tears."

When lead singer Ben E. King—who would record the solo hits "Spanish Harlem" and "Stand By Me"—departed, the Drifters remained successful with recordings such as "Up On the Roof" and "On Broadway," which featured Rudy Lewis singing lead. Following Lewis's death in 1963, Johnny Moore became the frontman for bestsellers such as "Under the Boardwalk" and "Saturday Night at the Movies."

By 1967 the hits had stopped coming, although the group continued to perform well into the 1970s. The act was revived in the mid-1970s to capitalize on the oldies circuit. Releases of both new material and updated versions of the group's old hits, however, failed to compete with regular reissues of the classic Drifters recordings.

Dr. Jeckyll and Mr. Hyde

Dr. Jeckyll and Mr. Hyde—the Bronx duo Andre Harrell (b. 1959) and Alonzo Brown, respectively, accompanied by DJ Scratch On Galaxy (b. George Llado)—was one of the earliest RAP acts to achieve commercial success in the recording medium. Brown recorded the first rap record (and second release overall) for the Profile label, "Young Ladies," as Lonnie Love. Their more notable singles included "Genius Rap," which utilized the Tom Tom Club's "Genius of Love" as the backing track, ultimately selling more than 150,000 copies, and "AM:PM"/"Fast Life," the latter cut produced by HIP-HOP trailblazer KURTIS BLOW.

The disappointing sales of their debut LP, *The Champagne of Rap* (Profile, 1985), spurred Harrell and Brown to focus on nonperformance avenues of the music business. Harrell launched UPTOWN, which released the work of Heavy D and Teddy Riley, among others. Brown held executive positions at COLD CHILLIN' and Warner Bros. prior to taking charge of the A&R department at A&M. While the two have not found time to make good on announced intentions to reunite, they did jointly sponsor Groove B. Chill.

DRS

Based in Los Angeles, DRS—standing for "Dirty Rotten Scoundrels"—have made a concerted effort to ride the gangsta rap bandwagon. The quintet's rude monikers—Blunt, Deuce, Endo, Jail Bait, and Pic—and hard-edged verses, however, are offset by frequent forays into old school R&B vocal harmonies and sometimes even A CAPPELLA. This identity crisis was self-evident in their debut LP, *Gangsta Lean* (Capitol, 1993)—the title referring to the burial mode of choice for their local homeboys—which was immaculately produced by Roll Wit It Entertainment, funded in part by squeaky clean silent partner M.C. HAMMER.

Dru Hill

Dru Hill consists of four high school friends—Jazz, Nokio, Sisqo, and Woody—who took their name from the Baltimore neighborhood where they were raised, Druid Hill Park. Formed in 1995, they were signed by ISLAND the following year after an eye-catching performance at the recording industry conference, Impact '96.

Their eponymous debut (Island, 1996) defined urban HIP-HOP, with lush harmonies and ample vocal gymnastics, set off by Keith Sweat's raw production work (with assists from Stanley Brown and Tim "Dawg" Patterson). Its most impressive track, the single "Tell Me," appeared on the soundtrack to the film *Eddie*, and achieved a gold record award. They continued in the same mold with *Enter the Dru* (Island, 1998), rising above comparisons with R&B crooners like BOYZ II MEN and Jodeci. *Dru World*

Order (Def Soul, 2002) followed two solo R&B chart toppers by Sisqo and the addition of Skola to make the group a quintet. Largely self-produced, their music now featured a gospel edge to offset the polished sheen of their rich harmonizing.

drum and bass

Drum and bass evolved out of the desire on the part of black British clubgoers to have a music with an identity apart from the then-prevalent African-American HOUSE and TECHNO styles. First appearing in London dance venues in the early 1990s, drum and bass—also known as JUNGLE—was a fast-paced, kinetic music featuring a predominance of drum loops. Emerging from the Ecstasy drug culture, it incorporated elements of hardcore techno, HIP-HOP, soul, jazz, and REGGAE afterbeats. Whereas house and techno were built around standard time signatures, particularly 4/4, drum and bass—like jazz—was founded on syncopation, that is, an emphasis on the offbeat. Furthermore, the focal center of the genre, its rhythmic groove, pre-empted the role of melody, with instrumental lines serving merely as ornamentation.

Drum and bass is generally believed to have evolved from the late 1980s to early 1990s work of Rage club deejays Fabio and Grooverider. Their approach consisted of melding the sped-up acid house (accompanying increased usage of cocaine and other chemical stimulants by club patrons) with the nuances of contemporary black music forms. These experiments were made possible by new developments in sampling and sequencing.

As drum and bass became more entrenched in British clubs, stylistic offshoots developed by the mid-1990s. The complex studio creations of LTJ Bukem—whose releases include the dance singles collection *Logical Progression* (Good Looking, 1996) and *Journey Inwards* (Kinetic, 2000)—were referred to as "intelligent drum and bass." The sub-genre was also mined by DJ Rap, the Singapore native Charissa Saveiro, who blended ethereal backdrops with pounding rhythms in *Learning Curve* (Columbia, 1998), and 4 Hero, a London duo achieving a fusion of jazz-rock, German synth-rock, and processed breakbeats in albums such as *Parallel Universe* (Reinforced, 1994) and *Two Pages* (Mercury, 1998).

GOLDIE helped pioneer a related form, "ambient jungle," utilizing symphonic flourishes that manipulated the listener's perception of time through a series of stretched and compressed musical samples. His breakthrough LP, *Timeless* (London, 1995), almost single-handedly stimulated heavy print and broadcast media coverage of the drum and bass phenomenon as well as countless imitators.

dub

Jamaican in origin, dub music consists of a disc jockey or Master of Ceremony improvising—generally in a free-form verse style—over recorded instrumental passages played through a sound system geared to either clubs or outdoor music events such as street dances. Closely related to the ska/rock steady/REGGAE axis dominant in that country from the 1960s onward, dub provided a forum for the stage host to exhibit his poetic facility and command of an audience without relying on a performing band, a resource in decidedly short supply at the time. Given this dearth of live musicians—arising in large part out of the absence of sufficient economic wealth to sustain a vital music scene—the onstage deejays (or "toastmasters," as they were often called) became stars in their own right, zealously guarding the identity of their soundtrack music by obliterating all label information on the record. The MC's presentation typically consisted of braggadocio, typically concerned with their alleged sexual prowess with women. Some musical events would pit the local talent in a competitive format, permitting the audience to voice their preferences as to the superior performance.

As reggae became an increasingly popular export around the world in the 1970s, LPs featuring Jamaica deejays such as Yellowman and Prince Buster became more widely available. The genre exerted a considerable influence on the emerging HIP-HOP movement based in New York City and other Eastern Seaboard music scenes.

Dubs, The

Although their string of minor hits lasted only two years, the Dubs were one of the finest harmonizing ensembles of the DOO-WOP era. Furthermore, lead singer Richard Blandon was a particularly sensitive song stylist and a first-rate songwriter to boot.

Whereas many rhythm and blues vocal groups came together as high school students while singing on street corners and local functions, music entrepreneur Hiram Johnson assembled the Dubs in early 1957 around Montgomery, Alabama, native Blandon, who'd recently been discharged from the Air Force. The other original members—all in their early twenties at the time—included first tenor Cleveland Still, from New York City; second tenor Cordell Brown, a Charlotte, North Carolina, native (later replaced by William Carlisle); bass Tommy Grate, hailing from Beaufort, South Carolina; and baritone James Miller. Their name came from the fact that they'd made many dubs (demo recordings) in an effort to attract industry attention.

Johnson, now their manager, managed to get the New York-based label Gone Records to pick up the Blandon-penned single "Don't Ask Me (to Be Lonely)." Another Blandon composition, "Could This Be Magic," inspired by a girl he'd known while in the military service, became a classic. The soaring "Chapel of Dreams" would crease the charts in 1959, but the group would disband in the early 1960s when further releases failed to capture the public's fancy. Blandon and Still would recruit new members in the 1970s and perform as the Dubs on the oldies circuit in the New York area.

Dupri, Jermaine (b. 1973) *rapper and producer*

Atlanta native Jermaine Dupri, born September 23, 1973, was one of the most successful R&B producers of the 1990s, nurturing new talent on his own label, So So Def Recordings, in addition to working with superstars like MARIAH CAREY and TLC. The son of talent manager/concert promoter Michael Mauldin, Dupri performed onstage with DIANA ROSS as a nine-year-old, and toured with the likes of Cameo and HERBIE HANCOCK in the mid-1980s. In 1987, he produced the trio Silk Tymes Leather, and secured a record contract for the group.

Dupri formed So So Def Productions in 1989, and reached the top of the charts with the debut album, *Totally Krossed Out* (1992), by Kris Kross, a teen duo he'd discovered the year before in an area shopping mall. He went on to produce tracks on TLC's first two LPs, which sold a combined total of more than 15 million copies. In 1993–94, he achieved platinum sales with the debut albums of two more So So Def acts, Xscape and Da Brat (he also assisted other label artists like Lil Bow Wow and Jagged Edge). By now, his services were in high demand; he would be recruited to work with Carey (the album, *Daydream*, which sold more than eight million units), JANET JACKSON, old school rappers RUN-D.M.C. and Whodini, and an up-and-coming R&B singer, USHER, whose resulting LP, *My Way* (1997), surpassed double-platinum sales within three months of its release, making the teenage heartthrob a superstar.

While continuing to collaborate with such notable rap acts as SNOOP DOGGY DOGG, OUTKAST, Slick Rick, NAS, and MASTER P, Dupri released his own single, "The Party Continues," in early 1998. The favorable response led to a debut solo album, *Jermaine Dupri Presents: Life in 1472* (So So Def, 1998), which featured a star-studded roster of guest artists. Although a polished package (as might be expected), his follow-up, *Instructions* (So So Def, 2001), was marred by mindless boasting and clichéd lyrics. As an accomplished producer and record label executive—*Billboard* ranked So So Def as the 12th most successful R&B/HIP-HOP label of 2004—Dupri continues to view his own solo recordings as little more than vanity projects.

Dyson, Ronnie (1950–1990) *singer*

Although moderately successful in the R&B market, Ronnie Dyson was best known as an actor in musicals and entertainment films. Born June 5, 1950, in Washington, D.C., he spent much of his youth in Brooklyn. His big break came when he landed a leading part in the landmark Broadway musical, *Hair*, in the late 1960s. His first hit single, "(If You Let Me Make Love to You Then) Why Can't I Touch You?" was taken from an off-Broadway musical, *Salvation*.

Dyson would place a dozen more recordings on the R&B charts through 1983, most notably "I Don't Wanna Cry," "One Man Band (Plays All Alone)," and "The More You Do It (The More I Like It Done To Me)." He would sign with Cotillion in the early 1980s, but failed to achieve the level of sales enjoyed in the previous decade. His biggest film role came with the satire on race relations, *Putney Swope* (1970). He died of a heart condition in Philadelphia on November 10, 1990.

Earth, Wind & Fire

One of the classic FUNK acts of the 1970s, the Chicago-based group was created in 1969 by vocalist/percussionist Maurice White, a former member of the RAMSEY LEWIS Trio and session man with the Chess label. Initially known as the Salty Peppers, the band—originally consisting of bassist Verdine White (Maurice's brother), keyboardist/vocalist Wade Flemons, pianist/vocalist Don Whitehead, guitarist Michael Beal, vocalist Sherry Scott, conga player Yackov Ben Israel, tenor saxophonist Chet Washington, and trombonist Alex Thomas—changed their name to Earth, Wind & Fire in 1970, and released their eponymous debut LP (Warner Bros.) in March of the following year. Their follow-up, *The Need of Love* (Warner Bros., 1972), was the first in a long string of charting releases.

Earth, Wind & Fire's fortunes took a quantum leap upward later that year with a wholesale lineup change—which featured the addition of velvet-voiced lead singer PHILIP BAILEY, saxophonist/flutist Ronnie Laws, and four other musicians to the White brothers core—and a shift to the Columbia label. The group's appealing formula of positive, pseudospiritual lyrics and polished funk grooves resulted in a string of Top Ten albums: the film soundtrack *That's the Way of the World* (Columbia, 1975), which included the chart-topping single "Shining Star"; the largely live *Gratitude* (Columbia, 1975); *Spirit* (Columbia, 1976); *All 'n' All* (Columbia, 1978); *I Am* (Columbia, 1979), featuring two Top Ten smashes, the disco-inflected "Boogie Wonderland" (with the EMOTIONS) and

"After the Love Has Gone"; *Faces* (Columbia, 1980); and *Raise!* (Columbia, 1981).

When the hits stopped coming, the group disbanded in 1984, with Bailey and Maurice White continuing as solo performers. The White brothers and Bailey reconstituted the act in 1987, augmented by countless session players. Their periodic releases continued to crease the charts well into the 1990s;

Earth, Wind & Fire (Frank Driggs Collection)

subsequently, the public—particularly in Great Britain—has exhibited a preference for reissues of the group's classic material.

Eazy-E (1963–1995) *rapper*

Eazy-E (born Eric Wright, son of soul-funk star Charles Wright, in Los Angeles) was one of the most successful entrepreneurial artists in rock history, bar none. In addition to forming the trailblazing gangsta rap group, N.W.A., and later achieving acclaim as a solo act, in 1985 he founded his own label, Ruthless Records (allegedly with illegal profits), which became a major force in the then-emerging West Coast HIP-HOP scene.

Eazy-E's first album project, *N.W.A. and the Posse* (Macola/Rams Horn, 1987), featured core members of N.W.A.—DR DRE, DJ Yella, and ICE CUBE—along with a supporting cast including, among others, the Doc and Arabian Prince. With the addition of MC Ren, N.W.A. released the landmark LP, *Straight Outta Compton* (Ruthless, 1989), which almost single-handedly launched the gangsta movement on the strength of incendiary tracks such as "Fuck tha Police" and was issued as a CD-single and 12-inch disc in April 1991, and "Gangsta Gangsta" (which charted in Great Britain in 1990). The album's notoriety helped propel the follow-up, *Efil4zaggin'* (Ruthless, 1991), to the top of the charts.

Shortly thereafter, internal differences caused N.W.A. to implode, with individual members all going on to solo careers. Eazy-E had a head start in this regard, having issued an album, *Eazy-Duz-It* (Ruthless, 1988), which almost predated N.W.A. His first post-N.W.A. release, the mini-CD *5150 Home for tha Sick* (Ruthless, 1993), was a pedestrian affair, apparently due to the distractions of administrative duties. The next release, the mini-CD *It's On (Dr Dre) 187 Um Killa* (Ruthless, 1993), revealed a greater concern for his artistic legacy; "Real Muthaphuckin G's," later released as a single, questioned Dr Dre's role in pioneering the G-funk sound.

Shortly after collaborating with Bone Thugs-N-Harmony on "Foe Tha Love Of" (Ruthless, 1995), Eazy-E was diagnosed as having HIV; a month later, on March 26, 1995, he died of AIDS. Two posthumous recordings, the compilation of previously released material, *Eternal E* (Ruthless, 1995), and the collection of unreleased tracks, *Str8 Off tha Streetz of Muthaphukkin Compton* (Ruthless, 1995), have been released.

Ebonys

The Ebonys might best be described as a poor man's version of the Dells. Like that group, they made lush, Philly soul–styled records featuring a baritone lead augmented by an answering falsetto as the second lead. Discovered by the Gamble-Huff production team, the Ebonys—comprised of David Beasley, Jenny Holmes, James Tuten, and Clarence Vaughan—enjoyed a brief run of commercial success in the early 1970s, most notably with "You're the Reason Why" and "It's Forever." They moved on to Buddah in the mid-1970s, but placed only one single, "Makin' Love Ain't No Fun (Without the One You Love) Part I," on the charts.

Edsels, The

The Edsels were one-hit wonders who twice rode the same recording, albeit with a slightly different title, to a measure of fame and commercial success. However, the song, "Rama Lama Ding Dong," with its propulsive beat and dynamic vocal interplay, revealed a group deserving of greater things.

Named after the highly touted new car line introduced by Ford, the Edsels—consisting of lead singer George Jones, Jr., brothers Larry and Harry Green, James Reynolds, and bass Marshall Sewell, all born in 1936 or 1937—began performing in their native Youngstown in the mid-1950s. Word of their popularity reached Youngstown music publisher Jim Maderitz in early 1958. He auditioned them in a local record store listening booth. Maderitz liked the song they performed A CAPPELLA—the Jones-penned "Rama Lama Ding Dong"—well enough to arrange for a recording session. After shopping the resulting master around to many record companies without a nibble, Foster Johnson's fledgling label, the Little Rock–based Dub Records, decided to release it in the summer of 1958.

Sporting an incorrectly printed label which identified the song as "Lama Rama Ding Dong," the recording would eventually become a local hit in the Baltimore area. Perhaps because its exaggerated vocal effects would not be in vogue until the early 1960s, the song failed to catch on elsewhere. Unable to make an impact in the marketplace with another record, the group would break up shortly thereafter.

In early 1961, the meteoric rise of the Marcels' "Blue Moon" to number one with an attention-grabbing bass intro, reminiscent of a similar effect employed previously by the Edsels, inspired a New York disk jockey to start playing "Rama Lama Ding Dong" again. When radio listeners responded favorably, Maderitz negotiated a new distribution arrangement with Sam and Hy Weiss, owners of the Old Town label. Released by the Twin subsidiary, the song became a bonafide national hit the second time around. The original group members, however, did not reunite to capitalize on this success. Jones sang with a group known as the New Affair during the 1970s, while the others worked at more conventional jobs in the Youngstown area.

Egyptian Lover *deejay and producer*

Egyptian Lover was the pseudonym for Los Angeles–based producer Greg Broussard, who recorded a string of influential electro-dance singles in the mid-1980s. Influenced by techno-pop pioneers Kraftwerk, old-school rappers like AFRIKA BAMBAATAA and Man Parrish, and the punk funk of PRINCE and Zapp, he began recording in 1983, breaking out the following year with the breakdance anthem "Egypt, Egypt." His debut LP, *On the Nile* (Egyptian Empire; 1984), was practically a greatest hits compilation of his high tech beats, blending

RAP, FUNK, and club music, with a dash of Middle Eastern and North African influences. *One Track Mind* (Egyptian Empire, 1986) and *Filthy* (Priority, 1988) mined similar territory, but his electro-hop style now appeared anachronistic in the face of the emerging gangsta rap trend. Following a hiatus of several years, he returned with *Back from the Tomb* (1994) and *Pyramix* (1995).

Elliott, Missy "Misdemeanor" (b. 1971)
singer and producer

Over the last 10 years, Missy "Misdemeanor" Elliott has risen to the first rank within the RAP industry, thanks to four platinum albums and her label and production company; her success has helped pave the way for women in rap and R&B.

Melissa Elliott was born July 1, 1971 in Portsmouth, Virginia. She recalls standing on her parents' roadside trash can, singing at the top of her lungs to passing motorists. It was this kind of determination that led Elliott to her first big break. She went backstage at a Jodeci concert and convinced Devante Swing (a member of Jodeci) to listen to her R&B group, Sista. Devante flew its members to New York to audition for Jodeci; the group was signed that day, along with Ginuwine (who later collaborated with Elliott). Sista recorded an album in 1994, but it was never released. Elliott began working behind the scenes, writing platinum tracks for Jodeci ("Want Some More," "Sweaty") and seven tracks for Aaliyah, including "If Your Girl Only Knew," "One in a Million," and the sultry "4 Page Letter." She also performed her "hee haw" rap on Gina Thompson's "The Things You Do."

In 1996, Elliott signed a deal with Elektra that allowed her to start her own label. She released her first album, *Supa Dupa Fly* (Gold Mind, 1997), which remains one of the highest debuting albums by a female HIP-HOP artist, eventually reaching number three on the *Billboard* album charts. *Supa Dupa Fly* was characterized by cranked JUNGLE beats and an irreverent style; it included a collaboration with childhood friend TIMBALAND. Her single, "The

Rain," was nominated for three MTV awards; its video was named the 15th Greatest Video of All Time by MTV. In 1997, Elliott became the first hip-hop artist to perform on the Lilith Fair tour.

Elliott continued to produce after the album's release, developing hits for stars such as WHITNEY HOUSTON, Paula Cole, DESTINY'S CHILD, and Christina Aguilera. In 1999, she released her second album for Gold Mind, *Da Real World*, a darker, more in-your-face recording. The single "Hot Boyz" spent 18 straight weeks at number one on *Billboard*'s Rap Singles chart, six weeks at the same position on the R&B charts, and almost a year in the Top 40. The album went platinum, and was nominated for four *Soul Train* awards as well as a Grammy.

Her third release, *Miss E . . . So Addictive* (Gold Mind, 2001), combined fierce dance beats, outrageous sampling, and powerful urban ballads. The album featured cameos by such artists as JAY-Z, Method Man, Redman, Da Brat, and LUDACRIS. It topped the *Billboard* R&B/Hip-Hop Chart for two weeks, and brought her a BET Award for Best Female Artist in 2002. The singles, "Get Ur Freak On" and "One Minute Man," hit the *Billboard* Top Ten immediately. In addition, "Get Ur Freak On" was awarded a *Soul Train* Lady of Soul Award for Best R&B/Soul Video and a Grammy for Best Solo Rap Performance (2002). The video for "One Minute Man" received six MTV awards nominations. A third single, "Scream aka Itchin'," earned her a second Grammy for Solo Rap Performance (2003).

This successful release was followed by an even bigger best seller, *Under Construction* (Gold Mind, 2002) which went platinum and made her the best-selling female hip-hop artist ever. The single, "Work It," led the *Billboard* R&B/Hip-Hop Chart for five weeks, was awarded a Grammy for Best Solo Performance (2004), won the *Soul Train* Best Song Award, and was named *Rolling Stone*'s Best Single of 2003; that magazine also named Elliott its Best Female Artist and Best R&B Artist that year. The song's video headed the MTV Top 20 Countdown and received two MTV and two *Soul Train* awards. Around this time, she dropped the "Misdemeanor"

tag from her name. Elliott's fifth album, *This Is Not a Test!* (Gold Mind, 2003), achieved platinum sales in short order.

—Emily Herring

Ellis, Shirley (b. 1941) *singer*

Born in the Bronx, New York, Shirley Ellis split her time between singing and songwriting in the 1950s. She joined a group called the Metronomes for a time and had one of her songs, "One, Two, I Love You," recorded by the Heartbreakers for the Vik label.

In the early 1960s, Ellis met and began collaborating with songwriter Lincoln Chase, whose compositions included "Jim Dandy," a hit for LAVERN BAKER, and "Such a Night," which was recorded by the DRIFTERS. Chase, who ultimately became both her manager and husband, wrote a dance song, "Nitty Gritty," especially for her. A number of publishers passed on it, including Hal Fein of Roosevelt Music and Bobby Darin at Trinity Music, before Galico Publishing agreed to put it out. Furthermore, the Congress label, located next door to Galico and newly acquired by Kapp Records, released the Ellis recording in fall 1963; it would reach number eight on both the R&B and pop charts.

The follow-up, "(That's) What the Nitty Gritty Is," got lost in the initial onslaught of British Invasion acts. Later that year, however, Chase came up with "The Name Game," which would ultimately become Ellis's biggest hit. Chase supplied her with one more hit in "The Name Game" mold, "The Clapping Song (Clap Pat Clap Slap)" (Congress, 1965). Despite the backing of a major label, she managed only one more minor hit, "Soul Time," during her lengthy entertainment career.

Eminem (b. 1973) *rapper*

Born Marshall Mathers (his initials inspiring the word play behind his stage name) in St. Joseph, Missouri, he grew up poor, splitting time between the Kansas City area and Detroit. He began freestyling at age 14, first attracting grassroots attention as part of the Detroit-based duo Soul Intent. Eminem's early independent label releases, *Infinite* (1996), followed by *The Slim Shady EP* (1997)—while suffering from poor distribution and promotion—made a splash within the rap underground, due both to his hyperactive, nasal voiced delivery and skin color, which earned him the moniker "great white hope."

Allegedly coming across Eminem's demo tape on the floor of Interscope label head Jimmy Iovine's garage, DR DRE went to see him perform at the 1997 Rap Olympics in Los Angeles, where he earned second place in the freestyle category. Dre signed him on the spot, and his major label debut, *The Slim Shady LP* (Interscope), was released in February 1999. Described by Stephen Thomas Erlewine as "an inspired, surrealistic parody of Jerry Springer–fueled pop culture and gangsta rap," the album rose to number two, selling two million copies during its first months in the marketplace. *The Marshall Mathers LP* (Interscope, 2000) rocketed to the top of the charts, its stark, often humorous depictions of violence, drugs, gay bashing, and the like, singling Eminem out for censure by the mainstream press and countless would-be social reformers. The rapper's next solo outing, *The Eminem Show* (Interscope, 2002), was more stridently political than prior works, focusing much of its invective on the perceived failings of the Bush administration.

Eminem played a key role in the emergence of D-12, a group vehicle in which he was supported by five black childhood friends. Their hard-edged album, *Devil's Night* (Shady/Interscope, 2001), also topped the charts, followed by the equally successful, *D12 World* (Shady/Interscope, 2004), named the 30th most popular LP of the year by *Billboard* in its "Year in Music & Touring" section (December 25, 2004).

Emotions, The

Few acts paid more dues than the Emotions prior to reaching the upper echelons of the music charts. At the time when their biggest hit, "Best of My Love," simultaneously topped the pop and R&B charts in 1977, the group had been active in show business for 20 years, having interpreted a variety of styles and taken on several different names in the process.

The group originated with three sisters, Sheila, Wanda, and Jeanette Hutchinson, who first sang as the Hutchinsons, and later, the Heavenly Sunbeams, in Chicago's Mt. Sinai Baptist Church. Guided by their father, Joe, they first performed on television in 1958, soon thereafter hosting a radio gospel program, followed by a Sunday morning TV series. Shifting to soul in the mid-1960s while still in high school, they recorded as Three Ribbons and a Bow for several Midwestern labels, including VEE-JAY.

The STAPLE SINGERS saw the sisters perform live, and referred them to STAX Records in 1968. They began calling themselves the Emotions at this time after a friend noted that their music was so powerfully emotional that it elicited spinal chills. Thirteen of their singles for the Stax subsidiary, Volt, made the R&B charts, most notably the ISAAC HAYES–produced "So I Can Love You" in 1969. They also appeared in the 1973 *Wattstax* documentary before the label went out of business in 1975.

The Emotions went on to sign with Kalimba Productions, fronted by Maurice White of EARTH, WIND & FIRE, who hooked them up with his band's label, Columbia Records. The initial product of this collaboration, *Flowers* (Columbia, 1976), proved to be their most successful album up to that point. The follow-up, *Rejoice* (Columbia, 1977), did even better, achieving platinum sales, due largely to the popularity of the funky "Best of My Love" (produced and co-written by White), which featured Wanda singing lead an octave higher than her usual register.

The Emotions would return to the Top 40 only one more time, backing Earth, Wind & Fire on the infectious dance number, "Boogie Wonderland," in 1979. They bounced around from one label to another in the 1980s, while achieving moderate success in the R&B market. The move from Red Label Records to MOTOWN in the mid-1980s coincided with the departure of Theresa, who'd previously taken a sabbatical from the group between 1970 and 1978; she was ultimately replaced by Adrianne Harris.

En Vogue

An early proponent of the R&B-rap fusion of the late 1980s, En Vogue enjoyed considerable success via highly marketable good looks and pop-crossover material that projected a hip, post-feminist perspective in tune with the times. Along with contemporaries like TLC, Jade, and SWV, it is closely aligned with the New Jill Swing movement.

Essentially an updated edition of the ages-old GIRL GROUP phenomenon, En Vogue formed in October 1988. They were the brainstorm of the Oakland-based duo, Denzil "Denny" Foster and Thomas McElroy (songwriter/producers previously successful as members of the Timex Social Club and CLUB NOUVEAU), who selected Terry Ellis (born 1966, in Texas), Cindy Herron (an actress and former Miss Black California, b. 1963, in San Francisco), Maxine Jones (b. 1962, in Patterson, New Jersey), and Dawn Robinson (b. 1965, in Connecticut) from a series of auditions.

Mainstream popularity came after joining MC HAMMER's 1990 tour and the release of *Born to Sing* (Atlantic, 1990), which included the hit singles "Hold On" and "Lies." They would build on this success with the release of the albums *Remix to Sing* (Atlantic, 1991) and *Funky Divas* (East West, 1992) before losing commercial momentum.

EPMD

The Long Island-based EPMD (standing for Erick and Parrish Making Dollars) first surfaced in 1987 with the single "It's My Thing"/ "You're a Customer." The record established their trademark sound, featuring laid-back, TRANCE-inducing grooves liberally punctuated by wide-ranging samples. The duo—comprised of Erick Sermon and Parrish Smith, a former tight end on the Southern Connecticut State

University football squad—followed with the classic *Strictly Business* (Fresh, 1988), which included the hit "You Gots to Chill." They released three more albums before breaking up in 1992 to pursue solo careers. Failing to achieve any commercial success of note, they reunited in 1997 to release *Back in Business* (1997), followed by *Out of Business* (1999). In addition to forming Def Squad with Redman and Keith Murray, Sermon has been enlisted as producer for many other HIP-HOP artists.

Eric B. and Rakim

Eric B. and Rakim—consisting of Elmhurst, New York–based disc jockey Eric Barrier and Long Island MC William Griffin—epitomize the East Coast RAP school. Their 1986 debut single, "Eric B. Is President" (billed as "Eric B. featuring Rakim"), helped establish the ground rules for the genre: well-crafted, often socially conscious lyrics backed by chunky rhythms, precision scratching effects, and heavy synth-bass. Signed to a major label, 4th & B'way, they continued to place singles on the R&B charts—including "I Know You Got Soul," "I Ain't No Joke," and "Paid in Full"—at a time when crossover rap hits remained a rare occurrence. The duo's LPs—*Paid in Full* (1987; reissued in a deluxe edition in 2003), *The Leader* (1988), *Let the Rhythm Hit 'Em* (1990), and *Don't Sweat the Technique* (1992)—established them as one of the most important HIP-HOP acts of all time, most notably for bringing JAMES BROWN drum loops and complex rhyme schemes into the mainstream. They parted company in the early 1990s, with Rakim releasing several solo albums, including the DR DRE–produced *Oh My God!* (2002).

Ertegun, Ahmet (b. 1923) *record company executive*

A son of the World War II–era Turkish ambassador to the United States, Ertegun—along with older brother Nesuhi Ertegun (1917–89)—developed a lifelong love of American jazz music as a youth. His passion for the genre led to the formation of Atlantic Records in 1947 in partnership with New York jazz collector HERB ABRAMSON; Nesuhi joined in 1956. Peter Guralnick, in *Sweet Soul Music* (New York: Harper & Row, 1986, 55), would note that the label "was nurtured by a combination of creative enterprise, cultural sophistication, business acumen, and good taste that would have been rare in any field but that has been practically unheard of in the music industry."

Following a series of unsuccessful jazz and jump band releases, Atlantic scored the first of many rhythm and blues hits with Stick McGhee's 1949 novelty cover, "Drinkin' Wine Spo-Dee-O-Dee." According to Ertegun biographer George Trow, Ahmet "did not seek to reproduce an older music exactly; rather he sought to introduce black musicians of the day to black musical modes older and more powerful than the ones they knew" (*The New Yorker*, May 29, 1978).

The label's success with R&B artists such as RUTH BROWN, the CLOVERS, the Cardinals, the DRIFTERS, BIG JOE TURNER, the COASTERS, LaVERN BAKER, and RAY CHARLES owed much to Ertegun's ability to find talented associates with similar musical values, most notably engineer Tommy Dowd (who worked on most important Atlantic sessions well into the 1970s), arranger Jesse Stone, producer-executive Jerry Wexler, and songwriter producers JERRY LEIBER AND MIKE STOLLER. Furthermore, he continued to utilize the same nucleus of New York–based session players and producers as R&B evolved into soul in the 1960s.

In addition to taking a considerable interest in artist development, Ertegun displayed great acumen as a deal maker, transforming Atlantic into one of the most powerful independent record companies through a series of distribution arrangements with recording studios and smaller labels such as STAX. He also expanded into the mainstream rock field, signing both high-profile British bands (e.g., Cream, Led Zeppelin) and hip West Coast acts (e.g., Buffalo Springfield, Crosby, Stills and Nash).

On November 24, 1967, Atlantic signed a merger agreement with Warner Brothers–Seven Arts, thereby providing Ertegun even greater financial and cultural clout. His accomplishments, combined with his wit and personal charm, enabled him to become a key record industry leader. His latter-day accomplishments included heading the drive for establishment of the Rock and Roll Hall of Fame Museum in Cleveland. He was inducted into the Hall of Fame in 1987; Nesuhi received the honor posthumously in 1991.

Esquires, The

The Esquires were one of the memorable one-hit wonders of the 1960s. They began as a Milwaukee-based DOO-WOP group in 1957. Originally consisting of siblings Gilbert, Alvis, and Betty Moorer, they added Harvey Scales, who was soon replaced by Sam Pace in 1961.

Following Betty Moorer's departure (her place was taken by Shawn Taylor), the Esquires relocated to Chicago, where they were signed by the Bunky label. They came up with an original composition in 1967, the infectious "Get On Up," which was helped by a catchy bass figure sung by Millard Edwards. Edwards became a permanent member of the group, but Taylor left prior to the release of a derivative follow-up, "And Get Away."

Taylor returned shortly before singing lead on the 1971 hit, "Girls in the City." The Esquires recorded one more chart entry, the reworked "Get Up '76," but continued to perform actively well into the 1980s. By then, Gilbert and Alvis Moorer were the only holdovers from the group's glory days.

Essex, The

The Essex owed their existence to the U.S. Marine Corps. The earliest version of the group featured a collaboration between Walter Vickers, born 1942 in New Brunswick, New Jersey, and Rodney Taylor, also born 1942 in Gary, Indiana, while both were stationed in Okinawa in the early 1960s. They recruited Billie Hill (b. 1942; Princeton, New Jersey) and Rudolph Johnson (b. 1942; New York City) following their return to Camp LeJeune, North Carolina. Things really started to jell, however, when the foursome came across Anita Holmes (b. 1941; Harrisburg, Pennsylvania), who was then singing at the Non-Commissioned Officers' Club. In 1963, shortly after bringing her into the group, the Essex were signed by Roulette Records. Their debut release, "Easier Said Than Done," became a nationwide Top Five smash while all members were still serving military tours. During their hit-making run, which spanned the follow-up singles, "A Walkin' Miracle" and "She's Got Everything," they were granted special permission to do promotional tours, which also helped enhance the Marines' profile, as the members wore their uniforms onstage. The British Invasion, however, pushed the group back into the periphery of the entertainment business the following year.

Eternals, The

The Eternals are remembered fondly for a couple of DOO-WOP novelties featuring prominent bass vocal lines and other loopy ensemble effects. The group developed a strong following around their home base in the Bronx in the late 1950s. Lead singer Charlie Girona convinced the other members that the key to commercial success lay with building up a reservoir of self-penned material. Acting on this logic, they recorded "Babalu's Wedding Day," a tribute to a neighborhood friend about to get married, as their debut single.

Shortly thereafter, they came to the attention of Bill Martin, who garnered them a recording contract with Hollywood Records after becoming their manager. Following several local hits with the label, they garnered national attention with "Rockin' in the Jungle," a 1959 single that incorporated animal sound effects into the arrangement. The group failed to build on this momentum, however, and soon slid back into oblivion.

Everett, Betty (1939–2001) *singer*

Betty Everett was one of the more underrated soul singers of the 1960s. Born November 23, 1939, in Greenwood, Mississippi, the vocalist/pianist started out performing in gospel choirs. Relocating to Chicago in her late teens, she first recorded for the Cobra label in 1958.

Everett became a commercially successful recording artist after signing with VEE-JAY in the early 1960s. Although her first hit single, "You're No Good," only reached number 51 on the *Billboard* Hot 100 and R&B charts in 1963, it would top the pop charts in 1975 when covered by Linda Ronstadt. Everett broke through with her follow-up, "The Shoop Shoop Song (It's In His Kiss)" (which reached number six on the pop and R&B charts), released on the outset of the British Invasion. She returned to the Top Ten that fall in a duet with labelmate JERRY BUTLER, "Let It Be Me," an update of a hit recording by the Everly Brothers in 1960.

While Everett reached the pop Top 40 only one more time—with "There'll Come a Time"—she would intermittently place singles on the charts through 1978. Her old-school soul style rendered dated first by the DISCO vogue, and then HIP-HOP, she has nevertheless remained active as a performer. She died in Beloit, Wisconsin, on April 19, 2001.

Everlast (b. 1969) *rapper*

Born Eric Schrody, he was one of the few rappers in the Los Angeles–based Rhyme Syndicate cartel. He learned both rapping and graffiti art while at a summer camp. When a friend hooked him up with a DJ named Bahal, he recorded a couple of tracks. The demos came to the attention of ICE-T, who took on the role of mentor, hiring him as a support act and helping him secure a recording contract. After issuing a string of singles beginning in 1988, Everlast recorded an album, *Forever Everlasting* (Warner Bros., 1990). Amid samples drawn from Bananarama, the Knack, Sly and Robbie, and Sly Stone, among others, he served up the usual gangsta rap cocktail: images of unremitting violence, raw language, and sexist depictions of women.

Everlast then spent much of the 1990s as a member of House of Pain, an eccentric trio that—in the process of releasing three albums—managed to overcome many of the stereotypes facing white rappers. When *Truth Crushed to Earth Shall Rise Again* (1996) failed to sell as well as its predecessors, Everlast returned to his solo career. After surviving open heart surgery needed to correct a birth defect, he recorded *Whitey Ford Sings the Blues* (Tommy Boy, 1998) which ran the stylistic gamut, from folk-rap and jazz to industrial metal. It achieved platinum sales and critical raves, leading to an appearance on Santana's Grammy-feted album, *Supernatural* (1999), and a sequel release that built on the ground first explored in his second LP, *Eat at Whitey's* (Tommy Boy, 2000). His third LP, *White Trash Beautiful* (Island/Def Jam), was released in 2004.

Exciters, The

The Exciters featured one of the more dynamic soul singers of the early 1960s, Brenda Reid (born 1945). Although the group had only one hit of note, "Tell Him," it remains one of the more distinctive and popular oldies from that period.

The Exciters were formed out of the ashes of two New York City area acts. A trio of Jamaica, New York, high school juniors—Carol Johnson (b. 1945), Lilian Walker (b. 1945), and lead singer Reid—began attracting attention in early 1962. In the meantime, record producer Herbert Rooney (b. 1941) was working with his own male ensemble. When Rooney's group disbanded, he hooked up with the girls to form the Exciters in mid-1962. Within a few months they had secured a contract with United Artists and recorded the Bert Russell–penned song, "Tell Him," which reached the Top Five on *Billboard's* Hot 100 early the following year. Follow-up singles, most notably, "He's Got the Power," "Get Him," "Do-Wah-Diddy," "I Want You to Be My Boy," and a spirited reworking of the Jarmels hit, "A Little Bit of Soap," failed to rise above the lower reaches of the pop charts. Ironically, as the Exciters struggled to find their way back into the public consciousness, a rather limp cover of "Do-Wah-Diddy" would become a number one smash for the British Invasion band, Manfred Mann, in late 1964.

Falcons, The

The Falcons are best remembered for the later solo success of members Eddie Floyd and WILSON PICKETT. Formed in early 1959 by baritone Mack Rice, the Detroit-based group originally included tenor Joe Stubbs, the brother of FOUR TOPS frontman Levi Stubbs; bass singer Willie Schoefield; guitarist Lance Finnie; and Floyd as lead vocalist. On the strength of their performances in local venues, they landed a recording contract in short order with Unart Records. Electing to record a Finnie-Schoefield composition, "You're So Fine," the Falcons found themselves with a nationwide smash right out of the box.

Finding a follow-up hit proved more elusive, but the group's fortunes improved with the addition of gravelly-voiced Pickett as lead singer in late 1961. His distinctive style was evident in their next single, "I Found a Love," released by LuPine in March 1962. Unfortunately, Pickett decided to strike out on his own later in the year, signing with the Double-L label in 1963, and ultimately achieving superstar status as an Atlantic artist in the mid-1960s. The group's commercial potential was effectively ended when Floyd also opted for a solo career, beginning a long tenure with the STAX roster in 1966.

Fascinations, The

The Fascinations are best remembered as the group that originally included Martha Reeves, who went on to star as the leader of the Vandellas. Formed in 1960 with Shirley Walker as lead singer, the Detroit-based female R&B act was first known as the Sabre-ettes. Following a series of personnel changes, the group, now consisting of Walker, Fern Bledsoe, new lead vocalist Bernadine Boswell Smith, and her sister Joanne Boswell Levell, relocated to Chicago, where their performing talent attracted the attention of the IMPRESSIONS. One member, Curtis Mayfield, produced the Fascinations' first two singles for ABC-Paramount in 1962–63; poor sales, however, caused them to be dropped from the label.

When Mayfield started his own record imprint, he signed the Fascinations. The quartet would go on to record five singles in the mid-1960s, the second of which, "Girls Are Out to Get You," was a solid chart hit. They disbanded, though, when Mayfield opted not to resign them in 1969. They would reunite briefly in 1971 for a British tour.

Fat Boys, The

The Fat Boys were the clown princes of rap in the 1980s. Their unthreatening, mass media–friendly approach helped to counteract the intimidating gangster image with which the HIP-HOP genre was saddled as it attempted to cross over to the pop mainstream.

The Brooklyn-born trio appeared on the music scene at the perfect time: the outset of the MTV-driven video age. Their humor was rooted in visual slapstick, accentuating their large size and awkward movements in a world that worshipped svelte, sexy physiques. The threesome—consisting of Darren "The Human Beat Box" Robinson, Mark Prince

"Markie Dee" Morales, and Damon "Kool Rock-ski" Wimbley—allegedly tipped the scales at more than 750 pounds combined.

The Fat Boys were only modestly successful at the outset; they first made the R&B charts in mid-1984 with "Fat Boys"/ "Human Beat Box," billed as the Disco 3. Taking the name of this single, they consolidated their success with such releases as "Jail House Rap," "The Fat Boys Are Back," "Sex Machine," "Falling in Love," "Wipeout" (featuring backing vocals by the Beach Boys), and "The Twist" (with CHUBBY CHECKER)—all assisted by promotional video clips that were frequently shown on various network and cable television channels.

By now idolized by young blacks and suburban white kids alike, the Fat Boys were seen in films such as *Krush Groove* (1985, which featured them along with RUN-D.M.C., SHEILA E., and KURTIS BLOW as the Krush Groove All Stars) and *Disorderlies* (1987), as well as countless fan magazines. By the 1990s, however, they had become passé. Any hopes of a return to favor were dashed by Robinson's death from heart failure on December 10, 1995.

5th Dimension, The

A soul counterpart to artists of the soft rock fad dominating the pop charts beginning in 1966, the Los Angeles–based 5th Dimension consisted of Billy Davis, Jr., Florence LaRue, Marilyn McCoo, Lamont McLemore, and Ron Townson. The group was formed as the Versatiles when McLemore and McCoo, who'd been members of the Hi-Fi's, hooked up with Townson and Davis, both veterans of the St. Louis music scene. The lineup was completed with the addition of LaRue, like McCoo, a former beauty queen intent upon a career in entertainment.

After concerns over legal rights to their name led to adoption of the 5th Dimension moniker, they signed with Johnny Rivers's fledgling Soul City label. The group's smooth harmony style did not immediately click with black audiences, and early pop hits like the cover of the Mamas & the Papas album track, "Go Where You Wanna Go," and "Up, Up

The 5th Dimension (Frank Driggs Collection)

and Away" failed to cross over to the R&B charts. Although they remained more successful within the pop mainstream, the 5th Dimension's recordings consistently sold well in the marketplace, beginning with "Stoned Soul Picnic," a mid-1968 release which rose to number three on the *Billboard* Hot 100 and number two on the Best Selling Rhythm & Blues Singles listing. In all, the group made the R&B charts 17 times through 1978.

Davis and McCoo, who married in 1969, left the group in the mid-1970s. Davis first enjoyed modest success as a solo act in 1975 before teaming with McCoo in 1976. While the duo ran out of steam in the early 1980s, McCoo was moderately popular performing and recording on her own. She became best known as the host of the long-running TV program, *Solid Gold*.

First Choice

Originally formed as the Debronettes, the Philadelphia trio included Rochelle Fleming, Annette Guest, and Joyce Jones. They placed a dozen singles on the R&B charts in the 1970s, beginning with "Armed and Extremely Dangerous." Their other Top 40 hits included "Smarty Pants," "Newsy Neighbors," "The Player—Part 1," "Guilty," and "Doctor Love."

Fitzgerald, Ella (1918–1996) *singer*

Dubbed "The First Lady of Jazz," Ella Fitzgerald was one of the great song stylists of the 20th century. In recognition of her unique status as a pop music interpreter, Verve reissued her classic songbook series (16 titles in all, one per song composer or team including Irving Berlin, Cole Porter, and Rodgers and Hammerstein) on CD—available separate and as a complete set—in the 1990s.

Fitzgerald was born April 25, 1918, in Newport News, Virginia, and raised in Yonkers, New York. After winning amateur contests at the Harlem Opera House and Apollo Theater as a 16-year-old, she made her professional debut with Tiny Bradshaw's band in February 1935. Fitzgerald moved on to Chick Webb's group (she had sung with them as early as 1932), staying on as bandleader for a year after Webb's death in 1941. Her breakthrough recording came in 1938 with the self-composed "A-Tisket A-Tasket." Going solo in 1942, she recorded 15 R&B hits through 1960, including the chart-toppers "Cow-Cow Boogie" (with the Ink Spots), "Into Each Life Some Rain Must Fall"/"I'm Making Believe" (with the Ink Spots) and "Stone Cold Dead in the Market (He Had It Coming)" (with LOUIS JORDAN). She became an American institution in the post–World War II era, with her LPs consistently achieving best-selling status, and appearances in a string of big-budget films, such as *Ride 'Em Cowboy, Pete Kelly's Blues, St. Louis Blues,* and *Let No Man Write My Epitaph.* She died in Beverly Hills, California, on June 15, 1996.

Five Discs

Although the Five Discs were virtually unknown outside the greater New York area, they deserved a better fate. Bounced around from label to label, the group suffered due to a lack of promotional and general support.

The Five Discs—featuring an interracial lineup consisting of lead singer Mario De Andrade, first tenor Paul Ablano, second tenor Tony Basile, baritone Joe Barsalona, and Andy Jackson (bass) all hailing from Brooklyn, New York—formed in early 1958. They initially developed their act performing mostly at high school events in their hometown.

They collaborated in the writing of "I Remember," which they promptly auditioned for Laurie Records executive Gene Schwartz. Impressed by the song's dynamic interplay of vocal parts, Schwartz decided to put it out in June 1958 on a Laurie subsidiary, Emge. When the record began to break out in New York, RCA purchased distribution rights, releasing it on the Vik subsidiary label. However, Vik went bankrupt shortly thereafter, placing the single in limbo just when it was beginning it attract nationwide attention. Laurie eventually re-released "I Remember" on Rust, another subsidiary, but by then the initial groundswell of interest had subsided and the record failed to generate much commercial interest.

The Five Discs toiled on, recording more singles for a succession of labels, most notably, "Adios," a Calo release in September 1958, and "Never Let You Go," issued by Cheer in 1961. As some members departed—D'Andrade was replaced by Eddie Pardocchi and Basile by Frank Arnone—and feeling their chance at big-time success had passed, the group eventually disbanded in the early 1960s.

Five Keys, The

The Five Keys followed in the footsteps of groups like the RAVENS and the Dominoes, who had led the way in creating a stylistic blend of mainstream pop and rhythm and blues that possessed broad-based commercial appeal. Although failing to achieve the stratospheric success enjoyed by the PLATTERS and post-1958 edition of the DRIFTERS, they were one of the most professional acts of the 1950s, featuring two exceptional lead singers: Maryland Pierce, who came out of the blues shouter mold, and satin-voiced Rudy West, who specialized in romantic ballads.

The Newport News, Virginia–based Five Keys began as the Sentimental Four in the late 1940s. The members included two sets of brothers: tenor Rudy (born July 25, 1933) and baritone Bernie (b. 1932) West and Ripley (b. 1933) and Raphael Ingram. They had adopted the Five Keys moniker by the time Raphael left in 1951 to join the army; his place was filled in short order by Maryland Pierce (b. 1933) and Dickie Smith. True to their name, the line-up also included a piano accompanist, Joe Jones.

The group's first big break came when ALADDIN RECORDS executive Eddie Mesner, who had caught their performance at New York's Apollo Theater in early 1951, offered them a record contract. Although the Five Keys' debut single, "With a Broken Heart" (Aladdin), released in the spring of 1951, failed to chart, the follow-up, "The Glory of Love," topped the rhythm and blues charts for four weeks.

After failing to build on this early success, the group tottered on the brink of disaster when Smith and Rudy West entered the Army in 1953. They were able to find serviceable replacements, however, in Ramon Loper and Ulysses K. Hicks. Hicks died in 1954; West rejoined the Five Keys following his discharge from the service in 1956. In the meantime, they became consistent hitmakers after signing with the Capitol label. Their charting singles included "Ling, Ting, Tong," "Close Your Eyes," "the Verdict," "Cause You're My Lover"/ "Gee Whittakers," "Out of Sight, Out of Mind," "Wisdom of a Fool," and "Let There Be You."

The group remained active for several years once their records stopped selling. Rudy West would assemble a new version of the Five Keys two decades later their biggest moment coming on October 3, 1981, when they headlined the Royal New York Doo Wop Show in Manhattan's Radio City Music Hall. Based in Hampton, Virginia—where they were all employed by the U.S. Postal Service—the group continued to perform on the oldies circuit in their spare time for many years.

"5" Royales, The

The "5" Royales are best remembered for the 1957 recording, "Dedicated to the One I Love," written by Lowman Pauling, the group's lead singer and guitarist. The song would become a major hit twice in cover versions by the SHIRELLES and the Mamas and the Papas.

They began in the late 1940s as a gospel group, the Royal Sons, signing with the Apollo label in 1951. Shifting to secular material, the quintet—originally consisting of three cousins, Lowman and Clarence Pauling and tenor vocalist Johnny Tanner, augmented by tenor William Samuels and bass vocalist Otto Jeffries—recorded a string of rhythm and blues hits in the mid-1950s, beginning with two chart-topping Lowman Pauling compositions, "Baby, Don't Do It" and "Help Me Somebody." The "5" Royales' popularity owed much to the down-home gospel feel that remained a part of their music.

"Think" brought modest pop crossover success in 1957. Various line-ups (one including tenor Johnny Moore, who went on to star with the DRIFTERS) continued to record for a succession of labels, including ABC, VEE-JAY, Smash, and Home of the Blues, but were unable to place any more records in the charts. They disbanded in 1965. Clarence Pauling (aka Clarence Paul) would go on to work with MARVIN GAYE, STEVIE WONDER, and other MOTOWN artists as a writer, producer, and A&R man for the company.

Five Satins, The

The Five Satins—including Al Denby, Jim Freeman, Eddie Martin, and pianist Jessie Murphy—were formed in New Haven, Connecticut, by Fred Parris (born March 26, 1936) in early 1956. Parris had been the leader of a moderately successful recording act, the Scarletts, beginning in 1954, and liked the vocal blend achieved by the Velvets; hence, the name he gave his new group.

Parris got the inspiration to write the Five Satins' first release, "In the Still of the Nite," one of the most celebrated R&B vocal group recordings of all time, while on guard duty at 3 A.M. in the U.S. Army. It was, ironically, designated as the B-side, backing "The Jones Girl." Recorded in a local church basement, the song has remained a perennial best-seller, selling millions of copies through countless retrospective compilations, according to Parris, who has been involved in a seemingly endless series of lawsuits trying to receive royalties due him.

Parris was stationed in Japan when the recording achieved hit status. In order to capitalize on this success, the Five Satins performed and recorded in the States with a substitute lead singer, Bill Baker. Baker possessed a lighter, sweeter voice and was featured on the group's next hit, "To the Aisle." Parris returned in January 1958, taking Baker's place in the Five Satins; the membership by this time included tenor Richie Freeman (born December 1940), second tenor West Forbes (b. 1937), baritone Lewis Peoples (b. 1937), and bass Sy Hopkins (b. 1938). However, the search for further hits proved elusive; the 1959 single, "Shadows," represented their only return to the charts.

By the early 1960s the group had dissolved, and the ex-members resumed lives in New Haven outside of the music business. They were lured back together in 1969, however, to perform in a rock 'n' roll revival show at New York's Madison Square Garden. The experience encouraged them to continue work together intermittently both live and in the studio. In search of a more contemporary—i.e., commercially marketable—sound, Parris assembled a new group in the mid-1970s consisting of Nate Marshall and ex–Five Satins Richie Freeman and Jimmy Curtis. They enjoyed one minor hit on the Buddah label, "Everybody Stand and Clap Your Hands (For the Entertainer)," before Parris returned to the nostalgia circuit with a new edition of the Satins.

Five Sharps, The

The Five Sharps' fame rests on one single, the 1952 release, "Stormy Weather"/"Sleepy Cowboy," the existence of which was questioned by many R&B vocal group enthusiasts. Far more than any intrinsic music qualities, the rarity of the disc—and legendary developments surrounding efforts to locate a copy—fueled interest in the group.

Formed in 1952 in the Jamaica section of Queens, New York, the Five Sharps—consisting of lead vocalist Ronald Cuffey (referred to as "Cussey" in some accounts), first tenor Clarence Bassett, second tenor Robert Ward, bass Mickey Owens (Cuffey's cousin), and baritone Johnny Jackson—started out singing at local venues such as school functions. Tom Duckett provided piano accompaniment (as well as sometimes singing) for the group as well as for other area acts like the Cleftones, the Harmonaires, the Heartbeats, and the Rivileers. Depending on the source, either their manager or an independent record producer facilitated the recording session with Jubilee. When the release elicited no public response, Ward and Duckett were encouraged to leave the group by their families. Cuffey, Bassett, and Jackson went on to form the Videos with second tenor Charles Baskerville and bass Ron Woodhall in the mid-1950s; following their first release in 1958, Cuffey died. Bassett and Baskerville would later hook up with James Sheppard as Shep and the Limelights.

The Five Sharps were all but forgotten when in 1961 R&B collector Bill Pensebini came across a 78-rpm copy of "Stormy Weather" in a Brooklyn record store. Times Square Records proprietor Irving "Slim" Rose agreed to play it on his WBNX radio show. The record broke before it could be broadcast, and Rose offered a reward to anyone who could produce a copy. When nobody came forward, Rose contacted Jubilee, who informed him that eighty of their masters had suffered irreparable water damage, including "Stormy Weather."

Later in 1961, collector John Dunn found another 78-rpm copy marred by a hairline crack in Brooklyn. He taped both sides and put it in storage until the management of the R&B vocal group periodical, *Bim Bam Boom*, purchased the record for $500 in 1972. Hiring a studio engineer to eliminate the ticking sound present during playback, they put it out on the Bim Bam Boom label, marketing it at the then premium price of $2.50. The reissue spurred a rash of counterfeits, many appearing on color vinyl 45-rpm discs. With purported offers of as much as $10,000 for a mint copy, another disc was found in California in 1977.

Five Thrills, The

The career history of the Five Thrills epitomizes the experiences of the rank-and-file DOO-WOP groups in the 1950s. They enjoyed a modicum of fame within the Chicago R&B scene during 1953–54 before lapsing into obscurity. Although their so-called original tunes were patchwork constructions of musical devices employed by other recordings from that era, their performing skills and emotional commitment to the material were such that collectors still place a premium on the group's singles.

All group members—Levi Jenkins (bass and piano), Oscar Robinson (baritone), Gilbert Warren (lead tenor), and brothers Fred (baritone) and Obie Washington (second tenor)—hailed from Thirty-first Street on Chicago's South Side. They began singing together in 1950 while attending Douglas Elementary School. After hearing them singing on a street corner, a local entrepreneur, Ted Daniels, offered to manage them. After shopping the Five Thrills to several area labels, he secured a recording contract from Parrot.

Their debut disc, released in December 1953, "Feel So Good," was a reworking of the Five Keys' "Serve Another Round" with Fred Washington singing lead, backed by "My Baby's Gone" (featuring Robinson doing the lead), actually "My Summer's Gone," first recorded by the Four Buddies. It was widely played in Chicago, but received little attention elsewhere due to the label's weak distribution network. In early 1954, the Sheppards, a much better known act, recruited Robinson in an effort to upgrade their vocal blend. That group's cast-off member, Andre Williams, proved useful to the Five Thrills in the short term due to his knowledge of stagecraft. Their second

single appeared in winter 1954: "Gloria," a ballad featuring Warren in the lead and high tenor wailing in the background, backed by "Wee Wee Baby," a perfunctory remake of a 1949 song by the ROBINS.

The Five Thrills frequently performed live in the Chicago area during 1953–54, touring for a time with noted jazz saxophonist Illinois Jacquet. According to Jenkins, the group's fall from favor arose out of feud between Parrot owner Al Benson and deejay McKie Fitzhugh. Benson had the Five Thrills pull out of a January 1954 Pershing Ballroom show featuring the DRIFTERS at the last minute. Although they submitted to Benson's demand, the group remained at odds with him from that point onward.

Unhappy with their state of affairs, group members decided to move on to other ventures later in the year. Warren organized a new group, the Orchids, shortly afterward; they recorded several songs for Parrot in the mid-1950s. Jenkins played piano for various acts up to his death in the mid-1980s. Williams appears to have had the greatest success in the music business among group members, working as a record producer and creating successful novelty records such as "Jail Bait" and "Bacon Fat." The appearance of previously unreleased recordings on a specialized reissue label, Relic Records (including a couple of tracks erroneously credited to the Earls), have added further luster to the group's legacy.

Flack, Roberta (b. 1939) *singer*

Born February 10, 1939, in Asheville, North Carolina, Flack was raised in Arlington, Virginia. As a 15-year-old, she earned a music scholarship to Howard University, where she met future collaborator Donny Hathaway. Signed by Atlantic Records in 1969, her velvety voice would be featured on 27 hit singles through the early 1980s. She was equally adept at placing recordings on both the pop and R&B charts; her number-one pop singles included "The First Time Ever I Saw Your Face" (1972), "Killing Me Softly with His Song" (1973), and "Feel

Like Makin' Love" (1974). The latter song also topped the R&B charts, as did "Where Is the Love" (1972) and "The Closer I Get to You" (1978).

Flamingos, The

The Flamingos were one of the truly great R&B vocal groups; they were without equal as ballad interpreters. The core of the group, cousins Zeke Carey (first tenor) and Jake Carey (bass), grew up in Baltimore, playing ball with neighbor Sonny Til, who went on to fame heading the seminal DOO-WOP ensemble, the Orioles. They relocated to Chicago around 1949, forming the Flamingos in 1952. Other members included another set of cousins, first tenor Johnny Carter and baritone Paul Wilson, and lead singer Earl Lewis. Lewis was fired early on for, in his words, missing rehearsals, spending too much

The Flamingos—one of the sweetest harmony groups ever (Frank Driggs Collection)

time with girls, and religious differences. He moved on to the Five Echoes and was replaced by Sollie McElroy.

In the meantime, the Flamingos began appearing regularly in nightclubs and won a series of local amateur contests. After a failed audition with United in early 1952, the group was offered a contract with the other notable Chicago R&B record company at the time, Chance. While the group allegedly never received any money, they cut six classic records for the label through 1954, most notably, "Golden Teardrops," believed by some fans to represent a junkie's letter to his girlfriend.

With Chance in financial trouble, the Flamingos switched to Al Benson's Parrot Records, releasing three singles for the label in 1954. This amounted to a transitional period, with McElroy departing due to personal differences (he would later sing with the Moroccos, Nobels, and Chanteurs) and his replacement by Nate Nelson, formerly with Chicago's Velvetones, and the death of manager Ralph Leon, making it necessary for group members to master his responsibilities.

They discovered that Leon had been negotiating a contract with Checker, where they would enjoy their earliest chart hits, "I'll Be Home," which failed to achieve major crossover sales due to Pat Boone's pop cover, and "A Kiss from Your Lips." The group temporarily suspended activities when Carter and Zeke Carey (the latter returned in 1958) were drafted in late 1956; they regrouped early the following year, however, adding Tommy Hunt, formerly with the Five Echoes, and Terry Johnson to the lineup. In 1957–58, they recorded at least four discs for Decca, although still legally tied to Checker as a result of Nelson's solo contract with the company.

In late 1958, the Flamingos moved to George Goldner's New York–based End label. With the sweet-voiced Hunt replacing Nelson as lead, the group enjoyed its greatest pop success with the likes of "Lovers Never Say Goodbye"; "I Only Have Eyes for You," with its ethereal arrangement of the 1934 Ben Selvin hit; the SAM COOKE composition, "Nobody Loves Me Like You"; and "Mio Amore."

When no more hits were forthcoming, the Flamingos returned to Checker in the mid-1960s. Nelson joined the PLATTERS in 1966; he died of a heart attack June 1, 1984. Now committed to the soul vogue, they managed to graze the charts with "The Boogaloo Party," "Dealin' (Groovin' with Feelin'")," and "Buffalo Soldier."

Flares, The

Formed in 1959, the Los Angeles-based Flares consisted of lead vocalist Aaron Collins, first tenor Willie Davis, second tenor Beverly Harris, bass George Hollis, and baritone Thomas Miller. Collins and Davis had previously been a part of the CADETS/THE JACKS organization, while Hollis was formerly a member of the Ermines and the Flairs.

Under Buck Ram's management, the group was signed by Felsted Records. Their first two singles, issued in 1960, failed to generate much sales action; however, the third, the dance craze classic "Foot Stompin' Part 1," became a crossover hit, despite a best-selling cover by the Dovells. The Flares switched to the Press label in 1962, but failed to place any of seven releases on the charts. The group underwent considerable turnover at this time; members at one time or another included Randy Jones, Eddie King, Robbie Robinson, and Patience Valentine.

Floyd, Eddie (b. 1935) *singer*

One of the mainstays of the Memphis-based STAX roster, he was born June 25, 1935, in Montgomery, Alabama. Much of his youth was spent in Detroit, where he became a founding member of the doo-wop group the Falcons in 1955. The Falcons produced hits for several labels, including Lu Pine, which was founded by Floyd's uncle Robert West.

Floyd embarked on a solo career in 1963, breaking through with the R&B chart-topper, "Knock on Wood" in 1966. He would enjoy intermittent success as a recording artist through 1977, most notably with the Top Five R&B singles "I've Never Found a Girl (to Love Me Like You Do)" and a remake of the SAM COOKE classic "Bring It on Home to Me."

Force MD's, The

Although largely forgotten today, the Force MD's (the latter portion of the name denotes "Musical Diversity") were an important link in the early evolution of RAP. Originally named the LDs, they performed in a street corner style known as DOO-WOP HIP-HOP. In short order, the group, whose members included TCD, Stevie D, Trisco, and Mercury, shifted to soul-tinged harmonies, punctuated by breakdance routines as well as impersonations of TV theme songs and pop culture celebrities, for performances, many of which took place on the Staten Island, New York ferry.

They were later joined by a DJ, taking on the name Dr. Rock and the MCs (he would later be replaced by DJ Shock). The Force MD's went on to record a best-selling ballad, "Tender Love," supplied by the JIMMY JAM AND TERRY LEWIS songwriting and production team. They also released a string of moderately successful LPs, including *Love Letters* (Tommy Boy, 1984), *Chillin'* (Tommy Boy, 1986), *Touch and Go* (Tommy Boy, 1987), *Step to Me* (1990), and *For Lovers and Others* (1992).

Four Tops, The

The Detroit-based Four Tops had one of the most distinctive sounds of the soul music era, driven by lead singer Levi Stubbs's raw lead vocals. The group's personnel—including Renaldo "Obie" Benson, Adbul "Duke" Fakir, and Lawrence Payton as well as Stubbs—remained unchanged for nearly a half-century following their formation in 1954 as the Four Aims. They first recorded for Chess in 1956, followed by stints with Red Top and Columbia prior to signing with MOTOWN in 1963.

Although their gospel-drenched sound always played better to an R&B audience than the pop mainstream, the Four Tops' 1960s singles—most

Mid-1960s publicity photo of the Four Tops (Frank Driggs Collection)

notably, "Baby I Need Your Loving," "I Can't Help Myself," "It's the Same Old Song," "Reach Out, I'll Be There," "Standing in the Shadows of Love," and "Bernadette"—sold well in both markets. While viewed as an anachronism by the 1970s, the quartet continued to regularly place records on the charts into the 1980s. They switched to the Dunhill label in 1972 (which was swallowed up by ABC in 1975), and then went over to Casablanca in the early 1980s where they hit again with "When She Was My Girl" (number one R&B, number 11 pop). In 1983, the group returned to Motown, although their chief appeal now was to the nostalgia crowd. They had a minor hit with "Sexy Ways" in 1985, before signing with Arista in 1988. In 1986, Stubbs supplied the voice for the man-eating plant in the remake of the film *Little Shop of Horrors*. Payton died of cancer in 1997, but the remaining members continued as a threesome, eventually bringing former Temptation Theo Peoples into the group. With Stubbs battling various health problems, Ronnie McNeir was brought in as a replacement in 2000. Nevertheless, the Four Tops continue to actively perform.

Four Tunes, The

Like many of the black vocal groups of the immediate post–World War II era, the Four Tunes were predisposed to record pop material as the surest route to success. They originated in the New York City area as the Brown Dots, formed by Deek Watson after leaving the Ink Spots in 1945. The members he had recruited—Pat Best, Jimmy Gordon, and Jimmy Nabbie—moonlighted along with Danny Owens to record as the Sentimentalists on the Manor label in 1946. The latter lineup changed their name to the Four Tunes shortly afterwards, and backed Savannah Churchill on the 1947 hit single, "I Want to Be Loved (but Only by You)."

The group members severed all ties with the Brown Dots in 1948, signing the following year with RCA. They finally broke through with "Marie," followed by "I Understand (Just How You Feel)." Effectively washed up as a hit-making entity from that point onward, they make their last recordings in 1956, breaking up for good in 1963. Their notable contributions would be revived during the rock 'n' roll era, with the G-Clefs releasing a smash version of "I Understand (Just How You Feel)" in 1961, and the British Invasion group, the Bachelors, covering "Marie."

Fowlkes, Eddie "Flashin'" (b. 1962) *techno deejay*

Part of the fabled postpunk Detroit TECHNO school, Eddie "Flashin'" Fowlkes (the nickname referred to his skills as a scratch and mix DJ) worked closely with such luminaries as Derrick May and JUAN ATKINS in the early 1980s. He recorded his debut single, "Goodbye Kiss," on

Atkins' Metroplex label. He continued to work the turntables at Detroit's The Alley into the 1990s, issuing critically acclaimed recordings such as the 1991 LP, *Serious Techno Vol. 1,* and the club singles, the Graeme Park–produced "Turn Me Out," and "Inequality," released by 430 West.

Foxxx, Freddie (b. 1969) *rapper*
More of a social activist than most rappers, Freddie Foxxx has produced videos depicting the horror of prison as a deterrent to potential gangstas, and had a hand in founding the Brooklyn-based Dream House, a charity dedicated to providing constructive alternatives for economically deprived youth. Born James Campbell, in Westbury, Long Island, he was already a performing in a RAP group at age 10. He first recorded as Freddie C. on a 12-inch single by Supreme Force in 1986. He was given the opportunity to record a solo 1989 LP for MCA, *Freddie Foxxx Is Here,* which proved to be a commercial bomb.

He slowly launched a comeback by collaborating with the likes of Kool G Ray & DJ Polo, Boogie By Productions, KRS-ONE ("Ruff Ruff") and NAUGHTY BY NATURE ("Hot Potato"). This led to a record deal with QUEEN LATIFAH's Flavor Unit, a subsidiary of Epic (Sony). His album, *Crazy Like a Foxxx* (Flavor Unit/Epic, 1994), would be shelved, with only a few promotional copies making it into public hands.

Refusing to give up, he contributed to records by GANG STARR and M.O.P. before starting his own label, Kjac, aided by a distribution tie-in with Landspeed. The ensuing LP, *Industry Shakedown* (Landspeed, 2000), featured his new moniker Bumpy Knuckles (based on an alter ego he developed after hearing a comment on his boxing technique), and production work from such HIP-HOP luminaries as DJ Premier, Diamond D, and Pete Rock. Resplendent with vibrant beats and even more vulgarities than normal for the genre, the work represented a nonstop attack on the evils of the record business.

Foxy
Although active from the late 1960s well into the 1980s, Foxy's greatest success occurred at the height of the DISCO craze. The Miami-based group consisted of lead singer/guitarist Ish Ledesma; clarinetist/percussionist Richie Puente, the son of legendary salsa bandleader Tito Puente; drummer Joe Galdo; keyboard/vibes player Charlie Murciano; and bassist Arnold Pasiero. They first reached the charts in 1970 with "Call Me Later," but then went six years without another hit. The group is best remembered for the dance club rave-up, "Get Off," which topped the R&B charts in 1978. After two best-selling follow-ups, "Hot Number" and "Rrrrrrock," they never returned to the charts again.

Franklin, Aretha (b. 1942) *singer*
Widely known as the "Queen of Soul," Aretha Franklin was a dominant force in American popular music between 1967 and 1974. Born March 25, 1942, in Memphis, she was raised in Buffalo and Detroit. Franklin's earliest musical influence of note was her father, the Rev. Cecil L. Franklin, one of the leading gospel singers of his day. Following a brief recording stint for JVB/Battle in 1956, she seemed poised for mainstream success when signed to Columbia by the legendary John Hammond in 1960. However, Columbia tried to harness Franklin's raw gospel roots, opting to place her amidst mannered jazz-oriented combos and big band–derived arrangements.

A label switch to Atlantic in early 1967 heralded a dramatic change in approach, resulting in unprecedented commercial success both on the pop and R&B charts. With producer Jerry Wexler helping facilitate her gospel-pop impulses, Franklin recorded such timeless classics as "Respect," "Baby I Love You," "Chain of Fools," "(Sweet Sweet Baby) Since You've Been Gone," "Think," and "Until You Come Back to Me (That's What I'm Gonna Do)." Her albums sold well, too; her double-LP tour de force, *Amazing Grace* (Atlantic, 1972), helped bring gospel music closer to the pop mainstream.

Aretha Franklin performing at the Martin Luther King Tribute, Madison Square Garden, New York City, on June 28, 1968 (Frank Driggs Collection)

Franklin moved to Arista at the onset of the 1980s, and while the hits no longer came as frequently, she remained a commercial force throughout the decade, collaborating with other artists such as GEORGE BENSON, the Eurythmics, and George Michael. Now a musical icon, she continues to record and perform, albeit at a more leisurely pace.

Friends of Distinction

Although generally grouped with pop-soul acts like the 5TH DIMENSION and the Supremes, the Friends of Distinction were influenced to an even greater extent by the soft-harmony rock of white groups like the Mamas and the Papas and Spanky and Our Gang. The vocal quintet included Harry Elston (born November 4, 1938, in Dallas), Floyd Butler (June 5, 1941, San Diego), Jessica Cleaves (December 10, 1948, Beverly Hills, California),

Charlene Gibson (May 6, 1947, Chicago), and Barbara Jean Love (July 24, 1941, Los Angeles). The group's composer/arranger, Elston, had already worked with Butler in the Hi-Fi's (whose members also included Marilyn McCoo and LaMonte McLemore, soon to become founding members of the 5th Dimension), best remembered for backing RAY CHARLES on a tour in the mid-1960s.

With the financial backing of Hall of Fame football player and film actor Jim Brown, the Friends of Distinction garnered a recording contract with RCA in 1968. Their first success came in 1969 with "Grazing in the Grass," originally a top-selling instrumental hit for African trumpeter Hugh Masekela in 1968. Several more chart singles followed, most notably "Going in Circles" and "Love or Let Me Be Lonely." With the group's commercial prospects seemingly on the wane, Love departed in 1971. They disbanded shortly thereafter, with Cleaves going on to join EARTH, WIND & FIRE.

Fugees, The

The Fugees derived their name from the fact that cousins Pras Michel (b. Samuel Prakazrel Michel, October 19, 1972) and Wyclef Jean (b. Jeannel Wyclef Jean, October 17, 1972) were Haitian expatriates. "Fugees" was short for "refugees." The two musicians hooked up with singer Lauryn Hill (b. October 19, 1975, in East Orange, New Jersey), fresh from a small film role in *Sister Act II,* in East Orange during the late 1980s. Although failing to chart, their debut album, *Blunted on Reality* (Ruffhouse, 1994), won kudos from the critical establishment for its socially conscious lyrics and cool RAP grooves overlaid with an eclectic blend of musical influences, including jazz, REGGAE, and African folk guitar phrasing. The intelligent HIP-HOP pop of their chart-topping, multi-platinum follow-up, *The Score* (Ruffhouse, 1996), helped undermine the primacy of the gangsta movement.

With Hill taking time out to have a baby, Wyclef Jean recorded a solo album, *The Carnival* (Ruffhouse, 1997), which reached number 16 on the *Billboard*

Top 200. Pras also began on his own project, *Ghetto Supastar* (Ruffhouse, 1998), with the title track making the U.S. Top 20 (and going as high as number two in the U.K.). Hill ultimately followed suit, releasing one of the most successful albums of the decade, *The Miseducation of Lauryn Hill* (Ruffhouse, 1998), not only topping the charts, but winning nine Grammys early the following year. With Wyclef Jean issuing a second LP, *The Ecleftic: 2 Sides II a Book* (Ruffhouse, 2000), which reached number nine on the pop charts, a reunion of the group appeared increasingly unlikely.

funk

Funk was a dance-oriented offshoot of soul music that originated in the late 1960s. (The term itself had been widely used in hip urban African-American circles since the early decades of the twentieth century; it carried several different off-color meanings.) It originated with JAMES BROWN's live jam sessions and by STAX groups such as BOOKER T. & THE MGS and the Bar-Kays. Sylvester Stewart, leader of the band SLY AND THE FAMILY STONE, was a notable pioneer of the genre. He developed his sound as a session musician in small San Francisco recording studios during the mid-1960s before going on to superstardom with hits such as "Everyday People" and "Dance to the Music."

By the time Sly experienced career burnout in the early 1970s, the chief features of funk were sharply delineated for the next generation of practitioners: a polyrhythmic, syncopated dance music usually centered around a repetitious, thickly-textured bass pattern, and a greater reliance on instrumental ensemble playing than had been typical of either rhythm and blues or soul. Classic exponents of the style who achieved significant success included GEORGE CLINTON's Parliament/Funkadelic combine, the OHIO PLAYERS, KOOL AND THE GANG, and EARTH, WIND & FIRE.

The genre dominated the black music scene throughout the 1970s, absorbing elements of DISCO and merging its heavy backbeat with punk's rebel-

lious attitude to create a new stylistic offshoot, FUNK PUNK. The most popular funk punk artists included PRINCE, RICK JAMES, and Morris Day and the Time. The innovative vanguard of funk was eventually co-opted by the RAP/HIP-HOP movement. Nevertheless, it provided the foundation for virtually every black-inspired and dance genre to emerge since 1980.

Funkadelic See CLINTON, GEORGE.

Funkdoobiest

Formed in Los Angeles in 1992, Funkdoobiest combined Latin-tinged HIP-HOP and soul elements with a plethora of marijuana references. The group consisted of MC Son Doobie (born Jason Vasquez, in Puerto Rico), MC Tomahawk Funk (b. Tyrone Pachenco, of Sioux Indian extraction), and DJ Ralph M. (b. Ralph Medrano), a former associate of Kid Frost.

They joined the Soul Assassins crew (other members included CYPRESS HILL and House of Pain), which became a springboard to an Epic record deal in 1993. Their debut album, *Which Doobie U B?* (Epic, 1993), produced by Cypress Hill's DJ Muggs, became an underground hit. *Brothas Doobie* (Epic, 1995), a more low-key affair, showed the trio venturing into social commentary. At this point, Tomahawk Funk departed to focus on his parental responsibilities. Carrying on as a duo, Funkdoobiest recorded *Troubleshooters* (Buzz Tone, 1998), which revealed an even greater emphasis on their Latin heritage. When no other releases were forthcoming, rumors abounded that Son Doobie was planning a solo LP project.

funk punk

Born out of the merger of classic 1970s FUNK and the abrasive, stripped down energy of the punk movement, FUNK PUNK first surfaced in the street-smart music of black artists like RICK JAMES and the P-Funk galaxy, featuring GEORGE CLINTON and Bootsy

Collins. James was particularly influential, having worked extensively with white rockers as far back as the 1960s (including Neil Young, when both were in a Toronto-based outfit called the Mynah Birds). His formula incorporated funk's propulsive bass lines, wailing lead guitar work, rebellious song lyrics, and outrageous stage attire owing something to the theatrical conventions of England's glam craze.

When drugs and other legal entanglements slowed James's career momentum, PRINCE assumed the funk punk's leadership mantle. Strongly conditioned by the prevailing punk ethic of the late 1970s, he recorded a comprehensive body of work that helped to define the genre's mature phase. Furthermore, he exerted a considerable influence as a songwriter, producer, and bandleader. Notable artists to emerge out of his Minneapolis-based school during the mid-1980s included Morris Day and The Time, ANDRE CYMONE, VANITY 6, and Wendy and Lisa (who played for a time in Prince's band, the Revolution). The scene ultimately was pushed into the background by the increasing popularity of HIP-HOP, particularly the crossover success of gangsta rappers, who seemed more in tune with the aspirations of African-American youth. Furthermore, Prince's growing disenchantment with the pressures of superstardom robbed the genre of its greatest innovator. He would periodically release new material in the 1990s and beyond, which typically revealed a more mannered performer, seemingly preoccupied with mining the R&B traditions at the core of his original sound.

Gangsta Pat *rapper*

The son of R&B session player Willie Hall, who played behind R&B greats like ISAAC HAYES, he was born Patrick Hall, in Memphis. Something of a studio wunderkind, he played all instruments, and handled the composition and production work on his recordings. The debut album, *#1 Suspect* (Atlantic, 1991), and two accompanying singles, "I Am the Gangsta" and "Gangsta's Need Love 2," broke out in the Atlanta-Memphis area. Like many other Atlantic HIP-HOP artists, he soon found himself shopping for a new contract as that label backed off from its ambitious plans to invade the rap scene.

Gangsta Pat's follow-up LPs, *All About Comin' Up* (Wrap/Ichiban, 1993)—which included the regional hits, "Gangsta Boogie," assisted by a promotional video clip that depicted the hip-hop dance fad of the same name, and "Stay Away from Cali"—and *Sex, Money and Murder* (Wrap/Ichiban, 1994), suffered to some degree from the industry-wide backlash against gangsta rap. However, he remains nothing if not persistent, continuing to issue trendy, competently executed—if blandly derivative—recordings, including *Homicidal Lifestyle* (Power, 1997), *The Story of My Life* (Redrum, 1997), *Tear Yo Club Down* (Redrum, 1999), and *Show Ya Grill* (Redrum, 2000).

gangsta rap   See RAP.

Gang Starr

Widely considered HIP-HOP's most intelligent, innovative act from both a musical and literary stand-point, Gang Starr consists of Guru Keith E (born Keith Allam, Roxbury, Massachusetts), vocals and lyrics, and DJ Premier (b. Chris Martin, Brooklyn, New York), musical accompaniment. The son of a Boston municipal and superior court judge, Guru worked as a counselor in a maximum detention home, an experience that greatly influenced his verses. After graduating with a business administration degree from Atlanta's Morehouse College, he relocated to Brooklyn, forming Gang Starr with rapper Damo D-Ski and DJ Wanna Be Down. Their notable early singles included "The Lesson" and "Bust a Move," both produced by DJ Mark The 45 King. Guru's cohorts, however, eventually decided to pursue projects closer to their home base of Boston.

At the time, DJ Premier was in Texas attending college, where he organized the Inner City Posse (not to be confused with INNER CITY). He was offered a recording deal with Wild Pitch, but only if a different rapper was brought aboard. The label put him in touch with Guru, and the duo recorded their debut LP, *No More Mr. Nice Guy* (Wild Pitch, 1990), in ten days while Premier was on vacation. One track, "Manifest," after garnering airplay on *Yo! MTV Raps*, spurred film director Spike Lee to recruit Gang Starr to cut Lotus Eli's poem on the history of jazz to a hip-hop rhythm for inclusion in *Mo' Better Blues*. Now recognized as pioneers in popularizing jazz-rap, they further advanced the form with *Step in the Arena* (Chrysalis, 1991), further consolidating their recognizable style—Guru's streetwise monotone, backed by spare, live jazz samples and cut-up scratching—in *Daily Operation* (Chrysalis, 1992).

In the meantime, both members became involved in a number of side projects, Premier producing for Big Daddy Kane, Fu-Schnickens, Heavy D, and KRS-ONE, and Guru melding rap with free-form jazz with Jazzamatazz. He also started the Gang Starr Foundation—including Big Shug, Felachi the Nutcracker, Jeru the Damaja, and Little Dap—which assisted in the hardcore-slanted *Hard to Earn* (Chrysalis, 1994). With the duo continuing to pursue solo paths, *Moment of Truth* (Noo Trybe, 1998) amounted to a comeback album of sorts. The next release, the two-disc retrospective compilation, *Full Clip: A Decade of Gang Starr* (Cooltempo, 1999), made it apparent that the act had reached an artistic crossroad and was trying to decide what step to take next.

Gap Band, The

The Gap Band was one of most successful and influential FUNK bands of the 1980s. Their promotional videos were widely copied within the rhythm and blues field, while their music continues to be sampled by many HIP-HOP artists.

The Gap Band was formed in Tulsa (the name refers to three hometown streets: Greenwood, Archer, and Pine); conflicting dates have been provided, ranging from 1967 to the early 1970s. At their peak during the post-punk era, the group included seven members, built around the Wilson brothers—Ronnie (vocals/keyboards/trumpet), Charles (vocals/keyboards), and Robert (vocals/bass)—cousins of P-Funk star, Bootsy Collins, whose father, a Pentecostal minister, encouraged them to sing during his Sunday services.

The Gap Band struggled throughout most of the 1970s with a sound heavily reminiscent of SLY AND THE FAMILY STONE's funk-soul hybrid. Their recording activity was sporadic at best, including an LP, *Magician's Holiday* (1974), for Leon Russell's Shelter Records; a gospel-styled single, "This Place Called Heaven," for A&M; and a self-titled album

for Tattoo in 1977. They finally found success with their Mercury debut, *Gap Band;* it was followed by eight more chart albums in the 1980s, the most popular of which, *Gap Band IV* (Total Experience, 1982), resided in the *Billboard* Top LPs & Tapes listing for 52 weeks and reached platinum level sales. Although not a fixture within the mainstream pop scene, their singles—typically, uptempo party numbers such as "Shake," "I Don't Believe You Want to Get Up and Dance (Oops, Up Side Your Head)," "Burn Rubber (Why You Wanna Hurt Me)," "Yearning for Your Love," "Early in the Morning," "You Dropped a Bomb on Me," "Outstanding," "Party Rain," "Beep a Freak," and "Going in Circles"—performed very well on the R&B charts.

The Gap Band did not record during the first half of the 1990s, earning a living through live performing and royalty payments from their extensive back catalog of recordings. Although remaining with the group, Charles Wilson collaborated with Dave Stewart on the soundtrack of the film, *Rooftops* (1990), and toured with the Eurythmics. He would also provide studio assistance for the likes of RAY CHARLES, Quincy Jones, Mint Condition, SNOOP DOGGY DOGG, and Zapp, as well as release solo recordings. With a revival of interest in funk and 1980s music in general, the group released its first album of original material in nearly six years, *Ain't Nothing But a Party* (Rhino), in 1995. They remain active in the music business up to the present day.

Gary G-Wiz *producer*

HIP-HOP producer Gary G-Wiz brought an unerring pop sense to his work with cutting-edge artists like PUBLIC ENEMY—most notably, the LPs *Apocalypse '91: The Enemy Strikes Back* (1991) and *Greatest Misses*—and RUN-DMC. He was also widely active as a remix specialist, working with Anthrax, Bel Biv Devoe, Peter Gabriel, Helmut, JANET JACKSON, Sinead O'Connor, and Lisa Stansfield, among others.

Born in North Carolina, G-Wiz relocated with his family to Freeport, New York at age six. He was exposed to R&B acts like the COASTERS and the

DRIFTERS, who played at his parents' nightclub. Teaching himself drums and, later, computer programming, he manned the decks for a New York rap group, 516. After becoming friends with Public Enemy's Chuck D in the mid-1980s, he was recruited to work with Eric Sader and Keith Schocklee as part of the Bomb Squad. He became the producer and manager for Young Black Teenagers, directing them to Schocklee's new label, S.O.U.L. By the 1990s, he was generally held to be one of the premier producers within both the RAP and pop-rock fields.

Gaye, Marvin (1939–1984) *singer and songwriter*

A leading proponent of the MOTOWN sound, a polished variant of 1960s urban soul music, he was born Marvin Pentz Gay, Jr., in Washington, D.C. The son of an Apostolic minister, he began singing in church as a youth in addition to teaching himself piano and drums. After graduating from high school, he sang with the Rainbows and Marquees before joining Harvey Fuqua's re-formed DOO-WOP group, the MOONGLOWS. When Fuqua was hired as a staff writer and producer by Motown, he brought Gaye along with him in 1960 to do session work.

At Motown, Gaye—who married Anna, the sister of label president, Berry Gordy, in 1961—was encouraged to develop a career as a solo vocalist. Beginning with "Stubborn Kind of Fellow," a Top Ten R&B hit in late 1962, he had 57 hits (including duets with a succession of female singers) for the label through 1981—most notably, R&B chart-toppers "I'll Be Doggone," "Ain't That Peculiar," "Ain't Nothing Like the Real Thing" (with Tammi Terrell), "You're All I Need to Get By" (with Terrell), "I Heard It Through the Grapevine," "Too Busy Thinking About My Baby," "What's Going On," "Mercy Mercy Me (The Ecology)," "Inner City Blues (Make Me Wanna Holler)," "Let's Get It On," "I Want You," and "Got to Give It Up (Pt. I)."

By the early 1970s, Gaye was chafing at the company's conservative production values. Faced with the threat of losing him to another label, Motown

Marvin Gaye live at the Apollo Theater, New York City, in the 1960s (Frank Driggs Collection)

allowed Gaye to explore more sophisticated sociopolitical themes in his compositions. *What's Going On?* (Motown, 1971)—which addressed civil rights, environmental, and Vietnam War issues—and the sexually explicit (for its time) *Let's Get It On* (Motown, 1973) are recognized as some of the earliest R&B concept albums.

Gaye's work fell out of favor somewhat during the DISCO era, but he returned to the spotlight with *Midnight Love* (Columbia, 1982), which included the Grammy-winning hit single, "Sexual Healing." However, his revival was cut short when he was shot to death by his father in a family dispute.

Gaynor, Gloria (b. 1949) *disco singer*

Until the rise of DONNA SUMMER, Gloria Gaynor carried the title "Queen of Disco" (an honor bestowed by the National Association of Discotheque Disc Jockeys in March 1975). Today, she is best known for the 1979 dance club anthem, "I Will

Survive," featuring a woman's defiant declaration of independence from an uncaring lover.

Gaynor was born Gloria Fowles, on September 7, 1949, in Newark, New Jersey. One of seven children, she grew up preferring the records of teen DOO-WOP singer Frankie Lymon as well as pop stylists like Nat King Cole and Sarah Vaughan. She was an accountant for a short time following high school before briefly joining a band based in Canada at age 18. Returning to New Jersey, she was recruited by the Soul Satisfiers in 1971 after a friend persuaded her to sing with them at a local club. After touring with them for a year and a half, she formed her own group, City Life, which achieved a measure of popularity along the East Coast.

Gaynor signed with Columbia in the early 1970s, and went on to release an early DISCO hit, "Honey Bee," in 1973. With the label providing minimal support, she switched to MGM, producing one of the earliest albums geared to dance clubs, *Never Can Say Goodbye* (1975). The title track, previously a hit single for both ISAAC HAYES and the Jackson 5, provided her commercial breakthrough, but follow-up records fared poorly.

Her fortunes reached a new peak with "I Will Survive," and the platinum-selling LP produced by Dino Fekaris and Freddie Perren from which it was culled, *Love Tracks* (Polydor, 1979). She continued to enjoy minor success through "I Am What I Am," a song originally introduced in the Act I finale of the Broadway musical, *La Cage Aux Folles*. With her career losing momentum, she denounced her prior substance abuse habits and embraced born-again Christianity in 1982. She has remained active as a performer and recording artist (focusing on post-disco dance music and gospel), and is still extremely popular in Europe. Her autobiography, *I Will Survive*, was published in 1997.

Gayten, Paul (1920–1991) *vocalist and bandleader*

Although unknown by all but the staunchest rhythm and blues fans, Paul Gayten remains one of the great pioneers of the genre. In addition to four Top Ten R&B hits between 1947 and 1950, the vocalist/pianist/bandleader accompanied countless other artists in the recording studio, most notably Bobby Charles, Sugar Boy Crawford, Clarence "Frogman" Henry, Annie Laurie, Chubby Newsom, and TV Slim.

Born January 29, 1920, in Kentwood, Louisiana, Gayten (the nephew of Little Brother Montgomery) had the good fortune to grow up within a musical family. He gained valuable experience organizing the Army base band during World War II in Biloxi, Mississippi. He signed with the DeLuxe label in 1947, and—billed as Paul Gayten & His Trio (consisting of Edgar Banchard, George Prior, and Robert Green)—promptly placed two singles on the charts: "Since I Fell for You" (lead vocal by Laurie), later a number four pop hit for Lenny Welch in 1963, and "True." After a brief dry spell, he regained his hit-making touch in 1950 with "I'll Never Be Free" and a cover of the Weavers' mega-smash, "Goodnight Irene."

He remained a force in the evolution of the New Orleans sound, appearing on Newsom's "Hip Shakin' Mama" (his band receiving credit as the Hip Shakers), Laurie's "Cuttin' Out," and Henry's seminal rock 'n' roll single "Ain't Got No Home" (later covered by The Band). He moved to Los Angeles in the late 1950s in order to take advantage of the growing prominence of the music industry there. He owned his own record company, Pzazz, for a time beginning in 1969. Due to his increasing involvement with the administrative end of the business, he effectively retired from the performing end at that time. Gayton died in New Orleans on March 29, 1991.

Georgio (b. 1966) *deejay and singer*

San Francisco native Georgio Allentini started out as a disc jockey in Los Angeles in 1986. He subsidized the recording of his debut single, "Sexappeal," which was picked up for distribution by MOTOWN. It became a nationwide hit, and was followed by the

Top Ten R&B hit, "Tina Cherry" (Motown). These and later releases—most notably, the 1987 LP *Georgio*—revealed a considerable debt to Prince, both his music and gender-bending sexuality.

girl groups

With the exception of the teen idols, girl groups were the only genuinely distinctive genre to peak in the early 1960s. The genre owed its success largely to the 1959 payola investigations, combined with increased attacks on rock 'n' roll's alleged bad influence on teenagers. These factors stimulated a change in image and musical focus among record companies and radio disc jockeys. Radio's efforts to clean house led to the concentration of power in the hands of the program director who, in turn, adopted national playlists and a tightened Top 40 format. There was a resulting decline in regional hits produced by small record labels; the pop music industry was driven by the ongoing search for the next big trend. Heavy reliance on proven formulas became the modus operandi, as the balance of power shifted to a select group of record executives, studio producers, staff songwriters, and media personalities.

Girl groups proved to be one of the more successful formulas, to be mined again and again by those labels committed to the youth market. Music historians have sometimes fallen prey to a revisionist perspective of that era which interprets the rise of girl groups—and female performers in general (e.g., Connie Francis, Brenda Lee, Lesley Gore)—as early evidence of the increasing assertiveness of women in the workplace and within society in general. In point of fact, however, girl groups were strongly manipulated by powerful men who were well-connected within the record industry. Successful girl groups were prized in large because they were easily pliable, generally submitting to outside control with a minimal display of rebellious attitude. The younger the performers, the more likely they were to accept the strict order of the system. This at least in part explains why few groups

were able to sustain a successful recording career beyond a hit recording or two.

The Chantels were the first girl group to rise above the one-hit wonder status, which had limited the impact of acts such as the Paris Sisters ("I Love How You Love Me"), the Teen Queens ("Eddie My Love"), and the Poni-Tails ("Born Too Late"). The group—originally a quintet whose members were all classmates at Saint Anthony of Padua School in the Bronx—were discovered backstage at an Alan Freed rock 'n' roll revue by Rama/Gee/Gone record producer Richard Barrett while waiting to meet their idol, Frankie Lymon (of the Teenagers). The Chantels' second release, "Maybe," proved to be a seminal event in the girl group genre, featuring lead vocalist Arlene Smith in one of the most searing and honest vocal performances ever. The disc's dramatic intensity and steady sales profoundly influenced musicians and producers for years to come.

The Shirelles were the first girl group to achieve both artistic and commercial success following in the stylistic path established by the Chantels. When the Shirelles' first few releases made little impact, producer Luther Dixon decided to sweeten up their heavily R&B sound through the use of strings. He first achieved success in 1960 with the West Indian–inflected "Tonight's the Night," followed by the Carole King–Gerry Goffin composition, "Will You Love Me Tomorrow." The latter song was a hit around the world, remaining number one for five weeks on the U.S. singles charts. The arrangement—featuring swirling strings accented by a snare drum figure that inverted the traditional rock beat and added a slight rhythmic shuffle—spurred record industry movers and shakers to try to incorporate and enlarge upon its techniques. In addition, its success drove home the idea that the right song, combined with the right singer and right arranger and right producer, represented the best blueprint for making a pop record.

While the Shirelles were recording a long string of hit singles (most notably, the chart-topper "Soldier Boy"), many other competitors were attempting to interpret the formula in their own ways. Producer Phil Spector was building his own roster of girl groups on the Philles label, while many of Berry Gordy's biggest hits for the MOTOWN-Tamla-Gordy (aka the Motown sound) combine were recorded by all-female aggregates. Don Kirshner and his Aldon publishing company, located in the heart of the Brill Building complex in Manhattan, supplied songs to many record companies who, in turn, matched them up with contracted girl groups. By 1962, his firm had eighteen writers on staff between the ages of nineteen and twenty-six, including the King-Goffin, Barry Mann-Cynthia Weil, and Neil Sedaka-Howard Greenfield teams. In addition, a number of smaller record companies achieved success in large part due to girl group recordings. These included Red Bird–Blue Cat, Cameo-Parkway, Chancellor, Jamie-Guyden, and Swan.

The decline of the girl group sound was a product of a complex chain of events. Although the British Invasion dominated the media in 1964, girl group and female performer records continued to sell well. MARY WELLS, the DIXIE CUPS, the Supremes, and the Shangri-Las resided at the top of the charts for twenty-five percent of that year, while major hits were recorded by the Ronettes, Martha & the Vandellas, Lesley Gore, the Jelly Beans, and numerous others. However, the innocent romanticism of the sound seemed out of step with an era colored by the JFK assassination, Vietnam, and the civil rights movement. With many of the key composers and producers turning to other pursuits, the public grew tired of the weaker girl group recordings flooding the market. Furthermore, psychedelic rock, soul, Motown, singer-songwriters, folk-rock, and the surfing sound provided stiff commercial competition.

Despite the relatively short duration of the girl group sound, its legacy continues to shine brightly. The classic songs of the genre—e.g., Little Eva's "The Locomotion," the Shirelles' "Will You Love Me Tomorrow," and the Crystals' "Da Doo Ron Ron"—have regularly been revived by contemporary stars, while its stylistic features have been recreated by

countless other performers. New wave girl groups (e.g., the Go-Gos, the Bangles), the riot grrrl movement, and pop confections like the Spice Girls all represent variations of the original mold.

God's Original Gangstaz

A Los Angeles–based Christian HIP-HOP duo, God's Original Gangstaz includes Preach D.O.G. and Mr. Reg N.I.C.E., both of whom flirted with drugs and gang activity as teenagers. After discovering a common commitment to their faith, they began spreading the gospel through the unlikely medium of gangsta rap. Their debut album, *True 2 Tha Game* (Grapevine, 1996), was highly derivative from a musical standpoint in addition to featuring lackluster arrangements. The truly unique nature of this gospel-rap fusion, however, made for an interesting listening experience. Follow-up releases—including *Resurrected Gangstaz* (Grapevine, 1997), *Pawns in a Chess Game* (Grapevine, 1999), and *Tha G Filez* (Grapevine, 1999)—served up more of the same, although the public reception proved to be increasingly apathetic.

Goldie (b. 1965) *drum and bass producer*

Born Clifford Price in Wolverhampton, England, Goldie spent his childhood drifting between foster families and children's homes. Inspired by New York graffiti culture and England's northern soul dance scene, which merged hard FUNK and lush melodies, he became a convert to the style of HIP-HOP espoused by AFRIKA BAMBAATAA. He began experimenting with the recording medium in the early 1990s, releasing a series of hardcore TECHNO dance tracks between 1993 and 1995.

His first album, *Timeless* (Sire, 1995), quickly sold more than 100,000 copies, bringing the ambient JUNGLE–DRUM AND BASS genre into the pop music mainstream. Now revered by British club followers and attracting the interest of Brian Eno, David Bowie, and other avant-garde artists, Goldie further refined his sensually symphonic approach in the double CD, *Saturnz Return* (Uni, 1998). Widely criticized for its length (over 150 minutes), he issued a truncated version, *Ring of Saturn* (Uni, 1998), later in the year.

As demand for his services continued to escalate, Goldie began working with an increasing number of musicians. A two-disc collection of his collaborations, *INCredible Sound of Drum 'n' Bass Mixed by Goldie* (Ovum Ruffhouse, 2000), was released in America by Columbia. In addition to administering a record label and dance club, Metalheadz, he was working in the film medium—both as an actor and producer—at the outset of the twenty-first century.

Goldstar Studio

Located in Hollywood at the intersection of Santa Monica Boulevard and Vine Street, Goldstar Studio was established by Stan Ross and Dave Gold in 1950. Built around a customized four-input console to permit recording directly to acetate disk, sessions ran the gamut in the early 1950s, including demos and broadcast air checks.

The facility became a music industry landmark when Phil Spector began producing his sessions there in 1962, resulting in hits such as the Crystals' "He's a Rebel" and "Da Doo Ron Ron," the Ronettes's "Be My Baby," and THE RIGHTEOUS BROTHERS's "You've Lost That Lovin' Feelin.'" Other notable projects were executed at Goldstar as well, most notably the best-selling albums by Herb Alpert and the Tijuana Brass and film soundtrack work by Dimitri Tiomkin.

The studio was razed by fire in the early 1980s. However, Spector's legendary "Wall of Sound" recordings have rendered it an icon of the "back to mono" movement.

Goldwax Records

The Memphis-based Goldwax label was founded in 1964 by former hardware salesman Quinton Claunch and pharmacist Doc Russell. Tishomingo, Mississippi native Claunch was born in 1922 and played in a country band on radio station WLAY, Muscle Shoals, Alabama. Following a move to Memphis in 1948, he continued to moonlight as a musician, playing guitar and composing for Sun Records. In 1957, he established the Hi label along with a number of associates before selling his interest in the company in 1959.

The initial Goldwax release, "Darlin'," recorded in 1964 by the Lyrics—already featuring the distinctive yellow label with black printing, the "o" being a 45-rpm drawing—was a regional hit. Focusing on soul music with distribution by New York's Bell Records, the company achieved its greatest success with O. V. WRIGHT and James Carr, both former members of the gospel trio, the Redemption Harmonizers. Wright recorded "That's How Strong My Love Is," which achieved classic status via covers by OTIS REDDING, the Rolling Stones, the Hollies, and other leading 1960s acts.

While the Houston-based Peacock label claimed to have Wright under contract as a member of the Sunset Travelers, Carr proved even more successful, scoring nine hits, most notably "You've Got My Mind Messed Up," the Dan Penn–Chips Moman standard, "At the Dark End of the Street," and "A Man Needs a Woman." However, the highly regarded singer—whose *James Carr* (Goldwax, 1967) and *A Man Needs a Woman* (Goldwax, 1968) were the only albums known to have been issued by the company—was unable to realize his full potential, suffering from bouts of mental illness.

Goldwax also reached the soul charts with the OVATIONS's "It's Wonderful to Be in Love" and "Me and My Imagination." The group would make a greater sales impact during the early 1970s with MGM.

The company shut down operations in 1969 because the owners had trouble working together. In the mid-1980s, Memphis businessman Elliott Clark acquired the master tapes of the 1960s material and re-formed Goldwax with Claunch as president. Claunch's skill in handling deteriorating tapes has much to do with the impressive sound quality of the reissued compact discs. In the early 1990s, the label opened a Nashville office, and moved its headquarters to Atlanta later in the decade.

G.Q.

The New York quartet—consisting of Keith "Sabu" Crier, bass/vocals; Emmanuel Rahiem LeBlanc, guitar/lead vocals; Paul Service, drums/vocals; and Herb Lane, keyboards/vocals—enjoyed considerable, albeit brief, popularity during the twilight of the DISCO era. Core members, however, had already enjoyed some measure of success prior to the formation of the group.

Crier and Emmanuel started out in such acts as Sabu and the Survivors, Sons of Darkness, and Third Chance, prior to forming the Rhythm Makers with Lane and drummer Kenny Banks. Signing with the De-Lite family of labels, they released the LP, *Soul on Your Side* (Vigor, 1976), which featured the TRANCE-like single, "Zone," a minor hit in Great Britain.

When Service was brought in to replace the departing Banks, they adopted the name G.Q. (meaning "Good Quality") at the prompting of manager Tony Lopez. After hearing one of their demo tapes, producer Beau Ray Fleming hooked them up with Arista Records. The debut LP, *Disco Nights* (Arista, 1979), earned a gold disc, due largely to the million-selling single, "Disco Nights (Rock Freak)." Although making the charts, the follow-up albums—*GQ Two* (Arista, 1980), which included the hit, "Standing Ovation," and *Face to Face* (Arista, 1981)—experienced a considerable drop-off in sales. Service left before the sessions for the third LP, and Crier, who went on to a successful solo career as Keith Sweat, did likewise after the release of a single on the independent Stadium label, "You Are the One for Me," prompting the group to call it a day.

Grandmaster Flash (b. 1958) *hip-hop deejay*
Grandmaster Flash, born Joseph Saddler in Barbados, West Indies, on January 1, 1958, played a major role in establishing the conventions of HIP-HOP recordings. Named for his lightning speed in manipulating record players, he pioneered the technique of "cutting" between discs on two separate turntables, in the process creating a continuous flow of beats punctuated by repetitive rhythmic "breaks."

Flash developed his skills playing records at local block parties in the Bronx during the 1970s. He was signed by the Enjoy label shortly after creating the Furious Five, a group of rappers—initially, Grandmaster Melle Mel, Kid Creole, Cowboy, Duke Bootee, and KURTIS BLOW, augmented with the addition of Scorpio on electronics in 1980—to complement his deejay pyrotechnics. Following several underground rhythm & blues hits, he became an industry-wide phenomenon in 1981 with the release of twelve-inch single, "The Adventures of Grandmaster Flash on the Wheels of Steel," a funky melange of sampling (most notably, Chic's "Good Times" and Queen's "Another One Bites the Dust"), scratching, breaks, and energetic rapping. The SYLVIA ROBINSON–Duke Bootee-penned "The Message" (issued by SUGAR HILL in both seven- and 12-inch configurations) remains one of the seminal rap recordings of all time, anticipating the gangsta subgenre with hard-hitting social commentary regarding ghetto life.

Unfortunately, Flash's career went downhill from there due to group infighting—Melle Mel, Scorpio, and Cowboy left in late 1983 to form a new version of the Furious Five—and cocaine addiction. Despite a legal victory over Melle Mel to use the group name, Flash's recordings in the mid-1980s—most notably, "Sign of the Times," "Girls Love the Way He Spins," "Style (Peter Gunn Theme)," and "U Know What Time It Is"—represented a less revelatory brand of electro–hip-hop that failed to cross over to the pop charts. With his approach rendered increasingly dated by the rise of such hard-edged rappers as PUBLIC ENEMY, ERIC B. AND RAKIM, and KRS-One, Flash, despite a reunion with Melle Mel for a charity concert in 1987, faded into obscurity.

Sugar Hill promo shot of Grandmaster Flash and the Furious Five (Frank Driggs Collection)

Grandmaster Slice (b. 1967) *rapper*

Grandmaster Slice was something of a child prodigy, rapping in public by age 11 and then moving on to do deejay work and dance for the group Ebony Express as a teenager. A native of South Boston, Virginia, Slice had formed his own ensemble and made early demo tapes by the time he was enrolled at Halifax Country Senior High School. Around this time, he joined forces with Charles Fulp (aka Scratchmaster Chuck T.), who became his road manager and DJ after the two had competed against each other in an extracurricular school talent show. This collaboration resulted in an independently distributed release, *The Electric Slide (Shall We Dance)* (Selecto Hits, 1991). The rap powerhouse Jive was sufficiently taken with the underground hit, "Thinking of You," to purchase rights to the album.

Grandmixer DST (b. 1960) *hip-hop deejay*

One of the leading underground pioneers in New York's emerging HIP-HOP scene in the early 1980s, Grandmixer DST—named after downtown Manhattan's Delancey Street, where his fashion sense was nurtured in the late 1970s—played a key role in the melding of that genre with traditional jazz. Born Derek Howells on August 23, 1960, in the South Bronx, he started out as a part of AFRIKA BAMBAATAA's street gang/sound system crew, the Zulu Nation. Going solo in 1982, his debut innovative single, "Grandmixer Cuts It Up," added further luster to his reputation. He was recruited to work with jazz great HERBIE HANCOCK on the LP, *Future Shock* (Columbia, 1983), supplying the scratching effects for the hit single, "Rockit," and other tracks.

DST's 1984 single, "Crazy Cuts," became an international club hit, and provided the impetus for a similarly titled LP (Celluloid, 1984). Producer BILL LASWELL, who had worked with DST on *Future Shock,* utilized his talents further with projects involving Deadline, Manu Dibango, Materia, and Foday Musa Suso. By the 1990s, however, he was pushed into obscurity by a new generation of DJs.

Grand Puba (b. 1966) *rapper*

Born Maxwell Dixon, in New Rochelle, New York, he was a founding member of the HIP-HOP groups Masters of Ceremony and, later, Brand Nubian. Going solo in the early 1990s, Grand Puba contributed a cut to the *Strictly Business* soundtrack prior to producing *Reel to Reel* (Elektra, 1992). The engaging collection consisted of RAP verse reflecting his Five Percent Nation Islamic upbringing set to a laid-back REGGAE accompaniment. It was also notable for a guest appearance by future star MARY J. BLIGE. He, in turn, would perform on "Watch The Sound," from Fat Joe's rap debut, *Represent.*

Granz, Norman (1918–2001) *producer and record company executive*

Although not a musician, Norman Granz was a major force within the record industry as a producer, label head, concert promoter, and artist manager. He was widely hailed as a visionary who never abandoned his social conscience, demanding equal pay for African-American musicians as well as equal rights for black concertgoers.

Born August 6, 1918, in Los Angeles, Granz first made an impact organizing a series of Jazz at the Philharmonic concerts both in the U.S. and abroad, placing a particular emphasis on championing the bebop style. He founded four record companies: Clef (1946), Norgran (1953), Verve (1956), and Pablo (1973). As a label executive, his artist roster included Louis Armstrong, Count Basie, Eddie "Lockjaw" Davis, Duke Ellington, ELLA FITZGERALD, Billie Holiday, Charlie Parker, Oscar Peterson, Zoot Sims, Art Tatum, Sarah Vaughan, and Ben Webster.

After selling Verve to MGM in 1960, Granz moved to Switzerland, concentrating on concert promotions and managing the careers of Fitzgerald and Peterson. He originally established Pablo as a mechanism for disseminating a 1972 JATP reunion concert. He built up a catalog of some 350 titles—including works by Roy Eldridge, Dizzy Gillespie, and Joe Pass—before selling the firm to Fantasy Records. He refused a lifetime achievement award from the National Academy of Recording Arts and Sciences in 1994, offering the rationale, "I think you guys are a little late" (*Los Angeles Times,* November 24, 2001).

Gravediggaz

One of the more interesting 1990s RAP supergroups, the Gravediggaz consisted of Prince Paul (born Paul Huston, formerly of Stetsasonic and rechristened "the Undertaker"), Fruitkwan (aka the Gatekeeper), Poetic the Grym Reaper, and RZA the Resurrector (a technical producer for the WU-TANG CLAN). Prince Paul conceived of the project to fill the void following the dissolution of his Doo Dew label. The foursome employed a gothic horror mode of presentation, best exemplified in the 1994 single, "Diary of a Madman," built around loop samples created by producer RNS. After touring with the Wu-Tang Clan, the Gravediggaz were indefinitely placed on hold due to other projects that occupied the attention of group members. Prince Paul did production work for De La Soul and Living Colour, while RZA concentrated on a solo career.

Greaves, R. B. (b. 1944) *singer*

R. B. Greaves is remembered as a classic one-hit wonder, although he deserved far better. Born Ronald Bartram Aloysius Greaves III on November 28, 1944, in Georgetown, British Guyana, he first made his name performing in the Caribbean and Great Britain (he broke into the latter scene as Sonny Childe, backed by the TNTs). One-half Native American and a nephew of SAM COOKE, Greaves was considered an important enough talent that Atlantic Records president AHMET ERTEGUN chose to produce his early work with the label. Ertegun pushed him to record his composition, "Take a Letter Maria," previously recorded by the likes of STEVIE WONDER and Tom Jones. The song—a gentle blend of ska and soul-pop—became an international smash, and was followed by two best-selling LPs, *Greaves* (Atlantic, 1969) and *R. B. Greaves* (Atlantic, 1970), and a series of moderately successful cover singles: Bacharach and David's "(There's) Always Something There to Remind Me," James Taylor's "Fire and Rain," and Procol Harum's "Whiter Shade of Pale."

When Ertegun's attention turned to other projects, Greaves switched to MGM; that label's brain trust, however, did not seem to understand how to bring the singer's considerable assets to the fore. He would later try to penetrate the country marketplace, but proved unsuccessful.

Green, Al (b. 1946) *singer*

Al Green has excelled in two widely divergent genres during his lengthy career—soul/R&B and gospel. Although the former has resulted in greater commercial success and public renown, he has gone on to earn the higher honors in the latter field. The Grammys awarded annually by the National Academy of Recording Arts and Sciences represent a case in point. Although rarely victorious as a pop artist ("Funny How Time Slips Away," a duet with Lyle Lovett, from the LP *Rhythm, Country, and Blues;* 1994 received a Grammy for Best Pop Vocal Collaboration), he has consistently won within the gospel sector, including Best Soul Gospel Performance, Traditional, in 1981 for the LP *The Lord Will Make a Way* (Myrrh), and in 1982 for the LP *Precious Lord* (Myrrh); Best Soul

Gospel Performance, Contemporary, in 1982 for the LP *Higher Plane* (Myrrh); Best Soul Gospel Performance, Male, in 1983 for the LP *I'll Rise Again* (Motown); Best Soul Gospel Performance by a Duo or Group, in 1984 for "Sailin' on the Sea of Your Love" (with Shirley Caeser); Best Soul Gospel Performance, Male, in 1986 for "Going Away" (Motown; album track from *Trust in God*) and in 1987 for "Everything's Gonna Be Alright" (Motown).

Influenced by SAM COOKE (then a member of the Soul Stirrers), Green—at age nine—joined a gospel group, the Green Brothers with siblings Robert, Walter, and William, that earned a measure of attention over the next half-dozen years. While in a Grand Rapids, Michigan, high school, he formed the pop-oriented Al Green and the Creations; after several years, the band was reconstituted as Al Green and the Soul Mates. His recording debut, "Back Up Train," reached number 41 on the *Billboard* Hot 100 in 1967, but a lack of quality follow-up material resulted in a return to the chitlin' circuit grind of the South and Midwest.

Green's singing at a Midland, Texas, club in 1969 impressed Hi Records vice president, bandleader, and chief producer, Willie Mitchell, who signed him to a recording contract. "I Can't Get Next to You," a cover of the 1969 TEMPTATIONS chart-topper, had all the elements of his signature sound: softly caressing vocals, subdued rhythm section, and an ethereal veneer of horns and strings filling background spaces. He followed with eight million-sellers between 1971 and 1974: "Tired of Being Alone," "Let's Stay Together," "Look What You Done for Me," "I'm Still in Love with You," "You Ought to Be with Me," "Call Me," "Here I Am," and "Sha-La-La." Much like the singles, his albums—most notably, *Al Green Gets Next to You* (Hi, 1971), *Let's Stay Together* (Hi, 1972), *I'm Still in Love with You* (Hi, 1972), *Call Me* (Hi, 1973), *Livin' for You* (Hi, 1973), *Al Green Explores Your Mind* (Hi, 1974), *Al Green/Greatest Hits* (Hi, 1975), and *Al Green Is Love* (Hi, 1975)—possessed sufficient polish to appeal to

Al Green publicity still (Frank Driggs Collection)

Green returned to pop in the late 1980s, recording a duet with Annie Lennox for the *Scrooged* soundtrack, "Put a Little Love in Your Heart." He devoted an entire album, *Don't Look Back* (RCA), to the exploration of his Memphis roots in 1993. Further validation of his early work came with his 1995 induction into the Rock and Roll Hall of Fame.

At the outset of the twenty-first century Green seemed as popular as ever. Not only were many of his classic soul recordings now available in CD editions, but he was touring regularly (performing a mix of gospel and pop material) and was part of the cast for the highly rated TV series, *Ally McBeal*. In fall 2000 HarperCollins published his autobiography, *Take Me to the River*.

Grits

A Nashville-based Christian rap act, Grits (standing for "Grammatical Revolution in the Spirit") have shown steady artistic growth, eschewing the P-Funk vogue of the present day in favor of plainspoken rhymes, propulsive bounce, and stylistic adventurism. Comprising Teron "Bonafide" Carter and Stacey "Coffee" Jones, the duo signed a recording contract with the DC Talk–owned label, Gotee, in the mid-1990s. Their promising debut album, *Mental Releases* (Gotee 1995), was followed by *Factors of Seven* (Gotee, 1997), *Grammatical Revolution* (Gotee, 1999), and *The Art of Translation* (Gotee, 2002).

Groove Corporation, The

An experimental synthesis of TECHNO and HOUSE-derived styles, the Groove Corporation grew out of Electribe 101 following the departure of lead vocalist Billie Ray Martin. Utilizing a Birmingham, England studio complex (Elephant House Sound Laboratory) as their home base, the creative core of Robert Cimarosti, Les Fleming, Brian Nordhoff, and Joe Stevens embarked on a series of collaborations

both pop and R&B listeners. His work was also acclaimed by the major trade publications; he was designated the Rock 'n' Pop Star of 1972 by *Rolling Stone,* while *Billboard, Cash Box,* and *Record World* all named him the Best Pop and R&B Vocalist for that year.

During the latter half of the 1970s, Green turned increasingly to his work as pastor of the Full Gospel Tabernacle in Memphis. In 1979, he declared his intent to focus exclusively on gospel material. His 1980s Myrrh/Motown releases included a combination of traditional hymns and self-penned religious songs, all imbued with a strong dose of Memphis soul.

with local talent, including the Original Rockers (DJ Dick and Nigel Blunt), resulting in the 12-inch "dub-clash" single, "Stoned," released by Cake in 1993; REGGAE proponents Captain Animal and Bim Sherman; and techno-oriented Reese Project.

After releasing an EP entitled *Passion,* and a club hit, "Summer of Dub," the group produced *Co-Operation* (Network, 1994), a concept LP depicting a fictional radio program, referred to as "Skunk FM," punctuated by snippets of static interference and dialogue. The Groove Corporation continues to explore the boundaries of avant-funk, with rest stops along the way to assist various collaborators on their own projects.

Hall, Rick (b. 1932) *producer and recording studio owner*

Rick Hall was the architect of the MUSCLE SHOALS sound, a country-funk brand of soul that enhanced the hits of such artists as CLARENCE CARTER, Arthur Conley, ETTA JAMES, WILSON PICKETT, and Candi Staton. Born January 31, 1932, in Franklin County, Mississippi, he first surfaced as a member of Carmel Taylor and the Country Pals. He formed the Hallmarks before joining the Fairlanes in 1958, which also included future producer Billy Sherrill, his partner in the formation of Spar Music and the Florence Alabama Music Enterprises (FAME).

Shortly after the two went their separate ways, another associate, Tom Stafford, referred soul singer/songwriter Arthur Alexander to Hall to do production work on "You Better Move On." Although Dot managed to pull Alexander out of Hall's orbit, the profits from the hit enabled the producer to lease a studio at Avalon Boulevard, Muscle Shoals. Located some distance from the distractions of major urban centers, artists who came to FAME were able to concentrate exclusively on the recording process, helped considerably by an inspired rhythm section that, in the 1966–67 period, included bassists David Hood or Junior Lowe, drummer Roger Hawkins, guitarist Jimmy Johnson, and keyboardist Spooner Oldham (later replaced by Barry Beckett). Oldham, along with Dan Penn and Donnie Fritts, wrote many of the classic soul songs that were recorded there.

One of the more notable sessions that took place there had ARETHA FRANKLIN recording her break-through single, "I Never Loved a Man (the Way I Love You)." Although Atlantic producer Jerry Wexler lured the Muscle Shoals house band to New York to record Franklin's follow-up records, the FAME studios continued to produce hits well into the 1970s for artists as diversified as PERCY SLEDGE, the Osmonds, Paul Anka, and Bobbie Gentry. After his core team of producers and musicians moved on, Hall enjoyed considerable success producing country music in the 1980s.

Hamilton, Roy (1929–1969) *singer*

A dynamic singer in the JACKIE WILSON mold, Roy Hamilton excelled in R&B treatments of pop ballads. Born April 16, 1929, in Leesburg, Georgia, he moved with his family to Jersey City, New Jersey, at age 14. In addition to his interest in singing as a youth—he received operatic and classical voice training and sang with the gospel group, the Searchlight Singers—Hamilton studied commercial art at Lincoln High School and boxed in the Golden Gloves heavyweight division.

Shortly after winning an amateur contest at the famed Apollo Theater in 1947, he embarked upon a professional career. Hamilton's recordings of two songs from the Rodgers and Hammerstein musical, *Carousel*, "You'll Never Walk Alone" and "If I Loved You," proved to be his commercial breakthrough. He followed with "Ebb Tide"; "Hurt"; "Unchained Melody," number one on the R&B charts for three weeks in 1955 and later a big hit for the RIGHTEOUS BROTHERS; and "Forgive This Fool."

Hamilton temporarily retired from the entertainment business between 1956 and 1958 due to exhaustion. He came back strong with "Don't Let Go" and "You Can Have Her." Although no longer a chart factor from mid-1961 onward, he continued to perform until his death from a stroke on July 20, 1969.

Hammer, M.C. (b. 1963) *rapper*

M.C. Hammer, born Stanley Kirk Burrell March 30, 1963, in Oakland, California's subsidized housing district, was the first rapper to achieve pop crossover superstardom. An ingenious songwriter/arranger, his material featured liberal samples of soul-FUNK hitmakers such as JAMES BROWN and Parliament. His considerable dance skills and expertly choreographed performances played a major role in his success. The fact that Hammer released several video titles during his peak period of popularity in the early 1990s attests to the strong visual orientation of his work.

Burrell was nicknamed "Little Hammer" while working as a batboy for the Oakland Athletics as a result of his resemblance to home run king, "Hammerin'" Hank Aaron. Baseball player friends lent him the money to establish his own record company; his Bay Area success led to a contract with Capitol Records. His second major label album, *Please Hammer Don't Hurt 'Em* (number one for 21 weeks in 1990), featured "U Can't Touch This" (based on an unauthorized sample from the RICK JAMES hit, "Super Freak, Part 1"); a RAP update of the CHI-LITES' "Have You Seen Her"; and "Pray," accompanied by a promotional video clip which melded religion, hip-hop, and a *West Side Story*–influenced dance sequence. High-profile tours, a children's cartoon (*Hammerman*), and endorsement deals with Pepsi and Kentucky Fried Chicken followed. However, the rise of gangsta rap (which rendered his flashy, slick approach dated), bad investments (e.g., horse breeding, real estate), and uneven follow-up LPs—*Too Legit to Quit* (Capitol, 1991) and *The Funky Headhunter* (Giant, 1994)—caused his career to stall.

In 1996, he had to declare bankruptcy with $13.7 million in debts. Since then, Hammer has attempted to resurrect his career, while devoting time to raising funds for his ministry.

Hancock, Herbie (b. 1940) *keyboardist*

Herbie Hancock is one of the seminal jazz figures of the second half of the twentieth century. But while his technical proficiency as a keyboard player and composing skills are of the highest order, he is best known as a jazz innovator, experimenting with synthesizers and electronic music in general. Furthermore, he has helped broaden the fusion movement, incorporating a wide range of pop, rock, FUNK, and classical music elements within a jazz framework.

Born April 12, 1940, in Chicago, Hancock studied both classical and jazz music at Grinnell College (Iowa) before joining Donald Byrd's band as pianist in 1960. His debut solo LP, *Takin' Off* (Blue Note, 1962) demonstrated his already well-developed compositional talents; one of his pieces, "Watermelon Man," would be covered by many other musicians. Other successful releases included *Inventions and Dimensions* (Blue Note, 1963), *Empyrean Isles* (Blue Note, 1964), and *Maiden Voyage* (Blue Note, 1965).

Hancock became a member of Miles Davis's group in 1963; during his five-year stay, Davis encouraged him to play an electric piano. The results of this experiment—*Miles in the Sky* (Columbia, 1968), *Filles de Kilimanjaro* (Columbia, 1969), and the elegiac masterpiece, *In a Silent Way* (Columbia, 1969)—defined the jazz-rock movement of the 1970s. During this period, he also contributed session work to other artists' recordings, made television commercials, and scored his first film, Michelangelo Antonioni's *Blow Up* (MGM, 1966; soundtrack).

Hancock continued to refine his electronic arrangements in the years immediately after leaving

Davis; one release, *Mwandishi* (Warner Bros., 1971), was designated one of the best albums of the year by *Time* magazine. With *Head Hunters* (Columbia, 1973), he employed synthesizers for the first time; its platinum sales inaugurated a wholesale trend within the jazz scene. As a host of jazz-inflected TECHNO-FUNK LPs flooded the marketplace, Hancock took on new challenges; utilizing a Vocoder voice synthesizer in his first recorded vocals for *Sunlight* (Columbia, 1978), and incorporating DISCO-oriented rhythms in *Feets Don't Fail Me Now* (Columbia, 1979).

The 1980s found Hancock divided between genre-bending experiments—most notably, *Future Shock* (Columbia, 1983), which included the Grammy-winning "Rockit" (Best R&B Instrumental Performance)—more traditional jazz fare featuring the V.S.O.P. Quintet, the Herbie Hancock Quartet, and collaborations with Chick Corea and Oscar Peterson. Further honors included a 1983 Best R&B Instrumental Performance Grammy for *Sound System* (Columbia), a 1987 Best Instrumental Performance Grammy for "Call Sheet Blues," and an Oscar for Best Original Score for the movie *'Round Midnight* (Columbia, 1986; soundtrack).

Hancock's recordings in the '90s were uneven at best. *Dis Is da Drum* (Mercury, 1995) represented a failed attempted at harnessing HIP-HOP within a fusion context, while his efforts to provide timeless settings for the music of the Beatles, Peter Gabriel, Prince, and others in *The New Standard* (Verve, 1996) comes across as both sterile and pompous. His best recordings from this period have been the countless reissues and retrospectives put out by Blue Note, Columbia, Warner Bros., and various smaller labels.

Harpo, Slim (1924–1970) *singer and guitarist*
Slim Harpo, a singer, songwriter, guitarist, and mouth harpist, is perhaps best known to rock fans for "I'm a King Bee," popularized by the Rolling Stones in 1964 (and included on their debut album). A leading exponent of swamp blues, he is closely identified with guitarist Lightnin' Slim, with whom he performed and recorded for two decades.

Born James Moore on January 11, 1924, in Lobdell, Louisiana, he moved with his family to nearby Port Allen soon thereafter. His parents died while he was still a youth, requiring him to leave school to help support the family. He was a longshoreman in New Orleans at 18, and later worked as a contractor and owned a trucking business (beginning in 1966) in Baton Rouge.

By the early 1940s, he had begun performing on the side in the bar and club circuit billed as "Harmonica Slim." He rarely strayed from this lifestyle until dying of a heart attack January 31, 1970, in Baton Rouge. His first studio sessions consisted of backing Lightnin' Slim in 1955–56 for Excello. He began recording as a solo for Excello in 1957, frequently employing his own material, typically cowritten with his wife, Lovell. He enjoyed intermittent hits, most notably "Rainin' in My Heart"; the laid-back swamp-rock classic, "Baby Scratch My Back" (number one on the R&B charts in 1966); "Tip On In, Part 1"; and "Te-Ni-Nee-Ni-Nu." His recordings have continued to be reissued on album compilations up to the present day.

Harris, Major (b. 1947) *singer*
Although relatively unknown to mainstream pop enthusiasts, Major Harris has been a fixture of the R&B scene for several decades. Born February 9, 1947, in Richmond, Virginia, he sang with the Jarmels in the late 1960s before moving on to the DELFONICS in 1971. Three years later, he formed the Major Harris Boogie Blues Band along with Karen Dempsey, Allison Hobbs, and Phyllis Newman.

Harris achieved his greatest success, however, as a solo performer. His 1975 Top Five pop hit, "Love Won't Make Me Wait," gained widespread notoriety for its incorporation of sound effects depicting a woman in the throes of sexual passion. He continued to enjoy intermittent success on the R&B charts through the release of "All My Life" in 1983. By the late 1980s, Harris had rejoined the Delfonics, even though that group's hit-making days were long since past.

Harris, Wynonie (1915–1969) *singer and drummer*

Wynonie Harris, known as "Mr. Blues," was one of the pioneer blues shouters of the post–World War II period. He was a dominant force on the R&B charts from 1946 to early 1952.

Born August 24, 1915, in Omaha, Nebraska, Harris worked for a time as a dancer and comedian. Relocating to Los Angeles in 1940, his first major break came when he was hired to front LUCKY MILLINDER's band in 1944. He first recorded Millinder's chart-topping R&B hit, "Who Threw the Whiskey in the Well," for Decca that same year; this song featured Harris as lead vocalist.

Going solo in 1945, he recorded a long string of R&B hits, including "Wynonie's Blues," backed by the Illinois Jacquet All-Stars; "Playful Baby," with the Johnnie Alston All-Stars; "Good Rockin' Tonight," a key precursor to rock 'n' roll, later recorded by ELVIS PRESLEY, among others; "Grandma Plays the Numbers"/"I Feel That Old Age Coming On"; "Drinkin' Wine Spo-Dee-O-Dee," accompanied by the Joe Morris Orchestra; "All She Wants to Do Is Rock"/ "I Want My Fanny Brown"; "Sittin' on It All the Time"; "I Like My Baby's Pudding"; "Good Morning Judge"; "Oh Babe"; "Bloodshot Eyes"; and "Lovin' Machine."

With his hit-making days behind him, Harris left the music business in 1953. He attempted a brief comeback in 1967 at the height of the blues revival, but to no avail. He died of cancer June 14, 1969.

Hathaway, Donny (1945–1979) *singer*

Donny Hathaway's musical talents spanned a wide range of fields, including songwriting, arranging, producing, and performing (both as a singer and keyboardist). Unfortunately, his potential was not fully realized; he committed suicide on January 13, 1979, jumping from the 15th floor of the Essex House, a New York City hotel.

Born in Chicago, on October 1, 1945, Hathaway spent most of his youth in St. Louis, where he began singing gospel at age three. He attended Howard University in Washington, D.C., on a fine arts scholarship; he laid the groundwork there for future collaborations with one of his classmates, ROBERTA FLACK.

Hathaway first reached the charts in 1969 as part of the duo, June (Conquest) & Donnie, with "I Thank You Baby," re-released three years later by Curtom following Hathaway's early rise to prominence as a recording artist. All of his biggest hits were duets with Flack, his down-home, funky style acting as a foil to her ethereal brand of soul singing. Their best-selling singles included "You've Got a Friend," "Where Is the Love," "The Closer I Get to You," and the posthumously issued "You Are My Heaven." He also earned praise during the 1970s as a producer/writer for many artists, most notably JERRY BUTLER, ARETHA FRANKLIN, the STAPLE SINGERS, and CARLA THOMAS.

Hawkins, Screamin' Jay (1929–2000) *singer*

Born July 18, 1929 in Cleveland, Ohio, Jalacy Hawkins focused on boxing as a youth, winning a Golden Gloves amateur championship. Shortly after defeating future Alaskan middleweight champ Billy McCann in 1949, however, he turned to singing full time. His nickname came from an incident onstage when a lady from the audience kept yelling for him to "scream the song." He finally relented, and a new persona was born.

Hawkins's 1952 recording debut on the Gotham label—"Why Did You Waste My Time," assisted by Tiny Grimes and His Rockin' Highlanders—was followed by stints with Timely and Mercury's Wing subsidiary, where his highly theatrical approach was first in evidence in his 1955 single, "(She Put the) Wamee (on Me)." After signing with OKeh Records in the mid-1950s, Hawkins was introduced to the ballad "I Put a Spell on You." During the recording session that followed, he and his session musicians—including guitarist Mickey Baker and sax player Sam "the Man" Taylor—drank heavily while searching for the appropriate mood. The outrageous reading that resulted, sounding much like a Hollywood horror flick, was released in November 1956. The record's success—although failing to crease the charts, it would sell steadily for decades despite creating outrage in some quarters and provide the centerpiece for countless album compilations—required Hawkins to adopt a similarly wild characterization onstage, complete with black cape, coffins, a flaming skull named Henry, and voodoo-inspired gesturing.

Hawkins had only modest success through 1958 with similarly crazed fare like "Hong Kong," "Yellow Coat," and the JERRY LEIBER AND MIKE STOLLER–penned "Alligator Wine" (all on OKeh), but remained in demand as a live performer. He continued recording into the 1990s, when he recorded three novelty-flavored albums—*Black Music for White People, Stone Crazy,* and *Somethin' Funny Goin' On*—for Bizarre/Straight Records. He also appeared in various films, most notably *Mister Rock 'n' Roll* (1957), *American Hot Wax* (1978), *Mystery Train* (1989), and *A Rage in Harlem* (1991). Hawkins received the Rhythm & Blues Foundation Pioneer Award in 1998. He died near Paris, France, on February 12, 2000, of multiple organ failure following surgery resulting from an aneurysm. A Web site was established shortly thereafter attempting to reach the 57 children he reportedly sired.

Hayes, Isaac (b. 1942) *singer, songwriter, and producer*

Isaac Hayes's work reflects an encyclopedic grasp of African-American music traditions. He honed his craft during the hegemony of soul as a session musician, songwriter, and producer for the STAX family of artists. He teamed with David Porter in the 1960s to write such classics as "Hold On! I'm a Comin' " and "Soul Man." After launching his own solo career, he specialized in extended-length, gothic ballads à la Barry White, film scores, and what later became known as SMOOTH JAZZ.

Signing with the Stax subsidiary, Enterprise, Hayes first charted with the double-sided crossover hit, "Walk on By"/"By the Time I Get to Phoenix" in late summer 1969. He remained commercially viable through the 1980s, recording the Top Ten R&B singles "Never Can Say Goodbye," the Hot 100 chart-topper "Theme from Shaft," "Do Your Thing," "Joy—Pt. 1," and "Ike's Rap." Unlike many of his fellow R&B artists, Hayes's albums sold well. He also garnered extensive radio play on both AM Top 40 and FM rock stations.

When Stax encountered financial difficulties in the mid-1970s, Hayes launched his Hot Buttered Soul label under the ABC umbrella. He switched to Polydor in the late 1970s, and then enjoyed a brief career revival after moving on to Columbia in the

Isaac Hayes at the peak of his popularity in the early 1970s (Frank Driggs Collection)

mid-1980s. He continues to perform and work on films.

Hearts, The   See ANDREWS, LEE, AND THE HEARTS.

Hebb, Bobby (b. 1938) *singer*

Born to a trombone-playing father and a mother proficient at both the piano and guitar in Nashville, Tennessee, on July 26, 1938, Bobby Hebb appeared to be destined for a career in showbiz. He got perhaps one of the earliest starts of any R&B musician when at the tender age of three Bobby was introduced to a national television audience in a variety talent show, *The Jerry Jackson Revue of 1942*, by his tap dancing older brother Hal, age nine. By the time the younger Hebb was preparing to enter the first grade, he and his older brother had become a regular fixture on the Nashville club circuit, appearing at clubs like The Paradise Club, Eva Thompson Jones Dance Studio, and The Bijou Theater.

The brother act split when Hal Hebb decided to pursue a recording contract under the Excello label and work under such artists as the Marigolds, the Solotones, and the Prisonaires. Bobby took this opportunity to join Roy Acuff's Smokey Mountain Boys; as Grand Master of the Grand Ole Opry, Acuff was able to provide Hebb with one of the largest stages of his young career. He was 12 at the time. This alliance also afforded Hebb the chance to learn to play the guitar under the tutelage of Chet Atkins. Looking to "advance [his] career," to use his own words, Hebb moved to Chicago in 1954, where he worked with Bo Diddley on a song, "Diddly Diddly Diddly Daddy," destined for a spot on a record by the MOONGLOWS and Little Walter being cut by Leonard Chess.

Hebb joined the U.S. Navy in 1955 working as a trumpet player in the Navy's USS Pine Island Pirates. Returning to the States in 1958, Hebb recorded "Night Train to Memphis," a Smokey Mountain Boys cover, for New York DJ John Richbourg's label, Rich Records. Though the song had no chart success to speak of, it was re-released in 1998 as part of a special commemorative box set by Warner Brothers Records. Richbourg also got Hebb a steady job working as the opening act at a New York nightclub for Mickey Baker and SYLVIA ROBINSON. After Mickey left for Paris he was replaced by Hebb in the duo and Bobby and Sylvia came under the management of Buster Newman.

Newman was responsible for the orchestrating the most successful run of Hebb's career. He shopped around the single, "Sunny," for Hebb, who contended that every label that he visited "turned the song down." Hebb had penned the song in memory of his old vaudeville partner and brother Hal Hebb, who had died only days after the assassination of JFK. When Newman did get Hebb a record deal for "Sunny" in 1966, the single turned into a full album, and the song nobody wanted turned into the biggest smash hit of Hebb's career. As one of the most widely covered songs in pop music history, "Sunny" has been performed or recorded by no less then the likes of Frank Sinatra, Cher, STEVIE WONDER, WILSON PICKETT, the FOUR TOPS, Duke Ellington, Dusty Springfield, ELLA FITZGERALD, Ernestine Anderson, Marvin Stamm, and electronic artist Boney M. Beyond. Having a hit single, Hebb stands in rare company as one of the few artists to co-headline with the Beatles.

Hebb's follow-up to "Sunny" would not be as lucrative, however, when "A Satisfied Man" failed to achieve much commercial success. Hebb then decided to shift his songwriting craft to a new venue. He began work on a Broadway musical with comedian Sandy Baron. Though the venture never came to fruition, it did supply fellow R&B star LOU RAWLS with "A Natural Man," one of his biggest records. Though Hebb would regain chart prominence in the U.K. in 1972 with the singles "Love Me" and "Love, Love, Love," (which was released six years prior as the flip side to "A Satisfied Man") his efforts on U.S. pop charts were less then stellar. He eventually tried re-tooling the song that had originally been such a success for him; the 1976 version, "Sunny '76," managed to crease the DISCO and R&B charts.

—Lowery Woodall

High Inergy

High Inergy was originally promoted as "the new Supremes." Although never coming close to that level of popularity, the group recorded a string of moderately successful recordings—albeit limited primarily to the R&B charts—in the late 1970s and early 1980s.

The foursome—consisting of Linda Howard, Barbara Mitchell, Vanessa Mitchell, and Michele Rumph—got together in April 1976 when all were enrolled in the Bicentennial Performing Arts Program in Pasadena, California. They were discovered by Gwen Gordy-Lupper, sister of MOTOWN Records owner, Berry Gordy. Signed to the Gordy label in 1977, High Inergy made an immediate impact with the engaging Top 20 single, "You Can't Turn Me Off (in the Middle of Turning Me On)." Vanessa Mitchell then departed to pursue a gospel career in 1979, but the group soldiered on until lead singer Barbara Mitchell opted to go solo in 1984. Her prospects appeared promising after achieving a measure of success in a duet with superstar SMOKEY ROBINSON, "Blame It on Love," but her debut LP, *Get Me Through the Night* (1984), failed to generate much public attention.

Hill, Lauryn   See FUGEES, THE.

Hinton, Joe (1929–1968) *singer*

Like SAM COOKE, ARETHA FRANKLIN, and many other 1960s soul singers, Joe Hinton started out singing gospel music before switching to more secular fare. He only had one bona fide hit, but might well have gone on to greater success if he had not died in a Boston hospital of skin cancer on August 13, 1968, while still in his 30s.

Little is known about Hinton's early life. He first attracted attention with the Chosen Gospel Singers. He was discovered by Don Robey, owner of the Duke and Peacock labels, while lead vocalist with the Spirits of Memphis. Robey persuaded him to record soul music.

Hinton's early singles failed to elicit much of a response. He finally made the charts with "You Know It Ain't Right" in 1963 on the Back Beat label. He followed with several more hits— "Better to Give Than Receive," the Willie Nelson-penned "Funny (How Time Slips Away)," and "I Want a Little Girl"—all of which featured his patented white-hot singing. Having faded into obscurity, his death received little media coverage.

hip-hop

RAP—and its cut-and-paste backing music and attendant subculture, hip-hop—might well be viewed as a form of musical piracy. The genre's live and recorded output are both built upon the sampling of existing source material with the record player and recording studio functioning as primary instruments. On the other hand, its emergence represents perhaps the most important cultural development within the rock scene over the past twenty years. Based largely on the urban black experience, it is a form of populist poetry drawn from the street vernacular and set to funky rhythms suited to dance venues.

The genre incubated outside the pop mainstream during the 1970s. Although commercial success eluded him, Kool DJ Herc is widely held to be the godfather of rap. His ideology would ultimately define hip-hop culture; he was a record collector, dedicated to finding jazz, rock, or REGGAE discs possessing a funky drum break ideal for dancing. Spinning records at Bronx venues, Kool DJ Herc attracted an African-American audience largely from the Bronx and Harlem. These so-called b-boys dominated club dance contests until Puerto Rican youth developed a new vocabulary of power moves: windmills, backspins on one hand, flairs (dance-floor gymnastics), and turtle crawls. This new dancing became known as break dancing.

GRANDMASTER FLASH provided the final impetus in making rap an art form; he specialized in playing breaks—the point when a DJ rapped or a b-boy displayed his flashiest moves. Flash was adept at extending breaks and then abruptly shifting records to the next break beat (the origin of "cutting"). He also perfected "scratching," the technique of taking the beginning of the beat, holding the record with a finger and making it go backward and forward with that finger. In this manner, he created a whole new rhythm, much like a musician.

In the meantime, rap culture had spread to other urban centers, with club or street dance deejays providing the impetus by speaking over a seamless blend of recorded snippets. The Sugarhill Gang's "Rapper's Delight," the first rap record to be a hit on the pop singles charts, brought the entire scene into the mainstream in 1979. Hip-hop pioneer, KURTIS BLOW, followed shortly thereafter with "The Breaks (Part 1)," the genre's first million-seller. Additional pop successes were slow to appear over the next few years, however, as many of the pioneer rap stars (e.g., AFRIKA BAMBAATAA, Grandmaster Flash, Grandmaster Melle Mel) tended to focus on harsh social commentary.

Rap truly achieved crossover appeal when RUN-D.M.C. ushered in the "new school" with the release of its debut album, *Run-D.M.C.* (Profile, 1984). By incorporating rock rhythms and instrumentation into the genre—most fully realized in its triple-platinum LP, *Raising Hell* (Profile, 1986), which included the hit single collaboration with Aerosmith, "Walk This Way"—Run-D.M.C. stimulated the appearance of a wide array of subgenres. These included (listed along with leading exponents):

Gangsta Rap: DR DRE, ICE CUBE, ICE-T, N.W.A., SNOOP DOGGY DOG, TUPAC SHAKUR
Bawdy Rap: Biz Markie, 2 Live Crew
White Rap: BEASTIE BOYS, Snow, 3rd Bass, VANILLA ICE
Political Rap: Boogie Down Productions, KRS-ONE, PUBLIC ENEMY
Jazz Rap: DIGABLE PLANETS, A TRIBE CALLED QUEST, UB3
Pop Rap: DJ Jazzy Jeff and the Fresh Prince, De La Soul, ERIC B. AND RAKIM, L. L. COOL J., M.C. HAMMER, P.M. Dawn, PUFF DADDY, SALT-N-PEPA, Roxanne Shante

Alternative Hip-Hop: Arrested Development, BASEHEAD, DISPOSABLE HEROES OF HIPHOPRISY, WU-TANG CLAN
"Screw Tape" Mixes: DJ SCREW, other Big Time Recordz mix-masters

Rap's diversity holds something for everyone. Nevertheless, the genre has continued to offend mainstream sensibilities due to its blatant sexuality, off-color language, spoken lyrics devoid of traditional singing, and the glorification of misogyny, lawless behavior, and the use of force to settle disputes. In this sense, rap appears to have much in common with early rock 'n' roll, punk, heavy metal, and other styles that have taken a strong anti-establishment stance.

Holland, Brian (b. 1941), Lamont Dozier (b. 1941), and Eddie Holland (b. 1939)
songwriters and producers

These three songwriter-producers, known collectively as Holland-Dozier-Holland, were all born in Detroit; they formed a working team as part of Berry Gordy's MOTOWN-Gordy-Tamla record company in the early 1960s. They quickly gained recognition as vital contributors to the label's polished, pop-soul output, known collectively as the "Motown sound." During 1963–66, they produced an unprecedented 28 Top Ten hits, including the FOUR TOPS's "Baby I Need Your Loving," "I Can't Help Myself," "It's the Same Old Song," and "Reach Out, I'll Be There"; Martha and the Vandellas's "Nowhere to Run" and "Jimmy Mack"; and the Supremes' "Where Did Our Love Go," "Baby Love," "Come See About Me," "Stop! In the Name of Love," and "I Hear a Symphony."

Motivated by a desire for more creative freedom and a greater share of the profits, Holland-Dozier-Holland departed Motown in 1967 to found Invictus/Hot Wax. In addition to producing such artists as the Chairmen of the Board, the HONEY CONE, and Freda Payne, all three harbored solo ambitions. Whereas Eddie Holland's success was

Martha & the Vandellas relied heavily on the songwriter and production skills of Lamont-Dozier-Holland. (Frank Driggs Collection)

limited to four charting singles in the early 1960s—including the Top Thirty hit, "Jamie"—his brother Brian and Dozier both released hit recordings in the 1970s. The trio disbanded in 1973 and Dozier continued his momentum as a recording artist with ABC-Paramount Records.

Honey Cone, The

Female R&B singing groups were not particularly popular as a whole between the glory days of MOTOWN soul acts such as the Supremes, the Marvelettes, and Martha and the Vandellas and HIP-HOP divas like TLC and DESTINY'S CHILD. The Honey

Cone represented one of the bright spots during this transitional period, releasing a string of classic singles in the early 1970s.

Prior to forming in Los Angeles in 1969, the Honey Cone's members—Carolyn Willis, formerly with the Girlfriends and Bob B. Soxx & the Blue Jeans; Edna Wright, sister of noted "Spector sound" exponent Darlene Love, who had a brief solo career in the mid-1960s as Sandy Wynns; and Shellie Clark, previously with the Ikettes and a regular with *The Jim Nabors Hour* TV series—were already well known as backup singers live and in the studio. They were encouraged to form a group by Eddie Holland, part of the Motown songwriting/production team of Holland-Dozier-Holland.

After several moderate hits—"While You're Out Looking for Sugar," "Girls It Ain't Easy," and "Take Me with You"—the group struck paydirt with the catchy "Want Ads," which topped both the R&B and pop charts. "Want Ads"—written by Chairmen of the Board leader, General Johnson, producer Greg Perry, and Barney Perkins—was first recorded on separate occasions by Invictus artists Glass House and Freda Payne, with less than satisfactory results, before the Honey Cone were brought into the studio to try it.

The Honey Cone remained on a roll through the following year with songs like "Stick-Up," "One Monkey Don't Stop No Show (Part I)," and "The Day I Found Myself." Although the trio would fall from favor in the trend-conscious R&B scene, they continued to perform for a number of years before ultimately calling it a day.

See also HOLLAND, BRIAN, LAMONT DOZIER, AND EDDIE HOLLAND.

Hooker, John Lee (1917–2001) *singer*

John Lee Hooker is known as the "father of the boogie"; he recorded many songs in this genre, featuring an insistent beat, typically emphasized by the clicking of hob-nailed shoes and his primitive, but expressive, staccato guitar lines. He was also a master of the slow blues form, possessing one of the most powerfully expressive voices ever recorded. According to blues historian Gerard Herzhaft (*Encyclopedia of the Blues*, 1997), he probably made more recordings than any other bluesman, considerably more than 500 tracks in all.

Born August 22, 1917, in Vance, Mississippi—part of the fabled Delta region native to many great blues interpreters—Hooker already possessed a mature style by the time he migrated to Detroit in 1943, in search of work. He began recording in 1948. "Boogie Chillen" and "Hobo Blues"/"Hoogie Boogie"—particularly popular in the black sections of Chicago and Detroit—led to further demand for recordings. He would work with many rhythm and blues labels of the period—including Modern, King, Chess, VEE-JAY, Sensation, Specialty, Chart, JVB, Savoy, Regent, Chance, Gotham, DeLuxe, Gone, Rockin', Prize, Staff, Swing Time, and Acorn—often using pseudonyms such as Birmingham Sam & His Magic Guitar, Delta John, John L(ee) Booker, John Lee Cooker, Johnny Lee, Johnny Williams, Texas Slim, and the Boogie Man.

Many of Hooker's classic recordings—including "Boom Boom," "Dimples," "I'm in the Mood," and "I'm Mad"—were covered by British Invasion artists in the 1960s; one band, the Groundhogs, took its name from his "Groundhog Blues." While still a top-selling R&B artist, he actively participated in the country blues revival beginning in the late 1950s, shifting back to acoustic guitar and folk material. Hooker's collaboration with the American blues revival group, Canned Heat, *Hooker 'n Heat* (Liberty, 1971; double-disc set), followed by an appearance in the hugely successful film *The Blues Brothers* (1980), broadened his appeal to rock fans. Although uneven in quality, his later albums—particularly *Endless Boogie* (ABC, 1971), *Never Get Out of These Blues Alive* (ABC, 1972), *The Healer* (Chameleon, 1989), and *Mr. Lucky* (Charisma, 1991)—typically featured a wealth of big-name guest artists and, as a result, sold moderately well. He was inducted into the Rock and Roll Hall of Fame in 1991. He died in Los Altos, California, on June 21, 2001.

Horne, Lena (b. 1917) *singer*

Lena Horne has enjoyed a long, distinguished career as a singer/actress, marked by frequent appearances in Broadway musicals, films (e.g., *Cabin in the Sky, Stormy Weather, Broadway Rhythm, 'Till the Clouds Roll By,* and *Words and Music*), radio, and television. Best known as a nightclub entertainer, she won the National Academy of Recording Arts & Sciences Lifetime Achievement Award in 1989.

Born June 30, 1917, in Brooklyn, New York, she became a member of the Harlem Cotton Club's chorus while still a teenager. This led to singing stints with bands led by Noble Sissle and Charlie Barnet. She began recording in the late 1930s; her hits included "Stormy Weather," "One for My Baby (and One More for the Road)," "Deed I Do," and "Love Me or Leave Me." She enjoyed even greater success with LPs, most notably, *Lena Horne at the Waldorf Astoria* (RCA, 1957), *Give the Lady What She Wants* (RCA, 1958), *Porgy & Bess* (RCA, 1959; with Harry Belafonte), *Lena on the Blue Side* (RCA, 1962), *Lena . . . Lovely and Alive* (RCA, 1963), *Lena & Gabor* (Skye, 1970; with Gabor Szabo), and *Lena Horne: The Lady and Her Music* (Qwest, 1981). The latter release was culled from her one-woman Broadway show, which led to a career revival and earned her a Tony Award.

Hot Chocolate

Hot Chocolate was something of an anomaly in the 1970s British pop scene; whereas punk and Caribbean-based styles such as ska, rock steady, and REGGAE tended to dominate, its members opted for more of a soul-FUNK direction. The interracial group was formed in 1970 by Jamaican-born lead singer Errol Brown; members included guitarist Harvey Hinsley (b. Mitcham, England), keyboardist Larry Ferguson (b. Nassau, Bahamas), percussionist Patrick Olive (b. Grenada), bassist Tony Wilson (b. Trinidad), and drummer Ian King (replaced by Romford, England, native Tony Connor in 1973).

Hot Chocolate first signed with the Apple label, releasing a reggae-inflected treatment of John

Lennon's "Give Peace a Chance" in 1970. With the assistance of legendary producer Mickie Most, the group recorded a string of successful U.K. singles in the early 1970s; one of their compositions, "Brother Louie" (a Top Ten English hit in 1973), was covered by Stories later in the year, topping the U.S. charts. Other Brown-Wilson songs were recorded by April Wine, Mary Hopkin, Peter Noone, and Suzi Quatro, among others.

Hot Chocolate finally broke into the American market in the second half of the 1970s with "Emma," "Disco Queen," "You Sexy Thing," and "Every 1's a Winner." Wilson exited in 1975, with Olive switching to bass.

The group continued to release hits in Great Britain well into the 1980s, but disbanded when Brown opted for a solo career in 1987. Interest in the group was revived in the late 1990s when "You Sexy Thing" was featured in the popular films *Boogie Nights* and *Full Monty* as well as a Burger King television commercial.

house

The genre originated as Chicago house, which featured electronic soul and Latin mixes created by deejay Frankie Knuckles at the Warehouse club during the late 1970s. Providing music for a predominantly gay audience known to use psychedelic drugs, he favored recordings built around aggressive bass patterns, looping drums, reverb, and sexually suggestive vocals by males in drag.

As the music took on a more cerebral tone, featuring extended instrumental breaks, area labels began placing a premium on studio innovation. Perhaps the most influential record of the time, Phuture's "Acid Tracks," released by Trax in 1987, employed minimalist, repetitive darting sound effects to pioneer a hypnotic spin-off style later known as acid house.

By the mid-1980s, the genre's creative center had shifted to Great Britain, where The Art of Noise's debut release, *(Who's Afraid Of?) The Art Of Noise!* (Island, 1984), anticipated ambient house in its use

of sampling and lush, synthesizer-dominated arrangements. However, London deejays tended to add psychedelic touches to the Chicago model, most notably spacey grooves and media sound bites. Genesis P-Orridge coined the term "acid house" while further refining the sound with *Jack the Tab: Acid Tablets Volume One* (Castalia, 1988) and a series of follow-up LPs. By this time, many British postpunk artists were releasing acid mixes of their hit recordings.

Like TECHNO, house continued to splinter off into new hybrid styles in the 1990s, including spiritual house, best exemplified by Enigma's platinum-selling *MCMXC A.D.* (Charisma, 1991), and progressive house. The latter form looked to Tangerine Dream's extended synthesizer washes for inspiration; notable proponents included Mixmaster Morris and The Future Sound of London, whose greatest success came with *Lifeforms* (Virgin, 1994).

Houston, Cissy (b. 1933) *singer*

Although better known as the mother of WHITNEY HOUSTON, Cissy Houston has had a highly successful music career in her own right. Born Emily Drinkard, in Newark, New Jersey, she started out performing in the family gospel group, the Drinkard Singers, which also included nieces Dee Dee and DIONNE WARWICK. The threesome later worked as backup vocalists for countless R&B and pop artists, most notably SOLOMON BURKE and WILSON PICKETT.

She became lead singer for the Sweet Inspirations, a quartet in high demand within the recording industry, particularly with Atlantic artists. She moved on to a solo career, although her recordings—including *Presenting Cissy Houston* (1971), *Cissy Houston* (1977), *Think It Over* (1978), *Warning — Danger* (1979), *Step Aside for a Lady* (1980), and *I'll Take Care of You* (1992; duet with Chuck Jackson)—did not sell particularly well. She ultimately returned to the gospel genre, operating from her home base with the New Hope Baptist Church Choir in Newark.

Houston, Whitney (b. 1963) *singer*

The daughter of soul/gospel singer CISSY HOUSTON and cousin of pop chanteuse DIONNE WARWICK, Whitney was destined for singing success. In addi-tion to possessing one of the truly distinctive voices within mainstream popular music, Houston's good looks have enabled her to secure starring film roles—most notably *The Bodyguard* (1992),

Famous early Arista promo photo of Whitney Houston (Frank Driggs Collection)

Waiting to Exhale (1995), and *The Preacher's Wife* (1996)—and a prominent part in the accompanying soundtrack albums.

Born August 9, 1963, in Newark, New Jersey, Houston burst onto the scene in the mid-1980s with a string of best-selling singles on the Arista label, including the number-one hits "Saving All My Love for You," "How Will I Know," "Greatest Love of All," "I Wanna Dance with Somebody (Who Loves Me)," "Didn't We Almost Have It All," "So Emotional," and "Where Do Broken Hearts Go." By the 1990s, despite chart-topping releases like "I'm Your Baby Tonight," "All the Man That I Need," "I Will Always Love You," and "Exhale," her career lost momentum due to mediocre albums encumbered with insipid material and routine synthesizer-drenched production work, and a slew of imitators (e.g., MARIAH CAREY, Toni Braxton, Brandy, and Celine Dion). Nevertheless, as the preeminent torch singer of her time, Houston's best recordings may still lie in the future.

Hues Corporation

The Hues Corporation helped define the DISCO sound as it emerged out of underground clubs and into the public mainstream. The vocal trio—consisting of soprano Hubert Ann Kelly (born April 24, 1947, in Fairchild, Alabama), baritone Bernard St. Clair Lee Calhoun Henderson (b. April 24, 1944, San Francisco), and tenor Fleming Williams (b.

Flint, Michigan)—formed in Los Angeles in 1969. Their debut single, "Goodfootin'," failed to make the charts when released in 1970.

The Hues Corporation's fortunes changed for the better after signing with RCA in 1973. The title track from their first LP with the label, *Freedom for the Stallion* (RCA, 1974), was modestly successful. However, the follow-up, "Rock the Boat," an obscure album track brought to the attention of radio programmers by popular demand, became a worldwide smash, topping the Hot 100 charts. Another single, "Rockin' Soul," made the Top 20, but the group failed to maintain their commercial momentum despite recording through the 1970s.

Hunter, Ivory Joe (1914–1974) *singer*

Born October 10, 1914, the Kirbyville, Texas, native first recorded, in 1933, a cylinder for the Library of Congress. Hunter worked as a disc jockey for KFDM-Beaumont in the early 1940s, before relocating to the West Coast in 1942. He released singles on his own labels, Ivory and Pacific, in 1944 but became a major R&B star shortly after signing with King Records in 1947. He produced 21 R&B hits over the next decade, including the chart-toppers "Pretty Mama Blues," "I Almost Lost My Mind," "I Need You So," and "Since I Met You Baby" (his only Top 40 pop success). His music took on a country flavor during the 1960s. He succumbed to lung cancer on November 8, 1974.

Ice Cube (b. 1969) *rapper*

One of the seminal gangsta rappers whose best work goes back to the 1980s, Ice Cube now appears to be directing his greatest energy toward record production work and film acting. Born Oshea Jackson on June 15, 1969, in the South Central section of Los Angeles, he grew up in a stable middle class environment. He wrote his first important RAP song while still in his teens, "Boyz 'n the Hood," later recorded by EAZY-E. He was a member of CIA

Ice Cube at a 2002 awards show (Fred Prouser/Reuters/ Landov)

before supplying material to N.W.A. After a brief interlude studying architectural draughtsmanship in Phoenix, he returned to the N.W.A. family to help record *Straight Outta Compton* (1988).

Ice Cube left the group in late 1989 to embark on a solo career. His debut LP, *Amerikkka's Most Wanted* (Priority, 1990), which utilized PUBLIC ENEMY producers the Bomb Squad, attracted considerable controversy over lyrics depicting homophobia, glamorization of violence, and overt sexism. Follow-up records—*Death Certificate* (Priority, 1991), *The Predator* (Priority, 1992), which featured the hit single, "It Was a Good Day," and *Lethal Injection* (Priority, 1993)—continued to dissect the underside of ghetto life, including the Los Angeles riots and the Rodney King beating. In addition, Ice Cube established a production company (Street Knowledge, which later spawned a subsidiary, Lench Mob) and, along with fellow rapper, ICE-T, a fashion line in 1993.

Ice Cube branched out into films in the 1990s, starring in the John Singleton vehicles *Boyz 'N the Hood* (1991) and *Higher Learning* (1993). He recruited Ice-T to appear in his own treatment of the L.A. riots, *Trespass* (1992), and remains active writing screenplays. Nevertheless, he has found time to foster the careers of up-and-coming rappers, including Yo Yo, Da Lench Mob, and Kam.

Ice-T (b. 1959) *rapper and producer*

Ice-T is one of the more problematic figures within the RAP world; capable of some of the most penetrating commentaries on ghetto life, he can revert to the glorification of sexism and gratuitous violence. He has been very successful crossing over to the hard rock audience, particularly with his heavy metal side project, Body Count.

Born February 14, 1959, in Newark, New Jersey, he relocated to southern California as a youth after his parents were killed in an automobile accident. He fell under the spell of rap while attending Crenshaw High School in South Central Los Angeles, recorded several forgettable 12-inch sin-

gles, and appeared in the low-budget HIP-HOP films, *Rappin', Breakin'*, and *Breakin' II: Electric Boogaloo,* prior to landing a major label contract with Sire in 1987. He helped usher in a West Coast hardcore sound with the release of his debut LP, *Rhyme Pays* (Sire, 1987). The follow-up, *Power* (Sire, 1988), revealed a much stronger sociopolitical bent. By now an acknowledged superstar, he shifted his focus from the gangsta milieu to First Amendment issues in *The Iceberg/Freedom of Speech . . . Just Watch What You Say* (Sire, 1989). He returned to life in the streets with *O.G.: Original Gangster* (Sire, 1991), widely considered to be his masterpiece.

Ice-T's rap metal release, *Body Count* (Sire, 1992), fueled a national controversy over the track, "Cop Killer," which was eventually pulled from the album. When the Time Warner company refused to put out *Home Invasion* (1993), due to its cover art, he switched to the Priority label; nevertheless, the tracks exhibited a tentative nature, perhaps resulting from the media notoriety arising out of his past work. By now, Ice-T was busy making feature films and starring in *Law & Order: Special Victims Unit* on NBC, and subsequent releases seemed to lack the hard edge that had initially built his reputation. He is now viewed as something of a hip-hop statesman, not entirely in step with the latest trends, but still capable of interesting work when the mood strikes him.

Imperials, The   See LITTLE ANTHONY & THE IMPERIALS.

Impressions, The

The Impressions were the archetypal Chicago soul group. Leader Curtis Mayfield (born June 3, 1942, in Chicago)—widely respected for his rich, falsetto voice, inventive guitar playing, socially conscious lyrics, and accomplished production work—was largely responsible for the group's distinctive sound.

Mayfield met JERRY BUTLER at age nine in his grandmother's Traveling Souls Spiritualist Church

Curtis Mayfield in the 1970s, after he left the Impressions (Frank Driggs Collection)

on Chicago's West Side. They would go on to sing gospel in the Northern Jubilee Singers before joining the Roosters, formerly based in Chattanooga and consisting of tenors (and brothers) Arthur and Richard Brooks and bass Sam Gooden, in 1957. The group first achieved success with "For Your Precious Love," erroneously credited to Jerry Butler and the Impressions. Butler would go on to a successful solo career later in the year, recruiting Mayfield for guitar accompaniment and songwriting.

The Impressions regrouped with the addition of tenor Fred Cash (born October 8, 1940, in Chattanooga) in 1959, moving briefly to New York City and signing with ABC-Paramount in 1961. They recorded a string of classic hits in the 1960s, including "Gypsy Woman," "It's All Right," "I'm So Proud," "Amen," and "People Get Ready," until personnel changes ultimately took their toll. The Brooks Brothers left in 1962 and Mayfield, who had composed most of their hits, struck out on his own in 1970. His replacement, Leroy Hutson, in turn went solo in 1973. Nevertheless, Cash and Gooden kept the Impressions together well into the 1990s. The group was inducted into the Rock and Roll Hall of Fame in 1991.

Inner City

Inner City—a TECHNO-dance act consisting of multi-instrumentalist/programmer Kevin Saunderson (born May 9, 1964, in Brooklyn, New York), whose mother was a member of the Marvelettes, and vocalist Paris Grey (b. Shanna Jackson, November 5, 1965, in Glencove, Illinois)—is responsible for one of the all-time great club hits, "Big Fun," released by the Ten label in 1989. The song was lying around unissued at Saunderson's home base in Detroit, when a friend came across it while searching for tracks to fill an LP compilation. The follow-up single, "Good Life," and debut album, *Paradise* (Ten, 1989), also sold well, the latter achieving sales of more than six million copies.

Inner City's third LP, *Fire* (Ten, 1990), revealed a tentative foray into RAP. Saunderson, a studio production wizard whose services were suddenly in great demand, established his own label, KMS, via a distribution deal with Network. That company also picked up the option to Inner City when the group's contract with Virgin ran out in the early 1990s.

Instant Funk

Latter day exponents of Philly soul, Instant Funk first attracted attention as the support band for producer/composer BUNNY SIGLER. Sigler helped them garner a recording deal with T.S.O.P. Records; their debut album, *Get Down with the Philly Jump* (T.S.O.P., 1976), was a modest commercial success, driven in large part by the hit single, "It Ain't Reggae (But It's Funky)."

After a brief lull spanning a change of labels, they returned with *I Got My Mind Made Up* (Salsoul, 1978), which earned a gold disc and contained the best-selling title track. Subsequent releases failed to do nearly as well, and another label switch, to Pop Art in the mid-1980s, failed to revive their plummeting fortunes.

Intelligent Hoodlum *rapper*

While serving 20 months at Riker's Island for a 1988 robbery conviction, New York City native Percy Chapman studied African-American culture and the Nation of Islam's religious tenets. Upon his release, he embarked on a career as rapper Intelligent Hoodlum, addressing the social ills of his environment, black politics, and other related issues. His albums, *Intelligent Hoodlum* (A&M, 1990) and *Tragedy: Saga of a Hoodlum* (A&M, 1993), featured deftly articulated observations of contemporary urban life—punctuated on occasion by seemingly incongruous light humor—and stylish production work by MARLEY MARL. No further releases appeared in the face of general public indifference.

Intruders, The

Formed in Philadelphia in 1960, the Intruders—consisting of Sam "Little Sonny" Brown, Eugene "Bird" Daughtry, Phil Terry, and Robert "Big Sonny" Edwards—were one of the mainstays of the Kenny Gamble–Leon Huff stable of artists. Although the distinctive soaring tenor lead possessed by notable Philly soul groups like the STYLISTICS with Russell Thompkins, Jr., and Harold Melvin and the Blue Notes with TEDDY PENDERGRASS, the Intruders—like their more successful contemporaries, the O'JAYS—focused on smooth harmonies generally set to easy rocking FUNK-pop grooves.

The group first signed with the Gowan label in 1961. After hooking up with Gamble and Huff in the mid-1960s, the Intruders released a decade-long string of hit singles, including six Top Ten R&B hits: "Together"; "Cowboys to Girls"; "(Love Is Like a) Baseball Game"; a redo of the 1961 Dreamlovers hit, "When We Get Married"; "I'll Always Love My Mama (Part 1)"; and "I Wanna Know Your Name."

Island Records

Chris Blackwell established Island/Blue Mountain Records in London as a vehicle for distributing the Jamaican music he'd grown to love while visiting the Caribbean islands. Early releases consisted of imported Jamaican recordings by Jimmy Cliff, Bob Morley (aka Marley), and the Skatalites, among others. Within two years the company scored its first international hit, Millie Small's "My Boy Lollipop."

After merging with B & C Records in 1968, the label began emphasizing the development of rock and folk artists, adding the likes of Fairport Convention, Free, Jethro Tull, King Crimson, Cat Stevens, Richard and Linda Thompson, and Traffic to its roster. However, Island's commitment to REGGAE reemerged with Blackwell's investment in the Jamaican film, *The Harder They Come* (1971). The soundtrack, featuring the music of Jimmy Cliff, became popular worldwide. Cliff would fail to equal this standard again, but the company continued to mine reggae via releases by BOB MARLEY—most notably, *Rastaman Vibration* (Island, 1976), *Exodus* (Island, 1977), and *Uprising* (Island, 1980)—the Maytals, and Steel Pulse.

Throughout the 1970s and beyond, Island remained a fixture within the fad-driven British pop scene, scoring its first number one hit in 1979 with the Buggles' "Video Killed the Radio Star." The following year, the label signed the youthful Irish band U2, which went on to the kind of stardom realized only by artists such as ELVIS PRESLEY, the Beatles, and the Rolling Stones.

Although Blackwell sold Island to Polygram in 1989, he continued to control major artistic decisions. The label continued to prosper into the 21st century, signing top alternative acts like the Cranberries, PJ Harvey, Pulp, and Tricky, and merging with rap-oriented DEF JAM. In 1999, Polygram sold Island/Def Jam to Seagram's/Universal Music.

Isley Brothers, The

One of the more versatile and lasting soul-FUNK bands to achieve recording success, the Isley Brothers—like singer SAM COOKE—provided an early template for minority artists with regard to taking creative and business control of career matters. In addition to establishing their own label, T-Neck, as early as 1964, they wrote timeless classics such as "Twist and Shout" and the Grammy-winning "It's Your Thing," and provided a forum for developing talented young musicians like guitarist Jimi Hendrix.

The group was originally comprised of three Cincinnati-based brothers—Ronald, Rudulph, and O'Kelly Isley—all of whom had roots in gospel singing. They recorded singles for several small labels in the late 1950s before achieving a minor hit with "Shout." Stints with Atlantic, Wand (Scepter), United Artists, and Tamla (MOTOWN)—while resulting in occasional chart successes, most notably "This Old Heart of Mine"—proved problematical, with these companies attempting to make the Isleys conform a preconceived formulaic sound. As a result, the trio re-launched their own label in

The Isley Brothers in the early 1960s (Frank Driggs Collection)

early 1969 and incorporated additional family members: brothers Ernie Isley (guitar, percussion) and Marvin Isley (bass, percussion) and cousin Chris Jasper (keyboards), who also composed many of their 1970s hits. Between 1973 and 1983, the Isleys released nine consecutive gold or platinum albums; their popularity was based on a seamless blend of pulsating dance rhythms, Ronald's soulful lead vocals (equally adept at silky-smooth ballads and hard-driving funk), and socially conscious lyrics, punctuated by Ernie Isley's Hendrix-inspired guitar riffs. Their most successful recordings during this period included *3 + 3* (T-Neck, 1972), which featured the sexy, uptempo workout, "That Lady"; *The Heat Is On* (T-Neck, 1975); *Harvest for the World* (T-Neck, 1976); *Go for Your Guns* (T-Neck, 1977); and *Showdown* (T-Neck, 1978).

With hit recordings becoming increasingly scarce in 1983, the group reverted back to the original trio following the departure of the younger family members to form Isley, Jasper, Isley. The Isleys became a duo in early 1986 following O'Kelly's death. In late 1988, Ernie and Marvin returned to the fold, the group now billed as the Isley Brothers featuring Ronald Isley. They were inducted into the Rock and Roll Hall of Fame in 1992, and continue to tour and record to the present day.

I-Threes

The I-Threes were formed in response to BOB MARLEY's need for backing vocalists after Peter Tosh and Bunny Wailer left to pursue solo careers. Comprised of Marcia Griffiths, Rita Marley, and Judy Mowatt, the trio added harmonic richness to Marley's spare REGGAE arrangements as well as providing a pleasing visual accent (complete with dance routines choreographed by Mowatt) in live performances. The three singers had all recorded previously in a solo capacity, and they resumed their careers when Marley died in 1981. Their trio work was limited to the Wailers' performances and recordings, with the exception of a 1983 12-inch single, "Music for the World," credited to Rita Marley, Mowatt, and Griffiths, and a small number of reunion concerts.

Jacks, The See CADETS/THE JACKS, THE.

Jackson, Bull Moose (1919–1989) *singer*
One of the pioneering rhythm and blues vocalists, Bull Moose Jackson was a highly successful recording artist during the late 1940s. He was also a multitalented musician, performing and recording on the saxophone, clarinet, and violin, among other instruments.

Born Benjamin Clarence Jackson, the Cleveland native formed the Harlem Hotshots with Freddie Webster while attending high school. He joined LUCKY MILLINDER's band in 1943, taking on vocal duties when WYNONIE HARRIS departed for a solo career in 1945.

Jackson first made the charts with an answer song to Millinder's number one 1945 hit, "Who Threw the Whiskey in the Well," entitled "I Know Who Threw the Whiskey in the Well." The following year, he assembled his own performing band from Millinder sidemen. His best-selling records included "I Love You, Yes I Do," his only crossover hit, backed by "Sneaky Pete"; "All My Love Belongs to You"/"I Want a Bowlegged Woman"; "I Can't Go on Without You," number one on the R&B charts for eight weeks; "Little Girl, Don't Cry"; and "Why Don't You Haul Off and Love Me."

Jackson made a brief return to the R&B Top Ten reinterpreting his classic single, "I Love You, Yes I Do," in 1961 for 7 Arts. His last attempt at a recording comeback was *Moosemania* (Bogus, 1984). He continued to perform live through the 1980s, touring Europe in 1985. Jackson died in Cleveland on July 31, 1989.

Jackson, Janet (b. 1966) *singer*
Although Janet Jackson's musical identity owes much to the slick FUNK-pop production work of ex–The Time members, JIMMY JAM AND TERRY LEWIS, her photogenic good looks and well-choreographed dancing skills have also been key ingredients in her commercial success. Now entering her third decade as a major recording artist, she has become an industry institution much like her older brother, MICHAEL JACKSON.

Born May 16, 1966, in Gary, Indiana, Janet started out singing with the Jackson 5 on their television variety show in the 1970s before garnering roles on programs like *Good Times, Diff'rent Strokes,* and *Fame.* She achieved marginal success with her first two albums, *Janet Jackson* (A&M, 1982) and *Dream Street* (A&M, 1984). However, the next LP, the chart-topping *Control* (A&M, 1986), made her a star, driven by several Jam and Lewis–penned hit singles like "What Have You Done for Me Lately," "Nasty," "When I Think of You," and "Control," aided by the accompanying high-energy video clips which appeared in heavy rotation on MTV, BET, and other cable TV stations.

With Jackson now sharing songwriting responsibilities and projecting a more mature sexuality, follow-up recordings—the number one albums *Janet Jackson's Rhythm Nation 1814* (A&M, 1989), *Janet* (Virgin, 1993), *The Velvet Rope* (Virgin, 1997), and *All for You* (Virgin, 2001), as well as a string of equally successful singles: "Miss You Much," "Escapade," "Black Cat," "Love Will Never Do (Without You)," "That's the Way Love Goes," "Again," and "Together Again"—have cemented her place in the pop music pantheon. With the fashion spreads and glitzy dance routines now balanced with lyrics addressing racism, inequality, and other forms of social consciousness, Jackson seemed intent on maximizing her core audience. However, this was all cast into the background by her notorious breast-baring episode during the halftime show

at the 2004 Super Bowl. Many industry observers interpreted this as an attempt to revive her slack commercial performance during the previous few years and to promote her newest release, *Damita Jo* (Virgin, 2004).

Jackson, Michael (b. 1958) *singer*

It appears more and more likely, with each passing year, that Michael Jackson's career will fall short of the expectations of music industry experts. By the mid-1980s, he was the most popular recording artist

Michael Jackson (front, second from right) as a member of The Jackson 5 (Frank Driggs Collection)

worldwide—his *Thriller* (Epic, 1982) was the top-selling album of all time—and on the cutting edge of the rapidly expanding video medium. However, a steady barrage of bad publicity surrounding his plastic surgeries, alleged sexual behavior with children, and other eccentric activities have substantially eroded his following over the years.

Born August 29, 1958, into a family of child prodigies, Michael became lead vocalist for the Jackson 5, with brothers Jackie, Tito, Jermaine, and Marlon. Following the release of a couple of singles for the local Steeltown label, the Gary, Indiana–based group signed with MOTOWN in 1969. They made an immediate splash when their first four singles for the label—"I Want You Back," "ABC," "The Love You Save," and "I'll Be There"—all reached the number one position. Their early album releases—*Diana Ross Presents The Jackson 5* (Motown, 1970), *ABC* (Motown, 1970), *The Third Album* (Motown, 1970), and *Maybe Tomorrow* (Motown, 1971)—also sold extraordinarily well for a black act at the time, due largely to an engaging, effervescent sound that incorporated elements of soul, pop, and bubblegum.

It was clear out of the box, however, that Michael's impassioned singing and showmanship was the most important ingredient behind the Jacksons' success. As a result, Motown decided to issue solo material by Michael alongside group releases beginning in October 1971. Among his more notable early singles were a dynamic remake of BOBBY DAY's 1958 hit, "Rockin' Robin," and the bizarre number one hit, "Ben," a sentimental tribute to a pet rat. He continued recording and performing with his brothers, who were by then writing much of their own material and returned to top form in 1974 with a proto-DISCO single, "Dancing Machine." However, the group's fortunes fluctuated wildly as Michael took frequent sabbaticals to pursue his solo career.

With the assistance of producer/arranger Quincy Jones, Michael hit the big time with *Off The Wall* (Epic, 1979), powered by four Top Ten singles: the pulsating "Don't Stop 'Til You Get Enough," the scintillating "Rock with You," the sentimental "She's

Michael Jackson publicity still (Frank Driggs Collection)

Out of My Life," and the title track. Despite this, the unprecedented quality and commercial staying power of Jackson's next LP, *Thriller,* caught the industry by surprise. The record gathered momentum slowly, first making an impact in the black market, before the heavy MTV rotation of "Billie Jean" and "Beat It" propelled it to a 37-week stretch at the top of the pop album charts; eventually, seven of its nine tracks reached the Top Ten.

Following his participation in the highly publicized *Victory* (Epic, 1984) album and tour with his brothers (the last time he worked with them as a group), Michael again collaborated with Jones on chart-topping *Bad* (Epic, 1987). It spawned seven hit singles, five of which—"I Just Can't Stop Loving You" (with Siedah Garrett), "Bad," "The Way You Make Me Feel," "Man in the Mirror," and "Dirty Diana"—reached number one. Despite their relative popularity, subsequent releases—including *Dangerous* (Epic, 1991), the partial retrospective *HIStory: Past, Present and Future Book 1* (Epic, 1995; double set), and a string of dance-oriented singles—have been poorly received by critics who consider anything falling short of his 1980s classics to be a letdown.

Jackson, Millie (b. 1944) *singer and songwriter*

Born July 15, 1944, in Thompson, Georgia, Jackson relocated to Newark, New Jersey, in 1958. After working as a model in New York City, she began singing professionally in 1964. She recorded initially for MGM in 1970 before moving on to the independent label Spring the following year. There, she became a fixture on the R&B charts, specializing in spicy love songs, typically from the vantage point of a strong-willed, independent woman who came of age in the post-feminist generation. Her biggest R&B hits included "Ask Me What You Want," "My Man, a Sweet Man," "Hurts So Good," "If You're Not Back in Love by Monday," "Hot! Wild! Unrestricted! Crazy Love," and "Love Is a Dangerous Game."

Jam, Jimmy (b. 1959), and Terry Lewis (b. 1956) *producers*

Minneapolis native Jimmy Jam (James Harris III) and Terry Lewis, born in Omaha, first gained attention as members of The Time, headed by Morris Day. Following the release of the group's debut FUNK PUNK LP, *The Time* (Warner Bros., 1981), produced by PRINCE, Jam and Lewis formed Flyte Time Productions. Their first success as producer-arrangers came with tracks from the S.O.S. Band's *On the Rise* (Tabu, 1983), most notably the hit, "Just Be Good to Me."

Fired from the Time by Prince, Jam and Lewis achieved further success in the mid-1980s working with R&B artists such as Patti Austin, Thelma Houston, GLADYS KNIGHT, and Klymaxx. Their trademark sound—richly scored yet streamlined, street-smart yet sophisticated—attracted the handlers of the then relatively unknown JANET JACKSON. The collaboration yielded a long string of successes, including *Control* (A&M, 1986), which sold more than five million copies and earned the duo a

Grammy as Producers of the Year; *Rhythm Nation 1814* (A&M, 1989), which quickly topped sales of six million; *Janet* (Virgin, 1993); and *The Velvet Rope* (Virgin, 1997).

Now in great demand, Jam and Lewis also worked on the Human League's chart-topping "Human," the FORCE M.D.'s' "Tender Love," Herb Alpert's "Keep Your Eye on Me" (with vocals by Lewis and Lisa Keith); NEW EDITION's platinum-selling *Heart Break* (MCA, 1988); Johnny Gill's eponymous debut album; Ralph Tresvant's *Ralph Tresvant* (MCA, 1990), and Karyn White's *Ritual of Love* (Warner Bros., 1991).

In 1991, they founded the A&M-backed label, Perspective; its first release, the Sounds of Blackness' *The Evolution of Gospel* (Perspective, 1991), won a Grammy. The team continued to freelance, working in the 1990s with the likes of MICHAEL JACKSON, BOYZ II MEN, MARY J. BLIGE, and Vanessa Williams.

James, Etta (b. 1938) *singer*

Etta James was born Jamesetta Hawkins on January 25, 1938, in Los Angeles. She began her singing career performing primarily gospel music in her local Baptist church. By age five, Jamesetta had began performing on a Los Angeles radio station. In 1950, her family relocated to San Francisco. She quickly formed a vocal trio with two other girls her age and, when she was 14, auditioned with them for Johnny Otis backstage in San Francisco.

Otis was particularly interested in a song the girls had written as an answer to HANK BALLARD AND THE MIDNIGHTERS' "Work with Me Annie." He recorded "Roll with Me Henry," with the group in Los Angeles to record with Otis. The song was rerecorded in 1954, with an additional, uncredited vocal by Richard Berry (composer of "Louis Louie"), for Modern Records. At this time, Otis rearranged "Jamesetta" to create the stage name Etta James, and dubbed the group the Peaches, after James's nickname. When "Roll with Me Henry" was released, its controversial title was changed to "The Wallflower" to appeal to a broader audience; the resulting publicity helped bring the song to the top of the R&B charts in 1955.

While the Peaches folded soon thereafter, James continued to record with Modern through most of the 1950s and produced a hit record, "Good Rockin' Daddy" (1955; R&B number six). In 1960, she signed with Argo (a subsidiary of Chess) and her career hit a new high. She recorded "If I Can't Have You," a duet with the MOONGLOWS' frontman, Harvey Fuqua (Chess, 1960; number six); that year she also had her biggest solo R&B hit to date, "All I Could Do Was Cry" (Argo; number two; number 33 pop). Chess decided she had great pop potential on top of her proven soul abilities, showering her with lushly orchestrated pop classics like "At Last" (Argo, 1961; number two R&B) and "Trust in Me" (Argo, 1961; number four; number 30 pop).

James's rougher side needed to be recognized. She released the tough, soulful "Something's Got a Hold on Me" (Argo 1962; number four R&B), followed by the live EP, *Etta James Rocks the House,* recorded at the famous New Era Club in Nashville (Argo, recorded 1963). Later hits for Chess included "Pushover" (Argo, 1963; number seven) and "Tell Mama," which she recorded at Muscle Shoals (Cadet, 1968; number 10; number 23 pop, her highest charting pop hit). She remained on the Chess label even after the death of its founder, Leonard Chess, in 1969 (to 1977). Her eponymous 1973 album won her a Grammy nomination for Best Female R&B Performance.

James's extensive drug use in the mid-to-late 1970s nearly took her life. The accompanying career slump ended in the 1980s, when she sang at the 1984 Olympic Games in Los Angeles, toured briefly with the Rolling Stones, and released the critically acclaimed *Seven Year Itch* (Island, 1988). *The Right Time* (Elektra, 1992), produced by the legendary Jerry Wexler, exhibited a slicker soul sound. *Mystery Lady: The Songs of Billie Holliday* (Private Music, 1994) earned her a Grammy for Best Jazz Performance; she would win another for Best Contemporary Blues Album (*Let's Roll,* 2004), following a Grammy Lifetime Achievement Award (2003). She was inducted into the Rock and Roll Hall of Fame in 1994. James continues to bring her soulful, risqué act on the stage, with a new audience that discovered her through the use of her interpretation of Muddy Waters's "I Just Wanna Make Love to You" in advertisements.

—Emily Herring

James, Rick (1948–2004) *singer and bandleader*
A leading PUNK FUNK innovator, Rick James merged the sprawling funk anthems of Parliament-Funkadelic and the OHIO PLAYERS with tight, radio-friendly arrangements and street-smart, sexually charged lyrics. His live performances borrowed heavily from Kiss, Queen, and other glam rockers of the 1970s.

Born James Johnson on February 1, 1948, in Buffalo, New York, he was raised by a single mother in a housing project. By the mid-1960s, he was fronting the Toronto-based Mynah Birds, which included Neil Young and Bruce Palmer, prior to their formation of Buffalo Springfield. Although the group recorded for MOTOWN, nothing was officially released.

James relocated to London, forming the band Main Line. By the mid-1970s, he was back to the United States, with a new support group, the Stone City Band. Signing again with Motown, his debut single, "You and I" powered the album, *Come Get It* (Gordy, 1978), to sales of almost two million copies. Anticipating gangsta rap with his incendiary tales of urban violence, drugs, and prostitution, James recorded a string of best sellers, including "Mary Jane," "Give It to Me Baby," "Super Freak (Part 1)," "Dance Wit' Me (Part 1)," "Cold Blooded," and a duet with rapper Roxanne Shante, "Loosey's Rap." In addition, he produced recordings for many acts, including Teena Marie, the Mary Jane Girls, and Eddie Murphy.

He regularly ran afoul of the law when the hits stopped coming. In 1991, he and his girlfriend, Tanya Hijazi, were accused of assaulting a woman following a drug binge. With James allegedly snorting $10,000 worth of coke per week at the time, a similar complaint surfaced the following year. After

Rick James was a fashion trendsetter in the late 1970s.
(Frank Driggs Collection)

serving two years in prison, he suffered a stroke in 1998 that severely impaired his speech and mobility. While planning a comeback, he died August 6, 2004, in his Los Angeles home, from a heart attack complicated by drugs.

Jamiroquai

Jamiroquai has survived media hype, brazen self-merchandising, and ill-conceived comments about the environment to become one of the more important British HIP-HOP acts around. The group, named after an Iroquois tribe, is centered around Jason

"Jay" Kay (born 1969, in London), who was raised by a jazz-singing mother who exposed him to FUNK and jazz pioneers such as Sly Stone, GIL SCOTT-HERON, and Roy Ayers.

After spending time as a breakdancer, he employed a sampler and drum machine to produce a single for Morgan Khan's Streetsounds label in 1986. He experimented with the emerging ACID JAZZ genre, which melded urban funk, improvisation, and new age mysticism. A highly regarded single, "When You Gonna Learn?" led to an eight-album deal with Sony Records. His first single for the label, "Too Young to Die," made the British Top Ten, and helped push the album, *Emergency on Planet Earth* (Sony, 1993), to sales of more than two million. The follow-up, *The Return of the Space Cowboy* (Sony, 1994), placed a greater emphasis on his vocals and hip-hop rhythms. At the onset of the 21st century, Kay remained one of the more promising artists within the hip-hop scene, and Jamiroquai's 2005 release, *Feels Just Like It Should* was anticipated by fans.

Ja Rule (b. 1976) *rapper*

One of the most successful crossover rappers in the early years of the 21st century, Ja Rule burst onto the music scene through his vocal contributions to JAY-Z's "Can I Get A. . . ." The Queens-based emcee's debut album, *Venni Vetti Vecci* (1999), was an immediate success, due largely to the hit single, "Holla Holla." He solidified his chart hegemony with four follow-up releases: *Rule 3:36* (2000), *Pain Is Love* (2001), *Clap Back* (2003), and *Blood in My Eye* (2003), which refined his hit-making formula: alternating gravel-voiced gangsta verses with R&B love jams, framed by Irv Gotti's punchy, club-oriented production work.

Jayhawks, The (The Vibrations; The Marathons)

Most acts have only one bona fide shot at fame and fortune. The Jayhawks had three, each following a radically different scenario from the others. All three paths, however, stopped far short of sustained commercial success.

The Jayhawks—originally consisting of first tenor James Johnson, second tenor Carl Fisher, baritone Dave Govan, and bass Carver Bunkum (later replaced by Don Bradley)—formed in Jefferson High School, Los Angeles, in 1955. Soon thereafter, they auditioned at a local Flash Record Store, performing the Johnson-penned "Stranded in the Jungle." The proprietors liked the song enough to release it on their label in mid-1956. Although the record's commercial impact was undercut significantly by the Cadets' more polished cover version, retail sales and jukebox activity were sufficient to boost it to number nine on the R&B charts and number 18 on the *Billboard* pop singles survey.

In an effort to secure the backing of a more established record company, the Jayhawks signed on with ALADDIN, a well-known West Coast independent label. Typecast as a novelty act, the group's subsequent singles failed to achieve any notable commercial success. By 1960, the quintet (augmented by the addition of tenor Richard Owens) felt a name change was in order, signing with the Checker label—a Chess subsidiary—as the Vibrations. With the Twist becoming a nationwide sensation on the heels of the chart-topping CHUBBY CHECKER hit, they came up with their own dance number, "The Watusi."

Back in the limelight, the group could not resist another foray into the novelty market, recording the humorous tribute song, "Peanut Butter" as the Marathons for Arvee Records. Checker was not amused, suing Arvee for breach of contract, consequently obtaining rights to the single and releasing it on another Chess subsidiary, Argo.

Almost three years passed before the Vibrations returned to the charts during the height of the British Invasion with "My Girl Sloopy." The song would fare even better the following year, topping the pop charts when reworked in a garage rock mode—and re-titled "Hang on Sloopy"—by the McCoys. The group regained the hit-making touch

intermittently throughout the 1960s with "Misty," the Beatles' "And I Love Her," "Pick Me," and "Love in Them There Hills." They disbanded in the 1970s, with Owens joining the TEMPTATIONS in 1971 for a brief stint.

Jaynetts, The

The New York–based Jaynetts recorded only one hit, but oh, what a hit: "Sally, Go 'Round the Roses," which reached number two on the Hot 100 with its ambiguous account of a young girl's descent into madness, delivered in chilling fashion. Songwriter Zelma "Zell" Sanders formed the group around her daughter, Johnnie Louise Richardson, formerly of the R&B duo, Johnnie and Joe (Rivers), whose most successful single had been the Top Ten crossover smash, "Over the Mountain, Across the Sea." Other members included Yvonne Bushnell, Ethel Davis, Ada Ray, and Mary Sue Wells.

Richardson left the Jaynetts to resume her work with Rivers; they performed at oldies concerts and recorded until her death on October 25, 1988. The group soldiered on, though follow-up releases such as "Keep an Eye on Her" and "Johnny Don't Cry" failed to chart. They ceased recording in 1965, and disbanded soon thereafter.

Jay-Z (b. 1969) *rapper, producer, and record company executive*

Born Shawn Carter in New York City, he became one of the most influential figures in the 1990s RAP scene due to his wide array of talents. Known as "Jazzy" while hustling on the streets near Brooklyn's Marcy Projects where he grew up, Jay-Z was inspired by a local rapper, Big Jaz, to start his own record company. Along with partners Kareem Burke and Damon Dash, he formed Roc-A-Fella in 1995.

In July 1996, he released his debut album, *Reasonable Doubt,* on the label; while content to appropriate the gangsta conventions then in vogue, his production skills helped boost it to number 23 on the *Billboard* charts. Taking a decidedly pop direction, his subsequent CDs—*In My Lifetime, Vol. 1* (Roc-A-Fella, 1997), *Vol. 2: Hard Knock Life* (Roc-A-Fella, 1998), *Vol. 3: Life and Times of S. Carter* (Roc-A-Fella, 2000), *Roc La Familia—The Dynasty* (Roc-A-Fella, 2000), and *The Blueprint* (Uptown/Universal, 2001)—all topped the charts (with the exception of his sophomore effort, which peaked at number three). Utilizing the Roots as his backing band, he tried a new direction with *MTV Unplugged* (Def Jam, 2001). The double-disc set, *The Blueprint2: The Gift & the Curse* (Def Jam, 2002) found Jay-Z still trying to push the envelope. No longer content to rely on his unparalleled rhyming skills and innovative beats, he worked a wide array of guest performers (including Beyoncé Knowles, Lenny Kravitz, Rakim, and Scarface) and outside producers (DR DRE, Heavy D, the NEPTUNES, TIMBALAND, and KANYE WEST) into his grand scheme.

By the late 1990s, Jay-Z had transcended musical stardom, becoming something of a cultural icon. In addition to producing some of the top R&B artists, he established his own clothing line, became a favorite subject of the paparazzi, and began dating DESTINY CHILD's Knowles. Obviously comfortable with the spotlight—as evidenced by the prefabricated feud with fellow New Yorkers NAS and MOBB DEEP, which he instigated by ridiculing them in the song, "Takeover"—Jay-Z is unlikely to relinquish his East Coast hegemony anytime in the near future. In 2005 he was named president and CEO of Def Jam Recordings.

Jean, Wyclef   See FUGEES, THE.

Jelly Beans, The

The Jelly Beans enjoyed their 15 minutes of fame at the tail end of the GIRL GROUP era. The group—consisting of Jersey City, New Jersey, high schoolers Alma Brewer, Diane Taylor, sisters Elyse and Maxine Herbert, and bass singer Charlie Thomas—was discovered by Bill Downs, who signed them to a management contract. He then introduced them to producer Steve Vanet, who in turn brought them to

LEIBER AND STOLLER's fledgling Red Bird label in early 1964.

Under the guidance of the Brill Building songwriting-production team of Jeff Barry and Ellie Greenwich, the Jelly Beans recorded their debut single, "I Wanna Love Him So Bad." The catchy, singalong song resonated with the public, as did—to a lesser extent—the follow-up release, "Baby Be Mine." For some inexplicable reason, however, the company decided not to issue any more recordings. The group switched to the Eskee label the following year, but—lacking a truly distinctive style or industry support—failed to repeat their earlier success.

Jive Bombers, The (Clarence Palmer & the Jive Bombers)

Although the Jive Bombers are remembered by R&B fans as one-hit wonders, they enjoyed a long career both as a performing and recording act. The New York–based group was formed in the mid-1940s from members of Sonny Austin & the Jive Bombers and the Palmer Brothers. They went on to record for Coral as the Sparrows in 1949, and for Citation as the Jive Bombers in 1952. In early 1957, the group—now consisting of Earl Johnson, Al Tinney, William "Pee Wee" Tinney, and lead singer Clarence Palmer—recorded their big hit, "Bad Boy" (reaching number seven on the R&B on the Savoy label), with its distinctive tongue-driven refrain: in fact, this was a cover of "Brown Gal," composed and recorded by Lil Armstrong in 1936. They remained active until the 1960s, but were unable to find the right hit-making combination again.

John, Little Willie (1937–1968) *singer*

Born William Edgar John on November 15, 1937, the Cullendale, Arkansas, native—the brother of Mabel John of the RAELETTS—was raised in Detroit. He recorded for Prize in 1953, before signing with the King label. His plaintive voice graced 17 R&B hits from 1955 to 1961, including the original versions of "Fever" (number one for five weeks in mid-1956) and "Tell It Like It Is." His biggest pop success,

"Sleep" (number 13 in 1960), was a best-selling 78 r.p.m. disc for Fred Waring's Pennsylvanians in 1924. His career had already lost momentum when he was convicted of manslaughter in 1966. John died of a heart attack while serving his sentence at Washington State Prison on May 26, 1968.

Johnny Moore's Three Blazers

Johnny Moore's Three Blazers is best remembered as the springboard to fame for rhythm-and-blues stylist Charles Brown. However, the group continued to produce R&B hits for seven years following Brown's departure.

The Los Angeles–based group—originally consisting of Brown on piano and lead vocals, guitarist Johnny Moore, and bassist Eddie Williams—was formed in 1944. It was one of the most successful R&B recording acts of the late 1940s; the trio's hits included "Drifting Blues," "Sunny Road," "So Long," "New Orleans Blues," "Changeable Woman Blues," the perennial classic "Merry Christmas Baby," "Groovy Movie Blues," "More Than You Know," "Where Can I Find My Baby," and "Walkin' Blues." The Three Blazers underwent a series of personnel changes at the height of their success. Moore's brother, Oscar (formerly guitarist with the King Cole Trio), joined in 1947, while Brown left the following year, and was replaced by Billy Valentine. Frankie Ervin would take over vocals in the early 1950s.

Moore and his band also collaborated successfully with a number of artists in the studio, most notably, with Ivory Joe Hunter on "Blues at Sunrise" and Floyd Dixon on "Telephone Blues." The group disbanded in the mid-1950s.

Johnson, Jimmy (b. 1928) singer

Born James Thompson, on November 25, 1928, in Holly Springs, Mississippi, Jimmy Johnson has explored a gamut of post–World War II styles, from gospel to Chicago blues and soul music. Moving to Chicago in 1950, he sang and played guitar in several gospel groups. In 1959, he began working with Magic Sam and FREDDY KING in much the same fashion as his blues-influenced brothers, Syl Johnson and Mac Thompson (aka Mac Johnson). After working in the soul scene during the 1960s, he reverted back to the blues, playing second guitar with Jimmy Dawkins and OTIS RUSH. Johnson began recording solo in 1975 for MCM. His well-crafted, gospel-inflected sound can be best appreciated on the albums *Johnson's Whacks* (1979), *Bar Room Preacher* (1983), and *I'm a Jockey* (1994).

Johnson, Johnnie (1924–2005) pianist

While Johnnie Johnson recorded a string of solo albums over the past two decades, he was best known as the piano accompanist on the bulk of CHUCK BERRY's classic Chess Records cuts in the 1950s and 1960s. Born in Fairmont, West Virginia, Johnson started playing piano by ear as a seven-year-old, listening to leading jazz and boogie-woogie musicians like Earl Hines and Meade "Lux" Lewis. Following a stint in the U.S. Army, he began a professional career in 1946. As leader of the Sir John Trio, he hired Berry to play guitar in 1952. Berry soon became the combo's de facto head, supplying song material and garnering a Chess recording contract in 1955. In addition to lending his idiosyncratic ragtime-oriented phrasing to hits like "Roll Over Beethoven," "Johnny B. Goode" (which Berry has alleged was written for the pianist), "Sweet Little Sixteen," and "You Never Can Tell," Johnson toured extensively with the guitarist.

Johnson went out on his own in the mid-1960s, working for such luminaries as blues guitarist ALBERT KING. He formed his own band in the 1970s, but reunited with Berry on occasion, most notably the film, *Hail! Hail! Rock and Roll* (1986), and guested on various LPs, including Keith Richards's debut, *Talk Is Cheap*. Johnson's solo releases included *Blue Hand Johnnie* (1987), *Rockin' Eighty-Eights* (1991), and *That'll Work* (1993), a collaboration with the country-rock band, the Kentucky Headhunters. He died in St. Louis on April 13, 2005.

Johnson, Lonnie (1889–1970) *guitarist*

Alonzo "Lonnie" Johnson's accomplishments are legion. He was the creator of the guitar solo played note for note with a pick, now a standard device in blues, country, jazz, rock, and other popular music styles. He inspired many 20th-century innovators—including jazz guitar creators Django Reinhardt and Charlie Christian and modern blues pioneers T-Bone Walker and B. B. KING—as well as many other musicians who copied his style (e.g., the St. Louis school exemplified by Henry Townsend and Clifford Gibson) and repertoire (most notably, Skip James's rendition of "I'm So Glad").

Born February 8, 1889, and raised in New Orleans, he worked the Storyville district from 1910 to 1917. Johnson also spent a considerable amount of time in St. Louis, Texas, New York, and Chicago while performing in theaters and on riverboats, strongly influencing the musicians based in each of these areas. He was very active recording during the first wave of blues recording, producing 130 sides between 1925 and 1932 as a session player for OKeh, including collaborations with Louis Armstrong (the 1928 OKeh release, "Hotter Than That") and Duke Ellington. A conflict with powerful Chicago producer Lester Melrose temporarily halted his studio work, but he became active again between 1937 and 1942 for Columbia, Decca, Bluebird, Disc, and other labels. Following World War II, he revived his career with a series of hits on the King label featuring his electric guitar playing, including "Tomorrow Night," "Pleasing You," "So Tired," and "Confused."

Dropping out of sight in the early 1950s, he was rediscovered at the beginning of the blues-folk revival in 1959, working as a porter in a Philadelphia hotel. Although consistently touring during the 1960s, his artistic and commercial impact did not approach that of many of his peers, primarily because his sophisticated, urban-based style—rooted in 1930s popular music—did not translate well to an audience most interested in the ethnic roots of the blues. Nevertheless, compact disc reissues of his work are widely available, including *Blues By Lonnie Johnson* (Prestige Bluesville, 1991), *Blues & Ballads* (Prestige Bluesville, 1990), *Another Night to Cry* (Prestige Bluesville, 1992), *Stompin' at the Penny* (Columbia Legacy, 1994), *The Complete Folkways Recordings* (Smithsonian Folkways, 1993), and *Steppin' on the Blues* (CBS/Sony).

Johnson, Marv (b. 1938) *singer*

Johnson was one of the earliest MOTOWN stars; he helped establish the company's place in the record industry before major acts like MARVIN GAYE, the SUPREMES, the TEMPTATIONS, and STEVIE WONDER appeared on the scene. Born Marvin Earl Johnson, in October 15, 1938, in Detroit, Michigan, he started out singing gospel as a member of the Junior Serenaders while still in his teens. In 1958, he teamed with Berry Gordy, then a songwriter/producer for JACKIE WILSON. After producing Johnson's early gospel-tinged R&B singles on Kudo, Berry chose his "Come to Me" to launch the Tamla imprint. Licensed to United Artists, it became a national hit, and was successfully followed by "You Got What It Takes," "I Love the Way You Move," and "Move Two Mountains."

Johnson's formula—gentle, upbeat love songs punctuated by a female gospel chorus—failed to click when he switched to the Gordy label in 1965. After a brief revival of his popularity in Great Britain in the late 1960s, he became a Motown sales executive. In the midst of the 1980s soul revival, Johnson returned to performing, touring with the "Sounds of Motown" troupe in 1987 and reinterpreting his old material for the Nightmare label. A strong comeback LP, *Come to Me* (Motor City, 1990)—produced by Ian Levine—was forced to compete with compilations of his classic 1960s singles.

Jones, Glenn *singer*

Glenn Jones was one of the few vocalists to make the successful transition from gospel to the pop genre (a commonly traveled path in the post–World War II era) in the 1980s. The Jacksonville, Florida, native began singing with the gospel group, Bivens Special, as an eight-year-old. He went on to form his own gospel act, the Modulations, at age 14. He appeared in the Broadway musical *Sing Mahalia, Sing,* and signed a solo recording contract with RCA in the early 1980s. He specialized in covers of R&B classics—including Johnnie Taylor's "I Am Somebody," the ISLEY BROTHERS' "Keep On Doin,'" JOE TEX's "Show Me," Robert Knight's "Everlasting Love," Maurice Williams' "Stay," and the CHI-LITES' "Oh Girl"—although his biggest success came from the easy listening pop field, the number two R&B hit "We've Only Just Begun."

Jones, Jimmy (b. 1937) *singer*
One of the truly distinctive R&B singers of the early 1960s, Jimmy Jones helped popularize the falsetto style later employed by the Four Seasons and countless soul groups. Born June 2, 1937, in Birmingham, Alabama, Jones started out as a tap dancer before joining in the DOO-WOP act, the Sparks of Rhythm, in 1955. In 1956, he formed his own group, the Savoys, renamed the Pretenders shortly thereafter.

Jones finally found success with the MGM subsidiary, Cub; his debut, "Handy Man" (reaching the top three on both the pop and R&B charts in early 1960), became a classic, later returning to the charts in covers by Del Shannon in 1964 and James Taylor in 1977. After one more smash, "Good Timin,'" follow-up releases—including the minor hits "That's When I Cried" and "I Told You So"—experienced a substantial drop-off in sales. However, he had even greater success in Great Britain, topping the charts with "Good Timin'" and reaching the Top 50 with five singles.

Jordan, Louis (1908–1975) *singer and bandleader*
Louis Jordan proved more successful than any other black artist in crossing over to the pop charts in the 1940s. He was equally adept at jazz, blues, R&B, and pop music, and his experiments in melding these styles played a major role in the emergence of rock 'n' roll.

The Louis Jordan Band live at the Strand Theatre, New York City, April 1952 (Frank Driggs Collection)

Born July 8, 1908, he mastered the saxophone during his formative years in rural Arkansas, before going on to accompany Ida Cox, Ma Rainey, Bessie Smith, and other major blues singers as a member of the legendary Rabbit Foot Minstrels revue. He first recorded with the Jungle Band for Brunswick in 1929, then moving to New York to play with Clarence Williams, among others, in the early 1930s. Joining Chick Webb's swing band on alto sax in 1936, he would also contribute vocals on blues and novelty material.

In 1938 Jordan struck out on his own, forming the Elks Rendezvous Band. Inking a record contract with Decca the following year, he changed the group's name to the Tympany Five. Mining the jump style of R&B, Jordan's sassy humor, punning, and driving rhythmic approach (further accentuated by his wordplay) were responsible for a long string of hits, including the following R&B chart toppers all on Decca: "What's the Use of Getting Sober," "Ration Blues," "G.I. Jive," "Mop Mop," "Caldonia," "Buzz Me"/"Don't Worry 'Bout That Mule," "Stone Cold Dead in the Market," "Choo Choo Ch'Boogie," "Ain't That Just Like a Woman," "Ain't Nobody Here but Us Chickens," "Texas and Pacific," "Jack, You're Dead," "Boogie Woogie Blue Plate," "Run, Joe," "Beans and Corn Bread," and "Saturday Night Fish Fry (Part 1)."

The rise of rock 'n' roll rendered his sound passé. Although no longer an important recording artist, he was still actively performing—particularly around his home base of Los Angeles—until suffering a fatal heart attack on February 4, 1975. His classic recorded work remains widely available today, most notably on Bear Family's monumental box set, *Louis Jordan: Let the Good Times Roll (1938–1954)*.

jungle

Jungle refers to a form of club music, combining breakbeats and samples, utilizing the staccato rhythms and subsonic bass of ragga (reggae with digital backing instrumentation). The tempo measures around 160 beats per minute. The genre grew out of HIP-HOP, with strong REGGAE influences as well; the name itself is widely felt to be a derivation of "junglist," Jamaican patois for a native of Trenchtown, the famous Kingston ghetto. Some music journalists have argued that jungle was a product of black's distaste for "white TECHNO." It was nurtured in clubs by the likes of DJ Ron, Randall, and Bobby Konders, and on both commercial (e.g., Jumping Jack Frost on Kiss-FM) and pirate radio (Kool FM, Transmission One, Don FM, etc.).

Pioneer recordings for the genre included Genaside II's "Narra Mine," Rebel MC's "Comin' On Strong," and virtually anything produced by Shut Up and Dance. Observers generally agree that jungle crossed over to the mainstream with SL2's 1993 hit, "On a Ragga Tip," followed by singles credited to Blame and Bubbles. Shortly thereafter, sampled chants were increasingly displaced by the practice—begun by traditional reggae acts—of voicing words over the rhythm figure; General Levy's "Incredible," released on the Renk label, was one of the earliest known examples of this phenomenon.

See also DUB; HOUSE.

Jungle Brothers

Eclectic RAP experimentalists, the Jungle Brothers have built their sound around elements of the full spectrum of African-American popular music genres, including R&B, soul, FUNK, and HOUSE. The group—which includes Mike G (born Michael Small, in 1969, in New York City's Harlem section), DJ Sammy B (b. Sammy Burwell, in 1968, in Harlem), and Afrika Baby Bambaataa (b. Nathaniel Hall, in 1971, in Brooklyn)—recorded first for the Warlock/Idlers dance label in October 1987 before moving on to Gee Street.

In addition to paying tribute to such seminal artists as JAMES BROWN, MARVIN GAYE (evident in their updated version of "What's Going On"), and HIP-HOP pioneer AFRIKA BAMBAATAA, they joined the NATIVE TONGUES POSSE with QUEEN LATIFAH, A

TRIBE CALLED QUEST, and others, which attempted to educate blacks regarding their role in history and African culture. Although mainstream commercial success has eluded them, LPs like *Straight Out the Jungle* (Idlers/Warlock, 1988), *Done by the Forces of Nature* (Warner, 1989), and *J Beez Wit the Remedy* (1993) garnered critical raves and a hardcore cult following.

Junior (b. 1961) *singer*

Born Norman Giscombe on November 10, 1961, the English-born singer was hyped in the 1980s as the future of UK soul. He made a big splash with the Top Ten British hit, "Mama Used to Say," which garnered a Grammy award. Although his other singles failed to do nearly as well—the exception being a 1987 duet with Kim Wilde, "Another Step Closer to You"—Junior has recorded a series of well-regarded albums, including *JI* (1982), *Inside Lookin' Out* (1983), *Acquired Taste* (1986), *Sophisticated Street* (1988), *Stand Strong* (1990), and *Renewal* (1992). He also joined forces with Billy Bragg, Jimmy Somerville, and Paul Weller in the formation of the vehicle for political activism, Red Wedge, in 1986.

Just-Ice *rapper*

Just-Ice (aka Justice) became famous overnight for decidedly nonmusical considerations. His name was prominently displayed alongside the *Washington Post* 1987 headline, "Murder, Drugs and the Rap Star." The text went on to say he'd been detained and questioned in connection with the murder of a drug dealer (although no charges were ever filed against him). The Washington, D.C., black community was sufficiently outraged by implied racism that they picketed the newspaper for a number of months.

Born Joseph Williams, Jr., in Ft. Greene, Brooklyn, he enjoyed a moderately successful recording career in the late 1980s. Notable albums included *Kool & Deadly* (Fresh, 1987) and *The Desolate One* (Sleeping Bag, 1989).

Juvenile (b. 1975) *rapper*

One of the leading exponents of the "dirty South" genre, Juvenile—born Terius Gray, in New Orleans—began performing as a teenager. His debut, *Being Myself* (Warlock, 1995), already exhibited the trademark bounce style—with club grooves and MC chatter front and center—for which he would become known. Although it revealed little of distinction beyond some tongue-in-cheek humor, the follow-up, *Solja Rags* (Cash Money, 1997), marked the beginning of Juvenile's longstanding association with Ronald "Suga Slim" and Brian "Baby" Williams's Cash Money combine.

No one was prepared for what came next. *400 Degreez* (Uptown/Universal, 1998) was a landmark album, built around tour de force wordplay and featuring two extraordinary tracks, the funky "Back That Azz Up" and "Ha" (supplemented by two remixes). Subsequent releases, however, were lackluster: *Tha G-Code* (Cash Money, 1999) was a highly derivative sequel, *Playaz of da Game* (D3, 2000) collects early 1990s tracks recorded prior to when Juvenile had fully realized his technical approach, and *Project English* (Uptown/Universal, 2001) represented a tentative effort to explore new musical territory.

Kam (b. 1971) *rapper*

Kam was a disciple of rapper ICE CUBE, drawing inspiration from the intergang scene in greater Los Angeles; however, rather than romanticizing the violence at the core of the Crips and Blood brotherhoods, he countered with pleas for unity in keeping with his Muslim beliefs. Born Craig Miller, in the Watts section of Los Angeles, he moved to Compton as a youth with his mother and brother. Ice Cube signed Kam as the first artist on his Street Knowledge imprint. His debut came with "Every Single Weekend" on the *Boyz 'n the Hood* soundtrack. He then guested on "Colorblind," a track on Ice Cube's *Death Certificate* (Priority, 1991), before releasing his own LPs, most notably, *Neva Again* (East West, 1992) and *Made in America* (East West, 1995).

KC & the Sunshine Band

KC & the Sunshine Band epitomized the infectious, dance-floor FUNK ascendant in the 1970s. Based in Miami, the group's punch pop sound represented a distillation of post-1960s soul (devoid of the sociopolitical agenda characterizing leading purveyors of the genre such as STEVIE WONDER, Sly Stone, and the O'JAYS) tinged with lilting Caribbean rhythms known as junkanoo.

KC—an interracial aggregate consisting of seven to 11 members—was the brainchild of vocalist/keyboardist Harry Wayne Casey and bassist Richard Finch. Together, they developed a strong regional reputation as a songwriting/studio production team, most notably with George McCrae, whose "Rock Your Baby" was named the top single of 1974 by *Rolling Stone.* The band released a string of top-selling hits during the latter 1970s, including "Get Down Tonight," "That's the Way (I Like It)," "(Shake, Shake, Shake) Shake Your Booty," "I'm Your Boogie Man," "Keep It Comin' Love," and "Please Don't Go." Although not considered an album act, their long-playing catalog (as well as twelve-inch singles) were solid sellers, particularly the debut, *KC and the Sunshine Band* (T.K., 1975), which remained on the *Billboard* Top 200 for 47 weeks.

Casey's involvement in a serious car accident in the early 1980s resulted in the cessation of the group's chart run. He would briefly return to the public eye billed as "KC" with the release of *KC Ten* (Meca, 1984), featuring the post-DISCO single "Give It Up," before fading back into obscurity.

K-Doe, Ernie (1936–2001) *singer*

Ernie K-Doe is seen by most popular music enthusiasts as a typical one-hit wonder. However, he knocked around the New Orleans rhythm and blues scene for many years, working with many of the local stars and producing a few best-selling singles under his own name.

Born Ernest Kador, Jr., on February 22, 1936, in New Orleans, he was the ninth of 11 children. Although raised by his aunt on his mother's side, he sang in the New Home Baptist Church, where his father served as minister. He toured with various gospel groups as an adolescent. At the age of

17, he relocated briefly to Chicago, recording his first secular tracks—four in all, none of which were released—as a solo artist.

Returning to New Orleans, he recorded for the legendary Savoy label in 1954 with the Blue Diamonds, whose membership also included Huey "Piano" Smith, Billy Tate, Frank Fields, and Earl Palmer. Going solo later in the decade, he recorded for both Specialty and Ember. Signed to Minit in the early 1960s, he would burst into national prominence with the tongue-in-cheek lament "Mother-in-Law" (which topped both the pop and R&B charts), featuring bass vocals by Benny Spellman. According to K-Doe, the song (composed by New Orleans producer Allen Toussaint) had special meaning to him. He allegedly retrieved it from a garbage can where Toussaint had thrown it, noting, "I was married 19 years, and it was 19 years of pure sorrow." Although moderately successful, his follow-up, "Te-Ta-Te-Ta-Ta," failed to establish him as a consistent hit-maker.

When his records stopped selling, K-Doe—typically wearing iridescent apparel and oversized gold rings—continued to offer a dynamic live show. He told Almost Slim (Jeff Hannusch), author of *Walking to New Orleans*, "I don't like to brag, but I still believe I can out-perform any man in show business. Ernie K-Doe can stop any show at the drop of a hat." He did return to the charts in the late 1960s with "Later for Tomorrow" and "Until the Real Thing Comes Along." By 1982, K-Doe was periodically hosting an R&B radio program on WWOZ, New Orleans. He continued to make music, contributing three new tracks to the mid-1989 compilation cassette *New Orleans: A Musical Gumbo*. He died in New Orleans on July 5, 2001.

Kelly, R. (b. 1969) *singer and producer*

Born Steven Williams in Chicago, R. Kelly emerged out of the New Jack Swing movement as frontman for the East Coast–based band, Public Announcement. They released two best-selling albums, *Born into the 90's* (Jive, 1992) and *12 Play* (Jive, 1993), which skillfully blended classic FUNK rhythms, updated HIP-HOP production values, and suave soul crooning. The latter record remains a benchmark work, selling more than five million copies; one track, "Bump n' Grind," logged 12 weeks as the number one R&B single as well as four weeks on top of the *Billboard* Hot 100.

Kelly opted to go solo in the mid-1990s. His recordings were mostly romantic ballads, and the most notable feature of his eponymous debut (Jive, 1995) was its carnal imagery. Nevertheless, it achieved sales of more than four million copies as well as including three platinum singles. He later won Grammy awards for Best Male R&B Vocal Performance, Best R&B Song, and Best Song Written Specifically for a Motion Picture or for Television—"I Believe I Can Fly," which appeared in the Michael Jordan film, *Space Jam* (1996). By then his crossover appeal was a foregone conclusion. In the meantime, he was in great demand as a studio producer, working with MICHAEL JACKSON, Celine Dion, and PUFF DADDY, among others. One of his biggest commercial successes came with Aaliyah.

Kelly's follow-up albums—the sprawling, experimental double-disc set, *R* (Jive, 1998), and the more radio-friendly *TP-2.Com* (Jive, 2000)—remained grounded in his core aesthetic: sinuous grooves and lush arrangements accented by soothing vocals that sugarcoat the explicit wordplay. More recent releases, however, have failed to match the success of his 1990s work. His collaboration with JAY-Z, *The Best of Both Worlds* (Universal, 2002), was something of an artistic and commercial disappointment, while the well-crafted *Chocolate Factory* (Jive, 2003) was overshadowed by the singer's legal difficulties, which included 21 counts of child pornography charges in Chicago and 12 additional counts in Polk County, Florida, as well as a number of other sex-related civil suits. Still, Kelly's career has displayed a resiliency that defies many industry observers; *Billboard*'s December 25, 2004, "Year in Music & Touring" issue listed him as 16th on its tabulation of Top Pop Artists.

Kendricks, Eddie (1939–1992) *singer*

Eddie Kendricks really had two careers, one as lead singer of the sweet soul juggernaut the TEMPTATIONS, and another in a solo capacity as a leading purveyor of 1970s FUNK. Within the MOTOWN stable of artists, only the great SMOKEY ROBINSON enjoyed comparable success as a recording artist in two guises.

Kendricks was born December 17, 1939, in Union Springs, Alabama, but was raised in Birmingham. Relocating to Detroit in the late 1950s, he joined the Primes, who later evolved into the Temptations. He remained with the group until 1971, when he opted for a solo career.

Kendricks's early records reveal a singer in search of his own trademark style; ranging from silky-smooth ballads to uptempo material, they were moderate hits at best. His breakthrough came with the propulsive dance track "Keep On Truckin' (Part 1)" (which reached number one on both the pop and R&B charts in 1973), followed by eight more R&B Top Ten smashes in succession, including the chart-toppers "Boogie Down" and "Shoeshine Boy."

The hits trailed off in the early 1980s, but Kendrick (who by now had dropped the letter "s" from his last name) returned to the public eye with a collaborative performance—along with former Temptations mate, David Ruffin, and the blue-eyed soul duo Daryl Hall and John Oates—at the re-opening of New York's Apollo Theater, released as an album entitled *Live At The Apollo with David Ruffin & Eddie Kendrick* (RCA, 1985). A Temptations medley culled from the concert, "The Way You Do the Things You Do/My Girl," was his last Top 20 single on the *Billboard* Hot 100. He continued to place duets with Ruffin on the R&B charts before succumbing to lung cancer on October 5, 1992.

Keys, Alicia (b. 1981) *singer*

Perhaps the most promising young R&B chanteuse of the 21st century, Alicia Keys was a childhood prodigy who began classical piano studies at age seven. While enrolled at the Professional Performing Arts High School in New York City, she met Conrad Robinson, who nurtured her considerable vocal talents. His brother, Jeff, would become her manager when Keys dropped out of Columbia University to focus on a music career.

Early record deals with Columbia, and then Arista, in the late 1990s did not result in any official releases. However, Keys struck paydirt in mid-2001 with her debut album, *Songs in A Minor*, on Clive

Alicia Keys and Usher perform at the 2004 MTV Europe Awards. (Alessia Pierdomenico/Reuters/Landov)

Davis's fledgling J label. A commercially savvy blend of soul, FUNK, jazz, and classical influences, it would reach number one on the *Billboard* Top 200, driven by two Top Ten singles, "Fallin'" and "A Woman's Worth," and net her five Grammy awards.

Subsequent recordings have done just as well. *The Diary of Alicia Keys* (J/RMG) was rated the fourth best album of the year in *Billboard*'s December 25, 2004 issue. She also earned the number two ranking in the Top Pop Artists and Hot 100 Artists categories, including three of the year's most successful singles: "If I Ain't Got You" (number three), "You Don't Know My Name" (number 29), and "Diary" (number 34), a collaboration with Tony! Toni! Tone! Further indication of her success came with the invitation to sing the National Anthem at the 2005 Super Bowl in Jacksonville, Florida. Keys took home four Grammy awards at the 2005 show, including Best R&B Album and Best R&B Song for "You Don't Know My Name."

Khan, Chaka (b. 1953) *singer*

A native of Great Lakes, Illinois, Yvette Marie Stevens grew up on Chicago's South Side. She first sang in a group at age 11, and went on tour with MARY WELLS with the Afro-Arts Theater troupe. She adopted her professional name in the late 1960s while working on the Black Panthers' Free Breakfast for School Children program. Dropping out of high school in 1969, she knocked around with a number of bands before bursting into the public consciousness as the lead singer of the FUNK ensemble, Rufus. Beginning with the 1974 Top Ten single, "Tell Me Something Good," Rufus produced a string of hit singles and albums until Khan's decision to go solo four years later.

Khan's debut, *Chaka* (Warner Bros., 1978), was a smash, propelled by popularity of the single, "I'm Every Woman." However, her next couple of albums got lost in the post-DISCO trauma of the early 1980s. She opted to record an assortment of jazz standards in 1982, *Echoes of an Era* (Warner Bros.), which won critical raves but left her even further from the pop mainstream. Nevertheless, she rebounded in spectacular fashion with the platinum-selling *I Feel for You* (Warner Bros., 1984); its RAP-tinged title track—a little-known Prince LP cut—won a Grammy. While rarely a factor on the pop charts, she has continued to be a major force within the R&B field up to the present day, winning another Grammy in 1990 for "I'll Be Good to You," a duet with RAY CHARLES. With the growth of interest in Khan's classic recordings, Warner Bros. has reissued much of her legacy both in the original albums and compilations such as *Epiphany: The Best of Chaka Khan, Vol. 1* (1996) and *I'm Every Woman: The Best of Chaka Khan* (1999).

Kid 'N Play

Kid 'N Play are one of the more pop-oriented HIP-HOP acts, parlaying an upbeat, Looney Tunes approach that led to their own TV cartoon series. The duo—consisting of Christopher Reid and Christopher Martin—first made a splash in the film, *House Party*, tempering their youthful braggadocio with middle class–friendly sentiments such as "Don't do drugs" and "Stay in school." Their albums—most notably, *2 Hype* (Select, 1988), which featured guest vocals by the REAL ROXANNE on "Undercover," *Kid 'N Play's Funhouse* (Select, 1990), and *Face the Nation* (Select, 1991)—featured slick, hook-laden production work by Hurby "Luv Bug" Azor.

King, Albert (1923–1992) *singer and guitarist*

At a time when even B. B. KING adopted a more soulful pop sound in order to achieve commercial success, Albert King was instrumental in keeping a traditional blues sound on the R&B charts. His raw, rootsy style—modeled on blues shouters like BIG JOE TURNER and Jimmy Witherspoon and bottleneck guitar specialists Elmore James and Robert Nighthawk—was a primary influence on a large number of late 20th-century blues musicians, including Robert Cray, Joe Louis Walker, and Donald Kinsey.

Born Albert Nelson on April 25, 1923, in Indianola, Mississippi, he performed live in Memphis area clubs as well as with the Harmony Kings gospel group between 1949 and 1951. By the early 1950s he had relocated to the Gary, Indiana–Chicago area, where he played occasionally on recording sessions for Chess. He would cut a series of tracks as a soloist for the label in the late 1950s and early 1960s, adhering closely to the prevailing Chicago blues style then being popularized by the likes of Muddy Waters and Howlin' Wolf. His first sessions as a leader, however, were recorded in St. Louis for the Parrot label (purchased by Chess in 1959); the surviving tracks—currently available on *Door To Door* (MCA, 1990)—include the self-penned "Bad Luck," "Merry Way," and "Murder." He was based in St. Louis by the mid-1950s, where his recordings for Bobbin brought him increased stature, but little commercial success.

King's first hit came in 1962 for the King/Federal firm (which owned his contract after purchasing Bobbin) with "Don't Throw Your Love on Me So Strong." As a result, the Memphis-based STAX label added him to its roster in the mid-1960s. Accompanied by members of the company's renowned house band, BOOKER T. & THE MGs, as well as the Bar-Kays and the MEMPHIS HORNS, he enjoyed a long string of chart successes, including "Laundromat Blues," "Crosscut Saw," "Cold Feet," "Everybody Wants to Go to Heaven," "I'll Play the Blues for You," "Breaking Up Somebody's Home," and "That's What the Blues Is All About." Many of his Stax albums—most notably, *Born Under a Bad Sign* (MFSL/Atlantic, 1967), *King Does the King's Things* (Stax, 1991), *Wednesday Night in San Francisco* (Stax, 1968), *Thursday Night in San Francisco* (Stax, 1968), *Years Gone By* (Stax, 1969), *I'll Play the Blues For You* (Stax, 1972), and *Blues at Sunrise* (Stax, 1973)—are still considered classics today.

King landed with Utopia/Tomato following Stax's descent into bankruptcy in 1974. His output, however, was marred by unsympathetic supporting players, bland arrangements, and a preponderance of brass and strings. His fortunes improved somewhat when he signed with Fantasy in the early 1980s. However, he was better appreciated live than on record during the decade preceding his death.

King, B. B. (b. 1925) *singer and guitarist*

When all has been said and done, it is likely that B. B. King will be recognized as the greatest figure in the history of blues music, bar none. Since first cutting tracks for Bullet in 1949, his recorded legacy stretches over seven decades; he continues to make vital music in the twenty-first century.

Born Riley B. King on September 16, 1925, in Itta Bena, Mississippi, he moved to Memphis in 1946, where he gained regional fame as a performing deejay. His moniker, "The Beale Street Blues Boy," would be contracted to "Blues Boy," and still later to "B. B."

B. B. King playing his guitar, Lucille (Frank Driggs Collection)

His success was largely confined to the R&B singles charts until the mid-1960s; his biggest hits—including the chart-toppers, "Three O'Clock Blues," "You Know I Love You," "Please Love Me," and "You Upset Me Baby"—came with RPM in the early 1950s. By the late 1960s, at a time when many black listeners considered his music to be anachronistic, he found a new audience among young white rock fans who'd been introduced to his work by British and American blues revival groups. As a result, albums became his primary focus, particularly following the highly successful ABC release, *Live at Cook County Jail* (1970). Over the years, he has earned a reputation as one of the hardest working performers in the music industry. On many occasions, he has explained that it has been necessary to spend 250–300 nights a years on the road in order to keep his musical organization steadily employed, something he has long considered his moral obligation.

King, Freddie (1934–1976) *singer and guitarist*
While overshadowed by the other bluesmen named King—ALBERT and B. B.—Freddie King was an emerging blues-rock star at the time of his premature death from a heart attack. His stinging guitar style, anchored by a propulsive rhythmic intensity and flawless technique, reflected the years spent perfecting his craft in the gritty clubs of Chicago's black districts.

Born Freddie Christian on September 30, 1934, in Gilmer, Texas, he moved to Chicago in 1950. Shortly thereafter, he began playing in area venues with bands headed by the likes of Little Sonny Cooper and Hound Dog Taylor. He also did session work for the local Parrot and Chess labels during the early 1950s. He eventually formed his own band, the Every Hour Blues Boys.

King's first solo recordings, for El-Bee Records in 1956, failed to have any commercial impact. By early 1961, however, he achieved success with the King/Federal label, due in no small part to the sure-handed guidance of producer–piano player SONNY THOMPSON. His biggest hits were divided between instrumental workouts—"Hide Away" and "San-Ho-Zay"—and searing vocal renditions—"Lonesome Whistle Blues" and "I'm Tore Down." By the mid-1960s King had recorded an impressive body of work for the Cincinnati-based firm; nevertheless, he signed on with Atlantic, which issued two LPs produced by the legendary saxophonist KING CURTIS.

Attempting to reach a mainstream audience in the early 1970s, he recorded three albums for Leon Russell's Shelter label. Although full of rock nuances, the raw vitality of classic cuts such as "Goin' Down" and "Big Leg Woman" revealed King at the height of his powers. His later work followed the then current vogue of placing American blues giants within a British framework (e.g., producer Mike Vernon and guitarist Eric Clapton), a formula already tried by Muddy Waters, Howlin' Wolf, and Bo Diddley, among others. The results were rather tepid, and any hopes of an artistic rebirth were dashed by his untimely death.

King is well represented on compact disc reissues. Both *Takin' Care of Business* (Charly) and *Texas Sensation* (Charly) compile the highlights of his King/Federal period. Also available are *Just Pickin'* (Modern Blues), a compilation of his instrumental tracks; *Texas Cannonball* (Shelter); and *Getting Ready* (Shelter).

King Curtis (1934–1971) *saxophonist*
Perhaps the best known saxophone soloist in rock history, King Curtis came out of the staccato, honking style of playing that evolved during the post–World War II R&B era. In addition to leaving his own recorded legacy, he worked with more than 125 other artists in the studio.

Born Curtis Ousley, on February 7, 1934, in Fort Worth, Texas, he performed in marching band and formed his own group while in high school. After graduation, he relocated to New York City, playing with such stars as Lionel Hampton and Horace Silver. He moved to a stint in Alan Freed's show band, and became a staff musician for Atlantic/Atco in 1958. There, he received wide recognition for his exciting solos on many of THE COASTERS' singles, most notably "Yakety Yak," and "Along Came Jones." Other artists wasted little time recruiting him to appear on their own recordings, including the Allman Brothers, RAY CHARLES, SAM COOKE, Eric Clapton, Bobby Darin, Delaney and Bonnie, SAM AND DAVE, and the SHIRELLES.

King Curtis balanced session work with his own prolific solo output, beginning with the LP, *Have Tenor Sax, Will Blow* (Atco, 1959). He recorded a major hit, "Soul Twist," in 1962 with his Noble Knights (later the Kingpins), and returned to the charts intermittently over the next decade, most notably with "Memphis Soul Stew" and "Ode to Billie Joe." He became more actively involved with production work in the late 1960s, and had just been appointed to be ARETHA FRANKLIN's musical director when he was stabbed to death in front of his New York apartment house on August 13, 1971.

Kirk, Rahsaan Roland (1936–1977) *saxophonist and flutist*

One of the most innovative musicians in jazz history, Kirk pioneered many unorthodox performing techniques, including circular breathing, playing two or three saxophones at once, and simultaneously singing and playing the flute. Beyond these novelties, his improvisational skills as a soloist and encyclopedic mastery of jazz styles, from Dixieland to free jazz, were of the highest order. In addition to incorporating many instruments rarely used within jazz (e.g., piccolo, harmonica, nose whistle), he designed the "trumpophone" (a trumpet with a soprano sax mouthpiece) and "slidesophone" (a down-scaled trombone/slide trumpet with sax mouthpiece).

Born August 7, 1936, Kirk lost his sight at the age of two when overmedicated by a nurse. Mastering a wide range of instruments as a youth, he cut the rhythm and blues-tinged *Triple Threat* (King, 1956), which featured his simultaneous playing of the tenor saxophone (fingered with the left hand),

the "manzello" (a modification of the saxello, itself a curved variant on the B-flat soprano sax) with the right, and the "stritch" (a modified E-flat alto) functioning as a drone. Relocating from Louisville to Chicago, he recorded *Introducing Roland Kirk* (Argo, 1960), which featured saxophonist/trumpeter Ira Sullivan. Although now securely within the jazz fold, he would retain a pronounced bluesy edge for the duration of his career.

Following a stint with Charles Mingus in 1961, Kirk did sessions for a variety of notable recording artists, including Quincy Jones, Roy Haynes, Tubby Hayes, Eddie Baccus, and Sonny Stitt. His own recorded output—much of which featured his backing group, the Vibration Society—was equally prolific. Critically acclaimed releases included *I Talk with the Spirits* (Limelight, 1964), an eclectic collection of material from musicals and seminal musicians like Django Reinhardt and Clifford Brown; the propulsive *Rig, Rig and Panic* (Limelight, 1965) and *Volunteered Slavery* (Atlantic, 1968), which reflected Kirk's pronounced commitment to African-American sociopolitical concerns. He died of a stroke in Bloomington, Indiana, on December 5, 1977.

Knight, Gladys (b. 1944) *singer*

Although never an innovator, Gladys Knight—with her backing group, the Pips (originally all close family members)—has enjoyed a long, successful career, first as a pop-soul singer, and, by the late 1970s, within the adult contemporary field. The Atlanta-based act began performing in the early 1950s, recording five chart singles (including the Top Ten R&B hits, "Every Beat of My Heart" and "Letter Full of Tears") for the independent labels Huntom, Fury, and Maxx, before signing with the MOTOWN subsidiary, Soul, in 1966. While not on a par with such commercial juggernauts as MARVIN GAYE, the FOUR TOPS, the TEMPTATIONS, and STEVIE WONDER, the group recorded a string of moderately successful hits with the company, including the original rendition of "I Heard It Through the

Grapevine," "The End of Our Road," "If I Were Your Woman," and "Neither One of Us," which peaked at number two on the *Billboard* Hot 100 in 1973, shortly before they switched to Buddah.

With Buddah they enjoyed a brief run in the upper echelon of the charts with best-selling singles such as "Midnight Train to Georgia," "I've Got to Use My Imagination," and "Best Thing That Ever Happened to Me." Always a highly capable outfit, effective at interpreting DOO-WOP–styled ballads, GIRL GROUP novelties, R&B/gospel rave-ups, and more conventional pop-soul fare, Gladys Knight and the Pips gradually took on more and more easy listening material once the mainstream hits stopped coming. They managed to top the R&B charts as late as 1987 with "Love Overboard." Not surprisingly for an artist who has been active for the better part of six decades, a wealth of anthologies are available that document all phases of Gladys Knight's career, most notably, *Anthology* (Motown,

1974), *Soul Survivors: The Best of Gladys Knight & the Pips 1973–88* (Rhino, 1990), *The Ultimate Collection* (Motown, 1997), and *Essential Collection* (Hip-O, 1999).

Kool and the Gang

While mainstream pop music fans were largely unfamiliar with Kool and the Gang when the effervescent "Celebration" topped the pop and R&B charts in 1980, they were the farthest thing from an overnight success. In fact, the band's core members had been working together for 17 years prior to the release of what would be their biggest record.

The origins of the group go back to frontman Robert "Kool" Bell's formation of a Jersey City–based combo, the Jazziacs, in 1964. The 14-year-old bassist started out doing session work and playing jam sessions on the Jersey circuit, complemented by brother Ronald Bell on tenor sax, trumpeter Robert "Spike" Mullins, alto saxophonist Dennis "D. T." Thomas, drummer George Brown, and lead guitarist Charles Smith. Later in the decade, the aggregate, now known as the SoulTown Band, began leaning increasingly in the direction of R&B and FUNK.

Shortly after renaming themselves Kool and the Gang in 1969, they garnered a recording contract with De-Lite. Their early releases, most notably, "Jungle Boogie," "Hollywood Swinging," "Higher Plane," "Rhyme Tyme People," and "Spirit of the Boogie," were heavily grounded in funk rhythms. The very "blackness" of such material made crossing over to the pop charts an unlikely proposition.

The onset of the DISCO era led to a discernable decline in their fan base; as a result, Kool opted to add lead singer James "J. T." Taylor, whose rich voice was well suited to ballads and other adult contemporary material, and SMOOTH JAZZ composer/producer, Eumir Deodato. The collaboration with Deodato resulted in two best-selling albums—*Ladies Night* (De-Lite, 1979), which included "Ladies Night" and "Too Hot," and

Gladys Knight and the Pips when they were part of the Motown roster in the late 1960s (Frank Driggs Collection)

Kool and the Gang during a performance on TV's Soul Train (Frank Driggs Collection)

Celebrate! (De-Lite, 1980). Although the group lost commercial momentum in the last years of the 1980s—their last chart hit was "Holiday" for Mercury in 1987—they have continued to perform up to the present day. In all, they placed 20 LPs and 44 singles on the charts.

KRS-One (b. 1965) *rapper*

KRS-One (Knowledge Rules Supreme Over Nearly Everyone) is best known for his humanistic leanings; he has promoted self-enlightenment and anti-violence through both his recordings and lectures on the college circuit. Known as "The Teacher" within the HIP-HOP community, he was the driving force behind the Stop the Violence Movement and 1991 H.E.A.L. (Human Education Against Lies) project, which featured contributions from a wide range of socially conscious artists, including Chuck D, QUEEN LATIFAH, R.E.M., and Billy Bragg.

Born Laurence Krisna Parker August 20, 1965, in the Bronx, New York, he teamed up with a social worker he met while staying at a local homeless shelter, Scott Sterling (aka DJ Scott LaRock), to form Boogie Down Productions. The duo's 1987 debut LP, *Criminal Minded*, remains a landmark recording, featuring a hard-hitting style that anticipated the gangsta RAP movement. Although Sterling was fatally shot in August 1987, KRS-One soldiered on with the additions of his brother, Kenny Parker, and D-Nice, releasing a string of albums—*By All Means Necessary* (Jive, 1988), *Ghetto Music: The Blueprint of Hip Hop* (Jive, 1989), *Edutainment* (Jive, 1990), and *Sex and Violence* (Jive, 1992)—notable for their innovative use of REGGAE stylings and social advocacy street verse.

Without changing his innovative approach to any discernable degree, KRS-One opted for a solo career in 1992. His CD releases—*Return of Da Boom Bap* (Jive, 1993), *KRS-One* (Jive, 1995), and *I Got Next* (Jive, 1997), which incorporated prominent DRUM AND BASS stylings—have enjoyed steadily increasing commercial success; as a result, at the onset of the twenty-first century he stood on the verge of superstardom.

K7

Blending Latin-tinged RAP with uptempo R&B arrangements, K7 became an overnight success with the catchy party anthem, "Come Baby Come" (Tommy Boy, 1993). The group—which consists of leader K7, DJ Non-Stop, LOS, Prophet, and Tre Duece—followed with an LP that focused on male bonding ritual, *Swing Batta Swing* (Tommy Boy, 1994). Given the mixed reception to this engaging, albeit uneven, set—ill-advised tracks included the bilingual "Zunga Zeng" and an awkwardly executed cover of "A Little Help from My Friends"—it is perhaps not surprising that K7 has been slow to issue any new material.

K-Solo *rapper*

K-Solo—which stands for Kevin Self Organization Left Others—is aligned with the now defunct Hit Squad, an EPMD spin-off that included Das EFX and Redman. Born Kevin Maddison, in Central Islip, New York, he worked with Parrish Smith

before the two contributed to EPMD's *Unfinished Business*. Smith oversaw production on K-Solo's debut LP, *Tell the World My Name* (Atlantic, 1990), which included the story-telling tour de force, "Tales from the Crack Side." Follow-up releases *Spellbound* (Atlantic, 1991) and *Times Up* (Atlantic, 1992) revealed increasing virtuosity as he gained the confidence to go his own way. K-Solo recorded an album with Death Row Records in 1996 that was never released, due to the legal troubles of the label.

Kurious (b. 1969) *rapper*

Kurious is one of the more articulate artists to populate the HIP-HOP scene, which is not surprising considering he attended Fairleigh Dickinson University in New Jersey. Born Jorge Antonio Alvarez, of Puerto Rican descent, he burst into the public consciousness in late 1992 with the underground hit, "Walk Like a Duck," which featured his associates, the Constipated Monkey crew. Based in uptown Manhattan, his improvisational style earned him the title, "Freestyle King."

His debut LP, *A Constipated Monkey* (Hoppoh, 1994), took several years to complete. Its release was held up in part due to protracted negotiations between Prime Minister Pete Nice's Hoppoh label and Russell Simmons of DEF JAM RECORDS; Alvarez had been hired as a messenger by the latter company in 1988, which led to a recording contract. However, Kurious instead chose to honor a verbal agreement with Nice while working on tracks with the Stimulated Dummies and the Beatnuts. The release experienced substantial crossover sales on the strength of the radio friendly single, "I'm Kurious."

Kwamé *rapper*

Growing up within the New York jazz scene, Kwamé appears to employ RAP conventions primarily to endow his work with a contemporary edge. Born Kwamé Holland, in East Elmhurst, Queens, he worked closely with the likes of Lionel Hampton and STEVIE WONDER as a youth. He recruited A New Beginning as his backing band both live and in the studio, resulting in a fluid spontaneity rare among HIP-HOP artists. His prolific output includes a string of hit singles—"Only You," "The Rhythm," "The Man We All Know and Love," "One of the Big Boys,"

"Nastee," and "Sweet Thing"—and albums: the Hurby "Luv Bug" Azor–produced debut, *The Boy Genius* (Atlantic, 1989); a loosely conceived concept set, *A Day in the Life—A Pokadelic Adventure* (Atlantic, 1990); *Nastee* (Atlantic, 1991); and *Incognito* (Wrap/Ichiban, 1993), which featured associates DJ Tat Money and A-Sharp.

LaBelle, Patti (b. 1944) *singer*

One of the most versatile and successful R&B artists ever in terms of career longevity, Patti LaBelle was born Patricia Holt in Philadelphia. She formed the Blue Belles, modeled after popular girl groups like the SHIRELLES and the Ikettes, in 1962. The quartet—including Nona Hendryx, Sarah Dash, and Cindy Birdsong—recorded a half-dozen charting singles between 1962 and 1967 for the Newtown, Parkway, and Atlantic labels, most notably, the Top 20 crossover hit, "I Sold My Heart to the Junkman."

The group soldiered on as a trio when Birdsong left to join the Supremes in 1967. In 1970, they hired British manager Vicki Wickham, who encouraged them to adopt a harder-edged FUNK sound as well as an updated moniker, LaBelle. Although failing to make the charts for a succession of labels—Warner Bros., RCA, and Track—in the early 1970s, they earned kudos for their collaboration with singer/songwriter Laura Nyro, *Gonna Take a Miracle* (1971).

Wickham instigated yet another makeover in 1973, with LaBelle taking on a glam-rock image accentuated by form-fitting, silver lamé space suits. They exploded into the limelight at the height of the DISCO era with the crossover number one smash about a New Orleans prostitute, "Lady Marmalade," which helped propel the accompanying LP, *Nightbirds* (Epic, 1974), into the Top Ten. Subsequent releases, however, failed to duplicate this success and the group splintered in early 1977 over creative differences between chief songwriters LaBelle and Hendryx.

All three members enjoyed a measure of success as solo vocalists. LaBelle far outpaced her former cohorts with two dozen hit singles through the 1980s, including the R&B chart-toppers "If You Only Knew" and "On My Own" (a duet with Michael McDonald, which also topped the *Billboard* Hot 100). Her best-selling album, *When a Woman Loves* (MCA, 2000), a collection of Diane Warren songs, revealed a new summit of artistic maturity, with LaBelle effectively negotiating a wide range of styles, including soul, HOUSE, and HIP-HOP.

Lance, Major (1942–1994) *singer*

One of the leading exponents of Chicago soul in the early 1960s, Major Lance, along with SMOKEY ROBINSON and the Miracles, who recorded the R&B and pop hit, "Mickey's Monkey," in 1963, is closely identified with the dance craze, the Monkey. Although he rarely creased the pop charts after 1965, Lance continued to produce rhythm and blues hits into the mid-1970s.

Born April 4, 1942, in Chicago, he started out as a professional boxer before signing with Mercury as a singer. His career took off after switching to Columbia's re-established OKeh subsidiary (famous as a "race" label in the 1920s), and hooking up with songwriter/producer Curtis Mayfield, then a member of the IMPRESSIONS. Lance's second release for the company, "The Monkey Time," with its distinctive horn-inflected orchestral arrangement, provided the template for later singles such as "Hey Little Girl" and "Um, Um, Um, Um, Um, Um."

Although squeezed off the pop charts by the influx of British Invasion artists, Lance remained active within the R&B field, moving on to Dakar Records in 1968, then Mayfield's Curtom label, Volt, Playboy, and Osiris. His last notable success—the last of 13 Mayfield compositions he placed on the R&B charts—was the 1970 single "Stay Away From Me (I Love You Too Much)." He died of heart disease in 1994.

Laquan (b. 1975) *rapper*

One of the great lost rappers, Los Angeles native Laquan revealed a considerable degree of sophistication in his youthful debut LP, *Notes of a Native Son* (4th & Broadway, 1990), particularly regarding its wordplay and treatment of sociopolitical concerns. Laquan's strident verses—e.g., accusing then President Bush of "living large while others starve"—belied the lush arrangements, built around a soul band and smooth backup singers, by producers Richard Wolf and Bret Mazur, perhaps best known for their work with Bel Biv Devoe. The release was greeted with indifference, however, and little has been heard of this promising artist in the intervening years.

Larks, The

The story of the Larks is really one of two different groups that possessed one common feature: lead singer Don Julian. The earliest manifestation of the act—which formed in 1953 and included tenor Ronald Barrett (later replaced by Glen Reagan), tenor Earl Jones, and bass Randy Jones—was known as Don Julian and the Meadowlarks. Although now revered as an R&B vocal group classic, their debut single for Dootone, "Heaven and Paradise," failed to make the charts. When it became evident that no hits were forthcoming, Julian moved on to other projects.

In the mid-1960s, Julian was inspired by the sight of a new teen dance to write "The Jerk." He recorded it in short order, naming his new group—comprised of Charles Morrison, Ted Waters, and himself—the Larks, while their backup band became the Meadowlarks. While the single, which reached number seven on the Hot 100, spurred a new dance craze, the Larks were unable to produce any follow-up hits. Nevertheless, the dance did inspire other best-selling records, most notably, the Capitols' "Cool Jerk" and the Miracles' "Come On and Do the Jerk."

LaSalle, Denise (b. 1939) *singer and songwriter*

A talented singer/songwriter, Denise LaSalle has also made an impact within the executive branch of the record industry. Along with husband Bill Jones, she has owned Crajon Productions since 1969.

Born Denise Craig on July 16, 1939, in LaFlore County, Mississippi, she moved to Chicago with her family in the early 1950s. LaSalle first recorded for Tarpen, a Chess subsidiary, in 1967, but switched to the Detroit-based Westbound label in the early 1970s, where she recorded a number one R&B hit, "Trapped by a Thing Called Love," shortly thereafter.

LaSalle consistently scored on the R&B charts in the 1970s, although crossover success for the most part eluded her. Her hits included "Now Run and Tell That," "Man-Sized Job," "Married, but Not to Each Other," and "Love Me Right." She would go to record for MCA and Malaco, among other labels, in the 1980s. After running out of steam by the mid-1980s, she chose to concentrate on the production side of the business.

Laswell, Bill (b. 1955) *producer and bandleader*

Bill Laswell has been termed a "postmodern Renaissance man," founding the Axiom label in 1988 through a partnership with ISLAND RECORDS, establishing Greenpoint Studio (1990), and pursuing new directions in the fusion of jazz, rock, and

FUNK, both as a producer and with his own band, Material.

Born February 12, 1955, in Salem, Illinois, and raised in Detroit, where he performed in funk groups, Laswell moved to New York City in 1978. Formed at the outset to accompany former Gong frontman, David Allen, on a U.S. tour, Material became a forum for Laswell musical experiments. Built around keyboardist Michael Beinhorn, drummer Fred Maher, and himself on bass, the group has negotiated many styles—including world music, avant-garde jazz, ambient music, HIP-HOP, and mutant rock—and collaborated with many artists (e.g., Nona Hendryx, Sonny Sharrock, Fred Frith, Henry Threadgill, Archie Shepp, Nile Rodgers, WHITNEY HOUSTON, and William Burroughs). Although outside the pop mainstream, Material's recordings—*Temporary Music* (Celluloid, 1981), *American Songs EP* (Red Music, 1981), *Busting Out EP* (ZE/Island, 1981), *Memory Serves* (Celluloid/Elektra Musician, 1982), *One Down* (Celluloid/Elektra, 1982), *Red Tracks* (Red, 1986), *Seven Souls* (Virgin, 1989), *The Third Power* (Axiom, 1991), *Live in Japan* (Restless, 1994), and *Hallucination Engine* (Axiom, 1994)—remain required listening for adventurous listeners.

Laswell has been widely sought after both as a session player and producer. He contributed bass on Laurie Anderson's *Mr. Heartbreak* (A&M, 1982) and has gone on to play with the Golden Palominos, Last Exit, the Last Poets, Brian Eno, David Byrne, Peter Gabriel, Fela Kuti, John Zorn, Bootsy Collins, and Buckethead, among others. In 1983 he cowrote and produced HERBIE HANCOCK's fusion hit, "Rockit," and won a Grammy for his work on Hancock's follow-up album, *Sound-System* (Columbia, 1983). His production of the HIP-HOP single "World Destruction," featuring AFRIKA BAMBAATAA and Johnny Lydon, also garnered considerable praise. Since then, he has produced a diversified array of artists, including Sly (Dunbar) and Robbie (Shakespeare), Mick Jagger, Motorhead, Iggy Pop, the Ramones, and Yellowman.

Latifah, Queen See QUEEN LATIFAH.

Lee, Julia, & Her Boyfriends

A veteran singer/pianist whose career predated the early days of blues recordings, Julia Lee (1902–58) enjoyed considerable success in the late 1940s specializing in risqué songs. Born October 31, 1902, in Boonville, Missouri, she performed with her father's band beginning at age four. She was a member of brother George E. Lee's band from 1920 to 1933, and first recorded for Merritt in 1927. Signed by Capitol Records in the aftermath of World War II and often utilizing the talents of jazz musicians like alto saxophonist Benny Carter, she placed ten singles on the R&B charts from 1946 to 1949, including "Gotta Gimme Watcha Got," "Snatch and Grab It," "King Size Papa," and "I Didn't Like It the First Time." Lee remained active until succumbing to a heart attack on December 8, 1958.

Leiber, Jerry (b. 1933), and **Mike Stoller**
(b. 1933) *songwriters and producers*
Jerry Leiber and Mike Stoller will be forever linked as pioneers of early rock 'n' roll. They met in New York City and, while still in their teens, wrote the classic songs "K.C. Loving"—a number one hit for Wilbert Harrison in 1959—and "Hound Dog," first a 1953 chart-topping hit for "Big Mama" Thornton, and one of the biggest hits of the rock era for ELVIS PRESLEY in 1956. They would become one of Presley's key sources for recording material, including the hits "Loving You" and "Jailhouse Rock."

Signing an independent production pact with Atlantic Records, Leiber and Stoller were responsible for string of chart successes by the DOO-WOP comedy group, the COASTERS, most notably, "Young Blood," "Yakety Yak," "Charlie Brown," and "Poison

Ivy." The duo would also produce many other artists (e.g., the DIXIE CUPS, the DRIFTERS, Peggy Lee, and Procol Harum), cutting across a wide range of musical styles.

Lewis, Bobby (b. 1933) *singer*
Born February 17, 1933, in Indianapolis, Lewis grew up in an orphanage before being adopted by a Detroit family at age 12. As a young man he worked at various jobs, including a traveling pot salesman, singing with a road show called Bimbo's, and as a part of the Soupy Sales organization.

Lewis first recorded for Parrot Records in 1952, followed by stints with Spotlight and Mercury later in the decade. In late 1958, JACKIE WILSON recruited him to be part of his New York–based band. There, he was able to secure a solo recording contract with Beltone in early 1961. His debut single, "Tossin' and Turnin' "—written by former Fireflies lead vocalist Ritchie Adams and accompanied by the Joe Rene Orchestra—resided at number one on the *Billboard* Hot 100 for seven weeks, becoming the top record of the year.

While his follow-up, "One Track Mind," sold well, only two other recordings—"What a Walk" and "I'm Tossin' and Turnin' Again"—managed to crease the charts. Nevertheless, Lewis continued to perform regularly in clubs and, later, as a member of rock 'n' roll revival troupes.

Lewis, Jerry Lee (b. 1935) *singer and pianist*
Jerry Lee Lewis was one of the great originals of 1950s rock 'n' roll, a dynamic showman possessing a lascivious vocal style, underscored by revved-up boogie-woogie piano playing that fairly leapt from the monaural grooves of his classic Sun records. The absence of a steady source of high-quality song material, combined with personal problems, severely curtailed his ability to sustain any kind of career momentum.

Born September 29, 1935, in Ferriday, Louisiana, Lewis grew up amidst a melting pot of music styles

(his cousins included gospel singer Jimmy Swaggart and country-pop star Mickey Gilley). Moving to Memphis, he soon signed a recording contract with the legendary Sun label. Alternating between honky tonk, rockabilly, rhythm and blues, and old folk standards in early recording sessions, Lewis struck paydirt with the talking blues–derived "Whole Lotta Shakin' Goin' On" in 1957, augmented by his superb improvisational gifts both as a singer and pianist as well as producer Sam Phillips's trademark echo. He stuck closely to this formula with the follow-up singles, "Great Balls of Fire" and "Breathless." By this time, Lewis was embroiled in controversies involving alleged bigamy and marriage to his 13-year-old cousin, Myra Gale Brown.

Arguably one of the most stubbornly egotistical and driven artists in popular music history, he soldiered on despite being virtually banned from important promotional outlets such as radio, television, and major performing venues. Signing with Smash (distributed first by Phillips, and then by Mercury) in 1963, Lewis released material focusing on his high-voltage live act and the growing nostalgia for early rock 'n' roll—e.g., *The Greatest Live Show on Earth* (Smash, 1964) and *The Return of Rock* (Smash, 1965)—before cultivating a country audience. However, despite a successful run of country and western singles—most notably, "What's Made Milwaukee Famous (Has Made a Loser Out of Me)," "To Make Love Sweeter for You," "There Must Be More to Love Than This," "Would You Take Another Chance on Me," "Chantilly Lace," and "Middle Age Crazy"—he kept on releasing albums aimed at a broader rock demographic. Moving on to Elektra in the late 1970s, and later MCA, Sire, and Warner Bros., Lewis—still dogged by controversy and exhibiting more attitude than most rappers—has continued producing new material in the face of significantly greater demand for his vintage Sun and Smash recordings. He was inducted into the Rock and Roll Hall of Fame in 1986, and was the subject of the 1989 biopic, *Great Balls of Fire,* starring Dennis Quaid.

Lewis, Ramsey (b. 1935) *keyboardist and bandleader*

One of the most consistently successful jazz-pop crossover artists, Lewis has continued to produce high-quality, albeit musically conservative, work for five decades. In addition to collaborating with drummer Max Roach, saxophonist Sonny Stitt, pianist Billy Taylor, trumpeter Clark Terry, vocalist Nancy Wilson, and many other established musicians, he helped nurture the careers of up-and-coming talent such as the Young-Holt Unlimited and drummer/vocalist Maurice White, who went on to found EARTH, WIND & FIRE. He has received countless awards for his contributions to the record industry, including Grammys for "The In Crowd" (a top five pop and R&B hit in 1965), "Hold It Right There" (from the 1966 Cadet album, *Wade in the Water*), and "Hang on Sloopy" (originally released as a best-selling single in 1965, it received an award in 1973 when reinterpreted for the 1972 Columbia LP, *Ramsey Lewis' Newly Recorded, All-Time, Non-Stop Golden Hits*).

Born May 27, 1935, Lewis was trained as a classical pianist at colleges based in his hometown of Chicago, while performing jazz and rhythm and blues professionally by his mid-teens. Forming the Ramsey Lewis Trio with bassist Eldee Young and drummer Isaac "Red" Holt in 1956, he released his debut LP, *Ramsey Lewis and His Gentlemen of Swing* (Argo, 1956). By the mid-1960s, he'd hit upon the lucrative commercial formula of reworking highly recognizable pop hits in a proto–SMOOTH JAZZ style. Hits in this mode included "A Hard Day's Night," "Wade in the Water," and "Up-Tight." His albums from this period also sold well, most notably *The In Crowd* (Argo, 1965), *Hang On Ramsey!* (Cadet, 1966), and *Wade in the Water*.

With progressive rock and fusion in vogue by the 1970s, Lewis incorporated a heavy, improvisational framework into his recordings. *Sun Goddess* (Columbia, 1974), augmented by STEVIE WONDER–influenced synthesizer touches and soaring vocals by Earth, Wind & Fire on the title track (a hit single in its own right), proved to be the biggest seller of his career. He continued to explore new musical approaches in the 1980s, most notably, orchestrated jazz in *Close Encounters with the Philharmonic Orchestra* (CBS, 1988). He has lightened his recording activities somewhat in recent years, due to the demands of hosting radio and television programs, the production of commercials with son Kevyn, and teaching at Roosevelt University in Chicago.

Lewis, Smiley (1920–1966) *singer*

Although he recorded a number of classic rhythm and blues tracks in the 1950s, he labored in the shadow of fellow New Orleans musician FATS DOMINO. They also shared songwriter/bandleader/producer Dave Bartholomew and local session players like Huey "Piano" Smith.

Born Overton Amos Lemons on July 5, 1920, in Union, Louisiana, he moved to New Orleans at age 11 with his parents. He began recording for DeLuxe in 1947, billed as "Smiling Lewis." His first hit came in 1952 with "Bells Are Ringing." Later chart smashes included "I Hear You Knocking," "One Night (Of Sin)," and "Please Listen to Me." At the height of his popularity, his "Shame Shame Shame" was included in the soundtrack of the 1956 film, *Baby Doll.* Although he never had a pop hit, other artists found mainstream success with covers of his songs, most notably TV sitcom star Gale Storm with "I Hear You Knocking," ELVIS PRESLEY with a sanitized reading of "One Night (of Love)," and British retro-rocker Dave Edmunds with yet another version of "I Hear You Knocking."

Seeking to rekindle his career, Lewis signed with OKeh in 1961. When no hits resulted, he moved on to the Nashville-based Dot label, then to Loma Records (where he worked with famed producer Allen Toussaint). He continued performing on the southern club circuit until his death from stomach cancer on October 7, 1966. His music remains available, however, via reissues such as a four-CD box set on the Bear Family label.

Lewis, Terry   See JAM, JIMMY, and TERRY LEWIS.

Lifers Group

This one-off project had inmates from New Jersey's Rahway State Penitentiary employing a gangsta rap format to warn those who were on a fast track to do prison time. The brainchild of Maxwell Melvins (inmate 660604), the set was recorded over a three-month period under the sponsorship of Disney-funded Hollywood Basic Records. The resulting album, *Belly of the Beast* (1991), and companion video, depicted a harrowing world defined by violence, cramped living quarters, and dull, controlled routines.

Liggins, Joe, & His Honeydrippers

Vocalist/pianist/composer/bandleader Joe Liggins—born in 1915 in Guthrie, Oklahoma—was known for the "big band" sound he achieved with his small combos. A fixture on the R&B charts from 1945 to 1951, he is best remembered for "The Honeydripper" (number one for 18 weeks in late 1945) and "Pink Champagne" (number one for 13 weeks in 1950). He continued to record and perform until his death from a stroke on August 1, 1987.

Lil' Kim (b. 1975) *rapper*

Born Kimberly Jones in the Bedford-Stuyvesant section of Brooklyn, Lil' Kim grew up in the area's federal housing projects. As a teen, her parents separated, and she went to live with her father. When he threw her out of the house, she became a street MC, eventually attracting the attention of the NOTORIOUS B.I.G. B.I.G. drafted her to guest on Junior M.A.F.I.A.'s hit single, "Player's Anthem," and 1995 album, *Conspiracy.* She followed with her own CD, the sexually explicit *Hard Core* (Undeas, 1996), co-produced by B.I.G. The record, which entered the pop charts at number 11 due in large part to its effervescent dance arrangements, represented something of a challenge

to the misogynistic posturing of male gangsta rappers.

Seemingly poised to become a superstar, Lil' Kim largely dropped out of sight following the murder of her good friend and mentor, B.I.G., the following year. With the exception of a Top 30 collaboration with MISSY "MISDEMEANOR" ELLIOTT, "Hit 'Em Wit da Hee," released in summer 1998, she did not issue any further recordings until *The Notorious K.I.M.* (Undeas, 2000), which shot up to number four on

Lil' Kim (Fred Prouser/Reuters/Landov)

Billboard's Top 200. She remains highly visible to the present day, a favorite of such fellow performers as Pink, Christina Aguilera, and Phil Collins, as well as paparazzi who lovingly document her outrageous fashion statements.

Lil' Louis *singer*

Lil' Louis specializes in progressive dance music, whether pushing the envelope within the realm of song lyric content or cross-genre fertilization. The son of Bobby Sims, a leading Chicago-based blues guitarist who has worked with the likes of B. B. KING and Bobby "Blue" Bland, Lil' Louis burst onto the pop scene with the 1989 club single, "French Kiss," which was banned by the BBC and at the New York venue featuring seminal DJ Frankie Bones, due to the presence of female heavy breathing. He handled the vocals, production, and most of the instrumental work on his debut LP, *From the Mind of Lil' Louis* (London, 1989), an eclectic affair which incorporated soul, jazz, and HOUSE influences. By the time of his second album release, *Journey with the Lonely* (London, 1992), he had relocated to New York and exhibited even more pronounced jazz influences. Later releases, however, attracted little in the way of sales or media attention.

Lil Soldiers

Perhaps the youngest rap act to record a HIP-HOP album, Lil Soldiers comprised brothers Ikeim and Freequon, who were ages nine and seven, respectively, when *Boot Camp* (No Limit, 1999) was released. The work was a disconcerting listening experience, not so much because youngsters were addressing gangsta themes, but rather the inability of the duo's lightweight voices to pack the punch needed for Beats by the Pound's hook-filled production work. Furthermore, their tag-team vocals rarely, if ever, seemed to be in synch with each other. Given this mediocre showing, it is not surprising that a follow-up has not been forthcoming.

Lipps, Inc.

One-hit wonders abounded during the disco era, but few enjoyed the degree of success Lipps, Inc. had with the Casablanca single "Funkytown." The group was a Minneapolis-based studio concept put together by songwriter/producer/multi-instrumentalist Steven Greenberg. "Funkytown" was more of an elongated dance club riff, featuring reverb-enhanced vocals by Cynthia Johnson, the 1976 Miss Black Minnesota U.S.A., and countless audio special effects. It spent four weeks at number one and 23 weeks on the *Billboard* Hot 100 (both rare feats at the time); although it failed to do quite as well on the R&B charts, it hung on at number two for five weeks.

Greenberg did have four more modest hits: "Rock It," "How Long," "Hold Me Down," and "Addicted to the Night." However, DISCO's retreat from the pop mainstream back to the clubs, combined with post-punk's increasing interest in dance-floor beats, spelled the end of the line for Greenberg's project.

Little Anthony & the Imperials

Few DOO-WOP groups had the long-term staying power of Little Anthony & the Imperials. They were able to assimilate the musical trends of three different decades—the R&B vocal group sound of the 1950s, 1960s soul, and the FUNK-inflected pop of the 1970s—in order to remain a commercially viable recording act.

Leader Anthony Gourdine (born January 8, 1940) first recorded as a member of the DuPonts in 1955 for the Winley label. He would form the Chesters in 1957; the Brooklyn-based group—who changed their name to the Imperials a year later—consisted of Clarence Collins, Tracy Lord, Glouster Rogers, and Ernest Wright, Jr. After signing with End, the Imperials recorded three hits in the late 1950s, featuring Gourdine's tremulous lead vocals: the classic "Tears on My Pillow," "So Much," and a tropical fantasy, "Shimmy, Shimmy, Ko-Ko-Bop."

Although they failed to reach the charts for almost five years, the Imperials continued to find steady work as performers, particularly the nightclubs across the country. They regained their hit-making touch in the mid-1960s with a more adult contemporary-oriented sound, first with the melodramatic "I'm on the Outside (Looking In)," followed by "Goin' Out of My Head," and "Hurt So Bad."

When things went sour with the DCP label, the Imperials moved on to United Artists in the late 1960s, and Avco in the mid-1970s. Despite their failure to release any popular recordings since 1975, they have remained box-office staples, from the oldies circuit to Las Vegas, on the strength of a slick stage routine and backlog of old hits.

Little Beaver (b. 1945) *singer and guitarist*
Little Beaver was something of the FUNK genre's version of a one-hit wonder. Born Willie Hale on August 15, 1945, in Forrest City, Arkansas, the singer/guitarist first performed professionally as a 13-year-old. He backed Birdlegs & Pauline in 1962, and was in demand as a session player beginning in 1964. His guitar work was a key ingredient in Betty Wright's crossover Top Ten hit, "Clean Up Woman." He first recorded as a solo artist for Phil-L.A. of Soul in the late 1960s. He placed five singles on the R&B charts in the 1970s, most notably, the uptempo "Party Down."

Littlefield, Little Willie (b. 1931) *singer*
Vocalist/pianist/guitarist Little Willie Littlefield enjoyed a brief run of popularity on the rhythm and blues charts in the late 1940s and early 1950s. He is best remembered for recording the original version for Federal of the R&B classic, "Kansas City," composed by JERRY LEIBER AND MIKE STOLLER in 1952 as "K.C. Lovin.'"

Born September 16, 1931, in El Campo, Texas, Littlefield first recorded for Eddie's in 1946. Relocating to Los Angeles in 1949, he produced several Top Ten R&B hits for the Modern label:

"It's Midnight," "Farewell," and "I've Been Lost." Although confined to the chitlin' circuit, he continued to perform and release recordings through the 1970s. After touring Europe in 1978, he settled in the Netherlands, and has continued to tour in Europe into the 21st century.

Little Richard (b. 1932) *singer and pianist*
One of the leading pioneers of early rock 'n' roll, Little Richard's frenetic singing style helped bring down the covering phenomenon, whereby the major labels assigned mainstream singers to record smoothed-over versions (often with sanitized lyrics) of original R&B hits geared to the pop charts. Although teen crooner Pat Boone garnered comparable sales with awkward covers of two early Little Richard songs—"Tutti Frutti" and "Long Tall Sally"—Little Richard's remaining hits faced no competition in crossing over to a mainstream audience.

Born Richard Wayne Penniman on December 5, 1932, in Macon, Georgia, his primary musical influences as a youth were singing in the church choir and playing saxophone in his high school band. When bluesman Buster Brown's singer failed to show up at a local concert, Richard—then age 14—filled in. While touring with the band, he began wearing his trademark pompadour and was billed as "Little Richard" for the first time. He was working variety shows when Zenas Sears—a WGST, Atlanta deejay—helped him get a contract with RCA. His first session on October 16, 1951, resulted in four recordings: "Every Hour" (a hit in the Georgia area due to on-the-air plugs by Sears), "Goin' to Get Rich Quick," "Taxi Blues," and "Why Did You Leave Me." He would cut four more tracks on January 12, 1952, but they failed to catch on with the public. He then recorded eight songs (with his group the Tempo Toppers) on February 25 and October 5, 1953, for the Houston-based Peacock label, again with negligible results.

Little Richard spent the next couple of years touring the Southeast with his new backup band, the Upsetters. A tip from R&B singer Lloyd Price led him to send a demo tape to Specialty Records in February 1955. Producer BUMPS BLACKWELL sensed his potential for communicating the same kind of gospel-blues blend that had made RAY CHARLES a star. The first session produced "Tutti Frutti," which reached number two on the R&B chart (and number 17 on the pop listing despite the Boone cover). Over the next three years, Little Richard recorded a prodigious number of hits (mostly his own compositions), including "Long Tall Sally"/ "Slippin' and Slidin'," "Rip It Up"/"Reddy Teddy," "She's Got It"/"Heebie Jeebies," "The Girl Can't

Help It," "Lucille"/"Send Me Some Lovin'," "Jenny, Jenny"/ "Miss Ann," "Keep A Knockin'," and "Good Golly, Miss Molly." His popularity was reinforced by appearances in three early rock 'n' roll films: *Don't Knock the Rock, The Girl Can't Help It,* and *Mister Rock 'n' Roll.*

Despite his wild performing antics and gender-bending lifestyle, Little Richard felt a calling to become a preacher. By the late 1950s he was only performing religious music; however, he decided to return to rock music in 1963. Subsequent recordings for a variety of labels— including VEE-JAY, OKeh, Reprise, and Green Mountain—failed to generate more than moderate sales. By the early 1970s he was appearing in rock 'n' roll revival shows and expanding into non-musical endeavors. His critically acclaimed acting role in the 1986 motion picture, *Down & Out in Beverly Hills,* represented his most notable post-1950s artistic achievement.

Little Richard looking debonair in 1957 (Frank Driggs Collection)

L. L. Cool J (b. 1968) *rapper*

Born James Todd Smith in Bay Shore, New York, L. L. Cool J (which stands for Ladies Love Cool James) began recording RAP demos while in high school, one of which attracted the attention of producer Rick Rubin. The ensuing 1984 single, "I Need a Beat," sold 100,000 units, providing the impetus for DEF JAM RECORDS and placed L. L. Cool J at the forefront of the East Coast school of rappers. His assertive, street tough style proved commercially viable on the mainstream pop charts. His debut LP, *Radio* (Def Jam, 1986), reached number 46 on the *Billboard* Top 200, while the follow-ups, *Bigger and Deffer* (Def Jam, 1987) and *Walking with a Panther* (Def Jam, 1989), made the Top Ten.

Although his collaboration with producer MARLEY MARL, *Mama Said Knock You Out* (Def Jam, 1990), garnered a Grammy, L. L. Cool J's effort to satisfy both pop and gangsta rap fans caused his early 1990s work to vacillate between clichéd hardcore posturing and macho self-parody. He revived his career, however, with the stripped-

Rapper L. L. Cool J performing (Albert Ferreira/Reuters/ Landov)

down FUNK of *Phenomenon* (Def Jam, 1997) and the chart-topping *G.O.A.T. Featuring James T. Smith: The Greatest of All Time* (Def Jam, 2000). Now something of an rap institution with a career spanning three decades, L. L. Cool J maintained his success with *The Definition* (Def Jam), ranked 125th in *Billboard*'s year-end compilation of the most popular albums in 2004.

L. L. Cool J has also pursued a successful acting career with major roles in movies such as *Any Given Sunday, Charlie's Angels, Deep Blue Sea, Halloween H20: 20 Years Later,* and *S.W.A.T.*

Lone Star Ridaz

A RAP supergroup comprising much of the Houston-based Dope House roster—including Baby Beesh, Fat Joe, Grimm, Russ Lee, Low G, Merciless, Max Minelli, Javi Picasso, Rasheed, and South Park Mexican—the Lone Star Ridaz were formed in the late 1990s. Enlisting producer Happy Perez, the predominantly Chicano act has released three polished, stylistically diverse albums: *Lone Star Ridaz* (Dope House, 1999), *Wanted* (Dope House, 2001), and *40 Dayz/40 Nightz* (Dope House, 2002). Each rapper—generally featured in combinations of two or three per song—possesses his own distinctive flow and dialect; the releases were also appended by chopped and skewed mixes of the strongest tracks. These works have been cited as proof that Houston has become one of the leading U.S. rap scenes.

Long, Shorty (1940–1969) *singer*

Born Frederick Earl Long on May 20, 1940, in Birmingham, Alabama, he relocated to Detroit in 1959. The singer/songwriter/pianist first recorded for the Tri-Phi label in 1962. Signing with the MOTOWN combine in the mid-1960s, he would release a couple of minor hits—"Function at the Junction" and "Night Fo' Last"—before breaking out with the novelty, "Here Comes the Judge." The Top Ten crossover hit would have been an even greater success if a competing version recorded by comedian Pigmeat Markham hadn't sold almost as many copies. Long drowned in Ontario, Canada, on June 29, 1969.

Love, Darlene   See BLOSSOMS, THE.

L.T.D.

The North Carolina group—first known as Love Men, Ltd., and then Love, Ltd.—first attracted attention backing Sam & Dave. After adding lead vocalist/drummer Jeffrey Osborne, they relocated to Southern California, working with singer Merry

Clayton, among others. L.T.D.—which stood for "Love, Togetherness, and Devotion"—signed with A&M in 1976, recording a string of hits through 1983, including the R&B chart-toppers "Love Ballad," "(Every Time I Turn Around) Back in Love Again," and "Holding On (When Love Is Gone)." Osborne's departure in 1980 for a solo career left a creative void in the group, despite the additions of Leslie Wilson and Andre Ray.

L'Trimm

The photogenic female RAP duo—consisting of Tigra (b. 1970, in New York City) and Chicago native Bunny D.—broke into the public consciousness with *Grab It!* (Time X/Atlantic, 1988), which included the title track hit, an answer song to SALT-N-PEPA's "Push It." Popular follow-up LPs, *Drop That Bottom* (Atlantic, 1989) and *Groovy* (Atlantic, 1991), continued to mine the same locker-room sexuality of the debut until the public lost interest.

Ludacris (b. 1977) *rapper*

The Atlanta-based Ludacris is a testament to the weaknesses inherent in the major labels' dominance of the record industry. Long before becoming the first artist signed to DEF JAM South, he found success with the private release, *Incognegro*, which featured the local hit, "What's Your Fantasy." He crossed over to the mainstream with *Back For the First Time* (Def Jam South, 2000), driven by the single, "Southern Hospitality." He continued his ability to balance intimate rhymes with street anthems with such Dirty South classics as *Word of Mouf* (2001), *Stand Up* (2003), and *The Red Light District* (2004). Now one of the most popular rappers around, he also made a play for the online file-sharing crowd with *Ludacris Live at Napster.*

Lutcher, Nellie (b. 1915) *singer*

The leading female rhythm and blues vocalist of the late 1940s, the multitalented Nellie Lutcher was also a first-rate piano accompanist and composer. The sister of singer and saxophonist Joe Lutcher, she was born on October 15, 1915, in Lake Charles, Louisiana. She joined Clarence Hart's band in 1930, before establishing her home base on the West Coast five years later. When Dave Dexter of Capitol Records heard her on a March of Dimes Benefit Concert broadcast in 1947, he offered her a record contract. She produced a string of hit recordings through early 1950, most notably "Hurry on Down," "He's a Real Gone Guy," "The Song is Ended (But the Melody Lingers On)," and "Fine Brown Frame." She was profiled on Ralph Edwards's television program, *This Is Your Life,* in 1953. She continued to record into the early 1960s and perform into the 1990s.

Lymon, Frankie, & the Teenagers

Frankie Lymon was one of the true greats of post–World War II R&B, a multitalented singer/songwriter/actor/dancer who electrified the pop music scene as a 13-year-old before falling on hard times. Born on September 30, 1942, in New York City, Lymon formed his back-up group, first known as the Premiers, in the Bronx in 1955. The group, known later as the Teenagers, whose members included tenors Herman Santiago and Jimmy Merchant, baritone Joe Negroni, and bass Sherman Gaines, recorded a half-dozen doo-wop-styled Top Ten R&B hits in an 18 month span beginning in February 1956. These included the chart-topper "Why Do Fools Fall in Love" (a number six pop smash as well), "I Want You to Be My Girl," "I Promise to Remember"/"Who Can Explain?", "The ABC's of Love," and "Out in the Cold Again." The group also appeared in two successful Hollywood films—*Rock, Rock, Rock* and *Mister Rock 'n' Roll*—while still a bankable commodity.

When the Teenagers lost their commercial momentum, Lymon tried to make it as a solo act. When success eluded him, he seemed to lose control of his life, dying of a drug overdose on February 28, 1968.

Madonna (b. 1958) *singer and songwriter*
It is easy to dismiss Madonna's superstar status as the product of her considerable flair for self-promotion. Beyond her physical allure, seemingly never-ending repertoire of fashion statements, and effective career moves, Madonna's success owed much to the irresistible pull of her dance-oriented rock recordings. In her best music, the elements—somewhat pedestrian arrangements, synthesizer lines, and programmed drum beats; competent, though not particularly distinguished singing; and hook-laden, if not profound compositions—added up to a much more impressive whole, with the emphasis on personality, an ingredient best showcased via the video medium.

Born Madonna Louisa Veronica Ciccone in Bay City, Michigan, on August 16, 1958, she burst into the public consciousness with her "Jellybean" Benitez–produced eponymous LP (Sire, 1983) which heralded the return of the DISCO ethic (sans that outré label) to the pop music scene. The chart-topping *Like a Virgin* (Sire, 1984)—produced by former Chic guitarist Nile Rodgers, and featuring the breakthrough hits, "Like a Virgin" and "Material Girl"—elevated her (at this juncture, in her Boy Toy manifestation) to iconic status. Her place in the pop culture pantheon now assured, she embarked upon a series of ambitious artistic statements—the eclectic tour de force, *True Blue* (Sire, 1986), best remembered for the anti-abortion plea in "Papa Don't Preach"; the remix collection, *U Can Dance* (Sire, 1987), featuring material first appearing on the three earlier albums; the socially conscious *Like a Prayer* (Sire, 1989); and a hits compilation, *The Immaculate Collection* (Sire, 1990), which included considerable studio editing of the originals (e.g., Q-sound remastering, faster tempos, earlier fade-outs, segueing of tracks)—punctuated by forays into film acting and book production.

Madonna's recorded output (and the public reception) was more uneven in the 1990s. *Erotica* (Maverick, 1992) was a sensual, pulsating workout; its comparatively poor commercial showing seems to have influenced her decision to produce a more intimate, low-key LP, *Bedtime Stories* (Maverick, 1994). Following her success in the movie adaptation of Andrew Lloyd Webber's *Evita,* and the album *Selections from Evita* (Warner Bros., 1997), which featured highlights from the original two-disc soundtrack, she attempted to update her sound by enlisting TECHNO producer William Orbit for *Ray of Light* (Maverick, 1998). She perfected her electronica-inspired approach in *Music* (Maverick, 2000), darting effortlessly from club grooves to trip-hop and synth-based ambient textures. Newly committed to a more domestic lifestyle in the 21st century, it appears likely that future recordings will continue to incorporate contemporary trends within a seamless, beat-inflected framework, emphasizing production values over image-making.

Magnificents, The
Although the Magnificents enjoyed only one real hit, "Up on the Mountain," they have long been recognized for a distinctive ensemble sound built

around an impeccable rhythmic sense. Although members of the group knocked around the edges of the music business for decades, the Magnificents were an active recording unit for barely a year.

The group—originally consisting of lead tenor Johnny Keyes, tenor Thurman "Ray" Ramsey, tenor Fred Rakestraw, and bass Willie Myles—formed in 1953 as the Tams to perform at an annual talent show sponsored by Hyde Park High School on Chicago's South Side. A local deejay known as the Magnificent Montague caught their act, and became their manager. Christening them the Magnificents, he was instrumental in eventually getting them a contract with local R&B label, VEE-JAY.

Their initial session in early 1956 yielded the number nine R&B single, "Up on the Mountain," which grew out of the bass-line motif from a widely sung street song, "Newborn Square." The resulting uptempo track, produced by Montague, was built around Myles's low-end scatting and Keyes's off-kilter lead vocal. Its success propelled the group into a nonstop touring grind, occasionally punctuated by rushed studio sessions.

The demise of the Magnificents was triggered by a dispute with Vee-Jay and Montague over money in the spring of 1957. With their label assigning prestigious gigs to other groups, the Magnificents—now including Keyes, Rakestraw, former Five Frenchmen tenor Reggie Gordon, and bass Rufus Hunter, formerly of the Five Bells—struggled through the summer before disbanding. Gordon hooked up with the Rays, who had recently hit with "Silhouettes," Hunter joined the Cameos, and Keyes and Rakestraw signed up as members of Thurston Harris's backup ensemble. In the meantime, Montague assembled another Magnificents group, who recorded for Vee-Jay without notable success in 1958.

The Magnificents would be resurrected in the 1960s by Ramsey to play the nightclub circuit and, later, in the 1980s, to appear at oldies concerts. Beginning in 1991, Keyes fronted yet another version of the group with former 1950s associates

Gordon, Hunter, and Julius Hawkins. He would also chronicle the R&B vocal group scene in his self-published book, *Du-Wop*.

Manhattans, The

The Jersey City–based Manhattans were one of the most successful soft soul groups of all time. Composed of lead singer George Smith (died of spinal meningitis in 1970 and replaced by Gerald Alston), tenors Edward Bivins and Kenneth Kelly, bass Winfred Lovett, and baritone Richard Taylor, they first recorded for Piney in 1962. Despite their mastery of the romantic ballad, only two of their more than 40 R&B hits spanning the mid-1960s through the 1980s cracked the pop Top 30: the crossover chart-topper "Kiss and Say Goodbye" (1976) and "Shining Star" (1980).

Marathons, The See JAYHAWKS, THE

Marchan, Bobby (1930–1999) *singer*

Due to the nature of record label credits and the marginal role of the rock press prior to the British Invasion, Bobby Marchan is virtually unknown to contemporary popular music fans. Nevertheless, he appeared on a number of seminal R&B hits in the late 1950s and early 1960s.

Born Oscar James Gibson on April 30, 1930, in Youngstown, Ohio, Marchan received musical training as a youth in the church choir. He began performing in the area while still attending East High School. His first recording was "Chick-A-Wa-Wa" in 1955. He was recruited to join Huey "Piano" Smith's New Orleans-based backup group, the Clowns, in 1958. He sang lead on a number of Smith's classic singles, most notably "Don't You Just Know It."

In early 1959, Marchan left the Clowns and formed the Tick Tocks. When that project failed, he signed a solo recording contract with the Fire label in 1960. Shortly thereafter, he produced a smash with the soulful "There's Something on Your Mind." Although Marchan continued to work on the periphery of the music business for many more years, he failed to have any further chart success. He died of liver cancer on December 5, 1999.

Mar-Keys, The

The Mar-Keys were one of the early proponents of the Memphis sound, a classic variant of 1960s soul that blended gritty, down-home country FUNK with a more urbane, uptown brand of rhythm and blues. They were also a precursor of the MEMPHIS HORNS, a loose group of studio players that placed their distinctive stamp on much of the music coming out of this recording center at the time.

The Mar-Keys formed in 1958 as a four-piece instrumental combo playing local dances in the Memphis area. Expanding to incorporate brass in 1960, the group's personnel—guitarist Steve Cropper, bassist Donald "Duck" Dunn, drummer Terry Johnson, keyboardist Jerry Lee "Smoochee" Smith, tenor saxophonist Charles "Packy" Axton, baritone saxophonist Don Nix, and trumpeter Wayne Jackson—became staff musicians for Satellite Records (owned by Axton's mother, Estelle, and rechristened STAX when threatened with a lawsuit by another similarly named label). Their first—and biggest—hit, "Last Night," with its repetitious, rock-steady brass riff, established a formula that the band milked for the better portion of the decade.

The Mar-Keys' momentum was slowed somewhat when Cropper and Dunn departed shortly thereafter to form BOOKER T. & THE MGs with organist Booker T. Jones and drummer Al Jackson. Nevertheless, the band continued to periodically place releases—most notably, "Morning After," "Pop-Eye Stroll," and "Philly Dog"—on the charts.

Marley, Bob (1945–1981) *singer and songwriter*

Although Bob Marley enjoyed limited commercial success in the United States, he remains the most important artist to have come out of the REGGAE movement. He was not only a wonderfully expressive vocalist and competent guitarist, but a first-rate composer; songs like "Stir It Up," "Guava Jelly," and "I Shot the Sheriff" were covered by Johnny Nash, Eric Clapton, and others, thereby facilitating the international acceptance of reggae. The uncompromising sociopolitical beliefs outlined in much of his later work—most notably, "Them Belly Full (But We Hungry)," "Revolution," and the title track from *Natty Dread* (Island, 1975), and his observations on the plight of Africa in *Survival* (Island, 1979)—continue to be instructive to listeners worldwide.

Born February 2, 1945, in St. Ann's, Jamaica, Marley's earliest singles from the 1962–63 period—"Judge Not (Unless You Judge Yourself)" and "One Cup of Coffee"—displayed a distinct preference for the emerging ska and bluebeat styles rather than the more established calypso. By 1964 he had formed the first edition of the Wailers, then a vocal quintet (initially billed as the "Wailin' Wailers") including Peter Tosh, Bunny Livingston (aka Bunny Wailer), Junior Braithwaite, and Beverley Kelso. Teaming up with seminal Jamaican producer Coxsone Dodd, they issued a string of successful singles on the Studio One and Coxsone labels during the mid-1960s. In 1967, following a brief stay in the U.S., he reunited the Wailers (now a trio including Tosh and Livingston) and formed his own record company with the assistance of American soul singer JOHNNY NASH. Strongly influenced by producer Lee "Scratch" Perry and Rastafarian doctrine, Marley and his cohorts (expanded in 1970 to include brothers Aston Barrett on bass and Carlton Barrett on drums) evolved from a ska/rhythm and blues vocal act to a pioneering reggae group over the course of several years.

By 1971 the Wailers had founded a label, Tuff Gong, and were producing their own material. It was the group's affiliation with Chris Blackwell's ISLAND RECORDS, however, that facilitated the distribution of their music worldwide. Although Island continued to issue their material on singles, albums became the band's creative focus. Although Tosh and Livingston departed for solo careers in

1974, Marley continued producing work of uniformly high quality, including *Catch A Fire* (Island, 1973), *Burnin'* (Island, 1973), *Rastaman Vibration* (Island, 1976), *Exodus* (Island, 1977), *Kaya* (Island, 1978), and *Uprising* (Island, 1980), until his death from brain cancer on May 11, 1981. Due to Marley's legendary status in parts of Europe, Africa, North America, and, of course, Jamaica, recordings spanning his entire career have been widely reissued, from the original Island LPs to varied anthologies.

Marl, Marley (b. 1962) *producer*

Born Marlon Williams, September 30, 1962, in Queens, Marley Marl is one of the most prolific producers on the HIP-HOP scene, combining old-school pop music values with cutting-edge sampling techniques (e.g., incorporation of the SP1200 synthesizer on the influential *Eric B for President*). His client list reads like a who's who of rap, including Big Daddy Kane, Biz Markie, Masta Ace, MC Shan, and Roxanne Shante, all of whom worked on his collaborative all-star team, the Juice Crew. He also played a seminal role in the development of the genre serving as host for the weekly WBLS-FM, New York radio show, *Rap Attack*.

Marl's recordings functioned as state-of-the-art samplers for COLD CHILLIN', the New York–based record company he founded in the mid-1980s after starting out as a mixer for the hip-hop/electro label Tuff City. *In Control, Volume I* (Cold Chillin', 1988) featured his then revolutionary repertoire of drum loops and JAMES BROWN samples on tracks built around Chuck D of PUBLIC ENEMY, Craig G., Heavy D, Kool G Rap, and L. L. COOL J, among other artists. *In Control, Volume II* (Cold Chillin', 1991) utilized a new wave of decidedly mediocre acts, including Kevy Kev, MC Amazing, and MC Cash. *House of Hits* (Cold Chillin', 1995) focused once again on major stars, ranging from hardcore selections by Kane and Kool G Rap to off-the-wall takes by Biz Markie and Masta Ace. *Re-Entry* (Beat Generation, 2001) was plagued by a predominance of lesser talents and faceless instrumentals, suggesting that Marl was essentially finished as a creative producer.

Marsalis, Branford (b. 1960) *saxophonist and bandleader*

The Branford Marsalis legacy has always been problematic to the jazz purist. Although widely held to be one of the most technically capable of the "new traditionalists"—the youthful vanguard in the contemporary scene dedicated to exploring the hard bop and modal jazz from the post–World War II era—he has also willingly immersed himself in the FUNK, rhythm and blues, and rock music currently in vogue with his peers.

Marsalis was born August 26, 1960, in New Orleans. Following stints with the Lionel Hampton Orchestra, Clark Terry, and Art Blakey's Jazz Messengers, Branford joined brother Wynton Marsalis's band in 1981. He played tenor and soprano saxophones on Wynton's recordings until leaving to work with ex-Police vocalist Sting in 1985. He appeared on Sting's *The Dream of the Blue Turtles* (A&M, 1985) and . . . *Nothing Like the Sun* (A&M, 1987) before starting his own quartet. Utilizing his group as a vehicle for serious jazz as his brother had done, Branford has released a string of critically acclaimed LPs over the years, including *Scenes in the City* (Columbia, 1984), *Royal Garden Blues: Romances for Saxophone* (Columbia, 1986), *Random Abstract* (Columbia, 1988), and *Requiem* (Sony, 1999), a tribute to his former keyboard associate, Kenny Kirkland.

Branford's collaborations with other artists, however, have spanned a wide range of popular music styles. He has contributed to recordings by PUBLIC ENEMY (political rap), the Neville Brothers (R&B/funk), TINA TURNER (black contemporary), the Grateful Dead (rock), and Bruce Hornsby (album-oriented rock), with whom he won a Grammy for Best Pop Instrumental Performance ("Barcelona Mona"). He has also supplied music to film soundtracks, most notably,

Spike Lee's *Mo' Better Blues* (Columbia, 1990), and has acted in *Bring on the Night, School Daze,* and *Throw Mama From the Train.* He was perhaps most criticized for serving as musical director of *The Tonight Show,* starring Jay Leno, between 1992 and 1995; he would eventually leave due to the creative limitations imposed upon him by the variety show format.

Martha & the Vandellas

Formed in 1960 by Martha Reeves and school chums Rosalind Ashford, Gloria Williams, and Annette Sterling (Beard), the group—originally called the Del-Phis—initially recorded a single for the Checkmate label. When the record failed to find an audience, they gravitated to MOTOWN. After doing back-up vocal for other artists, they were signed to the Gordy imprint.

Although Martha & the Vandellas never fit the so-called Motown mold—i.e., pliable singers that could be bent at the will of company songwriters and producers to achieve a desired sound—their dynamic, soulful approach resulted in a long string of 1960s R&B and pop hits, including "Come and Get These Memories," "Heat Wave," "Dancing in the Street," "Nowhere to Run," and "Jimmy Mack." The exit of the songwriting/production team Holland-Dozier-Holland from Motown in the late 1960s undermined the group's commercial momentum as much as changing trends and numerous personnel changes. Martha & the Vandellas remained active into the early 1970s before disbanding.

Marvelettes, The

An archetypal girl group, the Marvelettes—composed of Inkster (Michigan) High School friends Gladys Horton, Katherine Anderson, Juanita Cowart, Georgeanna Marie Tillman Gordon, and Wanda Young—formed in 1960. Signed to Tamla the following year, their debut single, "Please Mr. Postman," would become the first MOTOWN record to reach the top of the *Billboard* Hot 100. Although not considered one of the more distinctive Motown acts, the group enjoyed considerable success throughout the decade. It managed to soldier on when Cowart and Gordon departed in 1965. When Horton—who'd shared lead vocal duties with Young—left in 1967 (she was replaced by Anne Bogan), however, the Marvelettes were unable to maintain the creative chemistry that had previously sustained them. Following a few lackluster releases, the group disbanded in 1969.

Mase (b. 1977) *rapper*

Mason Durrell Betha, born in Jacksonville, Florida, relocated to Harlem with his family at age five. Following a couple of years in Florida during his early teens (where he had been sent due to concerns about peer pressure from unsavory elements), he started rapping in order to entertain friends on his high school basketball team. Shortly after being offered a scholarship to play at the State University of New York at Purchase, he adopted the name Mase Murder and joined the rap act, Children of the Corn. The group disbanded when a member died in an auto accident, and Mase hooked up with PUFF DADDY (Sean Combs) at an Atlanta music conference in 1996.

After appearing as a guest rapper on a string of Combs productions—most notably, with the NOTORIOUS B.I.G., MARIAH CAREY, Brian McKnight, and BUSTA RHYMES—he achieved superstardom with his debut album, *Harlem World* (Bad Boy, 1997), which topped the charts during the first two weeks following its release. Mase's distinctively simple, laid-back raps featured a wide array of guests, including Combs, Black Rob, DMX, Eightball & MJG, JAY-Z, Lil' Cease, LIL' KIM, the LOX, Monifah, 112, and Rhymes, and production by JERMAINE DUPRI, the Hitmen, and the NEPTUNES, among others.

Prior to the release of his second album, *Double Up* (Bad Boy, 1999), Mase remained in the news through collaborations with the likes of Brandy, Cam'ron, Harlem World, Blackstreet, and Mya, and an April 1998 arrest on disorderly conduct charges.

Although reaching number 11 and achieving gold sales, its commercial potential was severely undermined by Mase's pre-release announcement that he was retiring from the entertainment business in order to enter the ministry. He remained exclusively committed to his new course—working with inner city youth, giving inspirational speeches, and writing a memoir, *Revelations: There's Light After the Lime*—until the release of the relatively subdued *Welcome Back* (Bad Boy, 2004), rated one of the most popular albums of the year (number 152) by *Billboard*.

Masekela, Hugh (b. 1939) *trumpeter and bandleader*

Hugh Masekela is known as something of a one-hit wonder in the United States, despite a lengthy career marked by his experiments with jazz and various forms of ethnic African music within a pop context. He would later comment in *Rolling Stone* regarding his 1968 number one single, "Grazing in the Grass": "It was all very contrived. It happened because I came along about the time Herb Alpert was making it big with his 'South American sound,' so MCA figured that they would make me into a black Herb Alpert. I did it but it wasn't what I wanted—I wanted the fulfillment of playing something that was *me*."

Born April 4, 1939, in Wilbank, South Africa, Masekela—whose father was a noted sculptor—was raised by his grandmother prior to attending missionary schools. He began playing piano at age seven, but switched to trumpet when he saw *Young Man with a Horn* (1950), the Bix Beiderbecke biopic starring Kirk Douglas. He was a member of the Huddleston Jazz Band until leader Father Trevor Huddleston, a priest and anti-apartheid activist, was forced to leave the country. He then formed the Merry Makers of Springs, and toured in the late 1950s with the orchestra for the musical *King Kong,* the Jazz Epistles (reputedly the first band to record jazz in South Africa), Dollar Brand, and Miriam Makeba, his wife from 1964 to 1966.

In 1959, Masekela received a scholarship to the Royal Academy of Music, London, with the assistance of British orchestra leader, John Dankworth. A year later—with Harry Belafonte playing benefactor—he acquired a four-year scholarship at the Manhattan School of Music. He formed his own band in 1965, and released recordings on a designer label, Chisa. His instrumental albums were released to MCA's Uni subsidiary; *Hugh Masekela's Latest* (Uni, 1967), *Hugh Masekela Is Alive and Well at the Whiskey* (Uni, 1968), *The Promise of a Future* (Uni, 1968), and *Masekela* (Uni, 1969)—which featured the big R&B hit, "Riot"—would become nationwide best-sellers.

Masekela opted for a fusion sound in the 1970s, with *I Am Not Afraid* (Blue Thumb, 1974); *The Boy's Doin' It* (Casablanca, 1975); and a collaboration; *Herb Alpert/Hugh Masekela* (Horizon, 1978)—including the minor R&B hit, "Skokiaan"—which reached the pop LP charts (number 70). Although remaining active as a performer, his last commercial success came with the Jive single, "Don't Go Lose It Baby."

Master P (b. 1970) *rapper and record company executive*

Master P played a leading role in the explosion of the southern RAP genre into the pop mainstream during the late 1990s. Born Percy Miller in New Orleans on April 29, 1970, he grew up moving back and forth between the Louisiana Delta and Richmond, California. In an attempt to provide a greater diversity of hip-hop offerings at his California record store, No Limit, he formed the No Limit label in 1990. His early releases—*Get Away Clean* (In-A-Minute, 1991), *Mama's Bad Boy* (In-A-Minute, 1992), and *The Ghetto's Tryin' to Kill Me!* (No Limit, 1994)—were strongly influenced by the laid-back FUNK popular in the nearby Oakland area.

Master P relocated to New Orleans, where he joined forces with the local production team, Beats by the Pound, to adapt the prevailing gangsta genre to the southern vernacular and cultural milieu. The albums *99 Ways to Die* (No Limit, 1995) and *Ice Cream Man* (No Limit, 1996) sold well without the benefit of a notable radio or video hit. With his empire peaking in popularity, *Ghetto Dope* (No Limit, 1997) and *MP Da Last Don* (No Limit, 1999) topped the charts on the strength of straightforward verses espousing a materialistic lifestyle and toe-tapping, bass-heavy arrangements. Attempting to expand beyond his base gangsta constituency and shifting his attention to promoting the career of his son, Lil Romeo (and pursuing his dream to be a professional basketball player), Master P's more recent releases have lost a substantial market share to newly emerging rivals such as the Atlanta-based crunk acts and the New Orleans-based Cash Money Millionaires combine.

Mayfield, Percy (1920–1984) *singer, bandleader, and songwriter*

Vocalist/pianist/composer Percy Mayfield was one of the pioneering rhythm and blues bandleaders, bringing a new level of sophistication to a genre then dominated by its rustic Mississippi Delta and Carolina Piedmont blues roots. Born August 12, 1920, in Minden, Louisiana, he relocated to Los Angeles in 1942. In the days before crossover success was a viable goal, he recorded a string of a major R&B hits with the Specialty label in the early 1950s, including "Please Send Me Someone to Love"/ "Strange Things Happening," "Lost Love," "What a Fool I Was," "Prayin' for Your Return," "Cry Baby," and "Big Question."

He occasionally resurfaced with moderate sellers for Tangerine, RCA, and Atlantic in the 1960s and 1970s. In the meantime, he worked as a staff writer for the likes of RAY CHARLES (for whom he composed the classic "Hit the Road, Jack"). He remained active as a performer and recording artist until his death from a heart attack on August 11, 1984.

Mayfield, Curtis See IMPRESSIONS, THE.

McCoy, Van (1944–1979) *bandleader and producer*

Had he not died of a heart attack on July 6, 1979, Van McCoy might have made a far greater impact upon the music business. Nevertheless, during his short life he enjoyed some measure of success as a singer, pianist, bandleader, A&R man, producer, and record company owner.

Born January 6, 1944, in Washington, D.C., McCoy started out singing in rhythm and blues vocal groups in the late 1950s. Following a stint with the Marylanders, he formed his own ensemble, the Starliters; they would record briefly for End in 1959. McCoy established the record company, Rock 'N, in 1960 as a means of getting his material out to the public (by the mid-1960s he would own the more successful Maxx label). He was also an A&R man for Scepter/Wand from 1961 to 1964, and produced the likes of the SHIRELLES, GLADYS KNIGHT, the DRIFTERS, the STYLISTICS, and Brenda & the Tabulations. The demand for his services led to the creation of Van McCoy Productions in 1968. He wrote and produced most of the 1970s records for the most successful of his discoveries, Faith, Hope & Charity.

McCoy's own recording career took a while to gather momentum. Following a couple of minor R&B hits in the mid-1970s, he broke through with the chart-topping disco instrumental smash, "The Hustle," backed by the Soul City Symphony. He continued to enjoy moderate success with follow-up releases—most notably, "Change with the Times" and "Party"—prior to his death.

MC Lyte (b. 1971) *rapper*

Born Lana Moorer on October 11, 1971, in Queens, New York, MC Lyte was one of the earliest female RAP stars to project a hard-edged image. At age 12 she was trading rhymes with half brother Milk and his Audio Two partner, Gizmo. They achieved moderate success in 1987 with "I Cram to Understand You (Sam)," an indictment of crack addiction, released on First Priority, a label founded by her father, Nat Robinson.

Lyte made a substantial impact on the rap scene with her first two album releases, *Lyte as a Rock* (High Priority/Atlantic, 1988) and *Eyes on This* (High Priority/Atlantic, 1989), dissing—among others—rival rapper Roxanne Shante, game-show hostess "Vanna Whyte," dope-dealing hustlers, and sex-scamming homeboys. From 1991's *Act Like You Know* (First Priority/Atlantic) onward, she experimented with her established formula, attempting to incorporate new influences and stay abreast of current fashions. She remains an outspoken social and political activist, contributing public service announcements for the Rock the Vote movement and working continuously in the fight against AIDS.

MC Shy D *rapper*

Born Peter Jones in the Bronx, he is the cousin of HIP-HOP pioneer, AFRIKA BAMBAATAA. Although relocating to the Atlanta area, he would retain his New York City roots in his recorded work. Signing with Luther Campbell's Luke Skyywalker label in 1987, he released *Got to Be Tough* (Luke, 1987), a raw, hard-edged work built around boasting lyrics and music created by a drum machine, scratching, and extensive sampling. After two similar follow-ups, *Comin' Correct in '88* (Luke, 1988) and *Don't Sweat Me* (On Top, 1989), he dropped out of sight for a time. *The Comeback* (1993) was arguably his most mature work, featuring updated production values and a stripped-down rapping delivery. He disappeared again for several years before releasing *Recordnize*, featuring bass producer DJ SMURF. He also made guest appearances on several of DJ Smurf's late 1990s releases.

McFerrin, Bobby (b. 1950) *singer*

A one-of-a-kind talent, McFerrin possesses the ability to reproduce vocally the sound of virtually any musical instrument as well as many other natural sounds. Born March 11, 1950, in New York City, to opera-singing parents, he studied piano rather than voice at the Juilliard School in New York and Sacramento State College. Following stints playing piano with University of Utah dance workshops and singing in various journeyman bands, he was asked to join Jon Hendricks's jazz group. On the strength of highly acclaimed solo performances at the Playboy Jazz Festival (1980) and Kool Jazz Festival (1981), he was signed to a recording contract by Elektra.

From the beginning, McFerrin's releases ran contrary to traditional notions of jazz vocalizing. He performed without instrumental backup, combining his multitextured voice with rhythmic body slaps to simulate full-band accompaniment. His material—a blend of original compositions and covers—spanned the classical, jazz, soul, funk, and pop genres. After a series of moderately selling albums, he broke through with a chart-topping (and Grammy-winning) 1988 single, "Don't Worry Be Happy" (Capitol). By the late 1980s, he seemed to be everywhere: collaborating with jazz stars (HERBIE HANCOCK, the Manhattan Transfer, Chick Corea), classical musicians (Yo-Yo Ma), and film star narrators (Robin Williams, Jack Nicholson); recording the theme to *The Cosby Show;* and providing the accompaniment to a number of television commercials.

McGhee, Stick (1918–1961) *guitarist and singer*

The younger brother of folk/blues performer Brownie McGhee, Stick McGhee (sometimes known as "Globetrotter" or "Sticks") was an important R&B recording artist in his own right immediately following World War II. Born Granville H. McGhee on March 23, 1918, in Knoxville, Tennessee, the vocalist/guitarist became a national sensation with the crossover classic "Drinking Wine, Spo-Dee-O-Dee, Drinking Wine," which he recorded as Stick McGhee & His Buddies. It bested competing versions by WYNONIE HARRIS and Lionel Hampton and was later covered by JERRY LEE LEWIS (a Top 20 country hit), among others. He returned to the upper reaches of the R&B charts with an instrumental, "Tennessee Waltz Blues," before fading from the public eye. He died of cancer on August 15, 1961.

McGriff, Jimmy (b. 1936) *organist*

Like his contemporaries Jimmy Smith and Brother Jack McDuff, organist Jimmy McGriff played jazz with a decided R&B edge. Born James Herrell on April 3, 1936, in Philadelphia, he toured with Don Gardner, Arthur Prysock, and other R&B performers early in his career. He continued to release pop-oriented instrumentals as singles throughout the 1960s, achieving crossover hits with "I've Got a Woman, Part 1," "All About My Girl," "Kiko," and "The Worm." He has remained active through much of the century.

McNeely, Big Jay (b. 1927) *saxophonist and bandleader*

Tenor saxophonist/bandleader Big Jay McNeely was the creator of the unfettered honking style central to R&B and rock 'n' roll in the 1950s. Born Cecil James McNeely on April 29, 1927, in Los Angeles, he toured with a small combo (including, in his heyday, Melvin Glass, Leonard "Tight" Hardiman, and brothers Bob and Dillard McNeely) in the late 1940s and continued well into the 1980s. Although far more influential live than on record, he did have three notable R&B hits: "Deacon's Hop," "Wild Wig," and "There Is Something on Your Mind." He continues to perform and offers saxophone lessons.

McPhatter, Clyde (1932–1972) *singer*

Clyde McPhatter was a major force in the evolution of rhythm and blues toward mainstream pop music. He is also remembered for serving as lead tenor for a time in two seminal DOO-WOP groups: Billy Ward and the Dominoes and the DRIFTERS.

Born November 15, 1932, in Durham, North Carolina, the son of a Baptist minister, McPhatter first sang gospel in church. Following a move to Teaneck, New Jersey, at age 12, he developed an interest in R&B. In 1950, he was hired by an up-and-coming black vocal group, the Dominoes. His sexy, tremulous tenor voice elevated the Dominoes to the big leagues as steady R&B hitmakers with the Federal label, most notably "Sixty-Minute Man" (number one for 14 weeks), "Have Mercy, Baby" (number one for 10 weeks), and "The Bells."

In 1953, McPhatter moved on to form his own ensemble, the Drifters, in June 1953. Signed by Atlantic Records, the group immediately began producing a string of R&B classics, including "Money Honey" and the widely censored "Honey Love," which topped the charts for 11 and eight weeks, respectively. McPhatter's popularity was such that he was encouraged by label head Ahmet Ertegun to embark simultaneously upon a solo career. His career momentum was halted, however, when he was drafted into the army in 1954.

Discharged in 1956, McPhatter decided to focus on solo work, enjoying increasing crossover success with hits such as "Treasure of Love," "Long Lonely Nights," and "A Lover's Question." He remained popular well into the 1960s after switching to the Mercury label, most notably with "Ta Ta." However, the British Invasion spearheaded by the Beatles changed musical tastes and led to his fall from commercial favor. Stints with MGM, Amy, and Bell Records in the latter half of the 1960s produced little of note, and McPhatter's skills as a live performer were eroded by an ongoing battle with alcoholism. He reportedly died from a heart attack while visiting friends in Manhattan, June 13, 1972. Notable collections of his best work include *Deep Sea Ball: The Best of Clyde McPhatter* (Atlantic, 1991), *The Forgotten Angel* (2 CDs; 32 Jazz, 1998), and *A Shot of Rhythm and Blues* (Sundazed, 2000), the latter consisting of both sides of his five 1965–67 Amy singles plus four previously unreleased alternate takes.

Meaux, Huey P. (b. 1929) *producer and record company executive*

One of the prime movers in post–World War II Texas popular music, Huey P. Meaux was born March 10, 1929, in Kaplan, Louisiana. He started out as a music entrepreneur in the 1950s, acquiring masters for lease to various record companies. He turned to production work after establishing studios in Houston and Jackson, Mississippi, during the 1960s, achieving success with recordings such as Barbara Lynn's "You'll Lose a Good Thing," Roy Head's "Treat Her Right," and B. J. Thomas's "I'm So Lonesome I Could Cry." He also formed several record labels to help disseminate his efforts, including Tribe, which helped the Sir Douglas Quintet break out with "She's About a Mover" in 1965.

Meaux's career lost momentum following a conviction for violation of the Mann Act (transporting a minor across state lines for immoral purposes) in 1967. He returned in style by producing a series of Tex-Mex classics for Freddie Fender, including the 1975 number one single, "Before the Next Teardrop Falls." He began concentrating on roots music, doing production for bluesmen like Johnny Copeland, T-Bone Walker, and Johnny Winter, as well as Rockin' Sydney, who enjoyed a crossover smash in 1985 with the Cajun standard "My Toot Toot." David Byrne also hired him to play a deejay in the 1986 film, *True Stories*. His papers are housed in the Center for American History at the University of Texas, Austin.

Meco (b. 1939) *producer*

Meco proved to be the perfect prototype for a DISCO era producer. His recordings, both for other artists and under his own name, blended seamless pop production values (e.g., a rich palette of instrumental colors, strong melodic hooks) with a pulsating beat tailor-made for the dance floor.

Born Meco Monardo on November 29, 1939, in Johnsonburg, Pennsylvania, he started out doing arranging for the broadcast media. By the 1970s, he had branched out to the pop-R&B field, doing production for GLORIA GAYNOR's club classic "Never Can Say Goodbye" and Carl Douglas's "Doctor's Orders." Fascinated by George Lucas's blockbuster sci-fi film *Star Wars* (which he paid to see 11 times), he decided to adapt its theme music to the pop single format. In addition to hiring the requisite session musicians, he arranged, produced, and played piano and trombone on "Star Wars"/"Cantina Band" (which topped the Hot 100 in 1977), outselling the sound-

track version by the London Symphony Orchestra in the process. Meco continued to mine movie themes well into the 1980s, enjoying hits with reworked material from *Close Encounters of the Third Kind, The Wizard of Oz* (complete with Toto's barking and hysterical laughing from the Wicked Witch of the East), *The Empire Strikes Back,* and *Return of the Jedi.*

Memphis Horns, The

The Memphis Horns are best remembered as a key ingredient in the arrangements of many classic soul hits, particularly for AL GREEN, Al Johnson, Ann Peebles, and other artists on the STAX and Hi labels. A spin-off of the 1960s instrumental group the MAR-KEYS, the group's lineup—although constantly changing over time—was built around two core members, trumpeter Wayne Jackson and tenor saxophonist Andrew Love, and was typically supplemented by baritone saxophonist James Mitchell, trombonist Jack Hale, and tenor saxophonist Ed Logan (or Lewis Collins).

The group also achieved notable R&B success recording under its own name, releasing such albums as *Memphis Horns* (Cotillion, 1970), *Horns for Everything* (Million, 1972), *High on Music* (RCA, 1976), *Get Up and Dance* (RCA, 1977), *Memphis Horns Band II* (RCA, 1978), *Welcome to Memphis* (RCA, 1979), and *Flame Out* (Lucky 7, 1992). Having achieved legendary status by the 1980s, they were frequently recruited to play on mainstream rock LPs, most notably U2's *Rattle and Hum* (Island, 1988) and Keith Richards's *Talk Is Cheap* (1988). They also performed widely in live venues, supporting bluesman Robert Cray on tour in 1990 and appearing regularly at the prestigious Porretta Terme Soul Festival during the 1990s.

Meters, The

Formed in 1966, the New Orleans–based instrumental group consisted of Arthur Lanon Neville (formerly of the Hawketts), Joseph "Zigaboo" Modeliste, Leo Nocentelli, and George Porter. In addition to recording a string of hits singles, including "Sophisticated Cissy" and "Cissy Strut," and LPs, the Meters backed such performers as Fats Domino, Lee Dorsey, Betty Harris, Irma Thomas, Robert Palmer, and Paul McCartney. The group disbanded in 1977 when Arthur teamed with brothers Aaron, Charles, and Cyril to form the Neville Brothers.

Midnights, The   See BALLARD, HANK, AND THE MIDNIGHTERS.

Milburn, Amos (1927–1980) *singer and pianist*

Born April 1, 1927, in Houston, Texas, Milburn started his own band in 1945, following a stint in the U.S. Navy. Garnering a record contract with Aladdin in 1946, he would place 19 singles in the R&B Top Ten between 1948 and 1954, including the chart-toppers "Chicken Shack Boogie," "Bewildered," "Roomin' House Boogie," and "Bad, Bad Whiskey." His career was effectively placed on hold following a stroke in 1970. He died of another stroke on January 3, 1980.

Miles, Buddy (b. 1946) *drummer and vocalist*

Although always something of a bridesmaid, Buddy Miles played an important role in the emergence of progressive rock, particularly its intersection with the blues, funk, and fusion. Born George Miles, on September 5, 1946, in Omaha, Nebraska, he was already in demand as a studio session drummer in the New York area as a teenager. He tried to launch a career as lead singer of his own group, the Fidelitys, in 1958, but commercial success proved elusive. After a stint with the Dick Clark Revue during 1963–64, he was employed as a sideman by soul star WILSON PICKETT during 1965–66.

Miles burst into national prominence as the drummer and sometimes vocalist of guitarist Mike Bloomfield's blues-rock supergroup, the Electric Flag, in 1967. When the Electric Flag was torn apart by media-fueled hype, he recorded a solo album, *Electric Church* (Mercury, 1969), before hooking up

with guitarist Jimi Hendrix and bassist Billy Cox to form the jam-oriented Band of Gypsys in 1969. They released an eponymous live album (Capitol, 1970), culled from the 1969 New Year's Eve show at New York's Fillmore East, and have been represented on countless anthologies appearing after Hendrix's death in late 1970.

With Hendrix working again with drummer Mitch Mitchell again in 1970, Miles formed his own backup band, the Freedom Express (later renamed the Buddy Miles Express), releasing *Them Changes* (Mercury, 1970), which included his signature single, "Them Changes." He continued to release moderately successful singles and LPs—the most successful being a collaboration, *Carlos Santana & Buddy Miles! Live!* (Columbia, 1972), that achieved platinum sales—throughout the 1970s. After a period out of the public eye, he re-emerged in 1987 as the voice of television's claymation characters the California Raisins.

Millinder, Lucky (1900–1966) *bandleader*

Lucky Millinder helped many jazz and R&B stars—including ANNISTEEN ALLEN, Lockjaw Davis, Dizzy Gillespie, John Greer, WYNONIE HARRIS, BULL MOOSE JACKSON, and Rosetta Tharpe—gain a foothold in music industry by featuring them in his band between 1940 and 1952. His group was one of the more consistent hitmakers of the big band era, crossing over to the pop charts with regularity as well.

Born Lucius Millinder on August 8, 1900, in Anniston, Alabama, he was raised in Chicago, first attracting attention as an emcee during the late 1920s. Millinder's first experience as a bandleader came with an RKO theater tour in 1931. Stints heading the Mills Blue Rhythm Band in 1934 and the BILL DOGGETT Band in 1938 predated the establishment of his own ensemble. Although he was a singer in his own right, his hit records—"When the Lights Go on Again (All Over the World)" (with Trevor Bacon, vocal, and Gillespie, trumpet), "Apollo Jump" (instrumental), "Sweet Slumber" (vocal by Bacon), "Who Threw the Whiskey in the

Well?" (vocal by Harris), "Shorty's Got to Go" (vocal by Millinder), "D'Natural Blues" (vocal by Doris Davis)/ "Little Girl Don't Cry" (vocal by Greer), "I'll Never Be Free" (vocal by Allen), and "I'm Waiting Just For You" (vocal by Allen)—generally featured guest vocalists.

In addition to making records and performing live, Millinder's group did film work, most notably for *Paradise in Harlem.* When declining interest in big bands led to the demise of his unit, Millinder worked as a deejay in New York City and did public relations for a distillery. He died in New York on September 28, 1966.

Milli Vanilli

Few acts have fallen from grace as quickly as the German-based Milli Vanilli, named after a New York nightclub. The duo—Rob Pilatus and Fabrice Morvan, a trampoline athlete prior to a serious neck injury caused by a fall—worked as backup singers for an assortment of German artists before getting together to work out a blend of RAP and soul. They quickly achieved stardom on the strength of their 1988 hit singles, "Girl, You Know It's True" and "Blame It on the Rain," both driven by slick video clips that were heavily played on MTV and a host of pop music programs.

Milli Vanilli were victims of a large-scale consumer backlash when word surfaced that they were merely photogenic frontmen for a studio group fabricated by producer Frank Farian and had not sung on any of their recordings. The twosome took on a contrite public persona, returning all music awards, and expressing the desire to make a comeback on the merits of their own vocals. However, their efforts would never receive a widespread public hearing following Rob Pilatus's suicide in 1998.

Mills, Stephanie (b. 1957) *singer*

Stephanie Mills defined the black contemporary genre, effectively blending the 1960s classic soul tradition with Tin Pan Alley pop, particularly the American musical. Now in her fifth decade as a pro-

fessional entertainer, she stands on the brink of becoming a cultural institution.

Born in Brooklyn, New York, Mills was a precocious talent, singing in the Cornerstone Baptist Church choir by age three. She appeared in the Broadway show, *Maggie Flynn,* as a seven-year-old, and was chosen for the starring role of Dorothy in the musical *The Wiz,* eight years later.

Mills also began singing more soul-oriented fare during the 1960s, appearing at the Apollo Theater with the ISLEY BROTHERS for four weeks in 1967. She first recorded for ABC in 1974, and, following four years as a member of *The Wiz* troupe, embarked upon a solo performing career in earnest. Her more notable hit singles include "What Cha Gonna Do With My Lovin'," "Sweet Sensation," "Never Knew Love Like This Before," "Two Hearts," "The Medicine Song," "I Have Learned to Respect the Power of Love," "I Feel Good All Over," "(You're Puttin') A Rush on Me," and "Secret Lady." Married to Jeffrey Daniels of an R&B/dance group, Shalamar, for a short time in 1980, Mills has also been a successful album artist, placing nine releases (five of which were certified gold) on the *Billboard* charts, including *Whatcha Gonna Do With My Lovin'?* (20th Century, 1979) and *Sweet Sensation* (20th Century, 1980).

Milton, Roy (1907–1983) *singer*

One of the pioneers of the post–World War II rhythm and blues scene, Roy Milton was born July 31, 1907, in Wynnewood, Oklahoma. He was raised on a Chickasaw reservation where his grandmother lived; he would first be introduced to blues music when his family relocated to Tulsa.

Milton was hired as a singer for the Ernie Fields Orchestra in 1928; when the drummer was arrested during a tour in Texas, he filled in on that instrument. He moved to Los Angeles in 1935 and formed his own band. By the mid-1940s, the group was known as Roy Milton and his Solid Senders, with Buddy Floyd, pianist Camille Howard, and Hosea Sapp. Milton also doubled as a member of the Camille Howard Trio.

The Solid Senders first recorded for HampTone in 1945. They broke through with "R.M. Blues," followed by "Milton's Boogie." Milton had a series of designer labels in the late 1940s before signing with Specialty. His 17 Top Ten R&B hits for the company between 1947 and 1953—including "Hop, Skip and Jump," "Information Blues," and "Best Wishes"—helped establish it as a major player in the music business. In the late 1950s, he left Specialty, going on to record for the Dootone, King, and Warwick labels.

Milton's career was largely dormant throughout most of the 1960s due to changing fashions. With the blues revival of the late 1960s, however, he resumed touring in the U.S. and Europe. A stroke in 1982 confined him to his home; he would die in September 1983.

Mitchell, Willie (b. 1928) *bandleader, producer, and record company executive*

Although Willie Mitchell placed only eight recordings on the charts, his impact within the music industry cut across a wide range of roles. These included trumpeter, keyboardist, bandleader, composer, arranger, producer, and record executive.

Born in Ashland, Mississippi, Mitchell moved to Memphis as a youth. He worked with a number of area musicians, including Tuff Green and Al Jackson (whose son Al Jr. later became drummer for BOOKER T. & THE MGs). He first formed his own ensemble in 1954, which later served as the house band for the Home of the Blues and Hi labels. He recorded a string of instrumental hits between 1964 and 1969, most notably "20-75," "Buster Browne," "Bad Eye," "Soul Serenade," "Prayer Meetin'," and "30-60-90."

Mitchell went on to become the president of Hi Records. He produced many of the recordings for the company, the most successful of which were AL GREEN's classic 1970s soul singles and LPs.

Mobb Deep

Highly acclaimed for its graphic depiction of New York's street culture and complementary production values, featuring stark keyboard chords, shimmering dissonant strings, and passionate vocal outbursts, Mobb Deep rose above the stereotypical ranting of rank-and-file gangsta rap acts. The group formed in 1992 in Queensbridge, New York, after members Prodigy and Havoc met at Manhattan's Graphic Arts High School. Although largely confined to the East Coast HIP-HOP underground, their debut album, *Juvenile Hell* (4th & Broadway, 1993), garnered them a major label contract with Loud Records.

Released shortly after the groundbreaking success of *Illmatic*—recorded by another Queens-based poetic reality rapper, NAS—*The Infamous* (Loud, 1995), brought Mobb Deep to the brink of mass popularity. The next album, *Hell on Earth* (Loud, 1996), revealed the duo distilling their formula to a new level of refinement. Although this was perhaps their artistic summit, the next LP, the widely bootlegged *Murda Muzik* (Loud, 1999), became Mobb Deep's most commercially successful work—entering *Billboard*'s Top 200 at number three and quickly going platinum—due in part to the textural diversity resulting from guest appearances by Cormega, Eightball, Infamous Mobb, Kool G. Rap, Lil' Cease, LIL' KIM, and Raekwon.

Prodigy—long perceived to be the more politically outspoken member of the group—released a solo effort, *H.N.I.C.*, in late 2000. Although utilizing such notable producers as Alchemist and Rockwilder, the album retained Mobb Deep's distinctive style. At the same time, he was drawn into a feud between JAY-Z and Nas, when the former challenged Mobb Deep's street credibility. Rather than openly challenging Jay-Z, as Nas opted to do, the duo chose to move in the direction of pop-RAP with *Infamy* (Loud, 2001), thereby gaining a wider mainstream following.

Moments, The

The Philly soul–styled group was formed in Hackensack, New Jersey, in the late 1960s. The original lead singer, Mark Greene, departed after their first record and was replaced by William Brown (formerly in the Broadway and Uniques) and Al Goodman (ex-Corvettes and Vipers member). The

Moments struck paydirt in early 1970 with the crossover ballad "Love on a Two-Way Street." Shortly thereafter, Harry Ray left the Establishment to join the group. Following a long string of hits, Ray, Goodman, and Brown went off on their own in 1978, achieving considerable success over the next decade.

Monica (b. 1980) *singer*

Monica is often compared with another youthful R&B singer, Brandy; indeed the two collaborated on the 1998 mega-hit, "The Boy Is Mine." Although she has not enjoyed Brandy's level of commercial success, Monica is felt to possess a richer, more dynamic vocal style—the result of a professional singing career started as a 10-year-old.

Born Monica Arnold, in Atlanta, Georgia, on October 24, 1980, she first attracted attention as a member of the gospel group, Charles Thompson and the Majestics. Her performance of WHITNEY HOUSTON's "The Greatest Love of All" at a talent show at age 12 spurred producer/record executive Dallas Austin to offer her an Arista recording contract. Monica's debut album, *Miss Thang* (Arista, 1995), revealed a mature talent, equally at home with hot dance numbers and tender ballads. The follow-up, *The Boy Is Mine* (Arista, 1998), proved to be her commercial breakthrough, including two best-selling singles, the title track and "The First Night."

At the peak of success, Monica opted to take time off from career demands. She also spent time recovering from the harrowing experience of witnessing her boyfriend's shooting suicide in 1999. Plans for the release of the long-awaited *All Eyez on Me*, originally set for 2002, were shelved due to alleged Internet piracy. It was issued the following year, in reworked form, as *After the Storm* (J-Records), enjoying solid sales due in large part to heavy radio play for the engaging lead single, "So Long."

Montgomery, Wes (1925–1968) *guitarist*

Although Wes Montgomery first achieved renown as a mainstream jazz guitarist, he was actively moving in the direction of jazz-pop fusion at the time of his death on June 15, 1968, at age 43. Montgomery worked with many jazz notables in the post–World War II period. He played lead guitar on Lionel Hampton's biggest crossover hit, "Rag Mop," a 1950 Decca release. By the early 1960s, he had achieved success in the rapidly expanding LP market with the Wes Montgomery Trio, which also included his brothers Buddy on piano and Monk on bass, before going out on his own. His shift from the Verve label to A&M in the mid-1960s signaled a move in the direction of lush, easy listening song arrangements, many of which were instrumental covers of the pop hits of the day by artists such as the Beatles, the Mamas and the Papas, and the Association. The latter group's number one recording, "Windy," would be Montgomery's best-selling single. Despite his untimely death, jazz's flirtation with softer pop sounds continued unabated, peaking in the early 1970s.

Moonglows, The

Although enjoying few best-selling recordings, the Moonglows stood apart from the rank-and-file 1950s DOO-WOP acts in terms of their singing prowess, songwriting skills, and seamless production values. They played a key role in modernizing the rhythm and blues vocal group tradition, blending the blues, jazz, and old-time harmonies going back to minstrel music and the barbershop quartets with the emerging rock 'n' roll style. Their style and sound strongly influenced soul schools such as the Chicago sound (particularly the Dells and the IMPRESSIONS) and Motown (the TEMPTATIONS and the FOUR TOPS).

The founding members of the group—Harvey Fuqua (born July 27, 1929), whose uncle, Charlie Fuqua, was the Ink Spots' guitarist, and Bobby Lester Dallas (b. January 13, 1930)—met in their Louisville high school and began singing together at local school functions and dances, to Fuqua's piano accompaniment. After touring with Ed Wiley's jump blues band in 1950 they pursued different paths for a time. Relocating to Cleveland, Fuqua put together a vocal group with a military service friend, Danny Coggins, and bassist Prentiss Barnes, a gifted gospel singer (the brother of James "Pookie" Hudson of the Spaniels) born in Magnolia, Mississippi, in 1925. Fuqua recruited Lester, then back in Louisville, to complete the ensemble; known as the Crazy Sounds, they concentrated on "vocalese," improvised lyrics set to recorded jazz.

They received an early break in 1952 when a local bluesman, Al "Singin' Fats" Thomas, heard them at a Cleveland club, the Loop, and informed deejay Alan Freed about their potential. Freed encouraged them to adopt a new name—the Moonglows, a play on his broadcasting pseudonym, "Moondog"—and became their manager. Uncomfortable with the business arrangements Fuqua was making with Freed, Coggins departed; his replacement was tenor Alexander Walton (aka Pete Graves), born in Alabama on April 17, 1936.

Freed secured a recording contract for his group with Chicago-based Chance Records in October 1953. With Freed featuring them regularly in his stage shows and playing their records heavily on his radio broadcast, they became increasingly popular. They switched to Chess in October 1954, the most prominent Chicago R&B label at the time, and quickly hit a career peak as a recording act, releasing hits such as "Sincerely" (their most successful single ever, penetrating the pop Top 20 and topping the R&B charts), "Most of All," "We Go Together," "See Saw"/"When I'm With You," "Please Send Me Someone To Love," and "Ten Commandments of Love."

In mid-1955, Chess attempted to capitalize on the group's popularity by issuing some of their material under the moniker of the Moonlighters on the Checker subsidiary. The practice was quickly dropped when record buyers saw through the ruse. In the meantime, the Moonglows added guitarist Billy Johnson (b. 1924 in Hartford, Connecticut) to their lineup in order to enhance their onstage singles. Due to Freed's show business connections, the group appeared in a couple of feature films, *Rock,*

Rock, Rock (1956), starring 16-year-old Tuesday Weld, and *Mr. Rock and Roll* (1957).

By this time, hits were becoming harder to find, and Fuqua—clearly a talented songwriter and arranger—steered the Moonglows away from a cool sound (typically featuring Lester's mellow voice) to a rawer approach built around his own soulful emoting. When the rest of the group complained, Fuqua brought in a young outfit from Washington, D.C., the Marquees—including MARVIN GAYE, Reese Palmer, James Knowland, and Chester Simmons—as replacements. Billed as "Harvey and the Moonglows," the group had limited success before disbanding, with the new members going on to form the nucleus of the SPINNERS.

Fuqua flirted briefly with a solo career and production work for Chess before starting his own Detroit-based Tri-Phi label in 1962. Chess issued older Moonglows material up through 1962, and the group was revived in 1964 by Alex Walton, recording for the Lana, Crimson, and Times Square labels before breaking up. In 1970, Lester formed his own version of the Moonglows before reuniting with Fuqua. They recruited Walton, Doc Williams, and Chuck Lewis, and recorded an LP, *The Return of the Moonglows,* in Philadelphia for Big P in 1972. It was picked up by RCA—briefly entering the *Billboard* LP charts—while a single, "Sincerely '72," also grazed the charts. Shortly thereafter, the group called it a day, but Lester reassembled yet another edition in 1978, playing the revival circuit until his death from cancer on October 15, 1980.

Fuqua continued to write and produce for Anna, MOTOWN, and RCA, frequently working with SMOKEY ROBINSON. "Sincerely" earned a Grammy nomination in 1990 via a country rendition by the Forester Sisters, and the Moonglows's original release was included on the soundtrack of the popular gangster film, *Good Fellas* (1991).

Moore, Dorothy (b. 1946) *singer*

Dorothy Moore was a refined pop-soul stylist, whose success owed much to the judicious selection of old standards and material from widely respected contemporary songwriters like Bobby Goldsboro. Born in Jackson, Mississippi, she first attracted attention as the lead singer of the Poppies, formed while attending Jackson State University. Moore first made the charts in 1973 after embarking on a solo career with a redo of ARETHA FRANKLIN's Top 30 R&B hit, "Cry Like a Baby." She would disappear from view for more than two years before waxing a string of hits with the newly established label, Malaco, most notably, the mournful ballad first popularized by Joe Simon in 1972, "Misty Blue"; "Funny How Time Slips Away"; and "I Believe You." She would move on to Handshake in the early 1980s, before creasing the charts one last time in 1982 with "What's Forever For."

Moore, Melba (b. 1945) *singer*

The New York City–based singer/actress first achieved fame as a cast member in the Broadway production of *Hair*. While remaining active in musical theater (most notably, her award-winning interpretation of Lutiebelle in *Purlie*), she was a consistent hit-maker from 1975 through the 1980s for the Buddah, Epic, EMI America, and Capitol labels. She never broke into the pop Top 40, but reached the R&B Top Ten with "Love's Comin' at Ya," "Livin' for Your Love," "Love the One I'm With (A Lot of Love)" (with Kashif), "A Little Bit More" (number one; with Freddie Jackson), "Falling" (number one), and "It's Been So Long" (with Freddie Jackson).

Motown

The premier soul music substyle of the 1960s and the best-known African-American–owned record company, Motown was the product of Berry Gordy's vision and drive. Gordy was a prizefighter and car assembly–line employee before shifting his attentions to songwriting, record production, and artist management. After working with R&B great JACKIE WILSON briefly in the mid-1950s, he began producing Detroit area singer MARV JOHNSON, initially for the indie firm, Kudo, and then for Tamla, a label he established in 1959.

In addition to being an excellent judge of musical talent, Gordy had the good fortune to be in the right place at the right time. In short order, he hired such pivotal figures as singer/songwriters SMOKEY ROBINSON and MARVIN GAYE. By 1960–61, he had found the hit-making touch, most notably, with "Money," by Barrett Strong; "Shop Around," by Robinson's group, the Miracles; and the label's first pop chart-topper, "Please Mr. Postman," by the Marvelettes. He quickly added the Motown, Gordy, and Anna imprints to his roster. A hitherto unprecedented number of the artists he signed (many of them homegrown) went on to record hits, including MARY WELLS, STEVIE WONDER, Martha & the Vandellas, the Supremes, the TEMPTATIONS, the FOUR TOPS, and Junior Walker & the All Stars. Much of Gordy's success was the result of efforts to appeal to the mainstream pop marketplace. Besides maintaining songwriter/producers and a superb house band capable of consistently achieving crossover success (billed as "the Sound of Young America"), he had his acts meticulously dressed and groomed, drilled to execute polished stage routines, and given etiquette training. The company was astute enough to weather continued changes in musical fashion, sociopolitical upheaval, and countless imitators within the soul field during the 1960s.

Despite signing new stars like the Jackson 5 and the Commodores (with LIONEL RICHIE), Motown finally began losing momentum in the 1970s as established artists like Gaye, DIANA ROSS, and the Four Tops—dissatisfied with control being exerted over their respective careers—moved on to other labels. Other questionable moves at the time included the unsuccessful attempt to launch a rock imprint (Rare Earth) and the decision to relocate to Hollywood in 1973 as Gordy began focusing on making films. By the 1980s, Motown remained solvent largely through reissues of its back catalog (particularly on the newly emerging CD and video formats) and the production of musical revues for television. Gordy sold the company to MCA in 1988; the Universal Music Group continues to operate the Motown franchise to the present day.

See also JACKSON, MICHAEL.

Murphy, Eddie (b. 1961) *comedian and film actor*

Like Moms Mabley and Bill Cosby before him, Eddie Murphy not only was a successful stand-up comedian, but produced hit singles and albums as well. Born April 3, 1961, in Hempstead, New York, he first gained fame as a cast member in TV's long-running series, *Saturday Night Live*. Signing with Columbia, he made the charts with the following 1980s singles: "Boogie in Your Butt"; "Party All the Time," written, arranged, and produced by funk great RICK JAMES; and "How Could It Be." He would go on to become an even bigger film star, appearing in such box office smashes as the *Beverly Hills Cop* cycle, *Trading Places, 48 Hours, Coming to America,* and remakes of *The Absent-Minded Professor* and *Dr. Doolittle*.

Muscle Shoals

FAME Studio, an acronym for Florence Alabama Music Enterprises, is probably the most famous rural recording center in North America. Located approximately twenty miles from Tennessee, in Muscle Shoals, Alabama, the facility was, according to founder RICK HALL, "a cinderblock adobe shack" built in 1962 following the specifications of RCA's Nashville studio.

FAME's importance relates to the unique brand of earthy, gospel-inflected soul produced there. The foundation of its sound was the house band, which generally consisted of rhythm guitarist Jimmy Johnson, Junior Lowe or David Hood on bass, Spooner Oldham or Barry Beckett on keyboards, Roger Hawkins on drums, and an assortment of supporting players.

The studio's initial breakthrough came when Bill Lowery brought in his Atlanta-based stable of artists, including Tommy Roe, the Tams, Joe South, and Ray Stevens. In the meantime, FAME actively nurtured homegrown talent such as Arthur Alexander and Jimmy Hughes, whose Top 20 1964 hit, "Steal Away," established a template for all 1960s productions. FAME's success attracted the attention of established labels such as Atlantic, which sent down, among others, WILSON PICKETT ("Land of 1000 Dances" and "Funky Broadway") and ARETHA FRANKLIN ("A Natural Woman" and "Chain of Fools"), and Bell Records, which found success with JAMES AND BOBBY PURIFY's "I'm Your Puppet."

In April 1969, the FAME house band established their own studio, Muscle Shoals Sound, going on to record countless funk hits as well as working with Paul Simon, Art Garfunkel, Cher, Willie Nelson, the Rolling Stones (who cut the hits "Brown Sugar" and "Wild Horses" there), Bob Seger, and Rod Stewart. With Atlantic now recording most of its R&B artists in Miami, FAME focused on the pop mainstream, recording such chart-toppers as "One Bad Apple" by the Osmonds and Paul Anka's "Having My Baby," in addition to artists like Sammy Davis, Jr., Bobbie Gentry, and Tom Jones. Hall would be named *Billboard*'s Producer of the Year in 1973 after having his records hold the number one position on the Hot 100 for 17 consecutive weeks.

Mystikal *rapper*

One of the leading rappers in the Dirty South genre, Mystikal—born Michael Tyler, in New Orleans—comes across as a RAP-styled JAMES BROWN, utilizing spontaneous signature yelps and other hyperactive vocal effects to create a general funky feel. His debut LP, *Mystikal* (Big Boy, 1995), spurred a major record company, Jive, to sign him later in the year. Although a clichéd work overall, the follow-up, *Mind of Mystikal* (Jive, 1996), parlayed kinetic G-funk to underground success. Hooking up with MASTER P and his production team, he became a star on the strength of the stripped-down, thuggish, gangsta arrangements of *Unpredictable* (No Limit, 1997). Although the raucous rudeness remains, more recent releases—*Ghetto Fabulous* (Jive, 1998), *Let's Get Ready* (Jive, 2000), with its breakout single, "Shake Ya Ass," and *Tarantula* (Jive, 2001)—offered upgraded material and slick studio flourishes geared to packaging Mystikal as a pop star.

Nas (b. 1973) *rapper*

Born Nasir Jones in Queensbridge, New York, the son of a jazz musician, Nas began rapping at age 10 in a local ensemble, the Devastatin' Seven. After submitting a demo tape in the late 1980s to Main Source producer, Large Professor, he was subsequently featured on that group's album, *Breaking Atoms* (1991). His solo debut, "Half Time," was included in the film, *Zebra Head* (1992), which spurred Columbia to offer him a generous record deal. Assisted by noted producers like A TRIBE CALLED QUEST's Q-Tip and Premier (GANG STARR), he recorded the acclaimed masterpiece, *Illmatic* (Columbia, 1994).

Subsequent albums—the chart-topping *It Was Written* (Columbia, 1996) and *I Am . . . The Autobiography* (Columbia, 1999), followed by the less successful (albeit Top Ten best-sellers) *NAStradamus* (Columbia, 1999) and *Stillmatic* (Ill Will, 2001)—diluted *Illmatic's* literate lyrics and rich ghetto imagery, opting instead for catchy refrains and superstar posturing. At this point, Nas had lost much of his street credibility in his single-minded quest for fame and fortune, with hardcore rapper JAY-Z dissing him onstage and in the track, "Super Ugly."

While Nas was apparently going through a bout of soul-searching, Columbia reached into the vaults for *From Illmatic to Stillmatic: The Remixes EP* (2002) and *The Lost Tapes* (2002). His next album of original material, *God's Son* (Columbia), issued at the end of 2002, found him attempting to rise above the controversy regarding prior career moves. The work exhibited a decidedly spiritual perspective while relying on the talents of fellow performers EMINEM, ALICIA KEYS, and TUPAC SHAKUR as well as producers Ron Browz, Salaam Remi, Chucky Thompson, and the Alchemist.

Nash, Johnny (b. 1940) *singer*

Johnny Nash had been a fixture in show business for many years before he briefly became a high-profile recording star in 1972. Born in Houston, he started singing at the church attended by his Baptist parents. He performed on a local television program at age 13, which led to a regular slot on Arthur Godfrey's radio and TV network shows in 1956 (which continued for seven years).

The Godfrey connection helped Nash secure a recording contract with ABC-Paramount. The eponymous debut album, released in September 1958, was followed by a steady stream of titles for the label into the early 1960s. He switched to Argo before forming his own company, JoDa, in the mid-1960s. Primarily a nightclub entertainer specializing in middle-of-the-road fare up to this point, Nash became aware of the rock steady/REGGAE styles based in the West Indies. He began producing recordings—the first best seller of note being "Hold Me Tight" in 1968—that helped make this music more palatable to mainstream listeners. The breakthrough came with "I Can See Clearly Now" (which reached number one on the Hot 100) and "Stir It Up," followed by the album, *I Can See Clearly Now* (Epic, 1972). Although subsequent releases sold less spectacularly, he remained a fixture in the lower reaches of the charts through much of the 1970s.

Native Tongues Posse

A loose coalition dedicated to elevating awareness of black history, the New York–based Native Tongues Posse helped facilitate the rise of "Afrocentricity" within HIP-HOP culture. The participants—including De La Soul, the Jungle Brothers, Monie Love, QUEEN LATIFAH, and A TRIBE CALLED QUEST—were criticized in some quarters for their preoccupation with the superficial aspects of the movement. However, Afrocentricity generally reflected idealistic concerns, most notably that of realigning RAP's focus from self-absorption and unrestrained hedonism to a higher social consciousness.

Natural Four

An Oakland, California–based vocal act, the Natural Four enjoyed a string of moderate hits in a soft soul vein. Originally consisting of Al Bowden, John January, Allen Richardson, and leader Chris James, the group first recorded in 1968 for a local independent label, Boola-Boola. After signing with ABC Records, they hit the R&B Top 40 the following year with "Why Should We Stop Now." Follow-up recordings sold poorly, including a single released on Chess shortly before the group called it quits.

James put together a new edition of the Natural Four—including Darryl Canady, Steve Striplin, and Delmos Whitney—which signed with Curtis Mayfield's Curtom label in 1972. They would achieve crossover success (reaching number 10 on the R&B charts) with a Leroy Hutson composition, "Can This Be Real." They continued to enjoy intermittent chart success through 1976 before dropping out of sight.

Naughty By Nature

Naughty By Nature were one of the first RAP acts to enjoy major crossover hits without losing their street credibility among hardcore fans. Initially calling themselves New Style, the trio formed in 1986, while the members—MCs Treach (Anthony Criss) and Vinnie (Vincent Brown), and DJ Kay Gee (Keir Gist)—were attending the same East Orange, New Jersey, high school. At the onset of the new decade, they were discovered by QUEEN LATIFAH, who brought them to her management company and the TOMMY BOY label. Their eponymous debut (Tommy Boy, 1991)—featuring pulsating funk rhythms and clever wordplay—achieved platinum status out of the box, due in part to the Top Ten pop single, "O.P.P." (which reportedly referred to male or female genitals). Treach began receiving acting offers, appearing in the films *Juice, The Meteor Man, Who's the Man?* and *Jason's Lyric.*

Naughty By Nature's follow-up, *19 Naughty III* (Tommy Boy, 1993), also went platinum, driven by the hit single, "Hip Hop Hooray," with its catchy "Hey! Ho!" chant. Although *Poverty's Paradise* (Tommy Boy, 1995) found the group creatively treading water, it would win a Grammy for Best Rap Album. An extended recording hiatus followed with Treach landing an ongoing role in the HBO prison series, *Oz,* and Kay Gee producing records for the likes of Aaliyah, Krayzie Bone, NEXT, and Zhane. Other distractions included Treach and Vinnie's 1997 arrests in Harlem for illegal weapons possession, and the former's brief marriage to Pepa (of SALT-N-PEPA).

In 1999, the trio made a comeback, albeit not breaking any new ground, with *19 Naughty Nine: Nature's Fury* (Arista). At this point, Kay Gee exited to produce full-time; Treach and Vinnie decided to carry on as a duo, releasing *IIcons* (TVT) on March 5, 2002. The album made halting attempts at updating their signature sound, opting for spare production values and a series of guest collaborators, most notably, pop star Pink.

Nelly (b. 1978) *rapper*

Nelly was one of the most promising rappers at the onset of a new century. Almost single-handedly, the

Nelly performs at the 2002 Billboard Music Awards. (Ethan Miller/Reuters/Landov)

St. Louis–based performer made the Midwest a vital part of the HIP-HOP community.

Born Cornell Haynes, Jr., on November 2, 1978, in Austin, Texas, the youngest son of an Air Force sergeant, he spent his early childhood in Spain before moving to St. Louis. When he was eight his parents divorced; he attended eight different schools before his mother—concerned about the possible negative effects of peer pressure on her son—moved once more to suburban University City, Missouri.

As a 15-year-old, Nelly formed the St. Lunatics with brother City Spudd and high school friends Ali, Jason, Kyjuan, and Murphy Lee. They would record a regional hit, the self-produced "Gimme

What Ya Want," which sold over 7,000 copies but was not picked up any of the major labels. At the time, Nelly split his time playing shortstop in the St. Louis Amateur Baseball Association in hopes of becoming a big league ballplayer. Following the strategy used by the WU-TANG CLAN, the St. Lunatics encouraged him to secure a solo recording contract that might open the door for his associates. Signed by Universal, he burst onto the scene with *Country Grammar* (Universal, 2000), which debuted in the top five of *Billboard*'s album chart. Driven by the title track—featuring a sinuous bass figure, party atmosphere, and catchy refrain—the LP sold more than eight million copies and helped him capture the Best New Artist and Album of the Year awards from *Source* magazine in 2000.

Nelly went on to become a superstar the following year, introducing his Vokal and Apple Bottom clothing lines, recording a hit single, "#1," which was included in the motion picture *Training Day,* and costarring in another film, *Snipes.* He also repaid the St. Lunatics by participating on their first album, *Free City* (Universal, 2001), which was only moderately successful. Nelly rebounded to the top, however, with his next solo release, *Nellyville* (Universal, 2002), which topped the charts and quickly surpassed five million sales on the strength of smooth pop arrangements and infectious, sing-along choruses, especially those in the single, "Hot in Herre."

Neptunes, The

The Neptunes are one of the biggest behind-the-scenes names in music, and chances are that most radio listeners in recent years have heard something either produced by this pair or at least influenced by them.

Pharrell Williams was born in 1973 and grew up in Virginia Beach, California. The oldest of three sons, he showed a strong aptitude for music at a very early age. In his seventh-grade band class, he met Chad Hugo (b. 1974), who also grew up in Virginia Beach. Chad was the multi-instrumentalist of the duo, playing both drums and saxophone, while Pharrell played drums.

In 1992 Pharrell and Chad got their first break when producer Teddy Riley opened his New Jack Swing production company right next to their high school. Riley signed them and let them produce a song titled "Rumpshaker" for Wreckx N Effect. This collaboration opened the door for the Neptunes to begin producing RAP. Their next project was producing a track for MASE on his acclaimed 1997 album, *Harlem World,* on BAD BOY RECORDS. They also produced Blackstreet's debut album (Lil' Man Records, 1994) for Riley as well. The next two years were focused mainly on production, working with artists like SNOOP DOGGY DOG, Noreaga, JAY-Z, and MC LYTE.

After these successes in the rap industry, the Neptunes began producing outside the rap idiom by working with performers like No Doubt, *NSYNC, the Backstreet Boys, and Britney Spears. Soon the pair were well known throughout the industry for crashing musical barriers with their irreverent beats and their ear for all styles of popular music. Williams was named songwriter of the year in 2001 and again in 2002 for BMI. Hugo was named the R&B songwriter of the year in 2001 by ASCAP.

The NEPTUNES decided to release their own album in 2002. Along with another high-school pal, rapper Shae Haley, they dubbed themselves N.E.R.D (No One Ever Really Dies). *In Search Of . . .* (released on their own label, Star Traks) debuted to wide critical acclaim for its modern beats mixed with a hint of the 1970's sound. The album was awarded the prestigious XY Satellite Radio Shortlist Prize given for artistic achievement in music.

While releasing and touring to promote *In Search Of . . .,* the Neptunes continued their production work, producing eight tracks on Justin Timberlake's *Justified* (Jive, 2002), and producing platinum hits like NELLY's *Hot in Herre* (Universal, 2003). In 2002, the Neptunes were named Producers of the Year by both the *Source* and

Billboard. In that same year, they signed a deal to merge their Star Traks label with Arista Records.

Over the last decade, the Neptunes have established themselves as two of pop music's top producers; the release of their second N.E.R.D. album, *Fly or Die* (Arista, 2004) attracted even greater coverage from the mainstream media.

—Emily Herring

New Edition

While New Edition had a relatively short run as a hit-making entity, the vocal quintet nurtured some of the leading rhythm and blues artists of the 1990s. The group's original members—BOBBY BROWN, Ralph Tresvant, Ricky Bell, Michael Bivins, and Ronnie DeVoe—met in the early 1980s as junior high school students in Boston's Roxbury district. Promoter Maurice Starr, who discovered them performing at a local talent show, secured them a recording contract with the HIP-HOP label, Streetwise.

Following the release of two Top Ten R&B singles—"Candy Girl" and "Is This the End"—New Edition parted ways with Starr (who later formed New Kids on the Block) and signed with MCA Records. Their next album, *New Edition* (MCA, 1984) crossed over to number six on the *Billboard* Hot 100, propelled by the hit singles "Cool It Now" and "Mr. Telephone Man." Succeeding albums—*All For Love* (MCA, 1985), *Under the Blue Moon* (MCA, 1986), and *Heart Break* (MCA, 1988)—enjoyed moderate success, but the group's singles did not perform well on the pop charts.

New Edition was ultimately torn apart by the loss of key personnel to solo careers, beginning with Brown in 1986. His replacement, Johnny Gill, also struck out on his own in the late 1980s, as did Tresvant. In 1988, the remaining members formed a hip-hop trio, Bell Biv DeVoe. The group members have remained close, however, often working together in the 1990s as well as considering the possibility of reuniting to produce an album.

New Jack Swing/New Jill Swing   See
SWINGBEAT.

Next

Musically, Next combined the longstanding traditions of romantic crooning, as refined in the early 1990s by BOYZ II MEN, with the gospel fervor of 1960s classic soul singers. Their lyrics, however, pushed raw sexuality to new levels of explicitness, which required extensive editing for distribution in the mass media.

The Minneapolis-based trio formed in 1992 after brothers Terrance (aka T-Low; born June 7, 1974) and Raphael (aka Tweety; b. January 28, 1976) Brown were introduced by their uncle, a gospel choir director, to Robert Lavelle (R. L.) Huggar (b. April 2, 1977). Under the guidance of manager (and former gospel/R&B singer) Ann Nesby, Next recorded a demo at a Minneapolis studio run by the production team of JIMMY JAM AND TERRY LEWIS. Upon hearing it, NAUGHTY BY NATURE's Kay Gee signed them to his fledgling Divine Mill label, part of the Arista Records family. Powered by funky dance rhythms in the singles "Butta Love" and "Too Close," their debut, *Rated Next* (Arista, 1997), became a major hit. However, the formula had begun to wear a bit thin following the release of *Welcome II Nextasy* (Arista, 2000) and the *Next Episode* (J-Records, 2002).

Nice & Smooth

Based in New York City, Nice & Smooth—consisting of Gregg Nice (born Greg Mays) and Smooth Bee (b. Daryl Barnes)—specialized in FUNK-oriented music accented by their vocal pyrotechnics. Their eponymous debut release (Fresh, 1989) was issued shortly before the independent label ceased operations. However, the two moderately successful singles culled from the album, "More & More Hits" and "Funky for You," helped facilitate a shift to the RAP powerhouse, DEF JAM. The ensuing LP, *Ain't a*

Damn Thing Changed (Ral/Def Jam, 1991)—driven by the hit, "Sometimes I Rhyme Slow"—revealed an increasing preoccupation with HIP-HOP arrangements. *The Jewel of the Nile* (Ral/Def Jam, 1994) featured the talents of rap and dance stars such as BOBBY BROWN (they had supplied backup vocals on his tours, while Barnes had written lyrics for his *King of Stage* album), EVERLAST, Jo Jo Hailey of Jodeci, and Slick Rick. Uneven production and poor rhymes plagued *Blazing Hot, Vol. 4* (Scotti Bros., 1997), casting doubt on the duo's prospects for the future.

Notorious B.I.G., The (Biggie Smalls)
(1972–1997) rapper

Born Christopher Wallace in Brooklyn, New York, Notorious B.I.G. was a leading exponent of RAP's East Coast school in the mid-1990s prior to his tragic death. Initially performing in the greater New York area as Biggie Smalls, he was discovered by BAD BOY RECORDS owner, PUFF DADDY (Sean Combs), who provided him with cameo recording spots for established R&B artists like MARY J. BLIGE. His major label debut, *Ready to Die* (Arista, 1994), propelled him to the forefront of the gangsta rap genre, a lifestyle he knew first-hand, having been arrested on many occasions for assault, robbery, and weapon offenses. A string of successful singles followed, most notably, the 1995 Top Ten pop hits, "Big Poppa" and "One More Chance—Stay with Me."

B.I.G. found himself caught up in the East Coast/West Coast rivalry between Bad Boy and the Los Angeles-based DEATH ROW label. Eventually, threats exchanged in the press and on recordings led to TUPAC SHAKUR's death at the hands of unknown gunmen in Las Vegas on September 13, 1996. Although nothing could be substantiated, it is believed that B.I.G.'s murder on March 9, 1997, may well have been motivated by a desire for revenge. Released only days following his murder, B.I.G.'s second album, *Life after Death* (Arista, 1997), went straight to the top of the pop charts, fueled both by sensationalized media coverage and the fatalistic tone characterizing many of its songs. Two chart-topping singles, "Hypnotize" and "Mo Money Mo Problems," were released in short order, along with an equally successful tribute disc by Combs and B.I.G.'s wife, Faith Evans, "I'll Be Missing You." Although padded with the contributions of a stellar galaxy of rap stars—including LIL' KIM, EMINEM, SNOOP DOGGY DOGG, BUSTA RHYMES, MISSY "MISDEMEANOR" ELLIOTT, and ICE CUBE—his final album of original material, *Born Again* (Arista, 1999), also reached number one on the *Billboard* Top 200.

N.W.A.

A loose combine of rappers based in the Compton section of Los Angeles, N.W.A. (an acronym for the commercially indigestible moniker, Niggaz With Attitude) pioneered the gangsta RAP movement. Although the group fragmented shortly after the release of their third album, individual members continued to exert an influence on the evolution of HIP-HOP throughout the 1990s.

N.W.A. was formed in the mid-1980s when vocalist EAZY-E—aka Eric Wright, son of soul/funk artist Charles Wright, and founder of the seminal West Coast rap label Ruthless—combined forces with ex-C.I.A. vocalist ICE CUBE (O'Shea Jackson),

vocalist M. C. Ren (Lorenzo Patterson), and former World Class Wreckin' Cru members, producer DR DRE (Andre Young) and turntable maestro DJ Yella (Antoine Carraby). Along with Arabian Prince, The Doc, and other hip-hop artists, the group recorded *N.W.A. and The Posse* (Macola, 1987), which featured Eazy-E's harsh proto-gangsta diatribe, "Boyz 'N The Hood." The next LP, *Straight Outta Compton* (Ruthless, 1989), all but defined the gangsta rap genre, most notably in the biting social commentaries of "Gangsta Gangsta" and widely censored "Fuck Tha Police" (issued in the cassette, 12-inch, and CD singles formats). Although the heavily anticipated follow-up, *Efil4zaggin'* (Ruthless, 1991), was a smash hit (extremely popular with rebellious middle-class white youth), internal dissension caused group members to go their separate ways. Dr Dre found success with his G-funk innovations and the creation of the DEATH ROW label (funded in part by Interscope Records). Ice Cube enjoyed even greater commercial popularity both as a recording artist—his angry solo album, *The Predator* (Priority, 1992), which widely sampled black music innovators like GEORGE CLINTON and JAMES BROWN, would debut at number one on the pop charts—and Hollywood film star. M.C. Ren and Eazy-E also produced bestselling singles and LPs; the latter's career was cut short, however, when he died of AIDS in March 1995.

Oaktown's 3-5-7

Based in Oakland, California, the rap quartet included Sweat P, formerly an Oakland Raiders cheerleader; Sweet LD (b. Djuana Johnican); Terrible T (b. Tabatha King); and Vicious C. With M.C. HAMMER acting as their mentor, they landed a recording contract with Capitol Records. After releasing two undistinguished LPs—*Wild and Loose* (Capitol, 1989) and *Fully Loaded* (Capitol, 1991)—and Hammer's departure from Capitol, the group was dropped from the label roster. By late 1991, internal dissension would leave the act with only two members, Sweet LD and Terrible T.

Ocean, Billy (b. 1950) *singer*

With minimal media hype, Billy Ocean became one of the most consistent hit-makers of the 1980s. Rather than relying on a flashy image, he parlayed a judicious selection of pop-FUNK material and an extraordinarily soulful voice to stake his claim on the upper reaches of the charts.

Born Leslie Sebastian Charles on January 21, 1950, in Fyzabad, Trinidad, he moved to England with his family at age eight. Ocean worked for a time as a Savile Row tailor, before gravitating to studio session work in London. His MOTOWN-inflected "Love Really Hurts Without You" put him on the map in England. He relocated to the United States in the late 1970s as part of a concerted attempt to penetrate that marketplace.

Following several years of fitful commercial progress, highlighted by the release of "Night (Feel Like Getting Down)" (which reached number seven on the 1981 R&B charts), Ocean hit the bigtime with the chart-topping crossover smash, "Caribbean Queen (No More Love on the Run)." He continued his successful run throughout the decade, most notably with "Loverboy"; "Suddenly"; "When the Going Gets Tough, the Tough Get Going," helped by its inclusion in the soundtrack to the film *Jewel of the Nile*; "There'll Be Sad Songs (To Make You Cry)"; "Love Zone"; and "Get Outta My Dreams, Get into My Car." He has continued to record up to the present day, though without scoring any hits.

Ohio Players, The

Like most other notable FUNK acts, the Ohio Players' kinetic mix of percussion, loping bass lines, and stabbing horn flourishes owed much to SLY AND THE FAMILY STONE's progressive rock-soul fusion of the late 1960s. In terms of both recording productivity and career longevity, the group was unrivaled within the funk genre.

The band was formed in 1959, in Dayton, as Greg Webster and the Ohio Untouchables. Early on, they played behind the R&B vocal group, the FALCONS, appearing on recordings such as the hit, "I Found a Love." With the addition of three members from an area band, they became known as the Ohio Players.

Although they had first recorded on their own for Lu Pine in 1963, their stint as the studio group for Compass Records in 1967–68 proved to be

The Ohio Players during a performance on TV's Soul Train (Frank Driggs Collection)

something of a breakthrough. In addition to releasing singles under their own name, they produced a number of demo tapes, one of which was released as *Observations in Time* by Capitol in 1968. Moving on to Westbound Records in the early 1970s, the band enjoyed one big hit, "Funky Worm," which revealed their penchant for tongue-in-cheek humor. They also established another tradition during this period: marketing through provocative album covers typically featuring scantily clad women in sexually suggestive poses.

Signing with the Mercury label in 1974, the Players began a highly successful commercial run that included the following albums: *Skin Tight* (Mercury, 1974; featuring the single, "Skin Tight"), *Fire* (Mercury, 1974; featuring the chart-topping

crossover smash, "Fire"), *Honey* (Mercury, 1975; featuring the number one pop and R&B hit, "Love Rollercoaster"), *Contradiction* (Mercury, 1976), *Ohio Players Gold* (Mercury, 1976), and *Angel* (Mercury, 1977). By the time the group had switched to Arista Records in 1979, their popularity had dropped off considerably. They continued to record for a variety of labels in the 1980s—including Accord, Boardwalk, Air City, and Track—with only intermittent success. With the advent of compact discs, many of the band's classic albums were reissued (along with assorted hit collections such as PolyGram's *Funk on Fire: The Mercury Anthology,* released in 1995). Despite the deaths of two longtime members—saxophonist "Satch" Mitchell and trumpeter "Pee Wee"

Middlebrooks—in the 1990s, the band has continued to tour up to the present day.

O'Jays, The

The O'Jays are one of the more durable R&B acts of all time, making records for close to a half-century. Hailing from Canton, Ohio, the group—originally consisting of Bill Isles, Eddie Levert (whose sons later formed the R&B trio, Levert), Bobby Massey, William Powell, and Walter Williams—formed in 1958 as the Triumphs. After recording for King as the Mascots in 1961, they were given their present name by a Cleveland deejay, Eddie O'Jay.

Signing with Imperial, they first made the charts with "Lonely Drifter" in September 1963. They continued placing singles on the lower rungs of the R&B and pop charts throughout the 1960s, moving on to Bell Records in 1967 and then Neptune in 1969. Their fortunes took a significant upswing when they signed with Philadelphia International in the early 1970s; utilizing the songwriting and producing talents of Kenny Gamble and Leon Huff, the group (which carried on as a trio with the departure of Isles in 1965 and Massey in 1971) topped the R&B charts with "Back Stabbers," "Love Train," "Give the People What They Want," "I Love Music (Part 1)," "Livin' for the Weekend," "Message in Our Music," "Darlin' Darlin' Baby (Sweet, Tender, Love)," "Use ta Be My Girl," and "Lovin' You." Much like the ISLEY BROTHERS, the FOUR TOPS, and the TEMPTATIONS, the O'Jays seem impervious to the passage of time, still active as performers well into the twenty-first century.

One-derful Records

Established by George Leaner in 1962, One-derful Records was dedicated to disseminating the hard soul music of the local Chicago scene. Previously, Leaner had run a distribution company, United Distributors, with his brother, Ernie, from 1950. Utilizing producers like Monk Higgins (real name Milton Bland) and Andre Williams in addition to songwriters such as Otis Hayes, Larry Nestor, and Eddie Silvers, the label—along with its subsidiaries, Midas, M-Pac, and Mar-V-lus—recorded a string of national hits in its house studio at 1825 South Michigan, most notably Harold Burrage's "Got to Find a Way," Otis Clay's "That's How It Is," the Five Dutones' "Shake a Tail Feather," and McKinley Mitchell's "The Town I Live In." Learner's biggest success, however, came with Alvin Cash and the Crawlers, who were responsible for such rave-ups as "Twine Time," "The Barracuda," and "Philly Freeze." One-derful closed down in 1968, but Ernie and nephew Tony Leaner went on to form Toddlin' Town (which operated until 1971), signing a number of the former label's artists.

Organized Noize

Organized Noize played a key role in elevating southern RAP and the Atlanta record scene into the pop music mainstream. Melding the laid-back soul-funk of Parliament-Funkadelic with cutting-edge arrangements, the production team—consisting of Rico Wade (born February 26, 1972, in Atlanta), Pat "Sleepy" Brown, and Raymon Murray—opted to work entirely with original material rather than relying heavily upon samples of other artists' recordings, a common practice within the HIP-HOP community.

They first attracted attention for discovering and producing OUTKAST, whose debut, *Southernplayalisticadillacmuzik* (LaFace, 1994), achieved platinum sales. Organized Noize's success owed much to their ability to adapt to the demands of each client. Their production of TLC's "Waterfalls"—the third single from the trio's *Crazysexycool* (LaFace, 1994)—proved that they could appeal to mainstream listeners. The single's complex arrangement, incorporating elements of country, blaxploitation films, and sophisticated adult contemporary trappings, garnered 1996 Grammy nominations for Record of the Year and Best Pop Performance by a Duo or Group with Vocal. Although not as prolific as some other notable hip-hop producers, they went on to work with artists like EN VOGUE and LUDACRIS in addition to the Dungeon family, a group of Atlanta-based acts, including OutKast, Goodie Mob, Cool Breeze, and Backbone, utilizing their home studio, the Dungeon.

Orioles, The

One of the seminal R&B vocal groups, the Baltimore-based Orioles (first known as the Vibra-Naires), originally consisting of lead tenor Earlington Carl Tilghman (aka Sonny Til), tenor Alexander Sharp, baritone George Nelson, bass Johnny Reed, and guitarist Tommy Gaither, were formed in 1947. In addition, to recording the chart-topping R&B classics "It's Too Soon to Know" and "Tell Me So" in the late 1940s, the million-selling "Crying in the Chapel" (1953) is widely considered to be one of the first rock 'n' roll-styled recordings. Although the hits stopped coming in 1953, the group soldiered on until Til's death from a heart attack on December 9, 1981.

Orlons, The

The Philadelphia-based Orlons were one of the most successful pop-R&B vocal groups in the twilight of the Brill Building era. Consisting of neighborhood friends Shirley Brickley (born December 9, 1944), Steve Caldwell (b. November 22, 1942), Marlena Davis (b. October 4, 1944), and Rosetta Hightower (b. June 23, 1944), they were brought to the attention of Cameo-Parkway by Len Barry, then lead singer of the Dovells. Their biggest hits during 1962–63—"The Wah-Watusi," "Don't Hang Up," and "South Street"—were essentially snappy dance numbers given a GIRL GROUP reading, with Caldwell's bullfrog bass lines providing a distinctive accent in the refrains. Beginning in late 1963, their recordings experienced a substantial drop-off in sales, due in part to the advent of the British Invasion. Caldwell and Davis departed in the mid-1960s, but the Orlons limped on with the addition of Audrey Brickley. They finally

disbanded when Hightower relocated to England in 1968 to do session work.

Osborne, Jeffrey (b. 1948) *singer and songwriter*

Born March 9, 1948, the Providence, Rhode Island, native first gained fame as the lead vocalist of L.T.D. He left the group in 1980 to go solo, becoming one of the major recording stars of the 1980s. His notable crossover (R&B and pop) hits included "I Really Don't Need No Light," "Don't You Get So Mad," "Stay with Me Tonight," "The Last Time I Made Love" (with Joyce Kennedy), "You Should Be Mine" (The Woo Woo Song)," and "Love Power" (with Dionne Warwick).

Otis, Johnny (b. 1921) *vocalist, multi-instrumentalist, composer and bandleader*

Born John Veliotes on December 28, 1921, the Vallejo, California, native worked with various big bands before forming his own in 1945. He began recording later that year for Excelsior and became a major star when his 1950 Savoy single "Double Crossing Blues" topped the R&B charts for nine weeks. His two follow-ups for the label, "Mistrustin' Blues" and "Cupid's Boogie," would also go to number one, followed by more successes. Following a six-year hiatus from the charts, Otis returned with his only crossover hit, "Willie and the Hand Jive," in 1958.

As a bandleader (his group was referred to as the Quintette, Orchestra, Congregation, and Show in the 1950s), head of the Dig label, and co-owner of the Barrelhouse nightclub beginning in 1948, he helped discover such artists as CHARLES BROWN, ESTHER PHILLIPS, the ROBINS, and Devonia Williams. He also helped popularize R&B through his national tours with the Rhythm & Blues Caravan in the early 1950s. He would remain active as a performer and record producer through much of the century in addition to getting involved in politics and his own ministry.

OutKast

Formed as part of Atlanta's HIP-HOP underground in 1993 by teenage rappers Andre "Dre" Benjamin (Andre 3000) and Antoine "Big Boi" Patton, OutKast signed with the Arista subsidiary, LaFace, within a matter of months of their formation. Their debut album, *Southernplayalisticadillacmuzik* (LaFace, 1994), made the Top 20 and garnered a "Best Newcomer" Gong at the 1995 *Source* awards. Their sophomore effort, *Atliens* (LaFace, 1996)—which featured the chart-topping RAP singles, "Elevators (me & you)" and "Atliens"—rose to number two on the *Billboard* Top 200, boosted by world-class production values, innovative jazz-inflected instrumentation, and jagged rhythms reminiscent of British HOUSE music.

Aquemini (LaFace, 1998) and *Stankonia* (LaFace, 2000) were widely acknowledged to be hardcore dance masterpieces, built around the duo's distinctive interplay of rap verses. Their eclectic double-CD set, *Speakerboxxx/The Love Below* (LaFace/Zomba), released in 2003 and rated the second most popular album of 2004 by *Billboard*, elevated them to superstar status. The venerable trade magazine also designated them the top duo/group (and number three pop act) of the year; two OutKast releases, "The Way You Move" and "Hey Ya!," were included in the Top Ten singles of 2004. *Speakerboxxx/The Love Below* received the 2004 Grammy Awards for Album of the Year and Best Rap Album, while its hit "Hey Ya!" received the Grammy for Best Urban/Alternative Performance.

Ovations, The

The Memphis-based Ovations achieved success melding a smooth soul sound reminiscent of SAM COOKE with the southern gospel harmonies that had informed their upbringing. Featuring Cooke sound-alike Louis Williams, the group first surfaced with "It's Wonderful to Be in Love," which reached number 22 on the R&B charts in 1965. They followed with a string of regional hits on the GOLDWAX label, including "Me and My Imagination."

The failure to achieve national success ultimately caused the Ovations to disband. However, Williams went on to form a new edition of the group, recruiting Quincy Billops, Jr., Bill Davis, and Rochester Neal, all alumni of Ollie and the Nightingales. After signing with an MGM subsidiary, Sounds of Memphis, they returned to the charts. Their biggest hit came with their 1973 cover of the 1962 Cooke song, "Having a Party." With the black music scene then dominated by FUNK and the emerging DISCO sound, their style seemed dated. No more hits followed, and the Ovations soon disbanded for good.

Pablo, Petey *rapper*

Based in Greenville, North Carolina, Petey Pablo is closely identified with the southern RAP movement. He first attracted attention with guest appearances on MYSTIKAL's *Let's Get Ready* and the remix version of Black Rob's "Whoa." His debut album, *Diary of a Sinner: 1st Entry* (2001), which achieved modest success with the help of the infectiously energetic lead single, "Raise Up," featured the rapper's trademark characteristics: a dynamic mode of delivery and unrelenting rhythmic attack. The follow-up CD, *Still Writing in My Diary . . .* (2002), did even better, powered by the hit single, "Freek-A-Leek," produced by crunk star Lil' Jon.

Paradons, The

The Paradons, hailing from the country and western stronghold of Bakersfield, California, captured lightning in a bottle with their one notable hit, "Diamonds and Pearls," which reached number 18 in 1960. However, efforts to recapture the magic of that disc—the skewed harmonies, catchy vocal background riffing, and plaintive lead by the song's composer, West Tyler—all came up far short of the mark.

The Paradons—comprised of high school classmates Billy Myers, William Powers, Chuck Weldon, and Tyler—were discovered by former Louisiana rockabilly performer, Werly Fairburn, who had established Milestone Records along with Madelon Baker, a model allegedly being groomed by General Mills in the mid-1950s to become the next Betty Crocker. In January 1960, Fairburn brought the group into Hollywood's Audio Arts Recording Studio to cut "Diamonds and Pearls." Follow-up singles like "Bells Ring," "I Had a Dream," and one Warner Bros. release, "Take All of Me," failed to make the charts. The group disbanded, while Baker would go on to form the Audio Arts label and discover artists such as the Incredibles and Jimmy Webb.

Parker, Little Junior (1927–1971) *singer*

Although not considered to be a trailblazing artist, singer/mouth harpist Little Junior Parker was one of the most popular blues performers during the 1950s and 1960s. Born Herman Parker, Jr., on March 3, 1927, in West Memphis, he first attracted attention as a member of the Howlin' Wolf Band during 1949–50. After a brief stint with Johnny Ace's Beale Streeters, he started his own band, Little Junior's Blue Flames, in 1951. He would tour with the Johnny Ace Revue from 1953 until Ace died of a self-inflicted gunshot wound on December 24, 1954.

Parker first recorded for Modern in 1952, before achieving a Top Five R&B hit the following year with "Feelin' Good" on Sam Phillips's legendary Sun Records. Following a dry spell during the mid-1950s, he rebounded with a string of hits for the Houston-based Duke label, including "Next Time You See Me," "Driving Wheel," "In the Dark," and "Annie Get Your Yo-Yo."

Parker went on to produce modest hits for the Mercury, Blue Rock, Minit, and Capitol labels in the late 1960s and early 1970s. His career was cut short, however, by a fatal brain tumor on November 18, 1971, in Blue Island, Illinois.

Parker, Ray, Jr. (b. 1954) *singer, guitarist, and songwriter*

Born May 1, 1954, in Detroit, Michigan, Parker became a well-known session guitarist on the West Coast. After forming the pop-funk band Raydio in 1977, he became a major star on the strength of such crossover hits as "Jack and Jill," "You Can't Change That," and "A Woman Needs Love (Just Like You Do)." He continued his hot hand as a solo act, beginning in 1982, most notably with the number one pop and R&B single "Ghostbusters," the title track from the highest grossing film of 1984.

Parliament-Funkadelic   See CLINTON, GEORGE.

P. Diddy   See PUFF DADDY.

Peaches & Herb

The Washington, D.C., duo—originally consisting of Herb Fame (b. Herbert Feemster in 1942) and Francine Barker (b. Francine Hurd in 1947), who was succeeded by Marlene Mack in 1968—enjoyed a string of successful soft soul recordings in the late 1960s on the Date label. Fame would resurrect the act with Linda Green as his partner in 1977, deftly mixing disco-tinged fare like "Shake Your Groove Thing" and romantic ballads—most notably, the number one pop and R&B hit "Reunited"—strongly reminiscent of the first incarnation of Peaches & Herb.

Peebles, Ann (b. 1947) *singer*

Hi Records recording artist Ann Peebles began her career singing with her father's gospel group, the Peebles Choir. Peebles came from a musical family.

Her mother was a professional singer and her grandfather founded the gospel group that would provide a pathway for her fame. Born in St. Louis, Missouri, on April 27, 1947, the pivotal event in her career was a chance meeting with jazz instrumentalist Gene "Bowlegs" Miller.

Impressed with the unique quality to Peebles voice, Miller introduced her to Hi Records founder Willie Mitchell, for whom "Bowlegs" already worked. Peebles began writing R&B songs with Peebles's future husband Don Bryant, including her signature song "I Can't Stand the Rain," which reached number six on the R&B charts as well as the pop Top 40. She also enjoyed chart success with the subsequent album *I Can't Stand the Rain* (Hi, 1973). Other hit singles included "I'm Gonna Tear Your Playhouse Down" and "(You Keep Me) Hangin' On."

Though material released after 1974 sold poorly, Peebles continued working with Hi Records until the label changed hands in 1977. She continued working throughout the 1980s with such labels as Waylo, and guested on albums with soul singers such as Mavis Staples. Peebles hits have been covered in recent years by artists such as Bette Midler ("I Feel Like Breaking Up Somebody's Home") and Missy Elliot ("The Rain [Super Duper Fly]," which included a sampling from the original track).

Pendergrass, Teddy (b. 1950) *singer*

A premier balladeer whose velvety vocal delivery spanned the soul, funk, disco, and black contemporary eras, Teddy Pendergrass has also survived countless personal setbacks from artistic disputes, love affairs, and a serious automobile accident on March 18, 1982, that left him partially paralyzed.

Born March 26, 1950, in Philadelphia, Pendergrass honed his performing skills working in local clubs during the 1960s. He joined the budding Philly soul juggernaut, Harold Melvin & The Blue Notes, as a drummer in 1969; he became their lead vocalist the following year. Produced by Kenny Gamble and Leon Huff, the group enjoyed considerable success in the early 1970s, recording such crossover hits as "If You Don't Know Me by Now," "The Love I Lost (Part 1)," "Bad Luck (Part 1)," "Hope That We Can Be Together Soon," and "Wake Up Everybody (Part 1)."

Pendergrass left the Bluenotes in late 1975 under acrimonious circumstances. While it took a couple of years for his solo career to gain momentum, he ultimately established himself as a major R&B recording artist in the romantic soul-pop vein pioneered by the likes of Barry White. His chart smashes—always more popular with black listeners than the pop mainstream audience—included "I Don't Love You Anymore," "Close the Door," "Turn Off the Lights," "Can't We Try," "Love T.K.O.," "Two Hearts" (with STEPHANIE MILLS), "You're My Latest, My Greatest Inspiration," "Hold Me" (accompanied by a young WHITNEY HOUSTON), "Love 4/2," and "Joy." Shortly before his car accident, Pendergrass starred in the film, *Soup for One* (1982). He also worked with a supergroup comprised of Philadelphia International artists such as Archie Bell, DEE DEE SHARP, Gamble, the O'JAYS, Billy Paul, and LOU RAWLS; the profits of their sole hit, "Let's Clean Up the Ghetto," were contributed to an urban charity project.

See also BELL, ARCHIE, AND THE DRELLS.

Penguins, The
Named for the Kool cigarettes trademark, the Penguins—formed in Los Angeles in 1954—were composed of lead singer Cleveland Duncan, tenor Dexter Tisby, baritone Bruce Tate, and bass Curtis Williams. They recorded perhaps the most popular doo-wop song of all time, "Earth Angel," a Williams composition that topped the R&B charts (a number eight pop hit as well) in early 1955. When Mercury Records expressed an interest in buying their contract from DooTone, manager Buck Ram insisted that the company also take on another of his clients, the less highly regarded Platters. In one of the more ironic twists in pop music annals, the Platters became one of the most popular vocal groups of that era, while the Penguins failed to chart for Mercury. They would switch to Atlantic in the late

1950s, eventually disbanding when success continued to elude them.

People's Choice
Formed in 1971, Philadelphia-based People's Choice mined the same party FUNK vein as the OHIO PLAYERS and WAR. The group consisted of vocalist Frankie Brunson, Roger Andrews, Stanley Burton, Leon Lee, and Dave Thompson. Brunson sang with tenor saxophonist Lynn Hope's band before working with Andrews and Thompson in the vocal group, the Fashions. They first surfaced in 1971 with "I Likes to Do It," followed by nine more R&B hits through early 1981, most notably "Do It Any Way You Wanna" and "Nursery Rhymes (Part I)." Lee would depart for a solo career in 1974, releasing one minor hit, "He Was the Man, Part 1."

Persuaders, The
Formed in 1969, the New York–based soft soul group—originally consisting of lead vocalist Douglas "Smokey" Scott, James "B. J." Barncs, Willie Holland, and Charles Stodghill—struck gold shortly thereafter with the Atco single "Thin Line Between Love & Hate," an R&B chart-topper in 1971. Plagued by large-scale personnel shifts, the Persuaders had ceased to be a hit-making entity by 1974, when the line-up consisted of Scott, Willie Coleman, Richard Gant, and Thomas Lee Hill.

Persuasions, The
An A CAPPELLA quintet formed in 1966, the Persuasions spearheaded the movement to keep the DOO-WOP singing style vital and alive. Based in the Bedford-Stuyvesant section of Brooklyn, the group consisted of lead Jerry Lawson, tenors Joseph "Jesse" Russell, and Jayotis Washington, baritone Herbert "Tubo" Rhoad, and bass Jimmy "Bro" Hayes. Although their genre is considered marginal by record industry experts, they nevertheless issued a steady stream of LPs (whose tracks represent a

blend of original material and reworked rock 'n' roll classics) into the twenty-first century. While much of their following is based on the East Coast, two of their mid-1970s singles—"I Really Got It Bad for You" and "One Thing on My Mind"—became minor nationwide hits.

Phillips, Esther (1935–1984) *singer*

Esther Phillips was one of the first female rhythm and blues stars (she was the youngest female to have a number one single on the R&B charts). She was not only a dynamic vocalist, but a multi-instrumentalist as well.

Born Esther Mae Jones on December 23, 1935, in Galveston, Texas, she moved with her family to Los Angeles at age four. She was discovered by band-leader Johnny Otis in her early teens; joining his band, she became an overnight sensation, enjoying eight Top Ten R&B hits from 1950–52 (billed as Little Esther with the Johnny Otis Orchestra): "Double Crossing Blues," "Mistrustin' Blues"/ "Misery," "Cupid's Boogie," "Deceivin' Blues," "Wedding Boogie"/ "Faraway Blues," and "Ring-A-Ding-Doo."

From that point on, Phillips's career was frequently disrupted by bouts with substance abuse. She resurfaced periodically with hit recordings, most notably, the 1962 R&B chart-topper "Release Me," and "What a Diff'rence a Day Makes." However, drug problems ultimately led to her death from liver and kidney failure on August 7, 1984, in Los Angeles.

Pickett, Wilson (b. 1941) *singer*

Although Wilson Pickett spent a comparatively brief amount of time as a hit-making force, many considered him to be the classic soul singer. His rough, gritty voice was perfectly suited for uptempo material, melding a gospel fervor to a funky backbeat.

Born March 18, 1941, Pickett started out singing gospel music in church, first in his hometown of Prattville, Alabama, and then in Detroit between 1955 and 1959. In 1959, Willie Schofield invited him to join his R&B vocal group, the FALCONS, best known for the 1959 crossover hit, "You're So Fine." He would go on to contribute many compositions to their repertoire, most notably, "I Found a Love" (number six on the R&B charts in 1962).

Pickett's dual talents as a singer-songwriter made a solo career inevitable. His departure from the Falcons followed a successful audition with Double-L Records, headed by R&B legend Lloyd Price, in 1963. He immediately scored two successive R&B hits with the self-composed "If You Need Me" and "It's Too Late."

His breakthrough to a larger pop audience came shortly after his contract was purchased by Atlantic Records in 1964. Assisted by the label's marketing

Wilson Pickett at the start of his solo career (Frank Driggs Collection)

muscle and the decision to have him record with STAX—then affiliated with Atlantic in order to gain a wider market for its artists—Pickett found immediate success with such hits as "In the Midnight Hour," "634-5789," "Land of 1,000 Dances," "Mustang Sally," "Funky Broadway," "Sugar Sugar," "Engine Number 9," "Don't Let the Green Grass Fool You," "Don't Knock My Love – Pt. 1," and "Fire and Water." The tight, stripped-down rhythm accompaniment provided by members of the Stax house band, BOOKER T. & THE MGs (with production by Steve Cropper) proved to be the ideal foil for the dynamic tension communicated by Pickett's vocals. His albums also sold well in the latter half of the 1960s, including *The Exciting Wilson Pickett* (Atlantic, 1966), *The Wicked Pickett* (Atlantic, 1967), *The Sound of Wilson Pickett* (Atlantic, 1967), *The Best of Wilson Pickett* (Atlantic, 1967), *I'm In Love* (Atlantic, 1968), *The Midnight Mover* (Atlantic, 1968), *Hey Jude* (Atlantic, 1969), *Wilson Pickett in Philadelphia* (Atlantic, 1970), and *The Best of Wilson Pickett, Vol. II* (Atlantic, 1971).

Pickett's sales dropped off considerably in the early 1970s as soul was superseded by new black urban styles such as FUNK, DISCO, and REGGAE. He continued to tour extensively both stateside and abroad, although his new recordings—for RCA (1973–75), Wicked (1975–77), Big Tree (1977–79), EMI America (1979–mid-1980s), and Motown (late 1980s)—had trouble competing with reissues of his vintage soul material. He attracted considerable publicity in the early 1980s by uniting with JOE TEX, DON COVAY, and other 1960s black singers as the Soul Clan. His legend received added luster when the highly acclaimed film, *The Commitments* (1991), portrayed him as soul music's Holy Grail. Further recognition came with his induction into the Rock and Roll Hall of Fame in 1991.

Pieces of a Dream

Originally formed in 1975 as Touch of Class, this Philadelphia-based trio's brand of R&B-jazz fusion was an R&B chart fixture during the 1980s.

Adapting their name from jazz saxophonist Stanley Turrentine's 1974 Fantasy LP, *Pieces of Dreams,* the group consisted of drummer Curtis Harmon (born 1962), keyboardist James Lloyd (b. 1964), and bassist Cedric Napoleon (b. 1962). Their biggest hits included "Mt. Airy Groove," which was also released in a RAP version; "Fo-Fi-Fo"; and "Say La La." Pieces of a Dream also worked for a time as the house band for a television series, *City Lights,* airing on KYW-Philadelphia.

Platters, The

At the height of their career, the Platters were an anachronism, performing classic Tin Pan Alley material updated slightly to fit the rhythmic framework of the rock 'n' roll era. Founded by Herbert Reed in 1953, the group—which also included David Lynch, Paul Robi, and lead singer Tony Williams—initially recorded in a DOO-WOP style for the Federal label. Failing to achieve a hit record, members were working as parking lot attendants in Los Angeles when they met music business entrepreneur Buck Ram. Initially using them to make demonstration discs of his own compositions (which tended to fall within the crooning genre), Ram insisted that Mercury Records sign them in early 1955 as part of a package deal involving another of his clients, the Penguins, then on the verge of stardom with the recording, "Earth Angel." In one of the supreme ironies in recording history, the Penguins faded from the public eye without another pop hit, while the Platters (adding Zola Taylor in late 1955) became the top-selling vocal group of the second half of the 1950s. Their Top Ten singles included "Only You," "The Great Pretender," "(You've Got) The Magic Touch," "My Prayer," "Twilight Time," "Smoke Gets in Your Eyes," and "Harbor Lights."

The group's decline in the early 1960s has been attributed to a number of causes, most notably the morals arrest of the male members on August 10, 1959, the departure of Williams (one of the most gifted vocalists in pop) for a solo career in 1960, and

The Platters were sometimes described as "four guys and one lovely dish." (Frank Driggs Collection)

changing consumer tastes. The Platters continued to enjoy steady album sales with the release of titles such as *Encore of Golden Hits* (Mercury, 1960; 174 weeks on pop charts) and *More Encore of Golden Hits* (Mercury, 1960). By the early 1970s, the group, by now recording for Musicor, was considered a nostalgia act, sometimes performing in Richard Nader's rock 'n' roll revival shows. As copyright holder of the Platters' name, Ram continued to manage the official version of the group well into the 1980s. However, he was continuously forced to file lawsuits to keep pseudo-groups from using the

name. Greatest hits packages featuring the Mercury material have remained popular; Rhino issued a two-disc anthology and the Bear Family label released a nine-CD box set in the late 1980s.

Pointer Sisters

Sisters Anita, Bonnie, and Ruth Pointer started the Oakland-based group in 1971, with youngest sibling June joining shortly thereafter. Their early gospel-influenced style reflected an upbringing in which both parents were ministers. They first recorded for Atlantic in 1971, as well as doing session work for Elvin Bishop, Cold Blood, and Boz Scaggs, among others. They began appearing on the charts with increasing regularity adapting to a retro 1940s vocal group style with the Blue Thumb label in the mid-1970s. Following an appearance in the film *Car Wash* (1976), Bonnie left for a moderately successful solo career.

Continuing as a trio, the Pointer Sisters opted for a more contemporary pop-soul sound, producing a long string of hits—most notably Bruce Springstein's "Fire," "He's So Shy," "Slow Hand," "I'm So Excited," "Automatic," and "Jump (For My Love)"—through the 1980s. June and Anita would also make the charts in a solo capacity during that decade.

Positive-K (b. 1967) *rapper*
Born in the Bronx, Positive-K is best remembered as an advocate for the Nation of Islam within a gangsta-inflected, b-boy/breakbeat framework. He became fascinated with HIP-HOP as a youth after watching a GRANDMASTER FLASH show in Echo Park from his grandmother's window. After his inclusion on the *Fast Money* compilation at age 18, he was signed by First Priority. He appeared on another compilation, *Basement Flavor* (First Priority, 1988) and released a string of 12-inch singles, including "Quarter Gram Pam," "Step Up Front," and "I'm Not Havin' It," a duet with MC LYTE. He also contributed a duet with GRAND PUBA on Brand Nubian's debut album before switching to his own Creative Control label. He released two successful singles, "Night Shift," produced by Big Daddy Kane (whom he met during a RAP battle between New York and Philadelphia in the 1980s), and the boastful "I Got a Man" (a number one rap hit in 1993), and an accompanying album, *Da Skills Dat Pay Da Bills* (4th & Broadway, 1992), all of which were picked up for distribution by Island/4th & Broadway. However, his energy was increasingly given over to running Creative Control, signing and developing new talent such as Raggedyman.

Presley, Elvis (1935–1977) *singer*
Elvis Presley transcends categorization as the most important recording artist of the rock era; he may, in fact, be the most dominant cultural figure of the 20th century. Like the great heroes of Greek mythology, Presley's character has acquired a universality with which virtually everyone can identify. But it all began with his extraordinary voice, which fused gospel, black rhythm and blues, and white country-pop sensibilities in more convincing fashion than any performer up to that point in time.

Presley was born January 8, 1935, in Tupelo, Mississippi, the only child (a twin brother, Jesse, was stillborn) of working-class parents. He was raised in Memphis, Tennessee, within a tightly knit household; indeed, strong family ties played a role in his decision to record a couple of pop ballads at the Memphis-based Sun Studios as a birthday present for his mother. Brought to the attention of owner Sam Phillips, he was encouraged to forge that synthesis of black and white pop styles soon to be known as rockabilly and, in a broader stylistic context, as rock 'n' roll.

Following an apprenticeship period cutting demos for Sun, Presley was teamed with local session players, guitarist Scotty Moore and bassist Bill Black, and caught lightning in a bottle in July 1954 with a rave-up rendition of Arthur Crudup's R&B hit, "That's All Right, Mama," backed with Bill Monroe's bluegrass standard, "Blue Moon Of Kentucky." The A-side contains many of the features that made Presley, at least in an intuitive sense, deserving of the later appellation, "King of Rock 'n' Roll": his plaintive voice—literally dripping with teenage hormonal excitement—swoops and swoons over the spare accompaniment consisting of acoustic guitar chords (strummed by Presley himself), electric guitar flourishes, and propulsive upright bass. Phillips retained the split R&B-C&W format on the four remaining Sun releases during 1954–55, marketing Presley to a country audience (he became a regular on the *Louisiana Hayride* as well as appearing on WSM's *Grand Ole Opry*) because—as a southern white performer—no other viable options existed.

RCA's purchase of Presley's recording contract in late 1955 for the then princely sum of $35,000 can be attributed to two notable factors: Sun's need for cash to pay off existing debts as well as to develop new talent (e.g., Johnny Cash, Carl Perkins, Roy Orbison), and the management pact Presley signed with Colonel Tom Parker in mid-1955. Parker, whose business savvy proved instrumental in advancing Presley's career (notwithstanding revisionist interpretations to the contrary), had had a long history of working with the label, most notably as Eddy Arnold's manager.

Boosted by a series of TV appearances in early 1956 on the Dorsey Brothers, Milton Berle, and Ed Sullivan shows, Presley's first RCA single, "Heartbreak Hotel," reached number one on the pop charts (remaining there for eight weeks beginning April 21, 1956), as did the follow-up, "I Want You, I Need You, I Love You." The next single broke all existing precedents, with both sides—"Don't Be Cruel"/ "Hound Dog"—ascending to the top position on the pop (11 weeks), country (10 weeks), and R&B (six weeks) charts. The RCA recordings as a whole had thus far lacked the spontaneity and unadorned directness of the Sun material. They featured studied arrangements with Elvis's performing band augmented by professional session players, generally drummer D. J. Fontana, pianist Floyd Cramer, saxophonist Boots Randolph, and guitarists Chet Atkins and Hank Garland, and the ubiquitous harmonies of the Jordanaires. Worse still, the 45-rpm disc culled from Presley's film debut, "Love Me Tender" (number one for five weeks), introduced a maudlin element that would plague much of his subsequent output. The problem may have been that Presley, unschooled in either musical technique or the concept of good taste, always mimicked and integrated into his personal entertainment vocabulary the influences to which he was exposed. Consequently, the boy who'd chosen to sing the sentimental boy-and-his-dog tearjerker, "Old Shep" at the 1945 Mississippi-Alabama Fair (he placed second in the contest), grew up with the desire to interpret other singers diametrically opposed to the style that had made him famous in the first place.

Some popular music historians point to Presley's military stint from March 24, 1958, to March 1, 1960, as the pivotal event in his career. It is certainly true that the post-Army Elvis seemed more predisposed to record schlocky movie songs and romantic ballads perhaps better suited to middle-of-the-road performers. Presley did not interpret such mainstream material badly—gentler items like "Can't Help Falling in Love," "Good Luck Charm," and "Return to Sender" possessed a laid-back grace and charm that few popular artists of the period could have negotiated as convincingly. Because he was capable of so much more, however, the escapist fare he recorded for much of the 1960s gave the impression that he had sold out.

At the end of the decade, Presley provided a tantalizing glimpse as to what his recording career might have been. Motivated by criticism that he was out of touch with the tenor of the times—a politically mobilized era whose musical benchmarks included folk-rock, psychedelia, and idiosyncratic singer-songwriters—and stabilized by his May 1, 1967, marriage and birth of a daughter early the following year, he opted out of the moviemaking rat race and returned to live performing. Teamed with soulful session players from Memphis, he produced a string of tougher, more socially relevant hit singles, including "In the Ghetto," "Suspicious Minds," and "Don't Cry Daddy."

Although the quality of Presley's releases proved uneven in the 1970s—ranging from the spirited "Burning Love" to the perfunctory, exaggerated reading of "The Wonder of You"—he remained a major box office draw, with successes such as the 1972 Madison Square Garden concert and January 1973 Hawaii show telecast worldwide. Both were documented on disc: *Elvis As Recorded at Madison*

Square Garden and *Aloha from Hawaii via Satellite.* The increasing percentage of live and repackaged material among his album releases beginning in the 1970s owed much to his tendency to avoid the studio. This aversion seems to have been related to his heavy drug use, from amphetamines to the recreational types then in vogue with many of his Hollywood associates. His physical deterioration was evident in the dramatic weight fluctuations and erratic behavior during concerts. Therefore, his sudden death—from a heart attack induced by a drug overdose—at his Memphis home, Graceland, on August 16, 1977, did not come as a complete surprise to well-informed observers.

Beyond trying to accommodate the immediate rush on his recordings in the aftermath of his passing, RCA (sometimes in conjunction with subsidiary imprints such as Camden and Pickwick) has continued to release new Presley titles, virtually all of which have consisted of repackaged previously issued material. However, RCA's comprehensive retrospectives aimed at collectors—including *The King of Rock 'n' Roll—The Complete 50's Masters, Elvis: From Nashville to Memphis—The Essential 60's Masters I,* and *Walk a Mile in My Shoes—The Essential 70's Masters*—have earned universal raves from reviewers. Among the more dubious projects have been marketing gimmicks such as *The Elvis Presley Collection* (whose projected double-CD/cassette titles include "Country," "Rock 'N' Roll," "Love Songs," "Classics," and "Movie Magic"—each containing one "never-before-released bonus song"), leased to Time/Life Music in 2002. True rarities have surfaced over the years such as the *Louisiana Hayride* performances available on 10-inch open reel tape in the Louisiana State Library archives, in addition to material from Presley's early career release on albums, for example *Elvis: The First Live Recordings* (Music Works/Jem, 1984) and material culled from his legendary jam sessions with Jerry Lee Lewis and Carl Perkins at Sun Studios, the *Million Dollar Quartet* (Charly, 1985) and *The Complete Million Dollar Session* (Charly, 1988). But,

more typically, the new material has tended to be of a documentary (or infotainment) nature, in which music is a secondary consideration; e.g., *Elvis: One Night with You* (HBO), *Elvis Presley's Graceland* (HBO), *Elvis on Tour* (MGM/UA, 1984), and *Elvis Memories* (Vestron, 1987).

Recent estimates have placed the total number of legitimate Presley sound recordings sold worldwide at more than one billion. Given his status as an American institution, with something to offer virtually every popular music enthusiast, it's likely that the selling of Elvis Presley will continue unabated for many years to come.

Preston, Billy (b. 1946) *singer and keyboardist*

Born September 9, 1946, in Houston, Texas, Preston relocated to Los Angeles as a child, consequently finding work in films and the TV program *Shindig.* He became a high-profile session player in the 1960s, working with the likes of the Beatles, the Rolling Stones, and Sly & the Family Stone. He would go on to considerable success in his own right as a recording artist, with Top Ten crossover hits such as "Outa-Space," "Will It Go Round in Circles," "Space Race," and "Nothing from Nothing."

Price, Lloyd (b. 1933) *singer, pianist, composer, and record company executive*

Born March 9, 1933, the Kenner, Louisiana, native started his own band as a 16-year-old. His early string of hits—most notably, the R&B chart-topper "Lawdy Miss Clawdy"—was interrupted by a U.S. Army stint from 1953 to 1956. He would go on to form KRC Records in 1957 and become a major recording star with the ABC-Paramount label, with crossover best-sellers such as "Stagger Lee," "Personality," and "I'm Gonna Get Married." When the hits became harder to come by, the founded the Double-L label and shifted his focus to production and booking agency operations.

Prince (The Artist Formerly Known as Prince)

(b. 1958) *singer, songwriter and producer*

Prince may well be the most important R&B artist during the years following the DISCO era. He helped popularize many musical and fashion trends in addition to nurturing countless musicians—including SHEILA E., VANITY 6, Morris Day & the Time, and ANDRE CYMONE—at his recording studio/designer label complex, Paisley Park.

Born Prince Roger Nelson, on June 7, 1958, in Minneapolis, he formed his own band, Grand Central, while in junior high school. He signed with Warner Bros. prior to turning twenty, and soon became a chart fixture. His hits included the R&B chart-topping singles "I Wanna Be Your Lover," "When Doves Cry," "Let's Go Crazy," "Kiss," and "Sign 'O' the Times," in addition to a succession of platinum-selling LPs, most notably, the double-disk set, *1999* (Warner Bros., 1982), and the soundtrack to his first film vehicle, *Purple Rain* (Warner Bros., 1984), which spent 24 weeks at number one and reportedly sold more than 11 million copies.

Long at odds with Warner over his use of controversial lyrics and their attempts at slowing the prolific outpouring of Prince releases, he left to establish the NPG label (which was distributed by EMI). With his sales in a steady decline, Prince joined the Arista roster; however, sales continue to lag well below those of his 1980s work.

Public Enemy

Considered by many to be the most influential RAP act ever, Public Enemy appropriated RUN-D.M.C.'s rock-tinged arrangements and Boogie Down Productions' proto-gangsta verses, pioneering a politically astute—and incendiary—brand of hardcore HIP-HOP. It was formed by Chuck D (b. Carlton Ridenhour, August 1, 1960)—then studying graphic design at Adelphi University, New York, while DJing at the student radio station, WBAU—in 1982, along with friends Hank Shocklee (then actively recording demo tapes) and Bill Stephney, who had his own WBAU program. DEF JAM producer Rick Rubin signed them after hearing their track, "Public Enemy No. 1." After coming up with the concept of a socially conscious group, Chuck D added DJ Terminator X (Norman Lee Rogers, August 25, 1966), rapper Flavor Flav (William Drayton, March 16, 1959), and fellow Nation of Islam member, Professor Griff (Richard Griffin), who choreographed a troupe of backup dancers, the Security of the First World, to perform a classical soul revue complete with martial moves and prop Uzis.

Their debut LP, *Yo! Bum Rush the Show* (Def Jam, 1987), featuring strident rhetoric voiced over spare arrangements (provided by the production team, the Bomb Squad), was a modest success. The follow-up, *It Takes a Nation of Millions to Hold Us Back* (Def Jam, 1988), proved to be a breakthrough, garnering rave reviews from the rap and rock press alike and reaching number 42 on the pop charts (number eight in England). The group was also surrounded by controversy generated by the mainstream media as a result of such comments as "[rap was] the black CNN" (Chuck D) and "[Jews were responsible for] the majority of the wickedness that goes on across the globe" (Griff).

Public Enemy had become a commercial juggernaut with the release of *Fear of a Black Planet* (Def Jam, 1990) and *Apocalypse 91 . . . The Enemy Strikes Black* (Def Jam, 1991), both of which went Top Ten by tempering the militant verses with cleaner, slicker production values. However, continued media attacks, combined with Flavor Flav's legal entanglements (domestic charges, drug abuse), resulted in two critical disasters: *Greatest Misses* (Def Jam, 1992), a mediocre assortment of new material, remixes, and a live cut, and *Muse Sick-n-Hour Mess Age* (Def Jam, 1994), which seemed content merely to mine the group's old formulas.

With Public Enemy now rendered unfashionable by the mid-1990s G-funk craze, Chuck D decided to rethink the group's priorities, severing ties with Def Jam and ending their touring commitments. He recorded a solo album, *Autobiography of Mistachuck* (Mercury, 1996), and published a book on his life in fall 1997. He reassembled Public Enemy (along with the Bomb Squad) the following year, producing the soundtrack to Spike Lee's basketball saga, *He Got Game* (Def Jam, 1998), which utilized skeletal rhythm arrangements built around repetitive loops and bass lines. Initially available on mp3 form on the Web, *There's a Poison Goin' On* (Play It Again Sam, 1999) ushered a return to the group's classic format. Unfortunately, it sounded out-of-date to a new generation of hip-hop fans, and failed to register on the pop charts. *Revolverlation* (Koch, 2002) was another collection of new tracks, remixes, and live materials that—while failing to map out new stylistic directions—revealed Chuck D to be in complete command of his artistic powers.

Puff Daddy (Sean Combs, Diddy, P. Diddy)
(b. 1970) *rapper, producer, record executive*
Born Sean Combs in Harlem, New York, Puff Daddy was raised in the Mt. Vernon area. Securing employment at UPTOWN RECORDS—a label on the rise via hits by MARY J. BLIGE and Heavy D and the Boyz—through his childhood friend, Heavy D, he worked his way up from general gofer to A&R man, and then became executive producer of Father MC's hit album, *Father's Day* (1990). In 1992, however, Combs was fired due to undisclosed differences with the label. He decided to form his own record company, BAD BOY, and by late 1993 had signed Craig Mack and the NOTORIOUS B.I.G., both of whom went on to become major hit-makers. While continuing to run Bad Boy—whose roster included Faith Evans and Total in the mid-1990s—he also remixed tracks for R&B stars like BOYZ II MEN and MARIAH CAREY.

Signed to Arista, his Puff Daddy solo project was placed on hold in the wake of B.I.G.'s murder. He ultimately made a splash with the assertive anthem, "Can't Nobody Hold Me Down" (featuring MASE), which reached number one on the *Billboard* Hot 100 in early 1997. He also topped the charts in mid-year with a tribute to B.I.G., "I'll Be Missing You" (featuring Faith Evans, 112, and the LOX), followed by his equally successful debut LP, *No Way Out* (Arista, 1997), both of which won Grammys, for Best Performance and Best Rap

Album, respectively. While garnering considerable press for his relationship with actress Jennifer Lopez, he maintained his pop ascendancy with the reflective, melodic *Forever* (Arista, 1999) and—as P. Diddy & the Bad Boy Family—the somewhat lackluster *The Saga Continues . . .* (Arista, 2001). Puff Daddy officially changed his monicker to P. Diddy in 2001, after being acquitted of gun and bribery charges stemming from a shooting at a New York nightclub. He seems content at present to maintain a relatively low profile, focusing on the management of his record industry empire and clothing line.

Purify, James and Bobby
Although James and Bobby Purify had intermittent hits strung out over the course of a decade, they are best known for the classic soul recording, "I'm Your Puppet." If not for the abundance of talented soul acts in the late 1960s—particularly in such recording centers as Chicago, Memphis, MOTOWN, MUSCLE SHOALS, and Philadelphia—the duo might well have enjoyed much greater success.

Born James Purify (May 12, 1944, Pensacola, Florida) and Robert Lee Dickey (September 2, 1939, Tallahassee, Florida), the cousins started out performing in the early 1960s in a Florida-based band, the Dothan Sextet. They spun off as a duo in mid-1965, signing a recording contract with the Bell label shortly thereafter. The duo hit the pop and R&B Top Ten a year later with the ballad, "I'm Your Puppet," with their moody two-part harmonies set off by a horn choir and vibraphone lead filigrees. They followed up with a string of lesser pop-soul hits, including "Wish You Didn't Have to Go," "Shake a Tail Feather," "I Take What I Want," and "Let Love Come Between Us."

With their best days far behind them, Dickey departed in 1970. Purify continued to perform in a solo capacity until bringing in Ben Moore as the new "Bobby Purify" in 1974. They returned to the charts briefly in the mid-1970s, in America with "Do Your Thing," and in England with a remake of "I'm Your Puppet."

Queen Latifah (b. 1970) *rapper*

Born Dana Owens in Newark, New Jersey, she is widely held to be the earliest female rapper to communicate a feminist perspective in an intelligent, engaging manner. Her adopted name, Latifah, is of Arabic derivation, meaning "delicate" or "sensitive." After performing as a human beatbox with the group, Ladies Fresh, she achieved a measure of renown with the release of her assertive debut single, "Wrath of My Madness" (backed by the REGGAE-influenced "Princess of the Posse"), in 1988. The ensuing album, *All Hail the Queen* (Tommy Boy, 1989), was equally impressive, revealing her ability to interpret soul, HIP-HOP, dance pop, and reggae-derived DUB styles effectively.

Queen Latifah's follow-up LPs—*Nature of a Sista* (Tommy Boy, 1991) and *Black Reign* (Motown, 1993), which included the hit single and Grammy winner (Best Rap Solo Performance), "U.N.I.T.Y."—showcased increasingly more bellicose posturing tempered somewhat by commentaries on the social inequities of inner city life. Latifah's popularity was now at a peak, due in no small part to her high-profile acting career, which ranged from a regular spot on the Fox-TV sitcom, *Living Single,* to film roles like *Jungle Fever, Juice,* and *Bringing Down the House.*

After a long sabbatical from the music business, she issued *Order in the Court* (Motown, 1998), which attempted to meld hip-hop with old-school R&B in much the same fashion as the FUGEES, Faith Evans, and others during the mid-1990s. Her 2004 release, *The Dana Owens album,* featured Latifah singing covers from the 1920s through the 1970s. Although no longer a trendsetter, Latifah has continued to balance her music, acting, and celebrity-related activities up to the present day.

Raeletts, The

The Raeletts (spelled "Raelettes" for a time in the late 1960s) evolved out of the COOKIES, a GIRL GROUP, originally consisting of Ethel "Earl-Jean" McCrea, Margie Hendrix, and Pat Lyles, that recorded for Lamp (1954) and Atlantic (1956) in addition to backing artists such as BIG JOE TURNER and CHUCK WILLIS in the studio. They joined forces with RAY CHARLES in the late 1950s, and a new trio was christened the Cookies in 1962 to record for the Dimension label. As had been the case with their earlier manifestation, the Raelettes also recorded without a frontman, placing five singles on the R&B charts from 1967 to 1970, including "One Hurt Deserves Another" and "Bad Water." Driven by professional and personal considerations, the group's membership changed frequently. Personnel during 1967–69 included Gwendolyn Berry, Alexandra Brown, Clydie King, MINNIE RIPERTON, and lead singer Merry Clayton, while the 1970 edition included Vernita Amoss, Susaye Green, Mabel John, and Estella Yarbrough.

rap

Although the term is frequently used to encompass the entire HIP-HOP culture, rap is used by many experts to refer specifically to the improvised lyrics and mode of delivery employed by MCs on top of the beats, samples, and other elements comprising song arrangements. The genre had many stylistic antecedents, including talking blues, spoken interludes in gospel, and repeated refrains in countless pop novelties by the likes of Bo Diddley, Ray Stevens, Jerry Reed, the Shangri-Las, and the JIMMY CASTOR Bunch. More evolved links to rap can be found in the street poetry of the Last Poets, GIL SCOTT-HERON, and others set to stripped-down, heavily rhythmic R&B, jazz, FUNK, and DISCO arrangements. REGGAE toastmasters, or DJs, essentially provided the final link to rap, in creating DUB passages over instrumental backing tracks projected via mobile sound systems. Jamaican DJ Kool Herc is widely credited with originating the practice of mixing sounds from a battery of turntables, a trademark device in rap music.

The Sugarhill Gang's "Rapper's Delight," released in 1979, signaled the emergence of rap—no longer confined to clubs and house parties in the New York City area—into the recorded sound medium. As the genre evolved through old-school rap in the early 1980s—in turn, splitting off into the gangsta, pop rap, and Afrocentric/eclectic camps at the end of the decade—intellectuals, media critics, journalists, politicians, religious figures, and others joined in the growing controversy as to whether rap was a new art form, worthy of all the protections guaranteed by the First Amendment, or a morally reprehensible threat to the established moral and social order. Any thoughts of legal control, however, were undercut by the infiltration of the music—and its attendant lifestyle—into the very fabric of American popular culture. Despite the efforts of hardcore fans to pressure their favorite acts from straying into the pop mainstream, it could be argued that rap music is presently as popular with young suburban whites as it has been with inner-city African Americans. *Billboard*'s Top Pop Artists compilation, published in its December 25, 2004, issue, attests to this state of affairs, including 18 rap acts among the 50 positions.

Rascals/Young Rascals, The

Although best known as one of the most successful blue-eyed soul acts of the 1960s, the Rascals were also facile assimilators whose stylistic evolution mirrored the historical development of rock music. The individual band members cut their teeth on a wide range of genres, including jazz, rhythm and blues, DOO-WOP, pop, and rock 'n' roll. As the Rascals, they attempted to keep in step with changing fashions by veering from garage rock to soul, followed by psychedelia, progressive rock, and laid-back jazz fusion.

The band, originally called the Young Rascals, formed when drummer Dino Danelli, then supporting R&B artists like Willie John, hooked up with three members of Joey Dee's Starlighters—keyboardist/vocalist Felix Cavaliere, vocalist/percussionist Eddie Brigati, and guitarist Gene Cornish—to create a repertoire of songs for performance during the winter of 1964–65. Their exciting brand of dance-oriented rock led to a contract with Atlantic Records in late 1965.

The Young Rascals' first single, the up-tempo ballad "I Ain't Gonna Eat Out My Heart Anymore," was only a moderate seller; however, the follow-up, a cover of the Olympics' "Good Lovin'," topped the charts. The band's versatility—two strong lead singers, exceptional songwriting (often featuring Cavaliere's music and Brigati's lyrics) and arrangements, and equal command of slow and high-energy numbers—was largely responsible for their long string of hits. These included the Top 20 hits "You Better Run," "I've Been Lonely Too Long," "Groovin'," "A Girl Like You,' " "How Can I Be Sure," "It's Wonderful," "A Beautiful Morning," and "People Got to Be Free."

Unlike many rock bands in the 1960s, the Young Rascals' LPs sold nearly as well as their singles. They released both straightforward collections of songs such as *The Young Rascals* (Atlantic, 1966), *Collections* (Atlantic, 1967), *Groovin'* (Atlantic, 1967), and *Time Peace: The Rascals' Greatest Hits* (Atlantic, 1968) as well as later concept albums: *Once Upon A Dream* (Atlantic, 1968), *Freedom Suite* (Atlantic, 1969), *See* (Atlantic, 1970), and *Search and Nearness* (Atlantic, 1971). When the hits slowed to a trickle by the 1970s, the Rascals (the moniker used beginning with the release of *Once Upon A Dream*) regrouped, with Cavaliere and Danelli bringing in guitarist/pianist/vocalist/songwriter Buzzy Feiten, bassist Robert Popwell, and singer Ann Sutton to achieve a greater jazz orientation. The limited success of albums by the new configuration—*Peaceful World* (Columbia, 1971) and *The Island Of Real* (Columbia, 1972)—led to a breakup in 1972.

The original members have continued to work within the music industry; Danelli, Cornish, and Cavaliere got together in 1988 for a U.S. tour. However, the threesome became embroiled in litigation shortly thereafter regarding use of the band name. In 1997 the Rascals were inducted into the Rock and Roll Hall of Fame.

Ravens, The

The New York City–based Ravens were the first of the "bird groups" and played a key role in the evolution of post–World War II rhythm and blues. Formed in 1945, their original lineup included tenor Ollie Jones, tenor Leonard Puzey, bass Jimmy Ricks, and baritone Warren Suttles. With the inclusion of Maithe Marshall, who replaced Jones in 1946, the Ravens featured two leads, utilizing Marshall's soaring falsetto tenor to achieve heightened poignancy on ballads and Ricks's dynamic bass lines on mid-tempo material. The two singers also pioneered the switchover lead within a song, a device that was heavily copied by other vocal groups.

The Ravens initially recorded with Hub in 1946, but did not reach the charts until switching to the National label. Their lengthy hit run began in 1948 with "Write Me a Letter," and ran through "Rock Me All Night Long" in late 1952. Their hit renditions of "Silent Night" and "White Christmas," which was closely mirrored by the DRIFTERS's 1955 version, opened the door further to R&B-tinged interpretations of Christmas standards. The group moved on to the Argo label in the mid-1950s, but folded shortly after Ricks departed for a solo career in 1956.

Rawls, Lou (b. 1935) *singer*

Lou Rawls is living proof that popularizing the blues, jazz, and gospel can be accomplished without sacrificing musical values and good taste. Despite the polish and sophistication characterizing his approach, however, he remains capable of displaying the hard, soulful edge that attracted listeners in the first place. Many black contemporary singers popular in the 1980s and 1990s—most notably, Peabo Bryson and LUTHER VANDROSS—were strongly influenced by his singing style.

Born December 11, 1935, in Chicago, he progressed from singing in church choirs as a youth to a stint with the famed gospel group, the Pilgrim Travellers, in the late 1950s. After the group broke up, Rawls sang the blues on the chitlin' circuit. He developed a unique performing style consisting of an introductory monologue that would segue into a blues song. These numbers—half soliloquy, half RAP—effectively communicated the conditions faced by African Americans in the 1960s.

His vocal interplay with SAM COOKE in "Bring It on Home to Me" in 1962 led to a contract with Capitol. Rawls released a string of albums—28 in all—over the next decade with the label. Although much of this output featured somewhat overpowering production values, the warmth of his vocals and flawless phrasing, particularly on the million sellers *Lou Rawls Live!* (Capitol, 1966) and *Lou Rawls Soulin'* (Capitol, 1966), the latter of which

included the Top Ten single "Love Is A Hurtin' Thing," kept things interesting while consistently making the charts.

Rawls moved to MGM in 1971, immediately earning a Top 20 single, "A Natural Man." However, the company's insistence that he focus on middle-of-the-road material led to another label change, this time to Bell. When that association failed to click, Rawls asked Kenny Gamble and Leon Huff to add him to the roster of their Philadelphia International label. Their choice of material and arrangements reinvigorated his career. The up-tempo ballad, "You'll Never Find Another Love Like Mine," became his biggest crossover hit (hitting number two on the Hot 100), as well as providing the impetus for seven more best-selling albums over the next five years.

The hits stopped coming following a switch to Epic Records. However, a shift to Blue Note led Rawls back to a blues-inflected approach, most notably, in the albums *At Last* (Blue Note, 1989) and *Stormy Monday* (Blue Note, 1990), although commercial success has continued to elude him.

Real Roxanne, The *rapper*

Puerto Rican–born Adelaida Martinez, based in New York City, was one of the many MCs to owe her career to the flurry of answer songs recorded in response to U.T.F.O.'s raunchy "Roxanne Roxanne." The production team of Jam Master Jay, Howie Tee, and Full Force, who had assisted in the recording of that original hit single, discovered Martinez, who was then a waitress in Brooklyn. She released a promising debut LP, *The Real Roxanne* (Select, 1988), which revealed her skills to be the equal of any female rappers on the pop scene. Unfortunately, she was too closely identified with the Roxanne phenomenon, and when it died down, so did her commercial potential. Her follow-up album, *Go Down (But Don't Bite It)* (Select, 1992), attracted little attention, and she quickly faded from view.

Redding, Otis (1941–1967) *singer*

A one-of-a-kind soul stylist equally adept at rave-up houserockers and soft, caressing ballads, Otis Redding is remembered as much for his potential as for what he actually accomplished. Toiling for years on the R&B circuit before a breakthrough performance at the 1967 Monterey Pop Festival positioned him on the verge of mainstream stardom, he died tragically in a small plane crash on December 10, 1967, at age 26.

Born September 9, 1941, in Macon, Georgia, Redding did not seem destined for a recording career until given an audition at STAX RECORDS while serving as a chauffeur for an aspiring band headed by Johnny Jenkins. Redding's first release, "These Arms of Mine," reached the Top 20 in 1963 on the national R&B charts. Stax immediately signed him to a long-term contract. With BOOKER T. & THE MGs guitarist Steve Cropper serving as arranger/producer, Redding recorded a long string of R&B hits—many self-composed—including "Mr. Pitiful," "I've Been Loving You Too Long," "Respect," "Satisfaction," "My Lover's Prayer," "Try a Little Tenderness," "Tramp," and "Knock on Wood."

By the summer of 1967, when his Monterey appearance captured the imagination of white rock fans, Redding's singles were becoming fixtures on the pop charts. The widely acclaimed "Queen of Soul," ARETHA FRANKLIN, took one of his compositions, "Respect," to the top of the pop charts in 1967. A mere two-and-a-half weeks before his death, he recorded a song that close associates felt would propel him to mainstream success, the posthumously chart-topping crossover smash, "(Sittin' on the) Dock of the Bay."

Although only modest sellers during his lifetime, Redding's albums, all of which have been reissued as compact discs, have remained in demand up to the present day. The material from his original LP releases—*Pain In My Heart* (Atco, 1964), *The Great Otis Redding Sings Soul Ballads* (Volt, 1965), *Otis Blue/Otis Redding Sings Soul* (Volt, 1965), *The Soul Album* (Volt, 1966), *Complete & Unbelievable . . . The Otis Redding Dictionary of Soul* (Volt, 1966),

Otis Redding publicity still (Frank Driggs Collection)

King & Queen (Stax, 1967; with Carla Thomas), *Otis Redding Live In Europe* (Volt, 1967), *The Dock of the Bay* (Volt, 1968), *The Immortal Otis Redding* (Atco, 1968), and *Otis Redding in Person at the Whiskey A Go Go* (Atco, 1968)—is also available through countless retrospective compilations.

Reddings, The

The Reddings certainly possessed the bloodlines for stardom; the group comprised OTIS REDDING's sons Dexter (vocals/bass) and Otis III (guitar) and cousin Mark Locket (vocals/drums/keyboards). The Georgia-based trio made a big splash with their 1980 debut single, "Remote Control." Follow-up releases did not fare as well, although they reached the charts nine more times through 1988. Their greatest successes came with rehashes of Otis Redding's "(Sittin' On) The Dock of the Bay" and the Supremes' "Where Did Our Love Go" (part of a double-sided hit).

Reed, Jimmy (1925–1976) *singer*
Jimmy Reed outsold virtually every blues recording artist of the 1950s with the exception of B. B. KING. He had a considerable influence on the blues-rock acts of the late 1960s, including the Rolling Stones, John Mayall, and the Steve Miller Band.

Born September 6, 1925, on a plantation in Dunleith, Mississippi, he learned the fundamentals of guitar and harmonica from future sidekick Eddie Taylor. Following his discharge from the Navy in 1945, Reed relocated to Gary, Indiana, which provided close proximity to Chicago area clubs. He first recorded for Chance in 1953, and subsequently failed an audition for Chess before catching on with the fledgling VEE-JAY label, which he enjoyed a long string of hits between 1955–65. Utilizing a distinctive mumbled, slurring vocal style with unadorned guitar/harmonica accompaniment (assisted by the ever faithful Taylor), he not only enjoyed considerable R&B and pop crossover success with singles like "You Don't Have to Go," "Ain't That Lovin' You Baby," "Honest I Do," "Baby What You Want Me to Do," "Big Boss Man," and "Bright Lights Big City," but issued a string of moderately popular LPs, most notably, *At Carnegie Hall* (Vee-Jay, 1961), a double-disc set that was actually a studio re-creation of his live show.

Following the collapse of Vee-Jay, Reed moved on to Exodus and BluesWay in the late 1960s, but failed to sell well. Although introduced to a new audience via the American Folk Blues Festival tour of Europe in 1968 and the concurrent blues revival, his 1970s releases for a variety of labels met with public indifference. Beset with epilepsy and chronic alcoholism since early in his career, Reed died of respiratory failure on August 29, 1976, in Oakland, California. He would be inducted into the Blues Foundation's Hall of Fame in 1980 and the Rock and Roll Hall of Fame in 1991.

Reese, Della (b. 1931) *singer*
Della Reese was a polished pop-R&B stylist who appeared headed for superstardom in the late 1950s. Unable to maintain a high level of commercial consistency as a recording artist, however, Reese turned increasingly to acting, beginning in the 1960s.

Born Delloreese Patricia Early on July 6, 1931, in Detroit, she toured with Mahalia Jackson as a gospel singer between 1945 and 1949. Reese also worked with trumpeter/bandleader Erskine Hawkins in the early 1950s before going solo in 1957. She first made the charts with "And That Reminds Me." After signing with RCA, she opted for a more mainstream sound, finding immediate success with "Don't You Know" (which topped the R&B charts and reached number two on the Hot 100 in 1959) and "Not One Minute More." Subsequent releases, however, only reached the lower portion of the pop charts.

After acting and singing on countless television programs, Reese was offered her series, *Della,* in 1970. She was cast as Della Rogers in the popular TV series, *Chico & The Man,* from 1976 to 1978, and starred in *Touched by an Angel* (1994–2003). Since appearing in *Let's Rock* (1958), Reese has landed roles in many films as well. Through it all, she has continued to perform live and occasionally make new recordings.

reggae
Originally applied in 1968 to the latest in a rapidly evolving string of Jamaican dance rhythms, reggae would later become a collective term for various styles of Jamaican popular music, isolated examples of which have dented the U.S. Top 40 since the early 1960s. It is characterized by a loping beat, a strong dose of rhythm and blues, and recording techniques that have been simultaneously original in concept

and primitive in execution. It has had an impact on 1970s rock that was far greater than its moderate commercial success.

The genre was a product of a diverse array of influences, including African-derived children's games, the ecstatic Christian Pocomania cult, Garveyite Rastafarians, and New Orleans rhythm and blues, which was broadcast all over the Caribbean via clear-channel radio stations in the late 1950s. These forces did not converge until the appearance of transistor radios revived Jamaican interest in popular music recordings. Out of this state of affairs emerged the "sound system man," who operated a generator-powered hi-fi rig mounted on the back of a flatbed truck that would be driven to rural areas for dances. These operators, utilizing catchy handles such as "Duke Reid," generated large audiences of fans.

In the early 1960s, the dearth of New Orleans talent (and corresponding drop-off of available imports) forced sound system men to make their own records. Primitive studios sprang up around Jamaica. The first recordings were bad copies of New Orleans music; the Jamaican musicians could not seem to get the New Orleans rhythm right. This "wrong" rhythm became standardized, and "ska" was born, with its strict, mechanical emphasis on the offbeat (mm-CHA! mm-CHA!). One notable example of the ska style, Millie Small's "My Boy Lollipop," became a 1964 Top Ten hit in the United States.

By 1965, ska had been superseded by the slow, even more rhythmic "rock steady" genre. Sound system men began employing deejays, who would "toast" or talk over the instrumental B-side of a record. The DJ—prime exponents included Prince Buster, Sir Collins, King Stitt, and U Roy—improvised rhymes about his sexual prowess and the greatness of the sound system operator. This practice also became known as "dubbing"; some of it was "rude" (i.e., dirty—in Jamaican slang, "dub" is equivalent to sexual intercourse).

Poppa-top was the next link in the evolutionary chain; bubblier than rock steady, it loosened up the beat to the point where greater rhythmic division was possible. The leading exponent of the style, Desmond Dekker, reached the U.S. Top Ten with his 1969 release, "Israelites."

The release of the Maytals's "Do the Reggay," in 1968, served notice that a new form had entered the marketplace. Jamaican music had been expanding the role of the bass line for much of the 1960s; reggae brought the bass to the forefront, emphasizing the complex interrelationship between it, the trap drums, and the percussion instruments. The beat was interspersed with silences, the pulse could be divided as finely as 64 times, and cross-rhythms were in abundance. The bass appeared to be the lead instrument, with the guitar reduced to playing "change," merely scratching at a chord. Keyboard and horns were utilized to thicken the texture.

Despite the success of some reggae-styled material in the U.S.—e.g., JOHNNY NASH's "I Can See Clearly Now" and "Stir It Up," and Eric Clapton's "I Shot the Sheriff"—the genre remained relatively unknown to most Americans until the U.S. release of the film, *The Harder They Come*, starring Jimmy Cliff, in 1973. It became a cult favorite and opened the door to the American market for other reggae artists.

In contrast to its widespread acceptance in Europe, Africa, and South America, the genre's popularity in the United States was hampered by the scarcity of live reggae music. This was because most of the records used the same pool of studio talent, and most Jamaicans could not afford nightclubs or stage show performances. The most famous reggae performer was BOB MARLEY, whose recordings featured protest lyrics, first-rate melodies, high-quality production values, and a seamless blend of Jamaican roots and rock conventions that enabled him to please both his original followers and U.S. fans.

Marley's promising career was cut short by his death from brain cancer in 1981. Nevertheless, reggae has left a substantial musical legacy, including hip-hop (a RAP-inflected spinoff, "dancehall," was popular in urban clubs during the 1990s), DISCO

DUB with a DJ rapping over the track, and an expansion of the rhythmic possibilities in rock, as realized by artists as diverse as Jimmy Buffett, the Grateful Dead, the Clash, Police, the Flying Lizards, the Selector, Generation X, the Slits, the English Beat, Public Image Ltd., and UB40.

The genre continues to reflect the Jamaican lifestyle as well as supporting the world's most successful self-contained Third World record business. Homegrown artists such as Ziggy Marley, Musical Youth, Inner Circle, and Shabba Ranks managed to achieve international success in the 1990s within an updated reggae framework.

Reid, L. A., and Babyface *songwriting and producing team*

American songwriters and producers Antonio (L. A.) Reid and Babyface (born Kenneth Edmonds in 1959; nicknamed by space-funkster Bootsy Collins) first worked together in The Deele, an R&B group, before making a splash at the controls of Pebbles' 1988 hit single, "Girlfriend."

The team's distinctive sound, characterized by strongly melodic fare framed by hard, fast rhythms, has been employed by many lead R&B artists, including PAULA ABDUL, the Boys, Toni Braxton, BOBBY BROWN, the Jacksons, and Midnight Star. Babyface, in his own right, specializes in the release of smooth, romantic recordings—including *Lovers* (Solar, 1989), *Tender Lover* (Solar, 1989), *A Closer Look* (Solar, 1991), and *For the Cool in You* (Epic, 1994)—utilizing the vocal talents of such singers as Pebbles and Karyn White.

Rhymes, Busta (b. 1972) *rapper*

Born in the East Flatbush area of Brooklyn, New York, Busta—whose Jamaican heritage greatly influenced his style—moved to Uniondale in 1983, forming Leaders of the New School, with fellow MCs Charlie Brown, Dinco D., and Cut Monitor Milo at Uniondale High School. At age 17, his group signed with Elektra Records; before disbanding,

they made two albums, *Future Without a Past* (1991) and *T.I.M.E.* (1993), which reflected the Afro-centric leanings of their idols PUBLIC ENEMY and ERIC B. AND RAKIM.

Following a time out of the public eye, Busta resurfaced in 1996 with the Top Ten single, "Woohah! Got You All in Check" (featuring the late WU-TANG CLAN MC Ol' Dirty Bastard). Notable for its kinetic wordplay and funky beats, the track helped Busta's debut LP, *The Coming* (Elektra, 1996), achieve gold status. Subsequent releases—*When Disaster Strikes* (Elektra, 1997), *Extinction Level Event (The Final World Front)* (Elektra, 1998), *Anarchy* (Elektra, 2000), *Genesis* (J-Records, 2001), and *It Ain't Safe No More* (J-Records, 2002)—found him experimenting with innovative HIP-HOP fusions built around electronica, party FUNK, and eclectic sampling. One of the more prolific talents in hip-hop, capable of drawing inspiration from the most unlikely sources, he seems likely to remain an industry fixture for many years to come.

Richie, Lionel (b. 1949) *singer*

One of the major forces in black contemporary music in the 1970s and 1980s, Richie was a gifted songwriter and record producer, and played piano and saxophone as well as sang, which enabled him to achieve industry success in a number of guises. His ability to appeal to a broad-based audience was a result of an upbringing that included formal training in classical music as well as exposure to the pop, rhythm and blues, and country genres then popular in his native Alabama.

Born June 20, 1949, Richie joined a group that became known as the Commodores while attending Tuskegee Institute. Signed by MOTOWN in 1974, they negotiated FUNK and tender ballads with equal verve, releasing a string of hits that stretched well into the 1980s. By 1980, Richie was in great demand outside the group, writing and producing "Lady" (which topped the pop, adult contemporary, and country charts in 1980) for Kenny Rogers, as well as the title song to the film, *Endless Love* (1981). He

Motown promotional photo of the Commodores with Lionel Richie (second from right) (Frank Diggs Collection)

recorded the latter work, which reached number one on the pop, R&B, and adult contemporary charts, with DIANA ROSS; it became Motown's biggest-selling single ever, as well as top duet recording of all time. These growing commitments spurred him to go solo.

Richie's smooth, easy listening style immediately clicked with "Truly," which won a Grammy for Best Pop Male Vocal Performance; the accompanying album, *Lionel Richie* (Motown, 1982) would achieve quadruple platinum sales. The eight singles drawn from it and his second LP, *Can't Slow Down* (Motown, 1983; over eight million in sales),

all reached the Top Ten. The latter record also earned two 1984 Grammy Awards, for Album of the Year and Producer of the Year. He was also named Writer of the Year by the American Society of Composers, Authors and Publishers in both 1984 and 1985. While slow to appear due to Richie's full slate of activities, the third album, *Dancing on the Ceiling* (Motown, 1986), maintained his career momentum, selling more than four million copies.

Richie played a key role in the USA for Africa project, sharing writing credits with MICHAEL JACKSON and participating in the recording of both the record, "We Are the World" (which topped the pop, R&B, and adult contemporary charts in 1985), and its accompanying video release. He would also contribute music to a number of high-profile films such as *White Nights* (1985)—most notably the crossover chart topper, "Say You, Say Me"—and *The Color Purple* (1985). Although perceived as dated—his last Top Ten single came in early 1987 with "Ballerina Girl"—he has continued to issue moderately successful recordings that appeal to mainstream pop, adult contemporary, and rhythm and blues audiences.

Righteous Brothers, The

The Righteous Brothers were the best known and most commercially successful exponents of blue-eyed soul (i.e., whites displaying black gospel/blues/R&B influences in their singing style). However, during their peak period of success, between 1963 and 1967, they were able to transcend stylistic categorization, appealing to teenage music consumers, an older mainstream pop audience, and blacks alike. The duo's biggest hits—"You've Lost That Lovin' Feelin'," "Unchained Melody," and "Soul and Inspiration"—continue to top polls tabulating all-time favorite recordings.

Tenor Bobby Hatfield and bass singer Bill Medley—both of whom had sung in rock bands while attending high school in southern California—met at an area club in 1962. Finding that their voices and personalities meshed, they decided to work together. Moonglow Records signed them to a contract shortly thereafter, releasing *Righteous Brothers Right Now!* (Moonglow, 1964), *Some Blue-Eyed Soul* (Moonglow, 1964), *This Is New* (Moonglow, 1965), and *Best of the Righteous Brothers* (Moonglow, 1966).

While with Moonglow, the duo's work displayed a loose, funky edge highlighted by the call-and-response vocal interplay between Medley and Hatfield. One of the leading record producers of the day, Phil Spector, was sufficiently impressed to bring them over to his Philles label. The singles fea-

turing Spector's production work—"You've Lost That Lovin' Feelin'," "Unchained Melody," and "Ebb Tide"—instantly elevated the Righteous Brothers to the top of the music business (even their Moonglow albums charted for the first time). Although Spector considered singles to be the most important art form, the Righteous Brothers' albums—*You've Lost That Lovin' Feelin'* (Philles, 1965), *Just Once In My Life* (Philles, 1965), and *Back To Back* (Philles, 1965)—also sold well.

Aware of Spector's reputation for valuing the song over the artist, the Righteous Brothers signed with Verve Records. Their first hit for the label, "Soul and Inspiration," revealed a strong Spector influence. However, later album releases—most notably, *Soul & Inspiration* (Verve, 1966), *Go Ahead and Cry* (Verve, 1966), *Sayin' Somethin'* (Verve, 1967), *Souled Out* (Verve, 1967), and the live *One For the Road* (Verve, 1968)—attempted to showcase the duo's dynamic stage presence and affinity for pop standards.

Despite these efforts at creative growth, Medley felt the need to explore his options as a songwriter and solo performer. The decision to terminate the partnership was made public in early 1968, although Hatfield expressed a desire to continue the act with a new partner. When both floundered in their new career paths, they decided to get back together, allowing the official announcement to be made on a February 1974 broadcast of the *Sonny and Cher Comedy Hour*. The Righteous Brothers enjoyed another major hit in 1974, "Rock and Roll Heaven," but Medley retired for five years following the murder of his wife in 1976.

Medley and Hatfield performed together intermittently over the years after appearing on an *American Bandstand* anniversary TV special in 1981. Medley's top priority, however, continued to be his solo career. He signed with Planet Records in 1982, and later had a number one hit, "(I've Had) The Time of My Life," a 1987 duet with Jennifer Warnes (the song also earned a Grammy Award for Best Pop Performance by a Duo or

Group with Vocal). "Unchained Melody" returned to the charts in 1990 as a result of its inclusion on the *Ghost* soundtrack. A newly recorded version of the song on the Curb label achieved platinum status in 1990. The continued success of various compilations of the classic singles over the years—*Anthology (1962–1974)* (Rhino, 1990) earned a gold record, while *Best of the Righteous Brothers* (Curb, 1990) went platinum—have added further luster to the Righteous Brothers' legacy. The duo was inducted into the Rock and Roll Hall of Fame in March 2003; but Hatfield died in Kalamazoo, Michigan, on November 5 of that year during a tour.

Riperton, Minnie (1947–1979) *singer*

Despite a distinguished career during her relatively short life, Minnie Riperton seemed to be on the verge of even bigger things when she died of lymphoma on July 12, 1979, in Los Angeles. Nevertheless, she left a legacy of well-crafted group and solo recordings, notable for her breathtaking vocal gymnastics which featured a five-octave range.

Born in Chicago November 8, 1947, the youngest of eight children, Riperton began singing in church as a nine-year-old and enrolled at the Lincoln Center to study ballet and voice a year later. She was discovered performing A CAPPELLA at Hyde Park High School by Raynard Miner and Rose Miller, who were then actively promoting the Gems, a GIRL GROUP recently signed by Chess Records. They got her a position as receptionist for the label while she was with the Gems. While attempting to make it on their own as a recording act, the group backed Chess artists like Fontella Bass and ETTA JAMES prior to breaking up in 1966.

Still under contract to Chess, Riperton released singles as Andrea Davis before becoming a lead vocalist with Rotary Connection, a progressive rock-tinged R&B band that recorded six LPs before dissolving in 1970. She did a solo album, *Come to My Garden,* later that year for Janus, a Chess subsidiary. When it went nowhere she dropped out of the enter-

tainment field, adopting a more traditional lifestyle with husband, Richard Rudolph, until STEVIE WONDER talked her into returning as a member of his backing vocal group, Wonderlove, in 1973.

After appearing on Wonder's immensely successful LP, *Fulfillingness' First Finale* (Tamla, 1974), Riperton was recruited by Epic Records. Her initial Epic album, *Perfect Angel* (Epic 1974), included the first of nine R&B hits, "Lovin' You," best known for its high-pitched vocal refrains.

Riperton first discovered she had cancer in 1976. After undergoing a mastectomy and becoming a spokesperson for the American Cancer Society, she received the organization's Courage Award in a White House ceremony in 1977. Departing Epic for Capitol in 1978, she completed one more album, *Minnie* (Capitol, 1979), before her death. Capitol also released the posthumous *Love Lives Forever* (1980), featuring her taped vocals backed by various friends such as Wonder, GEORGE BENSON, Peabo Bryson, Roberta Flack, MICHAEL JACKSON, and Patrice Rushen.

RJD2 (b. 1976) *rapper*

Born May 27, 1976, in Eugene, Oregon, R. J. Krohn (RJD2), became a highly respected name among indie HIP-HOP producers and a leading force in the instrumental hip-hop underground. Though a native of the Beaver State, he spent many of his formative teenage years in Columbus, Ohio.

While in Columbus, he made his first long-term hip-hop contacts, becoming the DJ/producer for Megahertz, which was signed to Bobbito Garcia's New York label, Fondle 'em Records, in 1998. He contributed his efforts to two of their 12-inch releases that year and was also behind the Megahertz track, "This Year," that appeared on the regional record compilation, *Always Bigger and Better Vol. 1 (ABB)*. He went on to produce the debut solo single for Megahertz member Copywrite, "Holier Than Thou," on Rawkus Records. The hip-hop producer's early work was enough to afford him a nod from *Vibe* magazine in their "history of hip-hop" edition.

Opportunities for expansion arose for Krohn when hip-hop producer and instrumental enthusiast, EL-P, chose to form his own record label, Def Jux, after leaving Rawkus over creative differences. RJD2 would be one of the first acts signed on to the fledgling label, the name of which had to be changed to Definitive Jux after the threat of pending legal battles with established hip-hop trademark holders DEF JAM emerged.

RJD2 made his first appearance as a solo artist on the compilation, *Def Jux Presents I,* alongside label mates such as Company Flow, (EL-P's former musical project), and Aesop Rock. He followed with two 12-inch releases, "Good Times" and "June," a collaboration in which former Megahertz bandmate Copywrite lent his vocals to RJD2's composition.

Krohn finally put together a more fully realized effort with the release of his first LP in 2002, *Dead Ringer.* The album is widely referred to as "cinematic" music, a description given credence upon listening to the hodgepodge of tracks collected for the album, ricocheting between the tongue-in-cheek B-movie sampling of "The Horror" to the psychedelic undertones of "Ghostwriter" (featured in a Saturn ad). Though the record is virtually free of guest appearances, it did garner the praise of such hip-hop notables as Questlove (Roots) and art rock acts like Radiohead.

The producer split his time in 2003 between touring with a four-turntable setup in support of his album and producing/remixing tracks for such artists as Massive Attack, EL-P, the Polyphonic Spree, and Elbow. In 2004 he released his follow-up album, *Since Last We Spoke,* which takes on a larger use of synthesizers and a departure from his RAP roots to a more indie rock sensibility.

—Lowery Woodall

Robey, Don (1903–1975) *record company executive*

One of the pioneering entrepreneurs of the R&B scene, Robey was born November 1, 1903, in Houston. In 1945, he purchased a nightclub, the Bronze Peacock, which soon became a mecca for local R&B talent in addition to attracting major recording stars nationwide. Shortly thereafter, Robey started a record store, later the base of operations for Peacock Records, one of the earliest black-owned record companies. It developed into a leading R&B and gospel label, with a roster that included the likes of Johnny Ace, CLARENCE "GATEMOUTH" BROWN, the Dixie Hummingbirds, the Five Blind Boys, and Big Mama Thornton. Robey went on to acquire the Memphis-based Duke label, which attracted major R&B artists such as Bobby Bland and LITTLE JUNIOR PARKER. He also established a subsidiary gospel imprint, Songbird. He died in Houston on June 16, 1975.

Robins, The

The Robins are one of the more notable asterisks in rhythm and blues history. While they had limited success as a recording act, two members went on to form the core of one of the most popular DOO-WOP groups and arguably the finest R&B-oriented comedians of all time, the COASTERS.

Formed in Los Angeles as the Four Bluebirds, in 1947, the group originally included Bobby Nunn, Ty Terrell, Billy Richards, and Roy Richard. They were offered a recording contract by the legendary Savoy label in 1949, producing their debut hit, "If It's So, Baby," backed by the Johnny Otis Band, early the following year. Shortly thereafter, they contributed vocals, along with up-and-coming chanteuse, Little Esther (ESTHER PHILLIPS), to Otis's biggest hit, "Double Crossing Blues" (which topped the R&B charts for nine weeks).

As the R&B vocal group craze, which placed a premium on more sophisticated harmony arrangements, gathered momentum, the Robins added Carl Gardner and Grady Chapman in 1954. By the time they'd released the crossover hit, "Smokey Joe's Café"—originally appearing on the Spark label in the early fall, but reaching the R&B Top Ten the following year on Atco—lead singer Gardner and bassist Nunn had moved on to form the Coasters.

Robinson, Smokey (b. 1940) *singer,*
songwriter, and record company executive

Smokey Robinson possesses one of the truly distinctive voices in pop music, a pure tenor capable of soaring effortlessly into falsetto range. He has also been responsible for some of the most poetic verses ever put to pop music. These unparalleled talents, combined with his not inconsiderable skills as a record producer and label administrator, made him a primary architect of the fabulously successful MOTOWN sound.

Born William Robinson, on February 19, 1940, in Detroit, he formed an R&B vocal group, the Matadors, while attending Northern High School in 1955. Renamed the Miracles, whose original

Smokey Robinson performing as a member of the Miracles
(Frank Driggs Collection)

members also included tenors Emerson and Bobby Rogers, baritone Ronnie White, and bass Warren "Pete" Moore, the group first recorded for End in 1958. With Robinson's future wife, Claudette Rogers, replacing Emerson (who had joined the U.S. Army), the group signed with the Motown subsidiary, Tamla, and hit the jackpot in late 1960 with the R&B chart-topper, "Shop Around." The group placed 38 more singles on the charts before Robinson departed for a solo career in late 1972, including the number one R&B hits, "You've Really Got a Hold on Me," "I Second That Emotion," and "The Tears of a Clown."

Robinson remained a steady hit-maker through the 1970s and 1980s, although he did not click with a pop mainstream audience in a big way until the release of "Cruisin' " and "Being with You" at the tail-end of the DISCO era. His autobiography appeared in 1988 the year he was inducted into the Rock and Roll Hall of Fame. He was honored with a Grammy Living Legends award in 1990, followed by a Lifetime Achievement award in 1999.

Robinson, Sylvia (b. 1936) *singer and record*
company executive

Born March 6, 1936, in New York City, Sylvia Robinson (maiden name: Vanderpool) has left an indelible mark on the record industry in a variety of roles. In 1954, she teamed with session guitarist Mickey Baker to form the duo Mickey and Sylvia; their 1956 single, "Love Is Strange," remains an early rock 'n' roll classic.

She married Joe Robinson in 1956, and they founded a series of rhythm and blues labels, including All Platinum, Strong, Turbo, and Vibration. After splitting with Baker, she worked as a producer (her credits included IKE AND TINA TURNER's "It's Gonna Work Out Fine," the Moments' "Love On a Two-Way Street," and Shirley and Company's "Shame, Shame, Shame"), session musician, and songwriter. She continued to record intermittently as a solo artist, her greatest success coming with her number three hit, "Pillow Talk."

With All Platinum (soon to be reorganized as SUGAR HILL) involved in Chapter 11 proceedings, Robinson was introduced to the HIP-HOP scene by her son, Joey, Jr. She formed a studio group, the Sugarhill Gang, whose debut release, "Rapper's Delight," became the first mainstream rap hit in 1979. Despite efforts to add legitimate hip-hop performers to its roster—most notably, GRANDMASTER FLASH and Funky Four +1—Sugar Hill Records was unable to keep pace with TOMMY BOY, DEF JAM, Profile, and other street-smart labels, and went out of business in 1985.

Rob Roys (Norman Fox & the Rob Roys)

The Rob Roys were one of the more underrated classic DOO-WOP groups. They consisted of five DeWitt Clinton High School (Bronx, New York) friends—lead vocalist Norman Fox, bass Marshall "Buzzy" Helfand, second tenor Andre Lilly, baritone Bob Thierer, and first tenor Bob Trotman—who began performing as a unit in 1956. The group's black members, Lilly and Trotman, had sung with the Bronx-based Harmonaires.

A chance meeting between Trotman and Don Carter, New York account executive for Duke/Peacock Records, in a Bronx record store in 1957 led to a contract with its Backbeat subsidiary. The group's debut release, "Tell Me Why," was penned by Helfand, though Carter evidently arranged to receive coauthor credit, a common practice among industry executives at the time. It was back by "Audry," inspired by Lilly's girlfriend, and became a regional hit. It continues to pop up on radio playlists and album anthologies to the present day.

The Rob Roys recorded one more single for Backbeat, "Dance Girl"/"My Dearest One," which sold substantially fewer copies than its predecessor. Helfand departed in early 1959; his replacement, Paul Schneller, participated in the group's final recording, "Dream Girl"/"Pizza Pie." The record also experienced weak sales, and the Rob Roys disbanded shortly thereafter.

Ron C *rapper*

Born Ronald Pierre Carey, in Oakland, California, he relocated to Dallas as a 17-year-old. He showed early promise as a performer, which led to a recording contract with the Profile label. Two gangsta rap–styled albums—*"C" Ya* (1990) and *Back on the Street* (1992)—garnered critical raves, but generated little in the way of sales. Ron C's career was also compromised by a conviction for "possession of a controlled dangerous substance with intent" in the spring of 1990.

Ronettes, The

Classic exponents of the Spector Sound, the Ronettes parlayed massive beehive hairdos and an abundance of mascara to provide a tough, sultry accent to the GIRL GROUP genre. All three members—sisters Veronica and Estelle Bennett and cousin Nedra Talley—were born in New York City during the World War II years. They began singing together as the Darling Sisters and were performing a song-and-dance routine based on Hank Ballard and Chubby Checker's "The Twist" at the Peppermint Lounge by 1961. They went on to record for Colpix Records in 1961–62 as Ronnie and the Relatives as well as performing with disc jockey Murray the K's rock shows and singing behind of the era's top pop stars.

Signed by Phil Spector to his Philles label in 1963, the trio's first release, "Be My Baby," reached number two on the *Billboard* Hot 100. Although their follow-up singles continued to feature Spector's patented Wall of Sound production, none of them broke into the Top Twenty. By 1966 Spector lost interest in making records and married Ronnie Bennett. After a couple of failed attempts at launching her solo career (A&M, 1969; Apple, 1971), the couple divorced in 1974.

With the other Ronettes now married, Ronnie Spector continued to work with other prominent musicians during the 1970s and 1980s, including Steven Van Zandt, Bruce Springsteen's E Street Band, and Genya Ravan. Her greatest success came with "Take Me Home Tonight" (1986), a duet with Eddie Money which hit number four on the pop chart.

Roots, The

A Philadelphia-based RAP group well versed in old-school freestyling, the Roots also bring in jazz influences and rely on their own ensemble playing as opposed to a reliance on sampling or studio musicians. Their origins go back to 1987, when rapper Tariq Trotter (aka Black Thought) and drummer Ahmir Thompson (aka Questlove) were students at the Philadelphia High School for the Performing Arts. They joined forces with rapper Malik B and bassist Hob, performing on the busking circuit until their manager was able to set up a European tour. While performing in Germany, they came to the attention of the Geffen label, which signed them to a recording contract. A promising mini-album, *From the Ground Up* (Geffen, 1994), was followed by *Do You Want More ?!!!??!* (Geffen, 1994), which utilized high-profile jazz guests as well as the Roots' rap protégés, the Foreign Objects. More recent releases have continued to experiment with jazz/RAP fusion, garnering respectable sales and critical acclaim in the process.

Ross, Diana (b. 1944) *singer*

Born March 26, 1944, in Detroit, Diana Ross first gained fame as the lead singer of the Supremes. Ross's sexy, malleable voice, combined with the group's charm school image and photogenic good looks, enabled them to cross over to the pop main-

Diana Ross (far right) and the Supremes performing in the late 1960s (Frank Driggs Collection)

stream, a hitherto unprecedented achievement within the rhythm and blues/soul genre.

Her departure from the group seemed a foregone conclusion when, in 1967, it underwent a name change to "Diana Ross and the Supremes." MOTOWN Records owner Berry Gordy had long felt Ross possessed sufficient star quality to warrant a solo career in both the music business and motion pictures. Not only did her initial solo recordings—the singles "Reach Out and Touch (Somebody's Hand)" and chart-topping "Ain't No Mountain High Enough," and eponymous 1970 album—sell well, but she garnered high Nielsen ratings for her 1971 TV special (followed by a successful soundtrack LP) and an Oscar nomination for playing singer Billie Holiday in the film, *Lady Sings the Blues*. Ross maintained her momentum throughout the decade, appearing in another big-budget movie, *Mahogany* (1975), and releasing a string of best-selling, if artistically uneven, records, including *Touch Me in the Morning* (Motown, 1973), *Diana Ross* (Motown, 1976), *Diana* (Motown, 1980), and four number one singles— the bland ballads "Touch Me in the Morning" and "Theme from Mahogany," as well as the disco-flavored "Love Hangover" and "Upside Down."

By the time her collaboration with LIONEL RICHIE on the theme song to the film *Endless Love* (1981) achieved a nine-week run at number one on the Hot 100 charts, Ross had signed a contract with RCA. Despite regular appearances on the charts over the next half-decade, she moved back to Motown (now owned by EMI London) in 1987. Despite her high visibility in the entertainment tabloids, Ross, who took a considerable amount of time off to raise a family, failed to place a recording on either the singles or albums charts during the 1990s.

Roy C (b. 1943) *singer*
Roy C bounced around on the periphery of the R&B scene throughout the 1960s and 1970s, creating a notable legacy in the process. Born Roy Charles Hammond, in 1943, the New York City native started singing with the DOO-WOP group, the Genies, who were best known for the pop hit, "Who's That Knocking?" After going solo, he made the R&B Top 20 in 1965 with "Shotgun Wedding," which reached number six in Great Britain the following year, and then returned to the Top Ten in 1972. Later recordings never did quite as well, although "Got to Get Enough (Of Your Sweet Love Stuff)," put out on his own Alaga label, also made the R&B charts. While releases for labels like Black Hawk, Shout, and Mercury were commercial flops, his composition, "Honey I Still Love You," was a pop hit for Mark IV in 1972.

Ruffhouse
Formed in the late 1980s, the Columbia (later Sony) subsidiary, Ruffhouse, specialized in RAP music. Initially, the label roster was comprised largely of hardcore artists, most notably, pro-ganja revolutionaries CYPRESS HILL, Tim Dog, and NAS. Nevertheless, more pop-oriented HIP-HOP acts like the Goats and Kriss Kross were also actively courted. Ruffhouse's street credibility was considerably enhanced by the acquisition of pioneer gangsta rapper Schoolly D; its 1998 release of *The Miseducation of Lauryn Hill*, by the former FUGEES member, was extremely successful.

Run-D.M.C.
Run-D.M.C. was a rare commodity when it first became successful in the mid-1980s; whereas early RAP stars tended to come from economically repressed inner-city areas, Queens, New York rappers Joseph Simmons (Run) and Daryll McDaniels (D.M.C.) both grew up in a comfortable middle-class environment. A direct consequence of their combined backgrounds is that Run-D.M.C.'s recorded material lacks the harsh, bitter edge (e.g., profanity, violent images, and revolutionary dogma) typical of rank-and-file rap/HIP-HOP acts.

Simmons—a one-time protégé of hip-hop pioneer KURTIS BLOW—and McDaniels were involved in the New York city rap scene by their early teens. By the early 1980s they had hooked up with a club disc jockey, Jay Mizell, who adopted the moniker Jam Master Jay. Run-D.M.C.'s early records for the Profile label were popular in the New York area dance-rap scene; beginning with "It's Like That" in 1983, the group's singles consistently made the black charts.

Their recordings—particularly the albums *Run-D.M.C.* (Profile, 1984); *King of Rock* (Profile, 1985); *Raising Hell* (Profile, 1986), which achieved triple-platinum status, assisted in large part by the crossover hit single, "Walk This Way," a collaboration with Aerosmith's Steve Tyler and Joe Perry; and the film soundtrack *Tougher Than Leather* (Profile, 1988)—often crossed over to the pop charts, still a comparatively rare occurrence in the mid-1980s. This broader appeal was based in part on positive lyrics that emphasized the importance of education and urged listeners to avoid drugs and violence.

Run-D.M.C.'s clean mainstream image would prove to be something of a credibility problem by the late 1980s when changing public tastes seemed predisposed to prefer the political militancy and raw, street-smart message largely identified with gangsta rappers. The group's commercial momentum was also blunted by a protracted legal battle with Profile and its publishing company, Protoons, beginning in 1987. They released only one hit single in the 1990s, "Down with the King," while later albums—*Back from Hell* (Profile, 1990), *Greatest Hits 1983–1991* (Profile, 1991), and *Down with the King* (Profile, 1993)—documented their rapid fall from favor.

Rush, Otis (b. 1934) *singer and guitarist*

A solid second-line R&B vocalist/guitarist/harmonica player, Otis Rush was born April 29, 1934, in Philadelphia, Mississippi. He followed the path taken by many electric blues interpreters before him, relocating to Chicago in 1948. Originally known as "Little Otis" in the 1950s, he had one hit of note, the oft-recorded "I Can't Quit You Baby" (which reached number six of the R&B charts in 1956). He remained active for five decades as a performer and recording artist.

Sade (b. 1959) *singer*

Born Helen Folasade Adu, on January 16, 1959, the Nigerian native relocated to London at age four. Sade had already left her mark as a model and designer of menswear when she became an international pop music star in 1984. Her best known crossover hits include "Smooth Operator," "The Sweetest Taboo" "Never as Good as the First Time," and the 1988 R&B chart-topper, "Paradise." Her 1992 release, *Love Deluxe,* featured the single, "No Ordinary Love."

Salsoul Orchestra, The

The Salsoul Orchestra epitomized the blend of sweet arrangements and sinuous dance floor rhythms typical of DISCO era recording acts. The brainchild of Philadelphia producer/arranger Vincent Montana, Jr., the ensemble included vocalists Carl Hem, Philip Hurt, Phyllis Rhodes, and Ronni Tyson. Montana's concept was responsible for nine R&B hits from late 1972 through 1982, most notably a remake of Jimmy Dorsey's number one 1942 instrumental smash, "Tangerine," and "Nice 'n' Naasty." Guest artists such as gospel/pop singer Loleatta Holloway and Cognac were liberally employed to augment the group's sound.

Salt-N-Pepa

The first distaff rappers of note, they were instrumental in paving the way for other female acts in a male-dominated genre. They provided an assertive, more grown-up vision of African-American women in contrast to the wise-cracking, arrogant young teens most visible among the female MCs, and helped RAP cross over to mainstream pop acceptance.

Salt-N-Pepa were the brainchild of Hurby "Luv Bug" Azor, who enlisted his girlfriend, Cheryl James (Salt), and Sandra Denton (Pepa) to provide an answer song to Doug E. Fresh and Slick Rick's hip-hop hit, "The Show." The ensuing 1985 single on the Pop Art label, "The Show Stoppa (Is Stupid Fresh)," with the duo billed as Super Nature, was constructed around a sample from the *Revenge of the Nerds* soundtrack and had little trouble garnering massive airplay due to the limited number of rap releases then available for pop consumption. Its success led to a long-term deal with Next Plateau Records for the act, now known as Salt-N-Pepa from a line in "The Show Stoppa," in which they referred to themselves as "the salt and pepper MCs."

The platinum-selling debut album, *Hot Cool & Vicious*—with the DJ, Spinderella (Pamela Greene), rounding out the group—was dominated by Azor's vision. He wrote their lyrics, was credited with the studio production, and created the b-girl–derived visual image—basketball warm-up gear, large gold bamboo earrings, rope chains, and asymmetrical haircuts, as seen in their first video, "Tramp." Ironically, the single's B-side, "Push It," built around innocuously suggestive lyrics and an engaging go-go beat, proved to be the trio's commercial breakthrough, garnering a Grammy nomination and heavy MTV rotation. The follow-up LP,

A Salt with a Deadly Pepa (Next Plateau, 1988), went gold, emphasizing dance rhythms (best appreciated in Salt-N-Pepa's video clips) at the expense of the verses, which contained little of literary or social importance.

The platinum-selling *Blacks' Magic* (Next Plateau, 1990) featured greater creative control by the group, with four tracks produced by Salt and one by Spinderella. The music emphasized their rhythm and blues influences, including dead legends like Jimi Hendrix and Billie Holiday, while the verses covered mature themes such as self-esteem ("Expression"), predatory males ("Do You Want Me"), and loveless relationships ("Let's Talk About Sex"). *Very Necessary* (Next Plateau/London, 1993), which consolidated the artistic growth begun on the previous LP, elevated Salt-N-Pepa to the status of pop icons, selling more than five million copies on the strength of the hit singles "Shoop" and "Whatta Man." Released in the wake of prolonged record label maneuvering punctuated by the trio's decision to cut ties with Azor, *Brand New* (Red Ant, 1997) sold poorly. Much of the problem appeared to rest with the act, which came across as tentative, perhaps due to the rise of more youthful imitators such as TLC. At this point in time, Salt-N-Pepa's future seemed in question, with the three members (including Deirdre Roper, who had replaced Greene as Spinderella) all expressing interest in solo careers.

Sam and Dave

Sam Moore, born October 12, 1935, in Miami, and David Prater, born May 9, 1937, in Ocilla, Georgia, were the most popular black duo of the 1960s. Both grew up singing in church, and were veterans of the southern club circuit prior to meeting at Miami's King of Hearts club in 1961. When Prater forgot the lyrics to Jackie Wilson's "Doggin' Around" at an amateur night show, Moore—who was acting as MC—coached him through the song. They went on to become a fixture in the Miami club scene, eventually signing with Roulette Records.

They switched to Atlantic in 1965, where executive Jerry Wexler loaned them out to the STAX label. Their gospel fervor was effectively captured on recordings made by the Stax production/songwriting team of ISAAC HAYES and David Porter. While most readily identified with the rhythm and blues market, the team known as "Double Dynamite" nevertheless crossed over to the pop charts with hits such as "Hold On, I'm Comin'," "Soul Man," and "I Thank You."

At the peak of their success, Moore and Prater were barely speaking to one another. Although they broke up in 1970, there were several efforts at reunification. Following the Blues Brothers' hit remake of "Soul Man" in 1978, the duo was besieged with bookings from clubs across the country. Their last show together took place New Year's Eve, at San Francisco's Old Waldorf; Prater then began touring with Sam Daniels. In 1983 Moore told the *Los Angeles Herald Examiner* that the instigating factor in their feud was that he'd "lost respect" for his ex-partner when Prater shot his own wife during a 1968 domestic dispute. Prater died April 9, 1988, in a Georgia automobile accident. Moore continued his career, singing on Bruce Springsteen's *Human Touch* (Columbia, 1992). Later that year, Sam and Dave were inducted into the Rock and Roll Hall of Fame.

Scott, Jack (b. 1936) *singer*

Jack Scott followed in the tradition established by rockabilly stars like ELVIS PRESLEY, Carl Perkins, and JERRY LEE LEWIS, placing singles on all three major charts: country, pop, and rhythm and blues. Born Jack Scafone, Jr. on January 24, 1936, in Windsor, Ontario, the singer/songwriter/guitarist relocated to Hazel Park, Michigan, in 1946. He first signed with ABC-Paramount in 1957, before debuting on the R&B charts with the 1958 Carlton release, "My True Love"/"Leroy." Scott's vocals possessed a gospel quality, and he enjoyed notable success with the mournful 1960 ballads "What in the World's Come over You" and "Burning Bridges." Although no longer having hits after the early 1960s, he continued to perform well into the 1980s, particularly in the Detroit area.

Scott-Heron, Gil (b. 1949) *poet*

The leading jazz-R&B fusion poet of the 1970s, Gil Scott-Heron combined a rapier wit with a social consciousness that led him to address poverty, U.S. imperialism, the civil rights movement, and other topical issues of the day. The son of a librarian, he was also a literary figure of some note; his first novel was published in 1968, and his poems provided the impetus for his earliest attempts at songwriting.

Born April 1, 1949, in Chicago, Scott-Heron was raised in Jackson, Tennessee. While attending Lincoln University in Pennsylvania, he met bass guitarist Brian Jackson. They collaborated on a string of jazz–spoken word LPs in the 1970s, including *The First Minute of a New Day* (Arista, 1975); *From South Africa to South Carolina* (Arista, 1975), which featured the anti-apartheid protest rap, "Johannesburg;" *Secrets* (Arista, 1978), containing his most successful single, "Angel Dust"; and *1980* (Arista, 1980).

In 1980, Scott-Heron struck out on his own, although his basic approach changed little. He continued to place albums, most notably, *Reflections* (Arista, 1981), and singles on the lower reaches of the charts during much of the decade. Having earned a master's in creative writing, he taught for a time at Columbia University.

Shabazz, Lakim *rapper*

The New York City–based Shabazz utilized the recording medium to advance the Nation of Islam movement. An interest in poetry led to his discovery of rapping; he began actively performing while still attending school. His participation in a series of MC competitions led to a friendship with budding producer DJ Mark the 45 King. The two lost contact for awhile, but after hearing King mentioned on the radio, Shabazz got back in touch. With King man-

ning the boards, Shabazz made some demos, which led to the offer of a recording contract by Tuff City head Aaron Fuchs.

King continued to work with Shabazz on the latter's debut LP, *Pure Righteousness* (Tuff City, 1988), notable for its espousal of strongly Afrocentric views. The follow-up, *The Last Tribe of Shabazz* (Tuff City, 1990), was even more unrelenting in its pro-Muslim polemics. The resulting slack sales consigned Shabazz to obscurity.

Shaggy (b. 1968) *singer*

Shaggy was perhaps the leading dancehall (a REGGAE spin-off) artist of the 1990s. He was able to transcend that genre by means of universally appealing pop hooks and straightforward lyrics unencumbered by West Indian cultural and linguistic traditions.

Born Orville Richard Burrell, in Kingston, Jamaica, on October 22, 1968, he moved with his family to the Flatbush section of Brooklyn at age 16. Using the nickname (Scooby Doo's cartoon sidekick) he'd acquired as a youth, Shaggy took up singing and deejay work as a teenager. While still in high school, he recorded material with a local producer, Shaun "Sting" Pizzonia. After joining the Marines, he commuted from his North Carolina base to New York City on weekends to make records. His indie releases "Mampie" and "Big Up" topped the reggae charts, while "Oh Carolina"—a cover of a 1960s Jamaican hit—was a number one single in Great Britain. The latter hit would be included on his major label debut, *Pure Pleasure* (Virgin, 1993). The album set forth the sample-heavy melodic blend of pop and R&B that became Shaggy's trademark.

He achieved international superstardom despite a somewhat uneven commercial track record. His Grammy-winning (Best Reggae Album) second album, *Boombastic* (Virgin, 1995), and the title track were both million sellers. After a lackluster follow-up, *Midnite Lover* (Virgin, 1997), Shaggy returned with a career-defining release, the JIMMY JAM AND TERRY LEWIS–produced *Hot Shot* (MCA,

2000). The album sold more than six million copies and topped the *Billboard* charts for six weeks as well as reaching number one in other countries. It featured two of the year's most popular singles, the playfully raunchy "It Wasn't Me" and the crossover hit, "Angel," a remake of Merilee Rush's 1968 country-pop ballad, "Angel of the Morning." However, *Lucky Day* (MCA, 2002) failed to approach this success, providing ammunition to those detractors who felt Shaggy's best work was behind him.

Shakur, Tupac (2Pac) (1971–1996) *rapper*

Despite his tragic death in Las Vegas from a suspected gang-related shooting, Tupac Shakur remains one of the most popular RAP artists of all-time. His posthumously released recordings continue to garner critical raves and substantial sales.

Born Lesane Parish Crooks June 16, 1971, to Black Panther Party members in Brooklyn, New York, Shakur was active in theater during his teens. He joined the progressive rap combine, DIGITAL UNDERGROUND, as a dancer and roadie in 1989; he assumed a prominent role in their early releases, *This Is an E.P. Release* (Tommy Boy, 1990) and *Sons of the P* (Tommy Boy, 1991). He signed with Interscope as a solo artist in 1991; his debut, *2pacalypse Now* (Interscope, 1992), focused on the gritty underside of urban ghetto life. Alongside his growing prominence as a rap performer, he landed a string of film roles, most notably *Juice* (1992), *Poetic Justice* (1993), *Above the Rim* (1994), and *Gang Related* (1995).

Shakur continued to mine the gangsta rap genre with *Strictly 4 My N.I.G.G.A.Z.* (Interscope, 1993), which featured the hit singles "I Get Around" and "Keep Ya Head Up." His group vehicle, *Thug Life Volume 1* (Interscope, 1994) and the aptly titled *Me Against the World* (Tommy Boy, 1995) were released while he was in prison for sexual assault. Freed on parole with the assistance of DEATH ROW CEO Marion "Suge" Knight, Shakur signed with that label in late 1995. He issued the controversial double-disc set, *All Eyez on Me* (Death Row, 1996), which

included songs brimming over with invective against the East Coast HIP-HOP contingency (widely held to have led to a death sentence) as well as the Top Ten singles "California Love" (cassette only release) and "How Do U Want It."

His popularity has inspired the release of a steady stream of new material, including *The Don Killuminati: The 7 Day Theory* (Interscope, 1996; under the pseudonym Makaveli), *R U Still Down (Remember Me)* (Amaru, 1997), *Still I Rise* (Interscope, 1999; with the Outlawz), *Until the End of Time* (Interscope, 2001), *Loyal to the Game* (Amaru/Interscope, 2004; produced by EMINEM), and countless compilations and tribute recordings. A longstanding legal dispute between Shakur's estate and Death Row led to a 1998 settlement

Tupac Shakur (Wenn/Landov)

requiring the return of more than 150 unreleased master tapes to the former and the voiding of his contract with the label. Under the stewardship of Shakur's family and close associates, it appears likely that additional titles will continue to appear at regular intervals well into the future.

Shalamar

Formed in 1977 by Don Cornelius—the producer/host of the long-running television program, *Soul Train*—the black contemporary vocal group was a consistent hit-maker through the 1980s. Comprised of vocalists/dancers Jody Watley and Jeffrey Daniels (previously the husband of STEPHANIE MILLS) and Gerald Brown, Shalamar's most notable recordings included a medley of 1960s Motown classics, "Uptown Festival"; the R&B chart-topper "The Second Time Around"; "Dead Giveaway"; and "Dancing in the Sheets," which was featured in the 1984 film, *Footloose*. Although essentially a prefab construct, the trio would nevertheless be plagued by turnover problems, with Howard Hewett replacing Brown in 1978; Delisa Davis and Micki Free filling the slots vacated by Watley and Daniels, both of whom went on to solo careers in 1984; and Sidney Justin taking over for Hewett the following year.

Sharp, Dee Dee (b. 1945) *singer*

Most of Dee Dee Sharp's classic records have not been available for decades, due to legal issues surrounding the industry practices of her one-time label, Cameo/Parkway. Nevertheless, she remained active as a recording artist well into the 1980s, occasionally placing singles on the R&B charts.

Born Dione LaRue on September 9, 1945, in Philadelphia, she caught on as a backing vocalist for Cameo by 1961. Recognizing her ample attributes—photogenic looks and a dynamic voice combined with clear-cut diction, perfect for pop radio—the company began promoting her as a solo performer. Her debut release, "Mashed Potato

Time" (a number one R&B hit in early 1962), established her, along with label-mate CHUBBY CHECKER, as a leading interpreter of the dance craze fad. In addition to a rock-steady duet with Checker in "Slow Twistin'," she produced several more best-selling dance hits over the next year: "Gravy (For My Mashed Potatoes)," "Ride!," and "Do the Bird," the latter composed by Cameo-Parkway svengalis Kal Mann and Dave Appell.

By mid-1963, Sharp was a major pop star, appearing in teen films and on countless album compilations. As with many other American recording artists, however, the British Invasion—combined with Cameo-Parkway's late 1960s financial troubles—pushed her to the periphery of the music business. After two more Top 40 R&B hits, she disappeared from the charts for more than a decade. In the meantime, she married Kenny Gamble, part of the Philly soul songwriting-record production team of Gamble and Huff, in 1967. With his assistance, she revived her moribund career as part of the Philadelphia International roster in the mid-1970s and returned to the charts with a remake of the tongue-in-cheek 10cc smash, "I'm Not in Love." She would also participate in Philadelphia International's 1977 charity release, "Let's Clean Up the Ghetto."

Sheila E. (b. 1959) *singer and percussionist*

Although she has performed since age three, conga drummer/vocalist Sheila E. is best remembered for her slick video clips, which were broadcast in heavy rotation at the height of the MTV fad. Born Sheila Escovedo, on December 12, 1959, in Oakland, California, she joined the Latin-jazz fusion band, Azteca (led by her father, Pete "Coke" Escovedo), while still in her teens.

Her big break came when PRINCE enlisted her to sing on "Erotic City," the flip side of his 1984 chart-topper, "Let's Go Crazy." The exposure led to a Warner Bros. contract; her resulting LP, *The Glamorous Life* (Warner Bros., 1984), included the title single and the UK Top 20 hit, "The Belle of

St. Mark." The second album, *In Romance 1600* (Paisley Park, 1985), sold almost as well, driven by the single, "A Love Bizarre," with Prince supplying backing vocals. When her next LP, *Sheila E.* (Paisley Park, 1987), failed to catch on with the public, she enlisted as the drummer in Prince's touring band in addition to appearing in his concert film, *Sign 'O' the Times.* After an extended hiatus from solo recording, Sheila E. issued *Sex Cymbal* (WEA, 1991), self-composed and produced with an assist from brother Peter Michael and David Gamson, but again met with widespread public indifference.

Shirelles, The

Probably the most successful of the vintage GIRL GROUPS other than the Supremes, the Shirelles, comprising lead vocalist Shirley Owens, Addie Harris, Doris Kenner, and Beverly Lee, began singing together at school shows and parties. A classmate introduced them to her mother, music business executive Florence Greenberg. After the group-penned "I Met Him on a Sunday" reached number 49 on the pop chart, Greenberg formed Scepter Records in 1958. Spurred by the talents of writer-producer Luther Dixon, the Shirelles recorded a long string of pop/rhythm and blues hits, including "Will You Love Me Tomorrow" (number one on the Hot 100 in 1960), "Dedicated to the One I Love," "Mama Said," "Baby It's You," and "Soldier Boy" (a 1962 chart topper). Dixon's departure from the label slowed the group's momentum, although the first post-Dixon release, "Foolish Little Girl," reached number four in 1963. Heightened competition provided by British Invasion, folk-rock, soul, and surf music artists ultimately led to the end of their charting singles.

After breaking up in the late 1960s, the Shirelles re-formed (often without the original lineup) to perform at rock 'n' roll revival concerts. In 1994, the three surviving members (Harris died of a heart attack in 1982) sang together for the first time in 19 years; they have reunited on occasion in the following years.

Showbiz and AG

While in high school, AG started out working freestyle battles with Lord Finesse, who introduced him to Showbiz. Forming a team, the Bronx-based twosome tried without success to land a recording contract with one of the established companies in the greater New York City area. As a result, they decided to form an independent label, Showbiz Records, to distribute their 1991 EP, *Soul Clap.* The excitement created by the release, particularly the cut, "Diggin' in the Crates," led to a deal with London Records. The ensuing album, *Represent* (London, 1992), enjoyed a measure of success. From this point onward, however, the duo's career took a back seat to Showbiz's growing success as a producer. After overseeing a highly regarded remix of Arrested Development's "Tennessee," he went on to work closely with Big L and Deshawn, among others.

Early promo photo of the Shirelles (Frank Driggs Collection)

Showstoppers, The

The Showstoppers were formed in the mid-1960s by the younger brothers of soul star SOLOMON BURKE, Laddie (born 1950, in Philadelphia) and Alex (b. 1949, in Philadelphia). They were joined by another set of brothers—Earl Smith (b. 1949, in Massachusetts) and Timmy Smith (b. 1950, in Massachusetts)—who were also attending Germantown High School. Initially modeling their act after the VIBRATIONS, a soul group perhaps best known for having a hit with the original version of "My Girl Sloopy," the Showstoppers quickly developed a reputation as dynamic performers.

The group's contagiously vibrant rocker, "Ain't Nothing But a Houseparty" (which reached number 11 on the U.K. charts), became a major discotheque hit, returning to the charts in Britain in 1971. Follow-up recordings—most notably, "Eeny Meeny," another Top 40 hit in the UK, and "Shake Your Mini"—exhibited a similar uptempo excitement, but failed to maintain their earlier sales momentum.

Sigler, Bunny (b. 1941) singer

Bunny Sigler achieved a modicum of success as a soul journeyman at the height of the FUNK/DISCO era. Born Walter Sigler on March 27, 1941, in Philadelphia, the vocalist/multi-instrumentalist/composer/producer formed his own R&B group, the Opals, in the late 1950s. The Opals—whose membership also included Jack Faith, Ritchie Rome, and Sigler's brother James—first recorded for the V-Tone label in 1959.

By the mid-1960s, Sigler opted for a solo career. His earliest hit, a medley of Shirley & Lee classics, "Let the Good Times Roll & Feel So Good," was followed by an extended fallow period. Signing with Philadelphia International in the early 1970s, he continued to mine oldies for singles material, including "Tossin' and Turnin'" and "Love Train (Part One)." He switched to Gold Mind Records in the late 1970s, where he released a string of hits through 1979, most notably "Let Me Party with You (Party, Party, Party)—Part 1." Although he continued to perform and work with other artists in the studio, he failed to reach the charts again.

Silhouettes, The

One of the great one-hit wonder vocal groups, the Silhouettes, with their extraordinary vocal interplay and unerring feel for swing rhythms, deserved a better fate. The Philadelphia-based foursome formed in the mid-1950s as the Gospel Tornados. Originally comprised of lead singer Bill Horton, baritone Earl Beale, bass Raymond Edwards, and a tenor remembered only as Shorty, the group—with the encouragement of the Turbans's road manager, Richard Lewis, who took over the tenor slot in 1956—gradually began performing secular material during the week.

After a prolonged effort to obtain a recording contract from various Philadelphia and New York labels, they caught the attention of deejay Kae Williams at a local club in 1957. He became their manager and signed them to his Junior label with the proviso that they undergo a name change. Beale selected Silhouettes after a then current hit by the Rays, and "Get a Job" (a number one hit on both the pop and R&B charts) was released by the Junior label in late 1957. When it caught on with the public—thanks in part to the promotional efforts of Dick Clark on *American Bandstand*—Herald/Ember picked up national distribution rights.

The Silhouettes spent much of 1958 touring and, consequently, had little time to work on a strong follow-up record. Williams decided not to release covers of either the IMPRESSIONS's "For Your Precious Love" or the Spaniels' "Stormy Weather" due to his friendship with VEE-JAY head Ewart Abner. The second Ember single, "Headin' for the Poorhouse," received no support from Clark allegedly due to a falling out with Williams. Back on Junior, the group became disillusioned; Edwards and Horton moved on, being replaced by Cornelius Brown and John Wilson. They worked with a succession of labels—including Ace, 20th Century Fox, Imperial, and Grand (where they worked with

Jerry Ragovoy, who'd formerly managed the Castelles)—through 1963. The group ultimately disbanded, while Horton went on to record as Bill Horton and the Dawns for the Lawn label.

Simon, Joe (b. 1943) singer
Born September 2, 1943, in Simmesport, Louisiana, Simon was one of the more durable exponents of soul's golden age. Relocating to Oakland, California, in 1959, he would first record the following year for Hush with the R&B vocal group, the Golden Tones. Opting for a solo career, he would remain a fixture on the R&B charts from 1965 to 1981 with hits like the chart-topping "The Chokin' Kind," "Power of Love," and "Get Down, Get Down (Get on the Floor)."

Simone, Nina (1933–2003) singer
A jazz-oriented pop artist of the 1960s, singer/pianist/composer Nina Simone brought a refined sense of style to her recorded work unrivaled among her peers. Born Eunice Waymon on February 21, 1933, in Tryon, South Carolina, she went on to attend the New York City–based Juilliard School of Music. Her commercial breakthrough came with the 1959 release of "I Loves You, Porgy," culled from George and Ira Gershwin's folk opera, *Porgy and Bess*. Although she continued to enjoy periodic hit singles, most notably, "To Be Young, Gifted and Black," Simone made a significantly greater impact with albums. Her most popular LPs included *Nina at Newport* (Colpix, 1961), *Nina Simone in Concert* (Philips, 1964), *I Put a Spell on You* (Philips, 1965), and *Wild Is the Wind* (Philips, 1966). By the 1970s she was recording less and less frequently, concentrating instead on her commitments to political activism. She died at her home in southern France on April 21, 2003.

Sir Dyno rapper
One of the earliest Chicano hardcore RAP performers to achieve success on the West Coast, Sir Dyno first surfaced in 1996, with both a solo release, *Interview with a Chicano* (Explicit, 1996), and as a member of DarkRoom Familia, who produced *Barrio Love*. Originally formed in 1988, the Hayward, California–based group would continue to issue private releases at a prolific rate, including nine albums between 1999 and 2001 alone. Sir Dyno continued to balance his group activities with a solo career, depicting the bleak underbelly of barrio life in works like *Chicano Chronicles* (Dogday, 1999), *What Have I Become?* (Darkroom, 2000), and *Engrave These Words on My Stone* (Brown Power, 2002).

Sister Sledge
The North Philadelphia soul group—consisting of sisters Debra, Joan, Kathie, and Kim Sledge—first recorded for the Money Back label in 1971. The worked extensively as back-up vocalists before becoming consistent hit-makers in the mid-1970s. Sister Sledge are best remembered for the disco-styled "He's the Greatest Dancer" and "We Are Family"—both of which topped the R&B charts and crossed over to the pop Top Ten in 1979.

Sister Souljah (b. 1964) rapper
Sister Souljah had a brief flirtation with celebrity when Bill Clinton attacked her album, *360 Degrees of Power* (Epic, 1992), during the 1992 presidential election. Clinton accused the rapper of fomenting hatred—that blacks randomly targeted and killed whites based on Souljah's appeals to African Americans to stop destroying their own property and focus on white power brokers instead. As a result of the furor, she appeared on many talk shows and was covered in countless mass circulation periodicals. Her rather pedestrian record failed to receive much of a sales boost, however, and she was soon dropped from Epic's roster of artists.

ska/bluebeat revival
The ska/bluebeat revival was a retro movement concerned with recapturing the qualities of 1960s Jamaican music within a modern social and fashion

context. The first wave emerged in Great Britain during the late 1970s. The relocation of Caribbean natives to the London area provided the initial impetus for this revived interest in ska; however, skinheads and punks also became fans of the genre. Many "oi" and punk groups went on to make ska-styled records by the early 1980s.

The movement extended far beyond mere musical considerations. Like the mods and rockers who had preceded them, ska enthusiasts developed their own fashion statements. Clothing of choice included black-and-white checkered suits, skinny ties, and porkpie hats. Because the central message of ska revival songs was often one of racial unity, fans tended to exhibit a far greater degree of racial tolerance than was typically found in British society. Although ska music could be found in major British markets throughout the 1980s, it was no longer a force within the pop music mainstream. The sole exception was the watered-down, albeit highly popular, interpretations of the genre recorded by the likes of UB40.

The second wave, which arose in the late 1980s, featured a large number of American bands, including the Mighty Mighty Bosstones and the Pietasters. Whereas the first wave of ska artists were primarily promoted through televised video clips, the latter-day bands found that alternative rock radio stations were very receptive to their recordings. As a result, these acts have succeeded in sustaining their careers far beyond mere fad proportions.

See also REGGAE.

Skee-Lo *rapper*

Skee-Lo's work ran counter to the RAP scene norm, eschewing profanity and depictions of violence in favor of light-hearted tale-spinning augmented by self-deprecating humor. Born in Poughkeepsie, New York, he relocated to Riverside, California, at age nine. He became interested in HIP-HOP after listening to KURTIS BLOW's records. Skee-Lo surfaced with the funky pop-rap single, "I Wish," a smash radio and MTV hit, spurred by a video that parodied the film *Forrest Gump.* The ensuing

album, *I Wish* (Volcano, 1995), was engaging if somewhat lackluster. He seems to work at a very slow pace; only one album, *I Can't Stop* (2000), has appeared in the intervening years.

Sledge, Percy (b. 1940) *singer*

Sledge will be forever identified with the classic soul ballad, "When a Man Loves a Woman," which blended his intense, gospel-inflected vocal with an ethereal organ accompaniment. Success did not come overnight for the singer. Born November 25, 1940, he spent the first half of the 1960s performing in the region surrounding his native Alabama. He was a member of the Esquires Combo when he decided to go solo in 1966. Following the release of "When a Man Loves a Woman," which reached number one on both the pop and R&B charts, he scored Top 20 hits with "Warm and Tender Love," "It Tears Me Up," and "Take Time to Know Her."

Sledge's recording career stalled by the late 1960s, but he has continued to tour the U.S., Japan, and Great Britain through the 1990s. The appearance of "When a Man Loves a Woman" in the popular film *Platoon* (1987) spurred a revival of interest in Sledge. That same year the song was re-released in the United Kingdom, where it reached number two on the pop charts. In 1989 he won the Rhythm and Blues Foundation's Career Achievement Award.

Sly and the Family Stone

Sly and the Family Stone helped pioneer one of the dominant styles of the 1970s, FUNK music. Their variant fused the psychedelic rock of the late 1960s with classic soul; in that sense, it differed considerably from the bass-heavy grooves of mainstream funk. As popular on the pop charts as with urban black youth, the group greatly influenced the careers of later crossover giants such as GEORGE CLINTON, mastermind of the Parliament/Funkadelic collective; RICK JAMES; and PRINCE.

The creative core of Sly and the Family Stone, Texas-native Sylvester Stewart, developed an impressive music business résumé in San Francisco during the mid-1960s, excelling as a disc jockey (KSOL, KDIA), songwriter, and record producer for the likes of the Beau Brummels, Bobby Freeman, and the Mojo Men with Autumn Records. His first attempt at heading a group, the Stoners, failed in 1966; however, Sly and the Family Stone—including his brother, guitarist Freddie Stone; his sister, Rosie Stone, who played sang and played keyboards and harmonica; and a cousin, bassist Larry Graham, who would form Graham Central Station in the early 1970s—attracted sufficient local attention in 1967 to garner a contract with Epic Records.

The group's debut LP, *A Whole New Thing* (Epic, 1967), failed to make much of an impact on the public. However, the follow-up album, *Dance to the Music* (Epic, 1968), and the exuberant title song elevated them to the forefront of the rock scene. The group maintained its momentum with a steady stream of hit singles—most notably, "Everyday People," "Hot Fun in the Summertime," "Thank You (Falettinme Be Mice Elf Agin)," and "Family Affair"—and albums: *Life* (Epic, 1968), *Stand!* (Epic, 1969), *Greatest Hits* (Epic, 1970), *There's a Riot Goin' On* (Epic, 1971), and *Fresh* (Epic, 1973). The uplifting, anthem-like quality of Sly and the Family Stone's early work gave way to a decidedly more negative, militant tone in *There's a Riot Goin' On*; however, the uniformly high quality of Sly's musical ideas and production work made it the most artistically and commercially successful of his albums.

Sly's drug problems in the 1970s led to lackluster studio work and an increasing inability to meet concert commitments. He ceased to perform or record for several years, prior to attempting a comeback with the October 1979 release of *Back on the Right Track* (Warner Bros.). Unfortunately, the album lacked strong material and Stone spent much of the 1980s fighting drug convictions. Sly and the Family Stone were inducted into the Rock and Roll Hall of Fame in 1993. Rumors have periodically surfaced since then that the group would soon be releasing new material. In the meantime, their classic recordings have appeared in a host of

compilation releases, including *The Collection* (Castle Communications, 1991) and *Takin' You Higher—The Best of Sly & the Family Stone* (Sony, 1992; reissued on Epic in 1994).

Smith, Will (b. 1968) *rapper*

Born September 25, 1968, Philadelphia native Will Smith (aka the Fresh Prince) first found fame as a comical pop-rapper along with partner D.J. Jazzy Jeff (Jeffrey A. Townes). The duo's crossover success enabled Smith to become the first rap artist to make the transition to television success, a result of his landing the title role in the sitcom *The Fresh Prince of Bel-Air*, which ran for six seasons on NBC. A string of film roles (e.g., *Bad Boys, Independence Day, Men In Black, Wild, Wild West*) followed, which in turn have propelled Smith back to the top of the charts as a solo act.

D.J. Jazzy Jeff and the Fresh Prince's debut album, *Rock the House* (Jive, 1987), attracted considerable attention due to its innovative blend of samples (ranging from JAMES BROWN to the *I Dream of Jeannie* theme) and scratching, accented by the charismatic wit of Smith's humorous anecdotes. The follow-up, *He's the D.J., I'm the Rapper* (Jive, 1988)—driven by the hits "Parents Just Don't Understand" and "A Nightmare on My Street"—achieved unprecedented crossover popularity, ultimately selling more than 2.5 million copies. Subsequent LPs—*And in This Corner* (Jive, 1989); *Homebase* (Jive, 1991), which included the hit singles "Summertime" and "Ring My Bell"; and *Code Red* (Jive, 1993)—sold at platinum levels, but came across as rather silly and contrived.

Although never officially disbanded, the duo has not recorded since 1993, apparently due to the demands of Smith's media stardom. His first solo RAP recordings—two songs, including the title cut, which topped the *Billboard* Hot 100—appeared on the soundtrack, *Men In Black: The Album* (Columbia, 1997). The chart-topping album, *Big Willie Style* (Columbia, 1997), which included the number one single, "Getting' Jiggy wit It," validated efforts to place his recording career back on the front burner. The film title track, "Wild Wild West" (a chart topper in 1999, featuring DRU HILL and Kool Mo Dee), offered further proof that PG-rated HIP-HOP possessed considerable sales potential.

smooth jazz

The aging of the baby boomers has played a major role in the development of a number of musical genres, most notably adult contemporary, new age music, and smooth jazz. While jazz has always possessed a softer side, smooth jazz evolved out of the fusion movement of the 1960s and 1970s. From fusion—built on the intermingling of jazz and a wide range of styles, from the bossa nova to progressive rock—smooth jazz appropriated the rhythmic groove and instrumental riffing (as opposed to improvisation). The gritty, funkier aspects of many such hybrids, however, have been de-emphasized in favor of more polished arrangements. The dance-oriented sensibilities of the generation accustomed to DISCO and FUNK undoubtedly contributed to the notion that a steady backbeat could be tamed. Many smooth jazz recordings possess multilayered textures typically featuring synthesizers, guitars, and horns (saxophones, trumpets) to create a sound geared more to the subconscious rather than the intellectual domain.

The pop crossover success enjoyed by guitarist GEORGE BENSON in the mid-1970s—particularly *Breezin'* (Warner Bros., 1976), *Weekend in L.A.* (Warner Bros., 1978), and *Give Me the Night* (Warner Bros., 1980)—provided the template for the newly emerging genre. Saxophonist Kenny G is arguably the style's major star; hit albums such as *Duotones* (Arista, 1986), *Silhouette* (Arista, 1988), and *Breathless* (Arista, 1992) drew legions of new fans to smooth jazz. Other work falling at least in part within this field include Fattburger's *Livin Large* (Shanachie, 1994), Fourplay's *Fourplay* (Warner Bros., 1991), George Howard's *A Nice Place to Be* (MCA, 1986), and the Yellowjackets' *Mirage a Trois* (Warner Bros., 1985).

Snoop Doggy Dogg (b. 1972) *rapper*

Snoop Doggy Dogg (born Calvin Broadus on October 20, 1972) was a pop culture celebrity well before the release of his first album, the platinum-selling *Doggystyle* (Death Row/Interscope, 1993). He had already appeared on mentor DR DRE's chart-topping album, *The Chronic* (Priority/Interscope, 1992), in addition to being arrested in connection with the murder of an alleged Los Angeles gang member. Overnight, he had become a figurehead of the controversial gangsta RAP genre, his picture appearing on the covers of mass circulation magazines such as *Newsweek, Rolling Stone,* and *Vibe.*

Doggystyle was the fastest-selling debut LP in history, entering the pop album charts at number one and selling almost one million units alone in its first week of release. All issues of notoriety aside, the record's success owed much to Dr Dre's funky production work and Snoop's mesmerizing treatment of both the harsher side of hood life and partying. The commercial rise of rappers TUPAC SHAKUR and the NOTORIOUS B.I.G., combined with a weak follow-up album, *The Doggfather* (Death Row/Interscope, 1996), minus Dr Dre's studio support, pushed him into the background. Subsequent releases have resurrected his artistic credibility to some degree; however, the appearance of new creative forces—most notably, RZA, Method Man, and other members of the WU-TANG CLAN—have kept him from regaining the rap spotlight.

Solitaires, The

The Harlem-based Solitaires were unsurpassed at interpreting lush, romantic DOO-WOP material. Formed in 1953, the group consisted of R&B vocal group scene veterans Herman Curtis (lead singer, formerly of the Vocaleers), Buzzy Willis (tenor, formerly of the CROWS), Pat Gaston (bass, ex-Crows), Bobby Baylor (baritone, ex-Mellomoods), Monte Owens (tenor/guitarist, ex-Mellomoods), and Bobby Williams (piano).

Signing with Hy Weiss's Old Town label in 1954, the Solitaires recorded a series of regional hits built around Curtis's dreamy falsetto, including "Wonder Why," "Blue Valentine." "Please Remember My Heart," and "I Don't Stand a Ghost of a Chance." Curtis departed in 1955; his replacement, Milton Love, helped the group to even greater success in 1956–57 with hits like "The Wedding," "The Angels Sang," and "Walking Along."

The Solitaires remained with Old Town until 1960, at which time they had evolved into a COASTERS derivative. A succession of lineup changes sapped the group's vitality further, and they ceased recording in 1964. Nevertheless, a steady stream of Solitaires anthologies has appeared over the years, and various editions of the group have continued to perform on a rock 'n' roll revival circuit.

S.O.S. Band, The

Formed in Atlanta in the late 1970s, the S.O.S. Band—originally comprised of keyboardist T. C. Bryant, vocalist/keyboardist Mary Davis, flutist Billy Ellis, drummer James Earl Jones III, saxophonist Willie "Sonny" Killebrew, bassist John Simpson, and guitarist Bruno Speight—became one of the leading funk interpreters of the 1980s. The group's first chart single, "Take Your Time (Do It Right), Part 1" (number three pop and an R&B chart-topper for five weeks in 1980), would remain their biggest hit ever. The band lost considerable momentum when Davis, their acknowledged leader, went solo in 1987; she was replaced by Pennye Ford, formerly with the relativity unknown act Reach.

Soul Children, The

With soft rock a hot commodity in the late 1960s, STAX RECORDS attempted to cash in on the trend with the Soul Children. Formed by the label's resident songwriting/production team, ISAAC HAYES and David Porter, the group consisted of lead singer John Colbert (born in Greenville, Mississippi, and raised in Memphis), Shelbra Bennett, Anita Lewis, and Norman West. They recorded 15 R&B hits between 1968 and 1978, most notably "The Sweeter He Is—Part I," "Hearsay," and "I'll Be the Other Woman." When Stax went bankrupt, the Soul Children switched to Epic Records. Colbert went solo in the early 1980s, placing eight singles on the R&B charts as J. Blackfoot, the biggest of which was "Taxi," which reached number four in 1983.

Soul Survivors, The

The Soul Survivors were arguably one of the finest white soul bands to make recordings. Consisting of an expanded lineup whose members came from the New York City and Philadelphia areas, the group was originally formed by Kenny Jeremiah and brothers Charles and Richard Ingui. Assisted by Philly soul producers Kenny Gamble and Leon Huff, they surfaced with the 1967 crossover classic, "Expressway to Your Heart," which remains one of the most popular songs on oldies programming playlists. They had one follow-up hit, "Explosion in Your Soul," before internal conflicts led to a group breakup. The Inguis reactivated the Soul Survivors in 1972; they would crease the R&B charts in 1974 with one single, "City of Brotherly Love," before once again disappearing from view. Jeremiah hooked up with industry veteran Shirley Goodman as part of Shirley & Company in the mid-1970s.

Spinners, The

Although major success eluded them at the time, the Detroit-based Spinners—as opposed to the Pittsburg, California group of the same name—were one of the more sophisticated harmony groups of the 1960s. They emerged as one of the definitive soft soul acts of the 1970s, in a class with the best of the Gamble and Huff–produced artists, including the O'JAYS and the STYLISTICS.

Formed in the late 1950s, the group, originally comprised of former Ferndale High School students Bobbie Smith (tenor), George Dixon (tenor), Billy Henderson (tenor), Henry Fambrough (baritone), and Pervis Jackson (bass), was originally known as the Domingoes. They soon came under the tutelage of MOONGLOWS singer Harvey Fuqua, who helped create their distinctive lush vocal blend. In 1961, Fuqua spurred them to record a song he'd cowritten with Berry Gordy's sister, "That's What Girls Are Made For," for his Tri-Phi label. Fuqua allegedly sang lead on the Spinners's first two releases; experts such as Marc Taylor, author of *A Touch of Classic Soul,* have argued that this misunderstanding resulted from the fact that Harvey succeeded in getting Smith to emulate the Moonglows's sound and style.

In the early 1960s Dixon had departed (to be replaced by Edgar Edwards), and Tri-Phi was subsumed by the MOTOWN combine. From 1964 and 1968, the Spinners shifted to the Motown imprint, enjoying one hit of note, "I'll Always Love You." In 1966, Edwards left the group; his replacement, G. C. Cameron, was quickly elevated to lead vocalist. By 1969, they had been moved to Motown's V.I.P. label; the resulting hits—"It's a Shame" and "We'll Have It Made"—were produced by STEVIE WONDER, then barely in his 20s.

With the group no longer a priority at Motown, they followed friend ARETHA FRANKLIN's suggestion that they sign with Atlantic. When Cameron chose to remain with Motown, Phillipe Wynne was installed at lead in 1972. They recorded 33 hits with the label through the mid-1980s, including the chart-toppers, "I'll Be Around," "Could It Be I'm Falling in Love," "One of a Kind (Love Affair)," "Mighty Love—Pt. 1," "Then Came You" (with Dionne Warwick), "They Just Can't Stop It (Games People Play)," and "The Rubberband Man." Wynne, who died on July 14, 1984, opted for a solo career in 1977, touring with the likes of Parliament-Funkadelic. John Edwards took over his slot, with many personnel changes following over the next decade.

Staple Singers, The

The Staple Singers—consisting of Roebuck "Pop" Staples (born December 28, 1915, in Winona, Mississippi), along with his son, Pervis, and daughters Cleotha, Yvonna, and lead singer Mavis—represent one of the few acts to make the transition from gospel music to secular pop fare successfully. They were one of the most popular R&B groups of the 1970s, investing their anthems of racial pride and self-actualization with a soulful spirituality clearly derived from their church music roots.

"Pop" Staples performed as a blues guitarist while in his teens, relocating to Chicago in 1935. He joined the Golden Trumpets before forming his own gospel group in the early 1950s. They first recorded for United in 1953, but did not achieve major commercial success until opting for the pop mainstream. The group recorded an extensive string of hits for STAX with Al Bell as producer during the first half of the 1970s, including "Heavy Makes You Happy (Sha-Na-Boom Boom)," "Respect Yourself," "I'll Take You There" (which reached the top rung of the pop and R&B charts in 1972), "This World," "Oh La De Da," "If You're Ready (Come Go With Me)," "Touch a Hand, Make a Friend," and "City in the Sky."

After enjoying two major hits from the film, *Let's Do It Again*—the title track (number one on both the pop and R&B charts in 1975) and "New Orleans"—the group, now known as the Staples, switched to the Warner Bros. label, and later, in the mid-1980s, to Private I. Although they continued to place singles on the lower reaches of the R&B charts into 1986, they had ceased to be an important pop force over a decade earlier. Mavis, who had split her time between the family project and her own solo career since 1970, remained the most active, recording hits for Stax's Volt subsidiary, Curtom, Warner Bros., and Phono. "Pop" Staples died in Dalton, Illinois, on December 19, 2000.

Stargard

A female vocal trio specializing in DISCO music, Stargard consisted of Debra Anderson, Rochelle Runnells, and Janice Williams. Their first hit, "Theme Song from *Which Way Is Up*" (number one on the R&B charts in 1978), was also their biggest.

Their singles regularly made the R&B charts through 1981, although only one—"What You Waitin' For"—cracked the Top 40. They also appeared as "The Diamonds" in the film, *Sgt. Pepper's Lonely Hearts Club Band*. Anderson departed in 1980, but the group continued to record for Warner Bros. and perform well into the decade.

Starr, Edwin (1942–2003) *singer*

Edwin Starr is considered something of a one-hit wonder today. However, he had already been active as a performer, recording artist, songwriter, and producer throughout much of the 1960s before topping the Hot 100 with his snarling rendition of the anti-military anthem, "War."

Born Charles Hatcher on January 21, 1942, in Nashville, Tennessee, he moved with his family to Cleveland at age three. He began singing DOO-WOP in junior high school, eventually forming the Future Tones with four friends. They won a local television show talent contest, hosted by "Uncle Jake," five weeks in a row. Starr's musical activities were placed on hold during a two-and-a-half-year military stint. When discharged, he found that his associates were no longer interested in a professional music career. R&B bandleader BILL DOGGETT heard Starr singing in a Cleveland club shortly thereafter, and convinced him to join his tour.

Starr seemed poised to become a major star in the mid-1960s. He had several solo hits on the Ric-Tic label, including the spy flick parody, "Agent Double-O-Soul." The May 7, 1966, edition of the *Billboard* Hot 100 included the debut of three singles for which he was responsible: he recorded "Headline News" as a solo artist, sang lead for the Holidays on "I'll Love You Forever," and wrote and produced "Oh How Happy" for the Shades of Blue.

MOTOWN's purchase of Golden World/Ric-Tic in early 1966 led to a protracted contract dispute. As a result, Starr did not record again until some of the label's staff saw him in late 1968 on a local Detroit TV show, *20 Grand,* performing a song he'd written in 1965, "Twenty-Five Miles." They encouraged him

to record the song, and the single became his first major crossover hit. When follow-up singles failed to do as well, Motown producer Norman Whitfield asked Starr to record a Whitfield–Barrett Strong song, "War," which had originally appeared on the TEMPTATIONS's LP, *Psychedelic Shack* (Motown, 1970). Many fans, especially college students, had requested that the track be released as a single, but the label was already committed to issuing "Ball of Confusion (That's What the World Is Today)" as the Temptations's next disc.

Starr garnered a Grammy for Best Male R&B Vocal Performance for "War," but his next release, the Whitfield-Strong composition "Stop the War Now," stalled at number 26, due in part to the marked similarity with its predecessor. While he would retain a black following throughout the 1970s—placing 12 singles on the R&B charts during that decade, including "Funky Music," "There You Go," and "Contact"—he never placed a record in the pop Top 40 again. He died near Nottingham, England, in April, 2003.

Staton, Candi (b. 1940) *singer*

Born in Hanceville, Alabama, she started out singing in the Jewel Gospel Trio as a 10-year-old. Embarking on a solo career in 1968, Staton—who was married to soulman CLARENCE CARTER for a time—specialized in R&B remakes of country and pop hits like "Stand by Your Man," "In the Ghetto," "Nights on Broadway," "Listen to the Music," and "Looking for Love."

Stax Records

Stax Records, originally known as Satellite until another label with the same name threatened legal action, was created by Jim Stewart and his sister, Estelle Axton, in the late 1950s. After releasing a few country, rockabilly, and rhythm and blues recordings without success, "Cause I Love You," by Rufus and CARLA THOMAS, became a regional hit in 1960 and was picked up for nationwide distribution by

Atlantic Records. Carla Thomas reached the Top Ten with an ethereal, orchestrated follow-up, "Gee Whiz." The MAR-KEYS's funky R&B instrumental, "Last Night" (which peaked at number three in 1961), provided both a future stylistic direction and led to an expanded version of what would become the company's house band, BOOKER T. & THE MGS. William Bell's "You Don't Miss Your Water (Till Your Well Runs Dry)," with its understated eloquence and down-home gospel feel, anticipated other key ingredients of the company's self-proclaimed "Memphis sound."

By the early 1960s, Stax's chart success served as a magnet for area talent. The label's commercial track record (including subsidiaries such as Volt and Enterprise) during the decade was exceeded only by the MOTOWN-Tamla-Gordy conglomerate in Detroit. Leading Stax artists and their biggest hits included Booker T. & the MGs's "Green Onions" and "Time Is Tight," OTIS REDDING's "I've Been Loving You Too Long" and "(Sittin' On) The Dock of the Bay," SAM AND DAVE's "Soul Man" and "I Thank You," JOHNNIE TAYLOR's "Who's Making Love," and Rufus Thomas's "Walking the Dog."

By the 1970s, Stax had lost its most promising singer, Otis Redding, in a plane crash, and Booker T. & the MGs, who had provided a spare, rock-steady backup for many of the label's recordings, had broken up. Nevertheless, the company embarked upon an ambitious plan of expansion, developing comedy and gospel divisions as well as mounting Wattstax, a blend of rock festival and social consciousness. Although the hits continued—most notably, ISAAC HAYES's 1971 number one "Theme From Shaft" and a string of best-selling LPs, Luther Ingram's "(If Loving You Is Wrong) I Don't Want to Be Right," and the STAPLE SINGERS's "I'll Take You There" and "If You're Ready (Come Go With Me)"—the further loss of key artists and support personnel, combined with ill-advised financial practices, led to Stax's demise in the mid-1970s.

By the late 1970s, the label's classic recordings were being issued by Atlantic and Fantasy (which had obtained rights to the post-1968 catalogue).

By the 1990s, much of the Stax legacy had been reissued on compact disc, including virtually all of the 1960s albums, two exhaustive nine-CD compilations, *The Complete Stax/Volt Singles: 1959–1968* (Atlantic, 1991) and *The Complete Stax/Volt Soul Singles 1968–1971* (Stax, 1993), and the 10-CD *The Complete Star/Volt Soul Singles 1972–1975* (Stax, 1994).

Stereos, The

The Stereos typified the transitional phase of R&B vocal groups in the early 1960s that melded classic DOO-WOP harmonies and gospel-styled leads. This approach ultimately evolved into the style of soul popularized by groups like the TEMPTATIONS and the FOUR TOPS.

The core of the group—lead vocalist Bruce Robinson, bass Ronnie Collins, and first tenor Leroy Swearingen—came from the Buckeyes, who had recorded several songs for Deluxe Records in 1956. They hooked up with second tenor Sam Profit and baritone George Otis to form the Stereos in 1959. After cutting an unsuccessful record for Otis Blackwell's Gibralter label, Swearingen departed and was replaced by first tenor Nathaniel Hicks. Signing with the MGM subsidiary, Cub, in 1961, they achieved immediate success with the Swearingen composition, "I Really Love You" (reaching number 29 on the Hot 100, number 15 on the R&B charts), which featured a catchy bass figure. Two follow-up singles for Cub, and later stints with Columbia, World Artists, and Val, failed to produce any more hits. The group disbanded in 1965, but re-formed as a self-contained performing unit in 1967. After releasing two poorly selling singles for the Chess imprint, Cadet, during 1967–68, the Stereos called it a day once more.

Stevie B. *rapper*

Always something of a commercial opportunist, Miami-based Latino artist Stevie B. started out recording RAP, then SWINGBEAT, geared to the ethnic marketplace. He eventually shifted his emphasis to crooning ballads, one of which—"Because I Love You (The Postman Song)"—resulted in his first crossover hit. Although focusing on the club singles format, albums like *Party Your Body* (LMR, 1988), *In My Eyes* (LMR, 1989), and *Love & Emotion* (LMR, 1991) also reflect his stylistic evolution.

Stewart, Amii (b. 1956) *singer*

Amii Stewart recorded one of the most successful dance hits of the disco era, but never hesitated to say that her preferences leaned more toward adult contemporary fare. In the mid-1980s, she told *Record Mirror*, "You can't spend your life singing songs like 'Knock on Wood.' There's more melody now, you can dance as well as sit down . . . The DISCO era was a very good era for me, but it wasn't geared for melody."

Born Amy Stewart in Washington, D.C., Stewart was the fifth of six children; her father was engaged in classified activities for the Pentagon. She studied dance as a youth, and attended Howard University before joining the D.C. Repertory Dance Company, studying ballet and modern dance. Her first name was changed to "Amii" in her teens because someone with her name was already registered with Actor's Equity.

By 1975 Stewart had landed a part with the touring company of *Bubbling Brown Sugar*, which took her to Broadway and, later, London. While in London, she hooked up with record producer Barry Long, who helped her record the chart-topping "Knock on Wood," previously a gritty, Memphis soul–styled hit for Eddie Floyd in 1966. Promoted as a disco diva in much the same vein as DONNA SUMMER, Stewart failed to find strong follow-up material. Only two other singles reached the American pop charts, the medleys "Light My Fire/137 Disco Heaven" and "My Guy/My Girl," the latter a duet with Johnny Bristol. Remaining active in show business, she enjoyed modest success with the 1985 single, "Friends."

Stewart, Billy (1937–1970) *singer*

One of the great song stylists of the 1960s, Billy Stewart's career was tragically cut short by an automobile accident in North Carolina on January 17, 1970. His ability to belt out old standards in a truly innovative manner, complete with scats and trills, earned him the nickname "Motormouth."

Born March 24, 1937 in Washington, D.C., he performed in his family's gospel group, the Stewart Gospel Singers, as a teenager. He won a local amateur contest singing George Gershwin's "Summertime," which led to a series of club bookings. He also performed in a band led by his uncle, Houn' Dog Ruffin (the father of the TEMPTATIONS's David Ruffin).

Bo Diddley saw Stewart perform in 1956, and promptly recruited him for his band. Diddley also recommended him to his label, Chess, although Stewart's debut single, "Billy's Blues (Parts 1 and 2)," failed to make any notable commercial impact. He went on to sing with an R&B quartet, the Rainbows (which included future soul star DON COVAY), and record briefly for OKeh Records.

His dynamic vocal style began to catch on with the public in early 1960s; he had minor success with "Reap What You Sow" and "Strange Feeling." "I Do Love You" proved to be his breakthrough single, followed by a string of soul-pop hits, most notably "Sitting in the Park," "Summertime," "Secret Love" (a former number one hit for Doris Day), and "Everyday I Have the Blues," best known as B. B. KING's signature song.

Stoller, Mike   See LEIBER, JERRY, AND MIKE STOLLER.

Stylistics, The

One of the major acts within the Philly soul pantheon, the Stylistics were formed in 1968 out of two other Philadelphia-based groups: the Percussions—whose lineup included lead vocalist Russell Thompkins, Jr. (born March 21, 1951), Airron

Love, and James Smith—and the Monarchs (James Dunn and Herbie Murrell). They first signed with Sebring in 1969, before moving on Avco Embassy in late 1970.

The quintet placed 30 singles on the R&B charts through 1986, although none made the Hot 100 after early 1976. However, the Stylistics—propelled by Thompkins's soaring falsetto and lush orchestral arrangements—produced a string of memorable hits in the early 1970s, including "You Are Everything," "Betcha by Golly, Wow," "I'm Stone in Love with You," "Break Up to Make Up," and "You Make Me Feel Brand New."

Sugar Hill

The label responsible for bringing RAP into the American cultural mainstream, Sugar Hill remained a dominant commercial force well into the 1980s. Prior to the 1979 release of "Rapper's Delight," recorded by a group of studio rappers named the Sugarhill Gang, rap was disseminated largely on cassettes. As a result of this hit (number four on the R&B charts), HIP-HOP made the transition from New York City street dances to radio airwaves and dance clubs across the nation.

A result of the Chapter 11 reorganization of Joe and SYLVIA ROBINSON's All Platinum label, Sugar Hill's early recordings utilized house bands to approximate the breaks hip-hop deejays were using as sound-beds to frame MC raps. The later invention of sampling technology spelled the end for such warm, organic arrangements, resulting in a more synthetic feel.

The company also pioneered artistic statements and social commentary in rap recordings. Before GRANDMASTER FLASH garnered critical raves and crossover sales for the albums The Adventures of Grandmaster Flash on the Wheels of Steel (Sugar Hill, 1981) and The Message (Sugar Hill, 1982), the genre functioned almost exclusively to provide black party music.

Sugar Hill's early success led to many other signings, including Funky 4 + 1, Grandmaster Melle Mel, Spoonie Gee, and the Treacherous 3. Poor sales led to the label's demise in 1985. Its legacy, however, is widely recognized within the hip-hop community; gangsta rappers such as ICE CUBE and DR DRE as well as more pop-oriented artists (e.g., BUSTA RHYMES) have sampled classic Sugar Hill tracks. The Sugar Hill Records Story (Rhino, 1997), a five-CD compilation augmented by a twelve-inch vinyl disc featuring Grandmaster Flash & the Furious Five's "The Message" and souvenir booklet, does a thorough job of outlining the company's history.

Summer, Donna (b. 1948) singer

Donna Summer earned considerable renown as the Queen of DISCO during the later 1970s; however, few were aware of her ability to interpret a wide range of material, including pop, rock, blues, soul, and gospel. In addition, her talent encompassed acting, songwriting, and record production.

Born Adrian Donna Gaines on December 31, 1948, in Boston, Summer started out singing in European musicals in 1968. Her breakthrough as a recording artist came with a Giorgio Moroder–Pete Bellote production, the erotic "Love to Love You Baby" (a number two pop hit in 1975). Despite the predominance of disco songs in her early albums—Love to Love You Baby (Oasis, 1975), A Love Trilogy (Oasis, 1976), Four Seasons of Love (Casablanca, 1987), Once Upon A Time (Casablanca, 1977), Live and More (Casablanca, 1978), and Bad Girls (Casablanca, 1979), featuring the hit singles "Hot Stuff," "Bad Girls," and "Dim All the Lights"—she revealed an inclination to try other styles. I Remember Yesterday (Casablanca, 1977) served as a case in point, with an all-disco side and varied material on the other, including a chart-topping rendition of the Jimmy Webb classic, "MacArthur Park." Among her many awards were an Oscar for Best Original Song in 1978 with "Last Dance" (from Thank God It's Friday) and three American Music Awards that same year (Favorite Female Vocalist—Disco, Favorite LP—Disco for Live and More, and Favorite Single—Disco for "Last Dance").

This image was used to illustrate a 1978 Donna Summer LP.
(Frank Driggs Collection)

1997 Grammy for Best Dance Recording. She has concentrated on songwriting along with husband Bruce Sudano, particularly the country market. At the outset of the 21st century they were working on a musical.

Sunny and the Sunglows

Sunny and the Sunglows were one of the first Hispanic acts to succeed in both the pop and R&B markets. Formed in 1959, in San Antonio, the group originally consisted of Sunny Ozuna, Tony Tostado, Gilbert Fernandez, Alfred Luna, and the brothers Jess, Oscar, and Ray Villanueva.

Their approach consisted of interpreting R&B and pop standards in a laid-back, soulful manner. Their major hits included remakes of Little Willie John's "Talk to Me" (which reached number 11 on the Hot 100 and number 12 on the R&B charts in 1963), Tony Bennett's "Rags to Riches," and the FIVE KEYS's "Out of Sight, Out of Mind." Although they had few crossover hits from that point onward, Sunny and the Sunglows remained favorites of the Mexican-American community for several decades, scoring a succession of brassy polka instrumental hits, most notably, "Peanuts (La Cacahuata)" in 1965.

Wishing to make a more dramatic move away from her disco image, Summer signed with Geffen Records in 1980. Since then, her albums—most notably, *The Wanderer* (Geffen, 1980), *Donna Summer* (Geffen, 1982), *She Works Hard for the Money* (Mercury, 1983), and *Cats Without Claws* (Geffen, 1984)—have become increasingly diversified, with a particular emphasis on religious material. She won Grammy awards for Best Inspirational Performance in 1983–84, for "He's a Rebel" and "Forgive Me," respectively.

Following a succession of disappointing LPs, Summer was relatively inactive during the 1990s. Her biggest recording success came with "Carry On," a collaboration with Moroder that won the

swingbeat

Swingbeat, a genre also known as New Jack Swing (or New Jill Swing when involving female artists), originated in the late 1980s when a Harlem-based DJ, Teddy Riley, began grafting soul vocals to HIP-HOP rhythms. Although not embraced by either soul or hip-hop purists at the outset, early exponents like Guy and Today sold well to a largely young audience. In the early 1990s, New Jill Swing acts such as Riley's protégés, Gyrlz, Jade, and SWV, along with TLC, helped the style achieve mainstream success. By mid-decade, leading interpreters included MARY J. BLIGE, BOBBY BROWN, Jodeci, and Wreckx-N-Effect. Swingbeat also made a significant impact in Great Britain through acts like Rhythm Within and TCW (Twentieth Century Women).

Switch

Switch produced a dance-oriented soul, tailor-made for the clubs and discos of the late 1970s. They proved unsuccessful, however, at breaking into the pop mainstream.

Core members Bobby DeBarge (keyboards), Greg Williams (keyboards), and Jody Sims (drums) first got together as part of the Ohio-based funk act White Heat in the early 1970s. With Barry White serving as producer, the band recorded an eponymous LP in 1975, before the trio departed to form First Class along with vocalist Philip Ingram, bassist Tommy DeBarge, and guitarist Eddie Fluellen.

They took on the name Switch after Jermaine Jackson helped them secure a MOTOWN recording contract. He also produced their debut LP, *Switch* (Motown, 1978), and the group went on to release several big hit singles: "There'll Never Be," "I Call Your Name," and "Love Over and Over Again." Disappointed with the sales on the albums *Switch II* (Motown, 1979), *Reaching for Tomorrow* (Motown, 1980), and *This Is My Dream* (Motown, 1980), they left Motown in 1982. Bobby Debarge then departed to join the family group, DEBARGE, prior to his conviction for cocaine trafficking in the late 1980s. Switch struggled on for a time, enjoying a modest U.K. hit with "Keeping Secrets" in 1984.

SWV

Formed in the early 1990s, SWV, meaning "Sisters With Voices," consisted of Coko (born Cheryl Gamble, in 1974), Taj (b. Tamara Johnson, in 1974), and Lelee (b. Leanne Lyons, in 1976), all of whom came from the gritty inner-city sections of Brooklyn and the Bronx. Producer Teddy Riley groomed the trio to exude a streetwise look and attitude, with a sound on the harder side of the then hot New Jill Swing movement. Their debut LP, *It's About Time* (RCA, 1993), spanned a wide range of R&B-based styles, from A CAPPELLA to RAP, and included the Top 20 single, "I'm So into You." Follow-up releases continued to mine this vein with a notable degree of success.

t

Tairrie B *rapper*
A protégé of EAZY E, Tairrie B was promoted as the rap MADONNA. Despite Eazy E's guiding hand, and production work by Schoolly D on a couple of tracks, her debut LP, *The Power of a Woman* (Comptown, 1990), sold poorly. Critics attributed this to the fact that her delivery, despite being well executed, lacked conviction and authority. Whatever Tairrie B's potential may have been, a second chance at proving her mettle in the studio was not forthcoming.

Tampa Red (1903–1981) *singer and guitarist*
Although Tampa Red is generally placed within the pre–World War II country blues tradition, he was in actuality an essential link to the rhythm and blues era immediately preceding the rise of rock 'n' roll. The vocalist/guitarist (and sometimes pianist) developed an urbane style during his years in Chicago beginning in 1925, nurtured by his open-house jam sessions with the scene's leading blues musicians.

Born Hudson Woodbridge on December 15, 1903, in Smithville, Georgia, he took on his mother's maiden name (Whittaker) as a youth. His professional moniker came from a stay in Tampa during the early 1920s. Tampa Red's first recordings, done in acoustic blues styles, and featuring his vocals and guitar accompaniment, were made for the Chicago-based Paramount in 1928. He would go on to work with Georgia Tom Dorsey in the early 1930s.

He produced a series of seminal R&B singles, most successful of which included the suggestive "Let Me Play With Your Poodle," "Detroit Blues," "When Things Go Wrong With You," and "Pretty Baby Blues." He was also a prominent session player during this period, providing guitar accompaniment for hits like Big Maceo's "Things Have Changed," which reached number four on the R&B charts in 1945. He retired from performing in the early 1970s; as a result, his death in Chicago on March 19, 1981, attracted little media attention.

Tavares
Although lacking a distinctive lead vocalist or easily distinguishable style, Tavares enjoyed a run of smooth pop-soul hits in the 1970s. Formed in 1964, in New Bedford, Massachusetts, the group—consisting of brothers Antone "Chubby," Arthur "Pooch," Feliciano "Butch," Perry Lee "Tiny," and Ralph Tavares—were originally known as Chubby and the Turnpikes. Assuming the family's surname in 1969, Tavares first made an impact in 1975 with the chart-topper R&B hit, "It Only Takes a Minute," followed by the million-seller "Heaven Must Be Missing an Angel," "Don't Take Away the Music," "Whodunit," and "More Than a Woman," the latter culled from the soundtrack to the hit film, *Saturday Night Fever*. The group remained a fixture on the R&B charts until 1984, when its retro sound finally lost its following.

Taylor, Johnnie (b. 1938) *singer*

One of the leading exponents of Memphis soul, Taylor was born May 5, 1938, in Crawfordsville, Arkansas. He first surfaced as a member of the gospel groups, the Highway QC's and the Soul Stirrers, in the early 1950s. He also recorded for Sabre with the doo-wop-influenced Five Echoes in 1954. His earliest solo records were made for Sar in 1961. He placed two dozen singles on the R&B charts for STAX between 1966 and 1975, including the chart-topping "Who's Making Love," "Jody's Got Your Girl and Gone," and "I Believe in You (You Believe in Me)." He enjoyed his biggest success immediately after signing with the Columbia label, when "Disco Lady" topped both the R&B and pop charts in early 1976. He remained a chart fixture until the late 1980s with independent labels like Beverly Glen and Malaco.

techno

Techno originated as instrumental-based electronica in 4/4 time centered around hyperactive keyboard riffing and edgy, explosive drumming. It drew upon the synthesizer music of 1970s Euro-rock bands such as Kraftwerk, Faust, and Can and the postpunk industrial dance movement of the 1980s, spearheaded by Cabaret Voltaire, Throbbing Gristle, Ministry, and other largely British artists.

Although first centered in Detroit, the genre was imported by English clubs in the late 1980s. Closely aligned with HOUSE music and club raves—i.e., events characterized by lasers, mammoth sound systems, and countless dancers fueled by the designer drug Ecstasy—techno evolved from the neo-psychedelia of the Manchester-based Stone Roses and Scotland's Primal Scream into a diversity of hyphenated forms in the 1990s, including ambient techno and big beat.

The ambient school utilized samples of recording music, nature, and other extraneous noises to create richly textured, synthesizer-driven soundscapes; prime exponents included German classical composer Peter Namlook, England's Aphex Twin, and Australian avant-garde artist Paul Schütze.

Big beat, sometimes referred to as rock techno, combined pounding rhythms, synthesizer washes, and sampling within a more traditional rock format. This style owed much to the pioneering work of Prodigy, Underworld, and the Chemical Brothers, whose LPs—most notably, the British chart-toppers, *Dig Your Own Hole* (AstralWorks, 1997), and *Surrender* (AstralWorks, 1999)—were instrumental in making it the best-selling recorded dance music in British history.

Teena Marie (b. 1957) *singer, multi-instrumentalist, composer, and producer*

Teena Marie—born Mary Christine Brockert in Santa Monica, California—was a rarity within the record industry, a white artist whose success came almost exclusively within the R&B field. Signed by Motown's Gordy imprint, she burst upon the scene in 1979 with the Top Ten single, "I'm a Sucker for Your Love." Switching to the Epic label in 1983, she would enjoy her greatest success with "Lovegirl" (which reached number four on the pop charts in late 1984) and the 1988 R&B chart-topper, "Ooo La La La."

Despite the demands of a solo career, Teena still found time to produce other acts, most notably Ozone in the early 1980s, and take on various acting roles. As the first artist signed to Cash Money Classics, a new subsidiary of the southern rab label, Cash Money Records, Teena Marie released her first album of all new material in more than 10 years, *La Doña* in 2004.

Temptations, The

The most successful R&B vocal group of the post-World War II era, the Temptations were formed in 1960 out of two Detroit acts: the Primes, a trio including tenor EDDIE KENDRICKS and baritone Paul Williams, and the Distants, a quintet featuring tenor Otis Williams, bass singer Melvin Franklin,

The Temptations illustrating their hit single "I Wish It Would Rain" (Frank Driggs Collection)

and Elbridge Bryant (replaced by gospel-styled tenor David Ruffin in 1964). A successful Motown audition led to the formation of the Gordy imprint. After producing four minor R&B hits from 1962–64, they hit the big time with the single "My Girl," in 1965.

The quintet would reach the charts with 46 more singles and 33 albums in the next 15 years. They won two Grammys for "Cloud Nine" in 1968, and another for "Papa Was a Rolling Stone" in 1972. Despite the departure of Ruffin (1968) and Kendricks (1971) to develop solo careers, the Temptations managed to change with the times, relying heavily on funk and psychedelic influences beginning in the late 1960s.

The group lost momentum during the disco era, but Ruffin and Kendricks returned to the fold for a reunion LP and successful tour in 1982. They have remained active to the present day—despite the deaths of Paul Williams (1971), Ruffin (1991), Kendricks (1992), and Franklin (1995)—with a line-up featuring Otis Williams.

Terrell, Jean (b. 1944) *singer*

Jean Terrell had the unenviable task of succeeding DIANA ROSS as lead singer of the most popular GIRL GROUP within the R&B genre, the Supremes. The sister of heavyweight boxing champion, Ernie Terrell, she remained with the trio from 1970 to 1973. During her stint, they remained consistent, if less spectacular, hitmakers, recording singles such as "Up the Ladder to the Roof," "Stoned Love," and "Floy Joy." The Supremes temporarily disbanded when Terrell and Lynda Lawrence left in 1973, although Mary Wilson re-formed the group in 1975 with former member Cindy Birdsong and Scherrie Payne, sister of pop star/model Freda Payne. In the meantime, Terrell pursued a solo career, entering the lower reaches of the charts in 1978 with "Don't Stop Reaching for the Top."

Tex, Joe (1933–1982) *singer*

Although his records were far more popular with rhythm and blues fans than a mainstream pop audience, Joe Tex was one of the most successful soul singers of the 1960s and 1970s. In fact, Joel Whitburn's *Top R&B Singles 1942–1988* rated him 45th among all recording artists.

Born Joseph Arrington, Jr. on August 8, 1933, in Rogers, Texas, he started out singing in local gospel groups. He won a recording contract at a talent contest held at the renowned Apollo Theater in 1954. Although recording for King as early as 1955, he did not produce a hit until "Hold What You've Got" (which reached number five on the Hot 100 and number two on the R&B charts) a decade later. He remained a chart fixture for the next 14 years, including 11 more Top Ten R&B hits: "You Got What It Takes," "I Want To (Do Everything for You)," "A Sweet Woman Like You," "The Love You Save (May Be Your Own)," "S.Y.S.L.J.F.M. (The Letter Song)," "I Believe I'm Gonna Make It," "Skinny Legs and All," "Men Are Getting' Scarce," "Buying a Book," "I Gotcha," and "Ain't Gonna Bump No More (With No Big Fat Woman)."

Tex also recorded and toured with fellow Atlantic Records artists SOLOMON BURKE, Arthur Conley, DON COVAY, and Ben E. King in the late 1960s as part of the Soul Clan. He converted to the Muslim faith at the peak of his career, changing his name to Joseph Hazziez in July 1972. He died of a heart attack in Navasota, Texas, on August 13, 1982.

Thomas, Carla (b. 1942) *singer*

Prior to the rise of ARETHA FRANKLIN, Carla Thomas had been anointed the "Queen of Soul." "Gee Whiz (Look at His Eyes)," recorded while she was still a teenager, became the first Memphis soul release to receive national attention and provided the seed money for the launching of the fabled STAX label.

Carla Thomas was born in Memphis, December 21, 1942, the daughter of noted deejay and recording artist Rufus Thomas. She grew up performing in public, joining the Teentown Singers at the age of 10. Her first record, "Cause I Love You" was released on Satellite Records, which changed its name to Stax the following year in order to avoid a trademark infringement suit with another company. It consisted of a duet with her father, done during the summer break from college. Along with her father and the label's house band, BOOKER T. & THE MGs, she was an early star on the Stax roster. Her 23 chart hits—often appearing on the Atlantic label due to a distribution arrangement—included "A Love of My Own," later covered by the Average White Band on the best-selling *Soul Searching* album; the answer song to SAM COOKE's "Bring It on Home to Me", "I'll Bring It Home to You"; "Let Me Be Good to You"; "B-A-B-Y"; the first of a string of duets with OTIS REDDING, "Tramp"; "Knock on Wood" (with Redding); and "I Like What You're Doing (to Me)."

Although her recording career was effectively over by the time Stax went bankrupt in the mid-1970s, Thomas has remained semi-active as a club performer. She was appointed artist-in-residence for the Tennessee Arts Commission in the late 1980s, and received the Rhythm & Blues Foundation's Pioneer Award in 1993.

Thomas, Irma (b. 1941) *singer*

Although her career could be characterized as a series of near misses that became hits when covered by other artists, Irma Thomas had her 15 minutes of fame. Her soulful "Wish Someone Would Care" represented one of the few solid American hits at the peak of the British Invasion.

She was born Irma Lee on February 18, 1941, in Ponchatoula, Louisiana; her family moved to New Orleans when she was a child. She developed interest in music by listening to the rhythm and blues music pouring out of the Bell Hotel's jukebox located near her boarding house. Her singing, however, was nurtured at the Home Mission Baptist Church. Encouraged by her sixth-grade teacher, she won a local talent contest at the Carver Theatre singing Nat King Cole's "Pretend." These activities were temporarily terminated when she became pregnant as a 14-year-old.

During her second marriage and with three children already in tow, Thomas resumed singing publicly with bandleader Tommy Ridgley at the New Orleans Pimlico Club. Ridgley introduced her to Ron Records owner, Joe Ruffino; the resulting single, "Don't Mess with My Man," reached number 22 on the *Billboard* Hot R&B listing in 1960. After a follow-up failed to chart, Thomas switched to Minit Records, recording a series of intense, gritty singles (often backed by distinguished labelmates like ERNIE K-DOE, Jesse Hill, Aaron Neville, and Benny Spellman), most notably, "Ruler of My Heart," later reworked with great success by OTIS REDDING as "Pain in My Heart."

Shortly after Minit was acquired by Imperial in early 1964, Thomas had her biggest smash, "Wish Someone Would Care." The single's flip side, "Break-A-Way," also became a hit, albeit for British comedian Tracey Ullman in 1984. Her follow-up, "Time Is on My Side," failed to consolidate her mainstream success, but proved to be the break-though single within the American marketplace for the Rolling Stones. She later told Bob Shannon and John Javna, in *Behind the Hits,* "I stopped doing ["Time Is on My Side" in concert]. I really liked that song, and I put my heart and soul into it. Then along comes this English group that half-sings it, and gets a million-seller."

Thomas continued producing well-crafted, but by and large commercially unsuccessful, records for a variety of labels, including Chess, Roker, Fungus, RCA, and Maison de Soul. Into the new millennium, Rounder issued several albums of newly recorded material. Dubbed "The Soul Queen of New Orleans," she has remained a fixture in area clubs and the southern blues circuit.

Thomas, Timmy (b. 1944) *singer*

Although Timmy Thomas may strike pop music enthusiasts as something of a one-hit wonder, he remained a fixture on the R&B charts for as much as two decades. Born November 13, 1944, in Evansville, Indiana, the singer/songwriter/keyboardist performed with such notables as Donald Byrd and Cannonball Adderley early in his career. He was a studio musician in the mid-1960s for the Memphis-based GOLDWAX label. His first hit, "Why Can't We Live Together," topped the R&B charts and remained his biggest. While he only creased the *Billboard* Hot 100 two more times, a dozen more of his singles made the R&B charts through 1984. He also remained active as a session player, working with KC & THE SUNSHINE BAND and Betty Wright, among others.

Thompson, Sonny (1923–1989) *bandleader and pianist*

Bandleader/pianist Sonny Thompson attempted to achieve commercial success by smoothing out R&B's rough edges. Although he was a chart fixture between 1948 and 1952, pop music historians have tended to overlook his role in popularizing the blues.

Born Alfonso Thompson on August 22, 1923, the Chicago native first recorded for Sultan in 1946. The chart-topping R&B instrumental, "Long Gone, Pts. 1 & 2," was his first and biggest hit. He continued to record hits, most notably, the instrumentals "Late Freight," "Blue Dreams," and "Mellow Blues, I & II," as well as "I'll Drown in My Tears" and "Let's Call It a Day," which featured vocalist Lula Reed, while doing extensive session work for the King, Federal, and DeLuxe labels into the mid-1950s. He was loosely associated with Reed, for whom he provided backup from 1951 to 1961. Thompson died on August 11, 1989.

Thornton, Willie Mae "Big Mama"
(1926–1984) singer and multi-instrumentalist

Born December 11, 1926, the Montgomery, Alabama, native was a member of the Hot Harlem Revue from 1941 to 1948. She relocated in Houston in 1948 and first recorded for E&W in 1951. Thornton's only true hit, "Hound Dog," topped the R&B charts for seven weeks in early 1953. ELVIS PRESLEY would remake the song in 1956; coupled with "Don't Be True," it was the first double-sided number-one hit of the rock era. Thornton provided the soundtrack to the film *Vanishing Point* (1971) and continued performing until her death from a heart attack on July 25, 1984.

Tierra

Tierra stands as proof that movie star good looks, fortuitous timing, and ceaseless promotion are not the only roads to success in the music business. The Los Angeles-based group was formed in 1972 by the Salas brothers, Rudy (guitars) and Steve (trombone/timbales), both former members of the Latin rock–oriented El Chicano. Other members included percussionist Andre Baeza, bassist Steve Falomir, keyboardist Joey Guerra, drummer Philip Madayag, and reeds specialist Bobby Navarrete. Tierra broke through in 1980 with a lush ballad, "Together," at the peak of the DISCO/FUNK era. Follow-up releases—including a remake of the DELFONICS's "La La Means I Love You"—did not fare as well, and the group never made the charts again after late 1982.

Timbaland (b. 1971) producer and rapper

Producer/artist Timbaland was one of the most important figures within the HIP-HOP world in the late 1990s. His signature "bounces-and-beats" sound enabled many clients, most notably, Aaliyah, BOYZ II MEN, MISSY "MISDEMEANOR" ELLIOTT, Ginuwine, JAY-Z, and NAS, to enjoy crossover hits.

Born Tim Mosley, in Virginia Beach, Virginia, on March 10, 1971, he started out as a member of Da Basement, a continually shifting consortium of producers, songwriters, and deejays supporting Jodeci. He teamed up with rapper Magoo in Norfolk, Virginia, in the mid-1990s. The duo first attracted attention contributing songs and production expertise on Elliott's highly successful *Supa Dupa Fly* (1997). They recorded their own single, "Up Jumps Da' Boogie," featuring Elliott and Aaliyah, which helped push the ensuing album, *Welcome to Our World* (Blackground, 1997), to platinum sales.

While continuing to produce, write, and re-mix tracks for other artists, Timbaland began work on what would become his debut solo LP, *Tim's Bio: Life from da Basement* (Blackground, 1998). Heavily influenced by classic FUNK, the record also incorporated ensemble rapping, state-of-the-art R&B production values, and samples from a wide range of sources, including themes from *Spider-Man* and *I Dream of Jeannie*. His follow-up, *Indecent Proposal* (Blackground, 2001), delayed by legal issues, merged his prior dance club and soul-RAP influences with jazz, TECHNO, ambient, and world music flourishes. Guest performers included Aaliyah, Beck, Jay-Z, LUDACRIS, Magoo, SNOOP DOGGY DOGG, Bubba Spar, and Twista. Given his arsenal of skills, he seems likely to remain a major force within the R&B scene for many years to come.

TLC

A calculated blend of image and studio production, the Atlanta-based TLC would, in less than a decade, become one of the most successful female recording groups in history. Founded and managed by rhythm and blues singer, Pebbles, the HIP-HOP trio—consisting of Tionne "T-Boz" Watkins, Lisa "Left-Eye" Lopes, and Rozonda "Chilli" Thomas—exudes a spirited verve that has enabled them to transcend their playful, cartoonish image.

TLC's first album, the four-million-seller, *Oooooooohhh . . . On the TLC Tip* (LaFace, 1992), owed much of its popularity to the deft use of cutting-edge producers such as L. A. REID AND BABYFACE and Daryl Simmons for tracks like "Baby-Baby-Baby" and Dallas Austin for "Hat 2 Da Back." Another of the LP's tracks, the platinum-selling "Ain't 2 Proud 2 Beg," was a studio tour de force, incorporating samples from JAMES BROWN's "Escape-ism," KOOL AND THE GANG's "Jungle Boogie," Average White Band's "School Boy Crush,"

Silver Convention's "Fly, Robin, Fly," and Bob James's "Take Me to the Mardi Gras."

While generally considered less accomplished from an artistic standpoint, the follow-up, *CrazySexyCool* (LaFace, 1994), topped the *Billboard* LP charts and sold more than 10 million copies, driven by the singles "Creep" (which earned a platinum award), "Red Light Special" (gold record), "Waterfalls" (also achieving platinum sales), and "Diggin' on You" (gold record). The chart-topping third album, *Fanmail* (LaFace, 1999)—which included the million-sellers "No Scrubs" and "Unpretty"—maintained the group's commercial momentum. Lisa Lopes's death in a car accident in Honduras (2002) shortly after the album's release, left the group to carry on as a duo. The released *3D* in 2002.

TLC (from left, T-Boz, Left Eye, and Chilli) (Rose Prouser/Reuters/Landov)

Tommy Boy Records

Although best known as the home of many seminal RAP artists in the 1980s, Tommy Boy issued many dance-oriented rock and black contemporary titles as well. Established in 1981 by Tom Silverman, in short order the record company issued AFRIKA BAMBAATAA's "Planet Rock," which melded old-school HIP-HOP and the European TECHNO popularized by the likes of Can and Kraftwerk. Later signings of note included De La Soul, QUEEN LATIFAH, and Stetsasonic. One of the label's most innovative acts, the FORCE MD's, grafted contemporary hip-hop values onto updated 1980s soul.

Tommy Boy remained an industry force through the 1990s with such artists as Apache, DIGITAL UNDERGROUND, and House of Pain. When the latter group disbanded, member EVERLAST recorded the rap-inflected alternative rock classic, *Whitey Ford Sings the Blues* (1998), perhaps the label's greatest critical and commercial success. Tommy Boy has issued a number of compilations that effectively documented its role in the evolution of rap and dance music, most notably, *Tommy Boy's Greatest Beats 1981–1996*, a five-CD box set of hits, and near-hits, released on October 27, 1998.

Too $hort (b. 1966) *rapper*

Too $hort was one of the prime movers of the West Coast HIP-HOP scene. His harsh slice-of-life verses helped inaugurate the gangsta rap genre.

He was born Todd Anthony Shaw, on April 28, 1966, in the South Central section of Los Angeles. His parents, both accountants, moved the family to Oakland when he was 14 years old. Books by Iceberg Slim and Donald Goines on pimping spurred him to set that lifestyle to rap, and while producing and marketing his own songs, he was offered a recording contract by the indie label, 75 Girls. Dubbed "Too $hort" due to his diminutive size (five feet, two inches at the time), he attracted significant regional sales with the LPs *Don't Stop Rappin'* (75 Girls, 1983) and *Players* (75 Girls, 1984). He inaugurated his own label with the release of *Born to Mack* (Dangerous Music, 1986); its success in the San Francisco area caught the attention of Jive Records. The company reissued *Born to Mack,* enabling it to achieve gold status. The follow-up, *Life Is . . . Too $hort* (Jive, 1988), did even better, topping one million in sales.

Although his 1990s album sold well, he was increasingly relegated to the background by more sensationalized gangsta artists such as DR DRE and SNOOP DOGGY DOGG. Faced with more materialistic, pop-friendly rap competitors in mid-decade, Too $hort opted for retirement in 1996. After several years of inactivity, he decided to return, releasing *Can't Stay Away* (Jive, 1999), which featured collaborations with PUFF DADDY, JERMAINE DUPRI, and JAY-Z. Subsequent albums, however, have failed to go gold, prompting industry observers to posit that he had lost the hard edge much in evidence in the graphic depictions of violence and raw sexuality typifying his early career.

trance

Trance is a broad designation for various permutations of electronically generated dance music characterized by repeated crescendos featuring Doppler effects, sequencer riffs, and propulsive DRUM AND BASS patterns. It is built primarily on three prior traditions: synthesizer-driven postpunk industrial music, Detroit-based techno disco, and early 1970s psychedelia.

Closely related to ambient, TECHNO, and HOUSE, the genre originated in Germany during the late 1980s. Its earliest manifestation was marked by the merging of TB 303 synthesizers with mainstream dance material. Augmented by widespread use of the methamphetamine drug Ecstasy, trance spread to Goa and Thailand in the early 1990s, and then to the European club scene, most notably, Great Britain, the Netherlands, and Italy.

From the outset, trance has continued to evolve, providing the impetus for a considerable number of subgenres, including hard trance, acid trance, trancecore (heavily influenced by 1980s hardcore), psychedelic trance, and progressive trance. The artists and deejay producers most instrumental in shaping the style have included Paul Oakenfold, BT, Sash, Robert Miles, DJ Taucher, Paul Van Dyk, Tall Paul, Vincent de Moor, Ferry Corsten, Astral Matrix, Juno Reactor, and William Orbit.

Tribe Called Quest, A

Established in Queens, New York, in 1988, A Tribe Called Quest pioneered an innovative blend of acid jazz and Afrocentric HIP-HOP. The group comprised high school friends DJ Ali (b. Ali Shaheed Muhammed, August 11, 1970) and rappers Phife (Malik Taylor, April 10, 1970), Jarobi, and Q-Tip (Jonathan Davis, November 20, 1970). Q-Tip was already a music industry veteran, having worked with the likes of De La Soul and the JUNGLE BROTHERS.

The group's debut LP, *People's Instinctive Travels and the Paths of Rhythm* (Jive, 1990), offered sinuous jams punctuated by samples of classic tracks by Lou Reed, Carly Simon, Grace Jones, and others. It made the charts in both the U.S. and Great Britain, as did the follow-up, *Low End Theory* (Jive, 1991). With Q-Tip continuing to take on guest stints with other artists (e.g., Deee-Lite's "Groove Is in the

Heart"), A Tribe Called Quest achieved a commercial breakthrough with the chart-topping R&B album, *Midnight Marauders* (Jive, 1993). *Beats, Rhymes and Life* (Jive, 1996) did even better, ascending to number one on the pop charts. However, following the appearance of another Top Ten LP, *The Love Movement* (Jive, 1998), no more original material was issued by the group. Nevertheless, the individual members have remained active through collaborations with other RAP artists.

TTF

A Homestead, Florida–based vocal/instrumental band mixing dance club funk and 1960s smooth soul material, TTF was signed by Curtom Records when many of the members were still in high school. TTF—comprising Brett Brown, bass; Willie Brown, Jr., organ; Tony Gonzales, trumpet; Alton Hudson, drums; Tony Izquicrdo, saxophone; Andrew Most, guitar; and vocalist Deborah Peevy—had one hit single of note, the 1980 throwback ballad "(Baby) I Can't Get over Losing You." They also recorded two LPs—*Today, Tomorrow, Forever* (RSO/Curtom, 1979) and *Surprise! Surprise!* (Gold Coast, 1981)—before fading from the public eye.

Tune Weavers, The

The Woburn, Massachusetts–based Tune Weavers were fortunate enough to have one of the more notable lead singers of the early rock 'n' roll era, Margo Sylvia (born April 4, 1936). The group—whose other members included Margo's husband, bass Johnny Sylvia (b. September 8, 1935); her brother, tenor Gilbert J. Lopez (b. July 4, 1934); and her cousin, obbligato Charlotte Davis (b. November 12, 1936)—formed in 1956, and soon caught the attention of former big bandleader, Frank Paul.

Paul had them record "Happy, Happy, Birthday Baby," a song composed by Margo and Gilbert back in 1952. Initially released on Paul's Casa Grande label, Margo's warmly seductive voice enabled the single to appeal to audiences across a wide range of music formats (it was a top five pop and R&B smash). When no other hits were forthcoming, however, the group disbanded in 1961.

Turbans, The

The Turbans had one of the first rock 'n' roll hits, the mambo-styled "When You Dance" (a Top Three R&B smash in 1955). The song has achieved immortality due to its inclusion on countless LP anthologies, beginning with DJ Art Laboe's *Oldies But Goodies* series in 1960, and oldies radio programs. Nevertheless, the Philadelphia-based DOO-WOP group—whose members included lead vocalist Al Banks (born Andrew Banks; 1937–77), bass Andrew "Chet" Jones, tenor Matthew Pratt, and baritone Charles Williams—deserved better than being tagged "one-hit wonders." Although their other recordings failed to chart, many—most notably, the 1957 ballad "Congratulations," featuring Banks' dynamic falsetto lead—are prized by collectors. While the group disbanded in 1962, collections of their recordings continue to be issued on a regular basis to the present day.

Turner, Big Joe (1911–1985) *singer*

One of the leading shout blues interpreters of the 1930s and 1940s, Big Joe Turner—he was six feet, two inches in height, and weighed 300 pounds—later found a whole new audience as a rock 'n' roll trailblazer. Taken in its entirety, his career represented a synthesis of most major twentieth-century styles, including gospel, blues, swing, rhythm and blues, jazz, and rock 'n' roll.

Born May 18, 1911, Turner grew up in Kansas City, absorbing gospel singing in church, and folk, blues, and pop songs from local performers and sound recordings. In addition to selling papers and junk as a youth, he earned money singing with a blind guitarist in the streets. By the late 1930s, he had become a highly regarded blues singer, though limited to performing in rundown bars and theaters in the Midwest. He was also garnering attention as a songwriter; his compositions included "Cherry Red," "Hold 'Em Pete," "Lucille," "Piney Brown Blues," and "Sun Risin' Blues." His earliest known recordings—done in a boogie-woogie style that was back in vogue following his success at the December 23, 1938, Carnegie Hall "Spirituals to Swing" concert—were made for Vocalion on December 30, 1938, with Pete Johnson: "Goin Away Blues" and "Roll 'Em Pete."

The duo would work together at Café Society and Café Society Uptown in New York City for the next five years as well as recording for Decca in 1940. Turner continued to make records for the label's Race and Sepia series for the next four years, both solo and with Willie "The Lion" Smith, Art Tatum, Sam Price, and the Freddie Slack Trio. Turner cut 11 singles for National Records between 1945 and 1947, but with limited success. He spent the next few years recording for a wide variety of companies—including Freedom, MGM, Down Beat/Swingtime, Modern/RPM, ALADDIN, Rouge, Imperial, and DooTone—but making little impact due to declining interest in the blues.

Sensing his potential as an updated R&B belter, Atlantic Records added him to their roster in 1951. Now referred to as the "boss of the blues," Turner enjoyed his greatest success as a recording artist with hits such as "Chains of Love," "The Chill Is On," "Sweet Sixteen," "Don't You Cry," "Honey Hush," "Shake, Rattle, and Roll," "Flip Flop and Fly," "Hide and Seek," and "Corrine Corrina." When the singles stopped charting after 1958, he shifted his focus to albums, proving equally adept at classic blues, jazz, and R&B-inflected rock 'n' roll. Notable releases included *The Boss of the Blues* (Atlantic, 1956), *Joe Turner* (Atlantic, 1957), *Rockin' the Blues* (Atlantic, 1958), *Big Joe Is Here* (Atlantic, 1959), and *Big Joe Rides Again* (Atlantic, 1960).

Up until his death on November 14, 1985, he continued to record for many labels, including Arhoolie, United Artists, MCA, Black and Blue, Big Town, Spivey, Muse, Savoy, and Pablo. Many of his

classic recordings have been reissued on compilations, such as *His Greatest* Recordings (Atco, 1971), *The Big Joe Turner Anthology* (Rhino, 1994), and *Volume 1: I've Been to Kansas City* (Decca/MCA).

Turner, Ike and Tina

Although generally mentioned in relation to his former wife, Tina, Ike was one of the early pioneers of rock 'n' roll in his own right. His talents spanned many aspects of the music industry and also played a key role in furthering the careers of many other African-American artists.

Born November 5, 1931, Ike Turner formed a band while still in high school, the Top Hatters. Later known as the Kings of Rhythm, they worked the small clubs throughout the Mississippi Delta. He secured a recording session at Sam Phillips's legendary Sun Studios in Memphis, where his band cut the R&B chart-topper "Rocket 88," cited by many experts as the earliest rock 'n' roll recording. Due to obscure contractual considerations, however, Chess gave label credit to saxophonist JACKIE BRENSTON and the Delta Cats, thereby denying Ike an important place in pop music history. He also alleged that the company paid him only $40 for writing, producing, and recording the disc.

Turner continued as a highly regarded session guitarist, producer, and talent scout during the 1950s. His collaborations with the likes of Johnny Ace, Bobby "Blue" Bland, Roscoe Gordon, Howlin' Wolf, B. B. KING, and OTIS RUSH were released on Chess, Modern, and RPM. By the mid-1950s, he was a high-profile club attraction based in St. Louis. One night in 1956, Annie Mae Bullock (born November 26, 1939), who had moved from Knoxville, Tennessee, to St. Louis to try to build a career as a vocalist, was given a chance to sing with his band during a club date. Impressed with her performance, Turner asked her to join the group; they married in 1958.

The couple's recording breakthrough came unexpectedly in 1959 when a singer tapped to record Ike's composition, "A Fool in Love," failed to appear for the scheduled session. Tina (her adopted stage name) was substituted and the track reached number two on the R&B charts (number 27 pop) the following year. As a result, Ike decided to focus the act on Tina, bringing in a female backing group (the Ikettes) and working out arrangements and choreography to take advantage of Tina's dynamic voice and stage presence. In the 1960s, the group recorded a long string of R&B hits for a variety of labels, including Kent, Loma, Modern, Philles, Warner Bros., Innis, Blue Thumb, Minit, and Liberty, though few performed well on the pop charts. Producer Phil Spector had been particularly interested in packaging the duo for a wider audience through his renowned "wall of sound," but the commercial failure of his purported masterpiece, "River Deep—Mountain High," sung by Tina, reputedly led to his decision to retire from the music business.

The late 1960s, however, brought a change of fortune as roots-based sounds once again began dominating mainstream pop. They received invaluable exposure by touring with the Rolling Stones and performing on major television programs and Las Vegas venues. Among their best-selling singles were "I Want to Take You Higher," "Proud Mary," and "Nutbush City Limits." Their albums also regularly made the charts, most notably *Outta Season* (Blue Thumb, 1969), *In Person* (Minit, 1969), *River Deep—Mountain High* (A&M, 1969; recorded 1966), *Come Together* (Liberty, 1970), *Workin' Together* (Liberty, 1970), *Live at Carnegie Hall/What You Hear Is What You Get* (United Artists, 1971), *'Nuff Said* (United Artists, 1971), *Feel Good* (United Artists, 1972), and *Nutbush City Limits* (United Artists, 1973).

Despite their commercial success, the couple's marriage was in trouble. Tina ultimately decided to leave the act in Dallas during a 1975 tour; she obtained a divorce the following year. While she went on to both commercial and artistic success as a solo performer in the 1980s, Ike found nothing but problems. Not only did his recording activities fail to go anywhere, but he was dogged by a rash of drug and other personal problems. The one bright spot has been the public's continued interest in the classic work of the Ike and Tina Turner Revue, which has led to the release of many recorded anthologies as well as original albums such as *Dance* (Collectibles, 1996), *Don't Play Me Cheap* (Collectibles, 1996), *Dynamite* (Collectibles, 1994), and *It's Gonna Work Out Fine* (Collectibles, 1994).

Turner, Spyder (b. 1947) *singer*

Many artists within the rhythm and blues field as well as many other genres have earned the appellation "one-hit wonders." Spyder Turner's particular contribution, his version of "Stand by Me," is noteworthy, however, in that it not only was a big hit for a number of acts, such as Ben E. King (originally in 1961, and when reissued in 1986), John Lennon in 1975, and Mickey Gilley in 1980, but also because it was recorded merely as an audition tape featuring his impressions of JACKIE WILSON, David Ruffin, BILLY STEWART, SMOKEY ROBINSON, and Chuck Jackson.

Born Dwight Turner in Beckley, West Virginia, his family moved around quite a bit during his youth before ending up in Detroit in the late 1950s. He sang extensively in glee clubs and DOO-WOP groups during his teens. His eight-piece backing band, the Nonchalants, achieved a fair measure of success working local bars in the mid-1960s. When they broke up, Annie Gellen, host of the Lansing television program *Swing Time*, paved the way for Turner to submit an audition tape to MGM Records. They liked it so much they insisted on releasing it as a single, and it reached number three on the R&B charts and number 12 on the Hot 100 in 1967. While Turner did not like the recording, he went along with their wishes in order to get a record contract.

His follow-ups failed to generate much excitement, and Turner ended up writing songs and managing various acts. When his "Do Your Dance–Part 1" became a hit in a rendition by the R&B group, Rose Royce, he convinced the label to sign him as a recording artist. However, no hits were forthcoming, despite a label switch to Polydor in the early 1980s.

Twista

Chicago-based gangsta rap artist Twista goes by the title of "world's fastest rapper." He first surfaced in 1996 on Do or Die's platinum single, "Po Pimp," which led to a recording contract with Atlantic's Big Beat subsidiary. His debut album, *Adrenaline Rush* (Big Beat, 1997), was followed by *Mobstability* (Creator's Way/Big Beat, 1998), *Legit Ballin'* (1999), and *Kamikaze* (2003), which featured collaborations with Bone Thugs-N-Harmony, JAY-Z, and LUDACRIS, among others. Throughout, the formula consists of violent street imagery put across by Twista's rapid-fire delivery and an abundance of pop hooks.

U-Krew, The

Initially formed as the Untouchable Krew in October 1984, this Portland, Oregon–based RAP quintet, featuring lead vocalist Kevin Morse and programmer/producer Larry Bell, knocked around for years before breaking out with the romantic, R&B-tinged singles "If U Were Mine" and "Let Me Be Your Lover." An album, *The U-Krew* (Enigma, 1990), followed, but the group was unable to develd oped beyond its old-school roots and soon disappeared from view.

Undisputed Truth

Undisputed Truth was the brainchild of Norman Whitfield, the MOTOWN songwriter-producer who achieved major success in the early 1970s with MARVIN GAYE, the TEMPTATIONS, and EDWIN STARR. He decided to assemble a group to showcase his talents and recruited the Delicates—Billie Rae Calvin and Brenda Joyce, who were then singing backup in the studio for the FOUR TOPS, the Supremes, and others—to complement a recent acquaintance, Joe Harris.

Harris, who would remain the core of the group's continually shifting lineup, was born and raised in Detroit; he lived in the Brewster Projects along with other future luminaries such as Martha & the Vandellas and DIANA ROSS and Mary Wilson of the Supremes. While in high school, he sang with Little Joe & The Moroccos, a group best remembered for besting the SPINNERS in a local talent show. When the group's 1957 single for Bumblebee, "Bubblegum," failed to catch on, the act broke up.

Harris then teamed up with Richard Street—who later joined the Monitors and the Temptations—to form the Peps. Following a string of commercial failures on the Thelma and D-Town labels, Harris became lead singer for the OHIO PLAYERS in the late 1960s. He cowrote and produced much of their first Capitol LP, but departed when he found himself mired in an unfair production deal. After working briefly with the Stone Soul Children in Canada, he returned to Detroit and hooked up with Whitfield.

The second Undisputed Truth single, "Smiling Faces Sometimes," a Whitfield–Barrett Strong composition first recorded by the Temptations for their *The Sky's the Limit* album, hit paydirt, reaching number three on the Hot 100 and number two on the R&B charts in 1971. Its underlying paranoia struck a chord with listeners during an era disillusioned with the Vietnam War and social strife emanating from the civil rights movement. Follow-up singles, most notably, the original version of "Papa Was a Rollin' Stone," failed to sell well. Calvin and Evans then departed on the heels of the marginally successful "Law of the Land."

Bringing in the members of a Detroit-based bar band, the Magictones (Tyrone Berkley, Tyrone Douglas, Virginia McDonald, and Calvin Stevens), Undisputed Truth took on a more rock-oriented sound that reflected the influence of Jimi Hendrix and Sly Stone. The theatrical leanings of glitter rock artists and GEORGE CLINTON's P-Funk collective were also evident in the group's use of silver-painted faces, brilliant sequins, and oversized white Afros. Harris dispatched these musicians in the late 1970s in favor of a more R&B-flavored approach built around Melvin Stuart, Marcy Thomas, Hershel "Happiness" Kennedy, and CHAKA KHAN's sister, Taka Boom. Although occasionally creasing the R&B charts until mid-1979, they made their last appearance on the *Billboard* Hot 100 with "You + Me = Love," later reissued as a 12-inch single.

Unifics, The

Considered one of the finest soft soul vocal groups of the 1960s, the Unifics—consisting of lead singer Al Johnson (born 1948, in Newport News, Virginia), tenor Michel Ward, tenor Greg Cook, and baritone Harold Worthington—formed at Howard University. With Guy Draper providing the material and production work, the group enjoyed a few national hits for Kapp in the latter years of the decade, including "Court of Love," "The Beginning of My End," "It's a Groovy World," and "Toshisumasu," featuring their tender, but intense, ballad style. Ward and Worthington departed in 1970 following a prolonged dry spell and were replaced by Marvin Brown and Tom Fauntleroy, but the Unifics broke up shortly thereafter when their luck failed to improve.

Uptown Records

Uptown Records was established in Manhattan in 1986 by Andre Harrell (born 1959), formerly of DR. JECKYLL & MR. HYDE, who had four R&B hits between 1982 and 1986. He worked for a time with RAP entrepreneur Russell Simmons at Rush Management, but he allegedly departed after failing to convince Simmons that rapper Heavy D should be marketed as a sex object. Harrell initially used Uptown as a vehicle for Heavy D, who in turn brought them the proto–New Jill Swing act Gyrlz. Uptown soon developed into one of the leading

dance/HIP-HOP labels around, with a roster of artists that included Father MC, Guy, Jodeci, and MARY J. BLIGE. Not content to confine his energies to the record industry, Harrell branched out into movie production, achieving notable success with *Strictly Business*.

Urban Dance Squad

An Amsterdam-based RAP/rock collective, consisting of rapper Rude Boy (born Patrick Remington), Magic Stick, DNA, Silly Sil, and Tres Manos, the Urban Dance Squad enjoyed an international hit with the catchy "Deeper Shade of Soul" from the LP, *Mental Floss for the Globe* (Arista, 1990). The song hit number 21 on the *Hot 100*. After a lengthy lull, they followed with an equally engaging set, *Persona Non Grata* (Hut, 1994). However, the release failed to catch on stateside and the group disappeared from the public eye.

Usher (b. 1978) *singer*

Born Usher Raymond, in Chattanooga, Tennessee, on October 14, 1978, he started out singing in the church choir where his mother worshipped and participated in local talent shows. His mother moved the family to Atlanta when he was 12 in order to provide greater career opportunities. After winning a competition of TV's *Star Search*, Usher, still in high school, signed with LaFace, the label created by L. A. REID AND BABYFACE.

The debut album, *Usher* (LaFace, 1994), featuring the midtempo dance hit, "Think of You," produced by PUFF DADDY, barely hinted at Usher's future success. He became a major star with the release of *My Way* (LaFace, 1997), driven by the seductive dance floor lament, "You Make Me Wanna," which topped the R&B charts, produced by JERMAINE DUPRI. Usher took a break to do film and television acting, and fulfilled his legal obligations to LaFace by releasing *Live* (LaFace, 1999). He later re-emerged with *8701* (Arista, 2001), an uneven

Usher performing at the 2005 Grammy Awards (Gary Hershorn/Reuters/Landov)

affair highlighted by the chart-topping crossover single, "U Remind Me," built around an attention-grabbing synthesizer figure and pounding bass line.

U.T.F.O.

One of the earliest RAP groups to enjoy commercial success, U.T.F.O. (which stands for UnTouchable Force Organization) created a major recording industry phenomenon in 1984 with their second

single, "Roxanne, Roxanne." The song's lyrics, essentially a rant about a young woman who would not oblige the group sexually, and catchy arrangement, which producer Full Force had derived from Billy Squier's "The Big Beat," became an underground smash. Another artist, Roxanne Shante, immediately released a caustic response record, which became an even bigger hit. In short order, a slew of rappers—the REAL ROXANNE, the Original Roxanne, and Sparky D, among others—

weighed in with their takes on the ages-old male-female standoff.

The East Wimbush, Brooklyn–based act, consisting of Whodini breakdancers Doctor Ice and Kangol Kid as well as The Educated Rapper and, later, Mix-Master Ice, produced their own Roxanne follow-up, "Calling Her a Crab (Roxanne, Part 2)."

They next tried to find a fresh approach in order to remain commercially viable, including the rock/rap fusion of their third LP, *Lethal* (Select, 1987), and the raw sexual rhyming of *Bag It and Bone It* (Jive, 1991). In the face of public apathy, the group split, and Doctor Ice went on to issue several solo albums.

Vandross, Luther (1951–2005) *singer, songwriter, and producer*

Vandross enjoyed a very successful career as a session singer and recording commercials prior to becoming one of the preeminent R&B stylists of his generation, widely known for his impeccable phrasing and vocal control. Born April 20, 1951, in New York City, he began playing piano at age three. One of his compositions, "Everybody Rejoice (A Brand New Day)," was included in the Broadway musical, *The Wiz,* in 1972. His voice became a fixture on ad jingles for everything from the U.S. Army to Burger King.

His entrée to the pop music industry came when a friend, guitarist Carlos Alomar, introduced him to David Bowie. He contributed a song, "Fascination," to and sang on Bowie's highly successful LP, *Young Americans* (RCA, 1975), and later toured with him as well. While continuing to sing jingles and cutting two obscure albums under the name Luther, he quickly became one of the busiest backing vocalists and arrangers around, recording with Bette Midler, Ringo Starr, Carly Simon, DONNA SUMMER, Barbra Streisand, CHAKA KHAN, Chic, and Change.

With several labels expressing an interest in Vandross as a solo artist, he produced two demos, "Never Too Much" and "A House Is Not a Home." As a result, Epic Records signed him in 1981, granting him full creative control. Beginning with *Never Too Much* (Epic, 1981), he released a long string of platinum-selling albums, including *Forever, for Always, for Love* (Epic, 1982), *Busy Body* (Epic,

1983), *The Night I Fell In Love* (Epic, 1985), *Give Me the Reason* (Epic, 1986), *Any Love* (Epic, 1988), *The Best of Luther Vandross . . . The Best of Love* (Epic, 1989), and *Power of Love* (Epic, 1991). Although his singles had limited crossover appeal, they consistently reached the R&B Top Ten. Despite the demands ensuing from pop stardom, he continued to write and produce for other artists, most notably ARETHA FRANKLIN, Cheryl Lynn, Dionne Warwick, TEDDY PENDERGRASS, and WHITNEY HOUSTON. Furthermore, he made his acting debut in Robert Townsend's 1993 film, *Meteor Man.* Vandross suffered a stroke in 2003. In 2004 he won a Grammy Award for the album *Dance with My Father,* which had been recorded before the stroke. He died on July 1, 2005.

Vanilla Ice (b. 1968) *rapper*

Vanilla Ice was one of the first white rappers to court acceptance in the HIP-HOP community, openly. Born Robert Van Winkle, in Miami Lakes, Florida, on October 31, 1968, Ice became an overnight sensation when his debut single, "Ice Ice Baby," originally released as the B-side of "Play That Funky Music," topped the charts for 16 weeks. The success of the single propelled the accompanying LP, *To the Extreme* (SBK, 1990), to sales of more than seven million copies. Although Vanilla Ice's cool, hip pose and highly recognizable sample from the David Bowie/Queen classic, "Under Pressure," made the record hard to resist, his bland delivery and arrangements doomed follow-up releases.

Extremely Live (SBK, 1991), *Cool as Ice* (SBK, 1991), *Mind Blowin'* (SBK, 1994), *Hard to Swallow* (Republic, 1998), and *Bipolar* (Liquid, 2001) all failed to capture the same popularity. Furthermore, he suffered from backlash ensuing from overexposure—in addition to recordings and tours, the rapper appeared in two 1991 films, *Teenage Mutant Ninja Turtles II: The Secret of the Ooze* (which included his "Ninja Rap") and *Cool as Ice*—and criticism that he was simply smoothing out an inherently African-American genre to appeal to a mainstream pop audience. Soon rumors abounded that his childhood street experience were merely a publicist's prefabrication. Ice tried without success to redefine his image, from courting the drug subculture, to hardcore gangsta posing, to heavy metal-RAP fusion pioneer.

Vanity 6

The brainchild of R&B giant, PRINCE, this trio functioned primarily to add physical appeal and musical diversity to his stage shows in the early 1980s. Consisting of aspiring actress and model Denise Matthews (aka Vanity; born Niagara Falls, Ontario), Brenda Bennett, and Susan Moonsie, they enjoyed a blockbuster R&B hit, the sexually explicit "Nasty Girl." The eponymous album (Warner Bros., 1982) that followed engagingly blended GIRL GROUP pop and their mentor's trademark dance FUNK sound.

Prince had allegedly written the group into his film, *Purple Rain* (1984), when Vanity—who was determined to jump-start a solo career— signed with MOTOWN. She quickly recorded the funk-pop album, *Wild Animal* (Motown, 1984), which included the hit singles, "Pretty Mess" and "Mechanical Emotion," while the label promoted her as "Miss Audio-Visual 1984." The follow-up, *Skin On Skin* (Motown, 1986), attempted to showcase her more as a bravura pop chanteuse but failed. In the meantime, Prince reformed Vanity's old group as Apollonia 6, and continued to use them in much the same fashion as before.

Vee-Jay Records

According to Old Town Records executive Sam Weiss quoted in *Doowop: the Chicago Scene* by Robert Pruter,

> *Vee-Jay came the closest to being the number one black-owned pop label. . . . They penetrated the white market like a cannonball going through butter. Had they overcome the family and financial problems that ultimately destroyed them, they would have become as big as Motown.*

Deejay Vivian Carter and her husband, Jimmy Bracken, founded Vee-Jay in Gary, Indiana, in 1953, in order to provide an outlet for the kind of black rhythm and blues that was still hard to find on records. The label's first two singles, JIMMY REED's "High and Lonesome"/ "Roll and Rhumba" and the Spaniels' "Baby It's You"/ "Bounce" (the A-side was the first song recorded by the company), sold well, enabling Vee-Jay to adopt a more ambitious recording agenda. In addition to Reed and the Spaniels, the label found success in the 1950s with R&B acts such as the El Dorados, JERRY BUTLER, the Dells, DEE CLARK, the MAGNIFICENTS, JOHN LEE HOOKER, and Wade Flemons.

By 1955, Vee-Jay was successful enough to have established its own house band for use in the studio; key members included Lefty Bates on guitar, Quinn B. Wilson on bass, Paul Gusman or Vernel Fournier in drums, Horace Palm on piano, Red Holloway, Lucias Washington, and McKinley Easton on sax, Harlen Floyd on trombone, arrangers Von Freeman and Riley Hampton, and bandleader Al Smith. In 1957, the label began issuing albums and founded its first subsidiary, Falcon, in order to garner a greater broadcast share. The threat of a lawsuit from a southern label led Vee-Jay to rename it Abner; another subsidiary, Tollie, was created in the early 1960s. In 1958, the company formed a jazz department (signees included Eddie Harris, Bill Henderson, Lee Morgan, Wynton Kelly, and Wayne Shorter), and substantially expanded its slate of gospel releases the following year, the first group of

LPs featuring the STAPLE SINGERS, Swan Silvertones, Five Blind Boys, and Highway QC's.

By 1960, Vee-Jay had its own headquarters building at 1449 Michigan Avenue, Chicago, and had adopted its distinctive label design: a rainbow-colored band around a black and silver background which featured an inset red and white oval logo. In an attempt to garner a greater share of the mainstream pop market, the company issued Butler's "Moon River," the first time it scored on three national charts (pop, R&B, and easy listening) simultaneously.

Vee-Jay was a major force within the record industry by early 1963, having scored number one hits with GENE CHANDLER's "Duke of Earl" and the Four Seasons's "Sherry," "Big Girls Don't Cry," and "Walk Like a Man." Furthermore, they were given U.S. distribution rights to EMI artists Frank Ifield and the Beatles. Ifield's "I Remember You" reached number five, but a succession of releases by the soon-to-be famous Fab Four all flopped.

By late 1963, however, the label was threatened by a rash of lawsuits, many of which were instigated by artists such as the Four Seasons due to poor bookkeeping practices and the failure to keep up with royalty payments. Ultimately, the loss of its leading artists— and the failure to find new talent at the height of the British Invasion—caused Vee-Jay to close its offices and file for bankruptcy in May 1966. Beginning in the early 1990s, the company's classic material was being reissued by the New York–based Vee-Jay Limited Partnership.

Vibrations, The   See JAYHAWKS, THE.

Vontastics, The
Although not a major R&B vocal group in terms of commercial success, the Vontastics displayed a preference for gospel-inflected harmonies and soft, melodic material, and were the archetypal Chicago soul act. The Windy City quartet, consisting of Bobby Newsome, Kenneth Gholar, Jose Holmes, and Raymond Penn, was rewarded a recording contract with the local St. Lawrence/Satellite label after winning a talent contest sponsored by radio station WVON.

Employing a name derived from the station's call letters, the group had hits in the Chicago-Detroit area in 1965 with the energetic "I'll Never Say Goodbye," the languid "Peace of Mind," and the lightly grooving "I Need You." Their reworking of the Beatles's "Day Tripper" in 1966 enjoyed minor national chart action. At this point, the hits ceased, even though the band continued to record for labels like Toddlin' Town, Philadelphia-based Moonshot, and Chess.

Walden, Narada Michael (b. 1952) *singer and drummer*

Born Michael Walden on April 23, 1952, in Kalamazoo, Michigan, the drummer/singer/songwriter/producer was given the name Narada by spiritual mentor Sri Chimnoy. He toured with journeyman act Soul Revival early in his career before joining John McLaughlin's pioneering jazz-fusion group, the Mahavishnu Orchestra. Walden then embarked on a solo career, punctuated by studio session work for a wide range of jazz, R&B, and pop artists. In addition to achieving moderate commercial success in the album market, he placed 13 singles on the R&B charts, including the Top Ten hits "I Don't Want Nobody Else (to Dance with You)" and "I Shoulda Loved Ya."

Walker, Junior, & the All Stars

Saxophonist/vocalist Walker was born Autry DeWalt II in Blythesville, Arkansas, in 1942. He formed the group, consisting of guitarist Willie Woods, organist Vic Thomas, and drummer James Graves, in South Bend, Indiana, in the early 1960s. They initially recorded for Harvey in 1962 before landing a contract with Motown's Soul imprint in the mid-1960s. The All Stars specialized in funky, sax-driven remakes of soul and pop hits like "(I'm a) Road Runner," "How Sweet It Is (to Be Loved by You)," "Come See About Me," and "These Eyes." Ironically, their biggest hits—"Shotgun" and "What Does It Take"—were originals. Although remaining active as a performing unit, their charting singles had slowed to a trickle by the early 1970s.

War

Although early frontman Eric Burdon did not last past the second album, War remained one of the few successful interracial FUNK acts well into the 1980s. Although they did not record any new material for roughly a decade beginning in the mid-1980s, the band—whose work had been covered or sampled by many R&B and alternative rock artists, including JANET JACKSON, TLC, Korn, and Smash Mouth—was still releasing albums at the outset of the 21st century.

The band, originally billed as "Eric Burdon and War," consisted of the former Animals vocalist, a Los Angeles–area aggregate formerly known as Nite Shift, and a Danish harmonica player, Lee Oskar. Following several hits featuring Burdon's keening vocals, the LPs *Eric Burdon Declares "War"* (MGM, 1970) and *The Black-Man's Burdon* (MGM, 1970), as well as the million-selling single "Spill the Wine," the members of War decided to operate as a separate act, signing with United Artists. Emphasizing its strong rhythmic underpinning and first-rate songwriting skills, the band released a string of trailblazing recordings, including the gold singles "Slippin' into Darkness," "The War Is a Ghetto," "The Cisco Kid," "Why Can't We Be Friends?" and "Summer," as well as the albums *All Day Music* (United Artists, 1971), *The War Is a Ghetto* (United Artists, 1972), *Deliver the Word* (United Artists,

1973), *War Live!* (United Artists, 1974), and *Why Can't We Be Friends?* (United Artists, 1975). All of the albums went gold.

Beset by changing fashions, most notably, the rise of DISCO, personnel changes, and varying label support—Blue Note, MCA, RCA, Priority, Lax, Virgin, and Avenue have all released new material by the band since 1977—War has failed to match the commercial success enjoyed in the early 1970s. Nevertheless, the band, now dominated by keyboardist/vocalist Leroy Jordan and producer Jerry Goldstein, has continued to produce engaging work, ranging from film soundtrack and jazz experiments in the late 1970s to the eclectic *Peace Sign* (Avenue, 1994) and Hispanic-influenced *Coleccion Latina* (Avenue, 1997), both of which feature guest contributions from the likes of Oskar and guitarist Jose Feliciano. A competing version of War, featuring four original members of the band, began recording as Guerra ("war" in Spanish) and, later, Same Ole Band, in the late 1990s.

Warwick, Dionne (b. 1940) *singer*
Born Marie Dionn Warwick December 12, 1940, in Orange, New Jersey, she began singing in her church choir at age six. After a stint with the Drinkard Singers, she formed the Gospelaires, along with sister Dee Dee and aunt Cissy Houston. Warwick would attend the Hartt College of Music, in Hartford, Connecticut, before becoming increasingly involved with studio session work in the late 1950s.

Signed to Scepter Records, she became the mouthpiece for the Burt Bacharach/Hal David songwriting and production team from 1963 to 1971, recording some notable crossover hits, such as "Anyone Who Had a Heart," "Walk on By," "Message to Michael," "Alfie," "I Say a Little Prayer," and "This Girl's in Love with You." Warwick (who added an "e" to the end of her name for spiritual reasons) has remained successful in the performing and recording arenas up to the present day, most notably with the million sellers "Then Came You"

(with the Spinners; number one pop), "I'll Never Love This Way Again," and "That's What Friends Are For" (with Elton John, Gladys Knight, and Stevie Wonder; number one pop and R&B).

Washington, Baby (b. 1940) *singer*
Baby Washington's career as a recording artist spanned four decades and a multitude of changing fashions. Born Justine Washington on November 13, 1940, in Bamberg, South Carolina, she spent much of her youth in Harlem.

Something of a child prodigy as a vocalist/pianist, she joined a female R&B vocal group, The Hearts, in the mid-1950s. Her earliest solo recordings were made for J&S in 1957; she first charted in 1959 with "The Time," billed as Jeanette (Baby) Washington. Her biggest hits came in the first half of the 1960s, most notably, the R&B Top Ten singles "That's How Heartaches Are Made" and "Only Those in Love." She continued to have intermittent success with Cotillion in the late 1960s, Master 5 in the 1970s, and Casablanca in the early 1980s—in the latter case, singing with Parlet, the vocal trio within GEORGE CLINTON's Parliament/Funkadelic combine.

Washington, Dinah (1924–1963) *singer*
Although she failed to achieve prolonged crossover success, Dinah Washington was one of the most popular R&B singers of the post–World War II era, highly regarded for her vocal control and extraordinarily clear diction. She exerted a major influence on soul artists through her incorporation of gospel and jazz phrasing into an R&B-pop context.

Born Ruth Jones on August 29, 1924, in Tuscaloosa, Alabama, she moved to Chicago with her family as a child and first learned to sing in the St. Luke's Baptist Church choir, eventually becoming its director. She began appearing in local nightclubs after entering an amateur contest at the Regal Theater when she was fifteen. She briefly returned to gospel music as pianist and lead singer for the

Sallie Martin Singers in 1940–41, but from that point onward remained a fixture in clubs. Jazz bandleader Lionel Hampton heard her at the Garrick Club in 1943, and immediately hired her; she took on her stage name at this time, singing with Hampton until 1946.

Washington made her earliest solo records for Los Angeles–based Apollo in 1945, and then signed with Mercury the following year. After a number of near-misses, she broke through in the R&B market with "Am I Asking Too Much," achieving pop success as well with singles like "I Want to Be Loved," "Teach Me Tonight," "What a Diff'rence a Day Makes," and "Unforgettable." In addition to coming up big in duets with labelmate BROOK BENTON, she recorded jazz material on Mercury and EmArcy with a wide range of musicians, including Clifford Brown, Maynard Ferguson, Wynton Kelly, and Clark Terry.

Washington switched to Roulette Records in 1962, but garnered only a few minor pop hits. She died of an overdose of alcohol and drugs, in Detroit, on December 4, 1963. She was inducted into the Rock and Roll Hall of Fame in 1993.

Weather Report

Weather Report was the apotheosis of the 1970s jazz-fusion style. Core members Josef Zawinul, keyboards and synthesizers, and Wayne Shorter, saxophone, incorporated rock, classical, and Third World ethnic influences within a harmonic and improvisational jazz framework, enabling the group to achieve a mainstream commercial success that eluded most of its peers. The recordings resulting from this collaboration possessed an orchestral grandeur that greatly influenced later jazz developments, most notably European ambient labels like ECM and the SMOOTH JAZZ of Kenny G, Dave Grusin, and others.

Zawinul, an Austrian native, and Shorter first worked together in the Miles Davis aggregate responsible for the landmark LPs, *In a Silent Way* (Columbia, 1968) and *Bitches Brew* (Columbia,

1969). In 1970, Shorter left Davis (with whom he had worked since 1964) and Zawinul departed the Cannonball Adderley Quintet, after serving nine years as electric pianist and composer, to form Weather Report, along with Czech bassist Miroslav Vitous, drummer Alphonse Mouzon, and Brazilian Airto Moreira on percussion. The latter three musicians all moved on in the early 1970s, to be replaced by a rapid succession of jazz performers.

The group's eponymously named debut (Columbia 30661, 1971) established the mold for the emerging fusion movement, balancing richly textured instrumental pieces calculated to appeal to a progressive rock audience with adventurous arrangements and first-rate ensemble playing. The follow-up albums were: *I Sing the Body Electric* (Columbia, 1972), side two excerpted from a Tokyo performance released on two discs in Japan; the FUNK-influenced *Streetnighter* (Columbia, 1973), the first work to feature Zawinul's synthesizer leads; and *Mysterious Traveller* (Columbia, 1974), whose preoccupation with dance floor rhythms reflected the increasing industry profile of DISCO within the music industry. They solidified Weather Report's position as tastemakers within the jazz fraternity.

The addition of bassist Jaco Pastorius in 1976 ushered in the group's most popular phase. *Heavy Weather* (Columbia, 1977; gold record award), which featured the radio hit, "Birdland;" *Mr. Gone* (ARC, 1978); and *8:30* (ARC, 1979), with three of four sides culled from live 1979 dates, sold particularly well. By 1987, however, the group had lost its creative momentum, and the decision was made to disband. Pastorius died following a beating in 1987, and the other former members embarked on other projects, but compilations and reissues of the group's original albums on CD continue to sell well.

Wells, Jean (b. 1942) *singer*

Born August 1, 1942, in West Palm Beach, Florida, Jean Wells grew up in nearby Belgrade, where she sang in gospel ensembles. She first recorded in 1959, and released a string of unsuccessful R&B singles in the early 1960s while working in the Philadelphia club scene. Her career turned around when producer Clyde Otis helped her secure a recording contract with the New York–based Calla label in 1967. Wells enjoyed moderate success with several passionately rendered singles: "After Loving You," "I Feel Good," and "Have a Little Mercy." Although subsequent releases for a variety of labels failed to make the charts, she continued to record well into the 1980s, including *World! Here Comes Jean Wells* (Sonet, 1969) and *Number One* (Sunshine, 1981).

Wells, Mary (1943–1992) *singer*

On the strength of her cool, but sexy vocals, Mary Wells became MOTOWN RECORDS' first star. Born May 13, 1943, in Detroit, she arranged an audition with Berry Gordy, Jr. in order to pitch a song she'd written for his client, JACKIE WILSON. Gordy signed her, and that song, "Bye Bye Baby," was released in 1961 as her debut single. She was placed under the guidance of Smokey Robinson, whose understated production work helped launch a string of hits: "The One Who Really Loves You," "You Beat Me to the Punch," "Two Lovers," "Laughing Boy," "You Lost the Sweetest Boy"/ "What's Easy for Two Is So Hard for One," and the chart-topping "My Guy."

At the peak of her success, Wells sued Motown, arguing that the recording contract she signed at seventeen was invalid. She received a lucrative offer from 20th Century–Fox, along with promises that she'd be provided opportunities to appear in films. However, hits eluded her and acting roles did not materialize. Later stints with Atco and Jubilee failed to resurrect her career. She retired from music business, but returned in the 1980s when a revived interest in the classic Motown sound led to a demand for concert appearances. Wells had just completed an album for British release, *Keeping My Mind on Love,* when she discovered she had cancer of the larynx. A two-pack-a-day smoker without health insurance, Wells was forced to rely on friends and associates within the record industry to provide financial assistance during her final days.

Wesley, Fred, & the J.B.'s

Although the J.B.'s are best remembered as JAMES BROWN's funk-oriented support band in the early 1970s, they also were part of Parliament/ Funkadelic's extended family and recorded a string of hits under their own name. The group, headed by trombonist/ keyboardist Fred Wesley, featured various personnel over the years, most notably, bassist Bootsy Collins, drummer Nat Kendrick, and tenor saxophonist Maceo Parker.

The band recorded under a wide range of names. They first made the charts in 1960 with "(Do the) Mashed Potatoes (Part 1)" (which reached number eight on the R&B charts), billed as Nat Kendrick & the Swans (other members at the time included J. C. Adams, Fats Gonder, Bernard Odum, and Bobby Roach). Parker headed a spin-off act, Maceo & the Macks, who released four hits between 1970 and 1974, including "Parrty – Part I" and "Soul Power 74 – Part I." The Wesley-led ensemble would release best sellers from 1972 to 1980 as the J.B.'s, Fred Wesley & the J.B.'s, Fred & the New J.B.'s, Fred Wesley & the Horny Horns, and Fred Wesley. All of their *Billboard* Hot 100 hits—"Gimme Some More," "Pass the Peas," and "Doing It to Death"— were composed, arranged, and produced by Brown.

West, Kanye (b. 1977) *rapper and producer*

The Atlanta native began developing his keyboard and composing skills as a teenager, with the aim of eventually pursuing a music career. He attended Chicago's Columbia College for a very brief time before leaving to do production work on JERMAINE DUPRI's album, *Jermane Dupri Presents: Life in 1472* (So So Def, 1998). He was soon in high demand to work with other rap artists, producing hit singles for rap stars such as JAY-Z, ALICIA KEYS, Talib Kweli, and LUDACRIS.

Intent on making his own solo recordings, he signed with Roc-A-Fella in 2002. However, a serious automobile accident in October of that year left his jaw fractured in three places. His debut album, *The College Dropout*—which featured the chart smashes, "Through the Wire" and "Slow Jamz"—was released in early 2004. His clever wordplay, comfortable singsong flow, and distinctive rhythmic approach of pitched-up manipulation of often recognizable samples, complemented by a stutter-step drum-programming pattern, helped it become the 12th most popular LP of the year (*Billboard,* "Year in Music & Touring," December 25, 2004). He also received more 2005 Grammy Award nominations (10) than any other artist, ultimately winning for Best Rap Album and Best Rap Song ("Jesus Walks").

West's success has been considered a breath of fresh air for many who welcomed his sensitive take on human frailties as an anecdote to the preponderance of gangsta rap–styled releases dominating the marketplace. His album was initially on the ballot for the gospel Stellar Awards RAP/HIP-HOP CD of the year, but would be removed due to explicit language. In the midst of the media brouhaha surrounding his recent success, West has continued to divide time between production duties for Roc-A-Fella and his second album, *Late Registration* (Advance, 2005).

West Coast Rap All-Stars

The West Coast Rap All-Stars represented a coalition of California-based HIP-HOP artists dedicated to spreading the gospel of unity and raising funds for inner city youth programs. Notable participants included ABOVE THE LAW, Def Jef, DIGITAL UNDERGROUND, EAZY-E, M.C. HAMMER, ICE-T, King Tee, Michel'le, N.W.A., OAKTOWN's 3-5-7, Tone Loc, and YOUNG M.C. Despite the high principles involved, critics pointed out, with some irony, that many of those involved had contributed to these very social problems through their gangsta RAP posturing. Nevertheless, an album, *We're All in the Same Gang* (Warner Bros., 1990), and a single of the same name sold moderately well.

Weston, Kim (b. 1939) *singer*

Kim Weston was one of the serviceable second-stringers within the MOTOWN stable of artists during the 1960s. Born Agatha Natalie Weston, the Detroit native started out singing in gospel groups. Discovered by Motown songwriter/producer Eddie Holland, Weston was teamed with MARVIN GAYE (whose duet partner, MARY WELLS, had recently defected to the 20th Century-Fox label) when her own solo career failed to take off. Their debut single, "What Good Am I Without You" (which reached number 64 on *Billboard*'s combined pop and R&B charts in 1964), showed promise, but Motown shelved any further plans for the pairing when Gaye's solo recordings suddenly became consistent top sellers.

In the meantime, Weston found a measure of commercial success herself, most notably with "Take Me in Your Arms (Rock Me a Little While)," which was revived by the Doobie Brothers in the mid-1970s, and "Helpless." Another duet with Gaye, "It Takes Two," would become her only Top 20 hit. By this time, however, Weston had set her sights on a New York stage career, and Gaye hooked up with another up-and-coming singer, Tammi Terrell. Together they had 10 chart singles before Terrell's tragic death from a brain tumor in early 1970.

Weston continued to record for a succession of labels in the 1960s and 1970s, including MGM, People, and Pride, though she rarely made the charts. Later in her career, she organized a youth theater workshop in Detroit.

See also HOLLAND, BRIAN, LAMONT DOZIER, AND EDDIE HOLLAND.

Westside Connection

With ICE CUBE's career beginning to slide commercially and artistically, he formed Westside Connection with West Coast gangsta associates Mack 10 and WC, one of the earliest known HIP-HOP supergroups. Their one-off album, *Bow Down* (Priority, 1996), which included the hit single, "Bow Down," represented an impassioned apology for gangsta RAP, the tight production ranging from incessant hardcore beats to pure dance club FUNK. Subsequent releases, most notably, *The Shadiest One* (Def Jam, 1998), were released under WC's name.

Whispers, The

One of the most successful soft soul groups of all time, the Whispers—consisting of Nicholas Caldwell, Gordy Harmon, Marcus Hutson, and twins Wallace and Walter Scott—formed in 1964, signing a recording contract with Dore shortly thereafter. Despite limited pop success, they became a fixture on the R&B charts over the next two decades beginning in 1969, recording for the Soul Clock, Janus, Soul Train, and Solar labels. Their biggest hits included "And the Beat Goes On" (number one R&B), "Lady," "It's a Love Thing," and the L. A. REID AND BABYFACE–penned "Rock Steady" (another R&B chart-topper).

White, Barry (1944–2003) *singer, keyboardist, songwriter, producer, and arranger*

Born September 12, 1944, in Galveston, Texas, White was raised in Los Angeles. He got involved with recording studios at an early age, playing piano as an 11-year-old on Jesse Belvin's 1956 hit "Goodnight My Love." He was a member of the R&B vocal group, the Upfronts, who recorded for Lummtone in 1960. He would move on to Atlantic in 1964 as a solo act, and (as "Barry Lee") for Downey and Veep in 1965. He served as an A&R man for Mustang/Bronco from 1966 to 1967 and formed the female vocal trio Love Unlimited in 1969.

Completely in control of all aspects of his recorded output by the time he signed with 20th Century, White became a consistent crossover hit-maker beginning with the release of "I'm Gonna Love You Just a Little More Baby" (number one R&B, number three pop) in early 1973. Later successes would include the R&B chart-toppers "Can't Get Enough of Your Love, Babe" (number one pop as well), "You're the First, the Last, My Everything,"

"What Am I Gonna Do with You," and "It's Ecstasy When You Lay Down Next to Me."

Williams, Billy (1910–1972) *singer*

Billy Williams enjoyed a long career as a pop singer, finding success on radio and television as well as records. Born December 28, 1910, in Waco, Texas, he formed the Harmony Four along with Howard Daniel, Edward Jackson, and Ira Williams at Wilberforce College (Ohio) in 1930. The group, built around his lead vocals, achieved great success as the Charioteers on the radio program, *Kraft Music Hall,* with Bing Crosby. They began recording for Decca in 1935, achieving a Top Ten R&B hit with "A Kiss and a Rose" on the Columbia label in 1949.

In 1950, he formed the Billy Williams Quartet with John Ball, Eugene Dixon, and Claude Riddick. They became a fixture on early TV variety programs, particularly Sid Caesar's *Your Show of Shows.* Williams was also active as a recording artist; his biggest hit was "I'm Gonna Sit Right Down & Write Myself a Letter," which reached number three in 1957. His career ended in the early 1960s when diabetes eroded his singing skills. He relocated to Chicago, where he was a social worker until his death on October 17, 1972.

Williams, Deniece (b. 1951) *singer and songwriter*

Born Deniece Chandler on June 3, 1951, in Gary, Indiana, she first recorded for Toddlin' Town before reaching her teens. She was a member of Stevie Wonder's vocal backing group, Wonderlove, from 1972 to 1975. Embarking on a solo career in 1976, she signed with Columbia, where her smooth vocal style made her a consistent hit-maker through the 1980s. Her biggest successes included "Free" and the R&B chart-toppers "Too Much, Too Little, Too Late" (a number-one pop hit as well), "It's Gonna Take a Miracle," and "Let's Hear It for the Boy" (also number on the pop charts and included in the film, *Footloose*).

Williams, Otis   See CHARMS, THE.

Williams, Paul   (1915–2002) *bandleader and saxophonist*

One of the leading R&B bandleaders of the late 1940s, Paul "Hucklcbuck" Williams was born in Lewisburg, Tennessee, on July 13, 1915. He started out as a saxophonist with Clarence Dorsey's group in 1946, and first recorded with King Porter for Paradise in 1947. Later that year, he formed his own band, which included trumpeter Phil Guilbeau and tenor saxophonist Noble "Thin Man" Watts, as well as vocalists Connie Shaw, Jimmy Brown, Danny Cobb, and Joan Shaw. His first hit came with "35-30" (which reached number eight on the R&B charts in 1948). He remained a consistent hitmaker until the end of the decade, his most notable releases being "Walkin' Around," which featured Wild Bill Moore on tenor sax, and "The Hucklebuck," one of the most popular R&B songs of the post–World War II era (topping the charts for 14 weeks), later covered by CHUBBY CHECKER.

He continued to record into the 1960s as a house musician for Atlantic Records. He also served as director of the Lloyd Price and JAMES BROWN bands until 1964. He then retired from the music scene to work as a salesman in the New York area, although he went on to form a booking agency in 1968. He died in New York City on September 14, 2002.

Williamson, Sonny Boy (I)   (1914–1948) *singer and harmonica player*

Born John Lee Williamson on March 30, 1914, in Jackson, Tennessee, he is widely recognized as the first bluesman to utilize the harmonica as a lead—as opposed to accompanying—instrument. His work greatly influenced later blues harpists such as Little Walter Jacobs and Junior Wells.

Not much is known about Williamson's early career, although it is documented that he performed with seminal artists such as Sleepy John Estes and Homesick James. Also considered a trail-blazing blues singer, he relocated to Chicago in 1937, where he recorded classics like "Good Morning Little Schoolgirl" and "Sugar Mama" shortly thereafter for RCA's Bluebird imprint. He played for a time in a small combo featuring guitarist Big Bill Broonzy, but died June 1, 1948, a victim of an assault and robbery. He had two charting 78's (both on the Victor label in the late 1940s): "Shake the Boogie" and the posthumously released "Better Cut That Out."

Williamson, Sonny Boy (II)   (1899–1965) *singer and harmonica player*

Also known as Alex "Rice" Miller, he was born Aleck Ford on December 5, 1899, in Glendora, Mississippi. He was playing the guitar and harmonica by age five; he would become a major force in the evolution of blues playing on the latter instrument.

He first attracted attention as a performer on the Grand Ole Opry in the mid-1930s. With the fabled SONNY BOY WILLIAMSON (I) working largely in Chicago, he adopted that name for his KFFA–Helena, Arkansas, radio program from 1941 to 1945. Williamson did not record as a solo artist until 1947 with United Artists. He later recorded several R&B hits with the Chicago-based Chess company during the folk-blues revival: "Don't Start Me Talkin'," "Keep It to Yourself," and "Help Me." He seemed to be on the verge of even greater fame, having collaborated with the Yardbirds on a 1964 album, when he died on May 25, 1965 in Helena.

Willie D   (b. 1966) *rapper*

Born William Dennis, in Houston, he initially gained a measure of fame as a rapper on the Rap-A-Lot label. When two members of gangsta RAP group the Geto Boys departed in 1989, Rap-A-Lot brought in Willie D along with Scarface. The act earned considerable notoriety for their glorification of rape, mutilation, and violence on their debut LP as well as the widely reported incident in which member Bushwick Bill lost an eye when his girlfriend shot him after he threatened their baby. Internal friction caused all three members to focus on solo careers.

Willie D's debut LP, *Controversy* (Priority, 1992), included one of the most polemical tracks of the time, "Fuck Rodney King," depicting the police brutality victim as a sellout, traitor, and collaborator for asking, "Can't we all just get along?" during the L.A. riots. Subsequent albums—*I'm Goin' Out Like a Soldier* (Priority, 1992), *Play Witcha Mama* (Wrap, 1994), *Loved by Few, Hated by Many* (Virgin, 2000), and *Unbreakable* (Virgin, 2003)— sold well, but struck critics as disingenuous. While often coming across as theatrical and outrageous, Willie D was just as likely to appear intensely personal and confessional. He participated in a Geto Boys reunion LP, *The Resurrection* (1996), and channeled much of his energies into establishing his Wize Up subsidiary. He even made a guest appearance on the imprint's first release, Sho's *Trouble Man* album.

Willis, Chuck (1928–1958) *singer*

Although his career was tragically short due to his death on April 10, 1958, from peritonitis, Chuck Willis played a key role in popularizing the teen dance, the Stroll. An under-appreciated singer with a restrained, but soulful delivery, he is best remembered for a handful of classic songs, including "I Feel So Bad," "It's Too Late," "Hang Up My Rock and Roll Shoes," "Close Your Eyes," "Oh What a Dream," and "What Am I Living For." They were later covered by the likes of ELVIS PRESLEY, RUTH BROWN, Buddy Holly, JERRY LEE LEWIS, the FIVE KEYS, Delbert McClinton, the Animals, OTIS REDDING, the Band, and Foghat.

Born January 31, 1928, Willis made a name for himself as an R&B vocalist around his native Atlanta while still a teenager. A local disk jockey, Zenus "Daddy" Sears, helped him get a record contract with Columbia in 1952. He released a few successful singles for the label's subsidiary, OKeh, including "My Story," "Goin' to the River," "Don't Deceive Me," "You're Still My Baby", and "I Feel So Bad."

Known as the "Sheik of the Shake" in the early 1950s because he wore turbans on stage (he admitted to owning 54 of them at one point), Willis joined the Atlantic roster of artists in 1956. He immediately returned to the R&B charts with "It's Too Late" and "Juanita." Early the following year, he cut what many consider to be the definitive interpretation of the blues standard, "C.C. Rider," which reached number one on the R&B charts. With its sinuous groove, the single earned him a new appellation, "King of the Stroll." One of the few black artists to cross over successfully to mainstream pop up to that point, he seemed poised for even greater success at the time of his death. He had several posthumous hits, most notably "What Am I Living For"/ "Hang Up My Rock and Roll Shoes" (the A-track topping the R&B charts, while the flip side also made the Top Ten). Album compilations of his work have been released on a regular basis up to the present day.

Wilson, Cassandra (b. 1955) *singer*

Although generally categorized as a jazz artist, Cassandra Wilson incorporates a wide range of styles into her work, including rhythm and blues, soul, rock, and a more subdued approach typifying more adventuresome singer-songwriters such as Joni Mitchell and Van Morrison. Subtlety and restraint define her art, revealing a richly textured voice that effortlessly shifts from introspection to seductiveness and celebratory passion.

Born on December 4, 1955, the Jackson, Mississippi, native was musically influenced by both her parents; she sang with her mother in church and was exposed to the pop and jazz records owned by her father, a bassist and cellist who performed with RAY CHARLES, among others. After earning a bachelor's degree in communications, Wilson moved to New Orleans, where she sang on the side while employed in a more conventional job. After committing herself to music as a career, she went to New York in the early 1980s. Later in the decade she recorded a series of jazz albums for the independent JMT label.

By the time Wilson released *Blue Light 'Til Dawn* (Blue Note, 1993), her eclectic sound had found a mainstream audience. The record also revealed a predisposition to cover songs from unlikely sources, providing idiosyncratic interpretations of Ann Peebles's soul classic "I Can't Stand the Rain" and Morrison's "Tupelo Honey." She continued this practice in her follow-up, *New Moon Daughter* (Blue Note, 1996), ranging from the Monkees's number one hit, "Last Train to Clarksville" to the obscure Son House blues dirge, "Death Letter." While it would prove to be Wilson's most commercially successful album, she confounded fans and critics alike by opting for new challenges and releasing new works at a maddeningly slow pace. *Traveling Miles* (Blue Note, 1999) was a tribute to trumpeter Miles Davis; *Belly of the Sun* (Blue Note, 2002) mined the often overlooked blues contributions of Mississippi Delta musicians like pianist "Boogaloo" Ames. Her genre-bending work has been hailed from many quarters; *Time* magazine, for instance, referred to her as "America's best singer" in 2001.

Wilson, Jackie (1934–1984) *singer*

Jackie Wilson rivaled James Brown as one of the most dynamic performers of his generation, exuding a sexy athleticism capable of working his audience into a frenzy. He was also one of the most versatile vocalists in the rock era, ranging from the soulful, gritty style of a WILSON PICKETT to the smooth, gospel-inflected pop associated with SAM COOKE and CLYDE MCPHATTER.

Born June 9, 1934, and raised in a blue-collar section of Detroit, Wilson won his Golden Gloves weight division in the late 1940s. After high school, he began singing in local nightclubs. In 1953, Wilson joined Billy Ward and His Dominoes as a replacement for McPhatter, who'd departed to found the DRIFTERS. During his tenure the group recorded "St. Therese of the Roses," which reached number 13 on the pop charts in 1956.

Wilson went solo in late 1956, signing with Brunswick Records. Between 1957 and 1972 he recorded 49 charting singles, including the Top Ten hits "Lonely Teardrops," "Night," "Alone at Last," "My Empty Arms," "Baby Workout," and "(Your Love Keeps Lifting Me) Higher and Higher." When record sales dropped off, he was relegated to playing the oldies circuit. On September 25, 1975, as part of the Dick Clark revue at the Latin Casino in Cherry Hill, New Jersey, he suffered a major heart attack while singing "Lonely Teardrops." Emerging from a coma with considerable brain damage, he never performed again. He was inducted into the Rock and Roll Hall of Fame in 1987.

Winbush, Angela (b. 1954) *singer*

After first making a splash with the duo Rene & Angela, Winbush achieved even greater success as a soul chanteuse. She began tentatively, collaborating on an album with the ISLEY BROTHERS (she is married to Ronald Isley), *Smooth Sailin'* (Warner Bros., 1987). Her early solo LPs—*Sharp* (Mercury, 1987), *The Real Thing* (Mercury, 1989), and *Baby Hold On* (Mercury, 1990)—were geared to the popular trends of the day, most notably, urban dance music. Her first album for Elektra (1994), which she began recording in November 1992, revealed a far greater degree of personal control. It veered much closer to traditional R&B styles, as typified by the torchy ballad, "I'm the Kind of Woman," and "Baby Hold On," a duet with Ronald Isley that featured a string arrangement by Philadelphia soul producer THOM BELL.

Withers, Bill (b. 1938) *singer and songwriter*

Bill Withers was one of the more unique singer-songwriters of the 1970s, combining his gospel-soul roots with the spare folk style popular when he began his singing career in earnest. In addition to a long and distinguished recording career, his songs have been reinterpreted by countless artists covering a wide range of styles, including Michael Bolton, Joe Cocker, ARETHA FRANKLIN, Crystal Gale, Lionel Hampton, MICHAEL JACKSON, Mick Jagger,

ETTA JAMES, Tom Jones, Johnny Mathis, Liza Minnelli, Aaron Neville, DIANA ROSS, WILL SMITH, Sting, Barbra Streisand, Grover Washington, and Nancy Wilson.

Withers was born July 4, 1938, in Slab Fork, West Virginia. His father, a coal miner, died when he was 13, making it necessary for him to help support the family. During a nine-year stint in the navy, he began singing in public. He also took up songwriting in his search for suitable performance material.

Moving to Los Angeles in 1967 in order to pursue a music career, Withers made the rounds with his demo tapes until landing a recording contract with Sussex Records in early 1970. His debut album, *Just As I Am* (Sussex, 1971), featuring production work by Booker T. Jones, propelled him to the forefront of the music industry, earning a Grammy Award for songwriting with "Ain't No Sunshine" (which reached number three on the Hot 100). In the midst of heavy touring demands, he recorded a second LP, *Still Bill* (Sussex, 1972), which included two classic singles, the chart-topping "Lean on Me" and "Use Me" (number two on both the pop and R&B charts).

Withers's career momentum was slowed by a legal battle with Sussex in 1974. He managed to get back on track the following year after signing with Columbia Records. In addition to a total of 11 charting albums, he produced a steady stream of hits into the mid-1980s, most notably "Lovely Day" and his 1981 collaboration with fusion saxophonist Grover Washington, Jr., "Just the Two of Us," the latter of which earned him four Grammy nominations, winning one for songwriting. In 1987, he would receive his ninth Grammy nomination and third Grammy as a songwriter for Club Nouveau's reworking of "Lean on Me."

Although no longer a chart fixture, his songs and warm vocals continue to turn up in radio and television commercials, films, and TV programs. His material is not only covered by adult contemporary artists, but also widely sampled and reinterpreted by many HIP-HOP acts.

See also BOOKER T. & THE MGS.

Womack, Bobby (b. 1944) *singer, guitarist, and songwriter*

Born March 4, 1944, the Cleveland native knocked around the fringes of the music industry during the 1960s without making much of an impression on the public. His family's gospel group, the Womack Brothers, would record for the Sar label as the Valentinos and the Lovers from 1962 to 1964. He would also tour with Sam Cooke and work as a session guitarist for the likes of the Box Tops, Aretha Franklin, Janis Joplin, Wilson Pickett, and Joe Tex.

Womack's first solo recordings were done for the Him label in 1965. Although he would enjoy little success in the pop sector, he became a consistent R&B hit-maker in the 1970s and 1980s, most notably with the chart-toppers "Woman's Gotta Have It" and "Lookin' for a Love."

Wonder, Stevie (b. 1949) *singer and songwriter*

Stevie Wonder is one of the truly great figures of African-American popular music. Like his slightly younger contemporary, MICHAEL JACKSON, he literally grew up musically and physically in the public eye; although now approaching institutional status, he has remained a commercially successful recording artist for the better part of five decades.

Born May 13, 1949, in Detroit, he burst into the music business billed as a 13-year-old child prodigy; hence the moniker, "Little Stevie Wonder." His first hit, "Fingertips, Pt. 2," which topped both the pop and R&B charts in mid-1963, was a dynamic showcase for his wide-ranging talents—singing, harmonica playing, live performing, and songwriting. As Wonder settled into the role of perennial hit-maker, however, he rapidly transcended his novelty status. While the MOTOWN brain trust seemed hesitant to veer too far from the proven formula, his early releases displayed a surprising degree of diversity, including soul-inflected interpretations of folk-rock ("Blowin' in the Wind") and continental pop ("My Cherie Amour").

As he approached adulthood, Wonder, by now a talented multi-instrumentalist, insisted on greater control of his career, particularly in production and less reliance of studio session players. Already threatened with the imminent defections of superstars like MARVIN GAYE and DIANA ROSS, Motown loosened the reins somewhat, allowing him the kind of creative latitude that other labels were giving leading rock stars. If Wonder had not continued to produce commercially viable music, this freedom might have been short-lived. However, his singles, beginning with "Superstition," outperformed earlier releases while his albums went from marginal hit status to major bestsellers. Of even greater significance, his 1970s output won universal critical acclaim for its artistry. His legacy was guaranteed by three LPs—*Innervisions* (1973), *Fulfillingness First Finale, Pt. 1* (1974), and the expansive *Songs in the Key of Life* (1977)—which won a combined 13 Grammy awards.

After this peak, later releases were always somewhat unfocused and stylistically out-of-step with the prevailing trends, be it DISCO, FUNK PUNK, or HIP-HOP. By the 1980s, Wonder, just in his 30s, had assumed the mantle of elder statesman of the soul-FUNK nation. Mainstream pop-rock stars like Paul McCartney sought him out for collaborations, and large-scale, industry-wide projects like USA for Africa would be considered incomplete without him. Perhaps ironically, his increasing preoccupation with film soundtrack composition was blunted by the appearance of his older, vintage recordings in a host of big budget Hollywood features. His place in the pop music pantheon assured, the extremely likeable and decidedly noncontroversial Wonder, still seemingly in full possession of his creative powers, remains capable of breaking out of his commercial dormancy at any time.

Wright, Betty (b. 1953) *singer*
Born December 21, 1953, the Miami native began performing in the gospel group Echoes of Joy, in addition to sister Jeanette Holloway and brothers Phillip and Milton Wright, in 1956. She first recorded as a solo artist for Deep City in 1966. Wright went on to record a steady string of charting singles with the Alston label from 1969 to 1979, including "Clean Up Woman," "Baby Sitter," and "Let Me Be Your Lovemaker." Although failing to crack to pop Top 40 after 1972, she continued to crank out an occasional R&B hit through the 1980s for Epic, Jamaica, First String, and MS.B.

Wright, O. V. (1939–1980) *singer*
O. V. Wright was a highly regarded soul singer in the late 1960s and early 1970s. However, mainstream success by and large eluded him, due to a dark edge to his work and, later, drug abuse problems.

Born Overton Vertis Wright, October 9, 1939, in Leno, Tennessee, he started out singing gospel in church as a youth. He formed the Five Harmonaires before moving on to more successful groups as the Sunset Travellers, the Spirit of Memphis Quartet, and the Highway QC's. Singing with the GOLDWAX label, he broke into the pop field in 1964 with the classic "That's How Strong My Love Is," which he cowrote with Roosevelt Jamison. OTIS REDDING recorded the best-selling version of the song, but Wright followed with 17 R&B hits through 1978, most notably "You're Gonna Make Me Cry," "Eight Men, Four Women," and "Ace of Spades." Wright recorded for the ABC and Hi labels in the latter half of the 1970s. His drug problems brought on a fatal heart attack on November 16, 1980.

Wu-Tang Clan
Though most RAP groups are formed in hopes of being regarded as virtuoso musicians and MCs, the Wu-Tang Clan rallied around a much more tangible mantra when they formed under the leadership of Genius/GZA and Ol' Dirty Bastard in 1993. The motley nine-MC collective that made up the Clan saw themselves much more as a brand name to be extended than a rap group. With this ideology fueling their musical endeavors, the group

began shopping themselves around with the explicit stipulation that should a label sign them, each member of the Clan would have full authority to sign a solo deal at his own discretion with another label of his choosing.

This aversion to company loyalty was at least in part perhaps the result of several of the Clan's members having been burned by the flame of label producers and record executives' expert advice. RZA, who produced practically every Wu-Tang project in the 1990s, was one example of such treatment. In 1991, while working for TOMMY BOY RECORDS, producers convinced him to cut the joke single "Ooh I Love You Rakeem" which fell on deaf ears commercially and critically. Genius/GZA had suffered similarly at the hands of COLD CHILLIN' RECORDS, which among other projects had released his first full-length solo record, *Words from the Genius*.

Understandably, then, when RZA first met with two business conscious MCs, dissatisfied with their place in the rap arena and in need of a talented producer, the nucleus of the Wu-Tang Clan was quickly formed in 1993. The Clan, by virtue of their purpose, however, would require more then just three headstrong individuals. Indeed, in their 10-year career the Wu-Tang Clan has produced armies of rappers and MCs devoted to the paramount goal of diversification toward the maximization of assets.

Comprising the original Clan were: RZA (Robert Diggs), Ol' Dirty Bastard (Russell Jones), U-God (Lamont Hawkins), Raekwon the Chef (Corey Woods), Genius/GZA (Gary Grice), Ghostface Killah (Dennis Coles), Inspectah Deck (Jason Hunter), Method Man (Clifford Smith), and Masta Killa (Elgin Turner). Over the course of the next several years, the Clan expanded their list of inductees into a litany of offshoot groups.

Before they could multiply their numbers so immensely, however, the Clan had to make a name for themselves. In an effort to prove to labels that their talent was comparable to their unprecedented contracts, the Clan self-released their first group single "Protect Ya Neck," which generated enough underground interest that Loud/RCA agreed to the

Clan's unorthodox terms. The result was one of the biggest debut albums in rap history.

Enter the Wu-Tang (36 Chambers), released in November 1993, reached number eight in *Billboard*'s Top R&B/Hip-Hop Albums chart. Coming in at barely over half an hour, the album solidified the group's place in the HIP-HOP world as pioneers. The MCs split their time on the record evoking imagery of extreme violence and martial artistry, the latter of which is the basis of their name. The album's biggest success was the single "C.R.E.A.M.," which took almost a year to be released. The Clan seized upon their newfound popularity and began branching out into solo projects.

RZA took first advantage of his new freedom by forming an entirely new group, The Gravediggas, and producing their 1994 album, *6 Feet Deep*. He further extended his producing hand into the soundtrack genre that same year by completing Raekwon's single, "Heaven and Hell" (which also featured Ghostface Killah), and tried his hand at acting when he appeared in the film *Fresh*.

Method Man followed suit in 1994 by cutting his first solo album, albeit sans a separate backing group, with the release of *Tical*. In the following year, Ol' Dirty Bastard had RZA produce his first solo effort on Elektra, *Return to the 36 Chambers*, which included the best-selling singles, "Brooklyn Zoo" and "Shimmy Shimmy Ya." Both albums went gold. Other Clan members releasing solo albums in 1995 included Raekwon (*Only Built 4 Cuban Linx*) and Genius (*Liquid Swords*). Two others members— Inspectah Deck and Ghostface Killah—contributed tracks to the *Tales From the Hood* soundtrack.

Wu-Tang Clan's follow-up album, *Wu-Tang Forever*, was released in June 1997. The album included two CDs worth of material, and was the first appearance by then nonmember Cappadonna on an official Wu-Tang record (though he had appeared on numerous solo efforts tied to the group). The album sold over 600,000 copies in the space of only one week and went on to debut at the number one spot on the Top 200 chart. It included the hit single "It's Yourz."

In 1998, Clan cohorts, Cappadonna and Killah Priest, both released solo LPs. Many apprentice groups supported by the Clan began releasing their own material during this period, most notably, the Wu-Tang Killa Bees (*The Swarm Vol. 1*) and Killarmy (*Dirty Weaponry*).

Amid a host of legal difficulties stemming from fights breaking out on tour and the many run-ins with the law experienced by founder Ol' Dirty Bastard, the Clan still managed to have a highly productive second half of 1998, touring and releasing a new batch of solo albums from Wu-Tang members. Method Man released *Tical 2000: Judgment Day;* RZA issued a solo work under the alias Bobby Digital, *Bobby Digital in Stereo;* Inspectah Deck completed his debut LP, *Uncontrolled Substance;* Ol' Dirty Bastard produced *Nigga Please;* U-God, released *Golden Arms Redemption;* and Raekwon issued *Immobilarity.*

Spin-off releases in 1999 were limited to Ghostface Killah's *Supreme Clientele,* and RZA's compilation album, *RZA Hits,* which retraced the sonic landscape of the Wu-Tang members both as a group and individually.

The next Wu-Tang album, *The W* (which reached number five on the Top 200 as well as topping the R&B/Hip-Hop Album Charts), was released in 2000. During this period, film director Jim Jarmusch asked RZA to provide the soundtrack to a samurai movie he was currently filming, *Ghost Dog: Way of the Samurai.*

The Clan's fortunes have taken a plunge for the worse in recent years. Their album, *Iron Flag,* met with little critical praise and substantially lower sales. The number of solo projects involving band members have dropped off dramatically as well. Perhaps the biggest blow was the death of founding member Ol' Dirty Bastard in late 2004 due to drug intoxication; his body was found in a recording studio where he had been cutting what was to be his next solo project, following a jail stint for probation violation.

—Lowery Woodall

X-Clan

One of the most respected exponents of Afrocentric, politically slanted rap acts, X-Clan consisted of Grand Verbalizer Lesson "Brother J" (born Jason Hunter), Lumumba Professor X "The Overseer" (born Lumumba Carson, son of activist Sonny Carson), the Rhythem Provider "Sugar Shaft" (born Anthony Hardin), and Grand Architect "Paradise" (born Claude Grey). They were supported by MC Isis (aka Lin Que). Their two accomplished albums, *To the East, Backwards* (4th & Broadway, 1990) and *Xodus* (Polydor, 1992), both reached number 11 on the R&B album charts, but were somewhat overshadowed by their activist activities, which included membership in Blackwatch and outspoken endorsement of various pro-black organizations.

By the mid-1990s, Professor X and Isis had released solo LPs, which helped bring on the group's demise. Sugar Shaft died of AIDS-related causes, while Brother J started Dark Sun Riders, which released an album in 1996. X-Clan reunited in the late 1990s, although no commercial releases had appeared through 2004.

X-Ecutioners, The

The New York–based X-Ecutioners were the first all-DJ unit to release an album of "turntablism." Formed in 1989 by Roc Raida with Johnny Cash, Sean Cee, and Steve D, they took the name X-Men in anticipation of a competition with New York compatriots the Supermen, but the event never took place. They changed their name due to the threat of a copyright suit by Marvel Comics after signing with Asphodel in 1997. The group members, by now consisting of Mista Sinista, Rob Swift, Total Eclipse, and Roc Raida, won national and international titles for trick and battle DJing in addition to collaborating live and on recordings with the likes of Artifacts, the Beatnuts, Large Professor, and Organized Confusion.

The X-Ecutioners were prolific performers, working clubs, giving exhibitions, and participating in competitions on four continents. Their albums, including *X-Pressions* (Asphodel, 1997) and *Built From Scratch* (Relativity, 2002), consisted of new tracks constructed from bits and pieces of records manipulated by hand (as opposed to the use of a sampler and sequencer). The usual DJ arsenal of cutting, mixing, and beat juggling was punctuated by a renewed emphasis on scratching pyrotechnics. By 2004, the group was pioneering soundtrack music for video games as a means of gaining wider exposure for their creative work.

Xzibit (b. 1974) *rapper*

Born Alvin Nathaniel Joiner in Detroit on January 8, 1974, Xzibit first surfaced in the mid-1990s with the Likwit Crew, a loose association of West Coast hardcore rappers that included the Alkaholiks and King T. Relying heavily upon his Likwit cohorts, Xzibit's first two solo albums, *At the Speed of Life* (Loud, 1996) and *40 Dayz & 40 Nightz* (RCA, 1998), became underground hits on the strength of uncommonly proficient wordplay and richly diversified arrangements.

Dr Dre proved to be Xzibit's ticket into the mainstream. After being paired with Snoop Doggy Dogg to record the Dre-produced hit single, "Bitch Please," he was given a guest spot on "Some L.A. Niggaz," a track appearing on Dre's own highly successful album, *2001* (1999). He was also included in the prestigious Up in Smoke tour of North America during summer 2000, along with such luminaries as Snoop Dogg, Eminem, and Ice Cube.

Despite flashes of brilliance, Xzibit's next album, *Restless* (Loud, 2000), with Dre as executive producer, and featuring guest appearances by Eminem, Snoop Dogg, and Dre himself, was ultimately a lackluster affair. Although Dre and his Aftermath regime remained highly visible in *Man vs. Machine* (Columbia, 2002), Xzibit attempted to spread the production credits around, utilizing Rockwilder, Jellyroll, and Eminem as well as Dre. Nevertheless, the results were uneven at best, and major success continued to elude him.

Young Hearts

The Los Angeles–based Young Hearts, originally consisting of Earl Carter, Charles Ingersoll, James Moore, and Ronald Preyer, were typical of the R&B vocal groups of the early 1970s, featuring a falsetto lead singer and lush arrangements. Their biggest hits were "I've Got Love for My Baby," from the LP *Sweet Soul Shakin'* (Minit, 1968), and "Wake Up and Start Standing," culled from *A Taste of the Young Hearts* (20th Century, 1974). A move to ABC resulted in an album, *All About Love* (ABC, 1977), and several singles, but no hits. Something of an anachronism in an era dominated by DISCO and the punk revolution, the group eventually receded into oblivion.

Young M.C. (b. 1967) *rapper*

Young M.C. was born Marvin Young in London, England, on May 10, 1967, but was raised in Queens, New York. He first gained attention by composing lyrics for Tone Loc while attending school in southern California in the late 1980s. He garnered his own record contract, followed by the debut album, *Stone Cold Rhyming* (1989). It achieved platinum sales on the strength of the Grammy-winning hit single, "Bust a Move," a comic take on ill-fated attempts at winning over the opposite sex, framed by an unforgettable bass figure and effervescent arrangement. Although Young M.C. continued to release new material—*What's the Flavor?* (1993), *Return of the 1-Hit Wonder* (1997), *Ain't Going Out Like That* (2000), and *Engage the Enzyme* (2002)—featuring his trademark playful, upbeat verses, he has proven unable to move beyond the shadow of "Bust a Move," which regularly pops up on film soundtracks and HIP-HOP compilations.

Young Rascals   See RASCALS/YOUNG RASCALS, THE.

Zager, Michael, & the Moon Band (featuring Peabo Bryson)

The Moon Band—originally known as the Michael Zager Band—was a studio entity organized by composer/arranger Michael Zager (born 1943, in Jersey City, New Jersey). Zager's earliest success came with the hard rock group, Ten Wheel Drive, between 1968 and 1973. He then produced radio and television commercials prior to overseeing the recording activities of acts like Street Corner Symphony and the Andrea True Connection in addition to his own creations, Love Child's Afro Cuban Blues Band and the Moon Band. The latter group recorded hits for three different labels (Bang, Capitol, and Private Stock) over a three-year period beginning in early 1976, including "Do It with Feeling," "Reaching for the Sky" (which reached number six on the R&B charts in 1978), "Let's All Chant," and "I'm So into You" (which peaked at number two on the R&B charts in early 1979).

See also BRYSON, PEABO.

Appendixes

Appendix I

Discography of Recommended Listening

I. By Artist

Arrested Development.
3 Years, 5 Months & 2 Days in the Life Of . . . (Chrysalis, 1992; alternative rap)

Baker, La Vern.
Best of La Vern Baker (Atlantic, 1963)

Ballard, Hank, & the Midnighters.
What You Get When the Getting' Gets Good (Charly, 1987)

Berry, Chuck.
Chuck Berry's Greatest Hits (Chess, 1964)

Boogie Down Productions.
Criminal Minded (Sugar Hill, 1987; East Coast/hardcore rap)

Booker T. & the MGs.
McLemore Avenue (Stax, 1970; reissued, 1990)

Boyz II Men.
Cooleyhighharmony (Motown, 1991)

Brown, James.
At the Apollo (Polydor, 1987; two LPs on one CD)

Brown, Ruth.
Best of Ruth Brown (Atlantic, 1963)

Burke, Solomon.
The Best of Solomon Burke (Atlantic, 1965)

Butler, Jerry.
Best of Jerry Butler (Vee-Jay, 1962)

Carey, Mariah.
Mariah Carey (Columbia, 1990)

Chandler, Gene.
Duke of Earl (Vee-Jay, 1961)

Charles, Ray.
Modern Sounds in Country and Western Music (ABC-Paramount, 1962); *The Ray Charles Story* (Atlantic, 1962; two-LP set)

Checker, Chubby.
Chubby Checker's Biggest Hits (Parkway, 1963)

Clark, Dee.
Best of Dee Clark (Vee-Jay, 1962)

The Coasters.
Greatest Hits (Atco, 1959)

Cole, Natalie.
Anthology (Capitol, 2004; two-CD set)

Commodores.
Commodores (Motown, 1977)

Cooke, Sam.
The Man and His Music (RCA, 1986)

Domino, Fats.
The Best of Fats Domino (EMI America, 1987)

Dr Dre.
The Chronic (Death Row, 1992; West Coast/G-funk rap)

The Drifters.
Let the Boogie Woogie Roll: Greatest Hits, 1953–1958 (Atlantic, 1989; two-CD set); *1959–1965: All Time Greatest Hits and More* (Atlantic, 1989, two-CD set)

Earth, Wind & Fire.
The Collection (Sony, 2004; three-CD set, combining *That's the Way of the World* (Columbia, 1975); *Gratitude* (Columbia, 1975); *All 'n All* (Columbia, 1977)

50 Cent.
Get Rich or Die Tryin' (Interscope, 2003; East Coast/hardcore rap)

Floyd, Eddie.
Chronicle (Stax, 1979)

Four Tops.
Anthology (Motown, 1974; three-LP set)

Franklin, Aretha.
I Never Loved a Man the Way I Love You (Atlantic, 1967)

Gaye, Marvin.
Anthology (Motown, 1974; three-LP set)

Green, Al.
The Immortal Soul of Al Green (Capitol 2004; four-CD set)

Hayes, Isaac.
Hot Buttered Soul (Enterprise, 1969; reissued by Stax, 1978); *Shaft* (Enterprise, 1971; two-LP set, soundtrack, reissued by Stax in 1978)

Hill, Lauryn.
The Miseducation of Lauryn Hill (Ruffhouse, 1998)

Houston, Whitney.
Whitney Houston (Arista, 1985)

Ice Cube.
Death Certificate (Priority, 1991; West Coast/gangsta rap)

Ice-T.
O.G.: Original Gangster (Sire, 1991; West Coast/gangsta rap)

The Isley Brothers.
Greatest Hits, Vol. 1 (T-Neck, 1987)

Jackson, Janet.
Janet Jackson's Rhythm Nation 1814 (A&M, 1989)

Jackson, Michael.
Thriller (Epic, 1982)

Jackson 5.
Anthology (Motown, 1976; three-LP set)

James, Rick.
Street Songs (Gordy, 1981)

Little Richard.
18 Greatest Hits (Rhino, 1985)

Martha & the Vandellas.
Anthology (Motown, 1974)

Marvelettes.
Anthology (Motown, 1975; two-LP set)

M.C. Hammer.
Please Hammer Don't Hurt 'Em (Capitol, 1990; pop-rap)

McPhatter, Clyde, & the Drifters.
Rock and Roll (Atlantic, 1956)

Melvin, Harold, & the Blue Notes, featuring Theodore Pendergrass.
Wake Up Everybody (Philadelphia International, 1975)

MFSB.
Love Is the Message (Philadelphia International, 1973)

The Notorious B.I.G.
Ready to Die (Bad Boy, 1994)

N.W.A.
Straight Outta Compton (Ruthless, 1988)

Ohio Players.
Ohio Players Gold (Mercury, 1976)

The O'Jays.
Back Stabbers (Philadelphia International, 1972)

OutKast.
Aquemini (LaFace, 1998; southern rap)

Paul, Billy.
360 Degrees of Billy Paul (Philadelphia International, 1972)

Pickett, Wilson.
The Exciting Wilson Pickett (Atlantic, 1966)

The Platters.
Golden Hits (Mercury, 1986)

Prince.
1999 (Warner Bros., 1982; two LPs on one CD)

Public Enemy.
It Takes a Nation of Millions to Hold Us Back (Def Jam/Columbia, 1988; political rap)

The Rascals.
Time Peace: The Rascals' Greatest Hits (Atlantic, 1968)

Redding, Otis.
Dictionary of Soul (Atco, 1968; reissue of original Volt release); *The History of Otis Redding* (Atco, 1968; reissue of original Volt release)

Reed, Jimmy.
Jimmy Reed at Carnegie Hall (Vee-Jay, 1961; two-LP set. The title is misleading; the first disc consists of new material, while the second consists of Reed's earlier hits.)

Robinson, Smokey, & the Miracles.
Anthology (Motown, 1974; three-LP set)

Ross, Diana.
Lady Sings the Blues (Motown, 1972; 2-LP set)

Ross, Diana, & the Supremes.
Greatest Hits (Motown, 1967; two-LP set)

Run-D.M.C.
Raising Hell (Profile, 1986; hardcore rap)

Shakur, Tupac.
All Eyez On Me (Death Row, 1996; gangsta rap)

The Shirelles.
The Shirelles' Greatest Hits (Scepter, 1963)

Sly & the Family Stone.
Anthology (Columbia, 1989; two LPs on one CD)

Snoop Doggy Dogg.
Doggystyle (Death Row, 1993; West Coast/gangsta rap)

Staple Singers.
Chronicle (Stax, 1979)

Summer, Donna.
Bad Girls (Casablanca, 1987; two LPs on one CD, reissue of 1979 release)

The Temptations.
Anthology (Motown, 1973; three-LP set)

Turner, Big Joe.
Rock and Roll (Atlantic, 1957)

Turner, Ike & Tina.
The Best of Ike & Tina Turner (EMI America, 1987)

Walker, Junior, & the All Stars.
Anthology (Motown, 1974; two-LP set)

War.
Greatest Hits (United Artists, 1976)

Warwick, Dionne.
Make Way for Dionne Warwick (Scepter, 1964)

Wells, Mary.
Mary Wells' Greatest Hits (Motown M-616, 1964)

Willis, Chuck.
I Remember Chuck Willis (Atlantic, 1963)

Wilson, Jackie.
The Jackie Wilson Story (Epic, 1983; two LPs on one CD)

Wonder, Stevie.
Looking Back (Motown, 1977; three-LP set)

II. Compilations

Let's Clean Up the Ghetto. (Philadelphia International, 1977)

The Motown Story: The First Decade. (Motown, 1971; five volumes, also available separately)

Tommy Boy's Greatest Beats, 1981–1996. (Tommy Boy, 1988; five-CD set that spans the history of hip-hop better than any other collection, from old-school artists such as Afrika Bambaataa to dance tracks by the likes of Coldcut, 808 State, and Information Society. The first four volumes are also available as separate issues.)

Appendix II

Chronology

1942

Billboard begins charting the sale of records in the "Negro" market, employing the heading, "Harlem Hit Parade." The weekly listing is renamed "Race Records" in 1945.

1948

Atlantic Records is formed by Neshui and AHMET ERTEGUN and HERB ABRAMSON. The label has shown a flair for assessing performing styles and audience tastes that has been unmatched in the post–World War II era of popular music. Beginning with a roster of performers randomly collected from individuals without contracts, Atlantic acquired a succession of singers from various sources and with various styles. By the mid-1950s the company's artists included BIG JOE TURNER, RUTH BROWN, LAVERN BAKER, CLYDE MCPHATTER, RAY CHARLES, Ivory Joe Hunter, CHUCK WILLIS, the Cardinals, the CLOVERS, the DRIFTERS, the COASTERS, and Bobby Darin. With these performers Atlantic's share of the R&B market grew from three Top Ten records in 1950 to 17 (out of 81) in 1956. Though no longer a true independent, Atlantic continues to thrive as part of the WEA family.

1949

On June 25 *Billboard*, without any editorial comment, begins employing the term "rhythm and blues" (rather than "race records") in reference to the black charts.

1951

"Rocket '88'" (Chess), recorded by IKE TURNER's Kings of Rhythm and produced by Sam Phillips in his Memphis studio (although credited to vocalist/saxophonist JACKIE BRENSTON for contractual reasons), enters the R&B charts on May 12. It is widely recognized to be the first rock 'n' roll recording.

1952

Bob Horn's *Bandstand* is first broadcast on a local Philadelphia television station. Dick Clark would assume the host slot in July 1956, and ABC first aired it nationally on August 5, 1957. The program—renamed *American Bandstand*—provided a forum for many up-and-coming R&B artists in addition to becoming a template for *Soul Train* and other music programs geared to a predominantly African–American audience.

1953

The Orioles's "Crying in the Chapel" (Jubilee) enters the pop charts in September, eventually peaking at number 11, in the process becoming the first black R&B recording to achieve crossover hit status.

1957

SAM COOKE, widely considered to be the definitive soul singer, enters the R&B charts with his first hit, "You Send Me" (Keen), on October 21. The song, which reached number one on both the pop and R&B charts, enabled the multitalented Cooke to assume greater control over all aspects of his career, from songwriting to ownership of a production company.

1958

Jim Stewart establishes Satellite Records in Memphis. The commercial potential of one of his early signings, the father-daughter duo Rufus and CARLA THOMAS, led Atlantic producer Jerry Wexler to invest in a five-year option, which led to a long-term distribution pact. The label was later renamed STAX due to copyright concerns.

1959

"There Goes My Baby" is recorded by the DRIFTERS (Atlantic) and released on March 6. It was one of the first rhythm and blues discs to use strings. Its combined artistic and commercial success inspired an upsurge in the development of sophisticated recording techniques for black music, culminating in the "Golden Age of Soul" (1964–68).

1960

Cash Box combines its pop and R&B charts. In March 12 editorial appearing on the front page of that issue, the magazine justifies this decision by noting the similarity between the pop and R&B charts; i.e., the R&B listing was at that time almost 90 percent pop in nature. *Cash Box* evidently had second thoughts about this policy, and reinstated the separate R&B compilation on December 17, 1960 ("Top 50 in Locations"). *Billboard* used the same reasoning in deleting its R&B singles charts between November 30, 1963, and January 23, 1965. It, too, ultimately returned to the two-chart system.

1961

The Miracles's "Shop Around" (Tamla) reaches number one on January 16, remaining there for eight weeks. The song was the first major hit for MOTOWN.

1961

On August 26 the MAR-KEYS'S "Last Night" becomes the first STAX production to reach number one. Stax—and later in the decade, FAME, the MUSCLE SHOALS, Alabama, studio headed by RICK HALL—offered a rawer, more spontaneous, gospel-influenced alternative to the MOTOWN sound. The Mar-Keys (whose rhythm section also recorded as BOOKER T. & THE MGs) backed most of the label's artists, including SAM AND DAVE, OTIS REDDING, Eddie Floyd, Rufus Thomas, CARLA THOMAS, and Johnnie Taylor.

1962

On May 26 RAY CHARLES's country-influenced "I Can't Stop Loving You" (ABC) begins the first of its 10 consecutive weeks at the top of the R&B charts. The song typified in dramatic fashion—due to its incredible commercial success—the inclination of talented black performers to favor sweet and sentimental sounds over personal expression in order to achieve mainstream pop impact. Similar career moves were taken by SAM COOKE, JACKIE WILSON, BROOK BENTON, and others. Yet black singers such as WILSON PICKETT and ARETHA FRANKLIN were able to attain pop music success in the late 1960s while remaining true to their cultural roots.

1963

On October 12 "Cry Baby," by Garnett Mimms & the Enchanters (United Artists) begins the first of three weeks at number one. "Cry Baby" was among the earliest—and certainly the most commercially successful—gospel-styled songs to have an accompaniment that was not somehow adapted from another genre of music. In short, the song possessed all the prime ingredients characterizing the classic soul genre.

1967

Dyke & the Blazers's "Funky Broadway—Part 1" (Original Sound) enters the R&B charts on February 11, remaining there for four weeks, peaking at number 17. The word "funk" didn't become part of the legitimate radio jargon until the song had "bubbled under" for so long that disc jockeys were forced to play it and say the word. Though nobody knows who coined the term, "funk" simply was not a word used in polite society. But "Funky Broadway" changed all that.

1967

ARETHA FRANKLIN's "I Never Loved a Man" (Atlantic) reaches number one on March 25, remaining there for seven weeks. In a kind of soul-waltz time, the record built up from a quiet but dramatic opening organ figure into a hammering, screaming, but always firmly controlled yell of delight, as a brilliantly organized band fed more and more to support the singer's emotion. It was the first of Franklin's 18 number one songs on the R&B charts, more than any other artist between 1960 and 1985. Noteworthy commercial success combined with impeccable artistry earned her the sobriquet, "Queen of Soul."

1968

SLY & THE FAMILY STONE's first hit, "Dance to the Music" (Epic), enters the R&B charts on January 27, eventually peaking at number nine. The song shook off the assumptions about the separate roles of voices and instruments as sources of rhythm and harmony, alternating them and blending them, yet never losing either melody or dance beat. The adventurousness of the sound was recognized by the white audience, which had tended to deride soul arrangements as being overly simple. As Sly began employing increasingly personal lyrics, the social consciousness school of funk was created.

1968

"Say It Loud — I'm Black and I'm Proud" (King) by "Soul Brother Number One," JAMES BROWN, tops the charts on October 5. "Say It Loud" was merely the most successful of the wave of political slogan songs exploiting black pride.

1969

Billboard declares "rhythm and blues" officially dead by renaming its list of best-selling records for that market "Best Selling Soul Singles" on August 23. Ironically, there was every sign that this new euphemism for "black"—which had been widely used during most of the 1960s—would soon be musically outdated, and its successor defied prophesy.

1970

The Last Poets record an eponymous album on Douglas Records. Their mixture of spoken words with jazz rhythms and instrumentation was an early prototype of the HIP-HOP genre.

1971

ISAAC HAYES's "Theme From Shaft" (Enterprise) enters the R&B charts on October 16. The song, which graced Richard Roundtree's film *Shaft*, would garner an Academy Award, making Hayes the first African-American composer to be so honored. The double-disc soundtrack reached number one on the pop LP chart, achieving platinum sales and earning Hayes a Grammy.

1973

Kool Herc (real name: Clive Campbell) begins performing as a deejay at New York City block parties. Born in Jamaica, he relocated to the Bronx in 1967, bringing along his knowledge of the Kingston sound system scene. He focused on the "break" or "get-down" sections of R&B, soul, and funk records, the portion in which the "breakbeat" or percussion interlude appeared in its most dynamic form. Due to the short duration of most song breaks, he expanded them by employing two turntables with double copies of a given record. His "breakbeats" inspired the formation of the B-Boys (Break-Boys), dancers dominating the dancefloor during these passages, and future hip-hop innovators like Grandmaster Caz, AFRIKA BAMBAATAA, and GRANDMASTER FLASH.

1973

Manu Dibango's "Soul Makossa" (Atlantic) enters the R&B charts on June 23, eventually reaching the Top 20. Recorded by an African in Paris, "Soul Makossa" was imported into the U.S. when its enormous popularity in discos made domestic release seem like a good business proposition. Thus, the first disco pop hit was born.

1977

Frankie Knuckles becomes a DJ at the Chicago-based club, the Warehouse. His innovations included incorporating a reel-to-reel tape machine into turntable grooves that mixed soul recordings with DONNA SUMMER tracks and other contemporary disco fare.

1977

Los Angeles–based Shabba-Doo introduces "popping"—considered by many to be the first true HIP-HOP dance—to New York. In short order, local dance crews would add waves and smoother movements to popping.

1978

"Soft and Wet," the first hit by PRINCE, (Warner), enters the charts on July 29, eventually reaching number 12. Prince's combination of street-level hipness and musical inventiveness propelled him to the vanguard of black music in the 1980s. His seemingly boundless energy spawned a new school of stars, including the Time, Vanity, ANDRE CYMONE, and SHEILA E.

1979

"Rapper's Delight" (SUGAR HILL), recorded by a prefab ensemble, the Sugarhill Gang, enters the R&B charts on October 13 on its way to becoming the first notable RAP hit. With the genre clearly emerging from the underground, other labels spring up in an attempt to exploit HIP-HOP culture commercially.

1981

GRANDMASTER FLASH & the Furious Five's "The Adventures of Grandmaster Flash on the Wheels of Steel" (SUGAR HILL)—the first RAP record to feature live DJ scratching—enters the R&B charts on May 23.

1982

Cash Box first employs the term "Black Contemporary" in the heading of its black charts (i.e., "Top 100 Black Contemporary Singles"), starting April 10. For a time, the term gained nearly universal acceptance both inside and outside the music industry. Black Contemporary encompassed the full range of black pop music (dance music, easy listening, jazz fusions, etc.) as well as white releases that were expected to appeal to the black audience. However, the rise of postpunk styles expounding a more colorblind ethic (e.g., HOUSE, electronica) helped bring "rhythm and blues" back into vogue as a term referring to classic black pop music.

1983

RUN-D.M.C.'s "It's Like That"/"Sucker MC's" (Profile) enters the R&B charts on May 21. Built around a fusion of mainstream rock and RAP posturing, the single signaled the end of the road for old-school rap styles.

1984

KDAY, Los Angeles, becomes the first radio station to program RAP music exclusively.

1986

Schoolly D's independent release, "PSK—What Does It Mean" (included on the 1987 Rykodisc compilation, *The Adventures of Schoolly D*), ushers in "gangsta rap" or—as it was sometimes called at the time—"reality rap."

1986

The Ultramagnetic MC's—consisting of Kool Keith, Ced Gee, and DJ Moe Love—begin releasing singles like "Something Else" and "Space Groove." They were the first HIP-HOP group to employ a sampler as an instrument and to feature extensive live instrumentation.

1986

Derrick May's "String of Life" (under his moniker Rhythm Is Rhythm) becomes a huge British dance club hit. Featuring frenetic keyboard patterns, sampled orchestral strings, and a pounding drum track, it provided a launching pad for the spread of TECHNO far beyond its Detroit roots.

1988

Yo! MTV Raps goes on the air, playing a key role in bringing RAP a broad mainstream audience.

1988

N.W.A.'s *Straight Outta Compton* (Ruthless) goes platinum with no airplay, establishing gangsta RAP—and West Coast rap in general—as a sellable commodity. The track, "Fuck the Police," spurs widespread censorship in addition to denunciations from white politicians and black community leaders alike.

1995

Tricky releases the album, *Maxinquaye,* a post-house, trip-hop blend of RAP, sampling, and rock that lays groundwork for the rise of energetic club-based rhythms of DRUM AND BASS.

1996

Rapper Tupac Shakur dies in suspected gang-related shooting.

1997

Rap star Biggie Smalls (Notorious B.I.G.) is killed in a drive-by shooting in Los Angeles.

1999

On the strength of her debut solo album, *The Miseducation of Lauryn Hill* (Sony), Lauryn Hill becomes the first woman to be nominated for 10 awards in the history of the Grammys (winning five of them).

2001

DJ Qbert's animated film, *Wave Twisters,* is made an official selection at the annual Sundance Film Festival. It is adapted to a feature film by acclaimed graffiti artist, Dug-One, the first work of its kind.

2002

Superstar rapper Eminem makes his acting debut in the film *8 Mile,* directed by Curtis Hanson, which tells the story of a young Detroit rap artist from the bad part of town who's looking for his big break. The song "Lose Yourself," performed by Eminem, garnered the Oscar for Best Music, Original Song.

2003

Rap superstar Jay-Z announces his retirement from recording with a massive "retirement party" tour and a farewell concert at Madison Square Garden on November 25, but he remains active in the music business.

2004

The 2003 double album *Speakerboxxx/The Love Below* by OutKast takes the Grammy for Album of the Year. The first single off the album, "Hey Ya!," hits number one on the *Billboard* charts, only to be knocked from the top position by "The Way You Move," the second single released from the same recording, a feat last accomplished by the Beatles 40 years earlier.

Hip-hop celebrates its 30th birthday.

2005

Luther Vandross, who won a Grammy in 2004 for the album *Dance With My Father,* dies of a stroke.

Glossary of Music Terms

a cappella   Literally "in the chapel." Used generally to describe unaccompanied vocal music.

accent   Extra emphasis given to a note in a musical composition.

alto   (1) The lowest female voice, below mezzo-soprano and SOPRANO. (2) In musical instruments, an instrument with a range of either a fourth or fifth below the standard range; the viola is tuned a fifth below the violin, for example. (3) The alto CLEF (also known as the C clef) used for notating music for alto instruments and voices.

arpeggio   A broken CHORD; the notes of the chord played in succession, rather than simultaneously.

ballad   (1) In folk traditions, a multiversed song that tells a narrative story, often based on historic or mythological figures. (2) In popular music, a slow lament, usually on the subject of lost love.

bar   See MEASURE.

baritone   (1) The male voice situated between the BASS (lowest) and TENOR (highest). (2) Baritone is sometimes used to describe musical instruments that play an octave below the ordinary range.

barrelhouse   An aggressive two-handed piano style suitable for a piano player working in a noisy room, a bar, or a brothel. The same word is used to describe such a venue.

bass   (1) The lowest male vocal range. (2) The deepest-sounding musical instrument within a family of instruments, such as the bass violin. (3) The lowest instrumental part.

beat   The basic rhythmic unit of a musical composition. In common time (most frequently used in popular music), there are two basic beats to the measure; the first is given more emphasis, and therefore is called the *strong* beat, the second is less emphasized and thus is called the *weak* beat.

bebop   A form of jazz that developed in the late 1940s and 1950s played by small ensembles or combos, which emphasized rapid playing and unusual rhythmic accents. Many bebop musicians took common CHORD PROGRESSIONS of popular songs and composed new melodies for them, allowing the accompanying instruments (piano-bass-drums) a form that could be easily followed while the melody parts (trumpet, saxophone) improvised.

bending notes   Technique used on stringed instruments where the musician pushes against a string with the left hand, causing the note to rise in pitch. On an electric guitar, which has light gauge strings, the pitch may rise as much as a whole tone (two frets).

big band jazz   A popular jazz style of the 1930s and 1940s featuring larger ensembles divided into parts (brass, reeds, rhythm). Riffs, or short melodic phrases, were traded back and forth between the melody instruments.

"Blue Moon" progression   A sequence of four chords associated with the song "Blue Moon," popularized in 1935 by Benny Goodman and others. The chords are I, VI minor, IV (or II minor), and V. In the key of C, they would be: C, A minor, F (or D minor), and G. Each chord might be held for two, four, or eight beats, but they appear in sequence. The progression is very common in doo-wop music.

blues An African-American vocal and instrumental style that developed in the late 19th to early 20th centuries. The "blues scale" usually features a flattened third and seventh, giving the music a recognizable sound. The classic 12-bar blues features three repeated lines of four bars each, with the first two lines of lyrics repeated, followed by a contrasting line. The chord progression is also fairly standardized, although many blues musicians have found ways to extend and improvise around these rules.

boogie-woogie Boogie-woogie is a way of playing BLUES on the piano that was first recorded in the 1920s. Its chief characteristic is the left-hand pattern, known as eight-to-the-bar (a note is played on every one of the eight possible eighth notes in a measure of four beats), which provides a propulsive rhythm that seems to have been influenced by the sound of trains. Boogie-woogie became a fad after the 1938 and 1939 From Spirituals to Swing concerts, and was adapted into big band swing, pop, and country music. From there it became part of ROCK 'N' ROLL. To boogie in general slang (as in "I've got to boogie now") means to leave somewhere in a hurry. In musical slang, to boogie means to maintain a repetitive blues-based rhythmic foundation, particularly one associated with the style of John Lee Hooker, similar to the figure in his song, "Boogie Chillen."

brass Traditionally, musical instruments whose bodies are made out of brass (although sometimes today they are made out of other metals). Usually used to refer to members of the horn family, including trumpets and trombones.

British invasion Popular groups of the 1960s that dominated the American pop charts. The Beatles led the charge in 1964, but were quickly followed by many soundalike bands, as well as more distinctive groups like the Rolling Stones, The Who, the Kinks, and many others.

cadence A melodic or harmonic phrase usually used to indicate the ending of a PHRASE or a complete musical composition.

capo A metal or elastic clamp placed across all of the strings of a guitar that enables players to change key, while still using the same chord fingerings as they would use without the capo.

CD (compact disc) A recording medium developed in the mid-1980s that enables music to be encoded as digital information on a small disc, and that is "read" by a laser. Various forms of CDs have been developed since to contain higher sound quality and/or other materials (photographs, moving images, etc.)

chord The basic building block of HARMONY, chords usually feature three or more notes played simultaneously.

chord progression A sequence of chords, for example in the key of C: C, F, and G7.

chorus Most commonly used in popular songs to indicate a repeated STANZA that features the same melody and lyrics that falls between each verse. Perhaps because members of the audience might "sing-along" with this part of the song, it came to be known as the chorus (a chorus literally being more than one voice singing at the same time). See VERSE.

clef The symbol at the beginning of a notated piece of music indicating the note values assigned to each line of the STAFF. The three most common clefs used in popular music are the G clef (or treble clef), usually used to notate the melody; the F clef (or bass clef), usually used for harmony parts; and the less-frequently seen C clef (or tenor clef), used for notating instruments with special ranges, most usually the viola.

country and western (C&W) A category developed by the music industry in the late 1940s to distinguish folk, cowboy, and other musical styles aimed at the white, rural, working-class listener (as opposed to R&B, aimed at black audiences, and pop, aimed at urban whites). Later, the *western* was dropped.

cover versions The music business has always been competitive, and even before recordings were possible, many artists would do the same song, as can be seen by the multiple editions of the sheet music for certain hits, each with a different artists' photo on the front. In the 1950s the practice of copying records was rampant, particularly by bigger companies, which had more resources (publicity, distribution, influence) and which used their artists to cover songs from independent labels that had started to show promise in the marketplace. A true cover version is one that attempts to stay close to the song on which it is based. Interpretations of existing songs are often called covers, but when artistry is involved in giving an individual treatment to an existing song, that effort is worthy of being considered more than a cover version.

crescendo A gradual increase in volume indicated in music notation by a triangle placed on its side below the STAFF, like this <.

crossover record A record that starts in one musical category, but has a broader appeal and becomes popular in another category. For example B. B. King's "The Thrill Is Gone" started out as an R&B record, but crossed over to the pop category.

cut a record Recording a record.

decrescendo A gradual decrease in volume indicated in music notation by a triangle placed on its side below the STAFF, as in >.

Delta blues Blues music originating in the Mississippi Delta and typically featuring the use of a slide, intense vocal performances, an aggressive, sometimes strummed guitar style with bass notes "popped" by the thumb for a snapping sound.

diatonic harmony The CHORDS implicit in the major scale. The sequence of triads is I major, II minor, III minor, IV major, V major, VI minor, and VII diminished. Because the diminished chord is unstable, it is virtually never used in this context. Because major chords are more common, many songs use only them: I, IV, and V.

disco A dance form of the 1970s developed in urban dance clubs, consisting of a heavily accented, repeated rhythmic part.

Dixieland jazz Jazz style popularized in New Orleans at the beginning of the 20th century by small combos, usually including three horns: a clarinet, a trumpet, and a trombone. The rhythm section includes a banjo, a tuba, a simple drum set, and a piano, and occasionally a saxophone, string bass, or guitar is added.

DIY (Do-It-Yourself) An emphasis on homemade music and recordings, which began with the PUNK movement but outlived it. The message was that everyone could make their own music, and record and market it on their own, using simple, inexpensive instruments and technology.

DJ (deejay) The person who plays records at a dance club or on a radio station. DJs began to create musical compositions by stringing together long sequences of records, and then further manipulated them using techniques such as backspinning (rapidly spinning a turntable backward while a record is being played) and scratching (moving the turntable back and forth rapidly to emphasize a single note or word).

DVD (digital video disc) A form of optical disc designed to hold video or film, but also sometimes used for higher-quality music reproduction. See CD (COMPACT DISC).

easy listening See MOR (MIDDLE-OF-THE-ROAD).

eighth note See NOTE VALUES.

electronic music Music created using electronic means, including SYNTHESIZERS, SEQUENCERS, tape recorders, and other nontraditional instruments.

falsetto A high register vocal sound producing a light texture. Often used in soul music.

finger-picking A style of guitar playing that keeps a steady bass with the thumb while playing melody on the treble strings.

flat A symbol in music NOTATION indicating that the note should be dropped one-half step in PITCH. Compare SHARP.

flat pick A pick held between the thumb and first finger of the right hand that is very effective for playing rapid single note passages or heavy rhythm guitar.

flip side   The other side of a 45 rpm record, typically the nonhit song.

folk music   Traditional music that is passed down from one person to another within a family or a community. Often the original composer or songwriter is unknown.

45   A record that plays at 45 revolutions per minute (rpm). Developed in the 1950s by RCA, the 45 or "single" was the main way of promoting individual songs on the pop and R&B charts through the CD era.

gospel music   Composed black religious music.

half note   See NOTE VALUES.

harmony   Any musical composition with more than one part played simultaneously. In popular music the harmony is usually the accompanying part, made up of CHORDs, that complement the MELODY.

heavy metal   Rock style of the mid-1970s and later that emphasized a thunderous sound, simplified chord progressions, subject matter aimed to appeal to teenage boys (primarily), and flamboyant stage routines. Other variants (death metal, speed metal) developed over the coming decades.

hip-hop   The music (rap), dance (breakdancing), and visual expression (graffiti art) originating in urban areas in the mid-1970s.

holy blues   Songs that combine religious words with blues melodies and accompaniments.

hook   A recurrent musical or lyric phrase that is designed to "hook" the listener into a particular song or record. It is often also the title of a song.

interval   The space between two PITCHES. The first note of a SCALE is considered the first interval; the next note, the second; and so on. Thus, in a C major scale, an "E" is considered a third, and a G a "fifth." The I-III-V combination makes up a major CHORD.

jukebox   A machine designed to play records. Commonly found in bars (known as "juke joints" in the South), these replaced live music by the mid-1950s, and were a major means of promoting hit records. Customers dropped a "nickel in the jukebox" to hear their favorite song.

key   Indicates the range of notes (or SCALE) on which a composition is based.

key signature   The symbol at the beginning of a piece of notation that indicates the basic KEY of the work.

looping   Repeating a short musical PHRASE or RHYTHM. SEQUENCERs can be programmed to "loop" or repeat these parts indefinitely.

LP   A "long-playing" record, playing at 33 revolutions per minute (rpm). Developed in the late 1940s, the LP enabled record companies to present more or longer compositions on a single disc (the previous time limit of 78s was 3 to 5 minutes, while an LP could hold 20 to 25 minutes per side).

major   One of the two primary SCALEs used in popular music. The relation between the seven notes in the major scale is whole step (WS)-WS-half step (HS)-WS-WS-WS-HS. Each scale step has a related CHORD defining major harmony. Compare MINOR.

measure   A unit of musical time in a composition defined by the time signature. In 4/4 time, for example, each measure consists of four beats (and a quarter note is equal to one beat). The bar line (a vertical line across all five lines of the STAFF) indicates the beginning and end of a measure.

melody   Two or more musical tones played in succession, called the "horizontal" part of a musical composition because the notes move horizontally across the staff (as opposed to the HARMONY which is called the "vertical" part because the harmony notes are stacked vertically on the staff). In popular music the melody of a song is the most memorable part of the composition.

meter   The repeated pattern of strong and weak rhythmic pulses in a piece of music. For example, in a waltz, the oom-pah-pah meter is the defining part of the music's style.

MIDI (Musical Instrument Digital Interface)   A common programming language that enables SYNTHESIZERS, computers, and SEQUENCERS to communicate with one another.

minor   One of the two primary SCALES used in popular music. The relation between the seven notes in the major scale is whole step (WS)-half step (HS)-WS-HS-WS-WS. (There are two variations of this basic pattern found in scales known as the "harmonic" and "melodic" minor.) Each scale step has a related CHORD defining major harmony. Compare MAJOR.

minstrel   Performance of African-American songs and dances by white performers in blackface, burnt cork rubbed on their faces beginning in the mid-19th century. Later, black minstrels appeared. Minstrel shows included songs, dances, and humorous skits. Many of these skits and songs made fun of African Americans.

modes   A type of SCALE. The two common scales used today (the MAJOR and MINOR) are two types of mode. In the Middle Ages, a system of eight different modes was developed, each with the same intervals but beginning on a different note. The modes are sometimes still heard in folk music, some forms of jazz, and some forms of contemporary classical music.

MOR (middle-of-the-road)   Pop music aimed at a wide audience, designed to be as inoffensive and nondisturbing as possible. This term is often used pejoratively by critics. Also sometimes called "easy listening."

movement   A section of a longer musical composition.

notation   A system developed over many centuries to write down musical compositions using specific symbols to represent PITCH and RHYTHM.

note values   The time values of the notes in a musical composition are relational, usually based on the idea of a quarter note equaling one beat (as in ¾ time). In this time signature, a quarter note fills a quarter of the time in the measure; a half-note equals two beats (is twice as long) and a whole note equals four beats (a full measure). Conversely, shorter time values include an eighth-note (half a single beat), a sixteenth (¼ of a single beat), a thirty-second (⅛ of a single beat), etc.

octave   An INTERVAL of eight notes, considered the "perfect" consonance. If a string is divided perfectly in half, each half will sound an octave above the full string, so that the ratio between the two notes is expressed as 1:2.

opus   A numbering system used in classical composition to indicate the order in which pieces were composed. Some composers only give opus numbers to works they feel are strong enough to be part of their "official" canon.

percussion   Instruments used to play the rhythmic part of a composition, which may be "unpitched" (such as drums or cymbals) or "pitched" (such as bells, chimes, and marimbas).

phonograph   A mechanical instrument used to reproduce sound recordings. A phonograph consists of some form of turntable, needle, tone arm, amplifier, and speaker. A record is placed on a turntable, a disc that is set to revolve at specific speeds. The needle "reads" the grooves cut into the record itself. The vibrations then are communicated through the tone arm (in which the needle is mounted) into an amplifier (which increases the volume of the sound). A speaker projects the sound out so that it can be heard.

phrase   A subsection of the MELODY that expresses a complete musical thought.

Piedmont blues   A form of blues from the Carolinas, Georgia, Florida, and Alabama that uses a restrained style of fingerpicking and soft vocal performances. It also often uses ragtime CHORD PROGRESSIONS.

pitch   The note defined by its sound; literally, the number of vibrations per second (of a string, air column, bar, or some other vibrating object) that results in a given tone. Pitch is relative; in most tuning systems, a specific note is chosen as the pitch against which others are tuned. In modern music, this is usually A above middle C, defined as vibrating at 440 vps.

pop music   Any music that appeals to a large audience. Originally, the pop charts featured records aimed at white, urban listeners (as opposed to R&B, aimed at blacks, and C&W or country, aimed at rural, lower-class whites). Today, "pop" is applied to any recording that appeals across a wide range of listeners, so that Michael Jackson or Shania Twain could equally be defined as "pop" stars.

power chords   Played on the low strings of an electric guitar, power chords use only the root and the fifth (and often a repeat of the root an octave higher) of a triad, leaving out the third of the CHORD. With no third, the chord is neither MAJOR or MINOR. With only two notes, it is technically not even a chord, but an interval. The use of power chords was pioneered by Link Wray ("Rumble") and the Kinks ("You Really Got Me"), and used extensively in hard rock (Deep Purple's "Smoke on the Water"), heavy metal (Metallica), and grunge (Nirvana's "Smells Like Teen Spirit").

power trio   Three instruments—guitar, bass, and drums—played at loud volumes.

psychedelic   Popular ROCK style of the late 1960s-early 1970s that featured extended musical forms, "spacey" lyrics, and unusual musical timbres often produced by synthesizers. Psychedelic music was supposed to be the "aural equivalent" of the drug experience. See also SYNTHESIZER; TIMBRE.

punk   A movement that began in England and travelled to the United States in the mid-1970s emphasizing a return to simpler musical forms, in response to the growing commercialization of ROCK. Punk also encompassed fashion (including spiked hair, safety pins used as body ornaments, etc.) and sometimes a violent, antiestablishment message.

quarter note   See NOTE VALUES.

race records   Music industry name for African-American popular music recorded in the 1920s until around 1945.

ragtime   Music dating from around the 1890s and usually composed in three or four different sections. The most famous ragtime pieces were for piano, but the style was also adapted in a simplified form for the banjo and the guitar.

record producer   The person in charge of a recording session.

register   The range in notes of a specific part of a musical composition. Also used to define the range of an individual musical instrument or vocal part.

resonator guitar   Guitars with a metal front and back, often used in playing slide guitar, and prized during the 1930s for their volume.

rhythm   The basic pulse of a musical composition. In 4/4 time, the 4 beats per measure provide the pulse that propels the piece. Compare METER.

rhythm and blues (R&B)   Black popular music that emerged around 1945 and peaked in popularity in the 1960s. It usually included gospel-influenced vocal performances, and a rhythm section of piano, bass, and drums. The lead instruments were often guitar and saxophone.

riff   A short, recognizable melodic phrase used repeatedly in a piece of music. Commonly heard in big band jazz or in electric guitar solos.

rock   An outgrowth of ROCK 'N' ROLL in the 1960s that featured more sophisticated arrangements, lyrics, and subject matter. The BRITISH INVASION groups—notably the Beatles and the Rolling Stones—are sometimes credited with extending the style and subjects treated by rock 'n' roll. Rock itself has developed into many different substyles.

rockabilly   Mid-1950s popular music that combined BLUES and COUNTRY music.

rock 'n' roll   The popular music of the mid-1950s aimed at teenage listeners. Popular rock 'n' roll artists included Elvis Presley, Chuck Berry, Little Richard, and Carl Perkins. Compare ROCK.

royalties   Payments to recording artists based on the sales of their records.

salsa Literally "spice." A form of Latin dance music popularized in the 1970s and 1980s.

scale A succession of seven notes. The most common scales are the MAJOR and MINOR.

score The complete notation of a musical composition.

sequencer An electronic instrument that can record a series of pitches or rhythms and play them back on command.

78 The first form of recorded disc, that revolved on a turntable at 78 revolutions per minute (rpm). The first 78s were 10 inches in diameter and could play for approximately three minutes per side; later, 12-inch 78s were introduced with slightly longer playing times.

sharp A symbol in a piece of music indicating that a pitch should be raised one half-step in PITCH. Compare FLAT.

side One side of a recording disc.

slide guitar Style of guitar in which the player wears a metal or glass tube on one finger or uses a bottle neck to play notes. It creates a distinctive crying sound. Also called bottleneck guitar.

songster A turn-of-the-20th-century musician with a varied repertoire that included different styles of music.

soprano The highest female voice, or the highest pitched instrument in a family of instruments.

soul A black musical style developed in the 1960s that combined elements of GOSPEL MUSIC with RHYTHM AND BLUES.

spirituals Traditional religious music found in both white and African-American traditions.

staff The five parallel lines on which the symbols for notes are placed in a notated piece of music. The CLEF at the beginning of the staff indicates the pitch of each note on the staff.

stanza In poetry, the basic lyrical unit, often consisting of four or six lines. The lyrics to both the VERSE and CHORUS of a popular song follow the stanza form.

strings Instruments that produce musical sound through the vibration of strings, made out of animal gut or metal. Violins and guitars are stringed instruments.

suite In classical music, a group of dances played in succession to form a larger musical composition.

symphony In classical music, a defined form usually consisting of three parts, played Fast-Slow-Fast.

syncopation Accenting the unexpected or weaker BEAT. Often used in RAGTIME, jazz, and related styles.

synthesizer An electronic instrument that is capable of creating different musical pitches and timbres.

tempo The speed at which a piece of music is performed.

tenor The highest male voice.

theme A recognizable MELODY that is often repeated within a musical composition.

thumb picks and finger picks Guitar picks made of metal or plastic worn on the player's right hand fingers and thumb in order to play louder.

timbre The quality of a PITCH produced by a musical instrument or voice that makes it distinctive. The timbre of a guitar is quite different from that of a flute, for example.

time signature In notation, the symbol at the beginning of each STAFF that indicates the basic metric pulse and how many beats are contained in a measure. For example, in 4/4 time, a quarter-note is given one beat, and there are four beats per measure; in 6/8 time, an eighth-note is given one beat, and there are six beats in a measure.

Tin Pan Alley The center of music publishing on West 28th Street in New York City from the late 19th century through the 1930s (so-called because the clatter from competing pianists working in different buildings sounded to passersby like rattling tin pans). Used generally to describe the popular songs of this period.

tone See PITCH.

tremolo The rapid repetition of a single note to give a "quivering" or "shaking" sound. Compare VIBRATO.

turnaround   A musical phrase at the end of a verse that briefly outlines the CHORDS of the song before the start of the next verse.

12-bar blues   A 12-bar BLUES has 12 measures of music, or bars, and is the most common blues format, though eight bars and 16 bars are also used.

vamp   A short segment of music that repeats, usually two or four CHORDS. Two chord vamps are common in GOSPEL and ROCK, especially the I and IV chords (C and F in the key of C).

vanity records   Recordings that are conceived and financed by the artists involved. They are called "vanity records" because the motivation comes from the person or group themselves, not from a record company. The reason is to realize a creative project, to promote a career, or just to boost the ego. Previously, singers and musicians would pay to go into a studio and to cover the costs of backup musicians, mixing, mastering, and manufacturing. This continues, but with the rise of home studios, these steps can be done at home, with computerized recording and CD burning. Vanity records now represent perhaps the majority of recordings being made and are more likely to be called independent productions.

verse   The part of a song that features a changing lyric set to a fixed MELODY. The verse is usually performed in alternation with the CHORUS.

vibrato   A rapid moving up and down slightly in PITCH while performing a single note as an ornament. Compare TREMOLO.

walking bass   A style of bass playing that originated in jazz on the upright bass. The bassist plays a new note on every beat, outlining the CHORDS as they pass by in a CHORD PROGRESSION. Chord notes are primary, but passing notes and other decorations enliven the bass line, as well as brief rhythmic variations enliven the bass line. A rock example is Paul McCartney's bass part in the Beatles' "All My Loving" (1964).

whole note   See NOTE VALUES.

woodwinds   A class of instruments traditionally made of wood, although the term is now used for instruments made of brass or metal as well. Clarinets, flutes, and saxophones are usually classified as woodwinds.

Further Reading and Research

I. General Further Reading

Bond, Marilyn, and S. R. Boland. *The Birth of the Detroit Sound, 1940–1964.* Chicago: Arcadia Publishing, 2002.

Broven, John. *Rhythm & Blues in New Orleans.* Gretna, La.: Pelican Publishing Company, 1978, 1974.

Busnar, Gene. *The Rhythm and Blues Story.* New York: J. Messner, 1985.

Fox, Ted. *Showtime at the Apollo.* New rev. ed. Rhinebeck, N.Y.: Mill Road Enterprises, 2003.

George, Nelson. *The Death of Rhythm & Blues.* New York: Pantheon Books, 1988.

George, Nelson, et al. *Fresh, Hip Hop Don't Stop.* New York: Random House, 1985.

George, Nelson. *Hip-Hop America.* New York: Viking, 1998.

———. *Where Did Our Love Go?: The Rise & Fall of the Motown Sound.* New York: St. Martin's Press, 1987, 1985.

Gillett, Charlie. *Making Tracks; Atlantic Records and the Growth of a Multi–Billion-Dollar Industry.* New York: Dutton, 1974.

———. *The Sound of the City: The Rise of Rock and Roll.* 2nd ed.; newly illustrated and expanded. London: Souvenir Press, 1971; New York: Da Capo, 1996.

Gribin, Anthony J., and Matthew M. Schiff. *The Complete Book of Doo-Wop.* Iola, Wisc.: Krause Publications, 2000.

Groia, Philip. *They All Sang on the Corner; New York City's Rhythm and Blues Vocal Groups of the 1950's.* Rev. ed. Setauket, N.Y.: Edmond Publishing Company, 1974.

Groia, Philip. *They All Sang on the Corner; A Second Look at New York City's Rhythm and Blues Vocal Groups.* West Hempstead, N.Y.: Phillie Dee, 1983.

Hager, Steven. *Hip Hop: The Illustrated History of Break Dancing, Rap Music, and Graffiti.* New York: St. Martin's Press, 1984.

Heilbut, Anthony. *The Gospel Sound: Good News and Bad Times.* Updated and rev. ed. New York: Limelight Editions, 1985; New York: Simon and Schuster, 1971.

Jones, LeRoi (aka Imamu Amiri Baraka). *Black Music.* New York: Da Capo, 1998, 1968.

Keeley, Jennifer. *Rap Music.* San Diego, Calif.: Lucent Books, 2001. Geared specifically to young adults.

Keyes, Cheryl Lynette. *Rap Music and Street Consciousness.* Urbana, Ill.: University of Illinois, 2002.

Krims, Adam. *Rap Music and the Poetics of Identity.* New York: Cambridge University Press, 2000.

McGowen, James A. *Hear Today, Here to Stay: A Personal History of Rhythm and Blues.* St. Petersburg, Fla.: Sixth House Press, 1983, 1979.

McGrath, Bob. *The R&B Indies.* West Vancouver, B.C.: Eyeball Productions, 2000.

Merlis, Bob, and Davin Seay. *Heart & Soul: A Celebration of Black Music Style in America, 1930–1975.* New York: Billboard Books, 2002.

Mitchell, Tony, ed. *Global Noise: Rap and Hip-Hop Music Outside the USA.* Middletown, Conn.: Wesleyan University, 2001.

Neal, Mark Anthony, and Murray Forman, eds. *That's the Joint!: The Hip-Hop Studies Reader.* New York: Routledge, 2004.

Pruter, Robert. *Chicago Soul.* Urbana, Ill.: Universiy of Illinois, 1991.

———. *Doowop: The Chicago Scene.* Urbana, Ill.: Universty of Illinois, 1996.

Reed, Tom. *The Black Music History of Los Angeles, Its Roots: A Classical Pictorial History of Black Music in L.A. from 1920–1970.* Los Angeles: Black Accent on L.A. Press, 1992.

Warner, Jay. *Just Walking in the Rain: The Prisonaires.* Los Angeles: Renaissance Books, 2001.

II.   Reference Sources

All Music Guide to Hip-Hop: The Definitive Guide to Rap & Hip-Hop, ed. Vladimir Bogdanov. San Francisco, Calif.: Backbeat Books, 2003.

All Music Guide to Soul: The Definitive Guide to R&B and Soul, ed. Vladimir Bogdanov. San Francisco, Calif.: Backbeat Books, 2003.

Baptista, Todd R. *Group Harmony: Behind the Rhythm and the Blues.* New Bedford, Mass.: TRB Enterprises, 1996.

———. *Group Harmony: Echoes of the Rhythm and Blues Era.* New Bedford, Mass.: TRB Enterprises, n.d.

———. *The Last of the Good Rocking Men.* New Bedford, Mass.: TRB Enterprises, 2002. Surveys lesser-known gospel and R&B artists.

Gart, Galen, ed. *First Pressings: The History of Rhythm & Blues (1950–1959).* 10 vols. Milford, N.H.: Big Nickel, 1993.

Gregory, Hugh. *Soul Music A-Z.* New York: Da Capo, 1995, 1992.

Hildebrand, Lee. *Stars of Soul and Rhythm & Blues: Top Recording Artists and Showstopping Performers, from Memphis and Motown to Now.* New York: Billboard Books, 1994.

Kreiter, Jeff. *45 RPM Group Collector's Record Label Guide.* Fifth edition. Bridgeport, Ohio: self-published, 1994.

McCoy, Judy. *Rap Music in the 1980s: A Reference Guide.* Metuchen, N.J.: Scarecrow, 1992.

Music Hound R&B: The Essential Album Guide, edited by Gary Graff, Josh Freedom du Lac, and Jim McFarlin. Detroit: Visible Ink, 1998.

Nelson, Havelock, and Michael A. Gonzalez. *Bring the Noise: A Guide to Rap Music and Hip-Hop Culture.* New York: Harmony Books, 1991.

Pruter, Robert, ed. *The Blackwell Guide to Soul Recordings.* Cambridge, Mass.: Blackwell Publishers, 1993.

Rosalsky, Mitch. *The Encyclopedia of Rhythm & Blues and Doo Wop Vocal Groups.* Lanham, Md.: Scarecrow, 2000.

Vann, Kimberly R., assisted by David Martin et al. *Black Music in* Ebony: *An Annotated Guide to the Articles on Music in* Ebony *magazine, 1945–1985.* Chicago: Center for Black Music Research, Columbia College, 1990.

Westbrook, Alonzo. *Hip Hoptionary: The Dictionary of Hip Hop Terminology.* New York: Harlem Moon, 2002.

Whitburn, Joel. *Joel Whitburn Presents Top R&B Singles, 1942–1999: Chart Data Compiled from* Billboard's *R&B Singles Charts, 1942–1999.* Menomonee Falls, Wisc.: Record Research, 2000.

Whitburn, Joel. *Joel Whitburn's Top R&B Albums, 1965–1998.* Menomonee Falls, Wisc.: Record Research, 1999.

White, Adam, and Fred Bronson. *The Billboard Book of Number One Rhythm & Blues Hits.* New York: Billboard Books, 1993.

III. Discographies

Bartlette, Reginald J. *Off the Record: Motown by Master Number, 1959–1989.* Ann Arbor, Mich.: Popular Culture, Ink, 1991.

Beckman, Jeff, Jim Hunt, and Tom Kline. *Soul Harmony Singles, 1960–1990: A Discography of 45 rpm Recordings with the Black Vocal Group Sound.* Elizabeth, N.J.: Three-On-Three Publishing, n.d.

Ferlingere, Robert D. *A Discography of Rhythm & Blues and Rock 'N' Roll Vocal Groups, 1945 to 1965.* Fourth edition. Pittsburg, Calif.: Ferlingere, 1976.

Friedman, Douglas E., and Anthony J. Gribin. *Who Sang Our Songs? The Official Rhythm & Blues and Doo-Wop Songography.* West Long Branch, N.J.: Harmony Songs Publications, 2001.

Hayes, Cedric J., and Robert Laughton. *Gospel Records, 1943–1969: A Black Music Discography.* 2 vols. London: Record Information Services, 1996, 1993.

Neely, Tim. *Goldmine Standard Catalogue of Rhythm & Blues Records.* Iola, Wisc.: Krause Publications, 2002.

Propes, Steve, and Galen Gart. *L.A. R&B Vocal Groups, 1945–1965.* Winter Haven, Fla.: Big Nickel, 2001.

Sweeney, Michael J. *Single Artists, Groups and R&B Duets.* Second edition, 1993.

Editorial Board of Advisers

Duckworth is currently a professor of music at Bucknell University in Pennsylvania.

Kevin Holm-Hudson, Ph.D., received his doctorate of musical arts (composition with ethnomusicology concentration) from the University of Illinois at Urbana-Champaign. He is an assistant professor of music at the University of Kentucky and is an editor/contributor to *Progressive Rock Reconsidered* (Routledge). Dr. Holm-Hudson is also the author of numerous articles that have appeared in such publications as *Genre* and *Ex Tempore* and has presented papers on a wide variety of topics at conferences, including "'Come Sail Away' and the Commodification of Prog Lite," at the inaugural Conference on Popular Music and American Culture in 2002.

Nadine Hubbs, Ph.D., is associate professor of music and women's studies at the University of Michigan (Ann Arbor). She has written extensively on classical and popular music, particularly in relation to gender and sexuality. Dr. Hubbs is the author of *The Queer Composition of America's Sound: Gay Modernists, American Music, and National Identity* (University of California Press) and various essays,

including "The Imagination of Pop-Rock Criticism" in *Expression in Pop-Rock Music* (Garland Publications) and "Music of the 'Fourth Gender': Morrissey and the Sexual Politics of Melodic Contour," featured in the journal *Genders*.

Craig Morrison, Ph.D., holds a doctorate in humanities with a concentration in music from Concordia University (Montreal, Quebec). He is currently a professor of music at Concordia, where he teaches a course titled "Rock and Roll and its Roots." Dr. Morrison is the author of *Go Cat Go! Rockabilly Music and Its Makers* (University of Illinois Press) and contributed to *The Encyclopedia of the Blues* (Routledge). He has presented many papers on elements of rock and roll.

Albin J. Zak III, Ph.D., earned a doctorate in musicology from the Graduate Center of the City University of New York and is currently chairman of the music department at the University at Albany (SUNY). His publications include *The Velvet Underground Companion* (Schirmer Books) and *The Poetics of Rock: Cutting Tracks, Making Records* (University of California Press). Dr. Zak is also a songwriter, recording engineer, and record producer.

Index